W9-DEW-455

Novels for Students

Presenting Analysis, Context, and Criticism on Commonly Studied Novels

Volume 11

Elizabeth Thomason, Editor

Carol Jago, Santa Monica High School, Advisor
Kathleen Pasquantonio, Novi High School, Advisor

Foreword by Anne Devereaux Jordan, Teaching and Learning Literature

GALE GROUP

Detroit
New York
San Francisco
London
Boston
Woodbridge, CT

National Advisory Board

Novels
for Students

Novels for Students

Staff

Editor: Elizabeth Thomason.

Contributing Editors: Anne Marie Hacht, Michael L. LaBlanc, Ira Mark Milne, Jennifer Smith.

Managing Editor: Dwayne D. Hayes.

Research: Victoria B. Cariappa, *Research Manager*. Cheryl Warnock, *Research Specialist*. Tamara Nott, Tracie A. Richardson, *Research Associates*. Nicodemus Ford, Sarah Genik, Timothy Lehnerer, Ron Morelli, *Research Assistants*.

Permissions: Maria Franklin, *Permissions Manager*. Jacqueline Jones, Julie Juengling, *Permissions Assistants*.

Manufacturing: Mary Beth Trimper, *Manager, Composition and Electronic Prepress*. Evi Seoud, *Assistant Manager, Composition Purchasing and Electronic Prepress*. Stacy Melson, *Buyer*.

Imaging and Multimedia Content Team: Barbara Yarrow, *Manager*. Randy Bassett, *Imaging Supervisor*. Robert Duncan, Dan Newell, *Imaging Specialists*. Pamela A. Reed, *Imaging Coordinator*. Leitha Etheridge-Sims, Mary Grimes, David G. Oblender, *Image Catalogers*. Robyn V. Young, *Project Manager*. Dean Dauphinais, *Senior Image Editor*. Kelly A. Quin, *Image Editor*.

Product Design Team: Kenn Zorn, *Product Design Manager*. Pamela A. E. Galbreath, *Senior Art Director*. Michael Logusz, *Graphic Artist*.

010910

Table of Contents

The Informed Dialogue: Interacting with Literature

When we pick up a book, we usually do so with the anticipation of pleasure. We hope that by entering the time and place of the novel and sharing the thoughts and actions of the characters, we will find enjoyment. Unfortunately, this is often not the case; we are disappointed. But we should ask, has the author failed us, or have we failed the author?

We establish a dialogue with the author, the book, and with ourselves when we read. Consciously and unconsciously, we ask questions: "Why did the author write this book?" "Why did the author choose that time, place, or character?" "How did the author achieve that effect?" "Why did the character act that way?" "Would I act in the same way?" The answers we receive depend upon how much information about literature in general and about that book specifically we ourselves bring to our reading.

Young children have limited life and literary experiences. Being young, children frequently do not know how to go about exploring a book, nor sometimes, even know the questions to ask of a book. The books they read help them answer questions, the author often coming right out and *telling* young readers the things they are learning or are expected to learn. The perennial classic, *The Little Engine That Could, tells* its readers that, among other things, it is good to help others and brings happiness:

"Hurray, hurray," cried the funny little clown and all the dolls and toys. "The good little boys and girls in the city will be happy because you helped us, kind, Little Blue Engine."

In picture books, messages are often blatant and simple, the dialogue between the author and reader one-sided. Young children are concerned with the end result of a book—the enjoyment gained, the lesson learned—rather than with how that result was obtained. As we grow older and read further, however, we question more. We come to expect that the world within the book will closely mirror the concerns of our world, and that the author will *show* these through the events, descriptions, and conversations within the story, rather than *telling* of them. We are now expected to do the interpreting, carry on our share of the dialogue with the book and author, and glean not only the author's message, but comprehend how that message and the overall affect of the book were achieved. Sometimes, however, we need help to do these things. *Novels for Students* provides that help.

A novel is made up of many parts interacting to create a coherent whole. In reading a novel, the more obvious features can be easily spotted—theme, characters, plot—but we may overlook the more subtle elements that greatly influence how the novel is perceived by the reader: viewpoint, mood and tone, symbolism, or the use of humor. By focusing on both the obvious and more subtle literary elements within a novel, *Novels for Students* aids readers in both analyzing for message and in determining how and why that message is communicated. In the discussion on Harper Lee's *To Kill a Mockingbird* (Vol. 2), for example, the mockingbird as a symbol of innocence is dealt with, among other things, as is the importance of Lee's use of humor which "enlivens a serious plot, adds depth to the characterization, and creates a sense of familiarity and universality." The reader comes to understand the internal elements of each novel discussed—as well as the external influences that help shape it.

"The desire to write greatly," Harold Bloom of Yale University says, "is the desire to be elsewhere, in a time and place of one's own, in an originality that must compound with inheritance, with an anxiety of influence." A writer seeks to create a unique world within a story, but although it is unique, it is not disconnected from our own world. It speaks to us *because* of what the writer brings to the writing from our world: how he or she was raised and educated; his or her likes and dislikes; the events occurring in the real world at the time of the writing, and while the author was growing up. When we know what an author has brought to his or her work, we gain a greater insight into both the "originality" (the world of the book), and the things that "compound" it. This insight enables us to question that created world and find answers more readily. By informing ourselves, we are able to establish a more effective dialogue with both book and author.

Novels for Students, in addition to providing a plot summary and descriptive list of characters—to remind readers of what they have read—also explores the external influences that shaped each book. Each entry includes a discussion of the author's background, and the historical context in which the novel was written. It is vital to know, for instance, that when Ray Bradbury was writing *Fahrenheit 451* (Vol. 1), the threat of Nazi domination had recently ended in Europe, and the McCarthy hearings were taking place in Washington, D.C. This information goes far in answering the question, "Why did he write a story of oppressive government control and book burning?" Similarly,

it is important to know that Harper Lee, author of *To Kill a Mockingbird,* was born and raised in Monroeville, Alabama, and that her father was a lawyer. Readers can now see why she chose the south as a setting for her novel—it is the place with which she was most familiar—and start to comprehend her characters and their actions.

Novels for Students helps readers find the answers they seek when they establish a dialogue with a particular novel. It also aids in the posing of questions by providing the opinions and interpretations of various critics and reviewers, broadening that dialogue. Some reviewers of *To Kill A Mockingbird,* for example, "faulted the novel's climax as melodramatic." This statement leads readers to ask, "Is it, indeed, melodramatic?" "If not, why did some reviewers see it as such?" "If it is, why did Lee choose to make it melodramatic?" "Is melodrama ever justified?" By being spurred to ask these questions, readers not only learn more about the book and its writer, but about the nature of writing itself.

The literature included for discussion in *Novels for Students* has been chosen because it has something vital to say to us. *Of Mice and Men, Catch-22, The Joy Luck Club, My Antonia, A Separate Peace* and the other novels here speak of life and modern sensibility. In addition to their individual, specific messages of prejudice, power, love or hate, living and dying, however, they and all great literature also share a common intent. They force us to *think*—about life, literature, and about others, not just about ourselves. They pry us from the narrow confines of our minds and thrust us outward to confront the world of books and the larger, real world we all share. *Novels for Students* helps us in this confrontation by providing the means of enriching our conversation with literature and the world, by creating an *informed* dialogue, one that brings true pleasure to the personal act of reading.

Sources

Harold Bloom, *The Western Canon, The Books and School of the Ages,* Riverhead Books, 1994.

Watty Piper, *The Little Engine That Could,* Platt & Munk, 1930.

Anne Devereaux Jordan
Senior Editor, TALL
(Teaching and Learning Literature).

Introduction

Purpose of the Book

The purpose of *Novels for Students (NfS)* is to provide readers with a guide to understanding, enjoying, and studying novels by giving them easy access to information about the work. Part of Gale's "For Students" Literature line, *NfS* is specifically designed to meet the curricular needs of high school and undergraduate college students and their teachers, as well as the interests of general readers and researchers considering specific novels. While each volume contains entries on "classic" novels frequently studied in classrooms, there are also entries containing hard-to-find information on contemporary novels, including works by multicultural, international, and women novelists.

The information covered in each entry includes an introduction to the novel and the novel's author; a plot summary, to help readers unravel and understand the events in a novel; descriptions of important characters, including explanation of a given character's role in the novel as well as discussion about that character's relationship to other characters in the novel; analysis of important themes in the novel; and an explanation of important literary techniques and movements as they are demonstrated in the novel.

In addition to this material, which helps the readers analyze the novel itself, students are also provided with important information on the literary and historical background informing each work. This includes a historical context essay, a box comparing the time or place the novel was written to modern Western culture, a critical overview essay, and excerpts from critical essays on the novel. A unique feature of *NfS* is a specially commissioned overview essay on each novel, targeted toward the student reader.

To further aid the student in studying and enjoying each novel, information on media adaptations is provided, as well as reading suggestions for works of fiction and nonfiction on similar themes and topics. Classroom aids include ideas for research papers and lists of critical sources that provide additional material on the novel.

Selection Criteria

The titles for each volume of *NfS* were selected by surveying numerous sources on teaching literature and analyzing course curricula for various school districts. Some of the sources surveyed included: literature anthologies; *Reading Lists for College-Bound Students: The Books Most Recommended by America's Top Colleges;* textbooks on teaching the novel; a College Board survey of novels commonly studied in high schools; a National Council of Teachers of English (NCTE) survey of novels commonly studied in high schools; the NCTE's *Teaching Literature in High School: The Novel;* and the Young Adult Library Services Association (YALSA) list of best books for young adults of the past twenty-five years.

Input was also solicited from our advisory board, as well as educators from various areas.

From these discussions, it was determined that each volume should have a mix of "classic" novels (those works commonly taught in literature classes) and contemporary novels for which information is often hard to find. Because of the interest in expanding the canon of literature, an emphasis was also placed on including works by international, multicultural, and women authors. Our advisory board members—educational professionals—helped pare down the list for each volume. If a work was not selected for the present volume, it was often noted as a possibility for a future volume. As always, the editor welcomes suggestions for titles to be included in future volumes.

How Each Entry Is Organized

Each entry, or chapter, in *NfS* focuses on one novel. Each entry heading lists the full name of the novel, the author's name, and the date of the novel's publication. The following elements are contained in each entry:

- **Introduction:** a brief overview of the novel which provides information about its first appearance, its literary standing, any controversies surrounding the work, and major conflicts or themes within the work.

- **Author Biography:** this section includes basic facts about the author's life, and focuses on events and times in the author's life that inspired the novel in question.

- **Plot Summary:** a factual description of the major events in the novel. Lengthy summaries are broken down with subheads.

- **Characters:** an alphabetical listing of major characters in the novel. Each character name is followed by a brief to an extensive description of the character's role in the novel, as well as discussion of the character's actions, relationships, and possible motivation.

  Characters are listed alphabetically by last name. If a character is unnamed—for instance, the narrator in *Invisible Man*–the character is listed as "The Narrator" and alphabetized as "Narrator." If a character's first name is the only one given, the name will appear alphabetically by that name.

- Variant names are also included for each character. Thus, the full name "Jean Louise Finch" would head the listing for the narrator of *To Kill a Mockingbird,* but listed in a separate cross-reference would be the nickname "Scout Finch."

- **Themes:** a thorough overview of how the major topics, themes, and issues are addressed within the novel. Each theme discussed appears in a separate subhead, and is easily accessed through the boldface entries in the Subject/Theme Index.

- **Style:** this section addresses important style elements of the novel, such as setting, point of view, and narration; important literary devices used, such as imagery, foreshadowing, symbolism; and, if applicable, genres to which the work might have belonged, such as Gothicism or Romanticism. Literary terms are explained within the entry, but can also be found in the Glossary.

- **Historical Context:** This section outlines the social, political, and cultural climate *in which the author lived and the novel was created.* This section may include descriptions of related historical events, pertinent aspects of daily life in the culture, and the artistic and literary sensibilities of the time in which the work was written. If the novel is a historical work, information regarding the time in which the novel is set is also included. Each section is broken down with helpful subheads.

- **Critical Overview:** this section provides background on the critical reputation of the novel, including bannings or any other public controversies surrounding the work. For older works, this section includes a history of how the novel was first received and how perceptions of it may have changed over the years; for more recent novels, direct quotes from early reviews may also be included.

- **Criticism:** an essay commissioned by *NfS* which specifically deals with the novel and is written specifically for the student audience, as well as excerpts from previously published criticism on the work (if available).

- **Sources:** an alphabetical list of critical material quoted in the entry, with full bibliographical information.

- **Further Reading:** an alphabetical list of other critical sources which may prove useful for the student. Includes full bibliographical information and a brief annotation.

In addition, each entry contains the following highlighted sections, set apart from the main text as sidebars:

- **Media Adaptations:** a list of important film and television adaptations of the novel, including source information. The list also includes stage adaptations, audio recordings, musical adaptations, etc.

- **Topics for Further Study:** a list of potential study questions or research topics dealing with the novel. This section includes questions related to other disciplines the student may be studying, such as American history, world history, science, math, government, business, geography, economics, psychology, etc.

- **Compare and Contrast Box:** an "at-a-glance" comparison of the cultural and historical differences between the author's time and culture and late twentieth-century Western culture. This box includes pertinent parallels between the major scientific, political, and cultural movements of the time or place the novel was written, the time or place the novel was set (if a historical work), and modern Western culture. Works written after the mid-1970s may not have this box.

- **What Do I Read Next?:** a list of works that might complement the featured novel or serve as a contrast to it. This includes works by the same author and others, works of fiction and nonfiction, and works from various genres, cultures, and eras.

Other Features

NfS includes "The Informed Dialogue: Interacting with Literature," a foreword by Anne Devereaux Jordan, Senior Editor for *Teaching and Learning Literature* (*TALL*), and a founder of the Children's Literature Association. This essay provides an enlightening look at how readers interact with literature and how *Novels for Students* can help teachers show students how to enrich their own reading experiences.

A Cumulative Author/Title Index lists the authors and titles covered in each volume of the *NfS* series.

A Cumulative Nationality/Ethnicity Index breaks down the authors and titles covered in each volume of the *NfS* series by nationality and ethnicity.

A Subject/Theme Index, specific to each volume, provides easy reference for users who may be studying a particular subject or theme rather than a single work. Significant subjects from events to broad themes are included, and the entries pointing to the specific theme discussions in each entry are indicated in **boldface.**

Each entry has several illustrations, including photos of the author, stills from film adaptations (if available), maps, and/or photos of key historical events.

Citing Novels for Students

When writing papers, students who quote directly from any volume of *Novels for Students* may use the following general forms. These examples are based on MLA style; teachers may request that students adhere to a different style, so the following examples may be adapted as needed.

When citing text from *NfS* that is not attributed to a particular author (i.e., the Themes, Style, Historical Context sections, etc.), the following format should be used in the bibliography section:

"Night." *Novels for Students.* Ed. Marie Rose Napierkowski. Vol. 4. Detroit: Gale, 1998. 34–5.

When quoting the specially commissioned essay from *NfS* (usually the first piece under the "Criticism" subhead), the following format should be used:

Miller, Tyrus. Essay on "Winesburg, Ohio." *Novels for Students.* Ed. Marie Rose Napierkowski. Vol. 4. Detroit: Gale, 1997. 218–9.

When quoting a journal or newspaper essay that is reprinted in a volume of *NfS,* the following form may be used:

Malak, Amin. "Margaret Atwood's " 'The Handmaid's Tale' and the Dystopian Tradition," in *Canadian Literature* , No. 112, Spring, 1987, 9–16; excerpted and reprinted in *Novels for Students,* Vol. 4, ed. Marie Rose Napierkowski (Detroit: Gale, 1998), pp. 61–64.

When quoting material reprinted from a book that appears in a volume of *NfS,* the following form may be used:

Adams, Timothy Dow. "Richard Wright: "Wearing the Mask," in *Telling Lies in Modern American Autobiography* (University of North Carolina Press, 1990), 69–83; excerpted and reprinted in *Novels for Students,* Vol. 5, eds. Sheryl Ciccarelli and Marie Napierkowski (Detroit: Gale, 1999), pp. 59–61.

We Welcome Your Suggestions

The editor of *Novels for Students* welcomes your comments and ideas. Readers who wish to suggest novels to appear in future volumes, or who have other suggestions, are cordially invited to contact the editor. You may contact the editor via e-mail at: **ForStudentsEditors@galegroup.com.** Or write to the editor at:

Editor, *Novels for Students*
Gale Group
27500 Drake Road
Farmington Hills, MI 48331–3535

Literary Chronology

1840: Thomas Hardy is born, the son of a master mason, in Higher Bockhampton, in Dorsetshire, England, on July 2.

1850: Robert Louis Stevenson is born in Edinburgh, Scotland, on November 13 to Thomas, a civil engineer, and Margaret Isabella (Balfour) Stevenson.

1862: Edith Wharton (maiden name Edith Newbold Jones) is born to a wealthy family in New York City on January 24.

1878: Thomas Hardy's *The Return of the Native* is published. Meeting with mixed reviews at publication, the book becomes Hardy's sixth and perhaps best known novel.

1879: E. M. Forster is born in London on January 1 to Alice Clara Whichelo Forster (known as Lily) and an architect named Edmund Morgan, who dies of consumption in 1880.

1886: Robert Louis Stevenson's *The Strange Case of Dr. Jekyll and Mr. Hyde* is published. It becomes an immediate best-seller in Great Britain.

1894: Jean Toomer is born as Nathan Eugene Toomer on December 26 in Washington, D.C. His father, Nathan Toomer Sr., was the son of a slave and left Jean's mother shortly before the birth of Nathan Eugene.

1894: Robert Louis Stevenson dies on December 3 in Apia, Samoa.

1905: John O'Hara is born on January 31 to an Irish Catholic physician in Pottsville, Pennsylvania.

1908: E. M. Forster's *A Room with a View* is published. Begun in 1902 but not published 1908, the book is Forster's third novel.

1920: Edith Wharton's *The Age of Innocence* is published. Set in late nineteenth-century New York society, the novel becomes a best-seller and wins the Pulitzer Prize the following year.

1920: Richard George Adams is born May 9 in Newbury, Berkshire, England.

1923: Jean Toomer's *Cane* is published. The book comes to be considered a leading influence on the Harlem Renaissance.

1926: Margaret Laurence is born Jean Margaret Wemyss on July 18 in the small town of Neepawa, Manitoba, Canada, to Robert Wemyss and Verna Simpson Wemyss.

1928: Thomas Hardy dies on January 11. His ashes are buried in the Poet's Corner of Westminster Abbey, London, next to those of Charles Dickens. His heart is removed and buried separately in Dorset.

1934: John O'Hara's *Appointment in Samarra* is published. It becomes a popular and critical success, considered by many to be his best novel.

1936: Frank Conroy is born on January 15 in New York City to an absent, mentally ill father and a cold, unloving mother.

1936: Jean Auel is born in Chicago on February 18.

1937: Edith Wharton dies of cardiac arrest in France on August 11.

1946: Chris Crutcher is born in the small and isolated logging town of Cascade, Idaho, on July 17.

1948: Ntozake Shange, originally named Paulette Williams, is born on October 18 in Trenton, New Jersey.

1949: Dorothy Allison is born on April 11 in Greenville, South Carolina, to a poor, unmarried fifteen-year-old girl.

1961: Susan Power is born October 12 in Chicago, Illinois.

1964: Bret Easton Ellis is born on March 7 in Los Angeles, California.

1964: Margaret Laurence's *The Stone Angel* is published. Although Laurence had been publishing fiction for a decade, it is this novel that first wins her a wide and appreciative audience.

1967: Jean Toomer dies on March 30 in Doylestown, Pennsylvania.

1970: John O'Hara dies of a heart attack on April 11.

1970: E. M. Forster dies on June 7 from a series of strokes.

1972: Richard Adams's *Watership Down* is published. The book is originally published by a small press, then by a larger press. It becomes a huge success and wins both the Guardian Award and the Carnegie Medal.

1980: Jean Auel's *The Clan of the Cave Bear* is published. In 1986 the novel is made into a feature film directed by Michael Chapman, scripted by John Sayles, and starring Pamela Reed as Iza and Daryl Hannah as Ayla.

1985: Ntozake Shange's *Betsey Brown* is published. The novel portrays the small and large struggles of a thirteen-year-old girl while lovingly sketching the way of life in an all-black middle-class enclave at a time when the incipient Civil Rights Movement is agitating for integration.

1985: Bret Easton Ellis' *Less Than Zero* is published. It becomes a commercial success and is adapted to film in 1987.

1987: Chris Crutcher's *The Crazy Horse Electric Game*, a coming-of-age story, is published. Crutcher has received the prestigious Margaret A. Edwards Award for his young-adult writings.

1987: Margaret Laurence dies of cancer on January 5.

1992: Dorothy Allison's *Bastard Out of Carolina* is published. Allison's own experience of growing up in a poor, white, southern family, in which her stepfather sexually abused her for six years starting when she was only five years old provides background for the novel.

1993: Frank Conroy's *Body and Soul* is published. It becomes a best-seller in the United States.

1994: Susan Power's *The Grass Dancer* is published. The novel, written while Power's was in the creative writing program at the University of Iowa, receives immediate critical acclaim and also wins the 1995 PEN/ Hemingway Award for best first fiction of the year.

Acknowledgments

The editors wish to thank the copyright holders of the excerpted criticism included in this volume and the permissions managers of many book and magazine publishing companies for assisting us in securing reproduction rights. We are also grateful to the staffs of the Detroit Public Library, the Library of Congress, the University of Detroit Mercy Library, Wayne State University Purdy/ Kresge Library Complex, and the University of Michigan Libraries for making their resources available to us. Following is a list of the copyright holders who have granted us permission to reproduce material in this volume of *Novels for Students* (*NfS*). Every effort has been made to trace copyright, but if omissions have been made, please let us know.

COPYRIGHTED MATERIALS IN *NfS*, VOLUME 11, WERE REPRODUCED FROM THE FOLLOWING PERIODICALS:

Arizona Quarterly, v. 38, Autumn, 1982 for "Dr. Jekyll and Mr. Hyde: Anatomy of Misperception" by Daniel V. Fraustino. Copyright © 1982 by the Regents of the University of Arizona. Reproduced by permission of the publisher and the author.—*Black American Literature Forum*, v. 13, Winter, 1979. Reproduced by permission.—*Canadian Literature*, v. 93, Summer, 1982 for "A Feminist Reading of The Stone Angel" by Constance Rooke. Reproduced by permission of the author.—*Commonweal*, v. 120, November 5, 1993. Copyright © 1993 Commonweal Publishing Co., Inc. Reproduced by permission of Commonweal

Foundation.—*Extrapolation*, v. 27, Spring, 1985. Copyright © 1985 by Kent State University Press. Reproduced by permission.—*The Horn Book Magazine*, v. 49, June, 1973; v. 50, August, 1974; v. 64, May, 1988. Copyright, 1973, 1974, 1988 by The Horn Book, Inc., 11 Beacon St., Suite 1000, Boston, MA 02108. All rights reserved. All reproduced by permission.—*The Hudson Review*, v. XL, Winter, 1988. Copyright © 1988 by The Hudson Review, Inc. Reproduced by permission.— *Journal of Popular Culture*, v. 28, Winter, 1994. Copyright © 1994 by Ray B. Browne. Reproduced by permission.—*Ms.*, v. XIV, March, 1986 for "Speculative Fiction" by Lindsay Van Gelder. Copyright © 1986 *Ms.* Magazine. Reprinted by permission of the author.—*The Nation*, New York, v. 255, December 28, 1992. © 1992 *The Nation* magazine/ The Nation Company, Inc. Reproduced by permission.—*The New Republic*, v. 209, October 18, 1993. © 1993 The New Republic, Inc. Reproduced by permission of *The New Republic*.—*Publishers Weekly*, v. 240, August 23, 1993. Copyright © 1993 by Cahners Magazine Division of Reed Publishing USA. Reproduced by permission.— *School Library Journal*, v. 117, March 1, 1992. Copyright © 1992. Reproduced from *School Library Journal*, a Cahners/R. R. Bowker Publication, by permission.—*Telos: A Quarterly Journal of Critical Thought*, n. 76, Summer, 1988. © 1988 Telos Press, Ltd. Reproduced by permission.—*The Times Literary Supplement*, n. 4783, December 2, 1994. © The Times Supplements Limited 1994.

COPYRIGHTED MATERIALS IN *NfS*, VOLUME 11, WERE REPRODUCED FROM THE FOLLOWING BOOKS:

Baker, Jr., Houston A. From *Singers of Daybreak: Studies in Black American Literature*. Howard University Press, 1983. Copyright © 1974 by Houston A. Baker, Jr. All rights reserved. Reproduced by permission.—Carson, Edward Russell. From *The Fiction of John O'Hara*. University of Pittsburgh Press, 1961. Copyright © 1961 University of Pittsburgh Press. Reproduced by permission.—Davis, Terry. From *Presenting Chris Crutcher*. Twayne Publishers, Inc., 1997. Copyright © 1997 by Twayne Publishers, Inc. The Gale Group.—Fleishman, Avrom. From *Fiction and the Ways of Knowing: Essays on British Novelists*. University of Texas Press, 1978. Copyright © 1978 by the University of Texas Press. All rights reserved. Reproduced by permission.—Freese, Peter. From "Bret Easton Ellis, 'Less Than Zero': Entropy in the 'MTV Novel'?" in *Modes of Narrative: Approaches to American, Canadian and British Fiction, Presented to Helmut Bonheim*. Edited by Reingard M. Nischik and Barbara Korte. Königshausen & Neumann, 1990. © Verlag Dr. Johannes K. Königshausen and Dr. Thomas Neumann, Würzburg 1990. Reproduced by permission.—From *Twaynes Authors Series: Twayne English Authors*. Twayne Publishers, 1999. The Gale Group.—Geduld, Harry M. From an introduction to *The Definitive Dr. Jekyll and Mr. Hyde Companion*. Edited by Harry M. Geduld. Garland Publishing, 1983. Introduction © 1983, by Garland Publishing, Inc. All rights reserved. Reproduced by permission.—Grebstein, Sheldon Norman. From *John O'Hara*. Twayne Publishers, 1966. Copyright © 1966 by Twayne Publishers. The Gale Group.—Haralson, Eric. From *Queer Forster*. Edited by Robert K. Martin and George Piggford. The University of Chicago Press, 1997. © 1997 by The University of Chicago Press. All rights reserved. Reproduced by permission.—Hynes, Jennifer A. "The Age of Innocence: Overview" in *Reference Guide to American Literature. Third Edition*. Edited by Jim Kamp. St. James Press, 1994. Copyright © 1994 St. James Press.—O'Connell, Nicholas and Jean M. Auel. From an interview in *At The Field's End: Interviews with Twenty Pacific Northwest Writers*. Madrona Publishers, 1987. Copyright © 1987 Nicholas O'Connell. All rights reserved. Reproduced by permission of Nicholas O'Connell.—Scruggs, Charles and Lee VanDemarr. From *Jean Toomer and the Terrors of American History*. University of Pennsylvania Press, 1998. Copyright © 1998 by the University of Pennsylvania Press. All rights reserved. Reproduced by permission.—Walton, Geoffrey. From *Edith Wharton: A Critical Interpretation*. Fairleigh Dickinson University Press, 1970. © 1970 by Associated University Presses, Inc. All rights reserved. Reproduced by permission.

PHOTOGRAPHS AND ILLUSTRATIONS APPEARING IN *NfS*, VOLUME 11, WERE RECEIVED FROM THE FOLLOWING SOURCES:

Reproduced by permission.—Hannah, Daryl, Rory Crowley, Pamela Reed, in the film "Clan of the Cave Bear," 1986, photograph. Warner Bros. The Kobal Collection. Reproduced by permission.—Hardy, Thomas, photograph. Archive Photos, Inc. Reproduced by permission.—Home healthcare worker taking woman's blood pressure, photograph by Mark Gibson. Corbis-Bettmann. Reproduced by permission.—Ken Hill, 19th century English country house, photograph. © Clay Perry/Corbis Corporation. Reproduced by permission.—Laurence, Margaret, photograph. © David Laurence Photo. Reproduced by permission of the photographer.—Man reaching down into rabbit burrow, photograph. © Hulton-Deutsch Collection/Corbis. Reproduced by permission.—March, Frederic, in the film "Dr. Jekyll and Mr. Hyde," 1932, photograph. The Kobal Collection. Reproduced by permission.—O'Hara, John, photograph. The Library of Congress.—Pfeiffer, Michelle, and Daniel Day-Lewis, in the film "The Age of Innocence," 1993, photograph by Phillip Caruso. The Kobal Collection. Reproduced by permission.—Physical therapist administering balance and coordination tests, photograph. Custom Medical Stock Photo. Reproduced by permission.—Power, Susan, photograph. © 1994 Debi Milligan. Reproduced by permission.—Rabbits, scene from the animated film version of Richard Adams novel "Watership Down," directed by Martin Rosen. The Kobal Collection. Reproduced by permission.—Sands, Julian, and Helena Bonham Carter in the film "A Room with a View," 1986, photograph. The Kobal Collection. Reproduced by permission.—Shange, Ntozake, photograph. AP/Wide World Photos. Reproduced by permission.—Sioux dancers, wood engraving. © Corbis. Reproduced by permission.—Sioux war chiefs, photograph by Herman Heyn. The Library of Congress.—Skaters in Central Park, illustration. © Bettmann/Corbis. Reproduced by permission.—Stevenson, Robert Louis, engraving. The Library of Congress.—Toomer, Jean, photograph.—Venus of Willendorf, ca. 28,000-25,000 B.C. © Archivo Iconografico, S.A./Corbis. Reproduced by permission.—Waksman, Selman A., photograph. The Library of Congress.—Weathered house in rural South Carolina, photograph. © Peter Johnson/Corbis. Reproduced by permission.—Weeping willow tree, photograph. © Richard Hamilton Smith/Corbis. Reproduced by permission.—Wharton, Edith, photograph. The Library of Congress.

Contributors

Bryan Aubrey: Aubrey holds a Ph.D. in English and has published many articles on twentieth-century literature. Entry on *The Stone Angel.* Original essay on *The Stone Angel.*

Liz Brent: Brent has a Ph.D. in American culture, specializing in film studies, from the University of Michigan. She is a freelance writer and teaches courses in the history of American cinema. Entry on *Less Than Zero.* Original essay on *Betsey Brown.*

Jennifer Bussey: Bussey holds a master's degree in interdisciplinary studies and a bachelor's degree in English literature. She is an independent writer specializing in literature. Entry on *The Age of Innocence.* Original essay on *The Age of Innocence.*

Michele Drohan: Drohan is a professional editor and writer who specializes in fiction and nonfiction for young adults and children. Entry on *The Crazy Horse Electric Game.* Original essay on *The Crazy Horse Electric Game.*

Jeremy W. Hubbell: Hubbell has an M.Litt. from the University of Aberdeen, Scotland, and currently seeks a Ph.D. in history at the State University of New York at Stony Brook. Entry on *A Room with a View.* Original essay on *A Room with a View.*

David Kelly: Kelly is an instructor of creative writing and literature at several community colleges in Illinois. Entries on *Cane* and *Return of the*

Native. Original essays on *Cane* and *Return of the Native.*

Lois Kerschen: Kerschen is a grants coordinator for the Houston Independent School District, the author of *American Proverbs about Women,* and a freelance writer. Entry on *Body and Soul.* Original essay on *Body and Soul.*

Rena Korb: Korb has a master's degree in English literature and creative writing and has written for a wide variety of educational publishers. Entry on *Bastard out of Carolina.* Original essay on *Bastard out of Carolina.*

Caroline M. Levchuck: Levchuck, a writer and editor, has published articles on literature along with nonfiction essays and children's books. Entry on *Appointment in Samarra.* Original essay on *Appointment in Samarra.*

Tabitha McIntosh-Byrd: McIntosh-Byrd is an English Literature instructor at the University of Pennsylvania. Original essay on *Less Than Zero.*

Sarah Madsen Hardy: Madsen Hardy has a doctorate in English literature and is a freelance writer and editor. Entry on *Betsey Brown.* Original essay on *Betsey Brown.*

Wendy Perkins: Perkins is an associate professor of English at Prince George's Community College in Maryland and has published several articles on British and American authors. Entry on *Dr. Jekyll and Mr. Hyde.* Original essay on *Dr. Jekyll and Mr. Hyde.*

Michael Rex: Rex is an adjunct professor at the University of Detroit Mercy. Entry on *The Clan of the Cave Bear*. Original essay on *The Clan of the Cave Bear*.

Kelly Winters: Winters is a freelance writer and editor and has written for a wide variety of academic and educational publishers. Entries on *The Grass Dancer* and *Watership Down*. Original essays on *The Grass Dancer* and *Watership Down*.

The Age of Innocence

Edith Wharton
1920

Already a successful novelist in 1920 when she completed *The Age of Innocence,* Edith Wharton anticipated best-selling status for her new novel. *The Age of Innocence,* set in late nineteenth-century New York society, did indeed become a best-seller and won the Pulitzer Prize the following year. Wharton was the first woman to receive this high literary honor. The novel is both nostalgic and satirical in its depiction of old New York, with its often-stifling conventions and manners and its insistence on propriety. Wharton had written about old New York before in *The House of Mirth* and *The Custom of the Country,* but in *The Age of Innocence* she is less caustic in her criticism of its culture. Having worked diligently in relief efforts during World War I, Wharton recalled her formative years in New York society as a time of stability, even though that stability was the product of strict adherence to accepted rules of conduct.

Because of similarities between Wharton's style and that of her friend Henry James, *The Age of Innocence* is frequently compared to James' writing, especially his novel *A Portrait of a Lady.* Serious students are often encouraged to read the two titles in order to compare James's point of view to Wharton's distinctly feminine sensibility.

The Age of Innocence is regarded as a skilled portrait of the struggle between the individual and the community. It is also a work that explores the dangers and liberties of change as a society moves from a familiar, traditional culture to one that is less formal and affords its members greater free-

Edith Wharton

dom. The novel's staying power is generally attributed to its presentation of such universal concerns as women's changing roles, the importance of family in a civilized society, and the universal conflict between passion and duty.

Author Biography

Edith Newbold Jones was born to a wealthy family in New York City on January 24, 1862, and soon learned the manners and traditions of society life that would characterize her fiction. Because her family lived in Europe for much of her childhood, she was educated abroad and privately. She enjoyed travel and reading from a young age, and while her parents supported these interests, they disapproved of her ambitions to become an author. Her lifelong love of books, foreign places, and nature would figure into her successful career as a writer. Biographers depict her as a lively, congenial woman who made friends easily. This may account for her friendships with such notable men as author Henry James and Theodore Roosevelt.

In 1885, she married Edward (Teddy) Robbins Wharton, a banker who was thirteen years her senior. They lived in New York City; Newport,

Rhode Island; and Lenox, Massachusetts; and traveled to Europe often. As she became more serious about her writing, Wharton designed and built a home in Lenox, called "The Mount," as a writer's retreat. From 1900 to 1911, she often went there to escape social pressures and immerse herself in undistracted writing. Her marriage was unhappy, however, and because Teddy had numerous affairs, embezzled her money, and struggled with mental illness, Wharton divorced him in 1913. Wharton was independent and never remarried, although rumors persist about two important men in her life who may have been her lovers.

Published in 1905, *The House of Mirth* was Wharton's first critically acclaimed novel. By this time, she had become a good friend of Henry James, and she followed in his footsteps and became an expatriate in Paris, enjoying extended stays beginning in 1907. When she sold The Mount in 1911, she made Paris her permanent residence. Her talent responded well to the new environment, and she published volumes of short stories and novels, which earned her a faithful following, critical acceptance, and a Pulitzer Prize in 1921 for *The Age of Innocence*. In addition to being the first woman to win the Pulitzer Prize, Wharton was the first woman to be awarded the Gold Medal of the National Institute of Arts and Letters. She also received an honorary degree from prestigious Yale University in 1923, one of the few occasions that brought her back to the United States.

Wharton died of cardiac arrest in France on August 11, 1937.

Plot Summary

Book 1: Chapters 1–9

The book opens as members of old New York society gather at the opera. Although they have not come to the opera together, Newland Archer rests his gaze on his fiancée, May Welland. He considers her innocence and how he will educate and enlighten her, so that she can become his ideal woman. A stir is created when May's cousin, Countess Ellen Olenska, arrives in the Wellands' box. She married a Polish Count and lived in Europe until she left her husband, reportedly with his secretary. By inviting her to their opera box, the Wellands knowingly risk becoming the subject of gossip.

Newland thinks about the Welland family matriarch, Catherine Mingott, who is a powerful figure in New York society. Catherine is an enormous woman, whose weight prevents her from leaving her house. Still, she is a respected and animated member of her community.

During intermission, Newland visits May in her family's box, as a show of support in light of the scandalous appearance of Ellen. He suggests that they announce their engagement right away to restore dignity to the Welland family. After a brief conversation with Ellen, Newland is intrigued by her lack of regard for the rules and conventions of New York.

Regina and Julius Beaufort host a ball after the opera, where Newland and May announce their engagement. The newly engaged couple visits Catherine to seek her blessing, and as they are leaving her house, Ellen arrives with Julius Beaufort. Newland concludes that Ellen's European experience has rendered her unaware of the social impropriety of her behavior.

May's parents plan a dinner to be held as a formal introduction of Ellen. When almost everyone refuses to attend, the van der Luydens, an elderly, aristocratic couple, respond by inviting Ellen to their home for a formal reception. Because they are role models of propriety, New York society follows their lead. At the reception, Newland again talks to Ellen and is drawn to her. He visits her the next day and she admits her loneliness. Newland is sympathetic toward her and aware of being anxious in her presence.

Book 1: Chapters 10–17

As a lawyer, Newland is asked to help convince Ellen not to divorce her husband. Despite his opinion that she should be free to do as she wishes, he agrees and explains to her that although the law may support her divorce, New York society will not. While she may be happier divorced, her happiness will come at a cost to her family. Resigned, she agrees not to pursue the matter.

May and her family go to St. Augustine for the winter, and Newland sees Ellen at the opera. Soon after, he discovers that she has gone away with the van der Luydens to Skuytercliff, so he follows her. Once there, he finds Ellen and they speak in private until, to their surprise, Julius arrives. Newland realizes then that Julius is pursuing Ellen romantically, and he returns to New York. When Ellen sends a note asking to see him, he instead leaves for St. Augustine.

Newland asks May to move up their wedding date. May suggests that he is only asking because he loves another woman and is impatient to do the honorable thing. She adds that if he does truly love someone else, she will step aside for his sake. Newland denies loving anyone but her.

Returning to New York, Newland visits Catherine to persuade her to allow the wedding to be hastened. She agrees.

Newland visits Ellen the next evening. He tells her that she is the woman he should be marrying, if it were possible. They kiss, but when Newland offers to leave May, Ellen will not hear of it. She has learned from him that it is wrong to gain happiness at the expense of others.

Book 2: Chapters 19–26

May and Newland marry and go to an estate near Skuytercliff for their wedding night. While in London on their honeymoon, Newland meets a French tutor, Monsieur Rivière, who inquires about opportunities in New York. Newland sadly realizes that there is nothing for an intellectual like Rivière in New York.

After returning home, Newland hears that Ellen has gone to Boston, so he lies about a business trip in order to see her. She is surprised to see him and explains that she has just met with her husband's emissary. Although he offered a great deal of money for her to return, she rejected it. Newland and Ellen go to lunch, where he bemoans the fact that he married May because Ellen told him to do so. She agrees to stay close as long as they never do anything that would hurt May.

Back in New York, Newland runs into Rivière, who reveals that he was the emissary sent by the Count to speak to Ellen. After a very tense discussion, the men realize that neither of them thinks it is in her best interest to return to Poland. Newland secretly wonders if Rivière is the secretary with whom Ellen was reported to have run away.

At Thanksgiving, everyone discusses rumors of Julius' financial problems. Next, they gossip about Ellen, who has gone to Washington. When Sillerton Jackson suggests that Ellen is being "kept" by Julius, and therefore will be in dire straits should he lose his money, Newland becomes enraged. At home, Newland tells May that he has business in Washington. She assents to his leaving, adding that he should be sure to see Ellen while he is there, thus letting him know that she is aware of his real reason for making the trip.

Book 2: Chapters 27–34

Julius faces financial ruin and public scorn. His wife visits Catherine, the head of her family, to ask for help, but she is rejected. Catherine then suffers a mild stroke, after which she sends for Ellen. Newland cancels his Washington trip and offers to pick Ellen up from the station. In the carriage, he speaks openly of how he longs to find a way for them to be together. When she responds with talk of reality rather than dreams, he gets out of the carriage to walk home.

Catherine's condition improves, and she sends for Newland. She explains that Ellen has agreed to stay and take care of her, and she wants Newland to defend Ellen to the family. Thinking that Ellen has agreed to stay in order to be closer to him, he agrees.

Newland and Ellen meet at a museum. They talk of their helplessness in their situation, and Ellen insists that they not fall into the common trap of having an affair. That night, May is in good spirits and tells him that she visited Catherine and, while there, had a nice talk with Ellen.

A few nights later, Newland prepares to tell May about his feelings for Ellen. May interrupts and tells him that whatever he has to say makes no difference, since Ellen has decided to leave for Paris. Newland decides that he will follow her.

May hosts an elaborate going-away dinner for Ellen. Although Newland does not have the opportunity to talk to Ellen privately before she is driven home, he resolves to go through with his plan. After the guests have gone, he tells May that he has decided to travel. She responds by telling him that she will be unable to go with him because she is pregnant. She admits that two weeks before, when she reported having such a good talk with Ellen, May had told Ellen she was pregnant, even though she was not yet sure of it.

The novel's last chapter takes place twenty-six years later. May has given Newland three children (two boys and a girl) and has died of pneumonia two years previously. Newland has lived an honorable life, all the while harboring memories of Ellen. Called to Paris on business, Newland's older son, Dallas, insists that his father accompany him. There, Dallas arranges for a meeting with Ellen. In a frank conversation, Dallas admits that he knows something of his father's past with Ellen, as May had revealed to him that Newland had given up the thing he wanted most in favor of his family.

When Newland and Dallas approach Ellen's building, Newland tells Dallas to go in without him. Dallas asks what he should tell Ellen, and Newland responds, "Say I'm old-fashioned: that's enough." As Newland sits outside the building, he imagines the meeting going on inside and ultimately determines not to go in. He walks back to his hotel.

Characters

Janey Archer

Janey is Newland's unmarried sister. She lives with her mother and Newland. She and her mother grow ferns, do needlework, and seek out the latest gossip.

Mrs. Archer

Mrs. Archer is Newland's widowed mother. She and her daughter share a room upstairs so Newland can enjoy having more space to himself downstairs. Mrs. Archer follows social rules and manners to the letter, and tries to protect her grown daughter from certain topics because she is unmarried.

Newland Archer

The main character of the novel, Newland Archer is a young man who has grown up in New York society. He lives with his widowed mother and his unmarried sister, and is engaged to May Welland. Seeing her as an innocent, he imagines that he will educate her and show her the ways of the world. Because he reads a variety of books, he fancies himself erudite and well-educated, not realizing how much his own thoughts and experiences are limited by his immediate environment. In Chapter One, Wharton writes:

> In matters intellectual and artistic Newland Archer felt himself distinctly the superior of these chosen specimens of old New York gentility; he had probably read more, thought more, and even seen a good deal more of the world, than any other man of the number.

Newland has a position as a lawyer, but is not at all serious about his career. This is common in the society depicted, among young men whose families are wealthy.

When he meets Countess Ellen Olenska, Newland is drawn to her mysterious and unconventional ways. She helps him see the artifice of old New York, as he helps her understand the complex demands of decorum. He falls in love with her, but their love is doomed by propriety and responsibility. His struggle is essentially between his individual desires and the good of his community and family.

Newland chooses to stay with his wife, who is pregnant with their first child, but holds onto his memories and fantasies of what might have been. He creates a pleasant life for himself and his family, and even dabbles in politics at the insistence of Theodore Roosevelt. Twenty-six years later, he is a widower and finds himself in Paris, where Ellen is living. Faced with the opportunity to meet her and possibly renew their romance, he decides not to see her.

Julius Beaufort

Julius was not born into New York society, but is accepted because he has married into a respectable family. The details of his past are shady, a fact which is overlooked once he is a member of high society. His importance in the social arena is strengthened by the fact that he and his wife have the only private ballroom in their community. The annual ball becomes a major social event, and this is where May and Newland announce their engagement. For a short time, Julius pursues Ellen to be his mistress, but she is not interested.

When Julius' unscrupulous business dealings become public knowledge, he and his wife are quickly shunned by society. At the end of the book, Newland's son Dallas is engaged to marry the daughter of Julius and his second wife. The narrator notes that although Julius' ruin was a major event in its time, years later it is barely remembered.

Regina Beaufort

Regina is a relative of Catherine, head of the Mingott-Welland family. She marries Julius for the unconventional reason that he has recently become a millionaire. Because Regina's husband is considered an outsider, her peers take a little time to accept him.

Regina is beautiful but indecisive, and ignorant of her husband's financial decisions. When Julius' business dealings cause their ruin, Regina visits her mother to ask for help, but is refused. Catherine tells her that a wife's place is with her husband, in honor or dishonor.

Sillerton Jackson

Jackson is a bachelor who lives with his sister, Sophy. He has an incredible memory for old gossip and New York families. He is uniquely able

Media Adaptations

- *The Age of Innocence* was adapted as a silent film by Olga Printzlau, produced in 1924 by Warner Brothers. In 1934, Margaret Ayer Barnes, Victor Heerman, and Sarah Y. Mason adapted the novel as a film in a production by RKO Radio Pictures, Inc. Most recently, in 1993, Martin Scorsese directed a Columbia Pictures adaptation of the novel by Scorsese and Jay Cocks. The film starred Daniel Day-Lewis as Newland Archer, Michelle Pfeiffer as Countess Olenska, and Winona Ryder as May Welland.

- A well-received stage adaptation was performed on Broadway in 1929.

- Numerous audio adaptations have been made for listeners to enjoy the story on tape. These include releases by Books on Tape, 1982; Bantam Doubleday Dell Publishing Group, 1992; Bantam Books-Audio, and Random House, both 1993; Big Ben Audio, Blackstone Audio, Dove Entertainment (read by Joanne Woodward), and Penguin Audiobooks, all 1996; Bookcassette and Brilliance Corp., both 1997; and Audio Partners Publishing Corp., 1999.

to understand how all the pieces of history fit into the sprawling family trees of the upper class. Because he is caught up in gossip, he fails to recognize the goodness and decency in his fellow New Yorkers.

Lawrence Lefferts

Lefferts is New York's expert on good taste. He often lectures on the virtues of marital fidelity, even though everyone knows about his numerous affairs. Like Jackson, he prefers to focus on negative gossip than on the positive aspects of their social culture.

Medora Manson

Medora is Ellen's eccentric aunt, who took care of her orphaned niece throughout Ellen's childhood. Medora has been repeatedly widowed and her resources are almost spent, which has no effect on her lively and engaging spirit.

Catherine Mingott

Formerly Catherine Spicer of Staten Island, Catherine is the Mingott-Welland family matriarch. Widowed at the age of twenty-eight, she lives in a slightly unconventional house, which she never leaves because her obesity will not allow it. Despite her tendency to thumb her nose at established rules, she holds a great deal of social power in her family. The most important thing to her is the integrity of her family, and she is vocal in her criticisms and blessings. Unlike the rest of the family, Catherine likes Ellen very much, and is sympathetic to her.

Countess Ellen Olenska

Ellen is May's mysterious cousin, who arrives in New York and creates a stir merely by attending the opera. After marrying a Polish count and living in Europe for a number of years, she has determined that her husband is too much of a scoundrel to bear. She has left him, apparently with the help of his secretary, and has returned to New York to seek a divorce. In light of the rules of propriety, her situation is scandalous and risks the good name of her family. In contrast to May, Ellen represents sophistication, worldliness, and tragedy.

Having lived outside the New York milieu, Ellen has acquired "Bohemian" tastes, and she has become an independent woman. Her disregard of New York rules of conduct intrigues Newland, who is sent to talk her out of pursuing the divorce. They begin to spend time together, and realize they are passionately in love with each other. Ellen is unwilling to bring pain to her cousin May, however, so she refuses to run away with Newland. When May tells her she is pregnant, Ellen decides to go to Europe and cease being a distraction to Newland.

Monsieur Rivière

Newland meets Monsieur Rivière, a French tutor, while he and May are traveling in London on their honeymoon. Later, Rivière shows up in New York, telling Newland that he was sent by Ellen's husband to try to convince her to return to Poland. It is an odd twist of fate, but Newland is most interested to know if Rivière is the secretary with whom Ellen was reported to have run away. The answer is never made clear.

Mrs. Thorley Rushworth

A few years prior to the events of the novel, Newland had an affair with Mrs. Rushworth, a married woman. While the affair in no way marred his reputation, public knowledge of it tarnished her good name. The narrator describes her as "silly" and imagines that she was taken more with the secrecy of the affair than with Newland's charms.

Louisa van der Luyden

Louisa and her husband are the last of the true aristocrats living in New York. Their roots are European and their influence is great, despite their lack of socializing. When Ellen has been disgraced, Mrs. Archer pleads her case to the van der Luydens, who come to her rescue and encourage the other members of society to accept her.

May Welland

May is the sum of her New York society upbringing. She is beautiful, proper, and innocent. Although she enjoys "masculine" activities, such as sports, she is determined to be a perfect wife to Newland. May seems childlike and carefree, but the reader soon realizes that she is more knowledgeable about the complexities of relationships than Newland is. She knows that he will conform to the dictates of their community, and she uses this to manipulate him. Afraid of losing him to Ellen, her cousin, she tells Ellen that she is pregnant, knowing that Ellen is a decent and honorable person who would never allow herself to be the reason Newland left his wife and baby. She reveals her pregnancy to Newland just as she senses he is preparing to leave her.

May and Newland eventually have three children together. May dies of pneumonia after caring for their son, who recovers from the illness. After her death, Newland discovers that she knew of his love for Ellen and had told their older son that Newland had given up the thing he most wanted for the good of the family. As was proper, however, she never brought up the subject with her husband.

Ned Winsett

A friend of Newland's, Ned is a poor journalist who provides Newland with intelligent conversation and new ideas. Ned encourages Newland to go into politics, but Newland finds the idea laughable until he is much older.

Themes

Propriety and Decorum

The Age of Innocence is a detailed portrayal of social conventions and respectability in late nineteenth-century high society. Newland has grown up in this environment and has internalized all the manners that dictate behavior in old New York. Even intimate matters are subject to rules of etiquette, as when May lets Newland guess that she cares for him, which is the only declaration of love allowed a young unmarried woman. Gossiping is completely acceptable, yet members of society strive to uphold, above all things, their own reputations. Sillerton Jackson and Lawrence Lefferts are held up as experts on New York's family trees, proper form, and good taste.

Every event in old New York is subject to ritual. When May and Newland are engaged, they must make a series of social calls. On his wedding day, Newland wonders what flaws Lawrence Lefferts will find in the event. As Ellen prepares to leave for Paris, May hosts a formal dinner in her honor. As May and Newland's first occasion for entertaining on such a scale, the dinner is a milestone for them. At the same time, it serves an important social function, as Wharton writes in chapter 33: "There were certain things that had to be done, and if done at all, done handsomely and thoroughly; and one of these, in the old New York code, was the tribal rally around a kinswoman about to be eliminated from the tribe."

The novel's conclusion shows Newland refusing to see Ellen, even though they are both free to be together at last. Some critics argue that Newland's sense of decorum is so deeply ingrained that he cannot bring himself to realize the fantasy he carried around for so many years. James W. Tuttleton, writing in *Dictionary of Literary Biography, Volume Twelve: American Realists and Naturalists,* states that Newland forgoes the chance to have a romantic relationship with Ellen "out of respect for the memory of his marriage." Even as a widower, and even as the strict rules of conduct are passing out of style, Newland cannot bring himself to make decisions outside the parameters of propriety that have governed his life. It seems that things are as they were in chapter 1, where the narrator remarks that "what was or was not 'the thing' played a part as important in Newland Archer's New York as the inscrutable totem terrors that had ruled the destinies of his forefathers thousands of years ago."

The Role of Women

The contrast between Ellen and May is sharp. May is the pure and beautiful product of old New York and all of its elements. After she and Newland are married, he often observes how she is quickly becoming a younger version of her mother. May represents traditional womanhood in the New York social system. On the other hand, Ellen has been absent from New York for quite some time, and her time in Europe has changed her. She relies on Newland to help her navigate the treacherous social waters in which she finds herself upon her scandal-ridden return. She is mysterious and exotic, yet accessible. Unlike the other women in the community, Ellen has had experiences that are hers alone, not shared by an entire social set. She views herself differently than the other New York women view themselves, and as a result, she is seen as a completely different kind of woman.

In his introduction to the novel, Paul Montazzoli observes that a reader may approach the novel not as a romance, but as a "feminist thesis novel." He remarks:

> That May is mentally too lumpish a companion for Newland (at least according to his perhaps too-flattering self-image) he acknowledges as the fault of the old New York patriarchy that formed her. Ironically, Newland himself is a pillar of this patriarchy, with a few cracks here and there through which the charms of Ellen gain entrance. That rumors of an affair in Ellen's past damage her socially, while equivalent rumors about Newland damage him not at all, strikingly illustrates the double standard.

In the novel's setting, women, though their roles are slowly expanding, are still subject to such double standards. In chapter 7, Newland expresses his view that women should be as free as men are. Wharton adds:

> "Nice" women, however wronged, would never claim the kind of freedom he meant, and generous-minded men like himself were therefore—in the heat of the argument—the more chivalrously ready to concede it to them.

The Individual and Society

Newland desperately wants to follow his heart and be with Ellen, but his society would never accept such a decision. He is divided, but ultimately cannot abandon the conventions and expectations of the only society he has ever known. When he decides to run away to Europe with Ellen, May announces her pregnancy, and he knows that this turn of events seals his fate. He would never be such a cad as to abandon his wife and baby, so he learns to accept the life that is laid out before him. For the

Topics for Further Study

- Compare Wharton's depiction of New York society life with what you know about tribal societies, past or present. Do you think that Newland Archer's use of anthropological terms to describe his community is justified? If so, what can you conclude about human nature? If not, why do you suppose Newland thinks of his environment in this way?

- Compare and contrast Countess Ellen Olenska in *The Age of Innocence* and Hester Prynne in Nathaniel Hawthorne's *The Scarlet Letter.*

- Consider the novel's title, and make a case for why you believe Wharton chose it. Do you find that there are multiple meanings, or does the title refer to one specific character or event in the novel?

- Do you think Newland would have followed Ellen to Europe if May had not announced her pregnancy? Research three different psychological theories (i.e., behaviorism, gestalt, rogerian, etc.), and make a prediction based on each one.

- At the end of the novel, Newland muses on how things have changed between his generation and Dallas' generation. Research American history at the turn of the century to get a better idea of what major changes took place at this time.

- Draft a new ending for the novel in which Newland decides to meet with Ellen in Paris. As you imagine this turn of events, do you gain appreciation for the skill of novelists?

good of his family and social acceptance, he sacrifices his passion for Ellen. In his introduction to *Edith Wharton: Modern Critical Views,* noted literary scholar Harold Bloom observes that "Newland's world centers upon an idea of order, a convention that stifles passion and yet liberates from chaos."

Similarly, Ellen returns to New York at the beginning of the novel, expecting to file for divorce. She discovers, however, that New York will shun her unless she stays married to the count. Newland is sent to advise her, and he explains that her happiness must be secondary to the consequences that will be felt by her family if she disgraces them by divorcing. She unhappily agrees to stay married, even if she does not return to her husband.

Artifice

The reader soon learns that in old New York, reality is less relevant than appearance. In chapter 6, Wharton writes, "In reality they all lived in a kind of hieroglyphic world, where the real thing was never said or done or even thought, but only represented by a set of arbitrary signs." Careful phrasing, wearing appropriate clothing, and maintaining the illusion of a happy marriage are all examples of the habits adopted by members of New York society. As long as Julius keeps up the appearance of being financially responsible (even when everyone knows there are questionable details of his past), he is accepted, but as soon as his shady dealings become public, he and his wife are outcasts. Lawrence Lefferts, meanwhile, waves the banner of marital faithfulness in public, despite the fact that everyone is aware of his numerous love affairs. In her book *The Female Intruder in the Novels of Edith Wharton,* Carol Wershoven comments, "It is therefore not marital fidelity that is a value in New York, but rather the appearance of it."

Newland realizes after May's death that, in carrying out her role as wife, she maintained her own facade. He never knew that she understood the sacrifice he made in not following Ellen, and he is touched that she was sympathetic. Early in their marriage, May's interactions with Newland reveal a degree of artifice. She is fully aware of her husband's love for another woman, but rather than admit this openly, she pretends to be unaware, while at the same time saying seemingly innocent things to him that are understood by both parties as challenging. When Newland tells her he is going to Washington for business, for example, May knows he is going to see Ellen. When she tells him to be sure to see Ellen while he is there, they both know she is communicating that she knows why he is going and expects him to behave honorably.

Style

Setting

The setting is so dominant an element in *The Age of Innocence* that it almost becomes a character. Through detail and lush description, Wharton brings to life the social world of the wealthy in 1870s New York. The environment is so critical to the work that Wharton opens the novel with the grand scene in which everyone is dressed in their finery for the opera. This immediately alerts the reader to the novel's dramatic setting. Because the modern reader is unfamiliar with the "trappings" of old New York, details of the carriages, visiting practices, and attire provide a much-needed context for the story. James W. Tuttleton in *Dictionary of Literary Biography, Volume Twelve: American Realists and Naturalists* comments, however, that modern readers are less interested in the details of daily life in old New York than they are in "the spiritual portrait of the age," which is another component of the setting.

The society depicted is closed to outsiders and revels in its elite membership. Carol Wershoven in *The Female Intruder in the Novels of Edith Wharton* notes that the elimination of "undesirables" from the social circle is the product of a fear of reality. In this closed community, matters of reputation, manners, and decorum are valued highly, and the dignity of one's family name is of extreme importance. Every event, from a wedding to a night at the opera, is subject to the rigors of propriety. When May and Newland announce their engagement, they are expected to make a series of social calls because the "New York ritual was precise and inflexible in such matters." Subtleties of dress, gesture, and word choice can have enormous consequences, and gossiping is considered acceptable. This is the environment in which Newland has been reared and educated, and while he is comfortable in it, he regards it as stifling and narrow-minded.

Imagery and Symbolism

Throughout the novel, Wharton employs certain images to provide subtle cues to the reader. May's mud-stained and torn wedding dress clearly represents the problems in her marriage to Newland. Anthropological terms such as "clan," "tribe," and "totem" draw parallels between the strictly regimented social system of New York and less formal cultures of the past.

Newland's selection of flowers for May and Ellen provides insight into how he views the two women. To May, he sends pure white lilies-of-the-valley. They represent innocence and simplicity, which are traits he sees in May. On the other hand, he sends intense, fiery-yellow roses to Ellen, which reveals that he sees her as vibrant, sexual, and passionate. When Ellen and Newland are together, the narrator almost always mentions fire. Whether Newland lays his head on the mantle, a log in the fireplace snaps and flares, or memories burn in Newland's heart, the image of fire emphasizes their smoldering passion.

Humor

Known for her sharp wit and subtle use of irony, Wharton is equally capable of using outright exaggeration for the sake of humor. In her description of Catherine Mingott, one of society's most respected members, the narrator observes in chapter 4:

> The immense accretion of flesh which had descended on her in middle life like a flood of lava on a doomed city had changed her from a plump active little woman with a neatly-turned foot and ankle into something as vast and august as a natural phenomenon. . . . [In the mirror she saw] an almost unwrinkled expanse of firm pink and white flesh, in the center of which the traces of a small face survived as if awaiting excavation.

Explaining Mrs. Archer's delight at her son's upcoming marriage, Wharton writes in chapter 5 that Newland is entitled to marry someone like May, "but young men are so foolish and incalculable—and some women so ensnaring and unscrupulous—that it was nothing short of a miracle to see one's only son safe past the Siren Isle and in the haven of a blameless domesticity."

Irony

Wharton uses irony in *The Age of Innocence* to reveal the hypocrisies she sees in New York society. When May and her parents go to St. Augustine for the winter, Mrs. Welland arranges for a group of servants to help them make the best of it. As they all sit down to a sumptuous breakfast, Mr. Welland tells Newland, "You see, my dear fellow, we camp—we literally camp. I tell my wife and May that I want to teach them how to rough it." Later, in chapter 26, Mrs. Jackson condemns the vanity of wearing extravagant new dresses, when the proper thing is to buy dresses and wait a few years to wear them. She then describes another woman's dress that she remembers from the previous year, and how a panel has been changed to make it look new. She apparently cannot see that such minute attention to and memory of what ladies wear is exactly what feeds the vanity she berates.

Wharton also uses irony to make her main character, Newland Archer, especially tragic. Early in the novel he is sent to talk Ellen Olenska out of pursuing a divorce. Although he believes she should be allowed to make her own decisions, he

Compare & Contrast

- **1870s:** The United States is recovering from the Civil War and is not yet a world power. As a result, Americans focus on internal issues and resources, and tend to identify themselves in regional terms.

  Today: The United States has a major world presence, both economically and militarily. Americans are interested in both domestic and foreign issues and events. While people often retain a sense of pride in their regional culture, citizens of the United States generally think of themselves as Americans.

- **1870s:** The society described in *The Age of Innocence* strives to preserve itself against unpleasantness. Members of this society will not even consider allowing intellectuals, artists, or writers into their circle, as they are likely to bring with them new ideas and points of view.

  Today: "Unpleasantness" is not only pervasive, but is often sought out by average Americans. Movies and songs containing violent and profane content are routinely consumed by the American public. Individuals and families—not society—are responsible for censoring what they are willing to see or hear. Many parents

  make the effort to install blocking devices on their home computers in order to protect their children from the controversial material that is so readily available on the Internet.

- **1870s:** After dinner, wealthy men often retire to their private libraries to enjoy cigars together. In such comfortable surroundings, they are free to speak of sensitive issues and business matters that are not appropriate in mixed company.

  Today: Cigars have regained popularity, and bars, restaurants, and other social venues have become cigar-friendly. Just as in the past, people enjoy cigars and conversation together. The difference is that since the late 1980s, the number of women who smoke cigars has grown significantly.

- **1870s:** Women are expected to wear their wedding dresses at special events for up to two years after their weddings.

  Today: Some women spend thousands of dollars to buy an elaborate wedding dress that they will wear only once. After the wedding, women often have their dresses preserved to prevent damage, in hopes that one day the dress will be worn by another member of the family

---

agrees and explains to her that by getting a divorce, she would be buying her happiness and freedom with her family's pain. Later in the story, he falls in love with Ellen, but she is unwilling to be with him because doing so would deeply hurt Newland's wife. Newland has taught Ellen not to pursue happiness at the expense of others, and that lesson returns to haunt him. It is also ironic that Newland is pressured by May's family to approach Ellen about her divorce and support her. It is because of May's family that he gets to know Ellen, and it is because of her and her family that he cannot have a romantic relationship with Ellen.

Irony is used for comedy as well as tragedy. In the midst of a dramatic scene between May and

Newland in chapter 10, Newland is trying to convince her to move up their wedding date, and she flippantly remarks that maybe they should elope. When he responds favorably to this idea, she responds, "We can't behave like people in novels, though, can we?" Of course, they *are* people in a novel, and this is Wharton's use of tongue-in-cheek comic relief in an otherwise tense scene.

Historical Context

Wealth in the North

After the Civil War (1861–1865), the South was in ruins, economically and structurally, but the

North flourished. While wealth in the South declined by sixty percent, wealth in the North increased by fifty percent. As a result, there was a growing class of wealthy New Yorkers in the 1870s. This trend is represented by the character of Julius Beaufort, who has become a millionaire. Although the tight social circle of New York does not favor outsiders, he is allowed in by virtue of his marriage to Regina Mingott, a member of a very respectable family.

As people in the North gathered wealth, New York became especially showy. The upper class enjoyed attending the theater and the opera and hosting extravagant parties. A woman named Mrs. Stuyvesant Fish held a dinner party in New York City to honor her dog, who arrived at the party wearing a $15,000 diamond collar. In *The Age of Innocence,* this lifestyle is depicted in the lavish parties and luxuries the wealthy enjoy.

As the century came to a close, there was a growing lower class as most of the wealth was concentrated in the upper class. Forced to labor in sweatshops, factories, and mills, the underprivileged resented the lifestyle of the wealthy. Strikes and riots broke out and political corruption became rampant.

High Society

The Age of Innocence takes place during the last breath of New York high society, although its members did not sense the dramatic changes coming to their world. They gathered at the opera house, and they relied on an accepted canon of rules and conventions to direct their behavior. They flaunted their wealth and talked behind each other's backs, but remained respectful of convention. There were strict expectations regarding appropriate attire, events, home decor, and marriage.

Women

Although powerful in social terms, society women were dependent on men to provide for them. If a woman came from a wealthy family, she might be fortunate enough to have a sum of money to contribute to the marriage, but women expected their husbands to take care of all of their material needs. Women were expected to behave in certain ways, especially in the upper class. They were to master domestic skills, such as needlework, and they were never to challenge men or be unpleasant. A virtuous woman was one who was pretty, elegant, and compliant. In *The Age of Innocence,* May represents the New York society ideal, while Ellen hints at the strides being made for female independence outside the tightly knit New York community.

In 1869, Susan B. Anthony and Elizabeth Cady Stanton formed the National Woman Suffrage Association. Even before the Civil War, women had begun to assemble and demand to be heard. At the time Wharton's novel is set (1872), the women's movement had begun, although it had not reached the closed system of New York society. In fact, in 1872, Anthony went to the polls in Rochester, New York, demanding to be allowed to vote. Clearly, change within the traditional New York system was imminent.

Critical Overview

At the time of *The Age of Innocence*'s publication, Wharton was already a well-respected author. Her readers and critics expected much of her, and they were generally impressed with her new novel. They found the characters realistic and interesting, and Wharton's ability to capture the details, mood, and rigors of New York society life was praised by readers and literary critics alike. In a 1920 *New York Times Book Review,* William Lyon Phelps applauds the novel, noting, "I do not remember when I have read a work of fiction that gives the reader so vivid an idea of the furnishing and illuminating of rooms in fashionable houses as one will find in *The Age of Innocence.*" He adds, "New York society and customs in the seventies are described with an accuracy that is almost uncanny."

Besides providing a vibrant piece of social history, Wharton's novel told a compelling story complete with universal themes and comments on the complexities of human interaction. Margaret B. McDowell in *Twayne's United States Authors Series* writes that the novel is "at once a masterful evocation of a milieu and a masterful delineation of human beings caught between renunciation and passion." In *The Two Lives of Edith Wharton: The Woman and Her Work,* Grace Kellogg-Griffith remarks, "Mrs. Wharton portrayed the society of her young womanhood with a clarity and a firmness of outline that have given them life and permanent importance. *The Age of Innocence* is a flawless piece of artistry." Equally enthusiastic was Phelps, who concludes that "Edith Wharton is a writer who brings glory on the name America, and this is her best book." The critic went on to comment that this novel lacks the flaws typically found in Wharton's

Daniel Day-Lewis as Newland Archer and Michelle Pfeiffer as Countess Ellen Olenska in the 1993 film version of the novel.

novels, such as relentless witticisms, unbelievable coincidences, and seemingly rushed scenes. Critics noted that Wharton depicts New York with a sympathetic yet scolding tone that is wholly appropriate. One of Wharton's contemporaries, Carl Van Doren, author of *Contemporary American Novelists 1900–1920,* observes:

> From the first Mrs. Wharton's power has lain in the ability to reproduce in fiction the circumstances of a compact community in a way that illustrates the various oppressions which such communities put upon individual vagaries, whether viewed as sin, or ignorance, or folly, or merely as social impossibility.

Critics such as Cynthia Griffin Wolff of *Dictionary of Literary Biography, Volume Nine: American Novelists, 1910–1945* described *The Age of Innocence* as a *bildungsroman,* which is a novel that depicts a character's growth from adolescence into adulthood. Wolff argued that it is Newland whose growth into maturity is witnessed in Wharton's novel. She added that his experience is unique because of the narrow environment in which he matures. As a result, the restrictive setting can be viewed as meaningful, providing necessary structure to everyday life and to Newland's passage into manhood.

Some critics found notable flaws in *The Age of Innocence.* In fact, two of the members of the Pulitzer Prize committee thought the prize should have gone to another author in 1921 instead of Wharton. They believed the book to be overly specific to a time and place. As a result, they argued, the book lacked universal relevance. Other critics took this stance a step further, adding that the book is limited because it is about a community of people who were far removed from the norm, even in their own time and place.

Arthur Mizener in *Twelve Great American Novels* comments that *The Age of Innocence,* while "very nearly a great novel," is weakened by heavy-handed cleverness. He found the worst example to be May's muddied and torn wedding dress as a "crude and even sentimental symbol for the novel's feelings about Newland's marriage." Mizener is quick to add that, despite its flaws, the novel's depiction of the love affair between Ellen and Newland is "beautifully vivid and convincing," adding, "It would be hard to overpraise the dramatic skill and economy with which she brings these things [their love and frustration] about." Mizener was not the only critic voicing a mixed reaction. Blake Nevius, in the book *Edith Wharton: A Study of Her*

Fiction, writes, "*The Age of Innocence* is not Mrs. Wharton's strongest novel, but along with *Ethan Frome,* it is the one in which she is most thoroughly the artist. It is a triumph of style."

Criticism

Jennifer Bussey

Bussey holds a master's degree in interdisciplinary studies and a bachelor's degree in English literature. She is an independent writer specializing in literature. In the following essay, she examines Newland Archer's divided self and the three major decisions he faces in The Age of Innocence.

Edith Wharton's protagonist in *The Age of Innocence* is the ineffectual Newland Archer. He is a typical young man who is frustrated and angst-ridden and wonders if there might be more to life than what he sees. He is a product of the social world of old New York, and it is in this milieu that he is most comfortable. He fully understands and upholds the rules of etiquette and the essential artifice that make up his social reality. At the same time, he feels stifled by New York society's strict conventions that dictate behavior and decision-making. There is no room for individuality or trying new things. The society is so narrow that its members do not welcome intellectuals, artists, or writers, as they may bring with them disturbing new ideas and opinions. And money alone is not enough to win entrance. Newly minted millionaire Julius Beaufort is allowed into the circle only because he marries a woman who comes from a respectable family. His position in New York is cemented because he and his wife have the only house with a private ballroom, which makes them socially significant. While Newland fancies himself well-educated and a "man of the world," he cannot shake the feeling that there is a reality beyond the bounds of this insular community.

Countess Ellen Olenska and May Welland represent the conflicting forces in Newland's psyche. May is demure and proper, the golden daughter of old New York; Ellen is mysterious and scandalous. May is described in chapter 21 as "one of the handsomest and most popular young married women in New York" and "one of the sweetest-tempered and most reasonable of wives." On the other hand, Ellen's experiences in Europe with the Polish count exemplify what Newland imagines he

> While Newland fancies himself well-educated and a 'man of the world,' he cannot shake the feeling that there is a reality beyond the bounds of this insular community."

is missing in life. His neat, absolute categorizing of May and Ellen is evident in the flowers he sends them. Every day, he sends May a box of lilies-of-the-valley, which are pure white and signify innocence. In contrast, he sends brilliant yellow roses to Ellen, which demonstrates that he sees her as passionate, alluring, and sensual. That Ellen is leading the life he can only imagine heightens his attraction to her. In chapter 13, Wharton writes of Ellen's

> mysterious faculty of suggesting tragic and moving possibilities outside the daily run of experience. . . . The exciting fact was her having lived in an atmosphere so thick with drama that her own tendency to provoke it had apparently passed unperceived.

Newland thinks that if he can be with Ellen, he is sure to have exciting adventures. In fact, his thinking is borne out, as his pursuit of her throughout the novel provides his most stimulating experiences. By being in Ellen's orbit, Newland is able to have some excitement without having to create an exciting life of his own.

Newland's first major decision in the novel comes when he resolves to leave May and follow Ellen to Europe. He is motivated by his unwillingness to imagine his life without Ellen, especially when he is left with May, who is becoming more and more like her mother (and all the other society women, for that matter) every day. He is captivated by Ellen and completely bored with May. To be fair, the reader must realize that May is essentially the same person she has been all along; she is the woman Newland fell in love with. After meeting Ellen, though, Newland begins to compare the two and finds May lacking. Ellen knows this and tries to enlighten him in chapter 29, when he picks her up at the train station in the carriage. Newland tells Ellen he wants to run away with her to a place "where we shall be simply two human beings who

What Do I Read Next?

- Henry James's *Portrait of a Lady* (1881) is the story of Isabel Archer, a young American woman who comes into wealth and leaves for Europe, where she will test her mettle. This novel is considered by many to have been an inspiration for *The Age of Innocence*.

- Wharton's *The House of Mirth* (1905) vies with *The Age of Innocence* as Wharton's best work. Like *The Age of Innocence,* this novel is set in late nineteenth-century New York; here, however, she portrays Lily Bart's fall from social grace.

- Jane Austen's *Pride and Prejudice* (1813) is a classic novel of manners. Featuring one of literature's most memorable heroines, this novel depicts the struggles of romance in a time dictated by manners and class structures.

- Published in 1995, *The Gilded Age: Essays on the Origins of Modern America,* edited by Charles W. Calhoun, is a collection of essays about the United States between 1865 and 1898. Topics include politics, women, law, and the African-American experience.

love each other, who are the whole life to each other; and nothing else on earth will matter." She responds with a laugh and says, "Oh, my dear— where is that country? Have you ever been there?" She knows what he does not—that they can never be together the way he wants them to be.

Whether or not Newland might have followed through with his decision to pursue Ellen to Europe is a question little considered in criticism of the novel. A strong argument can be made that Newland would not have gone under any circumstances. Newland does follow Ellen to Skuytercliff and Boston, and these relatively nearby destinations represent the lengths he will go to in order to be with her. While these trips are somewhat thrilling in their clandestine nature, they also are quite safe for Newland. He can easily fabricate reasons for the trips. His home life carries on as usual while he sneaks off to see the woman he loves. On the other hand, actually following her to Europe would be a monumental act. Newland would be forced to wholly give up his safe and comfortable existence in New York, become an outcast, and bring shame on his entire family. He has seen firsthand what becomes of people who are evicted from "the clan," and, he would not really be able to put himself (and Ellen) in that terrible position.

Newland never tells Ellen he plans to leave May and go with her to Europe, which is another indication that he was not really prepared to go. It is exciting to think about and makes him feel alive, but if he were truly committed to taking action, surely he would have at least mentioned his intentions to Ellen. He hints, as when he tells her goodbye and adds, "[B]ut I shall see you soon in Paris!" Ellen responds, "Oh, if you and May could come—!" Newland never tells Ellen of his plans for two reasons. First, he needs to keep available the option of backing out, and perhaps knows all along that when the moment comes, he will not go. Second, he realizes that if he tells Ellen, she will not react with the delight he hopes for, but rather with outright refusal. She may even tell him that she never wants to see him again because the arrangement they made was that they would never do anything to hurt May.

As an interesting aside, it should be noted that early drafts of the novel showed Newland running away with Ellen. Wharton was unable, however, to figure out a way to create happiness for the lovers. With so little in common, and so few shared tastes, Newland and Ellen would be unable to find enough common ground to have a meaningful and lasting relationship. This demonstrates how, once characters are created, even the author cannot force them to be happy and satisfied in ways that are inconsistent with who they are.

When May tells Newland she is pregnant, he makes his second major decision. He knows that he cannot abandon May and the baby while he follows his passion to Europe. Just as Newland realizes what May is telling him, Wharton writes, "There was a long pause, which the inner devils filled with strident laughter." Newland knows that his decision has essentially been made for him, that he has been drawn back into his inescapable destiny as a society man in New York. Although he could technically still go to Europe, his sense of propriety and responsibility prevents him from doing so.

Once Newland realizes he is fated to be a family man in New York, he resigns himself to it and makes a pleasant life for himself and his family, carrying through his decision to stay with May. Rather than live a life filled with bitterness and resentment, he enjoys family life and enters politics for a short while at the insistence of Theodore Roosevelt. Reflecting on his life, he muses, "His days were full, and they were filled decently. He supposed it was all a man ought to ask." Perhaps the pleasant quality of his life indicates that Newland was relieved that he did not have to make the choice between the life he actually led and the life he might have led if he had chased after Ellen. Had May not given him the news of her pregnancy, he would have been forced to either go to Europe or talk himself out of it by conjuring up a compelling reason to stay.

In the last chapter, Newland makes his third and final major decision. Now a mature man, he makes this decision not from a sense of fancy or obligation, but from wisdom. He and his son are in Paris, and they are about to meet with Ellen, whom Newland has not seen for twenty-six years. His decision not to see her—and, therefore, not to see if there is still something left of their mutual passion—is confusing for many readers. On thoughtful reading, however, his reasons become clear.

At the age of only fifty-seven, the widowed Newland is fully aware that he has time for another romance in his life, which leads many readers to expect that love will triumph for Newland and Ellen after all. He kept her memory alive even as he grew to love May. In Paris, he walks through the city, seeing it as a context for Ellen's life. He imagines her walking here and visiting people there. For these reasons, a happy and romantic ending seems inevitable. So, why does Newland decide not to see her?

Newland is much wiser than he was twenty-six years ago, and he knows that the reality of a relationship with Ellen will never approach his long-standing fantasy. He has lived enough to understand what Ellen understood years ago—that people must live in the world of reality, not in the world of dreams. Wise enough now to grasp the difference, he chooses to preserve his dreams from the harshness of reality. Sitting outside her building, Newland imagines his son going in and meeting her, and he thinks, "It's more real to me here than if I went up." His fantasy far outshines anything reality can offer him, and he chooses not to risk losing it. This is by far his most courageous

decision because it is one that he makes for himself willingly and realistically.

Source: Jennifer Bussey, in an essay for *Novels for Students,* Gale Group, 2001.

Jennifer A. Hynes

In the following overview of The Age of Innocence, *Hynes explores Wharton's treatment of a changing society.*

The Age of Innocence, a reminiscent but satiric account of the time, place, and society in which Edith Wharton grew up, won for the author a 1921 Pulitzer Prize and was a best-seller when it appeared. Wharton had earlier taken up the topic of the society of the old New York, in which her wealthy parents played important roles, in novels such as *The House of Mirth* and *The Custom of the Country.* But, written after Wharton had experienced the horror and destruction of World War I, in a time during which old systems of beliefs and customs seemed to be collapsing, *The Age of Innocence* looks back to a time of apparent stability—a time in which the forms and conventions were understood, if sometimes repressive. The novel is typically read as a discussion of the conflict between the individual and society, and between the safety and order of old, familiar ways and the possible chaos and uncertainty of new ways. Thus the conflict is crystallized in Newland Archer's choice between May and Ellen, a choice that represents the split between the society of old New York in which his family holds a respectable place and that of the newly wealthy invaders of his society that were rising to prominence after the Civil War. Because *The Age of Innocence* subtly censures the values and actions of both respectable old New York society and the fashionable newcomers, it is generally considered among Wharton's finest works.

Although the title of the novel literally refers to a 1788 Sir Joshua Reynolds portrait of a little girl, the title can be interpreted in several ways. The innocent age might be the condition of New York society in 1872, the year in which most of the action of the novel takes place. This is a society that refuses to discuss any of the unpleasant facts of life, such as divorce, extramarital affairs among its members, or the possibility of marriages made for financial gain. At the same time, society insists upon the absolute innocence, purity, and ignorance of all sexual matters in its unmarried women. Newland's spinster sister Janey is the monstrous outcome of this insistence—an adult who is perpetu-

> The novel is typically read as a discussion of the conflict between the individual and society, and between the safety and order of old, familiar ways and the possible chaos and uncertainty of new ways."

ally forced to pretend a childish innocence. May Welland is another product of such an upbringing, and even her husband-to-be believes in her complete innocence; when observing his fiancee watching the seduction scene in the opera *Faust,* Newland boasts to himself that May "doesn't even guess what it's all about." But while May participates in presenting herself as an innocent maiden, she shows by her actions later in the novel that she understands the facts of life that motivate men and women—both in operas and in real life. Newland begins to suspect that his bride is not as shallow as he had suspected when he finds that she has lied to Ellen about being certain of her pregnancy in order to keep her marriage intact. Later, Newland finds that May has told their son on her deathbed that Newland gave up the thing he wanted most (Ellen) when May asked him to. "She never asked me," Newland recalls.

But the title *The Age of an Innocence* could also refer to Newland's own youthful belief that love between a man and a woman is all that is needed to secure their happiness. When he voices his desire to Ellen that they might live happily outside of all social constraints, Ellen replies that such a life is not possible since too many other people would be hurt by their actions. Newland's process of coming to terms with the realities of relationships is an education of irony. When he is called upon by his family to counsel Ellen not to seek a divorce, he states the case in terms of family responsibility: "The individual, in such cases, is nearly always sacrificed to what is supposed to be the collective interest: people cling to any convention that keeps the family together—protects the children, if there are any . . . It's my business, you know, to help you to see these things as the people who are fondest of you see them. The Mingotts,

the Wellands, the van der Luydens, all your friends and relations: if I didn't show you honestly how they judge such questions, it wouldn't be fair of me, would it?" But, ironically, it is these same reasons that Ellen forces Newland to consider when he later urges her to leave the stifling New York society to live in a world where such ugly designations as mistress and adultery do not exist. "Oh, my dear—where is that country? Have you ever been there?" Ellen asks Newland, attempting to make him realize that his dream is impossible.

May and Ellen represent different types of women to Newland. Even before becoming involved with Ellen he becomes interested in "the case of the Countess Olenska" rather than in Ellen as an individual. Since he is unaware of the depth of May's mind, Newland sees his fiancee and Ellen as contrasts, with May representing all that is safe, secure, and known in his society and Ellen all that is unknown and exotic in European society. May and Ellen can be read as the traditional light and dark heroines of literature, since Wharton portrays May as a wholesome blonde and Ellen as a seductive brunette. Newland thinks of May as representing "a Civic Virtue or a Greek Goddess"; her skill at archery reminds Newland of the goddess Diana. He notices May's eyes repeatedly as being transparent, serious, pale, limpid, and blue—all reminders of the extreme innocence he believes she possesses. In contrast, Ellen plays the role in Newland's mind as an exotic, European femme fatale who represents the threat of disorder that is descending upon old New York society. Her hands, described as being fragile and decorated with rings, are one of her most attractive attributes to Newland. The most sensual scene between Ellen and Newland is the one in which he takes off her glove in the carriage to kiss her hand. Newland learns few actual facts about Ellen's unhappy marriage and subsequent life, but is attracted by her mystery. Ellen is unconventional because of her desire to get a divorce from her cruel husband, her scandalous and shadowy past, her choice to live in a Bohemian section of New York, and her open friendships with men who are married or engaged. But while Newland mistakenly sees only the roles he ascribes to both May and Ellen, they are actually much more complex than these simple characterizations.

Although Wharton was perhaps more like Ellen than any other character in the novel (both are at once inside and outside of fashionable New York society, divorce their husbands, leave America to live in Paris, and greatly value stimulating conversation), the novel is more Newland's story

This 1875 print of ice skaters in Central Park, in which the women wear long skirts and skate separately from the men, illustrates the constrictive "Old New York" society of the late 1800s depicted in the novel.

than either May's or Ellen's. Just as Wharton did, Newland becomes interested in anthropology and is able to view his own society as an outsider and think critically of its rules and values. Wharton describes in detail the tribal rites that go on prior to a marriage between old New York families; May and Newland's schedule of prenuptial visits to relatives and friends follows a specific pattern. Even the decision to move up their wedding date must be approved by the family matriarch, Granny Mingott. In the opening scene of the novel Wharton refers to both Lawrence Lefferts, old New York's authority on form, and Sillerton Jackson, old New York's authority on family. But we see the hypocrisy of society since even Lefferts, a crusader for morality, has extramarital affairs. As Newland takes up the study of anthropology and begins to see such incongruities in his own society, he feels the impulse to break free from what he sees as stifling and meaningless conventions. However, Ellen's actions to save her cousin's marriage, May's maneuvers to keep Newland with her, and Newland's own inertia keep him from acting against his family's traditions.

By the end of the novel, when Newland's respectable son is about to marry the illegitimate daughter of Julius Beaufort, it is obvious that time and the invaders of old New York society have caused changes. Although little is mentioned of the twenty-six years between Newland's engagement to May and the closing scenes of the novel, we understand that he and his family have benefited from his (forced) decision to give up Ellen. Wharton depicts both the good and the bad sides of renunciation; the family is made stronger although the individual suffers from wondering what might have been. But since society has changed in spite of Newland's actions to maintain the old standards, it is clear that the suffocating old ways could not last.

Source: Jennifer A. Hynes, *"The Age of Innocence:* Overview," in *Reference Guide to American Literature,* 3d ed., edited by Jim Kamp, St. James Press, 1994.

Geoffrey Walton

In the following essay, Walton explores Wharton's nostalgic treatment of "Old New York" in The Age of Innocence.

Although Walter Berry prophesied that nobody else except themselves would be interested in the New York of her childhood, *The Age of Innocence,* 1920, was serialized in *The Pictorial Review* and was, almost inevitably, awarded the Pulitzer Prize

> The New York world is re-created in full and fascinating detail. This is the genuine old New York of the 70s, before the millionaires of *The House of Mirth* had built their mansions on Fifth Avenue."

and has become one of Edith Wharton's most widely read and admired works. It has all the ingredients of a historical best-seller, a richly detailed period setting, an emotional situation that the modern reader can flatter himself, or more important, herself would work out more happily at the present day and, combined with the appeal to critical superiority, a pervasive nostalgia for the past. It is, with all its faults, manifestly the product of a distinguished creative mind, if in a consciously relaxed mood, and it does not suffer from the wholly untypical rawness and nerviness of feeling, the uncertainty of tone and attitude that characterize *A Son at the Front,* which was being planned at the same time. The Puritanical element in the New York tradition comes out in *The Age of Innocence* much more strongly than in any part of *The Custom of the Country* and, remembering that Edith Wharton there uses the name Marvell, one is reminded in this later novel of *A Definition of Love.* There is, of course, no ground for supposing that she consciously took her theme from that poem, but the relationship between Newland Archer and Ellen Olenska has an air of being

. . . begotten by Despair Upon Impossibility. Everything in the situation is against them, the whole weight of a social and moral tradition. Nevertheless, as with the situation in *The Reef,* one finds it pathetic—and sometimes absurd—rather than tragic, and the elaborate moral solution and the epilogue rather heavily sentimental. The social conflict, of the individual against the group, is comparable to that of Lily Bart with a later New York Society, but it is muted and muffled by the mass of period upholstery. It is not merely that the age enthroned "Taste," that far-off divinity of whom "Form" was the mere visible representative and vicegerent; the whole story on both sides is especially fully visualized in terms of clothes and interior decoration, and documented with accounts of manners, customs, and social history. As

in the case of the fully historical *Valley of Decision,* Edith Wharton is, to put it simply, more concerned to recreate a past age than to say something she thinks important about life. There is a lack of emotional pressure and ironic tension; elegant as the writing undoubtedly is, it lacks the hard precision of the best earlier books. After all, the stimulus to such writing was not there in the chosen subject matter, except on one or two occasions.

The New York world is re-created in full and fascinating detail. This is the genuine old New York of the 70s, before the millionaires of *The House of Mirth* had built their mansions on Fifth Avenue. We are given illustrative examples to those early paragraphs in *A Backward Glance.* Book One brings before us the moral and emotional situation in relation to that wealthy but in every way thoroughly provincial and middle-class community, which is perhaps most strikingly and fantastically epitomized by the fact that women imported dresses in the latest fashion from Worth and then kept them for two years before wearing them. The pattern of this little "Society" had come to seem part of the order of nature, incredible as this may seem:

New York, as far back as the mind of man could travel, had been divided into the two great fundamental groups of the Mingotts and Mansons and all their clan, who cared about eating and clothes and money, and the Archer-Newland-vander-Luyden tribe, who were devoted to travel, horticulture and the best fiction, and looked down on the grosser forms of pleasure. . . .

Edith Wharton's use of the words "clan" and "tribe" is deliberate and recurring. The people who actually wrote books and painted pictures did not belong to either group. They did not want to, and Society was never sure whether hey were really "ladies" and "gentlemen." One moves on to note the finer distinction between the van der Luydens and two other families of aristocratic origin and the rest and, complicating the situation, the independent positions of old Mrs. Manson Mingott, a comic figure of monstrous obesity, and of Julius Beaufort, the rich financier, who is blatantly vulgar and openly disreputable. Two characters have a kind of choric function as representatives of the social spirit: they are Lawrence Lefferts who

. . . was, on the whole, the foremost authority on "form" in New York. He had probably devoted more time than anyone else to the study of this intricate and fascinating question; but study alone could not account for his complete and easy competence. One had only to look at him, from the slant of his bald forehead and the curve of his beautiful fair moustache to the long patent-leather feet at the other end of his lean and elegant person, to feel that the knowledge of "form" must be congenial in anyone who knew how to wear such good clothes so carelessly and carry such height with so much lounging grace. . . .

and old Mr. Sillerton Jackson, the authority on "family":

He knew all the ramifications of New York's cousinships, and could not only elucidate such complicated questions as that of the connection between the Mingotts (through the Thorleys) with the Dallases of South Carolina, and that of the relationship of the elder branch of Philadelphia Thorleys to the Albany Chiverse (on no account to be confused with the Manson Chiverses of University Place), but could also enumerate the leading characteristics of each family. . . .

It was an inflexible social pattern and it is very suitable that we should get our first panorama of it as Newland Archer, the hero, surveys the audience at the opera, an institution where all the traditional European social rituals were assiduously imitated. Ellen Olenska is conspicuous because her dress, though elegant, is not quite conventional. The Archer family, although belonging to the more intellectual section of Society, are shown as weighed down with conventional habits, and the implications of Newland Archer's gestures of rebellion are not always fully understood even by himself; sometimes he sees his marriage "with a shiver of foreboding becoming what most of the other marriages about him [are]: a dull association of material and social interests held together by ignorance on the one side and hypocrisy on the other." But he is "sincerely but placidly in love" with the "frankness" and "freshness," based of course on utter ignorance, of his bride, May Welland, and looks forward to guiding her vague cultural gestures. One can see that they are in fact predestined to become a typical New York couple, if of slightly wider interests than the majority. Newland Archer is too gentlemanly, too committed to the regime of doing the right things, of avoiding unpleasantness of all kinds and, especially, of ignoring the loose living of many of his associates. Presumably, in order to make life viable at all for a relatively small, wealthy, and leisured community, the moral atmosphere had been allowed to settle down in this way; only dishonesty in business or flagrant sexual irregularity was condemned. Yvors Winters sums up *The Age of Innocence* by saying that it illustrates an ethical tradition more ancient than Calvinist Puritanism, though modified by it:

. . . the characters are living in a society cognate and coterminous with those principles; the society with

its customs and usages, is the external form of the principles. Now the customs and usages may become unduly externalized, and when they appear so to become, Mrs. Wharton satirizes them; but in the main they represent the concrete aspect of the abstract principles of behavior. He goes on to discuss the relationship of Archer and Ellen Olenska in terms of their having to abandon a way of life that they in fact find satisfying and admirable, if they decide to rebel openly against its moral principles. This indicates the situation in the long run.

In the short run everything possible is done to absorb the Countess Olenska into Society and neutralize her possibly disturbing influence. Even the aristocratic van der Luydens are moved to lend her their prestige. Ellen Olenska, though a cousin, is a foreign and, at least potentially, a revolutionary force. She settles in a street between the purlieus of Society and Bohemia, has unusual decorations and unwittingly compromises herself by entertaining doubtful company—old New York snobbery did not extend to an English duke for his rank alone. The charm of Ellen Olenska is made very real. She is beautiful, smart, intelligent, original in her taste, generous and guileless; she is not a mere "made-over" version of the Baroness Munster, though the general idea of the book is, of course, related to that of *The Europeans*. The contrast between her and May Welland is brought out again when May goes so far as to cut church to walk with Archer in the Park, but causes him to say:

"Original! We're all as like each other as those dolls cut out of the same folded paper. We're like patterns stencilled on a wall Can't you and I strike out for ourselves, May?"

But Archer's subjection to convention comes out in his advice to Ellen to avoid a divorce with its risks of scandal and one reaches the point at which he has let his engagement to May go forward because he is not quite sure of Ellen's innocence and Ellen feels, "I can't love you unless I give you up"; in other words, she feels that she must accept the conventions of New York because its narrowminded community has after all made her feel happy and, paradoxically, even free. Fate has crowded itself betwixt them in the double guise of social convention, with its whole lineage of moral principle, and of family solidarity and generosity which, if they take effect a little slowly and grudgingly, nevertheless manifest themselves in very solid and material forms. The worst and best of old New York are inseparable. Everyone is too "nice" for the heights and depths of passion to have scope. The mere humbugs and the absurder customs are satirized, but in the rest of the picture Edith Wharton is resurrecting the historical types and evoking the scenes she remembered without her customary play of irony. The central situation is presented in all solemnity without seeming tragic; from Edith Wharton one would have expected something analogous to the wit of Marvell's poem.

Newland Archer's two relationships now develop rapidly. The fashionable wedding is described with much detail of dress and behavior, and, after this, his disappointing honeymoon in Europe, which shows up May as scarcely more cultivated than Undine Spragg is shown to be in similar circumstances, followed by a Newport season with all its archaic ritual. It is therefore inevitable that Archer should drift back toward Ellen A curious relationship is established depending on

> . . . the perfect balance she had held between their loyalty to others and their honesty to themselves that had so stirred and yet tranquillized him; a balance not artfully calculated, as her tears and her falterings showed, but resulting naturally from her unabashed sincerity. It filled him with a tender awe, now the danger was over, and made him thank the fates that no personal vanity, no sense of playing a part before sophisticated witnesses, had tempted him to tempt her. . . .

This relationship, with all the magnanimity it implies—it is a kind of "magnanimous despair" leading to a love of "divine" ideality—is offered for our unqualified admiration. May's conventionality and unsuitability as a wife for Archer are made painfully obvious; his throwing open a window on a cold evening symbolizes his feeling of claustration. Ellen's moral superiority to everyone around her becomes equally obvious in her demonstrative kindness to Mrs. Beaufort after the bank failure—old New York's human worst side was plainer than its commercial best on such occasions. Her clear-sightedness sees the frequent dinginess of the lives of unmarried couples where Archer has only his own sort of conventional romantic visions. But the alternative she offers of love in separation—"in reach and yet out of reach" or, at the most, "Shall I—once come to you; and then go home?"—lacks, for all the gratitude and generosity towards the feelings of her friends underlying it, a certain fundamental humanity. It is not in the context tantalizing and coy, as might appear in quotation, but very idealized. Her fineness has some of the rarefied quality of Anna Leath's, though none of the meanness, and she certainly does not suffer from Lily Bart's vein of frivolousness. Despite her past experience, she will not or cannot face the consequences of a break with social conventions. As Winters says, a formal social order, with all its re-strictions, seems to her to provide a more satisfactory way of life than freedom in isolation. The situation is wound up with the most meticulous regard for old New York conventions. Ellen Olenska has decided to return to Europe—we learn afterwards that May has precipitated this by a piece of deceit; the Archers give the farewell dinner, and the hypocrisy is an occasion for some magnificent satiric conclusions in Edith Wharton's most trenchant manner—here the writing really comes to life:

> There were certain things that had to be done, and if done at all, done handsomely and thoroughly; and one of these, in the old New York code, was the tribal rally around a kinswoman about to be eliminated from the tribe. There was nothing on earth that the Wellands and Mingotts would not have done to proclaim their unalterable affection for the Countess Olenska now that her passage for Europe was engaged.

> It was the old New York way of talking life "without effusion of blood"; the way of people who dreaded scandal more than disease, who placed decency above courage, and who considered that nothing was more ill-bred than "scenes," except the behaviour of those who gave rise to the to them . . .

Archer is made conscious of all the irony and the suspicions and of his helplessness in the grip of the genteel tradition, and we are shown a bitterly satiric picture of the victory of the two petty tyrants of Form and Family.

Nevertheless, the final solution can only be taken as a sentimental endorsement of the tribal code. Archer settles down as a model husband—he and May "compromise" by ignoring awkward realities to the end. In the epilogue he reemerges as a public-spirited citizen who has worked with Theodore Roosevelt, but he refuses the chance of a reunion with Ellen when it comes thirty years later. Though Archer has become a more active representative of old New York than Selden or Marvell, one is asked to reverence the persistence of tradition rather than admire its flexibility. The possible pointer toward the later chapters of *The Buccaneers* is not sufficiently followed up to make it truly significant. Edith Wharton apparently endorses both old New York and Ellen Olenska's and Archer's renunciation of each other, which indeed, in its idealism, also belongs to old New York; Ellen Olenska is not completely foreign after all. This is a rather sugary version of the kind of conflict that leads to Lily Bart's tragedy. To compare it with the brilliantly conic interplay of values and foibles that James creates in *The Europeans,* where the Baroness after doing so much to aerate the atmosphere of New England lets herself down with a fib, is to realize how leisurely and lacking in vitality *The Age of Innocence* is as a whole. One cannot help also realizing, however, that in its nostalgic escapism, which she admits to in *A Backward Glance,* is also personal to the author in other ways. One recalls, in connection with Ellen Olenska's attitude, Mrs. Wharton's exclamation quoted by Percy Lubbock, "Ah, the poverty, the miserable poverty, of any love that lies outside of marriage, of any love that is not a living together, a sharing of all!" These words, dating from about 1912, the year of her separation, and about two years after the end of her affair with Morton Fullerton, might have been spoken in the novel and one feels that, in creating Ellen Olenska and giving her human vitality and definition in a world of wax works, Edith Wharton may have been projecting an idealized vision of herself into the Society of her youth, where one knows she was in fact a rather colorless participant. Now that we know how far Mrs. Wharton in fact differed from Ellen Olenska, we see both the pathos and the irony of such an idealization. Anna Leath and, later, Rose Sellars are comparable, though older, types of elegant austerity; but they are more austere and also much more critically presented. Edith Wharton is surely in all three, partly idealizing and partly criticizing, in various combinations, her own complex nature, her refined puritanism, inherited and temperamental, and her sometimes concealed, sometimes repressed, capacity for human warmth and passion. It would be impertinent to speculate any further until more documentary evidence is available, but one also feels that the identification is supported by her creation of comparable types of elegant austerity in Anna Leath and, later, Rose Sellars. It is difficult to say how far this represents a vein of Puritan tradition and how far a temperamental compulsion, insofar as these could in any case be separated.

In the *Old New York* stories, 1922 to 1924, Edith Wharton goes back into reported history, beginning with the forties; their chief interest is social. *False Dawn* demonstrates how very middle class indeed the manners of the top layer of New York Society had been within the lifetime of Edith Wharton s older contemporaries, and *New Year's Day* gives us a very seamy picture of the age of innocence; Edith Wharton presents a situation of considerable pathos and implies a further and even more damning criticism of the pettier conventions of the time. The series brings to an end Mrs. Wharton's concern with the uneasy position of the individual in a closely integrated and exclusive social group where ordered and polished appearances are the expression of moral ideals and principles and the divergencies of errant reality may be not only ridiculous but also shocking.

Source: Geoffrey Walton, "Old New York," in *Edith Wharton: A Critical Interpretation,* Fairleigh Dickinson University Press, 1970, pp. 137–46.

Sources

Bloom, Harold, ed., *Edith Wharton: Modern Critical Views,* Chelsea House, 1986.

Kellogg-Griffith, Grace, *The Two Lives of Edith Wharton: The Woman and Her Work,* Appleton-Century, 1965.

McDowell, Margaret B., "Edith Wharton," in *Twayne's United States Authors,* G.K. Hall and Co., 1999.

Mizener, Arthur, "The Age of Innocence," in *Twelve Great American Novels,* New American Library, 1967, pp. 78–80.

Nevius, Blake, *Edith Wharton, A Study of Her Fiction,* University of California Press, 1953, pp. 185–7.

Phelps, William Lyon, "As Mrs. Wharton Sees Us," in *New York Times Book Review,* Vol. 53, October 17, 1920, pp. 1, 11.

Tuttleton, James W., "Edith Wharton," in *Dictionary of Literary Biography, Volume Twelve: American Realists and Naturalists,* edited by Donald Pizer, Gale, 1982, pp. 433–50.

Van Doren, Carl, "Edith Wharton," in *Contemporary American Novelists 1900–1920,* Macmillan, 1922, pp. 95–7.

Wershoven, Carol, *The Female Intruder in the Novels of Edith Wharton,* Fairleigh Dickinson University Press, 1982, pp. 91–3.

Wharton, Edith, *The Age of Innocence,* introduction by Paul Montazzoli, Barnes & Noble, 1996.

Wolff, Cynthia Griffin, "Edith Wharton," in *Dictionary of Literary Biography, Volume Nine: American Novelists, 1910–1945,* edited by James J. Martine, Gale, 1981, pp. 126–42.

For Further Study

Bell, Millicent, ed., *The Cambridge Companion to Edith Wharton,* Cambridge University Press, 1995.
  This book contains essays by established and new scholars evaluating Wharton's fiction. It is intended for readers who are new to Wharton's work, as well as for scholars of her writing.

Bloom, Harold, ed., *Edith Wharton: Modern Critical Views,* Chelsea House, 1986.
  Noted literary scholar Bloom reviews and evaluates Wharton's writing career.

Davis, Joy L., "The Ritual of Dining in Edith Wharton's *The Age of Innocence,*" in *Midwest Quarterly,* Vol. 34, No. 4, Summer 1993, pp. 465–81.

Davis demonstrates how the dining scenes in the novel serve to represent the larger action of the plot. At the dining table, the characters are able to assert their positions in the social hierarchy.

Godfrey, David A., "The Full and Elaborate Vocabulary of Evasion: The Language of Cowardice in Edith Wharton's Old New York," in *Midwest Quarterly,* Vol. 30, No. 1, Autumn 1988, pp. 27–44.

Godfrey examines Wharton's use of language and shows how it relates to norms of conduct and behavior by members of old New York society.

Hadley, Kathy Miller, "Ironic Structure and Untold Stories in *The Age of Innocence,*" in *Studies in the Novel,* Vol. 23, No. 2, Summer 1991, pp. 262–72.

Hadley describes the three different plots Wharton considered for *The Age of Innocence,* and examines the reasons for the chosen story line.

Hopkins, Viola, "The Ordering Style of *The Age of Innocence,*" in *American Literature,* Vol. XXX, No. 3, November 1958, pp. 345–57.

Hopkins provides a thorough review and explanation of Wharton's use of imagery in the novel.

Wharton, Edith, *A Backward Glance,* Appleton-Century, 1934.

This is Wharton's autobiographical work in which she considers her life and career. Critics of her work often refer to this important publication for contextual information about her work.

Appointment in Samarra

John O'Hara
1934

Appointment in Samarra, John O'Hara's debut novel, is situated in the small Pennsylvania town of Gibbsville, a fictional place whose occupants and mores mirror those of O'Hara's hometown of Pottsville, Pennsylvania. *Appointment* centers around the self-destruction of one of the town's more popular gentlemen, Julian English. Told from the viewpoints of several different characters, *Appointment in Samarra* is also a novel of manners in that it depicts the way in which one must abide by certain rules in order to gain acceptance or maintain one's social standing. While many seemingly scandalous foibles are often overlooked, a much smaller infraction could be perceived as completely unacceptable and topple the entire social order of Gibbsville's elite, letting unspoken truths and feelings rise to the surface.

Details abound of Julian's tenuous marriage, as well as his vulnerable financial situation; both are themes that were prominent in O'Hara's own personal life as he wrote *Appointment in Samarra* on the heels of his own failed first marriage. Furthermore, O'Hara was often subject to financial pressures as he had a great deal of trouble holding a job. The novel's main character, Julian, is also a rather heavy drinker, which closely mirrors O'Hara's own patterns of drinking to the point of excess.

The most critically acclaimed of all his works, *Appointment in Samarra* was an instant success, earning O'Hara popularity with the general public and critical praise for his ear for dialogue and his

John O'Hara

attention to detail. Ironically, the things that earned *Appointment in Samarra* accolades upon its publication are the very things that wrought harsher criticism of his subsequent works, according to Fran Lebowitz in her introduction to the 1994 edition of the novel. She writes, "[*Appointment in Samarra*] is the [book] generally considered to be his best, particularly by his detractors who tend rather showily to concede it and who almost invariably employ its virtues as a weapon with which to smite the rest of his work."

Author Biography

John O'Hara was a prolific author who produced an impressive number of novels, plays, short stories, and essays. Born on January 31, 1905, the son of an Irish Catholic physician in Pottsville, Pennsylvania, O'Hara grew up conscious of the class and religious lines that divided the small town. He alternately excelled and failed at school, his failures usually due to disciplinary problems. O'Hara's father punished his son by forcing him to perform hard labor as penance for his bad behavior. Before leaving Pottsville, O'Hara worked at the local paper, the *Pottsville Journal*, and became ro-

mantically involved with a woman who was beyond his reach socially. Her social status and his heavy drinking led to the demise of the relationship. The social dynamic of Pottsville and O'Hara's familial and romantic experiences would affect his writing in the years to come.

O'Hara's father passed away in 1925, leaving the family in a surprising amount of debt. Denied the opportunity to attend Yale because of financial concerns, O'Hara stayed with the *Journal* for a time before leaving to seek his fortune elsewhere. After brief stays in other regions, O'Hara made his way to New York in 1927, where he worked at various newspapers and magazines, including *Time*. However, he was fired from each post. At the same time, he began contributing stories to the prestigious *New Yorker*. It is during this period that he wed Helen R. Petit; it was a stormy union that ended in 1933.

With his failed marriage fresh in his mind, and in need of more money than selling short pieces to the *New Yorker* could provide, O'Hara isolated himself at New York City's Pickwick Arms Club Residence and penned *Appointment in Samarra*. While writing, he supplemented his income with freelance work. *Appointment in Samarra* was completed in April 1934 and was published in a speedy four months, that August. The book became so popular that three printings were required.

Armed with his newfound success, O'Hara went on to become a powerful force in the literary world, following *Appointment* with *Butterfield 8* and a number of other works, including screenplays and a libretto. He won the National Book Award for Fiction in 1956 for *Ten North Frederick* and wrote successful newspaper columns for the *Trenton Sunday Times-Advertiser, Collier's,* and *Newsday*. His second wife, Belle, passed away in 1954, and O'Hara married Katherine Barnes Bryan a year later. He continued to write until his death, which was caused by a heart attack on April 11, 1970. He left behind the beginnings of a novel, *The Second Ewings*.

Plot Summary

John O'Hara's novel *Appointment in Samarra* is the story of the rapid descent and demise of Julian English over the course of three days, due in large part to the complicated social order and manners that drive 1930 Gibbsville, Pennsylvania, where he lives. Julian, a well-known Protestant, was born into a privileged lifestyle. A member of Gibbsville's elite society, he resides at the most coveted address in town: Lantenengo Street, where he and his wife, Caroline, lead supposedly charmed lives.

Christmas Eve

Julian's undoing begins when he overindulges in alcohol at a Christmas Eve gathering at the Lantenengo Country Club. There, he throws a drink in the face of Harry Reilly, a *nouveau riche* Irish Catholic windbag (in Julian's opinion). Convinced that his social stature is more secure than that of Reilly, Julian is shocked to find that his drunken act has serious repercussions that lead almost immediately to his being cast out of polite society.

Christmas Day

On Christmas Day, Caroline is incensed by Julian's irresponsible gesture and urges him to apologize to Reilly, who, it is later revealed, was one of Caroline's suitors prior to her marriage to Julian. Reilly had generously lent Julian a formidable amount of money the prior summer to help rescue Julian's Cadillac dealership from financial ruin. In fact, Reilly has lent a number of Julian's peers money, a fact that indebts them all the more to him rather than Julian. After Caroline and Julian share a chilly Christmas celebration with Julian's parents, Dr. William Dilworth English and Elizabeth McHenry English, Julian attempts to call on Reilly to apologize. When Julian arrives, however, he is told that Harry won't see him. Caroline's response to Reilly's refusal is one of doom; she fears that because Reilly is a powerful member of the community and a Catholic, he will use his influence to adversely affect the flow of business to Julian's car dealership as well as threaten their place among Gibbsville's elite. Julian, however, is more concerned with the fact that Caroline and Reilly have flirted from time to time and share a past.

That evening, they attend yet another Christmas celebration at the club. There, Julian is met with snide remarks from several of his peers, who clearly disapprove of and take secret delight in his assault on Reilly. While Julian appears to take much of it in stride, when he is left in quiet contemplation in the men's locker room, it is clear that his peers' disdain is bothering him. He makes a mental laundry list of the foibles of his contemporaries but realizes the futility of such thinking as "the trouble with making yourself feel better by thinking of bad things that other people have done is that you are the only one who is rounding up the stray bad things." His spirits are momentarily lifted when he shares a drink with Father Creedon, the local Catholic monsignor. Creedon agrees in confidence that he thinks that "Harry Reilly is a horse's ass." Empowered by this, Julian rejoins Caroline, who then reneges on her promise to meet him for a "date" at midnight and he is put off. She is withholding sexual favors because she doesn't approve of his behavior or his heavy drinking. He makes comments that bring his jealousy of her to the surface and when it becomes clear that she isn't interested in having relations with him, he retreats back to the locker room to imbibe further.

The festivities then adjourn to the Stage Coach, a place where the second-tier society of Gibbsville often holds dances and dinners. Julian and Caroline and their set run into Lute Fliegler, who works under Julian at his dealership, and his wife Irma along with a number of their friends. Also in attendance are Al Grecco, yes-man to Ed Charney, the local gangster who oversees all illegal activities in and around Gibbsville, and Helene Holman, Ed's flirtatious mistress. After receiving the cold shoulder once more from Caroline, who is annoyed at how inebriated Julian is, Julian seeks solace in the company of Al and Helene. Julian and Al are friendly as Julian has something of a relationship with Ed (he gets his bootlegged liquor courtesy of Ed). However, drunken Julian is besotted with Helene and her revealing dress, and they hit the dance floor where all eyes watch the pair, waiting to witness something scandalous. While they merely dance, Julian and Helene deliver on the promise of a scandal when she escorts a wobbly Julian out to his car where it is implied that they make love, much to Caroline and Al's horror—Al is supposed to be keeping an eye on wildchild Helene for his married and otherwise-occupied boss Ed. Caroline and Julian's friends fetch the hopelessly intoxicated Julian from the car after Helene returns looking disheveled, and on the way home, through a drunken haze, Julian knows that he is truly in for trouble.

The Day After Christmas

The next day, an ashamed Julian heads to work before Caroline can confront him about his infidelity. There, he realizes that the dealership is once again headed for financial ruin as he has squandered much of the borrowed money from Reilly. He also receives a dressing down of sorts from Lute, who chastises him for straying from Caroline. Lute, though, also assures Julian that things will turn around. After Lute leaves, however, Julian pulls out a gun and ponders suicide. Caroline calls to admonish him for being rude to their servant that morning, which distracts him. He then heads off to the club for lunch where he almost immediately gets into a fist fight with Froggy Ogden, Caroline's cousin and supposedly one of Julian's best friends. Froggy confesses that he's never liked Julian but merely tolerated him and challenges Julian to a fight. At first, Julian declines because Froggy lost an arm in World War I, but when some other members join the fray, Julian gets physical with all of them and flees.

Julian meets up with Caroline at her mother's home, where Caroline has been unsuccessfully trying to inform her mother of the gravity of her marital woes. Her mother brushes off any suggestions of divorce and Caroline leaves but runs into Julian outside. He tells her of the melee at the club and she is horrified. He begs her to run off with him, but she refuses. She tells him that if he leaves to go drink, she'll leave him for good. She then tells him she won't be coming home that night and that she is canceling the party they are hosting at their home that evening. They exchange sarcastic remarks and Julian leaves.

Once home, Julian drinks himself into a stupor. For a time, he is joined by a young woman who writes the society column for a local paper; she had stopped by to confirm the guest list for the party. They kiss, but she leaves before anything more illicit transpires. Left alone, he plays old records and drinks heavily before retiring to the garage where he shuts the door behind him, gets in the car, and starts the engine. Some of his final thoughts while pondering his last moments on Earth are of a failed romance with Mary, a Polish girl he couldn't wed because of her poor social status. When Caroline learns of his suicide, she is hysterical and blames his parents but ultimately she comes to realize that "it was *time* for him to die."

As the book ends, Lute Fliegler winds up running Julian's Cadillac dealership and it is revealed that Julian's true beloved, Mary, becomes involved with Ross Campbell, one of Caroline's two true loves.

Characters

Ross Campbell

Ross had been one of Caroline's suitors just prior to her marriage to Julian. By the book's end,

he is with Julian's former love, Mary Manners, and working for Ed Charney.

Miss Alice Cartwright

Miss Cartwright is the society columnist from *The Standard* who arrives at Julian and Caroline's home on the last night of Julian's life in order to verify the guest list for the party that was to have taken place there that evening. After she is told of the party's cancellation, she winds up sharing several drinks with Julian and telling him her woes as an underpaid journalist. She and Julian kiss, but she leaves before anything more serious occurs. Miss Cartwright is the last person to see Julian alive.

Ed Charney

Ed is Gibbsville, Pennsylvania's answer to Al Capone. A minor gangster, Ed oversees all bootlegging, gambling, and prostitution activities between Reading and Wilkes-Barre. Unhappily married, Ed keeps a mistress, Helene Holman, under the watchful eye of his henchman Al Grecco.

Despite having little use for most of the Lantenengo Street crowd, Ed thinks highly of Julian: "I will take that English. He's a right guy." Although Ed does not often employ extreme violence as a means to an end, he is not above blackmail and his men are capable of carrying out his bidding.

Monsignor Creedon

Monsignor Creedon is the local Catholic rural dean, who had been denied the opportunity to turn his parish into a cathedral and become a bishop. Well-respected by all faiths in the community, Creedon is also a country club member who tells Julian in confidence on the night before Julian's suicide that he thinks "Harry Reilly is a horse's ass." He also listens to Julian's confession of sorts—that he never should have been a Cadillac salesman—and Creedon suggests that perhaps Julian is a failed literary man.

Carter Davis

A childhood friend of Julian's, Carter is also a member of the country club set. Once counted among Caroline's potential suitors, Carter attempts to save Julian from himself and the attentions of Helene Holman at the Stage Coach. Carter is also there to shuttle Julian home from the Stage Coach.

Caroline Walker English

Caroline is the thirty-one-year-old wife of Julian English. Married to him for more than five years, Caroline is a much-admired member of

Gibbsville's smart set. Despite her education at Bryn Mawr, Caroline is a rather naïve yet sexually manipulative woman who had grown "a little tired" of Julian, whom she had known since she was a child, by the time she fell in love with him in 1926. Although she had a few failed romances, Julian took her virginity and they wed and settled into a privileged lifestyle. The couple, however, never had any children and seem to have grown apart over the years.

As Julian's life begins its downward spiral, Caroline has grown weary of his drinking and reckless behavior. At one point, she even wishes him dead since he has killed something inside of her after apparently seducing Helene Holman. When Julian, at the end of his rope, requests that they both leave Gibbsville, she opts to remain, choosing the life of convenience she has always known rather than the unknown. While she is saddened by his death, she confirms the inevitability of it, saying, "It was *time* for him to die."

Mrs. Elizabeth McHenry English

Mrs. English is Julian's mother and the wife of Dr. English. She seems to hold Caroline in higher esteem than she does her own son, perhaps because of her husband's negative views of Julian and his character.

Julian McHenry English

Julian English is the thirty-year-old protagonist of the story. Born into a life of privilege, Julian begins a seemingly purposeful slide into oblivion over the course of three days. Ensnared in the complicated web of Gibbsville society, Julian has fallen into a trap of sorts, expected to fulfill the role of a businessman when he's not much of one at all. He also finds himself married to a well-admired woman of whom he does not always feel worthy. Julian indulges in heavy drinking and inappropriate behavior that leads to his self-inflicted downfall, which is perhaps a self-fulfilling prophecy of sorts as he follows his grandfather's fate of suicide.

Julian takes pride in his sexual prowess; however, this likely masks his greater insecurities and shortcomings as a husband and a son. Furthermore, he bears a certain degree of guilt over the fact the he was unable to serve in World War I. His outrage, too, at the hypocritical behavior of others is ironic in that he too is a hypocrite. He can barely comprehend that his so-called long-time friend Froggy never really liked him when Julian himself had turned to Harry Reilly in a time of need even though he didn't ever care much for the man. For

all his shortcomings, though, Julian has the capacity to be a regular guy, attempting to treat those around him with the same respect with which they treat him.

Ultimately, Julian feels stifled and takes his revenge by acting out with unacceptable behavior. His affair with a Polish girl who was beneath his social station is quashed, and this untraveled road haunts him until the end of his life.

Dr. William Dilworth English

Dr. English is Julian's father. A socially successful physician, his medical practices have been deemed murderous by some. He holds a certain amount of disdain for his son, having desired Julian to follow him into a career in medicine. Julian, however, never had any desire to pursue a medical degree.

Dr. English seems to note characteristics in Julian that were also present in Dr. English's own father, who committed suicide many years earlier amid a scandal involving misappropriated funds. At the novel's end, Caroline attempts to blame Dr. English for Julian's suicide, saying, "You did it. You, you don't like him. You did, too, you pompous old man."

Irma Fliegler

Irma Fliegler is the wife of Lute Fliegler. Content in her modest life with Lute on Lantenengo Street, she still strives for an improved position while noting that she wouldn't trade her life with Lute for that of Caroline and Julian. Proud and respectful of her hardworking husband, she is a pleasant complement to Lute, a fact that is not lost on Julian. He "knew that if there was one person to whom he would tell [his troubles], it would be Irma." Unfortunately for Julian, he opts not to turn to Irma for help, despite the fact that he'd grown up with her, as she is "the wife of one of his employees."

Luther LeRoy Fliegler

The underling of Julian English at the Gibbsville Cadillac dealership, Lute is something of a foil to Julian. His social position is not nearly that of Julian's; he is saving earnestly in order to join the Lantenengo Country Club. He lives a modest life with his wife, Irma, and their three children; their life, although much less glamorous than that of Caroline and Julian, has a happy and honest quality to it. Lute, however, is not one to pass judgment. When he speaks with Julian about his recent bad behavior, including Julian's supposed physical indiscretion with Helene Holman, he is chastising but also supportive and reassures Julian that things—and the business—will turn around in due time: "Aw, what the hell. We'll get by . . . it'll work out one way or another."

After Julian's death, Lute finds himself in a position to run the dealership and perhaps catapult into a higher social echelon.

Al Grecco

Al Grecco has been henchman to Ed Charney for four years. A Gibbsville native, young Al's real name is Anthony Joseph Marascho. He picked up the name Al Grecco while pursuing a career as a prize fighter. Only twenty-six years old, Al has accumulated a formidable amount of money overseeing Ed's bootlegging operations.

Al holds the rich of Gibbsville in a certain amount of disdain and, unlike others in the town, he has his doubts about the integrity of Caroline English; however, he does hold Julian in a higher regard. In fact, Al even goes so far as to follow Julian home one evening when he spies him weaving drunkenly on the road. After doing so, though, Al's true feelings toward the rest of the Lantenengo Street crowd become clear as he rolls down his window and shouts, "Merry Christmas, you stuck-up bastards!"

Al is present when Julian leaves the Stage Coach with Helene Holman.

Herbert G. Harley

Herbert Harley is Julian's next-door neighbor. After hearing the Cadillac's engine running inside the garage, Harley discovers Julian's lifeless body in the car. He pulls him out but is minutes too late to save him.

Bobby Herrmann

Bobby is a member of the Lantenengo Country Club and, as such, is part of Julian's extended circle of peers, although it is clear that he takes great delight in Julian's slipping status. He and Julian exchange words at the club on Christmas night and Bobby implies that Julian had purposefully avoided service in World War I while he and others braved the perils of going overseas.

Kitty Hofman

Kitty Hofman is the wife of Whit Hofman and a member of Caroline and Julian's inner circle of friends. Known for being frank, she first informs Caroline of how dire the consequences of Julian's

actions against Harry Reilly could be. Kitty has had her own run-ins with socially unacceptable behavior, having received a black eye from Carter Davis after she kicked him, and then getting into a cat-fight of sorts with another woman in the club. Kitty is present when Julian leaves the Stage Coach with Helene Holman.

Whitney Hofman

Whit Hofman is the ringleader of the Lante-nengo Country Club set, often presiding over the hub of action at the club. Whit remains decidedly neutral during Julian's foray into oblivion. Married to Kitty, he has been known to engage in childish, albeit harmless antics from time to time. Whit is present at the Stage Coach when Julian over-indulges and goes off with Helene Holman. He enters the country club as Julian is fleeing from his bout with Froggy; Julian thinks as he passes Whit, "Whit probably hated him and had hated him for years, just as Froggy had done." Whit is the only one of Julian's friends who had never made a pass at Caroline.

Helene Holman

Helene is Ed Charney's mistress and a professional singer of sorts. Al Grecco spends a good deal of time keeping tabs on Helene, but she winds up dancing with Julian one ill-fated night and leaves the bar to go out to a car with him. It is implied that she and Julian have sex, although Julian denies the charge to Lute.

Mary Klein

Mary Klein is Julian's secretary at the Cadillac dealership. A world-class worrier, she greets Julian each morning with a laundry list of woes; however, Julian notes, "you could stop her at any point and she would not be offended." She represents to Julian "precisely what she came from: solid, respectable, Pennsylvania Dutch, Lutheran middle class," something that raises insecurities and prejudices within Julian, who believes that she and others like her "secretly hated him and all the Lante-nengo Street people." He spends his last day of life at work trying to look busy in the hope that "he was making a good impression on Mary Klein."

Mary Manners

Mary Manners is the Polish girl who was the love of Julian's life. Because of their differing social positions, Julian was unable to pursue a real relationship with Mary. She was forced to "go away or her father would have killed her." The two shared a sexually charged relationship and Julian comes to the realization that she "had loved him and never would love anyone else the same way." She appears at the novel's end, sharing a drink with Ross Campbell, who describes her as "the prettiest girl I ever saw."

Joe Montgomery

Joe Montgomery is a playboy with whom Caroline fell in love just prior to leaving for an extended trip to Europe. He is the first man to see her unclothed as well as the first to seriously proposition her, an offer she declines. She does, however, accept his informal marriage proposal but is unable to see him again before she departs two days later, having made prior plans to get together with Julian, Jean, and Froggy. While Caroline is in Europe, Joe meets another woman and ends the long-distance affair. Caroline continues to remember him as "the man she had loved most in her life."

Froggy Ogden

Froggy Ogden, thirty-four years old, is a cousin to Caroline English and a member of Julian's social enclave. Froggy served in World War I and lost an arm in battle there. Froggy's presence reminds Julian of his lack of service in the war.

Froggy and his wife, Jean, who is Caroline's best friend, helped orchestrate the pairing of Julian and Caroline by planning a double-date the night before Caroline was to leave for her extended trip to Europe. Julian counts Froggy as one of his best friends, something that is an error in judgment as Froggy confronts Julian after his dalliance with Helene Holman and tells Julian that he's always hated him. Froggy then challenges Julian to a fistfight, something Julian tries desperately to avoid, but he winds up punching Froggy anyway.

Jean Ogden

Jean is married to Froggy Ogden and is Caroline's best friend. Many years ago, Julian and Jean had had a passionate love affair, one in which "everything that they ever could have been to each other, Jean and Julian had been." The affair ended amicably and left each "ready really to love someone else."

Harry Reilly

A former suitor of Caroline's, Harry Reilly is a member of Gibbsville's *nouveau riche*. A long-winded Irish Catholic, he shares his home with his widowed sister and her children. Harry has managed to social-climb in Gibbsville "by being a 'good fellow,' 'being himself,' and by sheer force of the money which everyone knew the Reillys had."

A member of several committees, Harry Reilly uses his money to get things done. Further, most of Julian's set are in personal debt to Harry as he has lent them money with the onset of the Depression. He lent Julian a formidable sum of money the previous summer, a fact that does not prevent Julian from hurling a drink in Harry's face the night before Christmas at the country club. Harry is hurt and humiliated by the gesture (he refuses to see Julian the next day when he comes to Harry's home to apologize) and word quickly spreads through the town that Harry could use his influence to hurt Julian professionally and socially.

While other townspeople concede that Harry Reilly is a bit of a blowhard, Julian's motivation may also come from the fact that he believes that "Reilly always danced a lot with and was elaborately attentive to Caroline English."

Constance Walker

Constance is Caroline's cousin and ten years her junior. She bears a striking resemblance to Caroline, and although she isn't as pretty, she is "fresher—to [Julian]." Constance isn't a virgin, but the boys at the club believe she is; although she has a gorgeous figure, those who bed her are ashamed to admit it because she is not considered a beauty. She attends Smith College and, in spite of her youth, is more worldly than Caroline, a fact that Julian notes as he shares a dance with her at the Christmas Day dinner at the country club.

Jerome Walker

Jerome is a distant cousin of Caroline's and her first love. A captain in the British army, he arrived in Gibbsville in 1918 at the age of twenty-five to teach modern warfare to the draft army after suffering a leg wound. He left Gibbsville without declaring his love for Caroline and succumbed to gangrene six months later.

Mrs. Waldo Wallace Walker

Caroline's mother, Mrs. Walker, is a well-dressed lady and the most attractive woman of her age in Gibbsville. She is decidedly shallow on many levels: "You would know her for all the things she was . . . [when] you expect her to say something good and wise about life, . . . what she would say would be: 'Oh, fish! I *must* have my *rings* cleaned.'"

Because someone once told her that Caroline had a great independence of spirit, Mrs. Walker took this to heart, raising Caroline in a very hands-off manner. A serious emotional distance exists between the two and when Caroline goes to her mother for sympathy over the terrible state of her marriage, her mother only offers vague advice and contradictions and refuses to hear any talk of divorce.

Themes

The Failure of Love

A theme common to most of John O'Hara's works is the failure of love and *Appointment in Samarra* is no exception. Although Julian English is ultimately responsible for his own demise, he may have indeed felt that his situation were less dire had he felt loved by those most important to him. The most basic love of all—parental love—eludes Julian. His parents, Dr. and Mrs. English, treat him with cold disregard; his father, in particular, sees in Julian the very qualities evident in his own father—weakness of character—which led to Julian's grandfather's suicide. It is because of this perception on Dr. English's part and this loathing that he cannot love Julian unconditionally. Caroline confronts Dr. English about his coolness toward Julian when he comes to inform her of Julian's death in the following passage:

> Ah, go away. You did it. You, you don't like him. You did, too, you pompous old man.

She continues her assault:

> Well, he never liked you. I guess you know that, don't you? So high and mighty and nasty to him when we went to your house for Christmas. Don't think he didn't notice it. You made him do it, not me.

Caroline's deflection of guilt is indicative of her lack of deep love for Julian. Although she claims to have fallen in love with him when she agreed to marry him, neither Julian nor Caroline are truly capable of actively loving the other unconditionally. When Julian begs Caroline to go away with him as he is nearing the end of his life, she refuses, choosing instead the life to which she'd grown accustomed. Clearly, she'd never grown accustomed to Julian in a meaningful way.

Fate versus Free Will

Fate is a common theme throughout *Appointment in Samarra*. The book's title, in fact, is taken from a legend having to do with fate and in-

Topics for Further Study

- Certain critics have accused O'Hara of misogyny in his writings. Research their claims and determine whether O'Hara's texts support or denounce their statements.

- Research the Great Depression and discuss the full effects this economic crisis would have had on a town such as Gibbsville, Pennsylvania, in the years following 1930.

- Research the philosophical concepts of fate and free will as outlined by different philosophers, such as Descartes and Nietzsche, and determine how each might have viewed Julian English's actions.

- In this novel, there is a clear-cut social order. Discuss whether or not class systems exist in current society and what impact they have on individuals today.

evitability. A man has a brush with Death in a Baghdad marketplace and leaves for Samarra in order to elude Death, only to again meet Death when he arrives in Samarra later that day.

Julian's self-destruction raises many questions with regard to fate and free will. His behavior may well have been part of his predetermined fate, springing from his familial legacy of suicide. Dr. English pigeon-holed Julian as being weak-willed when he was caught stealing as a boy:

> William Dilworth English was thinking of his own life, the scrupulous, notebook honesty; the penny-watching, bill-paying, self-sacrificing honesty that had been his religion after his own father's suicide. And that was his reward: a son who turned out to be like his grandfather, a thief.

Despite the fact that Julian never stole again, his father's perception of him never changed. As Julian grew older and had a few incidents in college involving being overdrawn at the bank, his mother warned him:

> Your father . . . is specially worried about you where money matters are concerned because he thinks it's in the blood, because of Grandfather English.

It is plausible, then, that these and other similar incidents contributed to Julian's ill-fated destiny. His own wife, after hearing of his suicide, conceded that Julian had actually outlived his usefulness:

> It was *time* for him to die. There was nothing for him to do today, there was nothing for him to do today.
>
> . ..

Conversely, though, Julian's behavior, so outrageous in the eyes of his fellow patricians, may be seen as his first exertion of free will in his life. The morning after he throws a drink in Harry Reilly's face, Caroline demands:

> Oh, God, Ju, why did you do it?

And when he comes to her after his fistfight at the country club, she cries out:

> Oh, Julian, what did you do? My God.

Each time she says these things, Caroline is crying hysterically, perhaps out of shock that Julian would do such unseemly and uncharacteristic things, things out of line with who he was supposed to be. These rebellious acts may have been Julian's efforts at exercising free will to free himself from a miserable fate in Gibbsville.

Style

Point of View

Appointment in Samarra features an omniscient narrator who tells the story from the points of view of several key characters intermittently. These characters include Luther Fliegler, Irma Fliegler, Julian English, Al Grecco, Dr. English, Caroline English, Mrs. Walker, Mr. Harley, Alice Cartwright, Harry Reilly, and Mary Manners and Ross Campbell. This technique allows O'Hara the ability to present characters through the perception of the other characters.

Setting

Appointment in Samarra is set in the fictional town of Gibbsville, Pennsylvania, in 1930. Gibbsville, according to the novel, is part of the anthracite coal region of the United States. As such, it is "a stronghold of union labor."

The story unfolds in different places around Gibbsville, including the Lantenengo Country Club, Julian's Cadillac dealership, and the homes of various characters. Another place where a great deal of action occurs is in or around the automobile. Cars, in general, play a large role in the story. In the beginning of the novel, Irma Fliegler listens to the comings and goings of her neighbors on Lantenengo Street while lying in bed, knowing each person by the specific sound of each family's automobile. Al Grecco's character is first introduced while driving and spends a good deal of time thinking about driving in general. Caroline and Julian have several rows, depicted or inferred, in their Cadillac; additionally, Julian's infamous indiscretion takes place inside a car.

As important as the region is to the story, Gibbsville's social structure drives the plot and provides the impetus for much of the novel's action. Inasmuch as *Appointment in Samarra* is the story of a man's self-destruction, it is also a study of the social hierarchy of a small-yet-affluent town in 1930 America. Race, religion, and wealth dictate position in the order; however, it seems that each tier of society has an equal interest in maintaining the social order as each seems to have a good amount of disdain for the other. The Protestants do not care for the Catholics; the Catholics bond together against the Protestants; and the solid, respectable, Pennsylvania Dutch, Lutheran middle class serves to act as a barometer of sorts for the self-indulgent behavior of the privileged Protestants.

Structure

The novel is told in the present tense from varying viewpoints; however, flashbacks play a large part of the tale in relating character histories, especially those of Caroline and Julian.

Historical Context

World War I

World War I began in 1914 because of a series of events triggered by the assassination of Archduke Francis Ferdinand, the presumed heir to the Austrian and Hungarian thrones, by Gavrilo Princip, a Serb nationalist. This single event may have prompted the war; however, tensions had long been building between several European countries. A strong feeling of nationalism existed in Europe, a feeling that spurred the desire for people who spoke the same language and shared the same culture to exist in independent states. This, of course, flew in the face of the imperialist activities taking place around the globe. European powers were clashing over colonial interests, specifically in Africa.

On top of this, two very powerful strategic alliances were formed, each of which had amassed enormous military power. First, the Triple Alliance

Compare & Contrast

- **1900:** The divorce rate for America at the turn of the twentieth century per 1,000 people is 0.7. Out of 76,212,168 people living in the United States at the time, only 55,751 couples are divorced.

  Today: The divorce rate in 1996 hovers at 4.3 per 1,000 people. Of a population sized at 265,283,783 people, 1,150,000 couples are divorced. In the last hundred years the population has increased at a rate of 250 percent, while the divorce rate has increased by more than 600 percent.

- **1930s:** The United States is in the midst of the Prohibition era, which began in 1920 and will last through 1933. Prohibition is the legal ban on the making and/or selling of alcoholic beverages.

  Today: Since the end of Prohibition in 1933, the manufacture and sale of alcohol in the United States has been legal; however, public concerns about overindulgence in alcohol have led to the growth of Alcoholics Anonymous (AA), a fellowship of people who follow a twelve-step program and support one another in their quest to abstain from drinking. Also, an increase in drunk-driving accidents and deaths resulting from those accidents led to the formation of Mothers Against Drunk Driving (MADD) in 1980. MADD helps increase laws against and penalties for drunk driving.

---

of Germany, Austria-Hungary, and Italy was formed. Great Britain, France, and Russia then bonded together to create the Triple Entente. When Ferdinand was killed, then, the Austrian-Hungary government viewed it as a hostile act from the Greater Serbian movement (which was a movement to take control of areas of Austria-Hungary inhabited mostly by Slavic peoples). Russia and Great Britain intervened and persuaded Serbia to attempt to pacify Austria-Hungary; however, when Serbia agreed to only eight of Austria-Hungary's ten demands, Austria threatened to march on Serbia. The Russian government then said it would take up arms against Austria if it did so.

On July 28, 1914, Austria declared war on Serbia. Russia quickly made good on its promise; however, the Russian response prompted Germany to threaten war on Russia if it did not demobilize immediately. When Russia refused, Germany declared war on Russia on August 1, 1914. France then mobilized against Germany, and on August 3, Germany declared war on France. When the government of Belgium, which was a neutral country, balked at Germany's plan to march through Belgium to get to France, Great Britain showed its support by demanding that it honor Belgium's request.

The Germans ignored the request, and Great Britain declared war on Germany on August 4. Italy broke its affiliation with the Triple Alliance several months later and entered the fray on May 23, 1915. Ultimately, then, France, Great Britain, Russia, and Italy were joined by Japan and the United States, the last nation to become involved on April 6, 1917. Turkey, long allied with Germany, had entered the war on Germany's side in late 1914.

World War I was a war fought on several fronts, using submarines, trench warfare, and fighter planes. It devastated Europe on many levels, directly claiming the lives of 37 million people, including many American soldiers. While Russia withdrew in 1917 (it was undergoing civil problems of its own that led to the toppling of the czar and the institution of communism), Germany was eventually defeated. Ordered to pay war reparations to the allied forces amounting to $186 billion, Germany's economy was ravaged and would never fully recover, a factor which led to the rise in power of Adolf Hitler and World War II.

The Great Depression

The Great Depression was a period of intense economic collapse that began in 1929 and ended in the early 1940s. While the depression began in the United States with the crash of the stock market, its effects were felt worldwide and soon most of the world's industrial nations were adversely affected.

While its onset may appear to have been sudden, conditions existed for years that led to the sudden collapse of the economy. First, in the United States, there was an imbalance in the distribution of income. The wealthiest 0.1 percent of American families had a combined income equal to that of the bottom 42 percent of American families. At the same time as this situation was building up, manufacturers of goods were producing products for consumers at an all-time high rate. To encourage people to buy these new products, such as household appliances and radios, advertising strategies that had been employed to get people to support the Allies' efforts in World War I were used to urge lower-income people that they needed these things. If people didn't have the money to purchase things, which most didn't, credit was extended to them, credit that allowed people to buy now and pay later.

At the same time that these things were occurring, the United States government was placing high tariffs on foreign-produced goods to encourage the sale of American-made goods. Unfortunately, though, many foreign economies had been weakened by World War I, especially Germany and France (whose male workforce was all but decimated in the war). The United States wound up being creditor to those countries and when the countries balked at the high tariffs, they lost product sales—and income—on goods that might have been sold in the United States. Decreased income meant that these countries began having difficulty paying their debt to the United States.

All of these situations were compounded when stock market investors began buying stock "on margin," which is similar to buying goods on credit. A small part of the stock's initial price is paid and the rest is borrowed against future profits the investors believe they will make when they sell the stock at a higher price—*if* they can sell the stock at a higher price. When confidence that the stock market prices would continue to rise waned, the stock market began to plummet as many investors began selling off their stock. On October 29, 1928, known as Black Tuesday, stocks lost from $10 to $15 billion of their worth; by mid-November there were losses of $30 billion. Entire fortunes were wiped out over the course of two weeks.

The stock market crash and its negative effects on the economy, coupled with all of the other negative economic conditions that existed, left people with little money to spend on disposable goods; further, many could not make good on the credit that had been extended to them for goods previously purchased. Manufacturers could not sell enough product and jobs were significantly cut. Banks closed as people began to attempt to withdraw all of their money; many people were unable to get to their savings before the closings and people were left bankrupt.

Unemployment rates skyrocketed to nearly twenty-five percent; almost fifteen millions Americans were jobless. Conditions worsened until the election of President Franklin Delano Roosevelt in 1932; Roosevelt implemented the New Deal, a variety of programs to assist the public and boost the economy. While some gains were made, however, the economy was not fully restored until government spending increased dramatically with the United States' preparation for entry into World War II, the groundwork for which began to be laid in 1939.

The Great Depression affected the level of government involvement in many aspects of daily American life. Banks began to be regulated closely and the Social Security Act of 1935 was passed. Furthermore, union activity, which had long been viewed as controversial and had many opponents, became protected under the National Labor Relations Act of 1935. This gave rise to the powerful labor unions that still exist in the United States today.

Critical Overview

The book underwent several rapid printings, a testament to its popularity with the public. O'Hara had found his audience and would go on to publish books for nearly the next four decades. His peers, too, praised his freshman effort. Ernest Hemingway wrote of *Appointment in Samarra:* "If you want to read a book by a man who knows exactly what he is writing about and has written it marvelously well, read *Appointment in Samarra* by John O'Hara." Dorothy Parker, who was something of a mentor to O'Hara, pointed out that "Mr. O'Hara's eyes and ears have been spared nothing, but he has kept in his heart a curious and bitter mercy." Parker's comments reflect the acclaim

A flapper defies prohibition at a speakeasy in the 1920s. The novel reflects the spirit of the "Roaring 20s."

given to O'Hara's descriptive flair and ear for dialogue that is especially sharp in his first novel.

Just as there were mixed reviews for *Appointment in Samarra* upon its release, contemporary times have not extinguished the ongoing debate over O'Hara's merits. For example, when the Modern Library released its list of the top 100 best twentieth-century English-language novels in 1998, *Appointment in Samarra* was ranked at No. 22, a fact that caused much furor and opened the door for ridicule of the list as a whole by a number of contemporary critics.

Ten years prior to the issuance of the Modern Library list, John Updike looked at *Appointment in Samarra* in hindsight in an article in the May 2, 1988, issue of *The New Republic* entitled, "Reconsideration: *Appointment in Samarra*—O'Hara's messy masterpiece." Updike tells of his first experience with the book:

> I first read *Appointment* as a teenager (because, I suppose, the scandal of it in Pottsville had stirred waves still felt in Reading [Pennsylvania], 40 miles away, 15 years later); this monstrous mad drink, and Julian's sodden retreat to the interior of his Cadillac, seemed to me then overwhelmingly dreadful—a liq-

uid vortex opening a hole in the workaday world about me. How surprisingly brief, on rereading, the sentences are! [Dorothy] Parker correctly spoke of the book's 'almost unbelievable pace.'

Despite the passage of more than fifty years (at the time of the article's publication), Updike insists:

> The 'slight' novel . . . has lasted. Though O'Hara wrote many more, and produced volumes of short stories as bulky as bulky novels, he never surpassed the artistic effect achieved by *Appointment in Samarra*. He belongs, with Hawthorne and Hemingway, to the distinguished company of American novelists whose first published novel is generally felt to be their best.

Several years later, Margo Jefferson, reviewing the re-release of *Appointment in Samarra* in 1995 in *The New York Times Book Review,* said of the novel (along with *Butterfield 8*) that they "deserve to be back in print: it's amazing how much [O'Hara] got right."

Finally, Benjamin and Christina Schwarz wrote in their article "John O'Hara's Protectorate" in the March 2000 issue of *The Atlantic Monthly:*

> Today's reader can still appreciate the taut *Appointment in Samarra* . . . even if he or she is puzzled by the enormous significance O'Hara placed on the differences between drivers of the comparably priced Buick and Franklin.

Criticism

Caroline M. Levchuck

Caroline M. Levchuck, a writer and editor, has published articles on literature along with nonfiction essays and children's books. In this essay, she focuses on O'Hara's Appointment in Samarra *as a portrait of the disintegration of a marriage.*

Appointment in Samarra has been viewed in many different ways. John Updike called it a "social panorama," while Ernest Hemingway dubbed it "a Christmas story." O'Hara himself, however, in a letter to his brother Tom prior to the novel's publication, referred to it as "essentially the story of a young married couple and their breakdown in the first year of the depression." Despite themes of fate and inevitability and the failure of parental love, then, *Appointment in Samarra* may be seen as an intimate look at the failings of a young union. Many of the truths evident in O'Hara's work hold true to this day, an age where divorce is almost as common as marriage.

Rather cleverly, O'Hara does not first present Caroline Walker English and Julian English; rather, he sets up their introduction by framing their relationship and the story itself within the solid bookends that are Lute and Irma Fliegler's marriage. Lute and his wife share a rather practical union, far less glamorous than that of Caroline and Julian. Their kindness and mutual respect and understanding of one another, however, is evident from page one. Lute awakens in the early morning desiring his wife but, realizing that she is probably too tired to be intimate with him, he decides to allow her to sleep, conceding that "Irma can say no when she is tired." He does caress her lovingly, though, and Irma wakes with a start but acquiesces to his amorous overtures and "for a little while Gibbsville knew no happier people than Luther Fliegler and his wife, Irma." After their romantic coupling, Irma rises from bed to commence with her holiday preparations. While doing so, she ponders Lantenengo Street, on which they live, and its inhabitants and the state of her and Lute's life together. They are not as well-off as Caroline and Julian; after all, Lute works under Julian at the Cadillac dealership. Irma and Lute are not yet members of the exclusive and expensive Lantenengo Country Club, although Irma is anxious to be. Still, she respects her husband's philosophy about such things; Lute believes that they should join when it is within their reach financially. Unfortunately, though, this means that they are missing out on the big Christmas Eve party being held at the club. Despite this, Irma is quite aware of the good man she has found in Lute: "Lute was all right. Dependable and honest as the day is long, and never looked at another woman, even in fun." This realization quells her momentary envy as she ponders the goings-on at the club and she reminds herself that "she wouldn't trade her life for that of Caroline English, not if you paid her."

It is then that the reader is thrust into the glamorous world of the country-club set that includes Caroline and Julian English. Against this backdrop of parties and privilege, O'Hara lays out the relationship of the golden couple. Almost immediately it is clear that Julian does not truly have a grasp on who his wife is as a person. He completely misses the mark in estimating what her reaction to his throwing a drink in Harry Reilly's face would be, guessing wrongly that she would simply exclaim, "Julian!" Despite this, when he realizes the growing gravity of the situation the morning after and

What Do I Read Next?

- Leo Tolstoy's *Anna Karenina*, published first in 1877, centers around a sophisticated woman and her demise as she pursues her true love despite the price to her family. She defies high society with her rebellious behavior and mentally disintegrates as a result, ultimately ending her own life.

- Edith Wharton's *The House of Mirth*, published in 1905, relates the tale of a woman and her descent down the social ladder. Fate and inevitability are both themes of this acclaimed classic story.

- *Ten North Frederick* is O'Hara's award-winning 1955 novel detailing the life and death of another of Gibbsville's prominent citizens, Joseph Benjamin Chapin. Trapped by societal constraints, Joe's life is marked by a series of unfulfilled desires and regret.

- F. Scott Fitzgerald's *Tender Is the Night* (1934) relates the story of the dissolution of a man's marriage and his entire life. Set against a jet-setter Depression-era backdrop, the tale of Dick Diver's destruction shares many common traits with O'Hara's work; in fact, O'Hara heartily endorsed this book as one of his favorites of Fitzgerald's.

---

is loathe to face the consequences of his actions, his affection for his wife is clear. He tells himself he'd be all right, "if I could just stay here for the rest of my life and never see another soul. Except Caroline. I'd have to have Caroline." This sentiment is sharply contrasted with Caroline's ominous response to Julian's impetuous act and her chilly behavior toward him for the remainder of the novel.

While each has a certain understanding of the mannerisms and preferences of the other, the premise of their very relationship appears to be rather shallow. Caroline is aware of Julian's idiosyncrasies, such as the precise manner in which he prefers his monogram. Julian, for his part, can pre-

> Despite this, Irma is quite aware of the good man she has found in Lute: 'Lute was all right. Dependable and honest as the day is long, and never looked at another woman, even in fun.' This realization quells her momentary envy as she ponders the goings-on at the club and she reminds herself that 'she wouldn't trade her life for that of Caroline English, not if you paid her.'"

dict some of Caroline's responses. Yet, there is an entire character living just under the surface that each possesses but of which the other is ignorant. When O'Hara reveals the history of Caroline's love life, it seems implausible that Julian is aware of any of the details of her past heartbreaks. Caroline, for her part, possessed a naiveté about the depth of Julian's feelings for Mary Manners, the Polish girl with whom he shared a doomed romance. Even when Julian was seeing both women at the same time, Caroline was "sure he loved Caroline the most." As evidenced by Julian's thoughts of Mary toward the end of his life, he actually loved Mary the most.

Although wed for nearly five years, Julian and Caroline are childless, having adhered to their initial five-year plan, which one can assume included purposefully not reproducing. Over the course of the story, this point is presented as a minor issue between the two, with Caroline impulsively deciding en route to the Christmas dinner at the club that they shall embark on building a family that very night. When Julian asks if she means it, she tells him insistently, "I never meant anything so much in my life." The fact remains, though, that Caroline never truly seems to be certain of anything. When she first recalls her and Julian's relationship, she says that she didn't fall in love with him until 1926. However, this is contradicted when Caroline,

in her ire over Julian's escapade with Helene Holman at the Stage Coach, wishing him dead, refers to a time "when I knew [him] in an Eton collar and a Windsor tie, and I loved [him] then." Of course, Julian wouldn't have worn an Eton collar and a Windsor tie as an adult but rather as a young boy. In her reverie, she also proclaims that Julian has "killed something mighty fine" in her; however, when she'd phoned him at his dealership earlier that morning, she merely chastised him for being cross with their housekeeper, concealing her true feelings about his supposed infidelity and public humiliation. It appears implausible that two people can truly love each other and have a successful marriage when neither is certain of his or her own feelings nor does either make an effort to convey their anger and outrage at the other.

The supposed depth of Julian's feelings, which he conveys with his "need" for Caroline, also are contrasted with his true understanding of Caroline as a person; perhaps, though, lack of understanding might best be the way to view Julian's perception of Caroline. On Christmas evening, as he dances at the club with Caroline's much-younger cousin Constance, her dissimilarities to Caroline bring him to a startling realization about Caroline of which he'd not been previously aware, despite the fact that they'd been married for several years and had known each other their entire lives. In contrasting Caroline with Constance, Julian realizes, "Caroline was an educated girl whose education was behind her and for all time would be part of her background." Excited over this new theory, Julian wishes to "tell Caroline about it, to try it out on her and see if she agreed with it." While he realizes that her reaction will be one of affirmation and she will point out that she's been "telling him that for years," this incident points to the fact that even though he is aware of her reactions, he hasn't much knowledge about who Caroline really is as an individual.

Another sticking point in their marriage is the tensions that surround their romantic couplings. Julian spends a good deal of time angling for "dates" with his wife, something for which she appears to have little desire. Although the book spans only three days, Julian asks Caroline to have relations with him several times and his request is indulged only once. When Julian returns from Reilly's house after trying unsuccessfully to apologize for throwing a drink in the man's face, Caroline comforts him physically and Julian refers to the experience as "the greatest single act of their married life. . . . It was the time she did not fail him." The latter part, which refers to Caroline's acquiescence to his needs, denotes that it was "the time"—in other words, the only time. This, of course, implies that Caroline has failed him on countless other occasions.

Much of the tension that surrounds their sexual relationship may be due to Julian's inflated sense of his physical appeal and his bravado in terms of his ability to physically satisfy a woman. While he may, in fact, satisfy Caroline on a physical level—after all, it is implied that she hadn't ever strayed physically from the marriage—he hasn't the first idea how to fulfill her emotionally. Compounding Julian's shortcomings is Caroline's skewed view of sexuality. When O'Hara details her past experiences, it is clear that she attached a degree of shame to sexuality and possessed a good amount of fear over it even when she was in her mid-twenties; she was embarrassed when suitor Joe Montgomery glimpsed her in her undergarments when they went swimming at the beach. She tells Montgomery later that she wishes to engage in a steamy physical affair and marry in a whirlwind; however, she never makes good on her desire. Further compounding her troubled perception of her own sexuality is the fact that she had been molested by a student while teaching when she was just out of college; and, following her failed fling with Montgomery, she was taken to a live-sex show in Paris and is left frightened by the entire incident. On top of all of these events, Caroline's mother cannot bring herself to speak of anything sexual with her daughter when Caroline comes to her mother for help. She tells Caroline, "I told you when you were married, I told you to take a firm stand on certain things." Caroline replies, "You never told me what things though." All of these things lead Caroline to be so out of touch with her own sexuality that she admits that she wants Julian most when she is not well more "than any other time." This impulse conflicts with the viability of their pairing, and her supposed desire for something when she knows she cannot have it can be taken as proof that while the desire is there, she is afraid of indulging it.

Before the book's end, Caroline fails Julian once again, on another, more crucial level. After his final faux pas at the country club in which he fights with several other members, Julian begs Caroline, "Listen, will you go away with me? Now? This minute? Will you? Will you go away with me?" Caroline refuses his desperate request and remains at her mother's home, effectively sealing the fate of their marriage and Julian's fate as an individual. As they trade parting barbs outside Caroline's mother's home and discuss how to handle the cancellation of that evening's party, Caroline suggests that she tell the invitees that the party is cancelled because Julian or she broke a leg. Julian tells her, "But it's nicer for us to be agreeable and sort of phony about it. You know what I mean?" His words are apropos of not only the situation but of their entire marriage.

After Julian's death, Caroline mourns not for Julian but rather for herself, for her loss, "because he had left her." While she insisted repeatedly throughout the tale that she loved Julian, she likened her love for him to having a cancer, a metaphor that is not likely used by truly happily married people. Certainly, there were moments of tenderness between the pair and an amicability that allowed them to live out their days together in a content state. Unfortunately, though, the pair held each other at arm's length, just as each did to their friends and family around them, swallowing their true feelings until they practically choked on them, withholding genuine affection and understanding until it was impossible to summon any sort of compassion.

At the novel's close, O'Hara affords his readers one last brief glimpse into the happily married lives of the Flieglers. While Lute frets about his financial obligations and their shaky future due to Julian's demise, Irma looks at him with genuine affection and wishes "daytime were a time for kissing [for] she would kiss him now." Their ability to come together in the face of adversity stands in direct opposition to Caroline and Julian who were so easily driven apart by the smallest adversity—a drink being thrown in the face of a tipsy club member.

Appointment in Samarra stands as an example of a marriage whose internal workings fly in the face of the external perceptions of it. The situation was both plausible and true-to-life in 1934 and cements the truth that lies in the old adage, "Times change but people do not." Almost seventy years after its publication, the world is undoubtedly full of married couples having relationships that parallel that of Caroline and Julian's.

Source: Caroline M. Levchuck, in an essay for *Novels for Students*, Gale Group, 2001.

Sheldon Norman Grebstein

In the following essay excerpt, Grebstein explores the emotional history of Julian English and its influence on his tragic circumstances in Appointment in Samarra.

> To Julian insolvency becomes more than a mistake, it seems a sin—one more added to the overwhelming burden of guilt and self disgust he already bears."

The tragedies of our time are very likely to be what Arthur Miller has called the tragedy of the common man. These are the tragedies of the mundane, the ordinary, the familiar: tragedies of men worn down by the everyday pressures of life or by their own inner pressures; pressures of earning bread; finding and maintaining an identity; of doing useful work; of keeping the love of one's wife, children, neighbors; of expressing one's simple human dignity; of remaining decent in the concrete jungle, the social jungle, the factory jungle, or the army jungle. So the tragedy of Julian English, of Gibbsville, Pennsylvania, who expires in his own garage during the evening of the day after Christmas, 1930, is a tragedy of the common man, a tragedy of the surrender to these attritive forces. It is, indeed, doubly a tragedy of the common man; for Julian's motivation for suicide derives partly from the belated discovery of his own commonness, of the terrifying recognition of his own susceptibility to the failures, pains, and defeats others had earlier confronted. The trials and disappointments which early come to ordinary men presented themselves to Julian during three packed days of a Christmas holiday; and he was not capable of absorbing the lesson. A few hours before Julian kills himself, he falls into a drunken sleep "wishing he knew more things," but it is too late for him to learn.

Appointment in Samarra thus seems to chronicle the unhappy history of a man wholly victimized by Forces, especially Fate and Society. Fate appears to operate through the compulsion which drives Julian to throw a drink into Harry Reilly's face, the event which begins the protagonist's swift slide to doom. Fate is presumably the theme of the novel's epigraph, which retells the ancient tale of man who seeks to flee death only to find that in his very flight he keeps his destined appointment with

it. Fate is also suggested in Caroline English's agonized reflection after her husband's death that "It was time for him to die."

Society, too, takes a significant part in Julian's history. As one recent commentator has interpreted the novel, " . . . place is agency, and the tragedy, depends upon the disguised impetus of the sociological forces." Another critic states: "What makes *Appointment in Samarra* remarkable . . . is not the story of Julian English; it is the story of Gibbsville. All the characters, even Julian English, are here for not their own sakes but because they represent significant social elements in Gibbsville."

Certainly these observations are pertinent, and no understanding of the novel would be complete without the recognition of the influence of Fate and Society upon the book's characters and action. Social status occupies an especially prominent position in the minds of O'Hara's fictional people; accordingly, much detail is given to family background, wealth, clothing—even to the social meaning of such seeming trivialities as the price of the various entrées on the country club's dinner menu. True, there exists in Gibbsville a delicate relationship between the various classes, religions, and ethnic groups. True, there is much snobbery both petty and vicious, notably the prejudices against Jews and Catholics. True, in Gibbsville one begins at birth with particular advantages and disadvantages. True, finally, O'Hara depicts all this with such convincing thoroughness and admirable subtlety that *Appointment in Samarra* would be a far weaker book without it.

But to his cognizance of these forces the sensitive reader must add a third element, one I believe to be crucial: free will. As I interpret the novel, Julian's tragedy derives less from fate, less from social pressure, than from a series of wrong choices, bungled acts, and misinterpretations which reflect his immaturity and defective character. He behaves as he is—a man who does not know himself. If a fatalism does operate, it is neither an occult power nor an exterior force but a fatalism in the way men are, of human nature. The tragedy, therefore, depends not so much upon circumstance but upon the failure of love, nerve, will. Or, to put it in another way, the tragedy could have been averted at almost any stage by the exercise of love, nerve, will. Even Julian's apparently uncontrollable impulse to attack Harry Reilly can be seen, like his other compulsions, as the outlet for an accumulation of past emotions. His impulses are, in fact, but one aspect of a destructiveness symptomatic of a life deficient in love, trust, and moral value. By the same token, as I will later argue, Julian's tragedy amounts to something more than a treatise about an individual who violates group protocols or an illustration of the rigidity of class structure in a small Pennsylvania city.

What, then, is the emotional history of Julian English; upon what foundations does his character at thirty stand? Most important—and this is a dominant and recurrent theme in O'Hara's fiction—is the failure of love between parents and children and, more specifically, between father and son. Because of one boyhood mistake, some petty larceny performed partly as a boyish prank and partly as a means for Julian to assert his place in the gang, Dr. English comes to think of his son as a thief and a weakling. The father's judgment, reinforced by his undemonstrative nature and by his stern, unbending righteousness, forever bends the twig of Julian's personality. To protect his own ego, already threatened by his own father's reputation as an embezzler and a suicide, Dr. English dissociates himself from his son at exactly the moment when Julian most needs assurance of his love. The father of another boy involved in the same escapade handles the matter with greater compassion. He severely punishes his son but continues to favor him. In contrast, by detaching himself from his son and his son's mistakes Dr. English cuts Julian adrift in a world without god, a world without authority, meaning, and hope of redemption; for to a boy god is manifested in his father.

This crucial rejection has several results, some of them ambivalent, as they often are in people. For one, Julian reacts against his father and all his father represents: a profession, an ordered life, respectability, restraint, politeness. Only to *Father Creedon*, Julian's father-surrogate, can he admit that he should have become a doctor. In his rebellion he releases his pent-up anger, the need to hit back and hurt and destroy, wishing subconsciously that he will be caught and punished. At the same time Julian wants to be liked, admired, accepted: to have from others what he cannot have from his father. He develops a charm which is enhanced by his good looks and supported by the family's prosperity, charm which he can exercise on those higher social levels of Gibbsville automatically open to him through the English name, money, and Aryan background. Accordingly, Julian becomes a "personality," but one without an identity; for in O'Hara's world the boy also first learns his identity from his father. Julian's mother might have compensated for the father's failure, as the mother

sometimes does in O'Hara's fiction, but we are told nothing about her except that she is a sweet, adoring woman, obviously without the strength or influence to fill the role of both parents.

Because Julian never fully assumes a stable identity, he can never grow up. He can never perform the adult function of understanding himself in relation to others; his own emotions remain of prime importance to him. All these sins of omission and commission return to torment him in the frantic days before his death. He has made few loyal friends to stand by him in his crisis. Rather, his country-club associates step back to see how well he can sail out the tempest he has himself blown up. Instead of appealing for help to the one person who could have been his salvation, his wife Caroline, he alienates her by making her the target for his anger and frustration. For a time a saving rapport is almost established, but at the club dance on the night following the Reilly episode—a dance they have come to in a mood of intimacy—he ignores her a little too long and violates her tender feeling. Then, rebuked, like the child he is, he takes revenge by humiliating her in public for what he has suffered in private.

Later, on the afternoon of the day culminating in his suicide, he says to Caroline: "This is a pretty good time for you to stick by me . . . Blind, without knowing, you could stick by me. That's what you'd do if you were a real wife . . . " As much as Julian needs such unquestioning loyalty and love—as much as he needed it from his father and, failing to get it there, goes on needing it from everyone else—Julian does not deserve what he demands. Even if given it, he would probably not repay it. And the final choice remains his. To gain Caroline's support, he has only to remain with her and tell her what troubles him; but arrogantly and pettishly he refuses, flaunting her warning: "Julian, if you leave now it's for good. Forever." Thus the second support for Julian's life, his beautiful wife in whom he takes pride, is lost, this time largely by his own action.

Yet another of the pillars shoring up his existence is demolished when Froggy Ogden tells Julian he has never liked him, a crucial admission to a man who had needed to think of himself as popular and well-liked because inwardly he had feared the contrary. And at this phase in the discussion of the protagonist, one must take into account the social realities of Gibbsville as they impinge upon character and behavior.

Of first importance is the fact that Gibbsville society is not a steel trap which, once sprung, relentlessly holds its victim. Rather, it is a shifting, fluid society, a society in transition in which old and rigid lines are being dissolved under the multiple impact of emergent elements in the town's population and the exigencies of the Depression. To note but two examples of this change, there is the upward mobility of Harry Reilly, the Irish Catholic with his crude manners and smutty stories, who pushes his way toward the top because he is tough, clever, and strong. Similarly, the lawyers of Polish background who are Julian's antagonists at the Gibbsville Club have made their way into this once-exclusive establishment because they are now too able and prominent to be suppressed. Even the Jews at the bottom of the Gibbsville scale have begun to climb, first to residence on Latenengo Street, and soon, one infers, to club membership—just as the Poles and the Irish have already made it.

Nor does Julian's conduct immediately cost him his social place. When Julian loses control with Reilly, his friends back away warily, but they neither turn upon him nor against him. He is not suspended from the club, not reprimanded, not even cold-shouldered; their final attitude and conduct toward him will depend upon his future behavior, just as other club members have acted foolishly in the past without suffering drastic punishment. Further, Julian's behavior looms much more horrendously in his own mind than in anyone else's. As O'Hara shows us at the end of the novel, Harry Reilly continues to think of Julian as a gentleman and to be proud that Julian likes him—despite Julian's humiliation of him. Froggy Ogden, despite his avowed dislike for Julian and his insults, takes his side against the Polish lawyers in the fist-fight (completely confounding Julian's antagonists). Father Creedon, spokesman for the Catholic community, offers him comfort. Lute Fliegler, representative of the middle class and of the strong Pennsylvania-Dutch element, continues to be Julian's friend and advisor. Ed Charney and Al Grecco, the bootleggers O'Hara uses to represent Gibbsville's lower class and *demimonde,* do not condemn Julian for the episode with the roadhouse-entertainer; time and an apology would have squared Julian with them also.

Of course, Julian's outrageous behavior will have social consequences. But in *Appointment in Samarra* society is neither the god nor the unknowable, juggernaut force that the plurality of critics have described. It has its stupidities, its cruelties, its excrescences; but it depends largely upon basic human needs and upon the observation of fundamental decencies. It sets forth only one strong rule that a violator breaks at his great hazard; one must not publicly offend the dignity of others, and even when this does occur, the transgressor can find ways to restore himself to good standing. Thus it is less a problem of "society" than of the verifies of human nature, of the ego. Some of Gibbsville's citizens may have an exaggerated sense of what that dignity means; but, although these may be the "best people," they are rarely the most admirable human beings. Dr. English is perhaps the prime example of this self-assumed superiority, and his snobbery is a function of his own inadequacies and anxieties.

Having remarked these social realities, we may return now to complete the inquiry into the novel's central character. Two final aspects of Julian's emotional history remain to be explored: the influences of sex and money, powerful determinants in O'Hara's work.

Learning that Froggy Ogden and perhaps others have always disliked him is the second great discovery in Julian's life. Had he lived, this discovery might have brought about a change in him toward the better—toward humility. His first great discovery, however, had been that of his own sexual power: his ability to control his physical passion so as to be able to give his sexual partner prolonged pleasure. (Doubtless it was O'Hara's daring in broaching such facts of human behavior which offended the early critics and which has continued to offend others.) While O'Hara does not explore all the ramifications of the subject, the reader arrives at the sure conclusion that Julian's discovery of his special ability had been essential to his jauntiness and self-assurance. With that power over women, he could think himself very much a man, at least in one basic sense; and the conviction of his own masculinity had produced the peculiar charm and insouciance which springs from a man's total self-confidence with women. It had attuned him to women as sexual creatures, leading him to the belief that he could have anyone he wanted and keep her as long as he wanted. Nor does O'Hara minimize this factor. As his work demonstrates again and again, his men and women are sexual creatures; and the men are especially subject to the urges of their sexual needs.

To O'Hara's credit, he does not let the issue drop just there; he has more respect for humans than to portray them as laboratory specimens reacting only to physical stimuli. As Julian learns to his chagrin—both with his own wife and then, just before his death, with the reporter Alice Cartwright—a self-respecting woman has her values and her times of strength which make her proof against the most accomplished lover. She insists upon recognition as a person, as an entity. Julian begins to realize this fact during the final three days of his life when he reflects that his physical intimacy with his wife has not also given him possession of her soul. Unfortunately, Julian fails to act upon this realization; nor is there evidence that he tries. He has too long depended upon charm and his body to begin to treat his wife, or any attractive woman, with full human decency. Ultimately, Julian's sexual power turns against him. It has given him one kind of perception at the expense of another, more important kind. His blindness costs him the only two women he ever loves: the Polish girl, Mary, who Julian realizes sometime during the drunken haze of the last few hours of his life, had also loved him; and the other, the fatal loss, his wife.

Just as the shallowness of Julian's sexual values assist in his crucial self-deception, so does his inability to manage money, to take it seriously, to understand its meaning (the same character flaw in another manifestation) mark a further milestone on the way to his collapse. Product of a boom time and a wealthy home, graduate of a college but possessor of no durable knowledge, skill, or talent, and without the maturing experience of combat in war, he slides along as owner of a Cadillac agency (presumably his father's gift), getting by, as he always has, on charm and luck. It had gone well enough in the prosperous years of the late 1920's, but it is 1930 and things are changing. He had needed $10,000 but had exploited his charm and once-superior class position to borrow $20,000 from Harry Reilly, indebting himself to precisely the wrong man.

Now Julian needs more. He will always need more. Despite his sexual self-confidence, he conceives a completely irrational fear of Reilly as a rival for Caroline's affections because, in Julian's fevered imagination, Reilly's money has invested him with a potency which his own looks, background, and manners cannot match. His ineptitude with money becomes increasingly one of his major fears and an irritant to his latent anger, and money in O'Hara's fictional world is power. Upon money depends respectability and social acceptance; its possession and wise use also testify to the virtue of its possessor. To Julian insolvency be-comes more than a mistake, it seems a sin—one more added to the overwhelming burden of guilt and self disgust he already bears. We see, then, that his suicide springs from no sudden compulsion, no quirk, no command of the gods. His fate flows, as it does in the creations of most serious novelists, from the wellsprings of his character.

With all these faults, what makes Julian important? Why is his end tragic, or at the very least poignant? We note something of its significance in the way Caroline thinks of him after his death: as a young officer who had died in the war, with his own inimitable gallantry of attitude, manner, and gesture. Moreover, he is considered a true gentle-man by the two men in Gibbsville least likely to romanticize about people, Al Grecco and Ed Charney, who trade in other men's vices, as well as by such other tough, experienced men as Harry Reilly, Father Creedon, and Lute Fliegler.

In other words, there is an indefinable winningness about Julian, a finer substance underneath the glitter. One might almost say that he has an aura of beauty about him, or of the potentially beautiful: a zest, a joy in living, a sense of the comic, a spontaneity. He reminds us in part of Fitzgerald's people, of Dick Diver in *Tender Is the Night;* like him, he has the gift of stimulating others by his very presence, of bringing them an illusion of happiness. Like him, too, his grace is curiously emphasized by his very flaws. For Gibbsville, Julian represents the glamor, the *noblesse oblige,* the easy carelessness of the high aristocratic life; and his spark glows all the more brightly against the grey Gibbsville backdrop overcast by the lengthening shadows of Depression. His tragedy, and by implication man's, is that he lacks the self-knowledge, the nobility of character, the moral stamina to sustain the surface beauty.

Just as the themes and events of *Appointment in Samarra* operate on several different levels, so does O'Hara's narrative method work toward the effect of simultaneity and felt life. We find in O'Hara's first novel one of his fundamental techniques: that of the concurrent use of varying points of view, or what will hereafter be called the *shifting perspective.* An analysis of the book's opening chapter will seek to describe this technique and to demonstrate how it interacts with other elements of the work.

The novel's first three words are: "Our story begins . . ." That is, the reader hears a narrator's voice and is guided by an impartial observer's cues. It is the familiar, traditional mode of the editorial

A 1919 advertisement for a New York City liquor store, urging people to stock up before Prohibition goes into effect. Several characters in the novel are involved in the bootlegging of liquor during the lively "Roaring 20s" era that is the novel's setting.

omniscient. However, O'Hara quickly removes his own obvious presence and melts into the selective omniscient; first briefly entering the mind of Lute Fliegler and then that of his wife Irma. Irma's thoughts become the narrative projection for the remainder of the scene. This technique resembles stream-of-consciousness but differs from it in that the reader does not directly confront the inchoate outpouring of Irma's thoughts and emotions, as he does with Joyce's Molly Bloom; instead, he hears them as they are first filtered through the mind of a nearly invisible neutral observer. Through Irma the reader gets the middle-class attitude of the not-yet-rich but socially ambitious family, replete with its prejudices and snobberies. Further, through Irma one is convinced of the quality of her husband, Lute, as a strong, loyal, sensible, stable man. Since Julian later measures himself against men like Lute, one must know what he represents. Finally, the spontaneous and affectionate sexuality which the Flieglers enjoy symptomizes the security and harmony of their marriage, conjugal *love* as well as desire—yet another contrast to the Englishes.

Scene I of Chapter One closes with Irma thinking about the country club dance and wondering whether Julian and Caroline English are fighting again.

Scene II shifts to the dance, rendered by means of a dual point of view: an unobtrusively editorial-omniscient depiction of the people at the dance and the introduction of Harry Reilly telling an off-color joke downstairs in the smoking room, followed by the shift into the mind of Julian English at the very instant it entertains the notion of throwing a drink into Reilly's face. O'Hara then momentarily returns to the dance upstairs, creating a brief but telling interval of suspense, before the reader learns that Julian has indeed surrendered to his absurd impulse.

Scene III shifts to Al Grecco, the young hoodlum who works for the local bootlegger and crime-boss, Ed Charney. From the mental processes of Grecco, the reader is apprised that Julian enjoys the liking and the respect of the Charney-Grecco element in Gibbsville. He is further apprised of the town's power-structure, and that every "respectable" man can be either bought or silenced if he dares oppose Charney. Through Al Grecco's eyes, the aftermath of Julian's disastrous act at the club is first presented. Grecco has always respected Julian for his expert handling of an automobile; now, on his way home, Julian wheels his car recklessly and abusively (a foreshadowing of his more general loss of control, already under way), while his wife sits furiously silent beside him. As Al drives down Latenengo Street, his greeting to the darkened houses of the prosperous fully represents his worm's-eye vantage point and serves as a fittingly ironic ending for the chapter: "Merry Christmas, you stuck-up bastards!"

Thus in Chapter One O'Hara has offered a representation of the novel's milieu, a synopsis of its situation, a foreshadowing of its outcome, and an insight into some of its characters and conflicts. The reader also knows through O'Hara's astonishing dexterity in his handling of point-of-view that he is in the hands of a craftsman. Certainly the placing of the crisis of the novel at its very start is a bold and effective gambit. The remainder of the novel continues to build one's admiration for O'Hara's skill; for, with the use of varying scenes and the shifting perspective, O'Hara employs yet other techniques.

For example, in Chapter Five O'Hara slows the action to insert a flashback summarizing the life, especially the romantic life, of Caroline, Julian's wife. Not only does this chapter serve the immediate purpose of exposition, of illuminating certain aspects of Caroline's character and of her marriage, but in the structure of the entire novel it also serves a vital esthetic function. In the first four chapters O'Hara has set down a series of swiftrunning episodes which build to an almost excruciating sense of gathering doom. Such rapid movement and cumulative tension could not be maintained, nor should they be, if the novel is to hold its reader to the end. Therefore, in the more leisurely told chapter recounting Caroline's past, a chapter shrewdly placed at exactly the halfway mark in the novel, O'Hara achieves stasis by changing the mood and pace and by pulling the reader away from the "now" of the action.

The same effect, the alternation of action and inaction, of dramatic scene with narration and description, of violence and stasis, is also maintained throughout the novel by O'Hara's strategic insertion of little anecdotes about the characters or items of local history. At times, in fact, *Appointment in Samarra* has something of the construction of the pattern or tapestry novel in which characters and events are at first presented individually, seemingly without the least relationship to one another, only later to be woven together into a whole, large, variegated fabric.

Finally, to O'Hara's accomplishment of a multi-layered rendition of reality, must be added his success in individual scenes, notably those in which he produces a completely convincing sense of lived experience: the sensation of hangover which seems to saturate the entire novel; the absurd wisdom of drunkenness; the almost Surrealistic scene of the events at the Stage Coach Inn; the tactile response to putting a gun in one's mouth; the flow of thoughts in the mind of a bereaved woman; and, most unforgettable of all, the montage of fear and self-disgust in Julian's whiskey-stimulated imagination just before his suicide, as he visualizes himself going down, down. One notes the adroitness with which O'Hara moves from external observation to interior monologue, altering the reader's stance from that of observer to participant. We begin by listening to O'Hara approximate Julian's thoughts about himself, but before we finish the passage we have witnessed Julian's conjuration of all the damning, humiliating whispers and rebuffs he fancies as his future:

> He didn't want to go back and make a more definite break with Caroline. He didn't want to go back to anything, and he went from that to wondering what he wanted to go to. Thirty years old. "She's only twenty, and he's thirty. She's only twenty-two, and

 O'Hara's intention, morally, is to render the anguish of the socially snubbed."

he's thirty. She's only eighteen, and he's thirty and been married once, you know. You wouldn't call him young. He's at least thirty. No, let's not have him. He's one of the older guys. Wish Julian English would act his age. He's always cutting in. His own crowd won't have him. I should think he'd resign from the club. Listen, if you don't tell him you want him to stop dancing with you, then I will. No thanks, Julian, I'd rather walk. No thanks, Mr. English, I haven't much farther to go. Listen, English, I want you to get this straight. Julian, I've been a friend of your family's for a good many years. Julian, I wish you wouldn't call me so much. My father gets furious. You better leave me out at the corner, becuss if my old man. Listen, you leave my sister alone. Oh, hello, sweetie, you want to wait for Ann she's busy now be down in a little while. No liquor, no meat, no coffee, drink plenty of water, stay off your feet as much as possible, and we'll have you in good shape in a year's time, maybe less."

Source: Sheldon Norman Grebstein, "Love, Failure and Death in the O'Hara Country," in *John O'Hara*, Twayne Publishers, 1966, pp. 34–45.

Edward Russell Carson

In the following essay excerpt, Carson explores the theme of "social snobbery'" in Appointment in Samarra.

Appointment in Samarra constitutes O'Hara's object lesson in the cruel side of social snobbery. Julian English, the novel's protagonist, affronts a social climber at a dance. In turn, English himself is made the subject of ridicule for this error in taste. Two days later English commits suicide in despair.

Two varieties of social snobbery exist here. One is that of the "smoking room of the Lantenengo Country Club" and the other is the kind of censure exerted upon English by the middle class populace of Gibbsville who "collectively . . . presented a solid front of sound Pennsylvania Dutch and all that it implied. . . What a pity it was that this business wasn't in the hands of one of their own men instead of being driven into the ground by a Lantenengo Street . . . wastrel."

F. Scott Fitzgerald. The novel's style is similar to that of Fitzgerald's novels, and Fitzgerald himself receives a mention in the story.

It is the snobbery of the Gibbsville *crème de crème* which displays first how the snobbery of Julian English's social milieu is turned back, ironically speaking, upon himself. Thus, English must suffer the same limitation as any person from another social group. He is reduced to humility by the censure of his clique. Whereas previously he might have relied upon his own social position in the "upper crust," he now becomes, like Harry Reilly (the Irish social sycophant whom English insults), equally despised. O'Hara's intention, morally, is to render the anguish of the socially snubbed. Julian English is the spokesman for most of us who at one time or another have been subject to the scorn of the *haute monde*—those of us who are excluded from the membership in the "better" college fraternity or the intimate circle of the Long Island garden party.

O'Hara's treatment of the finer points of class stratification appears meticulous, refined and precise in the expository part of his narrative. This is how O'Hara does it:

Any member of the club could come to the dance, but not everyone who came to the dance was really welcome in the smoking room. The smoking crowd always started out with a small number, always the same people. The Whit Hoffmans, the Julian Englishes, the Froggy Ogdens, and so on. They were the spenders and the socially secure, who could thumb their noses and not have to answer to anyone except their own families. There were about twenty persons in this group, and your standing in the younger set of Gibbsville could be judged by the assurance with which you joined the nucleus of the smoking room crowd.

In like fashion, O'Hara depicts the wrath of Julian English against Harry Reilly, who is not a member of "the smoking room crowd."

Reilly, had gone pretty far in his social climbing by being a "good fellow" and by "being himself," and by sheer force of the money which everyone knew the Reillys had. Reilly was on the greens committee and the entertainment committee, because as a golfer he got things done; he paid for entire new greens out of his own pocket, and he could keep a dance going till six o'clock by giving the orchestra leader a big tip. But he was not yet an officer in the Gibbsville Assembly.

In passages like these, O'Hara never falters in noting exactest gradations upon the social ladder.

Two days after insulting Reilly, English becomes subject to the same variety of malice and petty hatred which he has seen fit to exercise upon the Irishman. A fellow club member says to him, "I've done a lot of things in my life, but by Jesus if I ever sunk so low that I had to throw ice in a man's face and give him a black eye." The man's violence suggests a little ludicrously that English has committed an error in taste unbecoming to a member of the Gibbsville aristocracy.

That evening Julian English goes to a roadhouse with his wife. He becomes drunk and makes an attempt to sexually overcome Helene Hoffman, a singer there. By this time, he has done more than behave in bad taste, as with Reilly. He has attempted a major moral infraction. The chain of events is now speeding blindly toward the novel's fatal conclusion. When he appears at the Gibbsville Club for lunch the next day, he is insulted once more, and a quarrel ensues. Julian attempts a gentlemanly exit, but open violence follows:

Froggy swung on him and Julian put up his open hand and the punch made a slight sound on his wrist, and hurt his wrist.

"Gentlemen!"

"Don't be a God damn fool," said Julian.

"Well, then. Come on outside."

"Gentlemen! You know the club rules." It was [the steward]. He stood in front of Froggy, with his back toward Froggy, facing Julian.

A lawyer then insults English, who insults him in return by calling him a "Polack war veteran and whoremaster."

"Hey, you!" said the lawyer.

"Aw," said Julian, finally too tired and disgusted with himself and everyone else. He took a step backwards and got into position, and then he let the lawyer have it, full in the mouth.

Julian attacks both the lawyer and Froggy. Infuriated, he hurls a carafe at still another man and runs for his car. His doom has been sealed. As he drives away, he suddenly realizes that Whit Hoffman, another friend, has detested him just as Froggy had—for a long time, quietly. This last experience has cost Julian any chance to make amends for his bad behavior, and his reputation in the town of Gibbsville is now at an ebb.

English arrives home to discover that his wife has deserted him. His final act of status derangement occurs during an attempt to seduce Alice Cartwright, a visiting journalist. Julian knows that he has by this time committed the local unpardonable sin of marital disloyalty. Sooner or later, he must face the enmity of all Gibbsville for his several moral infractions: The drink thrown into Harry Reilly's face, the Stage Coach Bar misadventure, the fight with Froggy and the lawyer, and the attempted seduction. Finally Julian English climbs into his car and dies of carbon monoxide poisoning.

Morally speaking, *Appointment in Samarra* attempts to display the psychological effect upon an individual of rejection by an in-group coterie. The didactic function of this novel is thus to warn the reader of the iniquity of pressing class distinctions to so extreme an issue. While John O'Hara may be a snob in his own right "as sensitive to social distinctions as any *arriviste* ever was," to quote from Delmore Schwartz. O'Hara nevertheless takes time to display the person on the receiving end of class bigotry based upon a knowledge of "upper crust" ways. While one may detect in O'Hara's own motivation—at least as Delmore Schwartz sees it—an attempt to play vicariously the snob by writing about snobs themselves—*Appointment in Samarra* possesses a sympathy for English, and poses the question of just why such a calamity *was* necessary.

The novel of social criticism concerned with class mobility is no unusual phenomenon in American fiction. It has existed from Henry James through J. P. Marquand, as well as in the writers who constitute the chief influences upon O'Hara in this novel. "As for influences, here they are: Fitzgerald, Sinclair Lewis, Galsworthy, Tarkington, Owen Johnson, but chiefly Fitzgerald and Lewis." Yet, in none of these authors exists so stringent an emphasis upon the suffering endured by the snubbed, except possibly in Fitzgerald's characterization of Gatsby. O'Hara, as Delmore Schwartz shows in *Partisan Review:* . . . has a rich gift for social observation, for knowing how people are, what they are because of their background, and he has an acute, accurate ear which makes it possible for his characters to possess reality when they converse. But best of all, O'Hara is a snob; he is as sensitive to social distinctions as any *arriviste* ever was, and his snob-sensitivity provides him with inexhaustible energy for the transformation of observation into fiction. It was neither accident nor invention which made him call the scapegoat hero of his first novel, Julian English; for English is an Anglo-Saxon, he resents the Irish, he belongs to what is supposed to be the upper classes, and the tragic action which leads to his suicide is his throwing a drink in the face of a man with the choice name of Harry Reilly. It might just as well have been Murphy, O'Mara, or Parnell.

Merely to pinpoint O'Hara as a social commentator, however, or chronicler of the ways of the *haute monde* is to fall short of the mark. Edmund Wilson, writing in 1941 in *The Boys in the Back Room,* says this about O'Hara, but also considerably more. While maintaining that "to read O'Hara on a fashionable bar or the Gibbsville Country Club is to be shown on the screen of a fluoroscope gradations of social prestige of which one had not before been aware," Wilson also says, by way of certifying O'Hara's perception of class distinctions:

> [There is] no longer any hierarchy here, either of cultivation or wealth; the people are all being shuffled about, hardly knowing what they are or where they are headed, but each is clutching some family tradition, some membership in a selective organization, some personal association with the famous, which will supply him with some special self respect . . . eventually, they all go under. They are snubbed, they are humiliated, they fail.

O'Hara's characters cling to their illusions of superiority, their unvarying lot in the Gibbsville milieu, knowing only too well their own impotence and despair. Out of a hostility for this weakness and emotional apathy they will snub others and practice their kind of life before a mirror. Although O'Hara writes of "the cruel side of social snobbery" he does so from an even greater pessimism. It is a pessimism about the Very Rich, who perceive life only on the most sensate level possible, from one moment of indulgence to the next. As models for moral conduct, only a few of O'Hara's characters from the world of Julian English would suffice for most of us. It is a world which O'Hara describes with precision and insight. Because of O'Hara's restricting himself to describing only the visually real, the moral element in his novels becomes a thing of mundane but democratic necessity.

Source: Edward Russell Carson, "The Novels," in *The Fiction of John O'Hara,* University of Pittsburgh Press, 1961, pp. 9–14.

Sources

Jefferson, Margo, "Books of the Times; Reissues of 2 Novels by O'Hara," in *The New York Times,* January 18, 1995.

Schwarz, Benjamin and Christina, "John O'Hara's Protectorate," in *The Atlantic Monthly,* March 2000, p. 108.

Updike, John, "Reconsideration: Appointment in Samarra—O'Hara's Messy Masterpiece," in *The New Republic,* Vol. 198, No. 18, May 2, 1988, p. 38.

For Further Study

Bruccoli, Matthew J., *The O'Hara Concern: A Biography of John O'Hara,* Random House, 1975.
    Offers a detailed look at the author's life and works, including analysis and criticism.

Eppard, Philip B., ed., *Critical Essays on John O'Hara,* G. K. Hall, 1994.
    Early reviews and modern scholarship on John O'Hara can be found in this collection of articles and reviews by writers such as John Cheever and Malcolm Cowley.

Bastard Out of Carolina

Dorothy Allison
1992

In her discussion of Dorothy Allison's literary career in *Feminist Writers,* Deborah T. Meem writes, "For Allison, writing is a dramatic, life-affirming act in a world which consistently threatens death. A storyteller since childhood, Allison chronicles her discovery how . . . writing them [her most terrible stories] down gives her power of the experiences." Dorothy Allison has never been shy about the autobiographical background of her powerful first novel *Bastard Out of Carolina.* Allison was born to a poor, "white trash" southern family. Her stepfather sexually abused her for six years starting when she was only five years old, and her mother, whom Allison deeply loved, was unable or unwilling to deal with this issue. *Bastard Out of Carolina* is not Allison's first important piece of writing, but for many readers, it remains her truest.

Allison recounts the story of Ruth Anne "Bone" Boatwright, the illegitimate daughter of a fifteen-year-old, unmarried, uneducated waitress. Bone's mother, a child herself, desperately seeks love and familial stability, which she has never experienced in her own large, unorthodox brood of kin. Anney's need for love is so strong that she turns a blind eye to the abuse—physical, emotional, and sexual—that her second husband, Daddy Glen, heaps upon her young daughter. Before even reaching the age of thirteen, Bone has experienced a life's supply of disappointment, bitterness, self-hatred, and even hatred for her mother. If *Bastard Out of Carolina* sharply affects many readers because of the swell of truth behind the characters and their

Dorothy Allison

actions, that is partially Allison's intention. For Allison once explained what storytelling meant to her in an interview she gave to Alexis Jetter of *The New York Times Magazine:* "I believe that storytelling can be a strategy to help you make sense of your life. It's what I've done."

Author Biography

Dorothy Allison was born on April 11, 1949, in Greenville, South Carolina, to a poor, unmarried fifteen-year-old girl. Her mother soon married, and when Allison was five her stepfather began sexually abusing her. This situation lasted until Allison was eleven, at which time she finally brought herself to tell a relative. Allison's mother learned of the situation and put a stop to it, but the family still stayed together.

At the age of eighteen, Allison left home to attend college in Florida. At school she learned about and came to embrace feminism, finding that it gave her a completely different vision of the world. She lived in a lesbian-feminist commune for a period of time. She later attended graduate school in New York.

Allison began writing seriously in the early 1980s. She published poetry and short stories, many of which dealt with sexuality and sometimes shocking issues of abuse. Her 1983 poetry collection *The Women Who Hate Me* angered mainstream feminists in its praise of sexual promiscuity and sadomasochism. Despite the controversy her work generated, she established a name for herself among writers of gay fiction. Her success was solidified when her 1989 short story collection *Trash* won the Lambda literary awards for best small press book and best lesbian book.

Allison also began work on *Bastard Out of Carolina,* which has a strong and public autobiographical element. The novel, which was published in 1992, was an immediate success. It was a National Book Award finalist, received much positive criticism, and became a national bestseller. It was also made into a movie by Angelica Houston.

Allison followed up *Bastard Out of Carolina* with a collection of essays entitled *Skin: Talking about Sex, Class and Literature* (1994); *Two or Three Things I Know for Sure* (1995), a memoir of her family that included photographs; and a second novel, *Cavedweller* (1998). Allison currently lives with her partner and their adopted son in California.

Plot Summary

At fifteen years old, Anney Boatwright gives birth to her first baby out of wedlock. The child comes to be called Bone. Anney stubbornly tries to legitimize her child. She tries several years in a row to get a birth certificate that is not marked with the word "illegitimate." When Anney is seventeen, she marries a man who wants to be a good father to her child. Her first husband dies shortly thereafter, however, leaving her with yet another daughter, Reese, to care for. Anney comes from a large family, most of whom live in Greenville, South Carolina, and the family relies on each other for money, help, and comfort.

Through her brother Earle, Anney meets Glen Waddell. Glen promises to love and take care of her girls, which wins him Anney's love. Two years later, they marry. Glen, however, is a failure. He comes from a middle-class family but cannot hold a job. He is filled with rage against his own family, who make their dislike of him apparent, and he takes out his frustrations and anger on Bone. He first sexually abuses her less than a year after the marriage, masturbating against her while his wife gives birth to their stillborn baby.

As Glen finds it increasingly impossible to hold a job, the family moves constantly, and Bone and Reese are always hungry. One night Anney prostitutes herself to get money to buy her children food. When Bone is ten, Daddy Glen starts viciously and methodically beating her. He puts aside several belts, which he keeps well-oiled, for this purpose. The family witnesses the first of his savage beatings. Anney gets angry at Glen but forgives him. Bone quickly realizes that she must be careful around Glen to not invoke his rage. At times, however, she cannot keep herself from "sassing back." In reality, there is nothing Bone can do to prevent the beatings. Anney insists on deluding herself that Bone is simply "prone to accident," and gets furious when an intern at the hospital raises the specter of child abuse. She begs Bone to "be more careful" around Glen.

Around this time or perhaps even earlier, Glen's sexual abuse of Bone becomes a more regular practice. Bone tells no one what he is doing to her because she is ashamed and afraid of making him angry. She also has begun to masturbate, and her sexual fantasies center on violent scenarios. She imagines that a crowd of people watch as Glen beats her, but that she is defiant and unyielding. She feels great shame over these fantasies but does not stop them.

After a bad beating, Anney takes her children to Alma's, but two weeks later, they return home. Glen promises never to hurt Bone again, but she knows that he won't really change. Bone and Reese go over to Alma's after school, and Anney comes there to pick them up on her way home from work. Bone tells violent stories to her cousins, filled with rapes and murders. The family notices that she has changed, that her face is "scary" and that she is "almost mean-hearted." Bone starts going to the diner with Anney. She earns money washing dishes and spends most of it buying used books.

That summer, Bone goes to stay with and help out Aunt Ruth and Uncle Travis. Aunt Ruth has a debilitating illness and she has grown weaker. Bone realizes that Ruth is dying. Bone tells Ruth that Daddy Glens hates her, and Ruth agrees, noting that Glen is jealous of her and wants Anney all to himself. She asks Bone if Glen has ever sexually abused her, but Bone lies and says no. She does admit that he scares her, however. While Bone is at Ruth's, Glen gets a new job, and according to Anney, is "good as gold with Reese," but he never

mentions Bone; it's as if she no longer exists. Ruth tells Anney that Bone will never be safe around Glen, but Anney insists that he does love her. Bone overhears this conversation and decides to spend the rest of the summer with Ruth.

Bone becomes interested in gospel music and religion. She starts reading the Bible, going to Christian youth groups, and trying to save her family, particularly her uncles. She becomes friends with Shannon Pearl, an albino who starts attending her school. Bone recognizes Shannon from the revivals that Shannon also attends with her family— her father books singers for the circuit and her mother sews costumes for the singers. Bone goes with the Pearls to gospel revivals and when Mr. Pearl is searching for new talent in the small country churches. One day, while Bone and Shannon are walking around, Bone hears a beautiful voice singing gospel music, but it comes from a "colored" church. Bone and Shannon get into a fight when Shannon calls them "niggers." Abruptly, Bone loses her religious bent along with her friendship with Shannon. She starts to spend a lot of time at Aunt Raylene's, helping to pick vegetables and fish garbage out of the river for Raylene to clean up and sell. When Shannon invites Bone to a barbecue right before Thanksgiving, however, Bone goes. She sees Shannon burn to death when a can of lighter fluid explodes in her hand.

Bone comes up with a plan to break into the Woolworth store. Several years ago, the manager had forbidden her to come into the store after she had confessed to stealing Tootsie Rolls. Now, she and her cousin Grey sneak into the store via an air duct. While Grey runs around the store, gathering goods to steal, Bone waits for him, for suddenly everything the store offers seems cheap and useless. As the two children run up the main street, Bone yells that the Woolworth is open, knowing it will be looted.

The next morning when Bone wakes up, Anney tells her that Ruth has died. The day before the funeral, when Glen picks on her, Bone snaps and yells back at him. He takes her into the bathroom and beats her bloody, but for the first time, Bone does not scream. While Anney is washing her wounds, she asks why Bone started yelling at Glen. Bone spends that night with Aunt Raylene at Ruth's house, helping her clean up and cook some food. The family returns to Ruth's house afterwards. Bone's cousin gives her some liquor, and she gets drunk. She goes to the bathroom, and Raylene finds her in there. While helping her get up, Raylene sees that Bone's underpants are bloodstained. She pulls Bone's skirt up and sees the marks of Glen's beating. Raylene calls the uncles, who take one look at their niece and go find Glen to beat him up. Anney comes to the bathroom, and Bone apologizes, claiming it was all her fault because she made Glen mad. Later, one of the aunts takes Glen to the hospital. Meanwhile, Anney moves herself and the girls to an apartment. Everyone is miserable; Anney hardly speaks and won't even let the aunts in for a visit. Upset because Anney seems completely unfeeling, Bone runs away to Raylene's and stays there for a few days, but finally returns home.

A few days after Bone returns home, Alma's youngest daughter dies. Soon afterwards, Alma goes crazy. When Anney and Bone arrive at her house, they see that Alma has destroyed and tossed most of her belongings out on the lawn. Alma has cuts on her forearms and on her face from broken glass. She tells Anney that she is waiting for Wade to come back so she can cut his throat with the razor she has in her pocket. Alma explains that she wanted another baby, but Wade refused to sleep with her because she was "old and ugly and fat."

Bone and Anney stay at Ruth's. That night, Bone tells Anney that she is waiting for her to go back to Daddy Glen. Anney tells Bone that she won't do that if Bone will hate her and that she won't go back until she knows Bone will be safe. Bone, however, says she will never live with Glen, no matter when her mother goes back. She will stay with one of the aunts instead. Bone stays at Alma's house. She hears from Reese that Anney is talking with Glen again. Then one afternoon he comes over to the house. Alma is out in the garden, and Glen finds Bone alone in the kitchen. He says that Bone must tell Anney that she wants them all to live together again. Bone refuses, saying Anney can return to him if she wants, and she tells Glen to leave. Glen shakes her with rage, lifting her off the floor. Glen tells Bone that everything is her fault: that she makes him crazy and act the way he does, that she makes Anney ashamed of loving him, that Anney is only leaving Glen because of her. He looks at Bone with eyes filled with hate. He tells Bone that Anney has said she will come back, that she needs a little more time, but if she wasn't going to come back, he would kill Bone. Glen kisses Bone, and she tries to stab him with a butter knife. Glen throws her on the floor and kicks her. Then he jerks her arm and drops her back down, dislocating her shoulder. He curses at her, and Bone tells him that she hates him and won't let Anney go back to him. He tears her clothes off, all the while saying that

he should have done this a long time ago, that Bone always wanted it. He rapes her. Bone wishes only to kill him and die herself.

When Glen is finished, both he and Bone see Anney coming through the doorway. Anney starts to throw things at Glen, who swears that it isn't what it looks like. Bone wonders if Anney will think that she wanted him to do it. Anney helps Bone get up and takes her out to the car. All the while, Glen is begging Anney not to leave and saying that he doesn't know what happened and that he had only meant to talk to Bone. Anney puts Bone in the car. She hits Glen several times, and he drops to his knees in front of her telling her to kill him because he can't live without her. He begins to hit his head against the metal of the car door. Anney starts to cry and places her hands against his forehead to protect him. She holds his head against her belly. Watching them, Bone, for the first time, hates her mother.

When Bone comes back to consciousness, she is at the hospital with Anney, but her mother disappears. The sheriff comes to get her story. Suddenly the door swings open. Bone hopes it is Anney but it is Raylene. She kicks the sheriff out and spends the night in the hospital with Bone. The next day they return to Raylene's house. Raylene tries to explain that it is impossible for a woman to choose between her child and her lover; she made the woman she loved choose, and the woman chose the child, which just about killed them both. She tells Bone that no one knows where Anney has gone but that she loves her and that she will never forgive herself for what she let happen.

When Anney comes several days later, Bone is sitting alone on the porch. She tells Bone that she never thought Glen could do anything like that but that she loves Bone. Bone starts to cry, and Anney holds her. Anney draws away from the embrace, dropping an envelope in her lap. Then she leaves. Bone opens the envelope to find a copy of her birth certificate without the word "illegitimate" stamped on it. Bone thinks that at the age of only twelve, she has already developed into the person she is going to be: a Boatwright woman.

Characters

Aunt Alma Boatwright

Aunt Alma is married to Wade and has several children. She loves her husband, despite his numerous infidelities. The first time she learns that Wade has been unfaithful, she leaves him and moves with the children to an apartment. Bone notes at the time that she looks better than ever before and seems to relish her independence. However, when problems with the children arise, she returns home. Alma is devastated when her youngest child dies. Her husband refuses to have sex with her—and make another baby—and she physically attacks him. She is completely devastated because she has given her life, and all her love, to Wade. In her rage, she destroys many of their belongings and waits at home with a razor in her pocket to kill him. In time, however, she allows him to come home.

Anney Boatwright

Anney is Bone's mother. She is one of eight children born to a poor Southern family. Uneducated, underemployed, an unwed mother at the age of fifteen, a widow with two children at the age of nineteen, Anney is desperate for love and a stable family life. She marries Glen Waddell after she comes to believe that he will be a loving father to her two girls. Glen disappoints her—even sexually molesting Bone (though Anney does not know this) while Anney is in the hospital delivering their stillborn child. Anney, however, is determined to make the family work, and she refuses to acknowledge the cruelty that Glen openly displays toward Bone. Instead, she chooses to blame her own daughter for the violent attacks. She does not know of the sexual abuse at this time.

Like many of the novel's characters, Anney demonstrates conflicting aspects of her personality. She is independent and determined—as demonstrated by her multiple attempts to get a new and unmarked birth certificate for Bone, the length of her courtship with Glen, and her prostituting herself to earn money to feed her hungry children. At the same time she is weak, helpless, and even cruel—as demonstrated by her steadfastness in staying with Glen despite his abysmal treatment of her child. Her decision at the end of the novel—to leave town with Glen rather than stay with her child—is incomprehensible to her daughter (and to many readers). Before leaving, however, she does attempt to bestow upon her daughter a new identity by presenting Bone with a clean birth certificate, one that does not bear the damning stamp "illegitimate."

Media Adaptations

- An audiotape of *Bastard Out of Carolina,* read by Allison, was published by Penguin Highbridge Audio in 1993.

- Angelica Houston directed the movie version of *Bastard Out of Carolina* from a screenplay written by Anne Meredith. Jennifer Jason Leigh played the role of Anney, and Jena Malone played Bone.

Uncle Beau Boatwright

Like Bone's other uncles, Beau drinks too much and has a violent temper. He never cared for Glen, primarily because Glen doesn't drink. With his brothers, he soundly beats Glen after the family discovers his violence toward Bone. After Glen rapes Bone, Beau buys himself a new shotgun in case he finds Glen.

Aunt Carr Boatwright

Aunt Carr is the only Boatwright of her generation to leave South Carolina. She was in love with Wade, but he chose Alma instead. Carr quickly found a husband and persuaded him to move to Baltimore, Maryland, where he had family. She returns to South Carolina once a year to visit. She still occupies the role of outsider, for instance, taking Wade's side in arguments and going against her sisters.

Uncle Earle Boatwright

Uncle Earle is Bone's favorite uncle. When he is able, he helps Anney's family with much-needed money. He is known as Black Earle in three counties, and Raylene says it is because of his "black black heart." He is a man of extremes. For instance, he is devoted to his family, but his wife leaves him, taking their three children, because of his infidelity. Women find Earle attractive, and he is always involved with a young woman whom he eventually leaves. Throughout the course of the novel, he spends some time incarcerated in the "country farm," or jail.

Uncle Nevil Boatwright

Uncle Nevil is known as the quietest man in Greenville County. Early on, he recognizes that Glen could easily turn bad. After Bone's rape, he spends his nights searching throughout the county for Glen.

Aunt Raylene Boatwright

According to Bone, Aunt Raylene has always been different from the other Boatwright sisters. Raylene leads a private, solitary life and has few friends. She was wild when she was younger, running off to join the carnival, passing herself off as a man, and falling deeply in love with a woman. After returning home to South Carolina, she took up residence outside of town. She quit working at the mill after twenty years and makes a living by fishing trash out of the river, cleaning it up, and selling it by the side of the road. As Daddy Glen's abuse gets worse, Bone finds in Aunt Raylene a strong, comforting presence and spends increasing amounts of time with her. It is Raylene who discovers Bone's bloody bruises and shows her brothers, thereby inciting their beating of Glen. After the rape, Raylene takes Bone into her home. She tries to make Bone feel as protected as possible and also wants her to understand that her mother does love her despite making the choice to stay with Glen.

Aunt Ruth Boatwright

Ruth is the oldest of the Boatwright sisters, and she helped raise her younger brothers and sisters. She is a maternal woman but is somewhat estranged from her own children. Anney sends Bone to help Aunt Ruth as she grows increasingly weak from the disease that eventually kills her. Bone spends most of the summer with her aunt and uncle. Aunt Ruth shows real concern for Bone, asking if Daddy Glen ever sexually abuses her, but Bone cannot tell her the devastating truth. Ruth dies before the novel ends, and it is at her funeral that the extended family learns the physical extent of Glen's beatings.

Ruth Anne Boatwright

See Bone

Bone

Bone is the protagonist of the novel. The story focuses on her life between the ages of five and almost thirteen. Despite the poverty in which she grows up, Bone develops an intellectual curiosity. She is a born storyteller, entertaining her many cousins with the tales she makes up. She also loves to read, spending her dishwashing earnings on sec-ondhand books. She is briefly drawn to evangelical Christianity for the salvation it promises but comes to recognize its falsity.

Bone is an illegitimate child, born to the unwed, fifteen-year-old Anney. After her mother's marriage to Glen, she becomes the focus of his rage and jealousy. He soon begins sexually and physically abusing her. Partially because of Glen's actions, Bone develops into an independent, defiant, and sexually precocious child. At the same time, however, she blames herself for his unwanted attention and feels enormous shame. She acts out her ambivalence. For instance, she does not tell Aunt Alma about Glen's sexual abuse even when her aunt directly questions her, but she still deliberately provokes Glen. Bone's emotional predicament is not helped by the fact that Anney also places blame for Glen's actions on the child. When the family finally learns of Glen's savagery against Bone, the uncles beat him so badly that he must be hospitalized. Even then, however, Bone continues to apologize to her mother for what is happening to Glen.

After this beating, the family leaves Glen, but Bone is certain that her mother will go back to him. When Anney says that she will only take him back if she is sure that Bone will be safe, Bone, knowing the impossibility of that certitude, refuses to live at home: she will stay with Aunt Alma instead. It is Bone's determination that leads to Glen's final attack. When he comes to Alma's, he claims that he wants only to speak to her, but in his rage—and his desire to subdue Bone once and for all—he brutally rapes her. Though Anney witnesses the culmination of this act, she still decides to desert her daughter and stay with Glen. Bone returns from the hospital to Aunt Raylene's house, feeling like the events of her short life have already shaped her into the woman that she will become: a Boatwright woman.

Bone's Real Father

Bone knows very little about her real father, not even his name. Anney will not talk about him, and Granny chased him out of town after she learned that Anney was pregnant. He saw Bone only once, when he came to visit eight days after her birth. Granny tells Bone that he has a wife and six children, that he sells insurance to African Americans, and that he has never been in jail.

Deedee

Deedee is Bone's cousin, one of Ruth's daughters. She and her mother do not get along. She resents her mother's continuing illness, but she also is angry because she doesn't think her mother spent enough time with her or loved her enough. When Ruth becomes seriously ill, Travis only gets her to return home and help care for her mother by promising to make her car payments. After Ruth dies, Deedee refuses to go to the funeral, but Raylene makes her.

Granny

Granny tells Bone stories about the family. She moves back and forth among the houses of Alma, Ruth, and her sisters. She chased Bone's real father out of town.

Grey

Grey is Bone's cousin, one of Alma's twin boys. Bone likes Grey better than Garvey because he has a "sweetness" to him. Grey becomes Bone's accomplice for breaking into the Woolworth's.

Lyle Parsons

Lyle Parsons is Reese's father and Anney's first husband. He wants to adopt Bone and take care of his family—which will grow when Anney has their baby—but he does not earn enough money at the gas station, and Anney must continue to work during her pregnancy. To earn extra money, he gets a job at the stock-car races, and one day while returning home he has a car accident and dies.

Shannon Pearl

Shannon Pearl is a short, fat, ugly, half-blind albino, whom most of the children dislike. Shannon's father runs a religious store and books performers for the gospel circuit, and her mother makes costumes for gospel singers. Bone recognizes her from the revivals and befriends her, drawn to Shannon's stubbornness and self-sufficiency, both traits that she values in herself. She also thinks that Shannon will be saintly on the inside, but she soon discovers that—again like herself—Shannon is filled with rage against everyone who has ever hurt her. Eventually, Bone and Pearl have an argument, but months later, Shannon invites Bone to a barbecue at her house. There, Bone witnesses Shannon's death when the can of lighter fluid Shannon is holding explodes.

Reese

Reese is Bone's half-sister, younger by about five years. Until Glen ruins it, she maintains a relationship with her loving grandmother. Glen does not beat or molest Reese as he does Bone; in fact, along with other characters, Bone recognizes the kindness with which he treats Reese. Like her sister, however, Reese is sexually precocious, masturbating to violent fantasies at a young age. Reese and Bone are close as children, but as they grow older, they do not get along as well. Reese resents the tension that Bone's predicament with Glen introduces into the family.

Uncle Travis

Uncle Travis is Ruth's husband. He is an alcoholic, but he loves his wife. Bone claims that she never saw him sober until she was seventeen and he had to have his liver and half his stomach removed.

Daddy Glen Waddell

Glen Waddell is Bone and Reese's stepfather. He comes from a completely different background than the Boatwrights: his family is middle-class, not poor; his mother does not work outside of the home; family members are professionals, not blue-collar workers or manual laborers. Glen's father owns a dairy; one brother is a lawyer, the other a dentist. Glen is the black sheep of the family, failing at all his jobs, and—according to his brothers—marrying trash. His family looks down upon him, tolerating his presence at family events rather than welcoming him. He constantly tries to win the love of his family—particularly his father—but is unable to do so. According to many of the characters in the novel, it is this lack of love that leads him to desperately want Anney to himself and to treat Bone so cruelly.

Glen first meets Anney through Uncle Earle, and he is immediately drawn to her. He courts Anney diligently, waiting two years for her to accept his proposal of marriage. Though he promises to be good to her and her children, he reneges on that promise through his first act of sexual abuse against Bone. As he continues to fail in providing for his "family," he takes out his rage on Bone. As he continually assaults her, she acts more diffidently to him; thus the cycle of violence is perpetuated and escalated.

Many of the Boatwrights distrust Glen, seeing that propensity for violence in him. When they learn of his treatment of Bone, the uncles brutally attack him. Glen, fearing that Bone will keep him from Anney, rapes her.

Uncle Wade Yarnall

Uncle Wade is Alma's husband. He is continually unfaithful to her.

Themes

Child Abuse

From almost the beginning of his relationship with Anney, Glen abuses Bone. His first sexual abuse of her takes place shortly after he marries her mother but it occurs when he is looking forward to the future and the impending birth of their child. This action gains significance because it counters arguments raised by characters in the novel that Glen takes out his frustrations on Bone and shows that Glen has the proclivity, despite circumstances, to abuse the young girl, then only about eight or nine years old. The ensuing abuse all takes place while he is angry, but he still tells Bone "over and over again," often while he is beating her, how much he loves her.

At first, Anney knows that Glen is physically beating Bone. She hears, through the closed bathroom door, his first brutal attack on her. She cleans up Bone after this and subsequent beatings, all the while adamantly denying what her husband is doing: "I was always getting hurt, it seemed, in ways Mama could not understand and I could not explain. Mama worried about how careless I was, how prone to accident I had become." Yet, though Anney does leave him several times, she always goes back to Glen. In order to justify her actions, she must place the blame on Bone. She tells Bone that she knows better than to make Glen angry, that she must be more careful, that Daddy Glen really does love her. Anney's words are fitful protests, but Bone, only a child, internalizes these messages and feels herself to be at fault for Daddy Glen's treatment of her. Toward the end of the novel, Bone comes to realize that it is not her fault. When her family finds out how Glen is beating her, her uncles turn on him. Though Bone is upset by the friction this causes between her and her mother, her family's actions validate her own feelings of hatred for Glen. She also realizes just how dangerous he is and that he will never change. For this reason, she tells Anney that she will never live with Glen again. Hearing this, Glen comes to see Bone, but when she continues to defy him—which she has never done to such an extent—Glen violently rapes her.

Family

The importance of family is clearly demonstrated in *Bastard Out of Carolina*. The majority of the extended Boatwright family live in or around Greenville. The Boatwright sisters help each other out, look after each others' children, and serve more as surrogate mothers than aunts. Bone spends extended periods of time with her aunts Raylene and Ruth. Glen successfully places a wedge between Anney and her girls and the rest of the family by moving them to more distant areas in the town. The first time he does this, after the death of their child, Alma was "outraged he'd take us far away" but Glen is pleased because they will be on their own. He wants them to form a real family and rely on him, not on the aunts and uncles. He gets angry because the aunts are always telling the girls stories about the Boatwrights, which he attempts to counter with stories about his own family. In subsequent houses, they are sometimes so far away from the aunts that Bone and Reese cannot visit as often as they'd like.

Despite the genuine affection shared by the Boatwrights, Bone knows that they are not the "typical" American family. However, a healthy family is not seen anywhere in the novel. Travis and Ruth have raised children who demonstrate little care for their mother despite her fatal illness. Wade cheats on his wife Alma, and even tells her how disgusting she is. Carr, married and living in Baltimore, Maryland, still harbors feelings for Wade, whom she loved as a girl. Uncle Earle's wife leaves him, taking their three children with her, after she discovers his affairs. Thereafter, he forms relationships with much younger women, marries them, and soon thereafter deserts them.

Dysfunctional families, however, are not limited to the poor. Glen's parents and his brothers are middle-class. His parents and brothers live in nice homes, but they show no love for him nor genuine affection for each other. At family outings and parties, they constantly degrade Glen and his step-family, and the narrative clearly makes a link between this lack of familial love and Glen's violent rages against Bone. The Pearls, who also are much more financially stable than Bone's family, are similarly embedded in a web of family lies. Mrs. Pearl is unable to see the spiteful nature of her daughter Shannon, which contributes to her daughter's self-immolation.

Even the families that are tangential to the novel are not intact. Reese's father's family, the Parsons, has been destroyed. Grandmother Parsons has lost her three boys and is not close with her daughter. Her brothers are simply waiting for her to die so they can sell her land. Though Reese loves her grandmother, Daddy Glen ruins the relationship when he demands payoff money. The African-American family who share the apartment house with Alma lacks a father. He has gone up North to make money to support his family remaining in South Carolina.

Anney attempts to forge a nuclear family through her marriage to Glen, seeing in him a potential father for her girls, but this never happens. Instead of acting as a parental figure, Glen brings out feelings of rage, anger, and hatred in Bone. Yet, Bone continues to cling to the myth of the loving family, wanting "us to be like the families in the books in the library."

Poverty and Illegitimacy

Bone's family, as well as her extended kin, live in poverty. They exhibit all the stereotypical characteristics of those who inhabit a low socioeconomic class: too many children, worn-out homes and clothing, drinking, violence. Such an environment engenders instability. As Daddy Glen loses job after job, Bone's family moves so frequently that Anney stops even bothering to fully unpack. Bone and her sister are often hungry. Anney even prostitutes herself one evening in order to obtain money to buy her children food.

The poverty of the Boatwright clan causes Bone to feel shame. She knows that more well-off South Carolinians look down upon her, such as Daddy Glen's family and even Shannon Pearl. She understands that people are judged by how much money they have and that society deems poor people less legitimate than wealthier ones. This is graphically depicted when Aunt Alma and her children move into an apartment in a house shared with an African-American family, which draws the disgust of her husband and Glen. Alma, in deeper poverty since she left her philandering husband, has fallen as low as African Americans—the poor are as disenfranchised as African Americans in the pre-Civil Rights South.

Part of Bone's illegitimacy stems from this poverty, but her birth is truly an illegitimate one. Anney's mother is a fifteen-year-old unmarried mother. Bone's father's name does not even appear on her birth certificate; in fact, she never even learns it. Stamped across the document is the word *illegitimate,* hence the title of the novel. Anney recognizes the stigma that comes with this marking. For years, she tries to obtain a new, unblemished birth certificate for her daughter. She does not want her daughter to carry the mark of their class.

Love

The desire for love among the members of the Boatwright clan is strong and pervasive. The characters demonstrate a belief in the transformative powers of love. Anney, an unwed mother at fifteen and a widow at nineteen, accepts Glen's marriage proposal only after she comes to believe that he will make a good, loving father to her children, but she still wants him to fulfill her own needs. As Alma points out, "She needs him like a starving woman needs meat between her teeth." Anney and Glen are both desperate to be loved, Glen because of his family's scorn for him and Anney because of her desertion by the fathers of her children. Their codependency ties them together, causing Anney to allow the continued abuse of her child and her eventual desertion of Bone in favor of Glen. Anney is tortured by her conflicting needs. As she tells Raylene on the day the uncles beat Glen for beating Bone, "Sometimes I hate myself, but I love him."

The fine line between love and hate is seen in Anney's feelings. It is also seen in her sister Alma, who wants to kill her husband after he insults her and rejects her sexually. As she tells Anney, "That's why I got to cut his throat. . . . If I didn't love the son of a bitch, I'd let him live forever."

Ruth's need for love is seen both in the birth of her children and her death. Anney tells Bone that Ruth saw each pregnancy as proof that a man loved her. When she knows that she is going to die she makes her husband promise to delay her funeral until all of the boys have returned home.

Bone manifests a need to love her family and be loved. She rarely enunciates her feelings to her family, however. When she tells her favorite Uncle Earle that she loves him it is during a rare moment that she feels "fiercely proud, of him, and of myself"—in essence, she is proud of her family despite what others may think of them. She also yearns for a normal family love—though she knows this is impossible—"when I just wanted Daddy Glen to love me like the father in *Robinson Crusoe*." Despite the rampant abuse and denial that exists in her family, she still believes in the power of love. "[L]ove would make me beautiful:" she thinks, "a father's love would purify my heart, turn my bitter soul sweet, and light my Cherokee eyes."

Sexuality

Through her family morals and through Daddy Glen, Bone is introduced to human sexuality at a young age. She is only about eight or nine years

Topics for Further Study

- Imagine that you are Bone and you have just finished writing this book. You want to get in touch with Anney and tell her how you feel about your past and about her. Write a letter to Anney.

- Most of the people around them view the Boatwrights as useless and shiftless. What positive attributes do the Boatwrights demonstrate? Write a few paragraphs countering the argument that the Boatwrights are simply poor, white trash.

- Conduct research to find out more about how child abuse affects the family members involved and the victim. After you have finished your research, assess whether or not Bone and Anney are realistically drawn characters.

- Counselors often use creative outlets, such as art therapy, to help their patients heal from the trauma of sexual and physical abuse. What kind of art do you think Bone would create to express her feelings about what has happened to her in the past? Describe what a piece of Bone's work might look like.

- Bone narrates her story some years later, when she is at least past the age of seventeen. Judging from Bone's voice and the perceptions and wisdom she holds, how old do you think Bone is when she tells her story? Explain your answer.

- Write a short paper explaining why Bone might have decided to share her story and what she hopes to accomplish by doing so.

old the first time Glen sexually abuses her, masturbating against her body. Though Bone "knew what it was under his hand . . . this was a mystery, scary and hard." Daddy Glen and Anney have sex often, which Anney's young daughters are aware of. Bone agrees with Reese's assessment, that it is "mushy," but she also recognizes the power in sex. "Was that what Daddy Glen had been doing to me in the parking lot?" she wonders. Before she is ten years old, Bone has started masturbating. Her first sexual fantasies revolve around violence. She imagines that she is tied up while a fire rages around. Her fantasies evolve, and she masturbates while imagining that people are watching Daddy Glen beat her. As Glen continues to beat her with more force and more regularity, Bone's sexual fantasies become even more violent and complex. By the time she is ten years old, Bone already equates sex with violence and shame. Her shame and confusion is such that when Aunt Ruth asks her if Daddy Glen has ever sexually abused her, she says no.

Reese, growing up in the same environment, also starts masturbating at a young age. Like Bone, Reese makes up violent fantasies to go along with her masturbation. Bone sees her one afternoon enacting a scene in which she is attacked and raped. Watching her younger sister, Bone experiences her own sexual fantasy in which someone has beaten her, tied her to a tree, gagged her, and left her to starve. Bone orgasms while "pushing my thighs into the rough bark," while in the bed below her, "Reese pushed her hips into the leaves."

In the culture, children learn about and have sex at a young age. Anney is only fourteen years old when she becomes pregnant with Bone. As Bone points out, there is even a joke about it: "What's a South Carolina virgin? 'At's a ten-year-old can run fast." However, Bone's sexual curiosity is never turned outward. Even by the time she is twelve, she has demonstrated no interest in boys her age. At Aunt Ruth's funeral, her cousin Butch kisses her and uses his tongue. Bone is completely surprised at this behavior and pulls away "in surprise." This scene, though brief and underscored by Butch's order to not make " 'more out of this than there is,' " reminds the reader that for the Boatwrights and particularly for Bone, all sex is deviant.

Style

Symbolism

Bone's birth certificate is the primary symbol of the novel. Stamped with the word *illegitimate,* it decries the circumstances of Bone's birth. Symbolically, as long as the birth certificate takes that form, Bone is unable to escape her past history and her social illegitimacy. At the end of the novel, however, Bone must start her life over. Though this choice is forced upon her by Anney's desertion and by her own realization that "the child I had been was gone with the child she [Anney] had been," it still is a time of rebirth, a transformation physically signified by the birth certificate that Anney has somehow managed to obtain for her—one that lacks that accusatory and demeaning word.

The novel abounds with other symbols. The physical hunger that Bone feels when her family does not have enough to eat is a physical reflection of her spiritual hunger. She wants what other people seem to have: the ability to buy trinkets and candy at Woolworth, a grandmother with her hair in braids instead of hanging messily down her back, a house with a white picket fence. Bone notes that she feels a "dizzy desperate hunger edged with hatred and an aching lust to hurt somebody back." She wonders if this is the same hunger that causes her cousin Tommy Lee to steal money from his mother. She also feels this hunger "swell" when they visit Daddy Glen's family, who are lawyers and dentists, who have wives who stay home instead of working. This barrenness is also symbolically reflected in Bone's environment. The houses that Daddy Glen chooses for them are all cheap, dismal imitations of his family's houses. "The lawns were dry, with coarse straggly grass and scattered patches of rocky ground. There were never any trees or bushes . . . the houses always looked naked and abandoned." As Bone's cousin Temple astutely points out, Daddy Glen is "always finding your houses where it looks like nobody ever really wanted to live."

Point of View

The story is told from the first-person point of view of Bone. Because she relates her tale an undisclosed number of years after it happened, her voice is able to reflect a woman's maturity as well as an education. Through the use of such a narrative voice, Allison is able to home in on the true child's voice and experience, while at the same time reflect on the larger issues raised by the novel, such as poverty, social stigma, and the lure of religion. Allison's narrative includes pieces of information that Bone would not have thought of at the time, particularly a knowledge of her extended family's activities and motivations. The novel places Bone in the position of carefully looking back at the past, attempting to make sense of it in her effort to heal herself. The crucial question Bone tries to answer through her telling of the story is why her mother made the choices that she did, but she is unable to do so, perhaps because she—along with many readers—can never truly understand Anney's decision.

Setting

The story takes place in Greenville, South Carolina, in 1955, which Bone describes as "the most beautiful place in the world." The small-town southern setting has a strong influence on the story, for the Boatwrights and their kin are typical "white trash" as Bone identifies them upon reading *Gone with the Wind*. They epitomize the stereotypical poor white southerner: undereducated, alcoholic, and prone to violence and loose morals.

The physical setting of the South enhances Bone's story, for the heat is terribly oppressive. Bone describes a landscape filled with burned grass and baked dirt, and porches where the family sit holding large glasses of iced tea and damp hand towels. However, the South is oppressive in other ways. The story takes place at the beginning of the Civil Rights movement, and African Americans are hardly present, depicting the reality of segregation. The exception is the family with whom Aunt Alma and her children briefly share an apartment house. This momentary glimpse provides a convincing portrait of race relations. Alma's husband is displeased that his children are living side by side with African Americans, and Bone's cousin calls the family "niggers" and is proud that the children seem scared of him. For her part, Bone acknowledges that she has never had a normal conversation with an African American and feels nervous and shy around the children. The incident also shows the economic plight of African Americans. The father is absent from the family, instead working in the North where he can earn much more money.

Language

Many critics have pointed out Allison's deftness at capturing the rhythms of southern speech without resorting to the use of dialect. Her dialogue rings true and reflects the ungrammatical speech of the poorer American. Allison discussed her use of language in an interview she gave to Minnie Bruce Pratt for *The Progressive:*

> When I really started working on the writing of the language, I discovered that there is this conventional way to frame dialect on the page. Now, the language rhythms of the people I am writing about come entirely from gospel music, country music, and the church. But the way it is generally written down [is] barely intelligible and has an aura of stupid about it. And that I had to absolutely refuse, because the people whose voices I am using are very smart people. They are simply uneducated.

Allison creates a distinctive use of language in the novel, one unlike other novels that take place

Compare
&
Contrast

- **1950s:** A 1957 study determines that around forty million Americans live near or below the poverty line of $3,000 for a family four.

  Today: In 1995, 36.4 million Americans, which includes 27.5 million families, live in poverty. The average income cutoff level for a family of four at the poverty level is $15,569.

- **1950s:** Throughout the decade, an average of sixty-three percent of the U.S. population considers themselves to be church members. In 1958, 109 million Americans have an official religious affiliation.

  Today: In 1998, seventy percent of Americans claim to be members of a church or synagogue. Forty percent have attended a church or synagogue within the last week.

- **1950s:** By the end of the decade, thirty-nine percent of all women with children ages six to seventeen work for wages outside the home. Around 6.6 million women with children ages seventeen and under work outside of the home.

  Today: In the early part of the decade, seventy-one percent of married women hold jobs outside

the home. Around 18.2 million women with children ages seventeen and under work outside of the home.

- **1950s:** The birthrate in 1957 is 4.3 million, or 25.3 births per 1,000 Americans.

  Today: The birthrate in 1997 is 3.8 million, or 14.6 births per 1,000 Americans.

- **1950s:** The average age for the first marriage for women is twenty. The average age for men is almost twenty-three.

  Today: The average age for the first marriage for women is twenty-four. The average age for men is almost twenty-six.

- **1950s:** By the end of the decade, 125 million Americans live in urban areas and 54 million Americans live in rural areas. Throughout the decade, rural population drops by seventeen percent with an average of 1.4 million rural dwellers leaving each year for higher-paying jobs in cities.

  Today: Today, the majority of Americans— over seventy-five percent—live in urban areas.

---

among southerners and rely on the same type of transliteration of words, such as "Ah" for "I." For instance, she uses the word *ain't* and insists on the repetition of adjectives, as in Uncle Earle's "black black hair" and "black black heart."

Historical Context

A Prosperous Nation?

For many Americans, the 1950s was a decade of economic prosperity. Unemployment and inflation remained low, generally below 5 percent. By the middle of the decade, more than 60 percent of Americans earned a middle-class income, which at

that time was a salary between $3,000 and $10,000 a year. The number of homeowners increased by over 21 million during this decade, and people enjoyed material comforts and the benefits of household inventions and improvements. Government programs benefited many Americans. Social security and unemployment benefits also expanded in the mid-1950s, and the minimum wage increased. President Dwight D. Eisenhower also supported the largest increase in educational spending up to that time.

Nearly 40 million Americans, however, lived near or below the poverty line of $3,000 for a family of four, as determined by a 1957 study. As the middle class saw their incomes rise, poor Americans were increasingly earning a lesser portion of the nation's wealth. This was particularly true for African Americans and members of minority groups. Of poor Americans, almost one half lived in rural areas and suffered from inadequate medical care and a lack of education.

The South

Many rural Southerners moved to cities to search of a better life and higher paying jobs. African Americans made up the single largest group in the rural-to-urban movement. In a continuation of the Great Migration, which had begun during World War II, many African Americans left the South to find work in the industrial North. This movement peaked in the mid-1950s, when some northern cities saw their African-American population growing by about 2,000 each week.

A religious revival took place in the late 1950s, but was more pronounced in the South where many people attended outdoor evangelical revivals. The minister Billy Graham founded his Billy Graham Evangelistic Association in 1950, which promoted crusades, developed radio and television programs, and produced films.

Women in the 1950s

Many women in the 1950s stayed at home and took care of their families and households, though a large percentage worked outside of the home, often part-time. It had long been common for mothers of poor families to work for wages, but an increasing number of women joining the workforce were middle-class mothers. In general, women often faced discrimination and exploitation both at home and at work. Women often held jobs that were either part-time or low-level with little chance of career advancement. Fewer women were attending college, as well. Many women's colleges either closed during the decade or became coeducational institutions.

The Fledgling Civil Rights Movement

Protest movements took place in the 1950s to try to change discriminatory racial practices. In 1955, African-American citizens in Montgomery, Alabama, launched a bus boycott in an attempt to end segregation on public transportation. For almost a year, thousands of African Americans stopped riding the buses. In 1956, the Supreme Court declared Alabama's segregation laws unconstitutional. This struggle not only integrated the bus system, but it also brought a new civil rights leader to the forefront: Martin Luther King, Jr. Two years earlier, in 1954, the U.S. Supreme Court had ruled in the monumental decision *Brown v. The Board of Education of Topeka* that the segregation of school by race was unconstitutional. As a result of this decision, states throughout the South moved to desegregate their schools—most unwillingly, however.

A Society of Conformity

The 1950s society was generally dominated by the idea of conformity. For instance, in the suburbs, houses looked the same on the outside and had the same floor plan on the inside. Some teenagers challenged this conformity through literature that mocked the hypocritical adult world, as well as through rock 'n' roll, which many parents disliked. Adults also challenged the conformity of American life. John Kenneth Galbraith argued in his 1958 book *An Affluent Society* that Americans were ignoring pressing social issues in their pursuit of material possessions and comfort. A group of writers and poets known as the Beats challenged literary and lifestyle conventions of the middle class. Jack Kerouac's *On the Road,* one of the best-known Beat works, celebrated the search for individual identity. Other novelists such as Ralph Ellison discussed the experiences of those Americans who faced poverty and discrimination.

Critical Overview

Several years before the 1992 publication of *Bastard Out of Carolina* Allison had already established herself as a writer outside of the mainstream; her 1988 collection *Trash* won the Lambda Literary award for best lesbian book. *Bastard Out of Carolina* was her first novel and considered to be her "crossover" book. It drew immediate attention from critics and readers. George Garrett wrote in his review for *The New York Times,* "When I finished reading *Bastard Out of Carolina* I wanted to blow a bugle to alert the reading public that a wonderful work of fiction by a major new talent has arrived on the scene." That year as well, the book was selected as a finalist for the National Book Award.

Some reviewers saw *Bastard Out of Carolina* as a "southern" novel, rich in the gothic tradition of the grotesque and populated with a host of eccentric archetypes. Indeed, in Allison's novel are certain aspects strongly identified with the South, such as a tradition of oral storytelling, a marked interest in family history and lore, the power of evan-

Bone and her poor, working-class family live in a rundown house like this one in rural South Carolina.

gelical religion, and the class system and social status.

Randall Kenan, however, noted that Allison "skates uncomfortably near the thin ice of stereotype, a feat at once worrisome and brave." Kenan described the southern stereotypes: "poor white trash; liquored-up, malevolent, unemployed, undereducated, country-music-listening, oversexed, foul-tempered men; and long-suffering, quickly aging, overly fertile, too-young-marrying, hardheaded women." Kenan found that "[W]hen Allison succeeds [in her characterization], she succeeds

winningly." He particularly felt that Uncle Earle, Raylene, and Bone came across convincingly. Other characters—Anney, Glen, Reese, the cousins—hardly "ever come off as more than characters from a country music song." Garrett, however, would argue with this assertion; he found that the characters are "each distinct and memorable, each a recognizable physical presence."

Many critics also focused on the sexual aspect of the novel, which forms one of the major issues of Bone's young life. The character Bone had earlier appeared in Allison's short stories collected in

Trash, in which the young sexually abused girl initiates particularly masochistic forms of masturbation. For Allison, writing is closely tied to her lesbian identity, feminism, and politics. She has stated, "It is only as the child of my class and my unique family background that I have been able to . . . regain a sense of why I believe in activism, why self-revelation is so important for lesbians." Deborah Horvitz, in an article published in *Contemporary Literature,* takes up this theme. She argues that the abused Bone needs to integrate the past traumas in order to move into the future. Horvitz discusses ways that Bone attempts to do this: "She attempts to transform her nightmare into narrative as a means of coping with what she considers to be her 'damaged' and 'ruined' body, but that proves impossible since her stories themselves, along with her desires, wishes, and passions, are entrenched in sadomasochism." Only when everyone surrounding Bone acknowledges the abuse can Bone take steps to heal. Writes Horvitz, "At the close of the novel, Ruth Anne, though far from happy, is finally safe. Anney 'wakes up' to the truth regarding Glen's cruelty and simultaneously confronts her own inability to leave him. Only then can she leave Bone safely within Raylene's protection."

Allison early on acknowledged the autobiographical element in the novel. She had been sexually abused by her stepfather from the ages of five to eleven. In an interview with Lynn Karpen in *The New York Times Book Review,* Allison revealed that many of the introductory details are largely autobiographical, and further, that "a lot of the novel is based on real experience, but not the entire thing. The characters are modeled on members of my family and on stories I heard when I was growing up." However, Vince Aletti, writing in the *Voice Literary Supplement,* pointed out that even "if [the novel] is rooted in autobiography, it never takes on the obsessive tone of a confessional or the crusading fervor of an expose." Horvitz maintained that "in order to appreciate the importance of Bone's 'remembering' her past, one must 'read' her story within the context of Allison's life as, in her other work, she encourages us to do. . . . Allison transforms actual and remembered trauma into art."

On many levels, whether personal, biographical, or narrative, *Bastard Out of Carolina* is a resounding success. Kenan applauded the work as "a singular and important act of art and courage." Amber Hollibaugh, writing in *Women's Review of Books,* took an even more personal approach: "This is a book I had dreamed of reading since I first discovered Allison's writing . . . in the late seventies.

. . . She is right to say that her novel isn't easy to read, but neither are our lives. This is a book as consequential as our own stories: a novel that could save a life."

Criticism

Rena Korb

Korb has a master's degree in English literature and creative writing and has written for a wide variety of educational publishers. In the following essay, she discusses Bone's self-perception and how sexual abuse shapes her character.

Dorothy Allison's powerful first novel, *Bastard Out of Carolina,* drew enthusiastic response from readers and critics alike. Nominated for the National Book Award, the book and its success brought the author, previously known for her lesbian writing, into the mainstream. *Bastard Out of Carolina,* which depicts issues uncomfortable to some readers, such as the sexual molestation of children and preadolescents' violent masturbatory fantasies, has also had its share of controversy. When Angelica Houston faithfully reproduced Bone's story on film for a cable network, she was told to edit or it would not air; Houston did neither, instead selling it to another channel. Maine's Supreme Court ruled that local school boards could keep the book from being taught, a decision that has led to a counter-group determined to keep the novel in school libraries. Allison is equally outspoken; she makes no attempt to hide the fact that the novel is partially autobiographical, based on the sexual abuse she experienced at the hands of her stepfather from age five to age eleven. Her memoir/meditation *Two or Three Things I Know for Sure* presents a more personal discussion of the "Boatwright" family, particularly her mother, whom she introduces in *Bastard Out of Carolina.*

Readers respond to *Bastard Out of Carolina* so positively for myriad reasons. Allison raises a wealth of material and issues, so the reader is likely to find resonance in the novel. It is supremely well written. Allison also presents as a major theme the human search for love and acceptance, a topic that many people can understand and appreciate. At the time of its publication, critics responded to many of these attributes. A reviewer for *Publishers Weekly* talks about "Allison's remarkable country voice" and the way she "portrays [her 'white trash'

> After witnessing one of Glen's earliest beatings of Bone, Anney gathers her daughter in her arms. "'Baby,' she called me. 'Oh, girl. Oh, honey, Baby, what did you do? What did you do?'" With these words Anney establishes a convincing pattern of blame."

characters] . . . with understanding and love." In the *New Statesman and Society*, Elizabeth Young discusses Allison's hope "to illuminate aspects of a class that has been neglected and misunderstood." George Garrett, writing for *The New York Times Book Review*, praises specific characterization, analyzes the function of death in the novel, and raises ideas of literary symbolism. These reviewers also touch upon the crux of the novel: the abuse of Bone—mental, physical, and sexual. Young accurately notes that at one level, "the book traces the ways in which Bone's sexuality is twisted by abuse." Garrett comments that "the most inconceivable—and yet here the most clear—rendering is of how a mother would allow such abuse and how a child could learn to live with it." Anney's continuous assignment of blame for the abuse to Bone and her final decision at novel's end raises questions that perhaps no one can answer: How can a mother treat a child as Anney treats Bone? How can a mother stay with a man who has so severely damaged her child? Allison's exploration of these questions—Bone's attempts to comprehend her past and how it will affect her future—are finely-wrought and haunting.

On a basic level, *Bastard Out of Carolina* convincingly portrays a poor, white, "trashy" southern family living in the 1950s. The Boatwright clan is filled with women who pop out one baby after another, men who spend their lives drunk and unfaithful and in and out of jail, and undereducated children who will grow up to replicate their parents. Aunt Alma keeps a family scrapbook. What predominates, however, are the newspaper headlines and photographs detailing the legal and social trouble that surround the Boatwrights. Bone knows that Alma's "favorite is the four-page spread the *Greenville News* did when Uncle Earle's convertible smashed into the barbershop." Bone thinks that everyone in the scrapbook looks "moon-eyed, rigid, openmouthed, and stupid," and she recognizes her clan membership when her own picture earns a place in the scrapbook. The photograph captures her leaving the hospital after Daddy Glen has raped her. "I was a Boatwright there for sure, as ugly as anything. I was a freshly gutted fish, my mouth gaping open above my bandaged shoulder and arm, my neck still streaked with blood. Like a Boatwright all right—it wasn't all my blood."

In one scene, brief though it is, Uncle Earle gives voice to the feelings of rebellion and self-respect that the degradations of society can engender. Bone is visiting Earle in jail, and he shows her the leather wallet he has engraved using a mallet and razor blades.

> "They count 'em—the punches, the blades. If the count doesn't match at the end of the afternoon, we don't get out for dinner. Of course, sometimes they count wrong, and sometimes the razors break." He wiped sweat on his jeans and brought his hand up, palm open. A slender metal blade glinted in the sunlight.
>
> "They think they so smart." He spit in the direction of the fence. . . . Only his eyes were the same, dark and full of pain. Now those eyes burned in the direction of the guards walking the other side of the fence.
>
> "They think they so damn smart."
>
> My heart seemed to swell in my breast. His hand wiped again at his jeans, and I knew the blade was gone. He was my uncle.

In just a few lines, Allison succinctly demonstrates the disenfranchising of Bone and people of her class; they don't belong, they are, in fact, worthless. "We're smart, I thought. We're smarter than you think we are." She suddenly feels "mean and powerful and proud of all of us."

Such prideful feelings do not last long, however. For Bone clearly understands that other people in southern society look down upon the Boatwrights: they are good for nothing, knowing little and contributing less to society—except for more children they can't afford to properly care for. Anney rebels against this distinction, but she fulfills it nonetheless when she becomes an unwed mother at the age of fifteen. Bone's birth certificate is stamped with the word "illegitimate," which symbolizes for Anney her treatment at the hands of the rigid southern class system.

Mama hated to be called trash, hated the memory of every day she'd ever spent bent over other people's peanuts and strawberry plants while they stood tall and looked at her like she was a rock on the ground. The stamp on that birth certificate burned her like the stamp she knew they'd tried to put on her. *No-good, lazy, shiftless.*

Anney's numerous attempts to obtain an unblemished birth certificate form a pattern in the novel. At the novel's close, a clean birth certificate is all she can offer Bone. In this action, she attempts to communicate to her daughter that, despite all that has happened, she is a decent person. Bone need not bear the mark of illegitimacy, both through her birth and through her class, that society wants to bestow upon her.

Anney fails in her attempt to raise up the family through her marriage to Glen. His complete inability to hold a job coupled with his insistence on independence from her family actually bring Anney and her daughters to greater financial instability. Instead of trying to fight the social system that labels them as no good, Anney turns to a lifelong habit of denying the truth. At a young age, her daughters learn to turn bill collectors away with the lie that their mama is not at home.

> "We're not bad people," Mama told us. "We're not even really poor. Anybody says something to you, you keep that in mind . . . we pay our way. We just can't always pay when people want."
>
> Reese and I nodded earnestly, agreeing wordlessly, but we didn't believe her. We knew what the neighbors called us, what Mama wanted to protect us from. We knew who we were.

Attacks against Bone come from even closer sources. Daddy Glen's family are well-established members of the middle class, professional people who live in clean, well-kept homes that the wives stay home and maintain. At a family gathering, Bone overhears a conversation between Glen's brothers.

> "Look at that car. Just like any nigger trash, getting something like that."
>
> "What'd you expect. Look what he married."
>
> "Her and her kids sure go with that car. . . ."
>
> I pushed my black hair out of my eyes and looked in at one of my wide-mouthed cousins in a white dress with eyelet sleeves looking back at me, scratching her nose and staring like I was some elephant in a zoo—something dumb and ugly and impervious to hurt.

Bone reads the novel *Gone with the Wind* and identifies with the degraded and despised Slattery family. "Emma Slattery, I thought. That's who I'd

What Do I Read Next?

- *The Beans of Egypt, Maine* (1986) by Carolyn Chute tells the story of a poor, uneducated family from the backwoods of Maine.

- In Ursula Hegi's novel *The Salt Dancers* (1985) forty-one-year-old Julia, haunted by memories of her abusive father and the mother who abandoned her, returns home to see her father after twenty-three years. Unmarried and pregnant, Julia believes she must come to terms with her past in order to nurture her own child.

- *One or Two Things I Know for Sure* (1995) is Dorothy Allison's memoir of her family and childhood. The text draws on a spoken word performance and is embellished by photographs.

- Southern writer Bobbie Ann Mason's memoir, *Clear Springs* (1999), recounts the author's childhood growing up in rural Kentucky and the effect that her past had on her career as a writer.

- *To Kill a Mockingbird* (1960), Harper Lee's Pulitzer Prize-winning novel, is the story of a young girl's awakening to the racial prejudice of the 1930s South.

- Allison's second novel, *Cavedweller* (1999), tells the story of Delia Byrd who returns to the South to be a mother to her children years after leaving them in the hands of her abusive husband.

be, that's who we were. . . . I was part of the trash down in the mud-stained cabins, fighting with the darkies and stealing ungratefully from our betters, stupid, coarse, born to shame and death."

Because of the physical and sexual abuse that Daddy Glen heaps upon her, Bone has an even greater reason to feel shame. Judith Herman describes the victim of child abuse in *Trauma and Recovery*: "The child . . . develops the belief that she is somehow responsible for the crimes of her abusers. Simply by virtue of her existence on earth, she believes that she has driven the most powerful people in her world to do terrible things." In Bone's case, this shame is reinforced by the person she loves most in the world: her mother. After witnessing one of Glen's earliest beatings of Bone, Anney gathers her daughter in her arms. "'Baby,' she called me. 'Oh, girl. Oh, honey, Baby, what did you do? What did you do?'" With these words Anney establishes a convincing pattern of blame. By blaming her child, however, Anney is able to escape accepting any personal responsibility. She constantly tells herself and others that Daddy Glen really does love Bone as an explanation of why she stays with him. Bone comes to accept her mother's words, a belief underscored by Anney's complicity in the beatings. "When Daddy Glen beat me there was always a reason, and *Mama would stand right outside the bathroom door* [italics mine]. . . . I knew it was nothing I had done that made him beat me. It was just me, the fact of my life, who I was in his eyes and mine. I was evil. Of course I was." She later confides, "I lived in a world of shame. I hid my bruises as if they were evidence of crimes I had committed. I knew I was a sick disgusting person." Throughout the novel, she reinforces these feelings, at times noting that she is "nasty, willful, stupid, ugly" and again, that she is at fault for the beatings; "I made him mad. I did."

Prior to even entering puberty, Bone begins to masturbate with regularity. She develops perverse and sadomasochistic fantasies. She masturbates while imagining that she is about to burn to death in a fire or that an audience is watching Glen beat her. Her fantasies, however, which she acknowledges got "more violent and more complicated," can be seen as her attempt to take control of a situation that essentially renders her helpless. By masturbating to the "story I told myself about it [the beatings]" Bone is attempting to take ownership of her own body and the trials it undergoes. As quoted in Deborah T. Meem's article in *Feminist Writers,* Allison acknowledged as an adult, "Putting those stories down on paper . . . [enables Allison] to shape my life outside my terrors and helplessness, to make it visible and real in a tangible way." Meem further concludes, "Allison insists on the . . . equation Self-revelation = Life = Survival." Until Bone is able share her experience, she will not assert control.

After the uncles beat Glen following Ruth's funeral, Bone finally comes to accept the truth: "I can't go back to live with Daddy Glen," she tells Anney. Perhaps hearing her mother that day made her realize how helpless Anney was in the face of her desperate love for Glen—and how much danger that put Bone in. Anney told her sister, "I've

just wanted it to be all right. . . . For so long, I've just hoped and prayed, *dreamed and pretended* [italics mine]. I've hung on, just hung on." With these words come Anney's only acknowledgment of the delusional world that she has created around her family. Still, she returns to this false world of promise as the shock of the brutal events wears off. She swears to Bone, "I won't go back until I know you're gonna be safe," but even after she witnesses the aftermath of Glen's brutal rape of her daughter, Anney can't reject him. Significantly as well, she will not acknowledge her own culpability. With the bloody and beaten Bone in the car watching, Anney holds Glen's head to her belly and pleads, "Help me, God, . . . Help me." Anney turns over responsibility for what has happened to a greater power, which Bone recognizes as a weakness. "I'd said I could never hate her, but I hated her now for the way she held him, the way she stood there crying over him. Could she love me and still hold him like that?"

Bone's ultimate answer in the novel is unclear. As she acknowledges, "I didn't understand," but she also admits that "I didn't want to understand. Seeing Mama hurt me almost as bad as not seeing her had." For the first time, Bone looks at her mother as a separate being, which she later must do to tell this story. "Fourteen and terrified, fifteen and a mother, just past twenty-one when she married Glen." She recognizes her mother's strength, shame, desperation, and determination, neither applauding Anney for these attributes nor castigating her. Yet, at the very end of the novel Aunt Raylene comes to her. "I let her touch my shoulder, let my head tilt to lean against her, trusting her arm and her love." With this simple action, Bone wordlessly, yet not maliciously, indicts her mother. At the same time, she demonstrates that, despite all the violence and disappointment enacted upon her, she still holds faith in the redemption and power of love.

Source: Rena Korb, in an essay for *Novels for Students,* Gale Group, 2001.

Randall Kenan

In the following review of Bastard Out of Carolina, *Kenan says that while Allison's characters and plot sometimes cross into stereotype, she often exhibits fine skill nonetheless.*

Flannery O'Connor once observed of the "Southern School" of writing, in an essay called "The Fiction Writer and His Country," that "more often the term conjures up an image of Gothic monstrosities and the idea of a preoccupation with everything deformed and grotesque. Most of us are considered, I believe, to be unhappy combinations of Poe and Erskine Caldwell." Thirty-odd years later, despite the sparkling research centers, black Congressmen, skyscrapers galore and designer water by the barrelful, Southern writers are still haunted by these eccentric archetypes. And few works are more entrenched in that mythos than Dorothy Allison's latest effort, *Bastard Out of Carolina.*

This is not to say that her novel is hackneyed or grotesque; rather that, in dealing with the milieu Allison has chosen—poor white folk in small-town South Carolina of the mid-fifties—she skates uncomfortably near the thin ice of stereotype, a feat at once worrisome and brave.

Brave because in so many ways this far more bitter than sweet *Bildungsroman's* real subject is not "Trash" (the name of Allison's prize-winning collection of stories) but the explosive and often difficult to understand world of child abuse; it is also a Faulknerianly bold attempt to plumb the depths of one girl's emotional acceptance, initially, of such cruelty. Yet so closely linked to this story is a *particular* environment that engenders this *particular* tragedy that when this environment fails to convince thoroughly, Allison's overarching theme comes dangerously close to running aground. Luckily, she pilots her ship if not always masterfully, often with fine skill.

In this world where "black walnut trees dropped their green-black fuzzy bulbs," we have Ruth Anne (Bone) Boatwright, a girl-child born out of wedlock, whose daddy was run out of town by her grandmother just before Bone was born. Bone's mother, Anney, bore the child at 15; at 19 poor Anney had married another man, had his child (Reese), and lost him in a freak accident (" 'That's a handsome boy' one of the pickers kept telling the highway patrolman. 'He wasn't doing nothing wrong, just coming along the road in the rain' "); and by 22 she had married yet again. Such is the world of the Boatwright clan.

The Boatwrights—as Bone tells us in this first-person novel—are devilish, fun-loving, obstreperous, dirt poor, violent. Bone's three uncles are hell-raising fools who "had all gone to jail for causing other men serious damage." Liquor, women, gambling, brawling make up their nights and most of their days. Bone's Boatwright aunts—Alma, Raylene, Ruth, Carr—band together under the caustic but loving wing of their mother and are all (except

> **"** Perhaps it's a bit mandarin or churlish to demand that the parts always add up to the sum, for in this case the parts Dorothy Allison has created seem so flinty and true they sing loudly enough on their own. "

one) caught in that endless tension between love of a no-good man and rearing up their respective youn-guns, fighting off loneliness and hardship and the outside world's dim view of their affairs, aided only by grit, humor and each other. Add on the husbands and a passel of cousins and you can readily imagine this family populating a small county with ease.

Hence the danger. The stereotype of poor white trash: liquored-up, malevolent, unemployed, undereducated, country-music-listening, over-sexed, foul-tempered men; and long-suffering, quickly aging, overly fertile, too-young-marrying, hardheaded women. Of course, all stereotypes derive from some root of truth, but for the most part this band of sorry souls lacks the piss and vinegar, the quirkiness and subtleness, the unpredictability and the balm one truly encounters among farmers, mechanics, factory workers and waitresses who populate the Carolinas. Early on, it becomes clear that Allison is intimately involved with that world—she brings so much of her small postage stamp of Greenville, South Carolina, to life—but she seems to trust too often that we will see the charm, the hard faith and the rationale with which these folk operate and which operates them.

When Allison succeeds, she succeeds winningly. Uncle Earle in particular comes vividly to life. "Earle was good with a hammer or a saw, and magical with a pickax. He drove a truck like he was making love to the gears and carried a seven-inch pigsticker in the side pocket of his reinforced painter's pants . . . Moreover, Earle had a gift for charming people—men or women." Allison demonstrates throughout the novel how complex a character Earle is, generous and devoted to his family, coming through when he can; but violent to a deadly fault, addicted to teenage girls and of course overly fond of whiskey.

Weeping willow trees are abundant in Greenville County, South Carolina, where the novel is set.

Another character painted with a fine brush is Anney's older sister, Raylene, who had "always been different from her sisters." Something of a recluse, never married, she lives alone way off by the river, making her living by selling canned vegetables, fruit, chow-chow and whiskey, and by fishing refuse from the river and recycling it after a fashion. "'Trash rises,' Aunt Raylene joked the first afternoon I spent with her. 'Out here where no one can mess with it, trash rises all the time.'" Direct, no-nonsensical and disciplined, she has unexpected resources of compassion and a particularly painful secret—more so than her obvious lesbianism—which creeps out near the novel's end.

By drawing these characters so freshly, Allison gives us two beacons in an otherwise dim constellation for little Bone Boatwright. Neither her grandmother—witty, lovable and outrageous, though never fully seen; nor her mother, Anney, a wispy woman of mindless devotion who flickers in and out of focus, though rendered sharply in her annual bid to get "illegitimate" off Bone's birth certificate and in the annals of her coming to wed Glen Waddell; nor Bone's sister Reese; nor her bad cousins ever come off as more than characters from a country music song.

Nonetheless, Bone herself does march across these pages as more than a Southern-styled Dick-ensian bastard. Many of her scenes—after she has attained adolescence—are made quite literally of fire. Her stormy relationship with Shannon Pearl, a child so ugly the sight of her made someone exclaim, "That child is a shock to the digestion," is at first a case study in the real behavior of young girls, and ends in an unforgettable scene of horror. Another scene, in which Bone acts out her internalized rage by breaking into Woolworth's after dark, makes the reader fear for the child. And a particularly touching episode in which she visits her Uncle Earle at the "county farm" is perhaps the most moving and deftly handled of all. Brief, poignant, delicate, it comes close to making impalpable emotions palpable.

Of course, the most devastatingly real scenes are those between Bone and "Daddy Glen." Here, Allison is at her most convincing and disturbing. In fact, the scenes and their aftermath are so brutal one wants not to believe them—though a cursory glance at the newspaper or a local newscast confirms that as much and worse is done to children daily. And the most inconceivable—and yet here the most clear—rendering is of how a mother would allow such abuse and how a child could learn to live with it. And, ultimately, how it affects her.

Another of the key fashions in which Allison lets us know she knows from whence she writes is the way death functions in the novel—very like the way it functions in Southern life: to shape and structure the surrounding lives. The death of Bone's first stepfather moves her mother to marry the handsome, though vaguely menacing, Glen; the stillbirth of Anney and Glen's first child (and Anney's inability to have another) leads to Glen's increasing hostility toward Bone; the death of Bone's close friend Shannon leads to her closer and important relationship with hard-willed Aunt Raylene; the dying, death and funeral of Aunt Ruth sets the stage for Glen's exposure to the wider family as a child abuser; the death of Aunt Alma's baby—born with a bad heart—leads to her pyrotechnic mental collapse and to staging the novel's Roman candle of an ending, which—to Allison's credit—is handled not with melodrama, as it could easily have been, but with a calm and quiet understatement that goes far beneath the nauseating violence, and deeply into the complex skeins of love and hate and shame that compel and contort the hearts of those inextricably bound by both blood and heinous sin. Not only does the heart break during these final scenes but the mind expands to understand in a dark new way why the abused make the hard choices they often do; to understand a bit more the strange logic of the heart in the face of such unbelievable cruelty.

Perhaps it's a bit mandarin or churlish to demand that the parts always add up to the sum, for in this case the parts Dorothy Allison has created seem so flinty and true they sing loudly enough on their own. For this reason—pecan pie and gospel music, snuff-dipping grannies and kissing cousins notwithstanding—*Bastard Out of Carolina* is a singular and important act of art and courage.

Source: Randall Kenan, "Sorrow's Child," in *Nation,* Vol. 255, No. 22, December 28, 1992, pp. 815–16.

Kimberly G. Allen

In the following brief review, Allen posits that Allen creates "a rich sense of family" in Bastard Out of Carolina.

Set in the rural South, this tale centers around the Boatwright family, a proud and closeknit clan known for their drinking, fighting, and womanizing. Nicknamed Bone by her Uncle Earle, Ruth Anne is the bastard child of Anney Boatwright, who has fought tirelessly to legitimize her child. When she marries Glen, a man from a good family, it appears that her prayers have been answered. However, Anney suffers a miscarriage and Glen begins drifting. He develops a contentious relationship with Bone and then begins taking sexual liberties with her. Embarrassed and unwilling to report these unwanted advances, Bone bottles them up and acts out her confusion and shame. Unaware of her husband's abusive behavior, Anney stands by her man. Eventually, a violent encounter wrests Bone away from her stepfather. In this first novel, Allison creates a rich sense of family and portrays the psychology of a sexually abused child with sensitivity and insight.

Source: Kimberly G. Allen, Review of *Bastard Out of Carolina,* in Library Journal, Vol. 117, No. 4, March 1, 1992, p. 116.

Sources

Aletti, Vince, Review of *Bastard Out of Carolina,* in *Voice Literary Supplement,* June 1992, p. 7.

Garrett, George, "No Wonder People Got Crazy as They Grew Up," in *The New York Times,* July 5, 1992, p. 3.

Herman, Judith Lewis, *Trauma and Recovery,* Basic Books, 1992.

Hollibaugh, Amber, Review of *Bastard Out of Carolina,* in *Women's Review of Books,* July 1992, p. 15.

Horvitz, Deborah, "'Sadism Demands a Story:' Oedipus, Feminism, and Sexuality in Gayl Jones's 'Corregidora' and Dorothy Allison's 'Bastard Out of Carolina,'" in *Contemporary Literature,* Volume 39, No. 2, Summer 1998, p. 238.

Jetter, Alexis, Interview with Allison in *The New York Times Magazine,* December 17, 1995, p. 54.

Karpen, Lynn, Interview with Allison in *The New York Times Book Review,* June 26, 1994, p. 54.

Kenan, Randall, Review of *Bastard Out of Carolina,* in *The Nation,* December 28, 1992, p. 815.

Meem, Deborah, "Dorothy Allison: Overview," in *Feminist Writers,* edited by Pamela Kester-Shelton, St. James Press, 1996.

Review of *Bastard Out of Carolina,* in *Publishers Weekly,* January 27, 1992, p. 88.

Young, Elizabeth, Review of *Bastard Out of Carolina,* in *New Statesman and Society,* January 8, 1993, p. 41.

For Further Study

Jetter, Alexis, "The Roseanne of Literature," in the *New York Times Magazine,* December 17, 1995, p. 54.
　The author profiles Dorothy Allison's background.

Pratt, Minnie Bruce, Interview with Dorothy Allison in the *Progressive,* July 1995, p. 30.
　The author conducts an in-depth interview with Allison, focusing on her career and educational background and her views on politics and feminism.

Betsey Brown

Ntozake Shange
1985

Ntozake Shange is best known as the playwright who combined dance, poetry, and music in 1975's groundbreaking sensation *for colored girls who have considered suicide/when the rainbow is enuf.* In a change of gears and attitude, Shange published a conventional semi-autobiographical novel called *Betsey Brown* in 1985. *Betsey Brown* tells the story of a sensitive and thoughtful African-American girl as she struggles to understand her place in the world. While many of Shange's earlier works are both stylistically experimental and politically aggressive, *Betsey Brown* is accessible and understated. In it, Shange offers a richly descriptive coming-of-age story, taking place in 1959 St. Louis, whose universal themes of sexuality and morality are set against the backdrop of the school desegregation crisis. The novel also portrays the conflicts among family members, centering on the discontent of Betsey's mother, Jane. Like Shange's more radical works, *Betsey Brown* focuses on the difficulties of coming to terms with racial and feminine identity for black women. It is also often noted for being one of the few novels of its time to focus on black middle-class characters. In this novel Shange portrays the small and large struggles of a thirteen-year-old girl while lovingly sketching the way of life in an all-black middle-class enclave at a time when the incipient Civil Rights Movement agitated for integration. Though many critics find *Betsey Brown* lacking in literary power, it remains a favorite on high school reading lists.

Author Biography

Shange, originally named Paulette Williams, was born on October 18, 1948, in Trenton, New Jersey. She was the oldest of four children growing up in a materially comfortable, intellectually stimulating, and politically aware household. Her father, a surgeon, and her mother, a psychiatric social worker, were friends with some of the most notable African-American artists of the day. Jazz giant Miles Davis and race leader and educator W. E. B. DuBois were among the luminaries who were guests at the Williams home. Shange's parents were what "used to be called 'race people.' Life was dedicated to the betterment of the race," Shange explained in an interview with Serena Anderlini in the *Journal of Dramatic Theory and Criticism.* However, they were not radicals. Their aspirations for her included going to college and marrying a doctor.

Shange's family moved from Trenton to St. Louis, Missouri, when Shange was eight. There she was bused to a German-American school, where she faced the rejection of white classmates and gained a new firsthand understanding of racism. Shange fell back on the strength of her family's personal and intellectual support and eventually formed a strong bond with the city. When Shange was thirteen, the family returned to Trenton.

Shange married young and began Barnard College at age eighteen. The following year, having separated from her law-student husband, she made her first in a series of attempts to commit suicide. During radical times in the country, Shange felt ashamed of her middle-class background and, at the same time, was frustrated and alienated by the double discrimination she experienced as a black woman. Soon she began expressing her rage outwardly through her writing rather than directing it toward herself. She finished her B.A. at Barnard in 1970 and earned an M.A. in American studies from the University of Southern California in 1973. While there, she assumed her African name, which means "she who comes with her own things" and "she who walks like a lion."

After teaching, performing poetry, and dancing for a few years, Shange went back to New York, where her first play, *for colored girls who have considered suicide/when the rainbow is enuf,* was produced in 1975. The show's long Broadway run established Shange as a young artist to watch. It remains her best known and most highly acclaimed work. She has continued to teach while writing pro-

Ntozake Shange

lifically in the genres of drama, poetry, and fiction. She is the recipient of many awards, including an Obie Award for drama and a Pushcart Prize for fiction.

Shange had a second marriage which also ended in divorce. She has one daughter. A practicing Methodist Episcopalian, she also follows Santeria, a new-world hybrid of Catholic and Yoruba spirituality. She identifies herself not as an American, but as a "child of the new world"—that is, of the African diaspora. She told Anderlini, "Where there are black people, I know how to dance, I know the rhythms, I know the food, I know how to have camaraderie, and I can talk and sing."

Plot Summary

Set in 1959, *Betsey Brown* tells the story of a black thirteen-year-old as she confronts racial identity and inequality, developing sexuality, and family life in a middle-class African-American neighborhood of St. Louis. The novel opens by introducing the family and describing the rambling Victorian house where they live. The Brown family—including parents Jane and Greer, grandmother Vida, four children, and cousin Charlie—

get ready for a day of school and work. Betsey, Jane's oldest and favorite daughter, practices a poem by the famous black poet Paul Laurence Dunbar for an elocution contest at school. As the chaotic morning ends and the children go off to their all-black school, Vida airs her disapproval of the rising integration movement and cherishes the fact that her family lives in its "own world."

Betsey arrives at school and overhears two girls talking about Eugene Boyd, an older boy Betsey has a crush on. Though she is flustered when she arrives at class, she rises to the occasion and wins her elocution contest. After school she and two of her schoolmates go the house of a poor white friend. When one of her schoolmates leaves because the white girl's mother is racist, this triggers Betsey's thoughts about the integration crisis taking place in Little Rock, Arkansas.

That day Jane comes home from work and is met by police escorting Charlie and her son, Allard, who had been caught on the grounds of a local Catholic school. Jane is worried about the boys and angry with Greer for not being home to help her with the conflict. This precipitates a fight about how much Greer works. Chaos reigns in the house. Just then, a bedraggled woman, Bernice, approaches the house asking for work. She reveals Betsey's treetop hiding place in order to win Jane's favor, instead provoking Betsey's wrath. Betsey retaliates by getting all of the children to wreak havoc the next morning, and Jane fires the woman. At school Betsey is eager to tell her friends about her victory, but one of them, Veejay, reveals that her own mother works as a nanny for a white family and shames Betsey about her actions. Betsey returns home, eager to take the blame for the morning's misdoings, but it is too late—Bernice is already gone. Betsey goes to her tree and falls asleep. She is awakened by Charlie and his schoolmate, Eugene Boyd, throwing a basketball up at the tree. Eugene starts to flirt with Betsey and she goes inside to change her clothes. They spend the afternoon together and Betsey accepts her first kiss.

Bernice is soon replaced by Regina, a fun and sexy young woman from the poor side of town. Charlie has a crush on Regina, and gets her fired for kissing her boyfriend, Roscoe, in front of the children. Jane is upset to lose Regina, in part because this happens at the same time as laws enforcing school integration go into effect. "The neighborhood had saved them"—Jane and Greer—and now the children must venture out into the broader white culture where they all fear that they will be met with hostility.

The first day of school goes relatively smoothly for Betsey. She feels isolated, but is cheered when she knows all the answers to a geography lesson about Africa. Charlie fares less well; he returns home with a black eye, having fought with five Italian boys. Greer says he will go to school with Charlie the next day. Jane is agitated. Greer takes Jane upstairs to bed for sex, even though it is before dinnertime.

Betsey misses going to her old school and feels put upon by her new white classmates. One evening she makes a hopscotch board filled with racial slurs against whites. The neighborhood is outraged, and Betsey does not admit to the act, but offers to wash it away. This is a tense time in the Brown family, between the political stresses of enforced integration and the personal stresses of family life. Jane and Greer argue. Betsey feels isolated and misunderstood—confused about her racial identity and her budding sexuality. One night, while dancing to the radio and fantasizing about a famous husband, she resolves to run away.

The place Betsey heads is Mrs. Maureen's hair salon, a shop in a rough part of town where all of the middle-class black women get their hair done. She arrives there at dawn and is shocked to find that by night Mrs. Maureen runs a brothel. She is even more shocked to discover that Regina is living there and is pregnant. Roscoe has moved to Chicago and promised to send for her, but that seems doubtful. Regina reassures Betsey and affirms that she is special. Regina and Mrs. Maureen pamper her, doing her hair and make-up, before sending her home with cab fare. But Betsey instead takes a cab downtown, where she feels like she is the queen of the city.

Back at home the family waits anxiously for Betsey's return. Greer and Jane argue because Greer refuses to pray, choosing instead to go out and look for Betsey. He stops by the hospital to do his rounds, and there he finds Betsey, who had been taken there at her request by the police. Greer feels a connection to Betsey through their shared impulses toward black culture. He brings her home, where she is received joyously. Jane too feels a connection to Betsey, seeing in her a version of a younger self who wanted to "be somebody." The next morning Greer announces that the children will participate with him in a Civil Rights demonstration. Jane objects strenuously to placing her children at risk. He maintains his position, so Jane packs her bags and leaves.

In Jane's absence, a new housekeeper named Carrie comes to help the Browns. She is a rustic but wise country woman who organizes the household and teaches the children the value of work. They all pitch in to keep the house in order. Carrie takes up with the neighborhood gardener, Mr. Jeff, who courts her by bringing her flowers and alcoholic drinks, to which Vida strongly objects. One day Betsey comes home from school upset that her white teacher had never heard of Dunbar or other prominent black poets. Carrie confesses to never having heard of them either, then goes on to advise Betsey to "call her out"—that is, to "fight the teacher," not with her fists, but with her knowledge and words.

One day Jane returns home. The family celebrates her homecoming with a party and singing. Jane is uncomfortable with Carrie's behavior and confronts her in a conversation that Betsey overhears. Then Jane gives her three daughters a "facts of life" talk advising strict modesty, which makes Betsey wonder about her kisses with Eugene. Later, Carrie advises Betsey to "enjoy bein a girl," but, at the same time, to be careful. This makes Betsey feel better.

The Brown house goes on in relative harmony. Jane and Greer have time to rekindle their love as Carrie runs the house like a tight ship, with the children working together and taking pride in their chores. One Monday morning Carrie doesn't show up for work, and almost immediately chaos starts to break out again. Carrie calls from jail; she had knifed a friend of hers. Jane promptly fires Carrie. Betsey doesn't tell her mother how sad she is to lose Carrie, but instead carries on, doing things as Carrie would have done them. The novel ends with Betsey contemplating the issues that she has struggled with. Betsey "lingered over her city, making decisions and discoveries about herself that would change the world. In one way or another . . . [she] was surely going to have her way."

Characters

Eugene Boyd

Eugene Boyd is an older boy who plays basketball for the high school. Betsey has a crush on him, and her interest is soon reciprocated. Eugene is friends with Charlie, who brings him by the

Media Adaptations

- *Betsey Brown* was adapted for the stage as an operetta in a production by Joseph Papp's Public Theater in 1986.

Brown house, where he flirts with Betsey and gives her her first kiss. Though Betsey rarely sees him, she thinks of him as her boyfriend. He is a decent boy who seems to sincerely care for her. His interest in her and the strong feelings he evokes fill Betsey with ambivalence. Betsey's mother and grandmother also worry about her sexual involvement with Eugene, though this remains quite innocent.

Allard Brown

Allard Brown is the youngest of Jane and Greer's children and the only boy. Throughout the novel, his parents and siblings try to prevent him from setting fires, which he has a fascination with doing. Toward the end of the novel, he rechannels his antisocial interest in fire toward a healthy one in music.

Betsey Brown

The novel is named for Betsey and she is its protagonist, the center of the episodic events of its plot. She is an intelligent and spirited thirteen-year-old girl facing the pains and pleasures of growing up in a black middle-class neighborhood in St. Louis in the late 1950s. The events of Betsey's life are not particularly dramatic—she gets her first boyfriend, changes schools, forms and breaks friendships, briefly runs away, and experiences her mother's temporary abandonment of the family. But Betsey is a particularly sensitive and perceptive person who seriously contemplates the events of her life, often from a special spot at the top of an oak tree. Though many of the tribulations she faces—struggles for autonomy from her family, relationships with her parents and siblings, questions of morality and sexuality—are typical for any young girl, the political circumstances of her life add additional stresses. She is part of the first generation of African-American children to attend racially integrated schools—a step forward in the struggle for civil rights, but a difficult and sometimes dangerous situation for the schoolchildren. Betsey's journey toward learning who she is centers on her developing sense of female identity and African-American identity. The novel charts her consideration of various role models—including other girls, figures from popular culture, household help, and, most importantly, her parents—whose influences she admires, rejects, and eventually integrates.

Greer Brown

Greer Brown is Betsey's father. He is a strong and outspoken man, eager to instill in his children pride in and solidarity with their race. He is one of the few black surgeons in St. Louis—and, indeed, in the whole country. He has a political commitment to helping the underserved, so he works long hours—a decision that angers his wife. While Jane wants him to put family life before politics, Greer seeks to inject family life *with* politics. Afrocentric in his outlook, he plays the bongos and quizzes his children on significant facts of African and African-American culture before school each morning. He is in favor of the children attending St. Louis's newly integrated schools and insists on bringing them to a civil rights demonstration against Jane's strong objections, which causes her to temporarily leave him. Despite their differences, he has a passionate love for his wife.

Jane Brown

Jane Brown is Betsey's mother. She is an attractive and sophisticated woman, with the light skin and 'good' hair of her privileged African-American caste. In addition to raising her four children and her nephew, she also has a job as a social worker dealing with the mentally ill. She has a tense but passionate relationship with her husband, Greer, a surgeon. Her mother, who lives with the family, thinks Jane made a mistake in marrying Greer because of his dark skin and Afrocentric ways. Jane loves Greer deeply but shares some of her mother's snobbishness toward blacks of a lower class. Despite her considerable work and domestic obligations, Jane remains something of a free spirit and enjoys luxury wherever she can find it—in solitaire, coffee in bed, or sex with her husband before dinner. Because of these competing impulses, her household is often in chaos. She disagrees with her husband about religion and how much the children should participate in civil rights politics, over

which she leaves him for a time, hoping to retrieve some lost part of a younger self. She returns to the family certain she will not leave them again.

Margot Brown

Margot Brown is one of Betsey's two younger sisters. In the novel, she appears in tandem with Sharon. Both are sweet but boisterous girls.

Sharon Brown

Sharon Brown is one of Betsey's two younger sisters. In the novel, she appears in tandem with Margot. Sharon and Margot contribute to the general chaos of the Brown household.

Bernice Calhoun

Bernice is the first of three servants who come to help out in the Brown household. Betsey first sees her from her tree, observing her poor clothes and hearing her bluesy, autobiographical "Mississippi muddy song." She is, like Carrie, a simple country woman. She has just come up from Arkansas and needs work, so she rings the Browns' doorbell at a moment when Jane is feeling particularly overwhelmed. Jane hires her without first checking her references. Trying to win Jane's favor, she reveals Betsey's treetop hiding place. In revenge, Betsey arranges for the children to wreak havoc in the house the next morning, which results in Bernice's quick dismissal.

Carrie

Carrie is the third and most successful of the housekeepers who come to live with the Brown family. She arrives shortly after Jane has left, thus taking on a maternal role in the household. Carrie, however, couldn't be less like Jane. She is a stout and simple southern woman who has unstylish hair, wears a rope around her waist, and uses the latrine in the cellar rather than one of the bathrooms. She nevertheless wins the affections of Mr. Jeff, the local gardener, and offers the children a balanced view of love and passion. She also teaches them the value of hard work, instilling pride in them for helping to keep the house in order. Vida is snobbish toward Carrie and suspects her of practicing witchcraft. When Jane returns, she criticizes Carrie, feeling threatened by her important role in the family. Jane fires her after she is arrested for taking part in a knifing. Betsey maintains a strong bond with Carrie and tries to do what she would have done in the house.

Charlie

Charlie is the son of Jane's sister. He lives with the Brown family and they treat him like a son. He is in high school and is friends with Eugene Boyd, who becomes Betsey's boyfriend. Charlie is somewhat rebellious, which makes Jane worry about him. On one occasion he is brought home by the police for trespassing with Allard on the grounds of a Catholic school. On the first day at his new, integrated school, Charlie gets in a fistfight with five Italian boys.

Charlotte Ann

Charlotte Ann is Betsey's schoolmate at her all-black school and one of her closest friends. At school they hang around with another girl, Veejay, and after school they sometimes see Susan Linda, a poor white girl who shares their fascination with their growing sexuality.

Daddy

See Greer Brown

Grandma

See Vida Murray

Mr. Jeff

Mr. Jeff is a local man who earns his living as a gardener in Betsey's neighborhood. He falls for Carrie shortly after her arrival and courts her with flowers and sips of alcohol.

Mr. Johnson

Mr. Johnson is one of Greer's patients. He tends to him at a clinic after he is done with his regular job at the hospital because he feels a commitment to care for the most needy patients. Mr. Johnson has health problems and his whole family suffers from "too little of everything." Mr. Johnson and his family represent the privation of black life on the other side of the tracks from the Browns' middle-class neighborhood.

Regina Johnson

Regina Johnson is the second of the Browns' three housekeepers. She is the niece of Mr. Johnson, one of Greer's hard-luck charity patients. She has just graduated from high school and comes from an unprivileged background, but is hopeful for a future with Roscoe, her boyfriend, who wants to open his own gas station. Regina is popular with the Brown children because she is youthful, fun, and stylish. She offers Betsey a forward model of femininity and sexuality that intrigues her. Charlie

has a crush on Regina, which leads to her being fired when he resentfully tells on her for kissing Roscoe in front of the children. Later, when Betsey discovers Regina pregnant, apparently deserted by Roscoe, and living at Mrs. Maureen's brothel, Regina becomes for Betsey a cautionary tale about the dangers of sexuality.

Mrs. Leon

Mrs. Leon is Betsey's teacher at her new, integrated school. Betsey is reassured when the lesson on her first day involves African geography. Betsey knows all of the answers.

Liliana

Liliana is one of Betsey's classmates at her first, all-black school. She and Mavis talk knowingly about Eugene Boyd in front of Betsey. Liliana has been held back, so she is older and more sophisticated than Betsey. Though they are not friends, she is a figure of female sexuality to Betsey.

Mama

See Jane Brown

Mrs. Maureen

Mrs. Maureen runs a beauty salon on the rough side of town, one attended by all of the middle-class women of Betsey's neighborhood. When Betsey runs away, feeling misunderstood by her own family, it is to Mrs. Maureen's that she flees. To Betsey, Mrs. Maureen's shop represents a safe and supportive atmosphere that is distinctly black and distinctly female. When Betsey reaches Mrs. Maureen's early in the morning, she is shocked to learn that at night Mrs. Maureen runs a brothel. Despite this revelation, Betsey is affirmed by Mrs. Maureen's and Regina's attentions as they do her hair and make her feel special and grown up before sending her home.

Mavis

Mavis is Liliana's friend, another older girl who has been held back at Betsey's all-black middle school. She and Liliana talk about Eugene Boyd, which flusters Betsey. Betsey thinks of them both as models of adult femininity when she performs her poem in the elocution competition.

Mrs. Mitchell

Mrs. Mitchell is Betsey's teacher at her original, all-black school. She is a white woman who "hadn't reacted like some of the rest when the school turned over from white to black . . . she liked young minds." Mrs. Mitchell gives Betsey first place for performing a Dunbar poem in an elocution contest.

Frank Murray

Frank Murray was Vida's husband and Jane's father. Vida cherishes his memory and spends much of her private time in reverie, thinking about their courtship and past. Vida describes Frank as a "gentle man" who could pass for white, an implicit contrast to Greer.

Vida Murray

Vida Murray is Jane's mother. She lives with the Brown family, helping out with the children while Jane is at work. However, Vida has a heart condition that makes dealing with the rambunctious children difficult. Vida comes from a long line of middle-class blacks and is proud of her proper conduct, light skin, straight hair, and the fact that she is descended from freemen rather than slaves. She has reservations about Jane's husband, Greer, based on a snobbish application of skin-color hierarchy. Vida disapproves of the casual way the household is run and does her best to instill in the children a sense of propriety. She opposes the struggle for integration, believing that blacks do best in their own separate society. She is a religious woman who remains deeply devoted to the memory of her deceased husband.

Mr. Robinson

Mr. Robinson runs the local soda shop in Betsey's neighborhood near her school. He is part of the close-knit African-American community, reporting back to Betsey's parents when she skips her piano lesson and telling her that he is proud of her on the first day of busing.

Roscoe

Roscoe is Regina's boyfriend. She wears his ring on a chain around her neck and is in love with him, which is a source of fascination for the Brown sisters. He has plans to become a mechanic and open his own gas station, which would be a step up for him on the socioeconomic ladder. He also speaks of marrying Regina, though he worries about the extra responsibility that would entail. Later Betsey encounters a pregnant Regina; Roscoe has gone off to Chicago and says he is saving money to send for her and the baby. But given the circumstances, it seems unlikely that he will do this.

Susan Linda

Susan Linda is a poor white girl who, against the conventions of the time, is friends with blacks, despite the fact that she sometimes uses the offensive word "niggah." Her mother, who is openly racist, works long hours and does not know that Betsey and her friends come to the house. Susan Linda is fascinated with her developing sexuality and leads Betsey and Charlotte Ann as they explore their bodies.

Veejay

Veejay is one of Betsey's schoolmates at her all-black school and another of her best friends. Unlike Betsey and Charlotte Ann, she is not middle-class. She is something of a moral voice for Betsey, leaving when Susan Linda shows them her nipples and chastising Betsey for getting housekeeper Bernice fired. Veejay's mother is a housekeeper for a white family.

Themes

Identity and Self-Expression

The novel portrays Betsey's growth and development as she strives to understand who she is. Betsey is thirteen years old—an age sometimes considered as marking a passage from childhood to adulthood, or at least a passage into the independence of the teenage years. During this period of transition, Betsey seeks to learn to express her identity in a mature way. The first scene finds Betsey practicing for an elocution contest at her school. She has chosen to recite a Paul Laurence Dunbar poem written in African-American dialect in the voice of a sophisticated and confident woman. In practicing the poem, she strives to imitate the attitude of the adult woman she wishes she could be. She does this by looking to the people who are closest to her as role models, including her mother, women in the neighborhood, and older girls at school. The poem is not only a way for Betsey to try on a sexual, womanly persona, it is also a way for her to assert her connection to black culture. Early in the novel she masters the poem and wins the contest. Toward the end of the book, she returns to the poem's central idea of self-expression in order to help her assert her racial pride to a white teacher, integrating the power of the poem's message with a more authentic sense of her own voice and values.

Betsey is thoughtful and contemplative by nature, but not always able to act in a way that expresses her truest self. She looks to those around her for hints of the right way to behave as she faces difficult issues related to growing up. Betsey gauges her role models' reactions to different changes she is going through, from her first sexual feelings to her guilt about getting Bernice fired and the resentment she feels as a black girl integrating a white school. She tries on different attitudes and experiments with different approaches. The most dramatic scene of Betsey's attempt to figure out and express who she is comes when she runs away. She first fantasizes about changing her name, stringing together many different symbols of a wished-for adult self, then gets an elaborate makeover that makes her feel like a queen. After these experiments, she returns home more ready to take on the family responsibilities that fall to her when her mother leaves.

Race and Racism

Betsey's idea of herself as an African American is pivotal to the sense of identity she strives to attain throughout the narrative. Betsey has always been told that she is special, and her middle-class status also creates a distance between her idea of herself and many of the qualities she associates with blackness. Her sense of being different from others of her race derives mostly from her mother's and grandmother's influences. They are light-skinned and come from a long line of relative privilege. On the other hand, Betsey has grown up in a nurturing and protective black community. A sense of racial pride has been deeply instilled, particularly by her dark-skinned, politically outspoken father, who, as a surgeon, is a self-made success. Her grandmother, mother, and father all give her different messages about what her relationship to the rest of the race should be—and Betsey is confused. The situation is further exacerbated when Betsey is forced to leave her black enclave and attend a predominantly white school. This provokes her to write racist epithets on the sidewalk and to run away to the poor black side of town. While her parents seek, in their own different ways, to give her the strength to deal with racism, it is Carrie who helps her deal with a white teacher's ignorance in a mature and empowering way.

Sexuality

Betsey's explorations of what it means to be a woman are another important aspect of her quest for identity. Betsey is entering adolescence, her body is beginning to develop, and she has a crush on an older boy. Thus her new sexual feelings and the questions about love and moral conduct that they trigger further complicate Betsey's confusion over who she is. The novel shows Betsey accepting her first kiss and having her first boyfriend. But Betsey's relationship with Eugene Boyd makes up a relatively small part of the plot, and her interactions with him are not a very significant source of drama. Much more dramatic is Betsey's discovery of Regina, pregnant and reduced to living in a brothel while she hopes for her boyfriend Roscoe's return. The novel is also striking for how directly it deals with the sexual relationship between Betsey's parents. Central to Shange's portrayal of Betsey's questions about sexuality are the adult women Betsey carefully observes. It is through watching her parents' tumultuous but highly passionate marriage, questioning Regina and Roscoe about what it feels like to be in love, and listening to Carrie's cautionary tales about her past that Betsey absorbs complex and difficult lessons about what it means to be a sexual person—and about what this means, in particular, for a black woman.

Morals and Morality

Linking the issues of race and sexuality is the theme of morality. In terms of both African-American and female identity, Betsey receives mixed messages about what is the right way to act. Inherently moral in her way of thinking, Betsey takes criticism to heart and tries hard to figure out a code of morality that makes sense to her. A clearer sense of personal morality is key to Betsey's voyage toward maturity, independence, and self-love. Early in the novel, her friend Veejay stands as a voice of morality when she refuses to stay at Susan Linda's house because she disapproves of Susan Linda's sexual self-explorations and objects to the racist language used in the household. Betsey doesn't follow Veejay's example, but she does carefully reconsider her choice later. Veejay acts further as a moral voice when she criticizes Betsey for getting Bernice fired, revealing Betsey's snobbery and sense of entitlement to her and making her feel tremendously guilty. Both of Betsey's parents also offer her moral visions—with her mother emphasizing family life, self-respect, and proper conduct, while her father stresses racial solidarity and responsibility to the larger community. The novel ends with Betsey's sense of morality more firmly her own. Carrie helps her to take responsibility for the family and to stand up to a racist teacher. She also reassures her that her sexual feelings are

Topics for Further Study

- Research how different communities around the country dealt with the crisis brought on by the Supreme Court's decision to desegregate public schools. How do you think Betsey's experience of busing is affected by the fact that she comes from an educated middle-class background?

- Research the case of Emmett Till, which Jane mentions in Chapter 6. Why do you think Shange refers to this historical case in her novel? How does it shed light on the novel's themes of race and sexuality?

- Research the life and reputation of Paul Laurence Dunbar. Why do you think Shange chose the work of this black poet in particular for Betsey to recite? How does the Dunbar poem reflect the novel's larger themes?

- Music is important to many of the characters in *Betsey Brown.* Look for musical references in the novel and find out about the different artists, then compare the musical tastes of two characters. What does music represent to each of them? What does it say about their style, character, and morals?

---

okay—"Go on ahead and enjoy bein a girl, but be careful." Later, when Carrie is arrested and fired, Betsey refuses to be influenced by her mother's disapproval and makes her own moral judgment, confident that Carrie "wouldn't hurt nobody less they hurt her a whole lot."

Style

Point of View

The novel is narrated using an omniscient third-person narrator, one that is not a participant in the events described but has access to the characters' private thoughts and feelings. Though the focus of the novel is on Betsey and her development, the narrator explores the perspectives of various characters at different points in the narrative.

For example, the novel opens with a description of Betsey's house that reveals Betsey's individual thoughts about and experiences of living there. However, this alignment with Betsey's perspective shifts when her mother, Jane, awakens. "Something had to be done with all of these children," the narrator states, expressing *Jane's* inner thoughts this time. The chapter closes with grandmother Vida's private musings on the family and neighborhood. Thus this chapter, like the novel as a whole, shifts among different perspectives, often focusing on the generational differences between the Brown women. Shange's central interest is in Betsey and her inner life, but this portrayal is enriched by the contrasting perspectives of those who influence Betsey most strongly.

Setting

Shange's evocation of setting is one of the most significant aspects of *Betsey Brown*'s style. The sometimes joyful, sometimes stressful chaos of the Brown household, the atmosphere of Betsey's insular middle-class black neighborhood, and that of wider St. Louis all play key roles in Betsey's emotional and moral journey toward maturity. The novel opens by describing the Browns' large Victorian home, which "allowed for innumerable perspectives of the sun." Betsey intermittently looks out from the house or the tree in its yard onto the city beyond at moments when she is trying to understand her figurative place in the world.

The novel is set in St. Louis in the late 1950s, at a time of particular racial tension brought on by the Civil Rights Movement and, more specifically, by the national debate over school integration. Betsey's personal struggle with racial identity is thus strongly affected by the larger political debate shaking the country, as suggested by Shange's references to the integration crisis in Little Rock, Arkansas. But Betsey is also shielded from some aspects of the conflict by her family and community. Mr. Robinson, who owns the local soda shop, reflects the close-knit ties of the privileged black neighborhood. He expresses pride in Betsey and the other bused children while keeping a parental eye on their doings. In the face of Betsey's growing sense of independence as well as the external pressure of integration, she must learn to understand who she is in a context broader than that provided by her family or neighborhood. Betsey's sense of identity is mapped out on the city of St. Louis most explicitly when she runs away from home to Mrs. Maureen's beauty parlor in the poor black part of town. Rebelling against the pressures of being the only black girl at an integrated school, she seeks to flee the security of her home and neighborhood in favor of a stronger tie with black culture as well as with other women. After receiving personal confirmation and a makeover, she roams the city, feeling like its "queen" even though the police worry that a young black girl might not be safe there.

Structure

The plot of *Betsey Brown* is best described as episodic. Shange describes events not so much to gather them into the growing drama of a climax and resolution as to capture the quality and pace of everyday life. The plot does not center for too long on any one conflict—Betsey's mixed feelings about her romance with Eugene Boyd, the strife in Jane and Greer's marriage, or the threats to family members associated with integration and racism. Sometimes material that seems to signal catastrophe—for example, Allard's propensity for setting fires or Charlie's interest in white girls—fails to precipitate a full-blown crisis. Instead, the narration moves from one small, carefully sketched conflict to the next before any crisis comes to loom too large, showing how the different events of Betsey's thirteenth year create a kaleidoscope of questions regarding her sense of herself. The intent of the novel's structure is subtle character development rather than drama and denouement. At the novel's close, there is some resolution as a more mature Betsey is described as someone who is "surely going to have her way," but that way—with its pitfalls of racism and challenges of femininity and sexuality—is still left quite undefined.

Historical Context

Race Relations in the 1950s

Though Shange wrote *Betsey Brown* in 1985, she set the book in 1959, during the period of her own teenage years. The historical details of the novel are very significant, particularly as they relate to the issues of race relations and school desegregation.

In the 1950s African Americans lived in a society largely separate from whites. "Jim Crow" laws—in effect throughout the South and in other parts of the country as well—segregated public facilities, and blacks interacted with whites mostly as their workers or servants. One of the most significant arenas of segregation was in the educational system which, since the 1896 Supreme Court ruling of *Plessy v. Ferguson,* had been based on the principle of "separate but equal" facilities. In reality, facilities were not equal, and blacks received less and lower-quality education than whites, thus perpetuating their economic disadvantage when they entered the workforce. In the early 1950s there were a number of legal challenges to this doctrine, most notably the landmark case of *Brown v. The Board of Education of Topeka, Kansas,* in which the U.S. Supreme Court overthrew *Plessy v. Ferguson* as unconstitutional and ordered public schools integrated. This was a shock to communities across the country, particularly in the South. Since the court made no specifications regarding the time and manner of desegregation, a number of state governments strongly resisted the mandate, setting off controversy that flared throughout the decade.

In 1954 the State of Missouri required educational segregation by law, but it was relatively quick to accept the Supreme Court's decision and integrate its schools. By contrast, Arkansas and Virginia, among other states, resisted fiercely. In the most notorious example of state defiance—one that Shange refers to specifically—the governor of Arkansas ordered the National Guard to block nine black students from enrolling at the so far all-white Little Rock Central High School. When black students attempted to enter the school another day they were met by an angry mob. President Eisenhower then ordered the National Guard into federal service, commanding them to escort the students and thereby integrate the school. The students required protection throughout the school year and became a symbol throughout the world of America's racial strife.

Segregation did not only affect public education, but all kinds of public and private behavior. For example, social contact between blacks and whites was very limited, and sexual or romantic interaction was strictly taboo. Black men had long been categorized by racist stereotypes as sexual predators, and sexual aggression toward white women was often used as justification for vigilante violence against them. In the novel, Shange refers to the case of Emmett Till, with Jane drawing a worried parallel between Till and Charlie. Till, a fourteen-year-old African American from Chicago, was murdered by two white men in Mississippi after allegedly whistling at one of the men's wives. In what became an international scandal, the two men were acquitted by an all-white, all-male jury, only to confess the crime to a journalist shortly after the trial.

Compare & Contrast

- **1950s:** There are a series of legal decisions regarding equal access to educational opportunities for blacks, including the landmark 1954 case, *Brown v. Board of Education*, which lay the groundwork for the civil rights struggles for integration that shake the nation in the 1960s. However, these legal decisions are often resisted by localities, and the process of desegregation still lags at the decade's close.

  1980s: In keeping with the socially conservative tenor of the Reagan era, civil rights policies are attacked and, in some cases, reversed. The National Urban League calls the president's record on racial equality "deplorable."

  Today: African Americans make up President Clinton's strongest supporters. However, affirmative action and programs of busing for school integration are under fire in state courts across the country. Many districts are phasing out busing as a method of integrating schools. Legal challenges are being brought to universities that use race as a factor in deciding acceptance and financial aid.

- **1950s:** In an atmosphere of post-War conservatism and prosperity, many American women assume a traditional role in the family as supportive wives and mothers, and few have access to economic or other forms of public power.

  1980s: There is a backlash against the feminist ideologies of the 1970s that sought to alter traditional gender roles. The Equal Right Amendment (ERA) is defeated in 1982 and the anti-abortion movement is strong. However, the number of women in the workforce—including those in lucrative and powerful positions—continues to grow.

  Today: Sixty-one percent of married women have paid jobs, up from twenty-three percent in 1950. In a booming economy, more women seek flexible work arrangements such as job sharing and telecommuting to allow them to combine career and motherhood.

- **1950s:** American culture begins to show indications of a trend toward sexual liberation that will blossom a decade later. *Playboy,* which begins publication in 1953, makes pornography safe for the suburban coffee table. Alfred Kinsey publishes his study *Sexual Behavior in the Human Female,* with the shocking statistic that one-quarter of married American women report having had extramarital affairs.

  1980s: "Family values" and the rise of the AIDS epidemic lead to a new sexual conservatism in American culture. In May 1985, the government creates a special commission to find new ways to curb pornography. The conservative commission finds unusual allies among feminists when it concludes that pornography encourages violence and debases women. Convenience stores across the country temporarily stop selling soft porn such as *Playboy.*

  Today: Though the panic associated with the AIDS epidemic has subsided, a renewed emphasis on monogamy remains. There is a movement among young people to revalue virginity and some youth activists call themselves born-again virgins. Teen pregnancy is down. However, the Internet makes pornography vastly more accessible than it has ever been before.

- **1950s:** Half of all working whites describe themselves as middle-class, while only one-fifth of blacks who are employed say the same.

  1980s: Economic stagnation and inflation affect black families disproportionately, but many conservative social commentators attribute the erosion of the African-American family to social rather than economic factors.

  Today: In a strong economy, blacks have made small gains compared to whites. One scholar estimates that one-quarter to one-third of blacks can now be considered securely middle-class.

- **1950s:** Rock 'n' roll takes America by storm. Elvis Presley, who derives his style from little-known black blues artists, is rock 'n' roll's unrivaled king. With the popularity of rock, black

(continued)

performers such as Fats Domino and Chuck Berry begin to win a white "crossover" audience. However, parents fear that this new influence will seduce and corrupt their children.

1980s: Hip-hop culture, originating as a black, urban underground musical style in the 1970s, goes mainstream. In 1982 rap group Run DMC has a huge "crossover" hit with a song sampling from heavy metal. In 1985 the record industry introduces parental advisory labeling on music with "blatant explicit lyric content." Tipper Gore

founds the Parents Music Resource Center to warn parents about the sex and violence in popular music.

Today: In 1998 rap becomes the top-selling musical format in America, outselling both rock and country for the first time. Some rappers move to shake the genre's reputation for violence and obscenity, putting forth "positive messages" in their music. More than seventy percent of hip-hop albums are purchased by whites.

Little Rock and Emmett Till are symbols of racism in the 1950s and evidence of a deeply scarred and divided society. While the travails of integration are not nearly as sharp for Betsey and her family, these examples help explain the deep conflict and anxiety that the idea of integration brings to the Brown household.

Race Relations in the 1980s

The social climate in the United States in the 1980s, when Shange wrote *Betsey Brown,* bears some similarity to the 1950s, when the novel is set. Both decades were times of social conservatism and traditionalism, contrasting with the radical, tumultuous era that intervened. In 1980 Ronald Reagan ran for president on a platform of "trickle-down economics" and "family values." Winning two terms, he appealed to the white middle-and working-class voters, including many who had previously voted as Democrats. These voters seemed to agree with him that the social change of the 1960s and 1970s had been too extreme. Reagan was not considered an ally of African Americans. He came out against school busing and affirmative action, and during his presidency some important pieces of civil rights legislation were weakened or reversed. In response to blacks' feelings of disenfranchisement from national politics, Jesse Jackson, a black Civil Rights activist, ran an unsuccessful but nevertheless impressive campaign to be the Democratic challenger to Reagan in 1984, thus gaining stature as an important voice in American politics.

Despite the perception of many whites that African Americans now had equal advantages in American society, data shows that in the 1980s black students were still likely to be educated at predominantly minority schools whose facilities and funding were inferior to those of schools in white neighborhoods. The disparity between edu-

cational resources for blacks and whites was most marked in major cities and was virtually always paired with economic disparity. Studies found that African Americans were more likely to be suspended and put into special education classes and that teachers often treated black students with bias. On the college level, the number of blacks enrolled declined in comparison to the 1970s, a period of great progress for African Americans in higher education. Over the course of the decade the percentage of blacks in college and professional school dropped from 9.4 to 8.6. Against the generally conservative tenor of the period, college students protested against curricula that focused on "dead white men" and the canon was revised at many institutions to include works by more women, people of color, and non-Westerners.

In other realms, racial tension across the country was high. The Ku Klux Klan enjoyed a resurgence, and David Duke, a former grand wizard of the Klan, was elected to the Louisiana legislature. There were numerous racial incidents on college campuses and violent racial conflicts across the country, including the 1980 riots in Miami following the acquittal of four white police officers in the death of an black man. These and other conditions shaped Shange's perceptions of racial integration and race relations as she developed as a writer.

Critical Overview

Shange began her literary career as a poet and performer. Strongly influenced by jazz, she sometimes performed improvisational poetry at bars in New York and San Francisco. One such piece, a collection of twenty poems performed with dance and music by a group of seven women, impressed a New York theater director so much that he

An African-American girl at a segregated drinking fountain. The novel takes place in St. Louis in 1959, at a time when these types of divisions between the races were commonplace.

worked with Shange to develop it into an off-Broadway production in 1975. *For colored girls who have considered suicide/when the rainbow is enuf* quickly became a controversial sensation. The "choreopoem," as Shange terms this experimental work, was shocking to audiences not only for its unusual theatrical form, but for its outspoken message about the double oppression of black women. The play addresses rape, wife-beating, and single motherhood in the most raw and personal terms. "The work speaks of the physical and emotional abuse that black women experience at the hands of insensitive black men," writes Elizabeth Brown in the *Dictionary of Literary Biography.* "It is about the black women's ability to survive even after they have been knocked down repeatedly. . . . It is a tribute to black women who strive for and develop a sense of self."

Shange's portrayal of African-American gender relations drew public criticism from black male commentators, who accused her of undermining racial solidarity with her negative portrayals of men. She shared this controversial status with other black women authors of her generation influenced by feminism, including Alice Walker and Gayl Jones. *For colored girls* became a success on Broadway and remains Shange's most well-known work.

Shange went on to write several other experimental plays focusing with candor and sometimes rage on the relationships between black men and women. In the 1980s she began to work less in the theater, instead publishing several collections of poetry and, in 1982, her first novel, *Sassafrass, Cypress and Indigo.* This work tells the story of three sisters, each of whom reflects a different aspect of African-American femininity. Its experimental form includes recipes, poems, and nonstandard spelling and punctuation. *Betsey Brown,* published in 1985, is a more stylistically conventional book and arguably a more optimistic one. Set during the early Civil Rights Movement, it centers on the main character's unique position as a relatively empowered member of the middle class—an aspect of Shange's own experience that she had not emphasized in *for colored girls* or other writings. However, this semi-autobiographical coming-of-age story shares with Shange's earlier works a commitment to exploring the strife within the African-American female psyche as shaped by both racism and sexism, though here Shange's portrayal of oppression is considerably more understated. In *Black Women Writers at Work* Claudia Tate describes the changes the novel represents for the author, remarking that *Betsey Brown* "seems to mark

Shange's movement from explicit to subtle expressions of rage, from repudiating her girlhood past to embracing it, and from flip candor to more serious commentary."

Writer and scholar Sherley Ann Williams, writing for the feminist magazine *Ms.,* is most interested in *Betsey Brown*'s focus on black middle-class life. Compared to other contemporary novels that equate black authenticity with poverty, argues Williams, *Betsey Brown* "depicts an affluence that is not incompatible with black culture and community. . . . The book speaks to some of the deeper complexities and paradoxes that have helped sustain and perpetuate the positive aspects of the Afro-American experience." However, Williams is less positive about Shange's literary achievement. She finds fault with Shange's sentimental portrayal of servants and the fact that "the characters and the narrators all talk and think alike."

Overall, the popular press failed to embrace *Betsey Brown* as a major achievement for Shange. In a tepid *New Statesman* review, Marion Glastonbury comments that the "drama of political change" that the novel's historical setting evokes "is curiously played down." She notes that the novel, just published, was already slated for production as a musical and asks, "Will the lyrics sound better once we hear the tune?" Susan Schindehitte, writing for the *Saturday Review,* is more charitable about Shange's style, crediting *Betsey Brown* for its "lyricism and personality," while criticizing the fact that "there is no glue to bind [the novel's various] elements into a flowing whole." She too notes the plans to adapt the novel for the stage and goes on to diagnose the novel's weakness thusly: "This isn't really a novel after all. It is dramatist Shange's latest play . . . masquerading as a novel."

While critics tend to find fault with the novel, *Betsey Brown* is a popular choice for high school reading lists due to its relevant themes and accessible style. Furthermore, it remains a significant work in the context of the literary renaissance of black women writers of the 1970s and '80s and their struggles with representing feminist issues from an African-American point of view, as well as for its portrayal of the black middle class.

Criticism

Sarah Madsen Hardy

Sarah Madsen Hardy has a doctorate in English literature and is a freelance writer and editor.

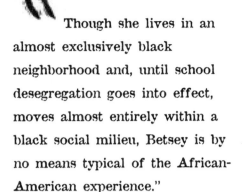

Though she lives in an almost exclusively black neighborhood and, until school desegregation goes into effect, moves almost entirely within a black social milieu, Betsey is by no means typical of the African-American experience."

In the following essay, she discusses how the protagonist's relationships with three domestic servants shape her developing sense of identity in Betsey Brown.

Betsey Brown has a loose plot, based on a series of episodes in the protagonist's thirteenth year. Betsey faces various trials and tribulations—some large and some small—as she negotiates the dilemmas of being black, being female, and just simply being a teenager in 1959 St. Louis. *Betsey Brown* may seem to lack structure. However, one thing that gives shape to its plot is the series of domestic servants who come to work for the Brown family. Though each woman works for the Browns only briefly, each one is symbolically significant to Betsey's moral and emotional development. Tracing Betsey's interactions with and ideas about Bernice, Regina, and Carrie outlines some of the most important aspects of Betsey's journey toward maturity and self-understanding.

One aspect of Betsey's developing sense of identity that a focus on the servants serves to highlight is her middle-class status. Though she lives in an almost exclusively black neighborhood and, until school desegregation goes into effect, moves almost entirely within a black social milieu, Betsey is by no means typical of the African-American experience. Her father is a doctor in an era when there were few black professionals of any sort and her mother, descended from free blacks rather than slaves, enjoys a long legacy of education and privilege. This special status reflects that of Shange's own upbringing. Until she wrote *Betsey Brown* Shange tended to focus on the hard-luck stories of emotionally and economically downtrodden characters. But in *Betsey Brown,* a semi-autobiograph-

What Do I Read Next?

- *For colored girls who have considered suicide/when the rainbow is enuf* (1975), Shange's groundbreaking "choreopoem" play, combines poetry, music, and dance to explore relationships between black men and women. This work, considerably more experimental than *Betsey Brown,* established Shange's international reputation.

- Shange's first novel, *Sassafrass, Cypress and Indigo* (1985), uses prose, poetry, letters, and recipes to portray the lives of three sisters, each of them a different kind of artist, as they confront dilemmas relating to love, feminism, racial politics, and art.

- *Brown Girl, Brownstones* (1959), by Paule Marshall, tells the story of a young Caribbean-American girl growing up in New York and learning about who she is in relation to her family, background, neighborhood, and the big city beyond.

- Gloria Naylor's *Linden Hills* (1985) is named for the affluent black suburb where its main characters, two writers, reside. In this novel Naylor explores the emptiness of wealth and the significance of social class among African Americans, borrowing imagery from Dante's classic *Inferno.*

- *Sarah Phillips* (1984), by Andrea Lee, is a coming-of-age story centering on a young, upper-middle-class African-American woman trying to reconcile her racial identity and her unusual economic privilege. This book offers a rare portrait of life in the high society of the black bourgeoisie.

- Jessie Fauset, a notable writer from the Harlem Renaissance era, focused most of her fiction on educated, middle-class black characters. Her 1931 novel *Chinaberry Tree* traces two generations of women and paints a portrait of life in an affluent and insular black community.

ical piece, she examines the particular tensions that arise out of being a *privileged* member of an doubly oppressed group, black women.

In her essay "Roots of Privilege," which appeared in *Ms.* in 1985, Sherley Anne Williams offers the historical context that until the 1920s, middle-class, educated, and light-skinned blacks tended to populate the fiction written by African Americans. With the rise of the literary movement known as the Harlem Renaissance, there was a revaluation of indigenous African-American art forms associated with "the folk"—the supposedly simple, often uneducated black masses. For example, Harlem Renaissance writers such as Zora Neale Hurston and Langston Hughes used dialect in their writing, celebrated the rich African-American oral culture of storytelling, and used motifs from the blues, a form of folk music.

In the mid-century, folk forms still dominated the black arts scene, and as the political radicalism of the Civil Rights Movement took hold, the situation of the common, working black person remained the most popular subject for black authors. "I was embarrassed to be a middle-class person at a time when the black proletariat was so active; the black people I was around were having bridge parties. Everybody in New York and Washington was burning down the city!," Shange admits in a *Journal of Dramatic Theory and Criticism* interview with Serena Anderlini. *Betsey Brown* shows how Shange came to terms with that shame.

The Browns' first servant, Bernice Calhoun, works for them less than one day and only appears in two short scenes, but her status in the novel is important to Betsey's moral development and her self-consciousness about her privileged status. Significantly, Bernice is introduced through a blues song—Shange's reference back to the Harlem Renaissance tradition of integrating African-American folk music into literary forms. Bernice's song serves as an autobiography. Shange provides little information about Bernice's background other than the lines of the soulful, improvised song, which begins, "well, my name is bernice & i come a long way / up from arkansas & i'm here to stay / i aint got no friends and i aint got no ma / but i'ma make st. louis give me a fair draw." Shange seeks to emphasize the cultural distance between Betsey and Bernice. Bernice embodies qualities associated with a common-folk definition of blackness that Betsey fails to understand or appreciate. Bernice "looks to [Betsey's] mind like a woman in need of some new clothes and a suitcase. Who ever heard of carrying one's belongings in two shopping bags while wearing a hat with five different colored flowers on it?" Betsey sees Bernice's poverty, but she fails to appreciate the richness in the song that "moved as if it weren't usedta having shoes on its feet."

At this point, early in the novel, Betsey—a middle-class city girl—lacks the experience and insight to perceive Bernice's "country honor." Disgruntled by the fact that Bernice has revealed her oak-tree hideaway, Betsey plots revenge against Bernice, rallying her siblings to wreak havoc in the household and get Bernice fired. Never having had to worry about material security herself, she is simply naïve as to the repercussions of her actions on Bernice's well-being. Then Betsey's classmate Veejay reveals that her mother is the household servant for a white family, "tak[ing] care of nasty white chirren who act up like y'all acted up this morning." Veejay, who Betsey is surprised to find she has angered, goes on to call Betsey "stupid" and to explain that her mother "don't do it cause she likes it neither. She does it so I could have clothes and food and a place to live." Betsey is suddenly filled with remorse. Veejay's condemnation comes as a revelation to Betsey about her own lack of insight and empathy. She had been "so busy seeing to herself and the skies, she's let a woman who coulda been Veejay's mama look a fool and lose her job." Betsey runs home, hoping to repair the situation, but it is too late—Bernice has hit the road, and she does not appear in the novel again. Betsey's treatment of Bernice stands as a moral error and a lesson to Betsey about the power that she, even as a young black girl, wields over the lives of others.

The next servant the Browns hire is Regina Johnson. Regina also faces Betsey across a cultural divide—she is from a poor and troubled family. But this is mitigated by the fact that she is herself from St. Louis and, more significantly, that she is an attractive young woman just out of high school, "fresh, neat and slender, with a heavy curl across her forehead, the fashion of the day." Furthermore, she is in love—a condition that Betsey is curious about and ambivalently aspires to. For these reasons, Regina is someone Betsey looks up to. With Bernice, all that Betsey perceives are her differences, ultimately failing to see her as fully human. With Regina, Betsey doesn't comprehend the significance of her differences enough.

If Bernice is associated with "Mississippi muddy" blues, Regina is associated with the new black pop stars of Motown. Regina's sexuality is part of the reason she initially fits in well at the Browns'. Charlie is obedient because he has a crush on her and the girls are fascinated with her. But her sexuality also leads to her downfall. Having few emotional or financial resources herself, she does what many women have done and puts all of her faith in her boyfriend Roscoe. A jealous Charlie reports one of Roscoe's visits to Vida. Proud of her love, Regina leaves. Betsey looks to Regina and Roscoe as she tries to understand her own budding feelings for Eugene. While Betsey worries that "when you're really in love, there's never enough to go around," Regina seems confident in both her love and her sexuality. "Regina took no mind of her body when she was with him. Her woman gave into his man and there was a hush, subduing her throbs and moans in the midst of the sepia rush that was Roscoe." However, when she meets Regina again at Mrs. Maureen's beauty parlor/bordello and learns that Regina is pregnant and living there, waiting for Roscoe's dubious return, Betsey must reevaluate her idol.

Betsey has run away to the bad side of town, feeling alienated from her family and tired of the white folks at school. She tells Mrs. Maureen that she plans to work for her until she can elope. She complains to Regina about her mother not letting her listen to popular music and goes on, "She doesn't want me to be like everybody else, Regina. She wants me to be special, like I lived in a glass cage or something." While Betsey claims that she "feels so much better when I'm just like everybody else," Regina explains to her that she is lonely because she *is* special—and different from women like her, whose options are limited. She helps Betsey see that she has broader resources to draw on than just her sexuality and warns her, "Don't you grow up too soon." Fortified by Regina's advice, she marches through the streets of St. Louis with a new appreciation for her uniqueness and the power that she possesses, feeling like the "Queen of the Negro Veiled Prophet."

Carrie, the third domestic servant, arrives at a crucial time in Betsey's development—just after Jane has left the family. Carrie helps Betsey to integrate what she has learned about herself from the hard lessons of Bernice and Regina and to carry on with a new maturity. Like Bernice, Carrie's appearance betrays her simple, rural background. She wears her hair unfashionably and ties her dresses with a rope. She also uses the latrine in the basement rather than any of the modern bathrooms in the house "cause that's what her mama had in Arkansas." This is an example of the "country

> Hearing her grandmother's 'Carolinian drawl,' Betsey thinks, 'There was a way about Vida that was so lilting yet direct that Betsey sometimes thought her grandma had a bloodline connection to Scarlett O'Hara.'"

honor" she shares with Bernice. By now, Betsey has learned enough to overlook appearances and appreciate the values that Carrie has to instill. Under Carrie's guidance, the Brown children learn the value of taking pride in hard work. While Bernice sings the blues and Regina has the girls mouthing along with the pop tunes of Mary Washington, Carrie helps them to make up their own song to sing as they work, expressing pride in their house: "this is our house . . . / we keep it shinin / spanking clean / if some white folks ever see it / they'll think they musta done it / but it's us colored kids that run it / this is ours." This responsible attitude is the exact inverse of what the children displayed on Bernice's catastrophic first day of work.

Like Regina, Carrie has a gentleman caller, Mr. Jeff, who comes by the house and stirs up trouble with Vida, but the older and wiser Carrie handles the conflict with aplomb. Discerning Carrie's womanly knowledge and warmth, Mr. Jeff is attracted to her despite the fact that she is overweight and odd-looking. Betsey watches her and learns how a woman can earn and enjoy a man's attentions without sacrificing her independence or risking her future. While Jane and Vida censure Betsey's sexuality and Regina gives her a glimpse into the consequences of thoughtless passion, Carrie teaches Betsey about moderating between caution and pleasure in matters of love: "Go on ahead and enjoy bein a girl, but be careful."

When Jane fires Carrie for getting arrested, Betsey has the quiet confidence that her role model acted with justice and reason, an opinion she is also now wise enough to keep from her mother. In Carrie's absence, "Betsey just took Carrie's place in the house." Betsey's optimism at the novel's close

that she was "surely going to have her way" can be attributed in part to her newfound ability to appreciate and understand a strong woman from a background so different from her own.

Source: Sarah Madsen Hardy, in an essay for *Novels for Students,* Gale Group, 2001.

Liz Brent

Brent has a Ph.D. in American culture, specializing in film studies, from the University of Michigan. She is a freelance writer and teaches courses in the history of American cinema. In the following essay, Brent discusses references to popular culture and African-American celebrities of the 1950s in Shange's novel.

The novel *Betsey Brown,* by Ntozake Shange, is set in St. Louis in the mid-1950s, during which the landmark Supreme Court ruling on *Brown vs. the Board of Education* led to the desegregation of schools in the South. Betsey Brown, the main character, is an adolescent African-American girl, from an educated, middle-class family, who is "bused" to a mostly white high school in the wake of this ruling. Throughout the novel, Shange addresses themes of desegregation and its effect on African-American families, especially children. The novel is also a look at the early period of the Civil Rights Movement, as seen from the perspective of an African-American girl. Throughout the novel, Shange makes references to several popular novels, films, and plays, as well as a number of African-American celebrities during the 1950s. These references to American culture of the 1950s function to expand upon Shange's theme of race relations in the United States and the historical and cultural roots of the Civil Rights Movement.

Betsey Brown makes reference to two classic titles, *Gone with the Wind* and *Imitation of Life,* both of which were originally novels by white women concerning racial issues, and both of which were adapted to film. Shange's novel also makes reference to the stage play, later adapted to film, entitled *The Green Pastures,* which was written by a white man, but includes an all-black cast. These references to popular American culture expand upon Shange's theme of racial desegregation and the early Civil Rights Movement. Written by white authors, but concerning characters and issues pertinent to African Americans, all three of these titles have met with a variety of interpretations as to their significance to race relations in the United States.

There are several references throughout *Betsey Brown* to the 1939 movie *Gone with the Wind,* directed by Victor Fleming, and based on the 1936 novel of the same title by Margaret Mitchell (1900–1949). *Gone with the Wind* is a romantic epic tale of the South before, during, and after the Civil War. It remains one of the most popular novels in American history; according to *Encyclopaedia Britannica*, "Within six months [of publication] 1,000,000 copies had been sold; 50,000 copies were sold in one day. It went on to sell more copies than any other novel in U.S. publishing history, with sales passing 12 million by 1965." The novel also won the Pulitzer Prize in 1937. The film version was equally popular, winning nine Academy Awards, and remaining the top-grossing film of all time for over fifty years after its initial release. *Gone with the Wind* stars Vivien Leigh as the Southern belle Scarlet O'Hara, and Clark Gable as romantic lead Rhett Butler, the source of one of the most famous movie lines in American cultural history: "Frankly, my dear, I don't give a damn!"

Although immensely popular, *Gone with the Wind* has come under fire for its racist stereotyping of African-American characters and its sympathetic portrayal of the pro-slavery South during the Civil War. The character played by Hattie Mc-Daniel, an African-American actress typecast as the "black mammy," represents a slave who is faithful to her white "owners" throughout the Civil War, and remains with them even after the Emancipation Proclamation abolishes slavery in the United States. In Shange's novel, reference to *Gone with the Wind* is used as ironic commentary on the story's racist elements, from the perspective of a pre-adolescent African-American girl during the early Civil Rights era of the mid-1950s. In one passage, Betsey Brown associates her grandmother with Scarlet O'Hara. Hearing her grandmother's "Carolinian drawl," Betsey thinks, "There was a way about Vida that was so lilting yet direct that Betsey sometimes thought her grandma had a bloodline connection to Scarlett O'Hara." The irony of this observation works at several levels. Whereas one might expect to observe a *contrast* between the fictional white Southern belle of a Southern slave plantation and an older African-American woman during the early Civil Rights era, Betsey finds in her grandmother a similarity between them. In stating that she thought her grandmother "had a bloodline connection" to the white character of Scarlett O'Hara, Betsey Brown, perhaps unwittingly, alludes to the fact that many African-American families are in fact descendants of white plantation owners. Because of the rampant rape of African-American slave women by white

male plantation owners in the South, it is in fact not unlikely that Betsey's grandmother could have a "bloodline connection" to a white Southern plantation-owning family. Through this allusion, Shange suggests that white and black Southerners share strong cultural, familial, and historical ties which are unfortunately obscured by the racism and segregation still practiced in the South during the 1950s.

In a second reference to *Gone with the Wind,* Betsey's grandmother is compared to the white Southern character of "Miss Pittypat," as well as, once again, to Scarlet O'Hara: "Vida hummed to herself, 'Lord, I wanna be a Christian in my soul,' and sat rocking on the pillared front porch. Miss Pittypat couldn't of done better." Again, Betsey Brown's grandmother is compared to a white Southern woman during the slavery era; she sits in a rocking chair on the porch of a large Southern home, humming a Christian hymn to herself. As she does so, Vida thinks, "Jane had never had to say 'I'll never be hungry again,' cause Vida'd seen to it that every one of her chirren ate. Every single one of em." This refers to one of the most famous lines from *Gone with the Wind;* after the South has lost the Civil War, Scarlet O'Hara returns to her family's plantation home, which has been devastated by the war. Formerly a pampered and spoiled Southern belle, accustomed to being waited on hand and foot, Scarlet O'Hara finds the inner strength to vow to herself that she will survive the devastation of her home, declaring dramatically, "I'll never be hungry again!" Shange's reference to this line from *Gone with the Wind* points out the irony of such a statement coming from a wealthy white Southern woman, when African-American women throughout American history have had to find the inner strength to struggle against great odds—such as slavery, poverty, and racist oppression—in order to see that their families will "never be hungry again."

A third reference is made to *Gone with the Wind* when Betsey enters her school in the morning: "Not only were the floors of the Clark School shining like the halls of Tara, but Betsey's brow was weeping with sweat, as were her panties and underarms. . . . She felt hot. And there was Mr. Wichiten with the razor strap at the head of the hallway, justa swinging and smiling." Tara is the name of Scarlet O'Hara's family plantation in *Gone with the Wind*. By comparing the hallway of her school to the halls of a Southern slave plantation, Betsey expresses her feeling of oppression upon entering school that morning. She is nervous and sweating because she is going to be reciting a poem in class and hopes to win a prize for the best elocution. But the white school official with the "razor strap" in his hands threatens her like a slave driver. Shange here is not at all implying that the school full of black children that is run by white teachers is anywhere near as oppressive as was a Southern slave plantation; however, she is expressing through hyperbole a young girl's feelings of oppression at the hands of her white school teachers. Finally, although Betsey Brown's white teacher treats her African-American students with the same interest and respect as she did her white students, Shange has chosen the name "Mrs. Mitchell" for this character; in conjunction with the nearby references to *Gone with the Wind,* it seems clear that Shange had in mind Margaret Mitchell, author of the original novel.

In addition to *Gone with the Wind,* Shange also makes reference to *Imitation of Life,* originally a novel by Fanny Hurst, adapted to film in 1959. This story is about two single mothers, one white and one black. The white woman (played by Lana Turner in the film), becomes a successful stage actress; the black woman (played by Juanita Moore) is hired as a maid who lives with her daughter in the white woman's house. The central drama of the story concerns the daughter of the black woman, who is so light-skinned that she can easily "pass" for white; as a teenager, she runs away from home, shunning her own mother in order to enter society as a white woman. *Imitation of Life* has been interpreted by critics both as racist, or as critical of racism, depending on the interpretation. In Shange's novel, Betsey's first day in an integrated school—which is predominantly white—includes meeting Mrs. Leon, her white teacher who treats her with kindness and respect, thus making a positive example for Betsey's white classmates to follow. Betsey is so impressed with Mrs. Leon's understanding treatment of her that she thinks, "maybe Mrs. Leon wasn't white at all, maybe she was passing, like in that book *Imitation of Life.* Or maybe she was what Jane called 'well-meaning white people.' At any rate Mrs. Leon broke the ice and the thrill of a new place and new faces came over Betsey as easily as the shadows had blackened her path." By comparing her white teacher to a fictional character who is African-American but "passes" for white, Betsey expresses a feeling of camaraderie—she imagines that her teacher is really African-American, like herself, and this helps her to better cope with the anxiety of her first day at a mostly white school.

When Betsey runs away from home for an entire day, her mother and father take very different approaches to addressing the crisis. While Jane gathers the family around her to kneel down and pray for Betsey's safety and return, Greer drives around St. Louis looking for her. Greer, Betsey's father, understands why she may have run away, while her mother does not. Greer thinks that he cannot possibly explain Betsey's desires to his wife, who remains "down there on her knees with Jesus." Greer concludes, "His whole family looked like a bad scene from *Green Pastures.*" *The Green Pastures* was a play by Marc Connelly, first performed in 1930, which consists of a reenactment of the stories of the Old Testament, in which all of the characters are African-American. The play, written by a white man, is made up of dialogue in what sounds to the modern reader like a highly stereotypical rendition of black English. While the play was extremely popular in the 1930s, it eventually came to be considered by many to consist of gross stereotypes of rural, Southern African Americans as ignorant and childlike, especially in terms of their religious devotion. When Greer says that his entire family, while kneeling together in their living room praying for the return of their daughter, looks like "a bad scene from *Green Pastures,*" he is expressing a degree of disdain for such a passionate expression of religious devotion. This sentiment demonstrates an important set of differences in value between Betsey's father and mother; Greer is much less traditional than his wife, and is disdainful of any behavior on the part of his children or family which suggests catering to white stereotypes of black people. Jane, on the other hand, resorts to prayer in a time of crisis, unconcerned with how her expression of faith might look to an outside observer.

Betsey Brown reads as a veritable *Who's Who* of African-American celebrities during the 1950s and the years preceding the Civil Rights Movement. The narrative refers to prominent and distinguished African-American athletes, musicians, singers, actors and actresses, and political figures. Shange's character of Betsey Brown fantasizes about marrying or emulating a wide range of African-American celebrities who were prominent during the 1950s. Through these many references, Shange celebrates African-American culture and history, as well as calling to mind the importance of such exceptional figures as important role models to a young African-American woman during the Civil Rights era.

Betsey's internal monologue, expressed through the third-person narrator, often takes flights of fancy, in which she imagines a romantic and illustrious future for herself. At one point, Betsey hears music which makes her think of getting married—but only "after she'd run away and made a career of her own, like her mama had and Madame C. J. Walker. Oh yes, Betsey Calhoun would be coming to the altar with something of her own to offer." In fantasizing that she will "make a career of her own," Betsey compares herself to her mother, and to Madame C. J. Walker. Madame C. J. Walker (1867–1919), also known as Sarah Breedlove, was the first black female millionaire in the United States. As a fantasy of a successful African-American career woman, Walker represents the epitome of success in the world of business. In 1905, Walker created a product and process designed for hair styling among African-American women. This process became known as the "Walker System," or "Walker Method," and was marketed by the Madame C. J. Walker Manufacturing Company, of which Walker herself was the president and sole owner. Walker's products were sold by door-to-door sales representatives who targeted African-American neighborhoods. Walker also became known as a philanthropist, donating extensive funds to such African-American causes as the National Association for the Advancement of Colored People, or NAACP. Betsey's choice of Walker as a role model is significant to the novel, in part because of its setting in St. Louis, Missouri, where Walker first developed her product. In addition, Walker's concerns with issues later associated with the Civil Rights Movement indicates the historical efforts of African Americans which led up to the dramatic changes in race relations which took place during the 1950s, in which Shange's novel is set.

References to famous black athletes in *Betsey Brown* include boxing champ "Sugar" Ray Robinson, tennis star Althea Gibson, and baseball player Jackie Robinson. In fantasizing about the kind of man she might marry, Betsey Brown thinks to herself, "I'm Miss Cora Sue Betsey Anne Calhoun Brown, soon to be married to a Negro man of renown." Betsey considers a wide array of African-American celebrities as potential husbands. Among them is "Sugar" Ray Robinson: "He's so handsome," Betsey thinks. "He's so sharp. Mrs. Cora Sue Betsey Anne Calhoun Brown 'Sugar' Robinson. Sounds good to me." "Sugar" Ray Robinson (1921–1989) was a widely admired professional boxer who held the world championship six times. Five of these championships were fought during the 1950s, when Shange's novel takes place. Ac-cording to *Encyclopaedia Britannica,* Robinson "is considered by many authorities to have been the best fighter in history." In addition, "his outstand-ing ability and flamboyant personality made him a hero of boxing fans throughout the world." Later in the novel, after Betsey has run away from home for a day, her father, Greer, drives around St. Louis looking for her. Having exposed his daughter to a wide array of African-American cultural heroes, Greer looks for Betsey in locations throughout the city which are associated with some of these his-toric figures. He looks "at the spot where 'Sugar Ray' liked the barbeque." This reference is also sig-nificant to the novel's setting in St. Louis—the African-American heroes Betsey fantasizes about are not just distant stars, but are, or have been, members of the African-American community in which she and her family live.

Later in the novel, Betsey discusses a white teacher who has put her down. Carrie suggests she "fight the teacher," not physically, but verbally. In response to the mention of "fighting," Betsey jumps up and down "like 'Sugar' Ray Robinson or Althea Gibson," thinking, "Betsey the champ. Humph. My, my, my." Althea Gibson (born in 1927) was the first African-American tennis player to win the Wimbledon and U.S. singles championships. The height of Gibson's career was during the 1950s, when Shange's novel takes place. In this passage of the novel, Betsey associates "fighting" for her dignity and rights against a white teacher with the physical fighting of a championship boxer, or the competitive physical effort of a famous tennis player. Shange also makes reference to Jackie Robinson, the first African-American baseball player in the U.S. major leagues. The effect of these references to successful black athletes is to paint a picture of America, particularly St. Louis in the 1950s, in which the early actions of the Civil Rights Movement went hand in hand with the success of a number of exceptional African Americans in such traditionally white domains as national and inter-national athletic competitions. The sense of em-powerment Betsey feels in calling to mind these successful African-American athletes is equivalent to the sense of empowerment among African Americans for which the Civil Rights Movement was striving.

In addition to athletes, Shange's novel makes reference to several prominent African-American singers, dancers, and actors of the first half of the twentieth century, including Paul Robeson, Dorothy Dandridge, and Eartha Kitt. When Betsey enters school hoping to win an elocution contest in

Dorothy Counts, the first African-American student to attend Harding Junior High School in Charlotte, NC, is escorted to school through a crowd of jeering white students in September 1957. Betsey faces similar prejudices when she is bussed to a white school.

her class, she fantasizes about what prize she might win, wondering if it would perhaps be a Paul Robeson record. Later, when she is fantasizing about what type of illustrious career she will have, she considers that of an actress, "like Dandridge or Eartha." All three of these singers/actors met with a significant degree of success, followed by unfortunate circumstances which led to the decline of their careers. Paul Robeson (1898–1976) became well-known for his stage and screen roles during the 1920s, '30s, and '40s. Robeson was also celebrated for musical recordings, particularly in the singing of spirituals. His most famous role was as Joe in the stage and screen versions of the musical *Showboat,* in which his leading number was "Ol' Man River." Robeson was also a left-wing activist, and his American passport was taken away in 1950 after he refused to deny his membership in the Communist Party. This led to general public condemnation of his character during the era of the "Red Scare," and a subsequent decline of his career prospects. Dorothy Dandridge (1923–1965) was known as the first black woman ever nominated for an Academy Award for Best Actress— for her performance in the 1954 *Carmen Jones.* This notoriety would have occurred in the same

year in which Shange's novel takes place, and Betsey's interest in her as a celebrity is historically accurate. However, Dandridge's film career was limited by the few opportunities for black women in Hollywood during this time, and her early success eventually led to disappointment. Eartha Kitt was well-known for her nightclub performances as a singer and dancer, as well as several film roles. Like Robeson, Kitt was eventually ostracized and her career virtually destroyed for her left-wing political views, after she publicly declared at a White House luncheon her disapproval of U.S. involvement in the Vietnam War. Through reference to these three figures, Shange reminds the reader of important African-American figures from American popular culture of the 1950s who expressed strong political sentiments, and whose careers were directly affected by the racism and the political climate of their time.

In addition to the many references to popular culture and African-American celebrities, *Betsey Brown* includes a number of references to prominent military and political figures such as Benjamin Oliver Davis, Gamal Abdel Nasser, and Kwame Nkrumah. In fantasizing that she will one day marry any of a number of famous men, most of them African-American, Betsey muses: "I'm Miss Cora Sue Betsey Anne Calhoun Brown, soon to be married to a Negro man of renown. There's Cab Calloway. Machito. Mongo Santamaria. Tito Puente. Colonel Davis. Nasser. Nkrumah. James Brown." While most of these figures are musicians, several were renowned for military and political accomplishments.

Mention of Colonel Davis could include both Benjamin Oliver Davis Sr. and Benjamin Oliver Davis Jr. Davis Sr. (1877–1970) was the first African American to reach the rank of general in the U.S. army. His son, Davis Jr. (born in 1912), was distinguished as the first African American to reach the rank of general in the U.S. air force. In Shange's novel, Betsey is most likely referring to Davis Jr., who was the organizer of the first air unit manned entirely by African Americans, which fought during World War II, after which he was promoted to the rank of colonel. Mention of Davis in Shange's novel is significant to the theme of desegregation and the beginnings of racial integration, because Davis was instrumental in planning the official desegregation of the U.S. air force after the war. In 1954, around the time in which Shange's novel is set, Davis Jr. was promoted to brigadier general (a one-star general). In 1959 he was made major general (a two-star general), and in 1965 he was promoted to lieutenant general (a three-star general). In 1998, after retiring, Davis Jr. was made a four-star general.

Shange also makes reference to an international diaspora of political leaders of African descent, as well as others not of European descent, through the mention of Gamal Abdel Nasser (1918–1970), who was prime minister and then president of Egypt between 1954 and 1970, and Kwame Nkrumah (1909–1972), the Ghanaian nationalist leader who led the drive for national independence from Britain and became the leader of Ghana from 1957 to 1966. In 1954, around the time in which Shange's novel is set, Nasser had just emerged as the new prime minister of Egypt, and Nkrumah had been prime minister of the Gold Coast (the name of Ghana during the era of British rule) since 1952.

Shange's many references to historically real texts and celebrities of American culture during the 1950s, in the context of her fictional novel, function to expand upon and enrich her central thematic concerns with desegregation and the early Civil Rights era.

Source: Liz Brent, in an essay for *Novels for Students,* Gale Group, 2001.

> " In the West we're terribly free to do whatever we want. We're free to associate with Asians and Latins at will, aesthetically as well as politically."

Henry Blackwell

In the following composite interview, Shange espouses her beliefs on what makes a poet and how geography influences poetic development.

One of the most articulate Black American artists to have emerged in the last few years, Ntozake Shange began the process of identifying and fulfilling her many talents in an academic milieu. An honors graduate of the American Studies program at Barnard in 1970, an NDEA Fellow at the University of Southern California, where she earned an M.A. degree in American Studies in 1973, Shange has lectured or taught at a number of colleges and universities, such as Brown, C.C.N.Y., Douglass, Howard, N.Y.U., Sonoma State, and Yale. Her book-length publications include *for colored girls who have considered suicide/when the rainbow is enuf* (1975, 1977), *sassafrass: a novella* (1976), *nappy edges* (1978), and *8 pieces & 'a photograph'* (1979). Individual poems, essays, and short stories of hers have appeared in numerous magazines and anthologies, including *The Black Scholar, Yardbird Ms., Essence, The Chicago Review,* and *Third World Women.* Theatrical credits, reflecting her work as a writer and a performer, include *for colored girls* (1976), *negress* (1977), *a photograph; a still life with shadows/a photograph: a study in cruelty* (1977), *where the mississippi meets the amazon* (1977–78), *from okra to greens: a different love story* (1978), *boogie woogie landscapes* (1978–79), and *magic spell #7* (1979). Her involvement in musical collaborations with David Murray, Oliver Lake, Jay Hoggard, Ramsey Ameen, and Cecil Taylor also reflects the range of her creativity, as does her role as a performing member of The Sounds of Motion Dance Company, directed by Diane McIntyre.

The following interview is a composite of conversations with Shange, recorded while she was visiting the University of Connecticut as a speaker. Shange supplied the answer to the last question by mail, and she has been kind enough to read and edit the typescript.

INT. You have indicated that you feel that Black writers from the East, West, South, and the Midwest represent separate groups, each with its own voice and perhaps a different aesthetic. Would you elaborate on that?

SHANGE. Sure. My craft was seriously nurtured in California and that probably has some influence on what my writing looks like. There's not a California style, but there are certain feelings and a certain freeness that set those writers off from those in the Chicago-St. Louis-Detroit tripod group. They're not the same. In the West we're terribly free to do whatever we want. We're free to associate with Asians and Latins at will, aesthetically as well as politically. And this is reflected in the kinds of things we do, so that the chauvinism that you might find that's exclusionary, in that triangle, you don't find too much in California. And if you do find it, it's in young poets who're just starting. Black, Asian, or Latin, they're only very nationalistic until they realize that all Third World people are working toward the same thing, which for us is the explication of our reality. I sometimes get the feeling that the writers in Chicago are at war, and that they are defending our reality. In San Francisco, that defensive stance isn't necessary, because the racism in California is so peculiar, they don't really attack us *immediately,* so we're able to do the particularly important job of simply exploring what our lives have been in the Western hemisphere, and making the exploration, not the defense, be the work of the poems. My kids and the people around me should know exactly who we are. And when someone speaks of Third World people's reality, there'll be no mistake about what that reality is. The poetry of the Black writer on the West Coast clarifies—migrations, our relationship to the soil, to ourselves in space. There is an enormous amount of space in the West, and you do not feel personally impinged upon every time you come out of your door, like you do in New York and in Chicago. So, there's a different attitude about being alive. I'm really glad that David Henderson and Ishmael [Reed] live there. I used to live there. It gave us a chance to breathe, to get away from the immediacy of oppression in the East and those particular political events, which all of us experienced, and which we sometimes deal with as a corrective group in our poetry. Black writers on the West Coast got out from under the heavy pressure

of those events, but that doesn't mean that we forgot them. It just means that we could deal with them from another angle. The Midwest people: If you see a poem you know where it came from, if it came from Chicago. Their sense of rhythm is almost limited to whatever it is that came up off the Delta. They seldom stray from particular rhythm sequences that I would associate with the blues and with inner-city urban life. This is all right, but it can become a trap. I think there is a tendency to assume that all Black people know that particular rhythm sequence, that all Black people migrated up the Mississippi River, and that is not true. They talk about the cities, about gangs, welfare—as opposed to opening it up and talking about Black folks in other places. There ain't no poems about nobody in the country in Indiana. Nobody knows what kind of life they live, because they are not a part of our scheme of what Black life is supposed to look like. And that means we're leaving out portions of our population in order to formulate some ideology of what we are. This monolithic idea that everybody's the same, that we all live the same lives. That the Black family, the Black man, the Black female are the same thing. A one image. A one something. It's not true, but it's very difficult to break through some of that. We ignore Black Catholics. They don't exist in literature. Maybe in the Renaissance a couple of people admitted to being Catholic, but everybody nowadays has become somebody who was nurtured in the Baptist Church. I don't know why we're trying to become some solid unit of something. Part of our beauty is the fact that we're so much.

INT. And New York?

SHANGE. I don't think poets in New York have ever gotten over. Whereas in California readings are a source of joy, readings in New York are almost scenario, because the impact of theatre, dance, and other art forms (and the fact that you need money to produce anything) has made the playwright, the novelist, and the musician the carriers of good news, as opposed to the poet. New York poets almost *have* to be miserable and unhappy to get over. Some are brilliant, absolutely brilliant. Some others are labeled poets, but I don't count them, I don't deal with them that way.

INT. Why not?

SHANGE. Because I don't think they know what they are doing.

INT. What makes a poet from your point of view?

SHANGE. A very conscious effort to be concise and powerful and as illusory as possible, so that the language can, in fact, bring you to more conclusions than the one in the poem, but that that one conclusion can't be avoided, even though there are thousands of others roaming around. And there should be wit and grace and a movement from one image to another, so that there's no narrowness to the body of your work. That to me would suggest someone is a poet.

INT. You seem to have very definite ideas about what it takes to be a poet. Does that definiteness reflect your academic training?

SHANGE. No. Poetry is my life. And actually, when I went to graduate school, and was studying Afro-American art, I was made to feel like a traitor, because there's a huge strain of anti-intellectualism not only in the new Black Arts movement, but in Black America in general. People think that you aren't doing anything: Studying don't mean nothing. I felt very bad, but I was determined that those people were going to hear from me. Just because I had studied didn't mean that I had lost my voice. The anger about my situation as a student propelled me to make doubly sure that I fulfilled *all* my obligations. I always went to my readings, even if I had a test the next day. Or, if I had to teach the morning after a reading, I *did* it. I have always appreciated my academic background, though not just for the usual reasons that you would expect. I went to Women's Studies, because in Women's Studies, I was at least able to discuss the anger and the awkwardness. I wasn't stifled or shut back.

INT. I can see from your experience why you would see not just richness but truth in our diversity. Do you think that Southern Black writers are shaped in distinctive ways by their experience in the South?

SHANGE. Yes. My sister and I were raised in the Midwest and the North, and we'd go to a lot of poetry readings together. At one reading, there were a lot of women who had formerly been raised in the South. And we were getting very upset by what, in our ignorance, we saw as their romanticization of Southern living. Instead of a streetcar, there would be hills and swamps and a porch and grandma and quilts and iron pots and Mr. So-and-So from down by the church. And I was saying to myself, if it was as wonderful as all that, why in the hell did you all come up here? It was really getting ridiculous. But I thought a little more, and I said, wait. If it's that severe a sense of loss, then

perhaps they're not talking about what we are talking about. To children of migrations, leaving the South may have engendered a stunning sense of loss, and that's something that should be respected and dealt with in its own right.

INT. So, were they merely romanticizing, or driving to the heart of a personal reality that you felt cut off from?

SHANGE. I think they were explaining. After a while, I wasn't paying attention to the romantic images. I was trying to deal with the motivation for those images, and I was wondering, why are they telling me this? Why is this supposed to be important to me? And I decided that it was because they wanted us to know what they thought they had lost. And what they thought they lost is, in fact, as important as what really did go away, because that vacuum has first to be identified and then filled with something. And those acts of identification and repair are going to be, or should be, increasingly personal. But mostly now you get just one picture. A lot of times, Black poets are expected to reflect immediate political need, or current political fashion. I think that tendency is behind the fact that you can't talk anymore about the South as a bad thing. It's like Heaven; you don't criticize it. Just as for a while, it was a terrifying and scary thing to write a poem which was not politically relevant, about yourself when you were a child. Nor could you speak critically of your mother and father; they worked so hard as Black people. So for a long time we didn't have strong poems dealing with *actual* Black family life; you couldn't do it. But, well, we've been here for as long as however we've been here—each of us, separately. And that is something that we're beginning to explore as we try to understand ourselves as mature adults. And some women are sort of easing away to address the real bludgeoning effects that any family has. Cover-ups, romantic or otherwise, are not endemic to us, but that doesn't matter. O.K., so I'm not from the South. I missed that big jolt that was a big thing in the fourth generation migratory Black person, who's been up North since 1917, or something, so I don't know nothing about that fund of experiences, and I just have to be quiet. So, I'm saying, all right, I'll be quiet, but I would at least like to know why those women glorified their losses. Usually, when people make something important, it's because it's not working. It's something that has to be dealt with. And they start addressing it however they can. I think critical explorations are beginning to happen, and in the next five years there will be some really marvelous work, like Black *Nashvilles,* like Black Black-fiction shows, and Black stories about the reality of our lives in the South, as opposed to our dream dimensions of that. It's too crazy now. Everybody had a grandma who was wonderful, or an uncle who came by and did the family errands. Cotton was nice to be picked. That is crazy to me, because it's the same thing that my grandma said she was tired of and the reason that she left. My experience poses not a simple difference but a contradiction to such depictions.

INT. Granting that differences are important to understanding our identity, are there similarities which it is crucial to examine? Are Black women writers, for example, connected by a common set of problems?

SHANGE. I worked exclusively with Black women in college, but since that time I've been working most in a Third World context, in terms of women, at any rate. I moved from New York in 1970 and went to California because at that time there was no space for an independent woman's voice; women were expected to be quiet and have babies, no matter what kind of training they had had. Where I came from, women existed for the pleasure and support of men. I began to wonder, What are we doing? What are we supposed to do when our men are gone? I started writing because I had to have an answer, I had to hear a voice. I absolutely had to hear something. And nobody was going to give it to me. So, I gave it to myself.

I left New York because I could not fight with them. In fact, I thought what they were doing was right. But I just could not live inside those roles. Those same male-oriented roles and expectations were imposed in our literature. As a young woman, I was starving for Black literature. I didn't care what they said, just so the writers gave me something. For years, I was able to tolerate being chastised and denigrated in American literature and any other kind of literature because that is where we were, and that's how women were regarded. But as my consciousness as a woman developed, I said, hey, you all are doing the same thing to women that you say Faulkner did to *you*. What the hell is going on? But even then I didn't take it as a personal affront, because that's how all of us were trained. I do now, though. I mean, after ten years of women saying, hey, we're people, we think, we feel—I don't expect the same kinds of attitudes. You can't blame somebody because salt wasn't refined when it wasn't refined. Now we know how to refine it, so let's do it.

INT. Do you think this habit of diminishment and neglect in and out of literature has forced Black women to look at life in a special way, has forced them to devise a special aesthetic?

SHANGE. To an extent. The same rhetoric that is used to establish the Black Aesthetic, we must use to establish a women's aesthetic, which is to say that those parts of reality that are ours, those things about our bodies, the cycles of our lives that have been ignored for centuries in all castes and classes of our people, are to be dealt with now. When women reach puberty, they menstruate. What does that mean? Women have relationships with their mothers that are incredibly full of pain and love. A mother functions as part of a husband, not as another woman for the child. Women have relationships to the world that have to do with whether you can *reach* things. Can you put a pan away? Can you lift stuff? Are you afraid of a corner at night—and other things that men do not deal with? And our poetry deals with that, and we use images that have to do with that. Some men have weird notions about women. The title of a manuscript that I have, "Dreams as Real as Menses," means to most women that their dreams are going to come true. Most men hearing that title either stumble over the word "menses" or go "ugh" because they can't see or accept that reality. So it's the same as the Black *man's* struggle, in terms of liberating our reality from the pits, from Hades, and making things we see everyday tangible and speakable. One has to speak about things inherently female. And that is my persona. A women. And she is going to talk the way she understands. Why must I use metaphors because men understand them? That's the same argument I have with Paul Laurence Dunbar. He knew that he could not be respected as a poet unless he wrote all those sonnets with the English corrected, and they are just awful. This is analogous to what women have been doing all along. Using male-identified symbols and myths to talk about ourselves. That's ridiculous. There are enough females in the world to be joyful, to be knowledgeable, to be loved. We don't have to go across the line. And if men don't understand it, then I would suggest, as I suggest to white students who say they don't understand Black literature, that they should get more serious about the subject. Learn something about women. I'm not going to change what I write to help a man understand it. They've been here as long as I've been here. They rule the damned world, they rule the household, if not the world, and they can certainly learn who their mother was, and who they sleep with at night.

INT. Does your position create friction with Black male writers?

SHANGE. Most of the Black men whose writing I respect, respect mine. And I have very good working relationships with them. I don't have good working relationships with some so-called critics and socio-political poets. They don't want idiom; they want ideology, and they can have it. They're seeing Black poetry as some kind of mammoth creature with four legs and a nose. And my leg is going over there, or over here. It destroys their idea. They don't want to deal with poetry, they want to talk politics. They want to make me run for office. Well, I'm not going to do that. Pablo Neruda did run for office, but he was a poet in the government. My politics, I think, are very correct. I do not have heroes who are not heroes.

INT. Who are some of your heroes?

SHANGE. Toussaint L'Ouverture. Denmark Vesey. Sojourner Truth. Nat Love. Albert Ayler. Jelly Roll Morton. Bessie Smith. Zora Neale Hurston . . .

INT. That's an interesting list. What makes them heroes? Politicians . . .

SHANGE. Politicians don't turn me on. When someone takes charge of your reality and does something to it that is satisfying for them, changing everything that comes after in some way or other, then that is, to me, being a successful and competent human being and a successful and competent Black person. When you take something you believe in and make it affect other people, you're doing a politically significant act. These people did things that changed the way all the rest of us were treated or thought of in the world. I think you have to stop looking to something called "the politician." They're there. That's their job, but it can't just be on them. What are we, sheep? We don't have no feet? No brains? We can't do anything ourselves?

INT. Are you stressing self-reliance, or . . .

SHANGE. The most important thing I know is that anything you want to do, especially pertaining to your work, you can do yourself. You don't have to wait on nobody. You don't have to wait on the Black world; you don't have to wait on Ishmael; you don't have to wait on Percy Sutton. If you want to do a show, you go to your little local bar, and tell them that on—whatever their night off is—you want to use their space. And you go and use it to the best of your ability, and get paid $1.37, but get known in your community. Send out your own little press releases. Meet a printer. Have

a printer do up just one page of your poems. Give them away, mail them to your friends. Give him fifty dollars and have him do a ten-page booklet. You don't have to wait. Learn how to print your goddamn self. This sense that we have to follow all the patterns established by the country and by our own habit is really quite unnecessary. And if we are, in fact, closer to developing a new way of thinking and new skills, we have no choice but to do for ourselves. Which is not to go back to Booker T., but to take him to the ultimate point of what he said in the first place. You can do what you have to, what you must. You don't have to be recognized by whites. Just go and do it. There's the anecdote: "They don't need to know we can build the Empire State Building, they just need to know we can clean floors?" I don't even care what they know. All I need to know is that Black people are not going to sit around waiting for the powers that be in the white community or in our community to take care of us.

INT. Did you have a Black audience in mind when you wrote *colored girls?*

SHANGE. It was meant for a women's audience, initially. In most of my work, I'm talking to women, because I'm talking to myself when I write. As for specifically Black audiences, I don't think like that. I write poems, and I take them where I think they'll work. I don't bar much. If I tried to stop a poem, because I don't have an audience for it, I'd be a fool. Poetry is like the only privacy in some areas that I have, so I can't jam it up because Black people might not like it. I write the poem because it's there, and I take it where I can take it. Maybe I can't take it anywhere, maybe I just have to leave it in the house. Some of them I do that with. But I have a right to think and feel what I want, and I can't stop feeling what I feel. Writing with me is a visceral thing. I have to get certain ideas out, or I will get sick, I will cry, I will become catatonic. I don't have a choice.

INT. You've spoken on other occasions about influences. Who among contemporary Black writers has had the most influence on what and how you write?

SHANGE. Ishmael. *Yellow Back Radio Broke-Down, Mumbo Jumbo,* "I Am A Cowboy in the Boat of Ra"—these have been terribly significant to me, because they said, look, you have the whole world to deal with. You do not have to deal with the block in New York City where there are no trees. And there's Baraka. Everything. All the essays. Everything. He's fabulous. I read the stuff out loud. The stories in *Tales,* in *Dante's Hell,* are just some of the most beautiful uses of language and imagery I've seen anywhere at all.

INT. Looking back at your work from *sassafrass* through *nappy edges* are you aware of any changes in the way you see the world or in the way that you express what you see and feel? Are you more concerned with technique? With broadening the scope of your vision? With exhausting your material?

SHANGE. Only the *way* I have to proceed has changed. As a recognized writer I face problems I never dreamed of as an unknown: expectations. I find that in order to work at all now I must virtually obliterate the outside world. I have to construct what I call a "creative myopia" because the wolves are at the door. People say, "How could *you* say *that?*" or "So many people pay attention to your ideas, you are responsible for . . . " All that sort of thing is burdensome and interrupts my relationship with myself. More and more I understand why Midwestern writers feel they are under siege. In certain parts of the country, the density of population and poverty surely exacerbate racism. This year the critics had a field day discussing whether or not Black and Latin actors *could* do Shakespeare! In such a world, one admittedly has to flex muscle not just lyricism. I have to do battle with myself to even present the fragile composites of a life—Black and fictional—before such barbarians. I sometimes doubt that I'd have been able to write *sassafrass* had I been aware of this situation. She's too precious to me to endure the wear and tear of this place (the Eastern literary establishment, Black and white). I am more concerned with craft at this point. To protect my characters and landscapes from unwarranted attacks, I make them taut and as lean as I can. Some whimsy is lost but I doubt anyone in the midst of an urban winter would miss it. There's little possibility of my exhausting my material. I'm still alive and feeling and seeing. I've started drawing and dancing again to make sure that I don't lose touch with the roots of my poetic vision. These roots have so much to do with actuality and yet so very little. But that begins another story.

Source: Henry Blackwell, "An Interview with Ntozake Shange," in *Black American Literature Forum,* Vol. 13, No. 4, Winter 1979, pp. 134–8.

Sources

Anderlini, Serena, "An Interview with Ntozake Shange," in *Journal of Dramatic Theory and Criticism,* Vol. 6, No. 1, Fall 1991, pp. 85–97.

Brown, Elizabeth, "Ntozake Shange," in *Dictionary of Literary Biography,* Vol. 38, edited by Thadious M. Davis and Trudier Harris, Gale, 1985, pp. 240–50.

Glastonbury, Marion, "Of the Fathers," in *New Statesman,* October 4, 1985.

Schindehette, Susan, Review in *Saturday Review,* May/June 1985.

Tate, Claudia, *Black Women Writers at Work,* Continuum, 1993.

Williams, Sherley Anne, "Roots of Privilege: New Black Fiction," in *Ms.,* June 1985, pp. 69–72.

For Further Study

Carroll, Rebecca, ed., with a foreword by Ntozake Shange, *Sugar in the Raw: Voices of Young Black Girls in America,* Crown, 1997.

This collection of nonfiction first-person narratives about the lives of fifteen girls, aged eleven to eighteen, from all across America, addresses issues of self-esteem, identity, and values, offering an authentic portrait of contemporary black girlhood.

Haskins, Jim, *Separate but Not Equal: The Dream and the Struggle,* Scholastic, 1997.

Tracing back from the 1957 crisis in Little Rock to explore the history of segregated education, Haskins sets a thorough context for the school integration crisis of the 1950s–1970s and also covers the landmark cases of the struggle. This book is aimed specifically at a high-school audience.

Landry, Bart, *The New Black Middle Class,* University of California Press, 1987.

In this in-depth academic study, sociologist Landry describes the rise of an elite and privileged class of African Americans since the Civil Rights Movement, offering insight into the social stratification of American blacks.

Shange, Ntozake, *See No Evil: Prefaces, Essays and Accounts, 1976–1983,* Momo's Press, 1984.

Shange's nonfiction writings, collected here, express her views on the state of black arts in her early career and illuminate the motivations behind her more experimental works.

Body and Soul

Frank Conroy
1993

Published in 1993, *Body and Soul* was the long-awaited first novel of the acclaimed author Frank Conroy. He had originally come into the literary spotlight with his autobiography *Stop-Time,* published a quarter of a century earlier. Critics and fans alike had eagerly awaited a book of stature equal to *Stop-Time* and were ecstatic to hear that at long last Conroy would be published again. *Body and Soul* was released with much hype and fanfare, yet the reaction from critics was mixed. Many were disappointed that *Body and Soul,* while very similar in subject matter to *Stop-Time,* was not as compelling as the autobiography had been. Others, however, were enthralled by the epic and weaving plot line, numerous and diverse characters, and rapid page-turning pace. Despite the mixed critical reaction, the book became a national best-seller and brought Conroy even more recognition. It even became a Delta Fiction Publisher's Choice book when it was reprinted in trade paperback format.

Body and Soul is the exploration of the life of a child prodigy, raised in poverty and neglect but achieving fame and fortune through his incredible musical gift. The saga chronicles his struggles with himself, his environment, his family, his ambition, and ultimately with the talent that has given him everything. It is, as Conroy himself put it, "a real old-fashioned novel—a big fat book with a lot of people and a lot of plot." *Body and Soul* encompasses not only the hopes and dreams of its protagonist, but of Frank Conroy fans as well.

Author Biography

While *Stop-Time* was Frank Conroy's autobiography, it is apparent that he continues to draw from his own childhood experiences to create the world in which his characters live. Born on January 15, 1936, in New York City, Conroy was the son of an absent, mentally ill father and a cold, unloving mother. He spent much of his childhood escaping from his loneliness by reading books and teaching himself to play jazz on the piano. Yet from this miserable childhood came the inspiration for the writing that would later make him famous.

Conroy attended Haverford College in Pennsylvania. While there he met Patty Monro Ferguson, whom he married in 1958, the same year he graduated. Patty introduced him to the world of New York's social elite. Then in 1967, at the age of thirty-one, Conroy published his first book, the uniquely styled autobiography *Stop-Time*. This story of his childhood in New York City was greeted with intense critical acclaim. The book was hailed as an extraordinary first work, and readers were eager to see what Conroy would produce next. However, the fans and critics would have to wait.

Conroy did not publish another work until 1985. During the interim, he divorced Patty and had to leave his two sons, Daniel and Will, and he left Manhattan for Nantucket, Rhode Island. In 1975, he married his second wife, Margaret Davidson Lee, and worked as a freelance journalist and a jazz musician. At the age of forty he began teaching and eventually served as the director of the literature program at the National Endowment for the Arts (1981–87). In 1985, Conroy published his second book, *Midair*. This collection of just eight short stories received mixed reviews. In 1993, Conroy became director of the renowned Writers' Workshop at the University of Iowa. That same year he published his third book and first novel, *Body and Soul*.

Today, Conroy, his wife, and his son Tim divide their time between their homes in Iowa City and Nantucket. He continues to work as an administrator and teacher.

Plot Summary

Part One

The novel begins when Claude Rawlings is six years old, living in a basement apartment on Third Avenue in New York City. While his mother,

Emma, drives a cab, Claude amuses himself on an old, out-of-tune piano in his dark, little room. He occasionally attends school, but sits in the back of class and goes virtually unnoticed. Fascinated by Weisfeld's Music Store, he ventures in one day. Aaron Weisfeld shows him how to read sheet music and gives him a beginner's piano book to learn. Claude devours the book in record time, mastering the lessons with very little difficulty. Weisfeld is astonished by the boy's talent and agrees to be his teacher.

Claude also chances to meet Al Johnson, a maintenance worker in an apartment building. Through Al, Claude earns the money to pay for his piano lessons. In the meantime, his mother becomes involved in the Communist Party, using her cab to chauffeur leaders of the movement. Detected by the FBI, she is pressured into testifying before the House Un-American Activities Committee. Traumatized by the experience, she slowly begins to lose her grip on reality.

Weisfeld arranges for Claude to practice on a concert grand piano in the home of the aged Maestro Kimmel. There the servants introduce him to gourmet dining, table manners, and strengthening exercises. When the Maestro passes away, he leaves Claude the Bechstein piano in his will and enough money in trust to pay for his music lessons. The piano is moved to the basement of Weisfeld's music store where Claude sets up a work studio. In the little time that Claude spends away from music, he goes to the movies and is enthralled with the glitzy, romantic adventures that he believes represent the world outside his narrow existence.

Claude then begins to study with a variety of music teachers, each one instructing him about a different technique or school of music. One of these teachers is the world-renowned Mozart expert Fredericks, who becomes a lifelong friend and mentor to Claude. As Claude moves into his teen years, he is hired to play at parties for the Fisks, a prominent, wealthy couple with two children, Catherine and Peter. Claude is immediately enraptured by Catherine, but she treats him with derision.

At the movie theater, Claude happens to find the notebook of Ivan Andrews, who attends The Bentley, a very exclusive private high school. Claude inquires about admission, and when they learn of his musical genius, he is admitted to the school with a full scholarship. Claude and Ivan become fast friends and spend much of their spare time together discussing music, physics, and life.

By this time Emma's emotional instability has reached its peak. Instead of driving her cab, she sits at home all day gathering evidence of what she believes to be a massive government conspiracy. Afraid they will be evicted from their apartment for nonpayment of rent, Claude tells Al of his dilemma. Al's understanding and support eventually bring Emma back to sanity. Then Al and Emma's relationship develops beyond friendship, and they begin living and working together on a permanent basis.

At school, Claude studies Schonberg's twelve-tone system of composition with his music professor Mr. Satterthwaite, and even manages to get invited to a social mixer by Catherine. When Catherine soon after elopes to Australia, Claude is confused and devastated, but does not have much time to dwell on it after he receives the opportunity to perform a Mozart Double Concerto with Fredericks at a music festival. It is Claude's debut, and he is a smashing success. Fredericks' manager, Otto Levits, signs on to manage Claude. By agreement among Levits, Mr. Larkin (the lawyer who handles Claude's trust), Weisfeld, and Claude, a scholarship is arranged for Claude to go to Pennsylvania to attend Cadbury College.

Part Two

Claude is in his senior year of college when he meets Lady Powers. They fall in love, and Claude discovers that Lady is Catherine's cousin. Lady's parents do not approve of Claude because he is a musician. Professionally, Claude's career is growing. He performs a concert tour with the famous violinist Frescobaldi, playing to enthusiastic audiences in several cities and even at Carnegie Hall. None of this, however, impresses Lady's parents, and her father hires a private investigator to look into Claude's past. There is no record of Claude's father, and Claude confronts his mother for the truth. Emma tells him that she does not know who his father is, and that Henry Rawlings was just a soldier she met two days before he was shipped out. Claude is not happy with this explanation, but there is nothing he can do but accept it. Lady is furious with her parents and refuses to go back to their house. Fortunately, she has a five-million-dollar trust fund, so Lady and Claude get married.

Part Three

Five years later, Lady and Claude are living the life of a normal married couple. Claude continues to build his music career while Lady flits from one project to another. Their world is shaken by the discovery that Claude is sterile. Lady desperately wants to have a baby, so they decide to adopt. The adoption falls through, however, and Lady is so traumatized by the bad experience that she closes the subject on adopting.

Claude comes into the music store one day to find Weisfeld in bed, very ill. He knows he is near death, so Weisfeld finally tells Claude the story of how he lost his family in the war. When Weisfeld passes away, Claude is absolutely devastated. He cancels all his engagements and goes into such a deep depression that he spends months lost in his own grief and completely out of touch with others. His marriage to Lady is falling apart, and she leaves to pursue a business venture with a friend in Florida. But when Claude learns that Weisfeld has left the music store to him and is reminded of Weisfeld's love for him, he is rejuvenated. He decides to move into Weisfeld's old apartment above the store and to begin to work again.

A big real estate development corporation wants to buy up the entire block, including the music store, and turn it into new apartment buildings. Claude refuses to sell, and finds himself the victim of corporate intimidation. He is harassed and even has his arm broken by hired corporate thugs. The intimidation comes to an end, however, when Senator Barnes, Lady and Catherine's grandfather, comes to Claude's aid.

Claude composes a concerto that wins the London Symphony competition. He leaves the store in the care of Emma and Al and goes to England. While there, Catherine, now a divorced single mother working on her doctoral degree, comes to see him. They become romantically involved, and Catherine confesses that during the time that Claude had known her in New York, she had been sleeping with her stepfather, Dewman Fisk. Claude asks her to marry him, but she does not want to marry again, and she knows that there is not room in Claude's life for anything but music.

While in a rehearsal, Claude meets a bassist named Reggie Phillips, who informs him of a nearby jazz club. Claude attends one evening and plays alongside Reggie's companion and bandleader, a black man named Lord Lightning. What Claude does not know is that Lord Lightning is his father. It is a secret that his parents, Al, and Reggie will take to their graves.

Claude's concerto, his debut as a major composer, creates a great demand for his performances, and Claude Rawlings leaves England for a whirlwind existence in the music world that will consume his life.

Characters

Ivan Andrews

Ivan is Claude's close friend from The Bentley School. He is an older student who has come from Britain to finish his war-interrupted schooling and teach Greek. He later moves back to England and teaches physics at Cambridge University. Years later, Ivan comes to the London opening of Claude's piano concerto.

Senator Barnes

Senator Barnes is Lady and Catherine's grandfather and a respected former U.S. senator. As a pillar of New York society, he is highly regarded and commands a great deal of power. Senator Barnes uses this power to push through the adoption of a baby for Claude and Lady. Unfortunately, ignoring some rules to rush the process causes disastrous results. The senator also helps Claude during a struggle with ruthless land developers, thereby allowing Claude to keep Weisfeld's store intact.

Dewman Fisk

Dewman Fisk is Catherine's stepfather and a prominent figure in New York government and the arts. He wrote a law that required a children's section in each movie theater to protect children from molesters. Ironically, he himself is a child molester who started an affair with Catherine when she was only thirteen years old.

Mildred Fisk

Mildred Fisk is Catherine's mother. Wealthy and shallow, she periodically becomes very ill, retreating to her room for weeks at a time. When she hears the news about Catherine's elopement, she is stricken with hysterical blindness and never recovers her sight.

Peter Fisk

Peter Fisk is Catherine's half-brother. He plays the violin very well, but has no real love for music. Sheltered and suppressed by his "delicate" mother, he becomes a shell without a soul and eventually takes his own life.

Mr. Fredericks

Mr. Fredericks is the best Mozart pianist in the world and a very expensive piano teacher who normally has students from only the wealthiest families. But he accepts Claude as a student on Weisfeld's recommendation, then befriends Claude and acts as his mentor. Fredericks gives Claude the opportunity to debut by playing with him at a music festival, and he helps to shape Claude into a world-class musician.

Mr. Frescobaldi

Mr. Frescobaldi is a world-famous violin player who invites Claude to perform with him. It is Claude's introduction into the world of professional music. They play Carnegie Hall together and go on to tour together at various times.

Al Johnson

Al Johnson is the black custodian who befriends Claude. They meet when he discovers the young boy digging around for bottles in the basement of the apartment building where Al works. A poor man just getting by, Al occasionally steals from the wealthy tenants. But he turns from trying to involve Claude in theft to becoming Claude's advisor on life. He even steps in to help Claude's mother out of her emotional upheaval. Al's kind heart and great patience cause a sudden and radical difference in Emma's mental state. Al soon moves in with her, and together they drive taxis to make a living until Claude invites them to run Weisfeld's store.

Maestro Kimmel

Maestro Kimmel is an elderly piano master who allows Claude to practice on a very special and magnificent Bechstein in his home. The maestro has his staff give Claude lessons in etiquette and sees that he exercises and eats well. When the maestro passes away, he bequeaths the Bechstein to Claude, as well as a trust fund to pay for all of Claude's future piano lessons.

Mr. Larkin

Mr. Larkin is the executor of Maestro Kimmel's will and is in charge of the trust left to Claude by the maestro. He is also on the scholarship committee at Cadbury College, and he is the reason Claude is accepted to that college with a full academic scholarship.

Otto Levits

Otto Levits is Fredericks' manager, and becomes Claude's manager as well, after the debut performance at the music festival.

Lord Lightning

Lord Lightning is a gay jazz pianist in London and Claude Rawlings's biological father. His one sexual relationship with a woman had produced Claude, but Emma wanted to handle the situation by herself. One-quarter black, he arranged for Emma to marry a gay white soldier who was shipping out to war, and Lightning purposely kept himself out of Claude's life after that to allow Claude the opportunity to grow up as a white American boy. Yet his absence is a major source of doubt and turmoil in Claude's life, and one of the major reasons behind Claude's paternal love for Weisfeld and his pursuit of music.

Catherine Marsh

Catherine Marsh is the unrequited love of Claude's youth and a modern-day version of Dickens's Estella. She is, on the surface, a rich, spoiled, precocious girl who enjoys tormenting the lovestruck Claude and flaunting her privilege and beauty. She treats Claude with disdain and a sort of superior bemusement, as if he were there merely for her entertainment. Even when she allows Claude to enter her world by letting him escort her to a school dance, it is not due to any great interest in Claude as a person, but rather because she knows she can. She knows the effect she has on him and she uses that to her advantage. When Catherine elopes with another boy without explanation, it is a slap in the face to Claude's unquestioning devotion. Yet such obliviousness is not unexpected from this self-involved girl.

However, when Catherine is reintroduced into the novel as an adult, it becomes obvious that there is more to her than was first revealed. She is a complicated woman, driven by her passion for academic pursuits, a fiercely independent, struggling single mother, but scarred from the molestation of her teenage years. The once superior, indifferent young girl is now a woman who cries when she thinks of how her daughter suffers on their meager income. Despite the hardships, however, Catherine has come to terms with her life and the path it has taken. She knows what she wants and where she is going, and she knows that ultimately her path will not be the same as Claude's. Catherine, for better or for worse, achieves her peace and in her own way shows Claude how to find his as well.

Media Adaptations

- Film rights for *Body and Soul* have been sold to Spring Creek Productions.

Reggie Phillips

Reggie Phillips is a bassist in Lord Lightning's jazz band and his ten-year companion. Reggie is the reason that Claude unknowingly meets and plays piano with his father, something he has been unconsciously yearning to do his entire life.

Lady Powers

Lady Powers is Claude's wife. Her real name is Priscilla, but Lady has been her nickname since she was a child. She and Catherine are cousins, but Lady has none of Catherine's pretentiousness. Instead, she is blasé about her wealth and, in most respects, very normal. Her major problem is that she has no direction. Lady has lots of ambition, and a driving need to do something "real" with her life, but she doesn't know what that something is. So she dabbles in a little bit of everything, from teaching to publishing to photography. She comes to believe that having a baby will bring meaning into her life, but when she finds out that Claude can never father her children, she is once again floundering for some sort of purpose. Lady carries a great deal of promise and integrity, but she is unable to bring her capabilities to fruition.

Claude Rawlings

Claude Rawlings, the protagonist of the novel, is a gifted and complicated young man. Without a father and neglected by his mother, he spends his childhood in the back room of his basement apartment slowly discovering the secrets of an old white piano. From this lonely and destitute beginning, he manages to take his life in all new directions including a wealthy marriage and concerts at Carnegie Hall. Yet through all this good fortune, he still has to struggle with finding himself.

Claude keeps a part of himself hidden from others, even those he loves dearly, and he allows them to keep things hidden from him as well. He tries to connect with people, to sustain meaningful relationships, but he fails because he puts too much distance between himself and others. The only thing he can rely on is his music. It has brought him everything he has ever hoped for, and it is only while playing the piano that he feels control and peace. Yet even his music can be difficult. He tries for years to compose and has some success, but it isn't until he emerges from the catharsis of his grief over Weisfeld's death that he finally writes something truly notable. His empty childhood has made the rest of his life sterile, so Claude finally resigns himself to living solely for and in his music. It is the only way for him to touch his soul and feel complete. Claude's gift saves him and ultimately becomes everything he has.

Emma Rawlings

Emma Rawlings is Claude's mother. Anything but the typical mother figure, she is a six-foot-tall, 300-pound cab driver by day and a withdrawn alcoholic by night. Emma cares for her son, but she does not have the ability or the strength to be the mother that he needs. As a young child, Claude is fascinated by this enormous figure who enters his sequestered world at the end of every day, orders him to get her a beer, and then goes off to bed, "not to emerge until morning." As he gets older and witnesses Emma's downward slide into controversy and emotional instability, he becomes ashamed of her behavior and lifestyle, afraid of what outsiders may think of her and, by proxy, him. Despite her flaws, however, she remains a constant part of his life, eventually gaining enough of Claude's trust to be able to look after his music store while he is away. Theirs is an unusual pairing, one that requires a great deal of patience, understanding and compassion.

Emma's life is not easy. She was a talented vaudeville singer, but had to give up performing when she got pregnant with Claude. Her greatest struggle, however, comes during the McCarthy era. In an effort to find friendship, importance, and a place to belong, she joins the Communist Party and becomes involved in smuggling one of the party's leaders out of the country. Her actions come under investigation by the House Un-American Activities Committee, and she nearly loses her hack license, her apartment, and her mind when she is pressured to cooperate. In an effort to compensate for the total lack of control she has over her life and the events affecting it, she begins to maniacally hoard newspapers and documentation in an effort to catch

the government in the gargantuan conspiracy that only she can see and understand. Her obsession nearly destroys her, but she is finally able to regain control of her life with the help and support of Al. It is through him that she is ultimately able to bring some normalcy into her world and develop a viable relationship with her son.

Anson Roeg

Anson Roeg is a writer and Mr. Fredericks' eccentric, constant companion. She is an unconventional woman, scandalizing the society ladies with her unorthodox attire and cigar smoking.

Mr. Satterthwaite

Mr. Satterthwaite is the music teacher at The Bentley School. He teaches Claude about Schonberg's twelve-tone system of composition.

Aaron Weisfeld

Aaron Weisfeld is Claude's first and most important piano teacher. Having discovered Claude's prodigious talent, he takes the young boy under his wing, arranges lessons from the best piano teachers, and launches Claude's remarkable career as a pianist and composer. Yet to Claude, Weisfeld is more than just a teacher. He is the father Claude never had. He takes Claude in from the streets and virtually raises him, not only teaching him the fundamentals of music, but of life as well. Weisfeld has a profound effect on Claude's life, and Claude loves him for it.

Weisfeld came to New York from Warsaw after his family was killed in a bombing in 1939. As a Polish Jew, he needed to escape Nazi Europe, so he established a new life with his music store on Third Avenue. But at night, the dreams still haunt him, the memory of his beloved family waking him up in a cold sweat. In Claude, he finds a new family, a son who makes him proud. Having been a promising composer himself as a young man in Poland, Weisfeld uses his connections to further Claude's education and career. But it is not until he is dying that Weisfeld tells Claude about his past. All the years that they know each other, Weisfeld's apartment, filled with photographs from his past, remains a no-entry zone. He keeps the pain of his past separate, just as Claude tries to hide the pain of his impoverished life with his neglectful mother. Claude and Weisfeld have a deep love and respect for each other, for they both fulfill what the other needs.

Themes

Appearances and Reality

The illusion of the public image versus the reality of private life is a prominent theme that appears throughout the novel. Weisfeld appears to be an ordinary, unassuming music store owner. Beneath the surface, however, he is an extremely talented composer whose career was cut short by the traumatic events of World War II in Poland. He is a man who has achieved much, suffered much, and experienced more than most people ever will.

The Fisks are another example of the power of appearances. To the outside world, they seem to live a charmed life: wealthy, happy pillars of the community. Inside, however, they are torn apart by incest, mental illness, and deceit. Their admirers do not see the darkness that lurks just behind the façade.

Claude himself is not all that he seems to be. His African heritage is a secret kept from him so that he can compete in the music world without the burden of racial stereotypes. He is also sterile, even though in every other way he is a healthy young man. In another sense, the depth of Claude's feeling for music belies the fact that he is emotionally shallow in all other aspects.

Fathers and Sons

The epigram before *Body and Soul* reads: "That which thy fathers have bequeathed to thee, earn it anew if thou wouldst possess it." Taken from Goethe's *Faust,* this quote is Conroy's way of telling the reader what the book is about. Claude's musical gift comes from his father, and he pursues the mysteries of music as fiercely as he would pursue the real man. Whether he realizes it or not, Claude spends much of his life searching for his father—perhaps not the actual man, but someone to replace him, someone to fill the hole in Claude's life. He finds others in his life to replace his father, namely Weisfeld, Al, and Fredericks. His father represents to him everything he does not have: a normal childhood, a past, the thing he cannot be himself. It is this one relationship, or the lack thereof, that keeps him from having a successful relationship with anyone else.

Salvation through Meaningful Life's Work

All of the characters in *Body and Soul* have some sort of obstacle to overcome. Most find the strength and the means to persevere through their life's work. For Claude it is his music that sustains him, for he can lose himself and his problems for hours in the midst of playing the piano. Catherine rebuilds her life through her passion for medieval history, finding meaning and contentment in her studies. Weisfeld also rebuilds his life after the Holocaust through music, owning the music store and teaching Claude. They find a path that makes them happy.

For those without a path, however, the prospects are dismal. Lady has loads of ambition, but no way to channel it into anything useful. So she meanders from project to project, desperately looking for something "real." Peter Fisk is also a victim of a passionless life. He has the skills to play the violin, but there is no love for the beauty of the music. There is an emptiness in him that consumes him to the point that he cannot live with it anymore. Emma also tries to find some meaning in her life, but by joining the Communist Party she only manages to create more upheaval. All the characters are searching for salvation, and the key in this novel is finding one's life's work.

Loneliness and Isolation

At the end of the first chapter, Claude is watching the crowd celebrate V-E day in the streets near his home. "Claude realized that all these strangers were caught up in something together, that an unseen force had wiped out all differences between them and made them one. They were joined, and as he clung tighter to the lamppost he felt his own tears starting because he felt entirely alone, entirely apart, and knew that nothing could happen to change it."

Through twenty-one more chapters, the reader waits to see if maybe there is something that could happen to change this poor little boy's loneliness and isolation. But Claude's talent continues to isolate him from ordinary people who can never know what it is to be so gifted. Although Claude does develop friendships and a comfortable relationship with the mother whose neglect started his life in loneliness and isolation, he does not ever really stretch beyond his self-centered world. That is why his marriage to Lady fails, and why Catherine will not marry him. Claude does not become one with others because he is one with music. Music is the soul he finds when he learns how to go beyond the "wall," and so with music he is complete.

The theme of loneliness and isolation carries over to many others in the novel. Mr. Weisfeld remains alone after he loses his family in the war,

Topics for Further Study

- Investigate the composer Schonberg and his twelve-tone system of composition. Discuss his impact on the history of music and future styles of composing.

- Research the Nazi concentration camps of World War II and their impact on European Jews. Discuss the aftermath of the Holocaust on those who survived—where they went afterwards, how they rebuilt their lives, and how they coped with the tragedy.

- Research the history of jazz and discuss its impact on American music. Who have been the most influential jazz musicians of the twentieth century? Who are the best jazz musicians playing today?

- Investigate the McCarthy era of the 1950s and the House Un-American Activities Committee. What were the committee's fears and goals? What was the impact on American society as a whole? How did it change our view of government and the political system?

- Research the psychological impact of the relationship between mother and child. What happens to the child's development when the mother is neglectful? How does it affect the child's future behavior and ability to interact normally in social situations?

- Research the Greek myth of Apollo, the god of music, then write and perform your own short play based on Apollo's life and adventures.

and he isolates his past from the rest of his life by never inviting anyone into his apartment. Peter Fisk is kept apart from a normal life by the needs of his mother and the shame of his family's sins. Lady keeps Claude at a distance and does not include him in any of her decisions, not even to discuss starting a family. Catherine chooses to isolate herself from her family by living abroad, alone with her child. Emma is set apart by her size, by being a single mother, and by being a female taxi driver

in a time when all of these features make her unusual. Until Al comes along, she uses beer, communism, and obsessive behavior to fill her life. It is sad that she cannot find fulfillment in mothering Claude, but instead continues the pattern of loneliness and isolation in his life.

Style

Bildungsroman

As several critics have noted, *Body and Soul* is a *bildungsroman,* a novel of formation. According to M. H. Abrams' *A Glossary of Literary Terms,* the subject of a *bildungsroman* "is the development of the protagonist's mind and character as he passes from childhood through varied experiences—and usually through a spiritual crisis—into maturity and the recognition of his identity and role in the world. . . . An important subtype of the *Bildungsroman* is the *Künstlerroman* ("artist-novel"), which represents the development of a novelist or other artist into the stage of maturity in which he recognizes his artistic destiny and achieves mastery of his artistic craft."

The subject of *Body and Soul* is the formation of Claude Rawlings as he passes from a six-year-old child through twenty years of varied experiences, including the crisis of the death of his teacher and father-figure, Aaron Weisfeld. Revived from his crippling grief by the strength of Weisfeld's love, Claude emerges with a new direction. Although Weisfeld could not find the heart to return to his life as a composer after all his work was lost in his flight from Nazi Poland, Claude begins anew and wins the London Symphony competition. Through Claude, Weisfeld passed on his dreams, and Claude fulfills them by becoming a masterful composer. In the process, Claude realizes that his destiny lies solely in his music.

Setting

The setting in *Body and Soul* is notable because the time and place in which the main character grows up are the same as that of the author. Both Frank Conroy and Claude Rawlings grow up fatherless and lonely in New York City in a time period beginning in the late 1930s. Those who knew New York City in the World War II and post-war era have said that this book captures the essence of a city that no longer exists and is a nostalgic reminder of a life that once was. Conroy heralds the change to modern times by including in the story the tearing down of the old buildings on Weisfeld's block to make way for a new development.

Symbolism

Tied into the setting is the most important symbol in *Body and Soul*. Weisfeld's music store is Claude Rawlings' safe haven. In his basement apartment, he is alone and full of questions about music. At Weisfeld's store, he finds a teacher, a father, and answers about the wonders of music. It is not by accident that the Bechstein will not fit into Claude's apartment. Conroy needs the concert grand piano to go into Weisfeld's store so that Claude's whole life stems from that place. The process is completed when even Claude's mother and Al work at the store.

At the end of the novel, Weisfeld's store stands completely surrounded by the new building development. In his grief, Claude thinks perhaps that he cannot exist as a musician without Weisfeld. He finally realizes that he can continue because he still has Weisfeld with him as long as he has Weisfeld's store. His fight to save the store is a fight for his very heart and soul and is a symbol of his devotion to Weisfeld. More powerfully, the store, standing alone among the modern changes, is a symbol of Claude's separation from the rest of the world, a symbol that his life is consecrated to music and none of the other events in his life will ever change that.

Historical Context

In *Body and Soul,* Frank Conroy, born in 1936, tells the story of Claude Rawlings, a boy who enters grade school during World War II. The novel progresses for twenty years until the mid-1960s. Thus, the author and his character grow up and enter adulthood in the same time period. Postwar America, full of confidence after victory, entered a time of enormous prosperity when anything seemed possible. The veterans of the war wanted to forget everything ugly they had just experienced and concentrate on building the family and country for which they had fought.

But the terms of the Allied agreement allowed Russia to build the Soviet Union through its occupation and subsequent rule of Hungary, Rumania, Poland, Czechoslovakia, and East Germany. The Iron Curtain came down and the Cold War began. Communism spread around the world into China, Africa, and Central and South America. The fear

of communism resulted in American participation in the Korean War and in the maniacal hearings of the House Un-American Activities Committee. Senator Joe McCarthy wielded great power as he searched for "a Commie under every bush" and ruined the careers of many in the arts and entertainment world who were suspected of being communist sympathizers. Conroy brings this element of the times into the novel through the involvement of Claude's mother in Communist Party meetings and her participation in the effort to get a well-known agent out of the country. Emma almost has a nervous breakdown after testifying in Washington, a reflection of the tremendous pressure put on people to implicate their friends and acquaintances.

The late 1940s and the 1950s are generally considered a time when America celebrated itself and pretended that it had no problems. On television, "I Love Lucy," "Father Knows Best," and "Ozzie and Harriet" portrayed perfect families in a blissful and moral society. The contrast between the ideal family life portrayed on the television and the dysfunctional home life that Claude had growing up further sets him apart from society and adds to his sense of isolation.

Women had left their wartime jobs in the factories to make way for the veterans who needed jobs and to resume their traditional roles solely in the home. But women's independence during the war was not forgotten, and after the pressure to return to domestic life in the 1950s, the women's movement demanding equal rights at work and at home began to develop in the 1960s. Emma Rawlings, as a single working mother, was an oddity for her time, particularly in a "man's" job like cab-driving. By the mid-1950s, the Civil Rights Movement was also coming into existence with the first attempts at desegregation of the schools and public facilities. This equal rights movement for blacks would climax in the 1960s with the signing of the Civil Rights Bill of 1964. Thus, the relationship between Claude's white mother and his black friend was highly unusual for the times and would normally bring scandal and violent repercussions.

The early 1960s also saw the election of John F. Kennedy as president, his assassination, and the subsequent presidency of Lyndon B. Johnson. The Camelot days of the Kennedy administration, when everyone felt young and most believed that the "best and the brightest" led our government, died with Kennedy and were replaced by a loss of innocence that led to an era of questioning everything and believing in little. Even as the country united

Compare & Contrast

- **1940s:** This is the Big Band Era and swing music is all the rage.

  1950s: The mellow sound of the crooners gives way to the rise of rock 'n' roll with Buddy Holly and Elvis Presley.

  1960s: Pop and rock rule the music scene. Folk songs played at "hootenannies," psychedelic rock, and the Motown sound have a phenomenal impact.

  Today: Swing music makes a big comeback while America's broadened, eclectic tastes make room for rap, country, rhythm and blues, jazz, and classical music all at the same time. Many stars of the 1950s and 1960s still perform in "classic" tours.

- **1940s:** Segregation is practiced in most of the country. Except for the Tuskegee Airmen, blacks may work only in menial jobs in the armed services.

  1950s: Desegregation begins in the schools, but any attempt at mixing the races is met with violent rejection.

  1960s: The Civil Rights Bill passes in 1964, but racial intermarriage is still banned in nineteen states until a 1967 Supreme Court ruling declares miscegenation laws unconstitutional.

  Today: All races have equal rights under the law, but only four percent of marriages are interracial.

- **1940s:** Hitler's attack on the Soviet Union forces Stalin to join the Allies during WWII, which leads to the postwar takeover of Eastern Europe.

  1950s: The Cold War ensues and communism spreads throughout the world. America joins in the Korean War against the communist Chinese in the North, and lives in the grip of fear of communist attack and espionage.

  1960s: The Cuban Missile Crisis in 1962 brings the Soviet Union and the United States to the brink of war.

  Today: The Soviet Union has broken up and communist governments exist in only a few places in the world.

- **1940s:** The Holocaust takes six million Jewish lives. Many survivors come to America and other countries, but the state of Israel is created in 1948 to provide a homeland for Jewish people.

  Today: After several wars over fifty years with its Arab neighbors, Israel is still working on peace agreements.

---

behind the early ventures of the space program, the turbulence of the 1960s left Americans shaken and unsure of their values. This loss of stability is reflected in Claude's life when Weisfeld dies and Claude loses his way. It is the only time that Claude expresses deep personal suffering, and he emerges from the experience with a new direction just as America did after the 1960s.

Critical Overview

The critics seem to be evenly divided into good, bad, and indifferent opinions of *Body and*

Soul. The phenomenal success of Frank Conroy's first book, *Stop-Time,* raised great expectations in the literary world. This autobiography of his youth demonstrated originality of style and masterful writing, so readers waited eagerly for a first novel. Conroy was only thirty-one years old in 1967 when he published *Stop-Time,* but he did not publish again until 1985 when he produced a somewhat disappointing collection of eight short stories. Finally, in 1993, at the age of fifty-seven, his first novel appeared to mixed reviews.

The main complaint of the critics who panned *Body and Soul* is that it is so similar to *Stop-Time.* Claude Rawlings is only a fictional version of

Duke Ellington. Conroy, himself a former jazz pianist, undoubtedly drew on the influence of the legendary musician in creating his protagonist.

Frank Conroy. Both grow up lonely and fatherless in poverty in New York City in exactly the same time period. Both pull themselves out of these circumstances through talent: Conroy is a gifted writer, Rawlings is a musical prodigy. However, according to critics, *Stop-Time* was innovative while *Body and Soul* seems to be a fill-in-the-blanks parade of stock characters, predictable outcomes, and hard-to-believe coincidences.

Perhaps the critics who complained that *Body and Soul* was too much like *Stop-Time* were actually disappointed that it wasn't exactly like *Stop-Time*. But it was never Conroy's intent to repeat the style and innovations of *Stop-Time* in his novel. Rather, as Conroy told Sylvia Steinberg in an interview for *Publishers Weekly,* "*Body and Soul* is a real old-fashioned novel—a big fat book with a lot of people and a lot of plot." Explaining Claude's "incredible string of good luck," Conroy concedes that he has made the novel "in many respects a fairy tale."

Joseph Olshan writes in his review for *Harper's Bazaar* that it is tempting to compare Conroy with Rawlings because of the similarities. But the important difference is that Conroy admits to being a merely competent pianist. Olshan reports, "Rawlings, to use one of the novel's central metaphors, attempts to get 'beyond the Wall,' to overcome his physical limitations to find his soul in his music," and he has the talent to be able to do so. Conroy described to Olshan the moment of his final breakthrough in writing *Body and Soul:* "Driving east from Iowa City, I suddenly came up with Fredericks, who tells Claude the secret of the Wall. That development affected the entire novel. If you listen carefully to the text, the way you listen to music, it reveals the answer to each problem it creates."

Perhaps the negative critics did not listen carefully enough to understand the story even though it was written in a "supple and elegant prose" according to a review in *Publishers Weekly*. This review calls Conroy's depiction of Claude "brilliant" and the explanations of musical theory "lucid." Nonetheless, *Publishers Weekly* found the second half of the book less successful because Claude's obsession with music that "makes him fascinating as a youth makes him hollow as a man." The review admits that Conroy is purposely trying to make Claude's life devoid of emotion, but feels that he fails to maintain an interesting character in the process.

Other critics agree that Claude is a flat character, although they often remark on the skill with which Conroy conveys the passionate feelings of an artist. But none of the critics seem to complain about the technical detail supplied when Conroy describes the music that Claude works on. One odd feature, however, is denounced by Stanley Kauffmann in his review for the *New Republic:* overarching comments. "This device not only jars our focus, not only makes us inappropriately aware of Conroy rather than Claude, it suggests a nervousness in the author, a worry that he isn't getting enough in, that he must enrich his book." By overarching comments, Kauffmann means the parenthetical glimpses into the future that Conroy inserts. For example, Catherine predicts that when Claude is forty-five he will be famous and have some fabulous young woman on his arm, and Conroy interrupts with a confirmation that that is exactly what happens. The reader is also told in a parenthetical note that Peter commits suicide in later years. If the author cannot think of a way to blend such character elements into the story, it is a crutch to use an intrusive author's comment.

Despite its faults, *Body and Soul* is a readable story, the kind that is hard to put down. Maybe it is only soap opera quality, but then soap operas are very popular, and there is occasionally some very good acting in the daytime dramas. So it is with *Body and Soul.* Critics and readers were expecting one thing and got another, and some could not adjust to the change. Others were open-minded enough to try to see what Conroy was attempting to do. Whether or not he succeeded is, as always, left up to the opinion of the individual reader and the connection made between reader and author.

Criticism

Lois Kerschen

Lois Kerschen is a grants coordinator for the Houston Independent School District, the author of American Proverbs about Women, *and a freelance writer. In the following essay, she discusses the themes of emotional distance and spirituality in* Body & Soul.

Distance is the ever-present element in Frank Conroy's *Body & Soul.* There is a distance between Claude Rawling's world and the world around him. While some critics have complained that Claude is a lifeless character with whom the reader cannot establish an emotional bond, it seems likely Conroy intended for there to be no link between reader and main character. Through the reader's own difficulty in getting a window into Claude's soul, it becomes apparent that Claude himself has never looked into his soul. Claude is totally self-absorbed, but there is no self-introspection. Separated from the outside world and human interaction, he lives on the surface of himself and expects no more than superficiality from others.

Claude's distance from the world around him begins with his childhood. His mother's almost total neglect leaves Claude locked in a basement apartment where his only knowledge of the outside world is his view through the basement window. When he finally is allowed to venture out, he feels as if he is in a dream because the sights and sounds are all so unreal to him. Fifty years ago there were no agencies like Child Protective Services to investigate Claude's home life, but today there are safeguards for children in our society because it is now known that such neglect and isolation can seriously and permanently damage a child emotionally. Is it any wonder then that Claude is an emotional cripple who cannot relate to others? He was kept at a distance from people until he was six years old. He had no playmates or extended family. There was no day-care, no play school, no pre-school, no Mother's Day Out to socialize Claude. Consequently, when he does go to school, he makes no friends, he remains a loner, and he doesn't even raise his hand and speak in class until the third grade.

Claude's brief encounters with the real world leave him with a distorted view of reality. He gets a glimpse of the lives of the wealthy tenants in Al's apartment building when he and Al attempt a few heists. He has glimpses into the life of the Fisk family and does not see the reality of the situation there at all. For years, he ventures outside his world only briefly to go to the homes of his various music teachers for weekly lessons. His first contact with sex is with girls he doesn't know in the dark balcony of the movie theater and with a girl he never sees again after the music festival. To Claude, the world is what he vicariously experiences in the movies. From that distance, he imagines a world that doesn't actually exist, so it is small wonder that he has trouble finding a connection.

Only through music is Claude able to reach outside himself to another person. The sole passion in Claude's life, his love of music, propels him into Weisfeld's store to ask about the piano and the sheet music he has found. Claude does develop an emotional attachment to Weisfeld, always feeling more comfortable with Weisfeld than others, always seeking his advice, but that relationship stemmed from Claude's need for a father and for the musical knowledge that Weisfeld could share with him. When Weisfeld dies, Claude enters a frighteningly deep depression whose intensity is perhaps the result of having used so few other outlets for emotion. It is as if he is using his life's quota of emotion in the grief he feels from the loss of Weisfeld. Nonetheless, Claude's devotion to Weisfeld never led to a curiosity about his mentor's life. Respecting Weisfeld's request for privacy in his quarters is one thing, but never inquiring about his past, his home country, his family, is quite another. Claude surely loves Weisfeld, but in many ways Weisfeld's importance to Claude lies only in what Weisfeld gives to Claude. It is a happy accident that in return Claude fills a void for Weisfeld after the loss of his family.

From Claude's perspective, virtually all the characters in the book are just vehicles that bring something into his world. He accepts everything that comes his way without question or interaction. Indeed, he is grateful, but he is never required to show gratitude or repay any debts. As a result, he expects good things to happen to him and never bothers to think about what it all means. For example, the maestro who allows Claude to play the Bechstein is another person who gives generously to Claude, but from a distance. The maestro listens to Claude's playing through partly opened doors. The only time that Claude sees the maestro, he is a shadow in the darkness.

Catherine kept Claude at a distance when they first met. Her aloofness appears to be a trait of snobbery, and then she puts actual physical distance between herself and Claude by eloping to Australia. It isn't until years later that Claude discovers the real reason for the distance Catherine kept from others: her illicit relationship with her stepfather. Catherine had to build a wall behind which she could hide the shame and horror of her situation. Her determination never to return to America is a manifestation of her need to distance herself from her family and the terrible memories of her early teens.

Although marriage is supposed to be an intimate relationship, Lady is just as distant as Claude when it comes to sharing her feelings. She does not include Claude in the decision to have a child, and he comes to realize that she tends to build elaborate defenses for herself. "Silence, privacy, and oc-

> Claude is totally self-absorbed, but there is no self-introspection. Separated from the outside world and human interaction, he lives on the surface of himself and expects no more than superficiality from others."

casionally secrecy were second nature to her. She could not share her sense of what was happening to her with him, could not reveal her sense of herself to him, and as a result he felt she didn't trust him." She makes so few demands on him that he feels almost lonely. When Claude sits by Weisfeld's deathbed, Weisfeld has to remind Claude to call his wife. It is something, one suspects, that Claude would not have thought to do because he and Lady did not truly share their lives. Ultimately, Claude and Lady permanently distance themselves from each other through divorce.

When Conroy writes about complex aspects of music that most readers will not understand, he is not just showing his own music education. He is distancing the reader from Claude by putting him on a different level of knowledge and understanding from the average person. The complexities of the music, the technical perfection that Claude can reach but others cannot puts Claude into a different realm from the rest of the world. A common problem of geniuses is that they often cannot relate well to others because there is just too much distance between the wavelengths on which they and others function. So, Claude's problem is somewhat understandable since being a genius in one aspect of life sometimes diminishes other abilities.

Claude's emotional life, then, is just as sterile as his body. The only connection between body and soul for Claude is through music. Here he virtually transcends his own body as the music carries him into an almost "out-of-body" experience. Fredericks taught him that going beyond the "wall" meant going beyond the body into the imagination. Children live in a world of imagination. If imagination takes one beyond the wall to spirituality, why

What Do I Read Next?

- Frank Conroy has written only three books. *Midair* (1985) is a collection of eight short stories dealing with the same themes of growing up and appearances that *Stop-Time* and *Body and Soul* explore.

- Claude Rawlings bears a striking resemblance to Pip in Charles Dickens' *Great Expectations* (1860–61). Both rise from abject, lonely beginnings to positions of prominence. The objects of their desire, Estella and Catherine, are both aloof, almost cruel, patricians.

- *The Great Gatsby* (1925), by F. Scott Fitzgerald, portrays an outsider who pursues and achieves great wealth to insinuate himself into society and get close to his obsession, Daisy Buchanan. This cautionary tale about the price of success is a good portrait of the 1920s Jazz Age.

- *Billy Bathgate* (1989), by E. L. Doctorow, made into a feature film, tells of another New York City boy's passage into manhood, but his mentor is a notorious mobster who teaches Billy about crime, love, life, and death in a 1930s decadent world that Billy comes to question.

- *Amadeus* (1981), the play that became a musical and an Academy Award-winning movie, is Peter Shaffer's interpretation of the life of a musical genius.

- *Ragged Dick and Struggling Upward* (1867) is a story about a kind and helpful New York City boy who lived on the streets until he followed his dreams to success. This is the first of the many famous rags-to-riches stories by Horatio Alger that chronicle the American Dream.

- *Solo Variations* (1997), by Cassandra Garbus, is a well-received first novel that examines not only the difficulties of a musician's life, but the personal relationships that are entangled and affected by a performer's career.

---

would one want to leave a child's world to face the realities of adulthood? Perhaps that is why Claude is so slow to mature. Fredericks remarks to Claude one day, when Claude is already out of college and married, that he seems to be slow to grow up. He asks Claude why that is, and Claude does not know. He admits that he does not know himself very well.

Possibly, Claude subconsciously refuses to grow up for fear of changing his relationship with Weisfeld. Considering Claude's deep depression following Weisfeld's death, it seems likely that Claude's emotional balance was dependent on the only stable thing in his life: Weisfeld. His mother was never there for him and his other teachers came and went. The only person who was a constant for him was Weisfeld. Without him, Claude lost his center and had to find himself again through another avenue of music. Fredericks has warned Claude that his talent would take him only so far. After that, he would have to depend on himself. Weisfeld's death brought him to that point.

In all of his writings, Frank Conroy expresses the belief that one can be redeemed through art. With enough self-determination, the pursuit of perfection in one's field of talent will be rewarded with a state of grace. Claude may not appear to be soul-searching, does not realize it himself, but his disciplined practice, his enjoyment of practice, is actually a determined effort to find his soul. Once beyond the wall, one finds spirituality. Once Claude determines that he can stand on his own feet after Weisfeld's death, and that he should follow his heart by becoming a composer, he is on the path to finding true satisfaction and fulfillment. Even though he makes an attempt to connect with Catherine, she senses what Claude will learn with time. He may never have a full relationship with another person, but he has connected his own body and soul through music.

Source: Lois Kerschen, in an essay for *Novels for Students,* Gale Group, 2001.

Stanley Kauffman

In the following review, Kauffman expresses disappointment with Body and Soul, *stating that is "affords almost no pleasure," and that Conroy fails to live up to his earlier promise.*

In 1967, at the age of 31, Frank Conroy published *Stop-Time.* It was his first book, yet it was an autobiography—so prismatically conceived in sharp facets, so intense in its view of experience and of words themselves, that it marked the appearance of an arresting writer. Admirers (like myself) then kept watching down the road for the next Conroy book. It didn't arrive until 1985: *Midair,* a slim collection of eight stories, most of which supported prior opinions of his talent without much advancing his career.

Where was the novel that, intentionally or not, he had promised? In *Stop-Time,* speaking of his seventeenth birthday, he said:

> It was around this time that I first thought of becoming a writer. In a cheap novel [that I had read] the hero was asked his profession at a cocktail party. "I'm a novelist," he said, and I remember putting the book down and thinking, my God, what a beautiful thing to be able to say.

He is now 57; at last the novel arrives, and, bitterly to report, it leaves this admirer bruised with disappointment. It's almost as if the publisher had made a mistake—sent out the wrong book with Conroy's name on it.

Body and Soul begins with a twinge of disappointment at its flat fide. (The previous two books had acute titles.) The first few pages aggravate the twinge, not because they are poorly written, though some of the subsequent book is, but because they don't read like Conroy or what might have grown out of the Conroy we knew. It may be unjust to expect that he further the style of 1967, but some of the stories in *Midair,* done in a subtle refinement of that earlier style, fueled the expectation. And if Conroy deliberately decided to abandon the artist's pointillist brush, why did he pick up, of all things, something closer to the house painter's roller?

> He was to walk Third Avenue for many years, until it became so much a part of him that he didn't see it anymore. But at first it was a feast. People moving on the sidewalks, automobiles threading through the columns of the El, trucks rumbling through the striated shadows—he drank it in, his eye leaping from image to image.

There's nothing grossly wrong with that writing, but there's nothing distinguished about it either. Would the author of *Stop-Time*—of even the

> **After all this, it can't surprise us that the dialogue is, to put it gently, not vibrant. Generally, the talk has a counterpoint of typewriter clatter or computer-screen blinking: it sounds written."**

first two pages of *Stop-Time*—have written "drank it in" and "leaping from image to image"?

I begin with the prose because Conroy's change of style almost predicates the choice of materials and the general approach. The story that he tells is long, complex and quintessentially familiar; the saga of an artist from childhood to manhood. Conroy has stepped into the line of the broad, full orchestral *Entwicklungsroman,* which today is not so much a choice of form as of generations.

Sometimes such a choice by an artist can be beautiful, amplifying, as for instance when the avant-garde R. W. Fassbinder decided to film Fontane's nineteenth-century novel. *Effi Briest.* But Fassbinder's old-style film showed us how much more there was to him, in sympathy and vision and technique, than we had thought. Conroy's retrospective choice, on the other hand, has diminished him: he seems murkier in perception, feebler in his language and almost devoid of the crackling electricity that made his work so welcome.

His protagonist, Claude Rawlings, is 6 when we meet him around 1944. (Rawlings was the name of a friend in *Stop-Time.*) He lives in a dingy basement apartment on Third Avenue in Manhattan with his mother, a six-foot, 300-pound woman who drives a taxi most of the day and hardly speaks to him when she is at home swilling beer. In their apartment is an old nightclub-size piano. After investigating it, Claude makes his way to a nearby music store run by Mr. Weisfeld, a Polish-Jewish refugee from Hitler. Weisfeld knows absolutely everything about music and a good deal besides.

Through his tutelage and care, Claude's life unfolds. Weisfeld knows an old, Hungarian composer, wealthy, and he gets permission for Claude to practice regularly on a fine piano in the old man's luxurious apartment. Claude never meets the old man; nevertheless, when the composer dies, he leaves Claude a trust fund that opens further education and opportunity to him. Directly if lengthily, this beginning leads to the conclusion—when Claude steps out on the stage or Festival Hall in London some twenty years later to play the solo part in the world premiere of his piano concerto.

Along the way, much else. His mother, an ex-show girl, turns out to be a Communist sympathizer whose taxi is used by Gerhardt Eisler, at the time a well-known Communist, to get himself aboard ship for Europe in an attempt to escape prosecution. (Conroy tells us in an afterword that he has juggled some dates. Eisler's escape is one of them.) In the basement of the composer's building Claude becomes acquainted with the black super, Al, who comes to figure in his mother's life in a way that prefigures later developments in London.

Along the way, too, of course, Claude meets girls. The first one of importance is Catherine, the attractive daughter of a very rich family, who dallies with him before she elopes at 17 with someone else. Claude meets the only other girl of importance in his final college year; nicknamed Lady, this Social Register belle turns out to be Catherine's cousin. Along the way Claude also encounters a very great deal of information, mostly but not only about music. These gobs of data are sometimes so thick that the narrative seems an armature on which hang explanations of, say, the valves of brass instruments and Schönberg's twelve-tone system.

When it's not delayed by data, the story moves on wheels lubricated with coincidence. The Catherine-Lady link is only one. Al has a black friend who teaches Claude a lot about the jazz that fascinates him throughout. Al happens to have been a taxi driver in the past so that he can help Claude's mother when needed. In the last pages Claude chances to go to a London jazz club that has connections with his past. And in the neatest of all the book's many arrangements, when Lady and Claude decide to marry, she tells him that she has a trust fund of $5 million. (Sometimes the book is close to a satire on classical serendipity.)

This sense of the author as guardian angel is heightened by Claude's excellence at virtually everything he tries. Musical theory, composition, piano playing—whatever it is, he excels at it. Balanchine compliments him on his playing, Copland on his composing. He's also good at basketball and

gin rummy; he can even turn "a spontaneous cartwheel." The only bad things that happen to him occur near the end. He sinks into despondency because of an incompetence that isn't his fault. Five years after his marriage to Lady, a doctor tells him that his sperm are lifeless. Eventually this leads to the breakup of the marriage and to some bleak weeks in London while his concerto is in rehearsal. But just then he meets Catherine, divorced, who is now able to respond to him. The tidiness with which he goes into and out of his slough of despond makes this penultimate episode seem like the dip-before-the-upward-finish that is a Hollywood staple.

Hollywood is otherwise manifest as well. Claude is passionate for films, and his fever seems to have infected his author. All the characters seem drawn from Movieland experience rather than from life. Claude himself is a dolled-up artifice. (We don't even really know what he looks like until late in the book.) The kindly, sagacious Weisfeld, the ignorant but deep Al, the elegant Fredericks who is Claude's principal piano teacher, the obese virtuoso violinist whom Claude accompanies on a tour, all of them seem remembered from Loew's balconies. The character whom Conroy works hardest to color, Claude's mother—gigantic, politically obsessed, once an errant show girl—is, after all the huffing and puffing, much less vivid than the father in the brief title story of *Midair*. The breath of life is not in the novel's people: Conroy merely gives them attributes that are like the springs in wind-up toys.

The author intrudes otherwise than as guardian angel. Most of the story is told from Claude's point of view, but Conroy breaks in frequently with overarching comments. For one example among many, Claude looks at a friend and thinks that he looks "like a dying man." Conroy then adds:

> (Which, in a sense, he was. Years later he was to leave home and go to the University of Chicago as a graduate student in history. In his small, luxurious off-campus apartment he would explode his brain with a German Luger pistol. . . . His body was not to be discovered for some time.)

This device not only jars our focus, not only makes us inappropriately aware of Conroy rather than Claude, it suggests a nervousness in the author, a worry that he isn't getting enough *in,* that he must enrich his book. This is quite the reverse of the earlier Conroy who exulted, quite rightly, in what he could leave out.

After all this, it can't surprise us that the dialogue is, to put it gently, not vibrant. Generally, the talk has a counterpoint of typewriter clatter or computer-screen blinking: it sounds written. Clichés float in. "You look like the cat that swallowed the canary," says Weisfeld at one point, and Conroy so likes the line that he uses it for someone else later in the book.

But the most painful dialogue, and it's plentiful, comes when Conroy tries to make the didactic material breezy. A discussion of physics:

> I mean, you go down and down, and there's the atom, protons, electrons and it doesn't matter if they're little bails or wave phenomena or whatever. Heisenberg comes in and you can't look at anything smaller because the beam of your fancy flashlight is going to knock the little thing away or change or something.

Leaden banter of this kind, applied to music and Marx and Gandhi and other topics, makes for almost physical discomfort in the reader.

Well, enough. It's a gray occasion, the arrival of this novel after such a long wait—a book that manifests no theme or point or purpose. What does Claude s story signify of character or the art he is engaged in or the epoch that he lives through? Virtually nothing. Worse, and more important whatever the aestheticians may think, the book affords almost no pleasure. It is possible to read it; but that's a dreadful thing to have to say about the Conroy we have been waiting on. His enthusiasts will have to wait still longer for the fulfillment of his career.

Source: Stanley Kauffman, "Wrong Notes," in *New Republic,* Vol. 209, No. 4109, October 18, 1993, pp. 47–49.

Sybil S. Steinberg

In the following Publishers Weekly *interview-essay, Conroy gives background on the creation of* Body & Soul.

Legions of authors have produced a shelf-full of books without coming close to the literary reputation that Frank Conroy earned with his first effort, his now-classic memoir of a miserable youth, *Stop-Time,* published when he was 37. Seventeen years elapsed before the appearance of a highly praised short story collection, *Midair,* Conroy is 57 now, and he seems surprised that his first novel, *Body & Soul* has been so eagerly awaited. He's somewhat stunned that it has thrust him into the limelight. In fact, commercial success, in the form of celebrity status, boffo rights sales and a perch on the bestseller ladder, appears imminent for this

Troops march through New York City's Washington Arch at the start of a WWII victory parade in January 1946. The atmosphere of post-WWII New York is a defining element in the novel.

book, out from Houghton Mifflin/Seymour Lawrence early next month.

A second major career is surely one reason why Conroy's literary output has been limited. He has a distinguished reputation as teacher and administrator, notably as the director of the renowned Writers Workshop at the University of Iowa. Another reason is that he is a slow writer and a careful one. "I have pretty high standards for myself," he tells *PW,* a statement borne out by his precise and resonant prose.

This time out, however, his ingrained caution may be blown away by fair-weather winds. Word of mouth preceded *Body & Soul* to the ABA and escalated there. With a 125,000-copy first printing, foreign rights sold in 10 countries, film rights picked up by Spring Creek Productions, and a tap by the BOMC, the novel is making beautiful music for its author, much as its protagonist finds transcendent joy in the music he plays and creates.

Body & Soul is a novel about a musical prodigy, a story that carries its young hero from his first exposure to music—fiddling with keys on an

> More than wish-fulfillment, the novel satisfied another need. 'The plot emerged from the two great preoccupations of my life, books and music,' Conroy says."

out-of-tune piano—through stages of increasing mastery of technique, concert performance and composition.

The boy, Claude Rawlings, is to some extent Conroy's alter ego, a fantasy of what his life might have been had he been rescued from his neglected childhood by a loving father figure. Conroy acknowledges that the key to the book is Claude's mentor, Aaron Weisfeld. The owner of a music store in Claude's 1940s Upper East Side New York neighborhood (a time and place evoked with fidelity and affection), Weisfeld makes himself responsible for Claude's welfare and his musical education. "He is the father I did not have," Conroy says simply.

More than wish-fulfillment, the novel satisfied another need. "The plot emerged from the two great preoccupations of my life, books and music," Conroy says. The idea came to him about five years ago as he was driving from Iowa to his summer home on Nantucket. Conroy confesses that he felt "a little leery—because music is very difficult to write about." Besides, he had given himself a difficult task, namely, "to recapitulate the history of piano pedagogy in Claude's teachers." Cognoscenti may recognize that Claude's professors represent Clementi, Beethoven and Chopin. But musical knowledge is hardly a requisite for appreciating the book.

For as Conroy himself says, " *Body & Soul* is a real old-fashioned novel—a big fat book with a lot of people and a lot of plot." He was inspired by the romantic writers he read as a boy: Dickens, Tolstoy, Stendhal. "Those books kept me from going crazy. I *like* that old stuff." He gives a deep, chesty laugh. "I'm sorry, but I just *do*."

The laugh is genuine, and frequent, but not simply mirthful. The effects of the childhood he de-

scribed in *Stop-Time* could not have rendered Conroy carefree. He is the son of an emotionally unbalanced man who spent most of his life in institutions, and a cold and irresponsible woman who withheld tenderness and love. The world of books was his solace and salvation, jazz improvisation his emotional therapy. His first wife, whom he met at Haverford College, took him into the milieu of New York's social register.

At 35, divorced after 12 years of marriage and "in bad shape emotionally," Conroy reluctantly left his two sons and Manhattan, and came to Nantucket. He supported himself (none too successfully) with freelance journalism and, during the summer months, by playing with jazz combos at island clubs. For a small price, he bought the five acres on which his house now stands, acquired the genuine barn beams from a farmer in Pennsylvania, and rounded up "eight hippies" to build it. Today, the gray-shingled house is weathered and snug, virtually one large open, high-ceilinged room with a view of woods and a pond. Comfortable and unpretentious, it is dominated by a beat-up piano that also serves as a haphazard bookshelf. Toys belonging to Tim, Conroy's six-year-old son from his second marriage, are scattered on the Oriental carpet.

Conroy and *PW* sit in canvas chairs looking into a well-used kitchen. His lanky six-foot frame is clad in a brightly hued sweater and jeans. A long lock of his once-blond hair, now faded to the color of coffee cream, falls across his forehead, and he brushes it back with an absentminded gesture. In a nearly two-hour conversation he uses a mild profanity twice, both times prefacing the vernacular expression with a courtly "excuse my French."

Though his name brings instant recognition in literary circles, Conroy considers himself primarily a teacher. He entered the profession when he was 40, a "late age" he regards as an advantage in preserving his enthusiasm. Even during the years (1981–1987) when he served as Director of the Literature Program at the National Endowment for the Arts, he insisted on teaching at least one class. And he finds working with students the most gratifying part of his job as head of the Writers Workshop. Houghton Mifflin has arranged his tour for *Body & Soul* so that he'll be back in Iowa for his classes each week.

To Conroy himself, it's quite logical that he has written only three books to date. "I really never thought of writing as a career. Although *Stop-Time* was a critical success (and has never been out of print in paperback), I never got any signals that I could make a living as a writer. So I had to look elsewhere to figure out how I was going to support myself."

Stop-Time sold only 7000 copies when it first appeared from Viking in 1967, despite a "terrific editor," Aaron Asher, who "did what he could," but could not surmount the '60s atmosphere. "Everybody was taking drugs and making love, and here was this sort of neoclassical memoir. It was just the wrong time for it to come out." In the wake of the excitement attending *Body & Soul,* Viking Penguin is now issuing new editions of *Stop-Time* and *Midair,* New foreign translations are in the works, too.

Much credit for the upsurge in his fortunes, Conroy claims, should go to his agent, Candida Donadio, and to Seymour Lawrence, his editor for *Midair* (published under his imprint at Dutton) and *Body & Soul.* Donadio "found" Conroy more than three decades ago, when a few chapters of *Stop-Time* appeared in the *New Yorker.* "She's the smartest person I know, both as a reader and as an agent," Conroy says. "What's nice is that now, finally, she will make a lot of money. She deserves it; she hung in with me for 30 years, when other people probably thought I was dead."

Sam Lawrence, whom Conroy calls "an impresario, the Sol Hurok of the publishing world," has been the guiding angel of *Body & Soul.* "Bob Stone and I were speaking at a conference in Key West," Conroy recalls, "and during lunch at Sam's house there, he gave me a tip about buying some stock. I told him I didn't have stock, or money to buy any, either."

"Sam is loyal to his writers. It's his hallmark virtue," Conroy continues. Determined to improve Conroy's fortunes, Lawrence and Donadio decided to show the first 200 pages of *Body & Soul* to a few people in Hollywood. "Then everything went crazy. It leaked from those four people to all the studios, from Hollywood to Europe. At Frankfurt, everyone came to Sam about it. He wasn't even planning to offer it; it was a long way from finished." After the feedback at ABA, Houghton Mifflin raised the initial printing of the book. Conroy still seems stunned by the hubbub. "I'm very heartened," he says.

Perhaps his cautious elation comes from his sense that he has pulled off a risky undertaking: into the form of a bildungsroman he has managed to pack a great deal of musical background. This entailed night courses at Juilliard and "a tremendous amount of reading and research. I wanted to

go back and learn everything over again—and learn it right," he says.

As indicated in the Author's Note, he is "deeply indebted" to Peter Serkin, who served as the book's unofficial vetter. The two met a decade ago when Conroy did a profile of the pianist for *Esquire.* "Once I was launched on the book, I thought of him," he says. "He's a very generous man, and very cultured. He looked at the manuscript, 100–150 pages at a time over the course of five years, made marginalia and sent it back to me. That allowed me to take chances that I otherwise would have been afraid to do."

Because of Serkin's enthusiasm, Conroy feels sanguine about readers' responses to the explanations of musical theory and descriptions of concertos, symphonies and jazz arrangements. "I think readers are interested in process," he says, "if it is *conveyed* as a process: the natural development of a child who's being taught by people who really care about music. As the child learns it, so can the reader."

While the title may suggest the familiar song, Conroy had other reasons for choosing it. "The concept of the body and the concept of the soul seemed to me to be what the book was really about. I knew that most people would immediately think of that song, but I also hoped that they would examine the phrase both in terms of the novel's musical component and in terms of the love story," he says.

What remains mysterious to Conroy is the manner in which the characters became so vividly alive to him. "Maggie [his wife] talks about last summer as the summer I wasn't here. I was so involved with the characters I walked around in a daze. That's every writer's dream, a situation when you don't have to push the story or flog it: you just have to follow it."

Another mystery is his choice of his protagonist's surname. Tobey Rawlings was the name Conroy gave to his boyhood friend in *Stop-Time.* He had originally used the boy's real name, Conroy recalls, "but the lawyers made me change every name in the book except my own." He says he has no idea why he elected to bestow it again on Claude in *Body & Soul.*

Though the resemblance between Conroy's youth and that of Claude Rawlings is hardly coincidental, Conroy's use of his boyhood memories was a far different emotional experience this time. The memoir resulted from an "almost therapeutic" need to exorcise his childhood. "Ted Solotaroff said the engine behind *Stop-Time* was anger. If *Stop-*

Time was anger, *Body & Soul* is love, largely because of the relationship between Claude and Weisfeld."

In granting Claude an incredible string of good luck, Conroy concedes that he has made the novel "in many respects a fairy tale." That was part of his pleasure. "The material was exhilarating. It was like being in a sailboat on a perfect day. The wind is going, the sun is shining, the ropes are tight. The boat is just *tearing* through the water."

Describing the serendipity of discovering the book's epigram—"That which thy fathers have bequeathed to thee, earn it anew if thou wouldst possess it"—Conroy bolts from his chair into the kitchen and takes down a well-worn copy of *The Joy of Cooking.* "I get sort of manic at the end of the day when I'm writing," he says, in what at first seems like a non sequitur. "My head is bouncing all over the place. I have a couple of beers, then I cook dinner. It helps me reenter." One day he happened to flip to the front of the cookbook and the epigram from Goethe's *Faust* leaped out at him.

"I felt a thrill go through me. I said: 'That's it, that's what I'm writing about!'" The loving protection of fathers, the ineluctable blessing of love, the empowerment of knowledge, the joy of music, that indeed is what *Body & Soul* is all about.

Source: Sybil S. Steinberg, "Frank Conroy," in *Publishers Weekly,* Vol. 240, No. 34, August 23, 1993, pp. 44, 46.

Rand Richard Cooper

In the following negative review, Cooper identifies clichéd characters and bad writing as two reasons why Body and Soul *is a "disappointment."*

Younger writers who've pulled off that rare feat, a wonderful first book, work on under a hefty burden of expectations. Frank Conroy was thirty in 1967 when he published *Stop-Time,* his memoirs of a childhood marked by the absence of a disturbed and alcoholic father. A collection of sharp images retrieved "from the very edge of memory," *Stop-Time* anatomized experience rather than judged it, setting forth episodes of boyhood—the thrill of scavenging an abandoned building with a best friend, the brutal beating of a helpless fat boy at boarding school—from a detached, almost amoral perspective that held out to readers the persistent illusion of breaking through adult sentimentality to see life as it "really" was.

Praised lavishly for its intelligent candor by such authorities as Norman Mailer and William Styron, *Stop-Time* went on to become that writer's dream, a true word-of-mouth book, remaining con-

tinuously in print decade after decade, winning new generation of readers and setting a standard for childhood narratives against which other talented practitioners—from Annie Dillard to Theodore Weesner to Alice McDermott to E. L. Doctorow—could be measured. Meanwhile, however, Conroy himself (who currently is director of the famed Writers' Workshop at the University of Iowa) managed but a single slim volume of stories in a quarter-century (*Midair,* 1984), invoking anxieties—shared, according to interview, by the author himself—of that nightmare of literary nightmares, a one-book career.

Now, at last, along comes *Body & Soul,* a sprawling *bildungsroman* taking up the youthful adventures of a musical prodigy named Claude Rawlings. Weighing in at 450 pages, the book clearly means to put all doubts to rest: "a big novel . . ." Conroy has called it, "a book [not] about me but about the world."

Such comments notwithstanding, it's hard not to read *Body & Soul* as an updated *Stop-Time.* Both books have as heroes a musically precocious boy growing up fatherless in postwar New York, and both explore, to a greater or lesser degree, the same terrain: isolation, imagination, and the redemptive power of art. Alas, however—I might as well say it right off—lovers of *Stop-Time* are in for a big disappointment. Slack where *Stop-Time* was startlingly fresh, *Body & Soul* rarely approaches the brilliance of its shimmering progenitor.

The novel begins promisingly enough. Following Claude Rawlings around from the dingy apartment he shares with his taxi-driver mother to the music store where his mentor, Weisfeld, teaches him piano, Conroy takes us on a guided tour through a long-lost New York. Food automats dispense franks and beans for a quarter, neighborhood saloons on V-E Day offer free beer for anyone in uniform, and in the background Rosemary Clooney sings "Come On-a My House." In the shadow of the Third Avenue el, Claude shines shoes, collect bottles, and indulges in a little petty larceny. He's like Doctorow's enterprising New York City boys, growing up clever and tough; but Conroy's version of the street urchin is softened by a quiet, baffled wonder:

> In the general torpor specific noises stood out in high relief—the wheezing of a bus, the clacking, rattling rush of the el, angry voices from inside a tenement, the crash of a storefront gate—thick sounds rising with an eerie clarity against the unnatural silence. On an empty street he might watch his own feet, as if to reassure himself that he was not dreaming. He might wipe the sweat from his face with the back of his

hand and then look at the back of his hand. He was often dizzy.

This is the quiet intensity that made *Stop-Time* so terrific, and it's what Conroy does best: carefully detailing the texture of consciousness, with its dizzying intimations of self and the formidable, sometimes terrifying otherness of the world. Conroy's boy protagonists, while preconscious, are nevertheless children; ideas come to them not abstractly, but with a taste, a shape, a sound. Their world is incorrigibly sensual, and in *Body & Soul,* as in his earlier memoirs, the author renders this sensuality superbly.

As soon as *Body & Soul* busies itself with the action of Claude's budding career, however, things start to go bad. Conroy knows a lot about music, and uses it in fashioning a successful career out of the dubious and scattered materials of Claude's circumstances. The problem lies in the characters with whom he surrounds his *wunderkind.* Dividing the boy's world neatly between mentors and antagonists, Conroy paints these figures with very broad strokes. There's the eccentric but kindly artist; the cold and shallow Upper East Side socialite, impervious to art; the shabby, soulful Eastern European Jew, tormented by Holocaust nightmares; the jovial black janitor with a heart of gold and a bottomless fund of folk wisdom ("You gotta decide if the mad runs you, or you run the mad"). These are not living character but types; worse, they're secondhand types, inherited from other New York writers, like Tom Wolfe or Bernard Malamud, who've done them far more compellingly.

Similarly, Conroy seems to have lost his ear for original language. The novel offers a full menu of bad writing, from bland straightforwardness ("A quiet idealism glowed on both of these small, protected campus worlds—islands of optimism within the larger security of calm, prosperous postwar America") to Mushy Love Writing ("As her soul welcomed him, his own was cleansed. As they ascended together in to the blue beyond blue, all else was trivial"). One searches *Body & Soul* in vain for the kind of pin-point-accurate insight into what makes people tick that made *Stop-Time* sing. But the new novel's characters remain stubbornly fuzzy and shallow. The are functional; less like real people than props furnishing the stage of Claude Rawlings's moral education.

The problem goes right to the heart of the differences between the two books. *Stop-Time* was both a reflection upon, and a recreation of, the extreme limitedness of a child's perspective. Its pro-

tagonist's deeply adolescent assumption was that life will never change, that it goes nowhere. "An adult [Conroy wrote] recognizes petty problems for what they are and transcends them through this higher preoccupations, his goals—he moves on, as it were. A child has no choice but to accept the immediate experiences of his life at face value. He isn't moving on, he simply is."

The lack of a redemptive *telos,* the refusal to discern or impose a "story" upon often painful and difficult events, gave *Stop-Time* its pessimistic cast—the narrative structure is framed by an account of the grown-up Conroy driving wildly through the night, drunk, heading for a crash—but also its vivid and penetrating honesty. The various people who pass through young Frank's life have no function, no part in a larger story, because from Frank's point of view there is no larger story. People aren't there to teach Frank anything he wants to learn; they're simply there to be seen in all their mysterious and sometimes tedious particularity. As its title implies, *Stop-Time* relies for its success upon stuckness. The mode of the book is the trenchant skepticism of an exceedingly intelligent young person convinced he isn't going anywhere.

Body & Soul, on the other hand, exudes progress and higher preoccupation. Life, it insists, is indeed a story, a series of peaks and valleys along a gradually rising curve toward enlightenment. Surprisingly, Conroy seems to have grown up into an optimist; but it's an optimism that strains and creaks in its dogged insistence on making everything fit together, on delivering every last lesson and missing piece. Nowhere does it creak more loudly than in the novel's climactic scene, when the author maneuvers his hero, by now an internationally known concert pianist in his midtwenties, into an unwitting and coincidental reunion with his long-lost father—who turns out (surprise!) to be a jazz pianist in a London nightclub. The two musicians play together four-handed, setting the house on fire with their shared passion for jazz, Claude unaware of the true identity of the man next to him, yet inexplicably drawn to him . . . . And so on. The scene has the sweetness of Hollywood product: "perfect" to the last detail.

Behind such sentimental manipulations lies a deep romanticism about creative genius and the nobility of art. *Body & Soul* is suffused by a longing for the purity of artistic devotion. It deals Claude (and the reader) chastening life lessons, ultimately offering salvation in a deep commitment to "the work." The tone of the novel is warm but powerfully earnest. "You're not a kid anymore," Weis-feld counseled Claude when the boy confesses be-wilderment at the twelve-tone system of modern music. "You're on your way to becoming a well-educated young man, and we're getting into deep stuff here." The substitution of Schoenbergian atonality for the birds and the bees in a standard coming-of-age moment might be hilarious, were there any irony to it; as is, we are asked to accept it, and other such moments, straightforwardly. With its hopeful messagizing, its sprawling all-inclu-siveness, its earnest profundity, *Body & Soul* reads like, well, a first novel: which, after all, it is. It's a good enough book, given what tends to get pub-lished. it just isn't a wonderful book. Harsh judge-ments are the reward for having once upon a time written a book a lot of people love.

Source: Rand Richard Cooper, "A Long-Awaited Encore," in *Commonweal,* November 5, 1993, pp. 44, 46.

Sources

Abrams, M. H., *A Glossary of Literary Terms,* 3d ed., Holt, Rinehart and Winston, 1971, pp. 112–13.

Kauffmann, Stanley, Review of *Body and Soul,* in *The New Republic,* Vol. 209, No. 16, October 18, 1993, p. 47.

Olshan, Joseph, Review, in *Harper's Bazaar,* October 1993, p. 130.

Review, *Publisher's Weekly,* Vol. 240, No. 25, June 21, 1993, p. 82.

Steinberg, Sybil, Interview in *Publishers Weekly,* Vol. 240, No. 34, August 23, 1993, p. 44.

For Further Study

Conroy, Frank, *Stop-Time,* Viking Press, 1967.
    The critics have noted that this stellar autobiography about Conroy's youth and the storyline in *Body and Soul* are very similar.

Decker, Jeffrey Louis, *Made in America: Self-Styled Success from Horatio Alger to Oprah Winfrey,* University of Minnesota Press, 1997.
    The achievements of a number of entrepreneurs from a variety of fields are examined in terms of how race, gender, and ethnicity fit into the American Dream.

Kenneson, Claude, and Van Cliburn, *Musical Prodigies: Perilous Journeys, Remarkable Lives,* Amadeus Press, 1999.
    The journeys from early youth to fame of forty-four musical prodigies from the eighteenth century to the present are chronicled in this book by a noted cello teacher and one of the world's most famous pianists.

Schoenberg, Arnold, ed., *Fundamentals of Musical Composition,* translated by Leonard Stein and Gerald Strang, Faber, 1982.
    This book provides basic information about composition terminology and forms.

Cane

Jean Toomer
1923

Cane is a haunting, lyrical book, one of the most influential works ever written by an African-American artist. Critics wrote of the book, when it was published in 1923, that it would endure for generations, that it heralded the advent of a new class of artist, the black intellectual. The book is in fact considered to be a leading influence on the Harlem Renaissance, a period of time in the 1920s and 1930s when there was a flourishing of creativity in the black community and white society became interested in the artistry produced by writers, painters, and musicians associated with the Harlem area of New York. The book's experiments with form brought respect from people around the world for its characters, including rural Negroes who acted from habit and superstition; women who were treated as objects in a culture that itself was struggling with its history of having been slaves; and intellectuals who sought to reconcile their love of their own race with the degradation in which they were forced to live.

One of the most fascinating aspects about *Cane* is what it failed to accomplish. Despite the glowing praise and anticipation of reviewers, the book only ended up selling two thousand copies. Jean Toomer, who was of mixed blood, decided to stop writing about the black experience, and he had a difficult time publishing works on other subjects. By 1930 he was no longer the promising new literary star, but a literary has-been, only occasionally publishing poems and reviews. He lived for almost forty more years in obscurity. It was not until a new edition of

Jean Toomer

Cane came out during the 1960s that the world realized what a stunning achievement the book represents, and it has been in print since then.

Author Biography

It is somewhat ironic that Jean Toomer is remembered as the writer of one of the greatest novels ever written by a black author, because during his lifetime he only published one significant book and he spent very little time among blacks. His mother's family was rich and powerful in Louisiana, where her father, Pickney B. S. Pinchback, had been the only African American ever to have served as acting governor. Toomer's father, Nathan Toomer Sr., was the son of a slave. His father left soon before Nathan Eugene Toomer was born on December 26, 1894, in Washington, D.C. The author was called Eugene Pinchback during his childhood, and was raised in affluent areas of New Orleans and Washington, where he hardly felt the effects of society's racist institutions until he was in high school.

In 1914, he enrolled in the University of Wisconsin to major in agriculture, but quit after he found himself unable to win the race for the class presidency. Following that, he attended the Mass-

achusetts College of Agriculture, then the American College of Physical Training in Chicago. In 1916, he became a devotee of socialism and gave lectures on the subject in a room that he rented out. Turned down by the Army during World War I in 1917, he became a Ford salesman in Chicago, then a substitute physical education teacher in the Milwaukee School System. In 1918 went to work for a manufacturing company in New York, where he began to socialize in literary circles.

From 1920 to 1922 Toomer wrote passionately, filling a trunk with poems, essays, short stories, and letters. During this time he made the acquaintance of Waldo Frank, a famous novelist of the time who became his friend and mentor. During March of 1921 Toomer filled in as an administrator at the Sparta Agricultural and Industrial Institute in Hancock County, Georgia, where he experienced the lives of rural blacks for the first time, an experience that strongly influenced *Cane.* That summer, feeling that he did not have enough material, he and Frank traveled the South together, with Frank posing as a black man: under the segregated laws of the early 1900s, they both could have been prosecuted or killed if people found out that a black man and a white man were travelling together.

After *Cane,* Toomer did not write about the African-American experience anymore. Being so light-skinned that he was often mistaken for being Indian, Oriental, or Mediterranean, he felt that the American black experience was not relevant to him: publishers, however, were only interested in his views regarding the black experience. His long friendship with Waldo Frank ended when he had an affair with Frank's wife. He became involved in different types of spiritualism, especially the teachings of Greek philosopher Georges Gurdjieff, whose Institute for Harmonious Development Toomer worked to popularize in America. His first wife died during childbirth a year after they married; his second marriage lasted more than thirty years, until his death on March 30, 1967, in Doylestown, Pennsylvania. Toomer published some poetry and essays, but never another novel.

Plot Summary

First Section

Cane is not organized like most novels are. It is an impressionistic piece, with many character sketches, stories, and poems that are similar in theme, leaving readers with an overall impression rather than an experience of having followed a unified narrative. Though the smaller parts of *Cane* do not follow a continuing plot, and only a few minor characters are carried over from one chapter to the next, the book still falls into three distinct sections, which Toomer envisioned as leading readers in a circular progression.

The first section takes place in rural Georgia, and concerns itself with the lives of poor blacks, especially focusing on women who live in this environment. It starts with the brief, poetic story of Karintha, a black woman who is noticeably beautiful from childhood on. The men all work hard for money to give to her, implying that their ignorance of who she really is and her naïveté work together to repress them all.

"Karintha" is followed by a poem, "Reapers," about a reaping machine with sharp blades being drawn through a field by black horses and cutting a field rat in half. The following poem, "November Cotton Flower," is about one winter, a time of drought, when cotton unexpectedly bloomed, giving hope that led to love.

The book then picks up with the story of Becky, a white woman who has two black children. Nobody in this small town knows who the father or fathers of these boys might be, and both blacks and whites ostracize Becky, although some charitable people try to help her out, donating land, lumber, and food that no one else wants. The boys grow up to be town bullies, ferocious to both blacks and whites. One day Becky's house is found collapsed, with her under the wreckage, unable to survive social disapproval like the rat mowed down by the reaper.

Two more poems follow: "Face," which gives a portrait of a sturdy old woman, and "Cotton Song," which provides a Biblical-sounding chant that might be sung by workers in the field.

The next story, "Carma," concerns a woman whose husband hears that his wife has been unfaithful, and he goes to confront her about it. After the ensuing argument, Carma runs out of the house and into the cane field. Hearing a gunshot, he gathers a group of neighbors to look for her, and when she turns out to be fine, he feels fooled, and, frustrated, slashes the nearest man with a knife. He ends up in prison, in what the story describes twice as "the crudest melodrama."

"Song of the Son" is a poem that presents the sun and earth, with Negro slaves, who sang, identified with nature. "Georgia Dusk" contrasts the previous poem by focusing on the people and machinery that have taken over the land in the decades since slavery. These lead into the story of "Fern," a girl of black and Jewish roots who is presented as almost totally a product of her environment. The story is lushly told, with little action: the unnamed narrator becomes infatuated with Fern and goes to her, asking her to walk with him in the cane fields, but once she is out there she is overwhelmed with her powerful feelings about the place and she faints.

The poem "Nullo" follows, giving an impressionistic picture of pine needles falling in the Georgia forest. "Evening Song" is a poem about a narrator and a woman, Cloine, who lazily dozes off in his arms as the moon rises.

The story "Esther" follows the maturation of a young woman, from nine to sixteen to twenty-two to twenty-seven. Early in life, she witnesses a man, King Barlo, fall into a religious trance in the street, and as years pass Esther becomes more and more convinced that Barlo is destined to be her lover. The story ends when, years later, she goes to offer herself to him, and he and the people he is partying with laugh at her.

There are two more poems: "Conversion" contrasting an ancient African religion with Christianity, and "Portrait in Georgia," which offers a physical description of a weathered woman who lives in this land. The last part of this section is "Blood-Burning Moon," a story about Louisa, who is courted by two men, one white and one black. When the white man attacks the black man, the white man is killed. A white lynch mob comes, captures the black man, and burns him alive.

Second Section

The second section, which was written at the request of Toomer's publisher in order to bring *Cane* to a decent book length, takes place in the North, in Chicago and Washington, D.C. It opens with the sketch "Seventh Street," a mix of poetry and prose that describes urban life in the section of Washington where black people live, emphasizing fast pace and the old-fashioned belief in God. "Rhobert," the following character sketch, shows a strong, suffering man, his legs bent by a childhood disease, who bears his hardships as if wearing his house around on his head.

The story "Avey" presents a girl whom the boys hanging around on the Washington street corner fantasized about, imagining what she does when she goes upstairs to visit her boyfriend. The narrator of the story finally manages to date her, and she seems only vaguely interested in returning his affection, leading him to the self-comforting conclusion that she is just too lazy for serious commitment. After years pass, he meets her again, and takes her out to a secluded spot in the park, but she falls into a deep, fatigued sleep.

Two poems follow: "Beehive," which compares the city to a beehive, with one bee wishing to fly away to "a far-off farmland flower," and "Storm Ending," which uses similar imagery of bees and flowers, but here they are victims of the violence of a beautiful thunderstorm. The story "Theater" is a brief piece of two upwardly-mobile urban blacks, John and Dorris: John is the brother of a theater owner, and Dorris dances in the chorus at the theater. She is attracted to him. Watching her dance, he dreams of being her boyfriend, but she thinks that the vacant look on his face while he is looking at her means that he does not care for her, so she leaves before he has the chance to talk to her.

The poem "Hot Lips Are Copper Wire" shows Toomer's amazement at the telephone, a relatively new invention then. "Call Jesus" presents a woman's soul as something separate from her, following her around like a dog. "Box Seat" is a relatively long story about a man, Dan Moore, who is dating a schoolteacher, Muriel. He is sure that she is repressing her true nature, and he tries to force himself on her: first physically, on the couch of her home, and then later by shouting to her in a crowded theater. It ends with Dan going out of the theater to fight with a man he has offended, but then wandering off, having forgotten his anger once he is out of doors.

The poem "Prayer," which follows, is a meditation on the nature of the human soul, followed by "Harvest Song," a poem that presents modern urban people as reapers of the harvest of the world's greatness. The last part of Section Two is the story of Bona, a white woman, and Paul, a mulatto: Bona is interested in dating Paul, and he likes her, but he is hesitant about a relationship because he cannot believe that Bona, raised in the South, would not look on him with some prejudice. In the end, he decides to cast his worries aside, but while he was deliberating she has left.

Third Section

The final section of the book is comprised entirely of the novella "Kabnis," the story of a man of mixed ethnicity, like Toomer, who has gone to Georgia to teach and finds himself attracted to the beauty of the land and repulsed by the ugliness of the way blacks are treated. At first, he is just lonely, working for a school that has strict rules for its teachers, with his behavior closely monitored. He sees the irony in this, noting that "where they burn and hang men, you cant smoke." In the second part of this section, Ralph Kabnis interacts with some of the local people, important men in town. They tell him stories about the lynchings they have seen, which makes him paranoid, afraid that the local whites will find him too bold and come to get him. He runs home to hide, and when his friends find out what is bothering him, they laugh and give him a drink, which gets him fired.

Kabnis ends up working in the repair shop of his friend, Halsey. The local values have dragged him down, making him give up his intellectual interests and take on physical labor, which was considered the place of black men in the South. While working at the shop, he sinks even further, spending the night drinking with some friends and the prostitutes that they bring over, so that in the morning, when it is time to go to work, he is helpless and cannot even stand up on his own. This leads back to the beginning of the book, with downtrodden Georgia blacks trapped by society into a cycle of ignorance, drink and lust.

Characters

Avey

Avey is a popular girl in Washington, D.C. The young men on the street corner pay attention to the fact that she goes to visit a man, and they talk about her and the fact that they would all like to date her. She is a mystery to them, and to the narrator of the story. He tries to impress her with his athletic ability, showing off to her in basketball, swimming, and dancing, but she remains aloof. Eventually, he has an opportunity to kiss her on a ferry boat, but while he wants their relationship to progress, she treats him like a little boy, holding his head in her lap. Later, he becomes physically involved with her, but decides that her sluggish response to his passions is due to her being lazy. The last time that they are together she falls into a deep sleep, indicating that she feels comfortable with him in a way that she does not feel with other people, and that it has been a long time since she felt she could let her guard down.

King Barlo

King Barlo is a man who Esther witnesses falling to the ground and writhing in a religious trance. The people in the streets who witness his trance shout their encouragement, but the white people are suspicious: "Wall, y cant never tell what a nigger like King Barlo might be up t," the sheriff says. Soon after, Barlo leaves town, and for years Esther fantasizes about being with him. When she approaches him upon his return he is not spiritual; he is drinking in a tavern with his friends and mocks her.

There is also a "Barlo" mentioned in the story "Becky," who may or may not be the same man. When he sees that Becky's house has collapsed into a pile of rubble, with Becky probably under it, Barlo throws his Bible onto the pile and leaves.

Becky

Becky is a white woman who is ostracized by her neighbors in a small southern town because she has a child by a black man. Toomer offers no information about the identity of the father. Both blacks and whites in the town turn their backs on Becky: the white people say that she is a "God-forsaken, insane white shameless wench," and the blacks say that she is a "poor Catholic poor-white crazy woman." Even though both groups reject her, there are still people from both groups who help her build her house and who donate food and provisions to Becky.

When her son is five years old, Becky has another son, again by a black man. They grow up to be troubled men: "They answered black and white folks by shooting up two men and leaving town. 'Godam the white folks; godam the niggers,' they shouted as they left town." After they are gone, Becky's house collapses at some undetermined time, with her in it.

Big Boy

See Tom Burwell

Tom Burwell

Tom Burwell is the black man who is in love with Louisa in the story "Blood-Burning Moon." Many of the black people in town know that Burwell is headed for trouble: as they remind one another, he has already been sentenced to work on the chain gang for injuring people in knife fights. When the white man who also likes Louisa, Bob Stone, attacks Tom with a knife, he kills Stone and is subsequently hunted down by the whites in town and burned alive.

Carma

Carma is a strong woman, "strong as any man," who drives a mule wagon. The narration of her tale describes it as "the crudest melodrama." She has a husband, Bane, but he is a prisoner on a chain gang. He came home once from working out of town and heard rumors about her having affairs with other men; when he confronted her about it, Carma ran out of the house, into the cane field. When he heard a gun go off, he assumed that, in her hysteria, she had killed herself, so he gathered other men from the neighborhood to search the field, where they found her lying. They carried her home and put her on the couch, and it was then that he noticed that she was not injured, and had probably just fired the gun to get his attention. Angry at being tricked, he cut one of the men from the search party with a knife. Now Bane is on a chain gang, and Carma travels the country roads freely.

Esther Crane

One of the few female characters in the first section of the book who is not admired for her beauty, Esther becomes enchanted with a suspicious man, King Barlo, and becomes convinced that he is an important part of her destiny. When she is nine, Esther sees Barlo fall into a religious trance in the street: he shouts phrases that have a Biblical sound as people in the crowd that gathers around him chant to encourage him. The whole town is captivated with his religious fervor, and when Barlo leaves town Esther remembers him for years afterward. The second part of Esther's story begins when she is sixteen, having a dream that is based on elements from the afternoon she saw Barlo: the store windows that were lit with sun are, in her dream, on fire; the people who had spit tobacco juice on the ground while he was rolling around spit their juice onto the fire; and the fire department rescues a baby, black as Barlo, which they give to Esther for safekeeping. When she is twenty-two, working at her father's grocery store, Esther remembers an affair that she had with a white boy and realizes that, even though her skin is pale enough to pass for white, she could never be accepted in white society. She decides that she is in love with Barlo.

Five years later, Barlo comes back to town, driving a big new car. Esther leaves her place at the store to go and see him. He is at a friend's house, where people are having a lively party. She tells Barlo that she has come for him, but he just laughs at her. A "coarse woman" who is with him thinks that Esther shows a lot of gall, coming into a place like that and claiming a man: the woman assumes that Esther is arrogant because her skin is so pale. Esther leaves, humiliated.

Dorris

In the story "Theater," Dorris is a chorus girl who dances at the theater that is managed by John's brother. John works the dancers hard, making them rehearse and correcting them when they make mistakes. While she is dancing, Dorris fantasizes about being in love with John, but when she is finished he is so involved with his own fantasy about her that he does not speak to her. She takes this as a sign that he does not care, and cries in the arms of her friend, Mame.

David Georgia

David is one of the field workers who cut cane and boiled its syrup from it. First mentioned in the "Becky" section as a man who brought her sugar sap, he appears again in the section "Blood-Burning Moon."

Bona Hale

Bona is a white girl who becomes infatuated with a mulatto boy, Paul. She is from the South, and he fears that she will not be able to get beyond the traditional racism of her society. Her story starts in a school gymnasium in Chicago, where she watches Paul and, in order to get closer to him, joins in a basketball game, even though she has already been excused from participating. Paul's roommate Art fixes them up for a date, and while Art and his girlfriend walk ahead and argue with each other, Bona confesses her love for Paul, although he is unable to return the sentiment. He is aloof to her throughout the date, and she leaves him just as he decides to open up to her.

Fred Halsey

Halsey is a friend of Kabnis. He owns a repair shop and is proud of his work, putting up with the degrading attitude shown toward him by whites when it is to his benefit. After Kabnis loses his teaching job, Hanby takes him on as an employee, hoping to show him a good life through working with his hands; Kabnis instead slides into drunkenness and subsequent ignorance.

Samuel Hanby

Samuel Hanby is the principal of the school where Kabnis teaches. He affects an attitude of superiority with blacks, but is subservient among whites.

John

John is the brother of the theater manager in "Theater." He is in love with Dorris, and has an elaborate fantasy about them being together, but he is also careful to make sure that none of the chorus girls like Dorris takes advantage of his position to further their positions. John puts on a gruff exterior, certain that Dorris would not want a relationship with him, when in fact that is her main desire. While watching Dorris dance he daydreams about what it would be like to be with her, but she, seeing the blank look on his face as he is daydreaming, assumes that he is uninterested in her.

Ralph Kabnis

Kabnis is the focus of a novella at the end of the book that is named after him. Like Toomer, he is an educated man, a teacher from the North living in a Southern town, where the people look at him with kindness tempered by the suspicion that he may try to think too much of himself. He feels lonely and afraid as he tries to sleep in the room that is provided to him by the school where he teaches, conscious of the stillness around him. He is uncomfortable in the South, unused to things like the chicken that makes noise outside of his door. The school he teaches for has rules of conduct for teachers that prohibit smoking and drinking, but with his friends Halsey and Layman he does both, discussing the best way for black men to behave in the hostile social environment. Their stories about blacks being lynched terrify Kabnis almost to insanity, although they laugh and tell him he has nothing to worry about.

After he is fired from the school, Halsey takes Kabnis on as an employee in his repair shop. He sees that black laborers are at the mercy of white people, who order them around without concern, and he falls deeper and deeper into despair. One night, while having a party with some prostitutes in the basement of the shop, Kabnis becomes drunk and rages against a silent old man who sits in the corner, accusing the man of passing judgments of sin against the entire Negro race. The next morning, he is too drunk to even stand up and go to work, and he realizes that his heritage, the social situation in the South, has sapped him of the intelligence and kindness he once had.

Karintha

Karintha, the focus of the book's first piece, sets the tone for the events that follow. Most of the first section is about men longing for women, and Karintha is a girl whom men find beautiful from her childhood onward. When she is very young, too young for them to have sex with, men already look upon with her in awe, and they excuse her faults because they are so enchanted with her beauty. For example, "Even the preacher, who caught her at mischief, told himself that she was as innocent as a lovely November cotton flower."

Because she has been raised in a small, two-room house, Karintha is exposed early in life to the sexuality of her parents, who slept in the same room as her. When she ends up being sexually active with men, they come to her with money, implying that she might have grown up using her beauty as a prostitute. She has a baby out in the woods, and the text implies that she buried it out there under a blanket of pine needles before returning home.

Louisa

Louisa is the object of affection for two men. She works for the family of Bob Stone, a white man, who likes her, and she is attracted to him as well. But she is also attracted to Tom Burwell, a black man.

> Separately, there was no unusual significance to either one. But for some reason, they jumbled when her eyes gazed vacantly at the rising moon, and from the jumble came the strange stir within her.

Although she likes them both, they each find it almost impossible to accept her attraction to the other. When Stone goes to Burwell, he is goaded into fighting, and he is killed. Burwell is killed by an angry crowd of whites. Louisa's story is told in the section titled "Blood-Burning Moon."

Dan Moore

Dan is a prominent character in the story "Box Seat." He is from the South, born in a cane field, a man with a violent and suspicious nature. When he visits the girl that he likes, Muriel, he discusses life as if it has to be miserable and painful, and he is bewildered when she sees it differently. He tells her,

> Your aim is wrong. There is no such thing as happiness. Life bends joy and pain, beauty and ugliness, in such a way that no one may isolate them.

He is so desperate for Muriel's love that he tries to force himself on her, but is stopped by her landlady. Later that night, at the theater, Dan shows up to keep an eye on Muriel. He thinks of her as a slave of society's pressures. He is fidgety, and disturbs the people around him. When one of the performers goes to the area of the stage below Muriel's box and sings to her, Dan becomes very agitated,

and shouts out, "JESUS WAS A LEPER!" Leaving after the performance, he steps on a man's toes, and there ensues a shoving match. The man and Dan go out into the alley to fight, but when they get there, Dan, forgetting what he is there for, wanders away.

Muriel

Muriel is a schoolteacher in the story "Box Seat." She lives in a boarding house, under the supervision of her landlady, Mrs. Pribby. Dan Moore, her suitor, sees the controlled life that she lives and assumes that Muriel is repressed, that society is holding her back from expressing her true self. When Dan becomes very physical with her in the living room of the boarding house, Mrs. Pribby, in the next room, makes noise to remind them of her presence:

> Muriel fastens on her image. She smoothes her dress. She adjusts her skirt. She becomes prim and cool.

Later, Muriel goes to the theater with her friend Bernice. They sit in a cramped box seat. During the show, one of the performers, a boxing dwarf, sings a song to Muriel and offers her a rose, causing Dan to jump up and shout out in the theater, which leaves Muriel embarrassed by him.

Paul

Paul is a mulatto from Georgia, living in Chicago, uneasy about living among white people and passing for white. When Bona, a white girl, courts him by engaging him in a competitive basketball game and then arranging a date with him through friends, Paul must deal with the question of whether he is going to become fully integrated into white society. They go to dinner and a dance, but he remains cold, which angers her. As they are leaving the dance, Paul notices a knowing look on the face of a dark-skinned black doorman, and he stops to correct the man's mistaken impression. "I came back to tell you, to shake your hand, and tell you that you are wrong," he explains. "That something beautiful is going to happen. . . ." When he finishes speaking to the doorman, however, he turns to find that Bona has gone.

Rhobert

The first character of the second section, Rhobert is described in symbolic terms as wearing a house. He has twisted legs from having rickets as a child, but he is also called strong because he bears the weight of the house on his shoulders.

Fernie Mae Rosen

Fern is the daughter of a black mother and a Jewish father. In the story bearing her name, she is described as being sexually attractive but cold:

> Men saw her eyes and fooled themselves. Fern's eyes said to them that she was easy. When she was young, a few men took her, but got no joy from it.

Later, she becomes so uninvolved with sexuality that "she became a virgin."

The narrator of Fern's story, smitten with her beauty, boldly walks up to her while she is standing around with her family and asks her to go for a walk in the cane fields with him. While they are out there, he puts his arms around her, and she is touched by some sort of religious revelation that she finds overpowering:

> Her body was tortured with something it could not let out. Like boiling sap it flooded arms and fingers till she shook them as if they burned her.

Overcome with powerful emotion, she faints in the field. After that, the people in town who had promised to protect Fern make some threats against the narrator, who leaves for the North soon after.

Bob Stone

Bob Stone is the white man whose family employs Louisa in "Blood-Burning Moon." He is in love with her, but conflicted because she is black. He already has a self-esteem problem because his family has lost much of their former social status, and he feels that he would be looked down on even more if word got out that he was involved with a black woman. At the same time, though, he is jealous of Tom Burwell, whom she is also dating, and is insecure about the idea of losing her in a competition with Burwell. He attacks Burwell with a knife, but the other man is an expert knife fighter and cuts Bob's throat.

Themes

Race and Racism

This book deals with the issue of race on several different levels. Most obviously, there is the way that blacks are treated within American society, both in the South and in the North. In the South, the element of danger is always present. For instance, Becky is rejected by both blacks and whites for the crime of having crossed the color line, having sex with a black man and becoming impregnated by him. There is suspicion of blacks by whites, such as the sheriff in "Esther" who keeps a close eye on the man

who is in the throes of religious ecstasy because "y cant never tell what a nigger like King Barlo might be up t." For the most part, this suspicion is enough to keep the blacks in their place. Kabnis sees Hanby, his employer, intellectualizing his own fear when he tells him that "the progress of the Negro race is jeopardized whenever the personal habits and examples set by its guides and mentors fall below the acknowledged and hard-won standard of its average member." He also sees his friend Halsey take commands from white men while believing that he is improving his life by limiting his personal growth to physical labor.

The tension between the races has some very real, dangerous ramifications in the South in the 1920s. There are, of course, the horror stories told Kabnis, about lynchings and beatings and about the pregnant woman whose fetus was stuck onto a post with a knife. There is the competition between Bob Stone and Tom Burwell for Louisa's hand: Burwell wins the fight between them, but that does not matter because he is immediately killed by whites who will not tolerate blacks putting on a fair fight.

Aside from hostilities between blacks and whites, the book also examines the problem of racism among blacks, who look down upon people of mixed heritage. This happens more within the Northern stories, where the uncertainty of the situation between the races is in some ways more frightening than the certainty of hostility in the South. The thing that separates Bona and Paul, who have a mutual attraction, is his fear of his black background being found out: in the end, when he decides that he can deal with this secret, he shows this by talking to a very dark-skinned doorman and shaking his hand. In "Theater," Dorris is all too willing to believe that John would have nothing to do with her when her friend tells her that he is "dictie," a word that Toomer uses over and again for light-skinned blacks who think that they are better than others because of their similarity to whites.

Sex Roles

Toomer devotes the first section of the book to isolated portraits of single women, showing society's varied attitudes and the passions that men often project upon them. The first example, Karintha, is a sad, obscure figure who does not develop a personality on her own, but is only presented in terms of her physical attractiveness. As a child, she is considered a sexual object even by the men who refuse to acknowledge that they think of her that way. She is left to run wild, to abuse animals and fight with other children, all without being scolded because of her beauty, and when she grows up she an object of lust, but not understood. After that, there is a succession of women who are misunderstood by men: Becky is left alone, so that no one even is sure when she died; Carma's husband jumps to conclusions about her fidelity and her suicide; Fern entrances the narrator of her story, although he can't say why and hardly cares to wonder; Esther is laughed at by the man she dreamed about for most of her life; and the two men fighting over Louisa use her as a status symbol against each other, with little said about who she really is.

In the second section, there is a little more interaction between the sexes, because the men in these stories long for the women without feeling that they have a right to them. This section is marked by missed connections, by love relations that do not work out because of assumptions made about the other sex. A prime example of this is in "Box Seat," which shows Dan Moore thinking that Muriel must be protected from society, which will otherwise take advantage of her passive nature, and becoming inappropriately aggressive because of it. The dominant symbol in this section is Mr. Barry, the dwarf who boxes himself bloody but then woos the woman with a beautiful song and a rose. Barry's diminutive size makes Dan's macho posturing ridiculous. At the end of this section, Bona and Paul provide the book's most well-balanced couple, as indicated by their equality on the basketball court. Even with their mutual respect, though, the relationship does not work out, mainly because of Paul's insecurity about his race.

The story of Kabnis hardly touches upon sex roles at all. Stella and Cora, the prostitutes, use the men in their lives just as much as they are used. Carrie K. ends up being one of the book's most levelheaded characters: surrounded by disappointment, she recognizes the dignity of the past that everyone else is trying to run away from. The book that started with a woman who was little more than a sex machine ends with a sensitive, enlightened woman.

Alienation and Loneliness

The theme of alienation does not become apparent until the book's second two sections, although once it is revealed there it becomes visible in hindsight in the earlier parts. The short prose piece "Seventh Street," which begins the second section, introduces the idea of urban isolation, showing the city street as the product of social inconsistency, a lonely place that is busy with people. The characters presented in this section have

Topics for Further Study

- Some critics have drawn a comparison between the views of Hanby in the "Kabnis" section of *Cane* and Booker T. Washington, an African-American educator prominent at the start of the twentieth century. Research Washington's views, and explain your feelings about his approach to the social positions of blacks.

- Many of Toomer's stories concern the distinctions made between dark-skinned and light-skinned blacks, while some people might tend to lump all African Americans together. Make a collage of pictures of black faces, showing as many hues as you can.

- The old man in the basement of Halsey's store only says a few words. Write a monologue for him, having him explain his history and what he thinks of his life.

- An underlying theme of the first section of this book is the violence that threatens blacks if they stand up for their rights. Report on modern hate groups and the methods that they use, such as the Internet, to spread their intimidating message today.

- In the Washington and Chicago sections of *Cane,* the characters would have listened to jazz music in the 1920s, but what kind of music would they have listened to in rural Georgia? Find some examples of the music they listened to and play it for your class.

- One of the reasons Jean Toomer never produced another novel is that he devoted much of his energy to working for the Institute for the Harmonious Development of Man, spreading the ideas of Georges Gurdjieff. Report on Gurdjieff's teachings.

less social pressure to stay segregated than exists in the segregated South, but even with that relative freedom, they find themselves unable to understand one another well enough to enter into satisfactory relationships.

Alienation is one of the major problems with Ralph Kabnis, a pale-skinned, educated black man who has gone to Georgia to find his roots, only to realize that his ancestral home wants nothing to do with the man that he has become. The first section of Kabnis' story is about his loneliness, as he sits in the still, quiet night in the room that has been provided him. He has insomnia because his mind has nothing to settle upon: the rules of life in Georgia prohibit the way of life he is used to. As he starts socializing more in the story, he becomes increasingly alienated from his former life. He mocks the idea of being a teacher and praises the local food, all in an attempt to fit in with the people around him, a strategy which is in fact a success. Halsey tells Professor Layman:

> He ain't like most northern niggers that way. Ain't a stuck-up thing about him. He like us, you and me, maybe all—its that red mud over yonder—gets stuck in it and can't get out. (Laughs)

The more Kabnis stays in the South, the more he fits in with the men around him, but his comfort comes at a price. In becoming like the men around him, he becomes bitter. He curses the old man who represents black history, and he drinks so much that he can hardly stand. Conformity requires shaving off the best things about his personality, in order to stave off loneliness.

Style

Narration

The narration of this book is uneven, changing from section to section, providing readers more with a feeling than with a direct story. Throughout the book, the language is very poetic, with words often chosen for their sounds and power. It even breaks directly into poetry, not only in the poems that hold their own pages but also sometimes within story segments, such as "Karintha," "Blood-Burning Moon," and "Box Seat." Because of this, critics have trouble with deciding what to call it. The critic Edward W. Waldron, for example, classified *Cane* as a "novel-poem." Others have called it an impressionistic piece or an imagistic novel.

The voices telling the stories vary greatly. There is often a third-person narrator, telling the story from an omniscient perspective, which means that the narrator has access to all of the characters' thoughts and can tell them to the reader. In "Blood-Burning Moon," for instance, the narration tells what Bob Stone is thinking, then switches to Tom Burwell's thoughts, then back to Stone's. There is

also a third-person narrator that is limited to one character's perspective, as in the novella "Kabnis," or in the story "Esther," which relies upon readers thinking like Esther but not knowing what King Barlo really thinks until the end.

The book also makes use of different types of first-person narration. The stories "Fern" and "Avey" both have straightforward narrators, with the person telling the story appearing in it as the main character. A more obscure first-person narrator tells the story of "Becky." Throughout most of the story, it is not at all clear that this piece is being told in the first person, until the last full paragraph, when the narrator begins referring to "we." Having presented himself as a member of the community, he then gives himself specific details, telling about a particular ride that he took on a particular day. Much of the book's voice has a communal feel to it, as if the thoughts presented are those of everyone living nearby, but sometimes the narration edges very close to Toomer's particular experiences.

Symbolism

Because of the poetic nature of this work, much of what is significant is relayed through symbolism. One example is the cotton plant, which is directly mentioned in the poems "November Cotton Flower" and "Cotton Song," and is alluded to in other places, such as "Kabnis." Because many whites owned slaves specifically to harvest cotton on their plantations prior to the end of the Civil War in 1865, cotton has come to represent enslavement to many black people in America. Another symbol used throughout the book is fire, such as the sawdust fire that permeates the whole area like guilt after Karintha loses her baby out near the mill, or the fire that Esther sees in the windows of the McGregors' notions shop.

The house that is said to be on Rhobert's head, "like a monstrous diver's helmet," is an example of symbolic use of language. Of course, he could not have a real house atop his head. This use of the word serves to show that the things a house usually reminds people of—stability, permanence, a place where one belongs—weigh on Rhobert like a burden.

In the basement of Halsey's shop sits an old man, in the darkness. He does not move or speak. He does not seem like a real person—he has no real function in this story other than his symbolic significance. Lewis even points this out within the story when he says, "That old man as symbol, flesh, spirit of the past, what do you think he would say if he could see you?" For Kabnis, the old man acts as a conscience, reminding him of the history of African Americans. He is old enough to possibly have been a slave, as someone suggests, and after Kabnis has shouted at him long enough that he is focused on sin, the old man finally speaks, and says "sin," over and over. He takes on the significance that people ascribe to him, but he also has no independent significance within the story: there is never a non-symbolic reason to explain why he is sitting in the basement.

Structure

Critics have a wide range of opinions regarding the structure of this book, from calling it "perfect" to denying that it has any structure whatsoever. Overall, there is no clear pattern, other than the clear fact that it is divided into three parts, each concerned with its own particular theme. The action of the various sections does not overlap, and the characters do not continue from one segment to another. In the first section, there are two poems before each prose piece, but this rule diminishes by the beginning of Section Two.

The book's most ardent supporters point to the progression of thematic concerns. It starts with lonely, isolated women who have been rejected by society but are used sexually, and by the end of Section One the stories are about women who are not rejected, but are desired. In Section Two, the emphasis is on men who desire women but have trouble acting on their desires, mostly because of their uncertainty of their place in Northern society. Section Three is about Kabnis, a Northern black man who goes to Georgia to learn about his history. Throughout Kabnis' story, he becomes more and more like the Southern men who distanced themselves from the women in the very first segments. Readers who follow this structure closely can notice that, even in the absence of a plot, each "chapter" of this book (including poems and character sketches) actually does respond to what came immediately before it, moving the main idea forward.

Historical Context

The Harlem Renaissance

During the 1920s, the artistic scene among blacks in the Harlem section of New York City prospered and gained national attention. It had been coming for a long time: black writers had been published in America for almost a century and a half, since Phillis Wheatley, a slave who had been born in Africa, published a book of poetry in 1773. In spite of the rich cultural heritage of African Americans and society's willingness to accept blacks as entertainers, there was a traditional reluctance to recognize the achievements of black intellectuals. In the later decades of the nineteenth century, the debate about social progress for African Americans split into two directions. Followers of Booker T. Washington, the founder of the Tuskegee Institute in Alabama, felt that blacks would gain more by working at whatever humble jobs they were offered and earning the trust of the majority. Followers of W. E. B. DuBois, one of the founders of the National Association for the Advancement of Colored People (NAACP), supported earning respect through intellectual growth and achievement. When the NAACP was founded in 1910, DuBois became editor of its magazine, *The Crisis,* which became an important forum for black writers.

World War I, which America fought in from 1917 to 1918, had a great influence in giving blacks confidence to find their own intellectual identity. Blacks participating in the war numbered 367, 000, with many leaving the rural settings that their families had been mired in for generations and gaining introduction to a wider world, where they found less hostility between the races than they were accustomed to in America. Returning veterans were much more aware of the injustices that they faced at home, especially in the South, where laws prohibited them from voting or owning land. Many moved north, and the greatest concentration of African Americans in the North was in Harlem.

It was in this context that the artistic community in Harlem blossomed, giving opportunity and encouragement to young writers, painters, and musicians. As always, America accepted the music of blacks first. The 1920s are known as the "Jazz Age," and black artists were the ones who invented this style of music. White Americans, disillusioned by the harsh suffering they had witnessed during the war, broke with convention by listening to Negro music in Negro nightclubs, giving Harlem a vibrant economy and increased visibility among the writers who influenced national tastes. Many of these whites who frequented jazz clubs were artists; still more followed an artistic lifestyle as a way of rebellion. As Harlem became the center of entertainment in the country's most prominent city, the people who lived in Harlem gained respect and attention.

Compare
&
Contrast

- **1920s:** The Ku Klux Klan, a post-Civil War terrorist organization that works to suppress blacks with threats, property destruction, and murder, is reorganized after having been disbanded for fifty years, and begins a new campaign of lynching.

  Today: The Ku Klux Klan still exists, but its violent activities are limited in favor of political activity.

- **1920s:** Artists like Pablo Picasso and Jean Toomer create works with a distorted sense of reality, working with the new artistic principle of modernism, which rejects traditional forms.

  Today: Postmodernism has rejected modernism by embracing traditional principles in an ironic way, mocking the humorless, serious "artistic" attitude of the moderns.

- **1920s:** The radio is a new form of entertainment, allowing people to enjoy professional performances without leaving their homes.

  Today: The Internet is the newest form of entertainment, allowing people to shop, do research, and download an endless supply of pictures, videos, and recordings, all without leaving their homes.

- **1920s:** African Americans are, by law, forbidden access to certain hospitals, schools, and neighborhoods in the South.

  Today: Laws threaten stiff penalties for businesses that discriminate because of race; still, most Americans live in segregated neighborhoods.

- **1920s:** Middle-class white Americans flirt with danger by listening to the exotic rhythms of jazz music, coming from a black culture that is mysterious to them.

  Today: Many middle-class white Americans listen to rap music that comes from a black culture that is mysterious to them.

- **1920s:** Blacks are regularly murdered in the South if there is even a suspicion of their being involved in an interracial affair.

  Today: Social disapproval still exists in many places, but America has become much more accustomed to the idea of blacks and whites marrying.

Ironically, the earliest writers associated with the "New Negro Renaissance" only lived in Harlem for a short time, and neither identified with the plight of American blacks. Claude McKay, a poet from Jamaica, drew national attention when he published his ground-breaking book *Harlem Shadows* in 1922, but by the following year he left to live in Europe. Jean Toomer lived in a number of places, with New York being only one of them. Soon after the publication of *Cane* in 1923 he left to become involved with the Gurdjieff Institute in France, and he never lived in Harlem on a regular basis again.

There were, however, many artists prepared to go through the door opened by Toomer and McKay. Other black writers introduced to the world during this period include Langston Hughes, Zora Neale Hurston, Arna Bontemps, and the historian Alaine Locke. Painters who made their name during the Harlem Renaissance include William H. Johnson, Lois Malliou Jones, Hale Woodruff, and John T. Biggers.

Segregation

From the end of the 1800s through the 1950s, many states in the South had laws on their books that left blacks at a severe social disadvantage, forcing them to rely on the mercy of whites almost as much as they had when they were slaves. These laws were collectively known as "Jim Crow laws," named so after a foolish black character in an 1832

An African-American family in front of their log cabin in North Carolina. The first third of the novel is devoted to the African-American experience in the Southern farmland.

minstrel show. Starting in the 1880s, states in the South began passing laws that required blacks to ride in separate railroad cars, stay in separate hotels, attend separate theaters, eat at separate restaurants, use separate rest rooms, drink at separate water fountains, and attend separate schools from whites. The U.S. Supreme Court upheld the rights of states to pass these laws in 1892, ruling in the famous case of *Plessy v. Ferguson* that it was acceptable for states to keep the races divided as long as the accommodations that were provided for blacks were, to use the famous phrase coined in that decision, "separate but equal."

The problem, of course, was that the facilities that were available for blacks to use were far from equal to those enjoyed by whites. Black schools were rare, and those that were run by teachers who were willing to work for practically nothing had almost nonexistent operating budgets. Public transportation in black neighborhoods was scarce, while laws prevented well-to-do blacks from moving to white neighborhoods. White landlords could neglect properties in black neighborhoods, knowing that their tenants had few options about where they could live. Medical facilities offered to blacks were primitive.

The situation caused by Jim Crow laws in the South did not change until the 1950s, when television made it possible for civil rights activists to draw the nation's attention to the injustice of segregation. In 1955 Dr. Martin Luther King Jr. led a boycott of public transportation in Montgomery, Alabama, when Rosa Parks, a black woman who refused to ride in the back of the bus, was arrested. In 1963 state officials of Mississippi caused a riot when they refused to uphold a court order allowing a black man, James Meredith, to enroll; the National Guard had to be brought out to defend citizens against the state militia. The Civil Rights Act of 1964 has set national standards for equal treatment of people of all races.

Critical Overview

Cane was a phenomenal critical success from its first printing, but it was a commercial failure, with fewer than 5000 copies published during Jean Toomer's lifetime. Some biographers and critics refer to this fact to explain why the author never followed it up with another novel. It was published in 1923, a time when the literary world was alive with writers like Toomer who experimented with traditional narrative styles, and the critics were very receptive to the novel's uniqueness, in some cases even overenthusiastic. Darwin T. Turner, who has written much about Toomer's career, captured some of the enthusiasm of the early praise in his introduction to the 1975 edition of *Cane:*

> Lola Ridge, editor of *Broom,* predicted that Toomer would be the most widely discussed author of his generation, which is remembered now for such individuals as Sherwood Anderson, Ernest Hemingway, F. Scott Fitzgerald, and William Faulkner. John McClure, editor of *Double Dealer,* had favorably compared Toomer's lyricism with Sherwood Anderson.

Anderson was an older writer, whose powerful artistic sensibilities and willingness to help other writers made him something of a mentor to many of the writers of the nineteen twenties, including some of those mentioned above. In a different book entitled *In A Minor Chord,* Turner quoted a letter from Anderson to Toomer praising his work: "You are the only negro . . . who seems really to have consciously the artist's impulse."

As Anderson's comment indicates, the critical reception of *Cane* was not just about Toomer's achievement as a writer, but as a Negro writer, which, in the 1920s was rare but increasingly important. He is often associated with the Harlem Renaissance of the 1920s and 1930s, but Toomer was, at best, on the outskirts of the intellectual scene in Harlem. Arna Bontemps, one of the most influential writers to have come out of that movement, captured the social significance of *Cane* in his introduction to the 1969 edition of the book, published by Perennial Classics. "Only two small printings were issued, and these vanished quickly," Bontemps wrote. "However, among the most affected was practically an entire generation of young Negro writers then just beginning to emerge; their reaction to Toomer's *Cane* marked an awakening that soon thereafter began to be called a Negro Renaissance." He went on to list such luminaries as Countee Cullen, Langston Hughes, Zora Neale Hurston, and Wallace Thurman as having been influenced by this book. Bontemps captures this critical response with the words of one writer, Charles S. Johnson, a distinguished scholar and sociologist. "Here was the Negro artist," he quotes Johnson saying, "detached from propaganda, sensitive only to beauty. Where [Paul Laurence] gave to the unnamed Negro peasant a reassuring touch of humanity, Toomer gave to the peasant a passionate charm . . . more than any artist, he was an experimentalist, and this last quality has carried him away from what was, perhaps, the most astonishingly brilliant beginning of any Negro writer of this generation."

Brian Joseph Benson and Mabel Mayle Dillard, in a 1980 book about Toomer's career, explain the novel's perseverance as resulting from the absolute dedication of its early readers. They wrote that "it is apparent that *Cane* became one of those classics kept alive by word of mouth and sheer admiration on the part of readership. This is a verifiable statement since, when it came time for those successful figures of the 1920s to write their memoirs, *Cane* is mentioned time after time as one book which stuck in the mind as an inspirational work."

Although the book was remembered by its fervent admirers, the rest of the world forgot it, as Toomer slipped from the public's consciousness each year that he did not publish a book. He only published sporadically, and refused to allow excerpts from *Cane* to appear in anthologies of writings by blacks, claiming that he was not a Negro. The novels that he did write were rejected by editors. According to Nellie Y. McKay, in her 1984 study of his career, "The editors and publishers who rejected Toomer's manuscripts for fifteen years did not do so capriciously, or with malice aforethought. The stories that issued from his pen during this time were turned down because they were tedious and described uninteresting people around whom he was unable to develop dramatic plots." In the years before his death, he published poetry and book reviews, but not fiction.

The revival of Toomer's reputation came soon after he died, in the 1960s. It was marked by racial turmoil, when blacks were, in the wake of the Civil Rights Movement and the deaths of Malcolm X and Martin Luther King Jr., being asked to raise their awareness of their identities. In this context, the richness of *Cane* was able to stand out. New studies of Toomer's life appeared in the 1970s, chronicling the tragedy of his early promise gone to seed. *Cane* has never been out of print since then.

Criticism

David Kelly

Kelly is an instructor of creative writing and literature at several community colleges in Illinois. In the following essay, he examines the circular design of Cane, *comparing the female characters who begin and end the book.*

One of the most impressive things about Jean Toomer's *Cane* is the way it gave fresh characterizations of African Americans at a time when existent literature about them was scant. Another is the complete freedom that Toomer exercised in his use of language, binding himself to neither traditional English nor the (now dated) black dialect that he used from time to time. His most sublime achievement, though, is in the area of structure. A casual reader—one who finishes the book with only a quick, shallow impression—might not see any overall pattern. Its individual parts don't fit together in any conventional sense of narrative.

It was Toomer's contention, though, that the book is designed as a circle, coming around to itself in the end, with final ideas bringing readers to beginning ones. If one focuses on the dissimilarities between the starting and finishing segments, this seems entirely unlikely. There could hardly be more difference than that between the educated, angst-ridden Ralph Kabnis, who has grown into adulthood without knowing what he is really about, and the spoiled nature-child Karintha, whose soul has "ripened too soon." There could hardly be more stylistic difference than that between her brief sketch and his novella.

It was Toomer's contention . . . that the book is designed as a circle, coming around to itself in the end, with final ideas bringing readers to beginning ones."

Cane is, however, a book that will not let readers rest assured with their feeling that they know the truth. In a linear sense, "Kabnis" is completely different than "Karintha," and so it is only fitting that the two should be at opposite ends of the book. But within "Kabnis" there is the story of Carrie K. She is the last female character in a book loaded with varieties of female characters, and she inverts the Southern values that the book begins with in Karintha's story. The story of Ralph Kabnis is interesting on its own, but it is Carrie K., mirror image to Karintha, who makes it part of a book.

The story of Karintha is a strange, disturbing place to begin, but it is appropriate for a book that is meant to circle back: it reads like an ending, not a beginning. By the end of this two-page segment, Karintha is old and worn out, even though she is only twenty. She "has been married many times," although this is most likely in a figurative, not literal, sense. She has had a child out in the forest and buried it there, under the pine needles, with the pine smoke from the mill following her back to town and, like a guilty conscience, infesting everything, even the water she drinks. She has men coming to her and giving her money, like a prostitute.

What makes this a strange place to start a book is that Karintha is irredeemable. She doesn't appear to have a shred of hope in her by the end, only misery and the memory of the promise she lost. Her childish misbehavior, which the men all indulged because they could not bear to handle such a beauty roughly, has forced her to find her own values, aging her soul—the end of "Karintha" marks an end, not a beginning. Sunrise is a likely place to start a book, because it represents a new start: by contrast, Karintha's story likens her to dusk in the beginning, the middle, and the end.

The book that follows keeps returning to the ideas that are touched on in this opening segment,

What Do I Read Next?

- Toomer's miscellaneous writings, including plays, letters, and reviews, have been collected in *The Wayward and the Seeking,* edited by Darwin Turner.

- Toomer's contemporary in the Harlem Renaissance, Arna Bontemps, was responsible for many works of poetry, fiction and criticism. One of his most compelling works is *God Sends Sunday,* a novel based on the old blues tradition.

- James Weldon Johnson was an African-American writer who preceded Toomer. Like Toomer, he struggled against being labeled and dismissed as a "black writer." His 1912 novel, *The Autobiography of an Ex-Coloured Man,* was more recently published with an introduction by Arna Bontemps.

- Among the many great works about African-American identity written since Toomer's time, one of the most influential and most stirring is Ralph Ellison's 1952 novel *Invisible Man.*

- Jean Toomer and Claude McKay are generally considered to be the first writers of the Harlem Renaissance. McKay gives today's readers a sense of what Harlem was like at that time in his 1928 novel *Home to Harlem.*

- Sherwood Anderson was considered one of Toomer's mentors, having encouraged him through the publication of *Cane.* Anderson's best-remembered work, *Winesburg, Ohio,* from 1919, bears similarities to the style Toomer used.

- *The Collected Poems of Jean Toomer* was published in 1988 by the University of North Carolina Press. It was edited by Robert B. Jones and Margery Toomer Latimer, the author's daughter.

- Toomer was known for refusing permission to reprint his works in anthologies of African-American writers, because he did not want to be categorized as black. One of the works from *Cane* that is anthologized is the story "Becky," which is included in Mentor Books' 1971 collection *Prejudice,* edited by Charles R. Larson.

---

as if to unravel the destruction of Karintha's life, to find some way to grant her amnesty for the crimes her circumstances have driven her to. In the subsequent stories, readers see men reacting to women's beauty; morality dictated by society; black characters wondering how their world has led them astray, how their childhoods steered them wrong. Carma's mannish appearance gives her a freedom from all the men (except the narrator) that Karintha will never have. Esther, too, has freedom from the men who are always around to pressure the characters with physical beauty, but her soul matures wrapped around the mistaken impression she has of one particular man, King Barlo. Avey, like Karintha, is the object of men's desires, and she ends up exhausted. Muriel might as well be from a different planet as Karintha, because it would be virtually impossible for them to understand one another—Muriel is concerned about her

reputation, both with her landlady and out in the public theater, which Dan Moore feels is an unhealthy suppression of her true sexual nature (unaware, of course, of the tragic results that leaving sexuality unchained caused for Karintha).

Toomer himself said that the true end of this book's circle was the story of Bona and Paul. Here, readers see the theme of sexual predation work itself out in healthy, robust competition: Bona is certainly Paul's match, not because she uses her feminine beauty to control him but because she puts an effort into being his equal. The theme of racial inequity, though, is not solved. There are two ways to read the ending. The most direct reading is that Bona, watching Paul shake hands with a black doorman, realizes the full implications of his racial identity, and leaves, implying that racial merging could never happen even for two people attracted to one another as these. The less simple reading, more in keeping with the sad tone of the book, is that Paul loses his chance at love because he has hesitated, taking too long deciding what he wants his identity to be. If Karintha is all response, giving the young and old men what they want, Paul is the opposite—all thought and little action.

The story of Kabnis, then, makes an excellent beginning. Like Toomer himself, Kabnis is a light-skinned educator seeking self-identity in the South—the character's quest begins where the author's did. And the mud of Georgia pulls Kabnis down. He starts off as a sophisticate, to some extent even a little snobbish about the locals' primitive beliefs, and he ends up a bib-overalled laborer: like the others only less skilled, and so infantilized by liquor that he is unable to stand on his own two feet.

In this, the largest section of *Cane,* there is much confusion, made worse by the jumbled rambling of the stream-of-consciousness narration, which brings Ralph Kabnis' confused thoughts to life. There is Kabnis' self-hatred, which if anything is fueled by the violence and callousness of the white community that surrounds him. There is religious mystery, in the form of Father John, who sits day and night at the table in the Hole; defiance in Louis; resignation in Halsey; and surrender in Hanby. The only character who is content and secure in this section is Carrie K.

Sister of Fred Halsey, she is considered an "adolescent." When Kabnis thinks about her, he does consider her body, shying away from thinking of her sexually the way that the old and young men tried to avoid thinking of Karintha when she was too young. "There is a slight stoop to her shoulders," Kabnis observes. "The curves of her body blend with this to a soft, rounded charm." His thought about the curves of her body indicates that he could easily sexualize her in the way that Karintha is sexualized in her youth.

Toomer shifts to Louis' point of view for the thought that Kabnis comes near to, the idea that young Carrie K. is wasting her virginity. Like Dan Moore, he worries that society is depriving her of life. "He sees the nascent woman, her flesh already stiffening to cartilage, drying to bone. Her spirit-bloom, even now touched sullen, bitter. Her rich beauty fading. . . ." The cause, Louis assumes, is the society around her. "The sin-bogies of respectable southern colored folk clamor at her: 'Look out! Be a *good* girl. Look out!'" In another context, readers might be tempted to go along with his fear, but not within a book that starts with the story of Karintha, who is ruined at an early age precisely because no one told her to look out.

Carrie is rooted to her society, not anchored by it or (as Louis assumes) oppressed by it. He mistakenly sees her caring for her brother and the silent old man as servitude, not realizing that her involvement with them gives her the sort of human interaction that most characters in *Cane* lack and sorely need. The old man, who they call Father John, might be a Christ figure, but this Christ is blind and deaf, and cannot communicate with people directly. What Carrie says of him—"He's deaf and blind, but I reckon he hears, and sees too, from the things I've heard"—does not make sense, except on a complex spiritual level. Few characters in this book have the spiritual complexity to see beyond the misery of their own lives.

Karintha has a baby and abandons it out among the pines. Stella, one of the prostitutes that Halsey and Kabnis bring down into the Hole where Father John lives, is described thinking: "She'd like to take Kabnis to some distant pine grove and nurse and mother him." It is hardly likely she could, with the bitter way her family has been destroyed according to the story she tells about a white man stealing her mother away. "Boars an kids an fools—that's all I've ever known," she explains. Instead of taking Kabnis and mothering him, she is claimed by Halsey as his sexual prize, and she goes off with him.

Carrie K. does mother him. Like a child, he finds it impossible to walk, and she helps him. She dresses him, or at least shows him when it is time to change out of his bathrobe and to dress to face the world. When he trips on the coal bucket and curses, she answers calmly with the last spoken words of the book: "Jesus, come." Her firm cool hands draw from him the fever of anger and confusion.

Carrie K. is the opposite of Karintha: the antidote to her sickness, the correction to what went wrong at the beginning of the book. The "Kabnis" story is about an educated man sinking to Karintha's level of instinctiveness, but it brings with it another black woman, one who is Karintha's social equal, her moral superior. Carrie K. is Karintha inverted. More than a circle, this book operates like a Mobius strip, a piece of paper that is twisted over before the two ends are attached, so that one can follow it continuously for infinity.

Source: David Kelly, in an essay for *Novels for Students,* Gale Group, 2001.

Charles Scruggs and Lee VanDemarr

In the following introduction to Jean Toomer and the Terrors of American History, *Scruggs and VanDemarr provide political background on* Cane *and its public rediscovery forty-five years after initial publication.*

Jean Toomer and the Terrors of American History is about a literary life and its complicated relationships to the social, political, and economic worlds in which the writer lived and worked. In particular it is about the African-American writer Jean Toomer and his major book, the hybrid short story cycle *Cane,* first published in 1923. For more than three decades a kind of subterranean text, not forgotten but unavailable, *Cane* had been a critical success rather than a popular one in 1923, and though its publisher reprinted it in 1927 (no doubt to capitalize on the rise of the Harlem Renaissance), it would not be reprinted again until 1969, two years after Toomer's death. In 1969, in the midst of a revival of interest in black writing, Robert Bone's review of the first paperback edition appeared in the *New York Times Book Review* with the headline "The Black Classic That Discovered 'Soul' Is Rediscovered after 45 Years," and *Cane's* revival was securely launched. The New York literary world's approval was something Toomer the author would have appreciated.

Cane became a canonic text rather late, but it was never quite a lost text; despite the *Times's* headline, *Cane* was "rediscovered" only in the sense that the mass-market edition made it available, as Bone remarked, "to the general reader." The importance of reprinting for a book's long-term survival should not be underestimated, but in this case the critical effort to remember *Cane,* which can be traced in Therman B. O'Daniel's excellent bibliography of Toomer, was equally important. Though excluded from "mainstream" anthologies of American literature, selections from *Cane,* a few poems and stories, were more or less continuously in print between 1927 and 1969—this despite the fact that Toomer himself sometimes declined to appear in "Negro" anthologies. Some critics of African-American writing also made sure Toomer's work was not forgotten: Alain Locke, Sterling Brown, J. Saunders Redding, Hugh M. Gloster, and particularly Bone and Arna Bontemps.

Since 1970 *Cane* has become an important text, and Jean Toomer has become the subject of biographies and book-length literary studies. After 1923 Toomer continued writing almost until the year of his death, accumulating a huge archive of unpublished work, most of it now collected at Yale University's Beinecke Rare Book and Manuscript Library. Understandably, much of the recent interest in Toomer has focused on this unpublished writing, particularly parts of his multiple autobiographies and the record of his "spiritualist" work after 1923; there has also been a tendency to read backward and interpret *Cane* in light of selected bits of this material. However, in part because of this concentration on the later writing, the now considerable body of scholarship about Toomer leaves important areas of his life and work untouched, especially the historical contexts within which Toomer began to write: the social and political milieus of the post-World War I period. Neglected in most previous commentaries, these matters are central to understanding *Cane* and cast light as well on Toomer's other works.

Two words in our title, "terrors" and "history," describe what we have found to be lacking from studies of Toomer and what we have tried to begin recovering. A significant project for recent critics of American literature has been the rediscovery of books and authors excluded from the New Critical canon, and a part of this work has also been to investigate the dimensions of literature which the New Critics were little interested in studying. Not coincidentally, the literary circles of Jean Toomer worked on a similar project; as Waldo Frank observed in *Our America,* criticizing the canon established by the "Genteel Tradition" and the "New Humanists": "Whatever consciousness we have had so far has been the result of vast and deliberate exclusions." Cary Nelson's critique of literary history as it has been written since the 1950s summarizes one kind of exclusion:

> The New Critics were at pains to point out that "literary history" generally omitted and obscured what was specifically *literary* about poetry and fiction, the textual qualities that distinguish literary language from other discourses. It may now, however, be more crucial to argue that literary history is typically (and improperly) detached from history as it may be more broadly construed—not only the familiar history of nations but also the still less familiar history of everyday life.

The background to *Cane* and the story of how Toomer came to write the book involve both "everyday" and national histories that had been "detached" from the text even as the complete text itself virtually disappeared for thirty years. *Contexts* have been there to be uncovered, but for various reasons they have remained hidden.

There is one obvious reason for the loss of historical—especially political—contexts for *Cane.* Toomer's life after 1923 turned away from the social circumstances and urgencies that led him to begin writing, and this move toward religious and personal concerns undoubtedly encouraged critics and biographers to regard him as a mystic and spiritualist rather than as a political writer. After 1923 Toomer formed a series of attachments to spiritualists like George Gurdjieff and religious groups like the Quakers which continued virtually until the end of his life. It seems clear that Toomer's commitment to a "spiritual quest" was serious and deeply felt, but our study is not concerned with that part of his career, except to point out that the political Toomer who wrote *Cane* resurfaced in later years. We have tried to outline the historical context from which *Cane* emerged, examining ignored or neglected evidence about the specific background within which Toomer wrote his book, and to show how that background helps explain the political meanings of *Cane.*

The politics of Jean Toomer the writer and of *Cane* have been obscured by intentional disregard (even by Toomer himself) and by scholarly neglect. Although we did not begin our work with the idea of revising Toomer's biography, in the process of writing we came up against serious errors and omissions in the scholarship dealing with Toomer's life through 1923; correcting this record has made us, in effect, involuntary biographers. The most complete biography of Toomer is Cynthia Earl Kerman and Richard Eldridge's *The Lives of Jean Toomer: A Hunger for Wholeness*—the subtitle of which indicates its concern with the "spiritual" Toomer. In fact, Kerman and Eldridge devote only two short chapters to *Cane,* whereas almost three-quarters of their book is given over to the religious quests of Toomer's later life. More important in our view, *Lives* contains factual errors and questionable interpretations and overlooks crucial biographical materials, particularly in its discussion of the writing of *Cane* and the social, political, and intellectual milieus that influenced it. We address specific errors in the notes to our main text, but the major problem is what has been omitted from the discussion of Toomer's life.

These omissions include a lack of attention to Toomer's earliest published writings, which are specifically political and which illuminate the crucial literary relationship between Toomer and his mentor, Waldo Frank. In *Lives* as, indeed, in all the published biographical writings on Toomer, there is no mention of the three articles he published be-

> To insist that *Cane* be a 'spiritual autobiography' is to disregard his text's most important enactment: the transformation of the isolated spectator into the witness of history."

tween 1919 and 1920 in the *New York Call,* a prominent socialist newspaper. Although Toomer avoided any mention of the *Call* essays in his autobiographies, references to these articles appear three times in Toomer's unpublished writings, twice in the correspondence between Waldo Frank and Toomer and again in the biographical sketch that Toomer wrote for Horace Liveright on the eve of *Cane's* publication.

Most of the writing about Toomer has understated, or even ignored, the essential contribution Waldo Frank made to *Cane,* and this problem becomes more troublesome when combined with critical misunderstandings about the meaning of Frank's own books, particularly his key work, *Our America.* Kerman and Eldridge, for instance, largely reduce Frank's significance for Toomer to the "spiritual" and the "religious," viewing *Our America* as a work focused on the idea of the nation's "organic mystical Whole." This phrase, however, offers little help in coming to terms with a book whose real foundation is political and social, as Toomer's defense of Frank in his final *Call* article, "Americans and Mary Austin," shows he well understood. Austin had attacked Frank as a Jew, condemning *Our America* because it presumptuously challenged the cultural hierarchy that Austin, as an Anglo-American, was determined to uphold, and Toomer defended Frank on precisely those issues of "race," culture, and politics that were at the heart of *Our America.*

In 1919, when *Our America* was published, Frank and others of his generation faced a repressive government. Bolshevik paranoia and war hysteria defined the national temper; anti-Semitism was at its zenith; civil liberties remained under "wartime" suspension; members of the liberal and radical Left were being harassed, jailed, or deported; major race riots (attacks by whites on black communities) erupted throughout the year. Randolph Bourne, Frank's friend and fellow contributor to the brilliant little magazine *The Seven Arts* (1916–17), wrote a brutal but unfinished satire on the tenor of the times called "The State." Published posthumously in the same year as *Our America,* it conceived of America's future as a totalitarian nightmare. Some of Bourne's politics found their way into *Our America* as part of an extended socialist critique of American history, but Frank's book placed hope for resistance more in the cultural arena than in the political one. This choice was not a retreat in his view: he believed the artist rather than the revolutionary could radically remake American society, just as marginalized groups (Jews, Hispanics, Native Americans, African Americans, immigrants from southern Italy and eastern Europe) might redefine an America as "ours" and not "theirs." Frank thought "culture" was a political force that might change society rather than simply reflect it, and his use of *religion* was tied to the social: art is "religious" (from *religare:* "to bind") because it serves in the creation of the Beloved Community.

Although by the end of 1923 Toomer was on his way to embracing Gurdjieffism, this future choice is largely irrelevant to *Cane's* meaning. The "spiritual" always appears in *Cane* within a political context, that is, within a context concerned with issues involving the American polis. Toomer's politics in the period from 1918 to 1923—roughly the time during which he was learning the craft of writing and then completing *Cane*—were centered on socialism and on the "New Negro"; his first published essays drew ideas from both movements, which were contemporary currents in postwar New York City and which coincided in radical African-American magazines like Cyril Briggs's *Crusader* and the *Messenger* of A. Philip Randolph and Chandler Owen.

Toomer criticism has largely dismissed socialism as a significant influence on his thought at the time he was writing *Cane.* Critics paraphrase Toomer's remarks in the 1931–32 version of his autobiography, that ten days of working in the shipyards of New Jersey in 1919 "finished socialism for me." But the shipyard experience did not finish socialism for Toomer. He continued to move in the world of the New York Left after 1919, and in 1936 he wrote another version of his autobiography which completely revised his understanding of those days in the shipyard. Where the 1931–32 autobiography is satirical, even cynical—the shipyard

workers "had only two main interests: playing craps and sleeping with women"—in the 1936 autobiography this satiric perspective shifts to the Gothic: Toomer admits his own fear of working-class life, that he did not want "to be confined in the death-house with doomed men."

The lot of these workers represented a brutal actuality that underlay society; working as a common laborer had shown Toomer "that the underlying conditions of human existence were ruthless and terrible beyond anything written in books or glimpsed in those forms of society wherein men, their behavior and manners, are veneered by the amenities of civilization. This is what the shipyard experience had done to me—and done for me." He was also convinced that socialism was a necessary solution to the soul-deadening, exhausting work of the shipyards: "I realized as never before the *need* of socialism, the *need* of a radical change of the conditions of human society." Like George Orwell—and indeed this part of the 1936 autobiography reads like *Down and Out in Paris and London*—Toomer would escape back to "normal" middle-class life, but the world of the shipyards would be present in *Cane,* in its keen social analysis of class and caste and in its Gothic portrayal of the terrors of American history.

Also missing from the biographical record are essential facts about Toomer's engagement with African-American politics and civil rights. The second *Call* essay Toomer wrote, "Reflections on the Race Riots," published in August 1919, raises important questions: Where was Toomer during the Washington, D.C., race riots of July 1919, and what was his reaction to them? Some of the worst fighting of July 21–22 took place in the streets virtually fronting the apartment Toomer occupied with his elderly grandparents, yet there is no mention of this in Darwin T. Turner's *The Wayward and the Seeking* or in Toomer's other autobiographical writings. Toomer's contemporary reaction, a militant leftist one, is evident from his *Call* essay, but his later decision to "forget" that public history points up how difficult it is to determine exactly what can be trusted in the autobiographies.

One of the problems in Toomer criticism has been the use of Turner's autobiographical collage in *The Wayward and the Seeking* as an accurate record of Toomer's life. Turner's book has been valuable as a source for long-unavailable portions of Toomer's published and unpublished work, and Turner himself was clear in his introduction about the selective nature of the autobiographical fragments he joined together to produce a narrative of Toomer's life through 1923. But inevitably the largest portion of the autobiographical writings were excluded from this anthology, and some of those excluded pages are of crucial significance for understanding Toomer's political life. It is absurd that the half-dozen lines about working in the shipyards from the 1931–32 "Outline of an Autobiography" should be quoted repeatedly even as Toomer's many pages of reflection on the same experience written in 1936 remain unmentioned.

To a considerable degree the difficulty in establishing the basic facts of Toomer's life has been due to his own evasiveness. The problem with Toomer's discussions of *Cane* and its composition presented in *The Wayward and the Seeking* is a matter not primarily of which documents were selected, but of Toomer's own deliberate misrepresentation of those circumstances. After comparing Toomer's extensive 1922–23 correspondence with Waldo Frank, Gorham Munson, and others against the record of the same period in "On Being an American," one becomes very cautious of Toomer's selective memory, especially in any matter involving his racial identity. Similarly, the exclusion of the *Call* articles from Toomer's autobiography was his own choice, a choice that successfully "buried" them for a surprisingly long time. Such was also the case with the events of his life during the summer of 1919, though it is now possible—with the *Call* article and various hints in Toomer's unpublished autobiographies—to piece together a probable narrative for those months.

Beyond mistaking specific facts of Toomer's life, scholarship about *Cane* has never adequately treated the intellectual and historical settings of that work, though there are important exceptions in the criticism of Vera M. Kutzinski, George B. Hutchinson, Michael North, and Barbara Foley, who have made valuable contributions to the recovery of *Cane*'s background. That background, the political circumstances behind *Cane,* was varied, and included Toomer's activist engagement in polemics ("Reflections on the Race Riots" and "Americans and Mary Austin"), the traumatic circumstances of his stay in Sparta, his attempt to understand the mulatto-elite milieu of his hometown, Washington, D.C., and its ideology of racial uplift, and his ongoing effort to define himself as an "American." Although he wrote about these experiences before he renewed his acquaintance with Waldo Frank in 1922, it was Frank's influence that led him to think of developing this diverse material into a book. The euphoria Toomer felt over being associated with

Waldo Frank and the group of intellectuals known during the Great War as "Young America" cannot be overestimated. The members of that group were to move in different directions after the war, but the ideas emanating from their vortex would give Toomer an intellectual context for *Cane.*

The brief mention of "Young America" in *The Lives of Jean Toomer* is the best available discussion of Toomer's relationship to this group, but it is sketchy and incomplete. Nor is it useful to characterize these people as part of the "Lost Generation." Whatever that phrase meant when Gertrude Stein dropped it to Ernest Hemingway in Paris, it has a very limited relevance to Toomer's circle of New York intellectuals. Lewis Mumford, a member of "Young America," put the difference directly:

> In contrast to the disillusioned expatriates of the "lost generation" who were travelling in the opposite direction, we [Mumford and Van Wyck Brooks] felt— as did Randolph Bourne, Waldo Frank, and Paul Rosenfeld—that this [task of reclaiming our American literary heritage] was an essential preparation for America's cultural "Coming of Age." For Brooks this remained a lifelong mission; and between 1921 and 1931, partly under his influence, I made it my concern too.

Mumford would say elsewhere that "what united me in comradeship" to this group was the idea of "re-discovery." Although he probably took that word from the title of Waldo Frank's *The Rediscovery of America* (1929), the sequel to *Our America,* he may have been thinking of Van Wyck Brooks's seminal article in the *Dial* (1918), "On Creating a Usable Past," in which Brooks saw American history, and especially American literary history, an "inexhaustable storehouse" of multiple pasts. Mumford, Frank, Hart Crane, and eventually Kenneth Burke came to see that America's usable pasts might be reclaimed in order to express a utopian future. The renewal of American life was also Toomer's concern, but Toomer's racial perspective on American society, past and present, complicated this theme in *Cane.* As much as he wanted to embrace the optimism of Frank and others, he came face to face in *Cane* not with a usable past but with the terrors of American history.

As Kerman and Eldridge's plural *Lives* suggests, and as most readers looking at *Cane* and the post-*Cane* work are likely to feel, Jean Toomer's life changed dramatically after 1923. Since we have read Toomer primarily because of *Cane,* we will look at only a few of his later writings, and those in light of the vexed question of what became of

Women skim boiling sugar-cane juice in preparation for making sorghum syrup. A pivotal scene in the novel takes place around a kettle for boiling sugar cane.

the author whom Waldo Frank at one time regarded as the most promising writer in America. Our sense of *Cane's* importance has led us to try to uncover the background for the book and to clarify its political meanings; we find little point in the current anachronistic tendency that attempts to link *Cane* with Toomer's New Age thinking after he came under the influence of George Gurdjieff and to read the book via Gurdjieffism or some other "spiritual" system. Fixing on the illusory search for "spiritual wholeness" in the text reduces, intentionally or not, its social and political dimensions, and ignores the historical background of the times and Toomer's intricate and evolving connection to them. To insist that *Cane* be a "spiritual autobiography" is to disregard his text's most important enactment: the transformation of the isolated spectator into the witness of history.

Source: Charles Scruggs and Lee VanDemarr, "Introduction: The Witness of History," in *Jean Toomer and the Terrors of American History,* University of Pennsylvania Press, 1998, pp. 1–7.

Houston A. Baker, Jr.

In the following essay excerpt, Baker asserts that with Cane, *Toomer transcended black Ameri-can literature of the 1920s to present a "thorough delineation of the black situation."*

William Stanley Braithwaite's "The Negro in American Literature," concludes with the rhapsodic assertion that "*Cane* is a book of gold and bronze, of dusk and flame, of ecstasy and pain, and Jean Toomer is a bright morning star of a new day of the race in literature." Written in 1924, Braithwaite's statement reflects the energy and excess, the vibrancy and hope of a generation of young black authors who set out in the 1920s to express their "individual dark-skinned selves without fear or shame." They were wooed by white patrons; they had their work modified beyond recognition by theatrical producers, and they were told time and again precisely what type of black American writing the public would accept. Some, like Wallace Thurman, could not endure the strain. Claude McKay absented himself from Harlem throughout most of the twenties, and Langston Hughes and Countee Cullen gained a degree of notoriety. Ironically, it was *Cane* (1923), a book written by a very light-complexioned mulatto, that portrayed—without fear of shame—a dark-skinned self that transcended the concerns of a single period and heralded much of value that has followed its publication. Arna Bontemps writes:

> Only two small printings were issued, and these vanished quickly. However, among the most affected was practically an entire generation of young Negro writers then just beginning to emerge; their reaction to Toomer's *Cane* marked an awakening that soon thereafter began to be called a Negro Renaissance.

The 1920s presented a problem for the writer who wished to give a full and honest representation of black American life; for him the traditional images, drawn from the authors of the Plantation Tradition and the works of Paul Laurence Dunbar, were passé. The contemporary images, captured in Carl Van Vechten's *Nigger Heaven* (1926) and Claude McKay's *Home to Harlem* (1928), were not designed to elucidate a complex human existence, for they were reflections of that search for the bizarre and the exotic that was destined to flourish in an age of raccoon coats, bathtub gin, and "wine-flushed, bold-eyed" whites who caught the A-train to Harlem and spent an evening slumming, or seeking some *élan vital* for a decadent but prosperous age. That only two small printings of *Cane* appeared during the 1920s is not striking: the miracle is that it was published at all. Toomer did not choose the approbation that a scintillating (if untrue) portrayal of the black man could bring in the twenties, nor did he speak *sotto voce* about the amazing progress the black man had made in American society and his imminent acceptance by a fond white world. *Cane* is a symbolically complex work that employs lyrical intensity and stream-of-consciousness narration to portray the journey of an artistic soul toward creative fulfillment; it is unsparing in its criticism of the inimical aspects of the black American heritage and resonant in its praise of the spiritual beauty to be discovered there. An examination of the journey toward genuine, liberating black art presented in *Cane* reveals Toomer as a writer of genius and the book itself as a protest novel, a portrait of the artist, and a thorough delineation of the black situation. These aspects of the work explain its signal place among the achievements of the Harlem Renaissance, and they help to clarify the reaction of a white reading public—a public nurtured on the minstrel tradition, the tracts of the New Negro, and the sensational antics of Carl Van Vechten's blacks—which allowed it to go out of print without a fair hearing.

The first section of *Cane* opens with evocative description and a lyrical question. The subject is Karintha, whose:

> . . . skin is like dusk on the eastern horizon,
> O cant you see it, O cant you see it,

"*Cane* is a symbolically complex work that employs lyrical intensity and stream-of-consciousness narration to portray the journey of an artistic soul toward creative fulfillment; it is unsparing in its criticism of the inimical aspects of the black American heritage and resonant in its praise of the spiritual beauty to be discovered there."

> Her skin is like dusk on the eastern horizon
> . . . When the sun goes down.

The repetition and the simile bringing together the human and the nonhuman leave a memorable impression. The reader is directly asked to respond, as were the hearers of such spirituals as "I've Got a Home in Dat Rock": "Rich man Dives he lived so well / Don't you see?" From the outset, the atmosphere is one of participation, as the reader is invited to contemplate a woman who carries "beauty, perfect as dusk when the sun goes down."

"Karintha," however, offers more than rhapsodic description and contemplation. It is a concise, suggestive sketch of the maturation of a southern woman: from sensuous childhood through promiscuous adolescence to wanton adulthood. The quatrain that serves as the epigraph is repeated twice and acts as a sharp counterpoint to Karintha's life, which is anything but beautiful: "She stoned the cows, and beat her dog, and fought the other children . . . " In a sense, "Karintha" is a prose "The Four Stages of Cruelty," and its exquisite style forces some of its more telling revelations into a type of Hogarthian background, where they are lost to the casual observer.

There are elements of the humorous black preacher tale in the narrator's comment that "even the preacher, who caught her at mischief, told himself that she was as innocently lovely as a November cotton flower," and grim paradox appears after Karintha has given birth to her illegitimate child near the smoldering sawdust pile of the mill:

Weeks after Karintha returned home the smoke was so heavy

you tasted it in water. Someone made a song:

Smoke is on the hills. Rise up.

Smoke is on the hills, O rise

And take my soul to Jesus.

The holy song that accompanies an unholy event is no less incongruous than the pilgrimages and the fierce, materialistic rituals in which men engage to gain access to Karintha. For the heroine is not an enshrined beauty but a victim of the South, where "homes . . . are most often built on the two room plan. In one, you cook and eat, in the other you sleep, and there love goes on." Karintha has been exposed to an adult world too soon, and the narrator drives home the irony that results when biblical dictates are juxtaposed with a bleak reality: "Karintha had seen or heard, perhaps she had felt her parents loving. One could but imitate one's parents, for to follow them was the way of God." While some men "do not know that the soul of her was a growing thing ripened too soon," the narrator is aware that Karintha has been subjected to conditions that Christianity is powerless to meliorate. Her life has been corrupted, and the mystery is that her beauty remains.

The type of duality instanced by Karintha's sordid life and striking appearance recurs in Part One and lends psychological point to the section. The essential theme of "Karintha" is the debasement of innocence. Men are attracted to the heroine but fail to appreciate what is of value—the spirituality inherent in her dusky beauty. They are awed by the pure yet wish to destroy it; evil becomes their good, and they think only in terms of progressive time and capitalistic abundance—"The young fellows counted the time to pass before she would be old enough to mate with them" and ran stills to make her money. These conditions result, in part, from a southern Manichaeanism; for the land whose heritage appears in "Karintha" stated its superiority and condoned an inhumane slavery, spoke of its aristocracy and traded in human flesh, lauded its natural resources and wantonly destroyed them to acquire wealth. Good and evil waged an equal contest in a South that contained its own natural harmonies but considered blacks as chattels personal, bound by no rights that a white man need respect. In such an instance, love could only be an anomaly, and the narrator of Part One seems fully aware of this. When black women are considered property (the materialism surrounding Karintha and Fern) and white women goddesses (the recrimina-tion that accompanies Becky's sacrilegious acts), deep relationships are impossible; the evil of the encompassing universe and the natural compulsion of man to corrupt the beautiful inform the frustrating encounters of Part One.

The two poems—"Reapers" and "November Cotton Flower"—that follow "Karintha" offer a further treatment of the significant themes found in the story. The expectations raised by the title of the first poem are almost totally defeated by its text. There are sharpened blades, black men, black horses, and an inexorable energy; but wearying customs, indifference, and death are also present. "I see them place the hones/In their hip-pockets as a thing that's done," the speaker says, and goes on to depict the macabre death of a field rat that, "startled, squealing bleeds." This event does not halt the movement of the cutters, however: "I see the blade, / Blood-stained, continue cutting. . . . " An abundant harvest is not the result of the poem's action, and the black reapers, with scythes in hand, take on the appearance of medieval icons of death—an appropriate image for those who help to corrupt the life of Karintha. "November Cotton Flower" with its images of scarcity, drought, dead birds, and boll weevils continues the portrayal of a grim environment. Against this background, however, stands a beauty like Karintha's. The heroine of the first sketch was compared to a November cotton flower, and here the appearance of the "innocently lovely" flower brings about the speculation of the superstitious. "Beauty so sudden for that time of year," one suspects, is destined to attract its exploiters.

While exploring the nature of Karintha's existence, the author has been constructing the setting that is to appear throughout Part One. The first story's effect is heightened by the presence of the religious, the suggestive, and the feminine, and certain aspects of the landscape linger in the reader's mind: a sawmill, pine trees, red dust, a pyramidal sawdust pile, and rusty cotton stalks. The folk songs convey a feeling of cultural homogeneity; they are all of a religious character, rising spontaneously and pervading the landscape. The finishing details of this setting—the Dixie Pike and the railroad—are added in "Becky," which deals with a mode of interaction characteristic of primitive, homogeneous societies.

"Becky" is the story of a white woman who gives birth to two mulatto sons, thus violating one of the most rigid taboos of southern society. As a consequence, she is ostracized by the community.

William Goede (following the lead of Robert Bone) describes her plight as follows:

> Becky is, like Hester Prynne, made to pay for the collective sense of guilt of the community: after whites and Negroes exile her, they secretly build her a house which both sustains and finally buries her. The house, on the other hand, built between the road and the railroad, confines the girl until the day when the roof falls through and kills her.

Unlike Karintha, Becky is seldom portrayed in physical terms. The narrator has never seen her, and the community as a whole merely speculates on her actions and her changing appearance. She is primarily a psychological presence to whom the community pays an ironical homage: a spectral representation of the southern miscegenatory impulse that was so alive during the days of American slavery and was responsible for countless lynchings even in Toomer's own day. As early as the seventeenth century, southern legislatures were enacting laws to prevent sexual alliances between blacks and whites; hence, the community in "Becky" reacts in a manner sanctioned by law and custom.

"Becky" presents a further exploration of the duality theme encountered in "Karintha," and here the psychological element seems to predominate. The heroine's exile first calls to mind repression; she is set apart and finally buried. A more accurate description of Becky, however, is that she is a shaman. Among certain Asian groups and American Indian tribes, a person who engages in unsanctioned behavior (homosexuality, for example) is thought to have received a divine summons; he becomes a public figure and devises and leads ritualistic ceremonies that project his abnormal behavior. The function of the shaman is twofold; he enables the community to act out, by proxy, its latent abnormalities, and he reinforces its capacity to resist such tendencies. He is tolerated and revered because of his supernatural power, yet hated as a symbol of moral culpability and as a demanding priest who exacts a penitential toll. The most significant trait of the shaman, however, is that—despite his ascribed powers—he is unable to effect a genuine cure. Georges Devereux explains this paradox:

> Aussie ne peut-on considérer que le chaman accomplit une "cure psychiatrique" au sens *strict* du terme; il procure seulement au malade ce que L'École de psychoanalyse de Chicago appelle une "expérience affective corrective" qui l'aide à réorganiser son système de défense mais ne lui permet pas d'attendre à cette réelle prise de conscience de soimême (*insight*) sans laquelle il n'y a pas de véritable guérison.

It is not surprising that analysts consider the shaman a disturbed individual; he is often characterized by hysteria and suicidal tendencies, and he remains in his role because he finds relief from his own disorders by granting a series of culturally sanctioned defenses to his followers.

Becky has engaged in a pattern of behavior that the surrounding community considers taboo, and she is relegated to a physical position outside the group but essentially public. Her house is built (by the townspeople) in a highly visible location, an "eye-shaped piece of sandy ground. . . . Islandized between the road and railroad track." The citizens scorn her and consider her deranged ("poor-white crazy woman, said the black folks' mouths"), but at the same time they pray for her, bring her food, and keep her alive. Becky, in turn, continues her activities; she has another mulatto son and remains in the tottering house until it eventually crumbles beneath the weight of its chimney. In essence, we witness the same dichotomy presented in "Karintha"; the South professes racial purity and abhorrence of miscegenation, but the fundamental conditions of the region nourish a subconscious desire for interracial relationships and make a penitential ritual necessary. It seems significant, moreover, that Becky—who is a Catholic and in that respect also one of the South's traditional aversions—assumes a divine role for the community. Attraction toward and repulsion by the spiritually ordained are as much a part of the landscape in "Becky" as in "Karintha."

The narrator is swayed by the attitudes of the townspeople, but he is by no means a devout shamanist. He duly records the fact that Becky's house was built on "sandy ground" (reflecting the destructive and aggressive feelings that are part of the shamanic experience), and he points out that Becky is a Catholic. Moreover, he sets up a contrapuntal rhythm between the natural pines that "whisper to Jesus" and the ambivalent charity of the community. The most devastating note in this orchestration is that Sunday is the day of Becky's destruction, and the vagrant preacher Barlo is unwilling to do more than toss a Bible on the debris that entraps her. In short, the narrator captures the irony inherent in the miscegenatory under-consciousness of the South. The town's experience with Becky provides a "corrective, affective experience" but not a substantive cure; as the story closes (on notes that remind one of the eerie conjure stories of black folklore), one suspects that the townspeople are no more insightful.

At this point, Toomer has set forth the dominant tone, setting, characters, and point of view of the first section. Women are in the forefront, and in both "Karintha" and "Becky'" they assume symbolic roles that help to illustrate the dualities of a southern heritage. The beauty of Karintha and the beneficent aspects of Becky's existence are positive counterpoints to the aggressiveness, materialism, and moral obtuseness of the community as a whole. The omnipresent folk songs and the refrain in the second story bespeak a commitment to spirituality and beauty, while the animosity of the townspeople in "Becky" and the ineffectiveness of Christianity in "Karintha" display the grimmer side of a lyrically described landscape whose details pervade the whole of *Cane.* The point of view is largely that of a sensitive narrator, whom Arna Bontemps describes:

> Drugged by beauty "perfect as dusk when the sun goes down," lifted and swayed by folk song, arrested by eyes that "desired nothing that you could give," silenced by "corn leaves swaying, rusty with talk," he recognized that "the Dixie Pike has grown from a goal path in Africa." A native richness is here, he concluded, and the poet embraced it with the passion of love.

The narrator speaks in a tone that combines awe and reverence with effective irony and subtle criticism. There are always deeper levels of meaning beneath his highly descriptive surface, and this is not surprising when one considers Toomer's statement that in the South "one finds soil in the sense that the Russians know it—the soil every art and literature that is to live must be embedded in."

The emblematic nature of the soil is reflected in the tone and technique of the narrator and particularly in the book's title. Throughout Part One there is an evocation of a land of sugar cane whose ecstasy and pain are rooted in a communal soil. But the title conveys more than this. Justifications of slavery on scriptural grounds frequently traced the black man's ancestry to the race of Cain, the slayer of Abel, in the book of Genesis. Toomer is concerned not only with the Southern soil but also with the sons of Cain who populate it. In a colloquial sense, "to raise Cain" is to create disorder and cacophony, and in a strictly denotative sense, a cane is an instrument of support. Toomer's narrator is attempting to create an ordered framework that will contain the black American's complex existence, offer supportive values, and act as a guide for the perceptive soul's journey from amorphous experience to a finished work of art.

The third story of Part One. "Carma," is called by the narrator "the crudest melodrama," and so it is—on one level. When Carma's husband, Bane (surely an ironical name to set against *karma*), discovers that she has been unfaithful, he slashes the man who has told him, and is sentenced to the chain gang. This is melodramatic to be sure, but only (to quote the narrator) "as I have told it." Beneath the sensational surface is a tragedy of black American life. Bane, like Jimboy in Langston Hughes's *Not Without Laughter,* is forced by economic pressures to seek work away from home; thus, his wife is left alone in an environment where (again, according to the narrator) promiscuity is a norm. But Carma is also a woman who flaunts her sensuality, and can hardly be said to possess a strong sense of responsibility.

As in the previous stories, there are positive and redeeming elements in "Carma." The heroine herself is "strong as any man," and, given her name, this at least implies that her spirituality—that which is best and most ineffable in her—is capable of enduring the inimical aspects of her surroundings. This is particularly important when one considers that "Carma" introduces a legendary African background to the first section: "Torches flare . . . juju men, greegree, witch-doctors . . . torches go out . . . The Dixie Pike has grown from a goat path in Africa". The passage that introduces this reflection reads: "From far away, a sad strong song. Pungent and composite, the smell of farmyards is the fragrance of the woman. She does not sing; her body is a song. She is in the forest, dancing". The folk song is linked to the African past, and a feeling of cultural continuity is established. The atavistic remains of a ceremonial past have the fragrance of earth and the spirituality of song and dance to recommend them, and at the center of this drama is Carma. She is strong (as Karintha is beautiful) despite southern conditions, and she endures in the face of an insensitive Bane, who is enraged because he cannot master his destiny.

"Carma" is also the first story in which the narrator clearly identifies himself as a conscious recounter ("whose tale as I have told it"), and the poems that follow read like invocations to the heritage that he is exploring. "Song of the Son" states his desire to sing the "souls of slavery," and "Georgia Dusk," which makes further use of the legendary background encountered in "Carma," evokes the spirits of the "unknown bards" of the past. It is not surprising, then, that the story of Fern should follow.

Fern is a woman whom men used until they realized there was nothing they could do for her that would modify her nature or bring them peace. She is an abandoned Karintha, and in a sense a more beautiful and alluring Esther, staring at the world with haunting eyes. The narrator seeks out this beautiful exile who is free in her sexuality and unmoved by the all-pervasive cash nexus of her environment. However, when he asks himself the question posed by former suitors—"What could I do for her?"—his answer is that of the artist: "Talk, of course. Push back the fringe of pines upon new horizons". The others answered in solely materialistic terms, coming away from their relationships with Fern oblivious to her fundamental character and vowing to do greater penitence: "candy every week . . . a magnificent something with no name on it . . . a house . . . rescue her from some unworthy fellow who had tricked her into marrying him". The narrator, on the other hand, aspires to project a vision that will release Fern from her stifling existence; she thus becomes for him an inspiration, an artistic ideal. She is a merger of black American physical attractiveness and the unifying myth so important in black American history and in the creation of the spirituals.

"If you have heard a Jewish cantor sing, if he has touched you and made your own sorrow seem trivial when compared with his, you will know my [the narrator's] feeling when I follow the curves of her profile, like mobile rivers, to their common delta," and Fern's full name is Fernie May Rosen. The narrator is thus making use of the seminal comparison between the history of the Israelites and that of black America, which frequently appears in the religious lore of black American culture. In effect, the slaves appropriated the myth of the Egyptian captivity and considered themselves favored by God and destined in time to be liberated by His powers; this provided unity for a people who found themselves uprooted and defined by whites—historians and others—as descendants of wild savages on the "dark continent" of Africa. Despite the fact that she dislikes the petty people of the South and apparently needs to express an underlying spirituality, Fern seems to act as a symbolic representation of the black man's adoption of this myth. When the narrator has brought about a hysterical release from her, however, he fails to comprehend what he has evoked. The story ends with an injunction to the reader to seek out Fern when he travels South. The narrator feels that his ideal holds significance, but that his aspirations toward it are unfulfilled. There is some naivety in this assumption; for the

teller of Fern's story has explored the ironies inherent in the merger of white religion and black servitude. The religion of the Israelites is out of place in the life of Fern. While she captures—in her mysterious song like that of a Jewish cantor— the beauty of its spirit (and, in this sense, stands outside the narrow-minded community), she is imprisoned by the mores it occasions. Like Becky and Karintha, Fern is a victim, and the narrator skillfully captures her essence. The apparent naivety at the story's conclusion is in reality an act of modesty; for the art the narrator implies is humble actually holds great significance (in its subtle didactic elements) for the culture he is attempting to delineate.

"Esther" is a story of alienation and brings an inquietude that grows into the concluding terror of the book's first section. Apocalyptic images abound as the heroine dreams of King Barlo (a figure who first appeared in "Becky") overcoming her pale frigidity with a flaming passion that will result in a "black, singed, woolly, tobacco-juice baby—ugly as sin". Edward Waldron points out that "beneath this superficial level . . . lie at least two more intense and, for Toomer, more personal interpretations. One deals with the relationship of a light-skinned American Negro to the black community in which he (she) must try to function, and the other has to do with a common theme of the Harlem Renaissance, the relationship between the American Negro and Africa." But one can make excessive claims for King Barlo. While it is true that he falls into a religious trance and sketches, in symbolic oratory, the fate of Africans at the bands of slave traders, it is also true that he is a vagrant preacher, a figure whom Toomer sketches fully (and with less than enthusiasm) in Layman of "Kabnis." And though Barlo is the prophet of a new dawn for the black American, he is also a businessman who makes money during the war, and a lecherous frequenter of the demimonde. It thus seems an overstatement to make a one-to-one correlation between Barlo and Africa, or Afro-America. It is necessary to bear in mind that Esther Crane is not only a "tragic mulatto" repressed by Protestant religion and her father's business ethic ("Esther sells lard and snuff and flour to vague black faces that drift in her store to ask for them"), she is a fantasizer as well. Esther's view of Barlo is the true presented to the reader through most of the story; hence, when she retreats fully from reality at the conclusion, the reader's judgments should be qualified accordingly.

Esther's final state is described as follows: "She draws away, frozen. Like a somnambulist she wheels around and walks stiffly to the stairs. Down them. . . . She steps out. There is no air, no street, and the town has completely disappeared". The heroine is enclosed in her own mind; the sentient objects of the world mean nothing to this repressed sleepwalker. Given the complexity of Barlo's character, it is impossible to feel that such an observer could capture it accurately. Just as we refuse to accept the middle-aged and sentimental reflections of Marlowe as the final analysis of Kurtz in Conrad's "Heart of Darkness" and exercise a qualifying restraint before the words of Camus' narrator in *The Fall,* so we must recognize the full nature of Esther's character if we are to grasp her story and the role of King Barlo in it. Barlo does contain within himself the unifying myth of black American culture, and he delivers it to the community, in the manner of the most accomplished black folk preachers. In this character, however, he paradoxically contributes to Esther's stifled sensibility, which continually projects visions of sin. As a feat hero (the best cotton picker) and a skillful craftsman of words (his moving performance on the public street), he contains positive aspects, but the impression that remains—when one has noted his terrified and hypocritical response in "Becky" and his conspicuous materialism and insensitive treatment of Esther—is not as favorable as some critics would tempt us to believe.

The feelings of alienation and foreshadowing generated by "Esther" are heightened by the poems that follow. "Conversion" tells of a degraded "African Guardian of Souls" who has drunkenly yielded place to white religiosity, and seems intended to further enlighten the character of Barlo. "Portrait in Georgia" is a subtle, lyrical protest poem in which a woman is described in terms of the instruments and actions of a lynching. The second poem's vision prefigures the horror of the last story in Part One, "Blood-Burning Moon."

"Blood-Burning Moon" stands well in the company of such Harlem Renaissance works as Claude McKay's "If We Must Die" and Walter White's *The Fire in the Flint.* It is a work that protests, in unequivocal terms, the senseless, brutal, and sadistic violence perpetrated against the black man by white America. The narrator realized in "Carma" that violence was a part of southern existence, and the shattering demise of Becky, Barlo's religious trance, and Fern's frantic outpouring speak volumes about the terror of such a life. But in "Blood-Burning Moon" the narrator traces southern violence to its source. Tom Burwell—strong, dangerous, black lover of Louisa and second to Barlo in physical prowess—is only one of the black Americans whom the Stone family "practically owns." Louisa—black and alluring—works for the family, and Bob Stone (who during the days of slavery would have been called "the young massa") is having an affair with her. Tom reacts to hints and rumors of this affair in the manner of Bane; he turns violently on the gossipers and refuses to acknowledge what he feels to be true. Wage slavery, illicit alliances across the color line, intraracial violence—the narrator indeed captures the soul of America's "peculiar institution," and the results are inevitable. In a confrontation between Stone and Burwell, the black man's strength triumphs, and the white mob arrives (in "highpowered cars with glaring search-lights" that remind one of the "ghost train" in "Becky") to begin its gruesome work. The lynching of Tom, which drives Louisa insane, more than justifies the story's title. The moon, controller of tides and destinies, and a female symbol, brings blood and fire to the black American.

Part One is a combination of awe-inspiring physical beauty, human hypocrisy, restrictive religious codes, and psychological trauma. In "Fern" the narrator says: "That the sexes were made to mate is the practice of the South". But sexual consummation in the first section often results in dissatisfaction or in a type of perverse motherhood. Men come away from Fern frustrated; Karintha covertly gives birth to her illegitimate child in a pine forest; Esther dreams of the immaculate conception of a tobacco-stained baby, and Becky's sons are illegitimate mulattoes, who first bring violence to the community then depart from it with curses. The women of Part One are symbolic figures, but the lyrical terms in which they are described can be misleading. With the exception of their misdirected sexuality, they are little different from the entrapped and stifled women of the city seen in Part Two. In short, something greater than the pressure of urban life accounts for the black man's frustrated ambitions, violent outbursts, and tragic deaths at the hands of white America. The black American's failure to fully comprehend the beautiful in his own heritage—the Georgia landscape, folk songs, and women of deep loveliness—is part of it. But the narrator places even greater emphasis on the black man's ironical acceptance of the "strange cassava" and "weak palabra" of a white religion. Throughout Part One, he directs pointed thrusts—in the best tradition of David

Walker, Frederick Douglass, and William Wells Brown—at Christianity. Although he appreciates the rich beauty of black folk songs that employ Protestant religious imagery ("Georgia Dusk"), he also sees that the religion as it is practiced in the South is often hypocritical and stifling. The narrator, as instanced by "Nullo," the refrain in "Becky" ("The pines whisper to Jesus"), and a number of fine descriptive passages throughout the first section, seems to feel a deeper spirituality in the landscape. Moreover, there seems more significance in the beauty of Karintha or in the eyes of Fern (into which flow "the countryside and something that I call God") than in all the cramped philanthropy, shouted hosannas, vagrant preachers, and religious taboos of Georgia. The narrator, in other words, clearly realizes that the psychological mimicry that led to the adoption of a white religion often directed black Americans away from their own spiritual beauties and resulted in destruction.

But the importance of white America's role cannot be minimized. King Barlo views the prime movers behind the black situation as "little white-ant biddies" who tied the feet of the African, uprooted him from his traditional culture, and made him prey to alien gods. The essential Manichaeanism of a South that thrived on slavery, segregation, the chattel principle, and violence is consummately displayed in the first section of *Cane,* and Barlo realizes that a new day must come before the black man will be free. The brutality directed against the black American has slowed the approach of such a dawn, but the narrator of Part One has discovered positive elements in the black Southern heritage that may lead to a new day: a sense of song and soil, and the spirit of a people who have their severe limitations but cannot be denied.

Source: Houston A. Baker, Jr. , "Journey toward Black Art: Jean Toomer's *Cane,*" in *Singers of Daybreak: Studies in Black American Literature,* Howard University Press, 1983, pp. 53–67

Sources

Benson, Brian Joseph, and Mabel Nayle Dillard, "Lifting the Veil," in *Jean Toomer,* Twayne Publishers, 1980, p. 50.

Bontemps, Arna, "Introduction," in *Cane,* Perennial Classics, 1969.

McKay, Nellie Y., *Jean Toomer, Artist,* University of North Carolina Press, 1984, p. 9.

Turner, Darwin T., "Introduction," in *Cane,* Liveright Publishing Corp., 1975.

———, in *In a Minor Chord: Three African-American Writers and Their Search for Identity,* Southern Illinois University Press, 1971.

Waldron, Edward W., "The Search for Identity in Jean Toomer's 'Esther,'" in *CLA Journal,* Vol. 14, March 1971, p. 227.

For Further Study

Byrd, Rudolph P., *Jean Toomer's Years with Gurdjieff: Portrait,* University of Georgia Press, 1990.
    A biographical study of Toomer, following his life from the time he first heard Georges Gurdjieff lecture in New York City in 1924.

Kerman, Cynthia Earl, and Richard Eldridge, *The Lives of Jean Toomer,* Louisiana State University Press, 1987.
    This biography is useful in offering documented corrections to earlier misconceptions about Toomer's mysterious life.

Lewis, David Levering, *When Harlem Was in Vogue,* Oxford University Press, 1979.
    This book is very readable, and tells the full story of the Harlem Renaissance, including literary and social perspectives.

Woodson, John, *To Make a New Race: Gurdjieff, Toomer, and the Harlem Renaissance,* University of Mississippi Press, 1999.
    Woodson does a thorough, credible job of showing the connections between the ideologies of Gurdjieff, the religious leader, and his follower, Toomer. This book is required reading for understanding Toomer's career after *Cane.*

The Clan of the Cave Bear

Jean Auel

1980

The Clan of the Cave Bear was initially met with reluctance by publishers when Jean Auel approached them with her plan for a series of novels set in prehistoric times. Although meticulously researched, the sheer length of the original manuscript made many publishers unwilling to take the risk on the untried author. Indeed *The Clan of the Cave Bear* is one of those novels that is either loved or hated.

The story concerns a young girl named Ayla who is orphaned by a natural disaster and then adopted by a group known as the Clan. Ayla is very different from the Clan: physically, she is blond and blue-eyed and the people in the Clan are stocky and dark; she is expressive, sensitive, and smart and they are dour, plodding, and cold. Historians and anthropologists immediately reacted to Auel's book, maintaining that her assumptions about Neanderthal life were not realistic. In fact, Auel seems to be basing her view of the Neanderthal on the racially motivated "bad" science of late nineteenth-century French anthropology. It is precisely this "bad" science and overt racism that has prompted many anthropologists to denounce the novel.

However, the reading public truly seems to enjoy the novel that sold over one hundred thousand copies in the first three months after its publication. *The Clan of the Cave Bear* is an original work of fiction that explores the world of human beings in prehistoric times. Her novel has even inspired fans to write sequels about the Clan available on the World Wide Web (www.onebridgehome.com/altauel)

Jean M. Auel

Author Biography

Jean Auel was born in Chicago on February 18, 1936. She moved to Oregon and attended Portland State University, receiving her M.A. from the University of Portland in 1976. It was not until after she had raised five children that she began to write poetry and fiction. In fact, *The Clan of the Cave Bear* started as a short story exploring Auel's interest in Paleolithic humans. As Auel asserts, "the story lead to research, the research fired my imagination, and the wealth of material made me decide to write a novel." The original manuscript was almost one half-million words long and was rejected by several publishers.

In the mid-1970s, Auel began revising her mammoth manuscript. She rewrote *The Clan of the Cave Bear* four times. Finally, in 1978, she found a publisher willing to devote the time and resources to publishing the series. The novel was finally published in 1980. Over the following twenty-two years, she published three more novels in the series: *The Valley of the Horses* (1982), *The Mammoth Hunters* (1985), and *The Plains of Passage* (1990).

Although she continues to work on the Earth's Children Series, Auel admits that she wants to

tackle something lighter next time. She currently lives in Oregon with her husband.

Plot Summary

Part I

Jean Auel's *The Clan of the Cave Bear* chronicles the story of a prehistoric girl, named Ayla. As the novel opens, Ayla is a young child when her parents are killed in a violent earthquake. She wanders aimlessly for days, starving and alone. In her delirium of hunger, Ayla wanders into a valley that is home to massive cave lions. She survives a lion attack by hiding in a rock crevice, but a lion is able to scratch her left thigh. Ayla's thirst finally drives her from her hiding place and she is found by the Clan woman, Iza. The woman rescues the child.

Iza belongs to the Clan, a group of humans that are looking for a place to live after the earthquake had destroyed their home too. Brun, the leader, is worried that the spirits are angry with him. After several weeks, Brun decides that they should turn back. Just before he makes this announcement, Iza tells him that Ayla has found a home for the group. The new cave is large and convenient in terms of water, weather, and food sources.

Brun decides to let the oldest son of his mate, Broud, join in the hunt for the first time. The successful hunt allows Broud to become a man and allows the Clan to move into the cave. However, Broud must share his coming-of-age ceremony with naming ceremonies for the two Clan infants and Ayla. He is resentful of her presence right away, foreshadowing later problems.

At the ceremony, Iza's brother, Creb, names her as if she were a normal Clan child. Iza is stunned, because this means that Ayla is her daughter. However, Creb goes even further: for her totem, Creb names the Cave Lion one of the most powerful male totems known to the Clan. The people are shocked by the adoption and floored by the totem. Ayla has become Clan and it is Creb's and Iza's responsibility to train her to be a good Clan woman.

Part II

After the disastrous Cave ceremony, life begins to settle down for the Clan. With great difficulty, Ayla learns to speak in the Clan hand gestures and stops making most sounds. Besides communication, Ayla has other problems. She stares into the hearth areas of other families and at men (strictly forbidden). She runs and does not show the proper fear of men, especially Broud. Creb and Iza are very concerned about Ayla's future with the Clan. Ayla slowly begins to understand the ways of her new people—but she is still the outsider, the strange one.

Iza gives birth to a daughter named Uba. Since Uba was not a boy, Iza could stay at her brother's hearth and raise her two girls. Ayla loves her little sister; always treated as an outsider, now she has a companion and friend. As she grows, she develops an interest in healing from her mother. This causes some concern at first, but the Clan soon accepts Ayla's strange healing nature.

While out gathering wild cherry bark one day, Ayla watches the men practice hunting. An old hunter is trying to teach a young boy how to hunt with a sling, a difficult task for Clan men since they cannot fully rotate their arms. In fact, Broud cannot work the slingshot well, which pleases Ayla. After the men abandon the practice area Ayla goes and picks up the discarded sling. Slowly, she teaches herself how to use the weapon and she develops an excellent shot.

Once when she is not as attentive as she should have been, Broud beats her to a bloody pulp. He is punished and, for a time, Ayla becomes more arrogant and disrespectful. When she realizes that the Clan was going to let Broud beat her when they felt she needed it, Ayla's fear turns to rage and she kills a porcupine. In that moment, Ayla feels power and regret. Ayla becomes determined to behave in proper Clan manner. All through that winter she works as hard as she can to be the ideal Clan woman. After the winter, Ayla decides to hunt predators, since she could not help her Clan any other way. She even develops a double-loading system for the sling that makes her a much more deadly hunter.

Part III

By the time Ayla is nine years old, she has become accepted by many members of the Clan as a medicine woman in training and as a good luck charm. Ayla's role in helping her people grows with each major event. First, she heals Brun's burned arm with snow, an action Iza would not have thought of. Second, she saves Ona from drowning when the Clan is out catching sturgeon.

Yet her most impressive act is when she saves Braec, Broud's son, from a hyena during the mammoth hunt. Without even realizing what she has

done, Ayla kills the hyena with a quick fire from her sling. She kills the animal before Broud and the other hunters can even react. For saving Braec's life, Ayla is condemned to death for one month. Ayla's death sentence forces Creb and Iza to destroy all of her possessions and she is traumatized. For several days she really believes that she is dead, but she clings to Brun's words that she can return in a month. Ayla makes sure she will survive to return.

After she returns from the dead, Ayla's status in the Clan is even higher. Broud cannot stand that Ayla has yet again stolen the spotlight from him. She is even allowed to hunt, much to Broud's displeasure. This is when he decides to start sexually assaulting her. Within Clan culture, Ayla cannot refuse any Clan male; Broud's delight in her hatred and disgust for what he is doing to her only fuels his desire more. She has overcome everything else about him, but her unwilling consent to his sexual assaults only makes them more frequent. Only when she discovers that she is going to have a baby does Ayla become ambivalent to him. He soon stops assaulting her after that.

Ayla's son, Durc, is born after a difficult pregnancy and birth. When the Clan thinks her baby is deformed, she takes her baby and flees. If a baby lives for seven days, then it must be accepted as Clan. Brun does not want a woman to force him to do anything and will kill Ayla and her child when she returns. Ayla finally realizes this and returns early, begging Brun for his forgiveness and mercy on her child. Brun forgives and life returns to normal as the Clan prepares to go to the Great Clan Gathering.

Part IV

The last section of *The Clan of the Cave Bear* describes the Great Clan Meeting and its aftermath. Once every seven years all the Clans in the area get together for a grand festival where they kill a captive Cave Bear raised by the host Clan from a cub as way of communing with the Great Bear Spirit. At these meetings the medicine women of Iza's line prepare a special narcotic drink for the Mog-urs and the other men. However, Iza is too ill to make the journey and the other Clans do not accept Ayla as a woman of Iza's line. It is not until she risks her life to save a young warrior wounded by the angry Cave Bear that the Clans accept her.

She prepares the drink, but accidentally swallows some. The narcotic effects cause Ayla to wander into the cave and observe the men's ceremonies. Particularly damaging is that Ayla, a woman, becomes a witness to the most sacred of all Clan ceremonies. She watches in horror as the Mog-urs eat the brains of the warrior slain by the Cave Bear earlier that night. Creb recognizes her presence and realizes that all the old ways are at an end.

When the Clan returns to the cave, they discover Iza on the verge of death. Ayla frantically tries to save her, but she is too late. At the age of twenty-nine, Iza dies an old woman and is buried inside the cave with the highest Clan honors.

Brun and Creb decide that they are both too old for their jobs and pass them on to a new generation with disastrous consequences. Broud agrees to take Ayla as his second woman, but will not let her keep her son. The Clan is shocked. He then insists that Creb move his hearth to a much colder, windier place in the cave. Although Ayla was able to suppress most of her anger at being separated from her child, she will not let Broud punish Creb. She verbally attacks him and defies his orders. Broud reacts in characteristic anger and orders the new Mog-ur, Groov, to curse Ayla with death. Groov hesitates, but complies.

At that moment the earth begins to shake much like it did at the beginning of the novel. Ayla is cursed and the cave is destroyed. Creb is found dead lying over Iza's grave. Ayla slowly and calmly packs her belongings to leave forever after she has Brun's and Uba's promises to take care of Durc. Ayla's last act is to force Broud to acknowledge her presence even though she is dead. Ayla leaves the Clan.

Characters

Ayla

The Clan of the Cave Bear chronicles the early life of Ayla. As a young Cro-Magnon girl, Ayla's parents are killed in an earthquake at the beginning of the novel when she was just five years of age. She is rescued by Iza, the Clan's medicine woman, and she is brought into the Clan. However, Ayla is uncomfortable with the rules and customs of her adopted people and she makes a series of costly mistakes that eventually lead to her exile.

Ayla is adopted by The Clan and trained by Iza to be a medicine woman. This is difficult for Ayla, but she has a quick mind and a natural curiosity. She teaches herself to hunt with a sling

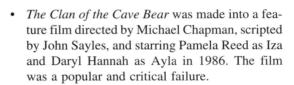

Media Adaptations

- *The Clan of the Cave Bear* was made into a feature film directed by Michael Chapman, scripted by John Sayles, and starring Pamela Reed as Iza and Daryl Hannah as Ayla in 1986. The film was a popular and critical failure.

(hunting is forbidden to Clan women) and only hunts predators since she could not bring her kills back to the cave. When she saves the life of Broud's child on the mammoth hunt, she is cursed with death for a month. Ayla survives this exile and earns the respect of The Clan. Her return confirms to Iza, Creb, and Brun that she is protected by her Cave Lion totem and is lucky for the Clan. However, her accomplishment only increases Broud's irrational hatred for her. At the end, Ayla is exiled from the Clan, but she leaves in peace because she knows that she doesn't belong there.

Broud

Broud is the son of Brun's mate, Ebe, and is therefore destined to become the next leader of The Clan. He is also shallow, vain, egotistical, impatient, and illogical. Yet he is a brilliant dancer, a fearless hunter, and a great storyteller. His resentment of Ayla begins early on, and grows stronger as they grow up; he resents her strength, resourcefulness, and the fact that she does not respect him. His obsessive anger toward Ayla is the driving force of the novel; he progresses from verbal abuse to physical beatings and finally to sexual assault. It is only when Ayla discovers that she is pregnant and no longer cares if Broud "relieves his needs" that his daily rapings of her stop.

After he becomes leader he is even more tyrannical with Ayla. Since she has no mate, Broud agrees to take her as his second mate, but will not allow her to keep her son. He also insists that Creb leave his comfortable place in the cave to a colder, more exposed area. Ayla attacks him and he curses her with death. At that moment, an earthquake destroys the cave and The Clan must wander once more.

Brun

Brun is the leader of The Clan. He is a very traditional ruler and does not like to upset the old ways. However, he is very concerned about doing whatever is necessary to help his people survive. His only blind spot is for Broud. He knows that Broud is a vain, selfish boy—but Brun cannot bring himself to break the tradition of giving power to the son of his mate. However, he does realize the mistake he has made after Broud has sentenced Ayla to permanent death. By the end of the novel Brun is the only "old" one left.

Creb

Creb (also known as The Mog-Ur) is a great holy man and a respected member of the Clan. He is the brother of Brun and Iza. Born deformed, Creb was later horribly scarred in an attack by a cave bear. This attack cost him his right eye and heightened his ability to speak to and interpret the sayings of the "spirits": the supernatural entities that The Clan believed surrounded them. Creb's birth defect prevented him from hunting, and so kept him from being a real man in the eyes of his people. He agrees to train Ayla as a good Clan woman once his sister, Iza, has adopted her. He also finds Ayla intriguing because she does not look at him in fear and disgust, but trust and love. Creb feels deeply wounded whenever Ayla is unable or unwilling to conform to the Clan ways.

Creb is not just the holy man of his particular group; he is The Mog-ur, the holiest and most powerful holy man among all the clans of his species. He believes that his species has reached the height of their evolution and will soon die out. He realizes that Ayla's half-breed son, Durc, will be the salvation of his people and their kind. Creb also shows touching devotion to Iza and finally dies during the second earthquake on top of her grave.

Durc

Durc is Ayla's son. Born when his mother was only eleven years of age, he is half Neanderthal and half Cro-Magnon. The Clan decides that he is deformed and must die, but Ayla forces the Clan to accept him by hiding for seven days. Creb realizes that Durc is the future of the Clan people and during Iza's final illness, he becomes the child of the entire Clan.

Iza

Iza is Ayla's adopted mother and the sister of both Creb and Brun. She is also the greatest medicine woman of the entire species, her status being handed down in an unbroken chain from mother to daughter for countless generations. It is Iza who discovers a starved, scared, half-dead, five year-old Ayla and nurses her back to health. She also decides to train Ayla as a medicine woman. After the earthquake that kills her mate, Iza sets up a hearth with her brother, Creb, and raises Ayla and her biological daughter, Uba, as sisters. Her final illness and death devastate Ayla.

The Mog-ur

See Creb

Uba

Uba is Iza's biological daughter and Ayla's adopted sister. She and Ayla are devoted to each other and she silently agrees to raise Durc when Ayla is cursed with death at the end of the novel.

Themes

Nature versus Nurture

One of the most prevalent themes in *The Clan of the Cave Bear* is the idea of "nature versus nurture"; in other words, is the way one behaves more controlled by genetics or environment? Auel insists that The Clan survives only by following the traditional rules and gender roles to the point where they have become incapable of change and cannot adapt to new situations. For example, Clan women do not hunt simply because women do not hunt: they do not *want* to hunt. She also describes the Clan woman as naturally submissive and physically unable to learn new things.

Ayla's presence forces the Clan to question their society and their traditions. Ayla seems driven to rebel against the Clan's traditions because she cannot logically understand them. Although she behaves as a model Clan woman, there is a bounce to her step and a refusal to bend her will to the patriarchal culture. Although the Clan punishes her for her transgressions, other Clan women see that a female *can* hunt, heal, and can stand up to abuse and exploitation. Therefore, because she represents such a danger to the patriarchal Clan structure, she is exiled at the end of the novel.

Individual and Society

Ayla's inability to assimilate into Clan society exposes another of Auel's themes: what happens to the wants and desires of the individual when those wants and desires clash with the needs of the individual's society? Ayla wants love from Creb and Iza and acceptance from the Clan, yet her individual needs to be free, to think, to experience life, and to wander alone are incompatible with the Clan's need to control all of its members for the good of the community. Ayla is beaten, raped, and cursed because she puts her own feelings and the needs of the individuals in her life above the needs of the community for order and harmony.

Auel is directly criticizing contemporary American society which, on the one hand, champions the rights of the individual and yet culturally teaches citizens to be obedient and law-abiding. This conflict between the individual and societal needs is clearly defined by the character of Broud. Broud is driven by revenge and does not think about the good of his community or the individuals that make up that community. In the end, he drives out a gifted medicine woman and brings down the retribution of the spirits who destroy the cave, killing Creb and forcing Broud's people to become wanderers again.

Cultural Stagnation Equals Extinction

Arguably the most problematic part of Auel's novel is her creation of Neanderthal culture. Most anthropologists would argue that Auel's science is weak and inaccurate. There is no scientific evidence that the Neanderthal were bowlegged, that they did not have a full range of motion in their arms, or that they could not speak, cry, or laugh. These are all ideas that Auel created out of thin air. She then uses these reasons to explain why the Neanderthal died out. She suggests that cultural stagnation—the inability of a people to change and adapt—leads to extinction. Auel's narrator insists that the Clan cannot learn anything new because their brains would then have to get bigger, making childbirth more dangerous. She also suggests that because the Clan people cannot share domestic tasks or develop new inventions or new ways of hunting their society will die.

This is Auel's perception of American culture in the mid-1970s. Failed economic plans, social agendas, and cultural ideology that refused to change had led the country into double-digit inflation and record high unemployment. Using the Clan as a metaphor, Auel is maintaining that American society must be flexible and welcome new influences in order to survive and prosper in the future.

Problems with Patriarchy

For many readers, the strict gender roles of the Clan are puzzling and offensive. Writing at the

Topics for Further Study

- Research the anthropological and archeological evidence about the origins and the extinction of the Neanderthals and compare the scientific evidence with the way Auel portrays the Clan's physical and cultural appearance. Is Auel's portrayal accurate?

- After investigating different kinds of religious ceremonies, including ritual cannibalism and Native-American ceremonies, compare these religions to those Auel describes in her novels.

- Using contemporary feminist literary theory, discuss Ayla as a feminist heroine.

- Auel provides a considerable amount of technical material in *The Clan of the Cave Bear* about flint-knapping, arrowhead making, medicinal plants, and leather tanning. After trying out Auel's directions, describe the experience. Were the directions easy and accurate?

height of the feminist movement, Auel explores the problems associated with a male-dominated culture. Patriarchy leads to a host of social and political problems in any society and it is these problems that Auel wants to expose through her fiction. For example, the Clan women have no rights, no say in the power structure, and must be completely subservient to men in all ways.

Broud epitomizes the dangers of a patriarchal culture. He is so out of control that he beats Ayla almost to death and brutally rapes her on a daily basis for months afterwards. The physical and sexual violence that permeates the Clan social structure contribute as much to their extinction as does their cultural stagnation. In a bizarre twist, Auel makes the two truly good men—Creb and his trainee—Groov, sterile. Broud has three sons and a daughter by the end of the novel. However, the extremes of patriarchal culture eventually leads to the destruction of the cave and the displacing of Broud's people.

Style

Point of View

The Clan of the Cave Bear uses a third-person, omniscient narrator to explain Ayla's difficulties in assimilating into her adopted culture. The readers know exactly what is going to happen before the characters do. Because Broud's jealous feelings and Ayla's bewildered compliance are clearly drawn by the narrator, Ayla's exile from the Clan is inevitable from the moment she received her totem and stole Broud's thunder. The narration is so heavy-handed and thorough that it drains the novel of any dramatic irony or suspense. This point of view also allows Auel to develop fully her fictional ideas about Clan culture and to overload the reader with information on flint-knapping, medicinal plants, and hunting techniques. The narrator often intrudes into the novel with sociological tangents on why the Neanderthal people died out.

Symbolism

Auel uses symbolism in two major ways: the spirit/totem world and traditional epic conventions. The Clan worships a collection of invisible spirits who inhabit the natural world and can cause illness, death, and bad luck if they are angered or ignored. These spirits generally take the form of totems or animal guides. Each Clan member is given a totem at his/her naming ceremony; the symbol for these totems are painted onto the infant's skin with a paste made of powdered red stone and bear fat. Later, when a boy becomes a man, the symbol of his totem is carved into his chest with a sharp stone knife. When women find mates, their man's totem symbols are painted over their own in a yellow paste. This process obviously symbolizes the dominance of the male over the female and the subsequent loss of identity of the female in the mating process.

In addition to the idea of totems and spirits, Auel also uses more traditional literary symbols from Biblical and epic literature. Ayla represents many different literary types. Not only is she the Eve figure whose actions, according to Broud and Creb, would cause the end of the Clan, she is also a Virgin Mary figure who gives birth to the savior of the Clan, i.e. Durc. Compounded with this image is the image of Christ returning from the dead and being forever changed. When Ayla returns from her one-month death sentence, she becomes "She Who Hunts." Like the great epic heroes Achilles, Beowulf, and Ulysses, Ayla represents the only force that can save the Clan—but only

through her self-sacrifice and exile. Auel cleverly combines these images to give her fiction depth and meaning.

Setting

Auel has stated in several interviews that she started writing about prehistoric peoples because it was a place and time that did not get much literary attention. Her story is set on the shores of the Black Sea roughly 25,000 years ago. However, she is forced to describe plants, animals, and land formations as they are currently known so that readers would have some idea what she is talking about. Many of the plants that she describes in meticulous detail are modern and there is no physical evidence that they existed then.

The harsh realities of the time provide much of the novel's energy. The need for community, safety, and traditions are essential for survival, so Ayla's behavior threatens the Clan in ways that a modern heroine could not. At the same time, Ayla's ability to innovate and adapt shows that humans are still evolving. Most of Ayla's inventions and discoveries are only significant because no one has ever thought of them before.

Ancient Science Fiction

No one can read Auel's novel without being amazed at her copious and thorough research. However, Auel's information is not always accurate and the line between the physical evidence and her own creations is blurred. Auel does a remarkable job of incorporating some anthropological evidence and should be credited with sparking people's interest in prehistoric peoples. However, she has a tendency to "core dump": when an author goes into vivid detail of some scientific or technical operation that has little or nothing to do with plot or character development. Most of Auel's descriptions of flint-knapping, medicine production, plant gathering, and butchering of game does not have any real relevance to the novel as a whole. Although *The Clan of the Cave Bear* does not fit the usual description of science fiction, Auel's use of modern plants, her blurring of fact and theory, and her tendency to core-dump show that the novel bears all the usual traits of a first-time science fiction novel.

Historical Context

What Happened to the Neanderthals

Perhaps the people most frustrated with the commercial success of *The Clan of the Cave Bear* are anthropologists and archaeologists. The problems revolve around Auel's physical descriptions of the Clan—whom she never calls Neanderthals—and her wholesale creation of their culture. While the theories surrounding the disappearance of Neanderthal peoples from Europe and Asia are still the subject of much scholarly debate, the vast majority of anthropologists and archaeologists agree (and agreed even at the time Auel was doing her research for the novel) that there was not an exaggerated physical difference between Neanderthal and modern humans.

William Straus and A. J. E. Cave stated in 1957 that "If [Neanderthal Man] could be reincarnated and placed in a New York subway—provided that he were bathed, shaved, and dressed in modern clothing—it is doubtful whether he would attract any more attention" than anyone else. In fact, the image of a hairy, bent-over, brutal race of cave dwellers is more a creation of Hollywood and a few nineteenth-century French anthropologists than any modern science.

For example, Auel describes the Clan as having bowed legs and arms, brown shaggy hair, and dark eyes. Quite a number of Neanderthal skeletons have been found and only a few have the bowed limbs as Auel described them, suggesting that this was a vitamin deficiency (rickets) rather than something common to the species. She also suggests that Clan members are old by the time they are thirty years of age, yet the majority of Neanderthal adult skeletons are adults in their fifties and sixties. Auel buys into Hollywood and the racist stereotypes when she portrays the Clan as a dark-haired, dark-eyed people—when there is no physical evidence for either their hair or eye color. The same goes for their inability to laugh, cry, or speak.

Cultural Problems

However problematic her science is, Auel's real problems with anthropologists and social scientists come from her fabrication of Neanderthal culture. The problem is not that she creates a culture for these people, but that she does not make it clear where fact ends and her theories begin. Cultural anthropologists particularly object to the brutal nature of the Clan—especially since there is no evidence for it. They also object to the almost absurd theory that the Neanderthal race died out because their brains were wired to remember the past rather than plan for the future. The reason for the criticism is that while Auel does not claim that her fiction is true, it is usually the only exposure most people have to prehistoric peoples and so her dis-

tortion of scientific evidence and wholesale fabrication leaves many scientists cold. While most critics will admit that she did a considerable amount of research, many anthropologists and archeologists would argue that her research is shoddy and culturally biased.

Racial Issues

Many people find the overt racism in *The Clan of the Cave Bear* unsettling. The Clan, comprised of Neanderthals, is described as primitive, dark, and without the ability to laugh or to cry. The Others—comprised of Cro-Magnon, the modern humans—as characterized by Ayla, are blond, blue-eyed, white-skinned, and beautiful. Even though the Clan thinks Ayla is ugly, the narrator lets the readers know that Ayla is an extraordinarily beautiful woman by Western standards. Auel says that she wanted to create a character that looks like "us" being raised in a completely alien environment. However, by casting her novel as stories about the earliest people, Auel seems to be suggesting that only blond, blue-eyed Aryan Euro-Americans can be "us."

The Feminist Movement

On a positive note, most critics applaud Auel's creation of a strong female character at a time when American culture was looking for female heroes. The women's movement grew in earnest in the 1970s on the heels of the Civil Rights movement. Issues such as reproductive rights, equal pay for equal work, sexual harassment, and gender discrimination became part of the national debate. The Equal Rights Amendment showed signs of passage and many women joined the workforce in high-profile professional positions.

By 1980, with films like *9 to 5* and *Norma Rae,* a novel about a prehistoric female hero seemed quite logical. Auel uses Ayla to show contemporary Americans that a society that insists on subordination of one gender cannot survive. While many histories of prehistoric peoples focus on the accomplishments of the male half of the species, Auel tries to show how important women's contribution to survival was. Even though she has her hero banished at the end of the novel, Auel does not end Ayla's story there. Instead it is the repressive society of the Clan that is not heard from again in any of the other novels.

Critical Overview

Jean Auel's novels have met with much popular success. Yet most literary critics and scholars

Daryl Hannah as Ayla, Rory L. Crowley as Durc, and Pamela Reed as Iza in the 1986 film version of the novel.

have problems with her work on several different levels. Some reviewers find her work lightweight in terms of character, plot, and style. In addition, many popular culture scholars, who seem to be the only ones who will address Auel's work directly, find her foreshadowing heavy-handed and boring.

There are similar problems with her mixture of fact and fiction. Lindsay Van Gelder questions Auel's commitment to both feminism and racial equality. She is particularly troubled with the idea that boys become men when they do something (hunt) yet girls do not become women until something is done to them (menstruation begins for Clan women and lose of virginity for Other women). Bernard Gallagher also suggests that Auel failed to create a truly feminist female hero because she allowed the Clan to break and destroy her. Clyde Wilcox contends that Auel's feminism does not fail outright nor along the lines Gallagher describes, because Auel is looking at a bigger picture than just one girl in one unhappy situation.

Many of the standard anthropology works published after 1980 address *The Clan of the Cave Bear.* James Shreeve mentions Auel's novel in the introduction to *The Neanderthal Enigma,* but he does not go into specifics. He does refute many of

the scientific and cultural claims Auel makes about Neanderthal and Cro-Magnon society.

Other anthropologists do give Auel credit for increasing the popularity of prehistoric peoples, particularly woman. However, some cringe at the Hollywood overtones in the novel. For example, the Clan wears animal hide wraps that have no form of sewing or weaving in them. Yet, as Elizabeth Wayland Barber asserts, woven textiles have been found in salt mines that date to the periods that Auel is writing about. Other archeologists and anthropologists have found evidence of domesticated animals and woven textiles thousands of years older than Auel's Clan. Olga Soffer says that the old way of looking at prehistoric cultures has changed since the early 1980s, and suggests that the type of fiction Auel writes might be an influence.

There are times that Auel seems to outguess the scientists. In 1998, researchers suggested that, according to DNA evidence, the Neanderthal race did not contribute to modern human genetics and therefore are not related to modern humans in any real way. Not five months later, archeologists made two discoveries: one, a child's skeleton that had both Neanderthal features and Cro-Magnon features (much like Durc in the novel) and two, that

Neanderthals and Cro-Magnons coexisted in Europe for over 10,000 years. The evidence of interbreeding between the human species was not available to Auel in the 1970s—she made it up. As Wilcox suggests, Auel is much more interested in exploring contemporary society than accurately investigating prehistoric cultures.

There is no dismissing the popular appeal of *The Clan of The Cave Bear*. It sold over one-hundred-thousand copies in its first three months. Auel's popularity, particularly among women, has grown in the years since the first novel's publication.

Criticism

Michael Rex

Rex is an adjunct professor at the University of Detroit Mercy. In the following essay, he explores how the social structure of The Clan of the Cave Bear *reflects Auel's concerns for contemporary American society.*

Jean Auel's *The Clan of the Cave Bear* has been embraced as the most popular work of prehistoric fiction in American culture. Readers love getting caught up in the story of Ayla and how she tries to be true to herself and yet fit into the new culture. Many people see the novel as a possible, if not probable, depiction of life in the world of the Neanderthal. However, Auel creates the vast majority of Clan culture on no actual evidence. Instead, she creates a culture that is very much like the American society that Auel saw around her with a healthy dash of high Victorian culture mixed in with it. Auel does not really care about "truth" or accuracy in the way she is constructing Neanderthal culture. She is using the mask of this culture to critique how Americans in the late 1970s view religion, sex, and family.

Religion has always had a large influence on American culture. The pilgrims, who left England due to religious persecution, are celebrated every year at Thanksgiving. Alfred Smith lost the presidency in the 1920s because he was Catholic, while John F. Kennedy had to promise the American people that he would not "obey" the pope if he was elected. The Pledge of Allegiance says that America is "one Nation under God." However, our culture has inherited some interesting religious biases that Auel chooses to attack in her creation of religion in this novel; primarily the religious structure,

> *Auel does not really care about 'truth' or accuracy in the way she is constructing Neanderthal culture. She is using the mask of this culture to critique how Americans in the late 1970s view religion, sex, and family."*

the ceremonies, and the lack of participation by women.

The structure of the Clan's religion is highly illogical and tends to be more threatening than comforting. Clan members are not faithful because the spirits are good to them, generally they are faithful out of fear. Auel is drawing a direct parallel between this religious structure and contemporary religions that use fear and punishment as ways to coerce the behavior of the faithful. This idea can be seen in descriptions of Hell as a place of everlasting torment. Brun makes it very clear that he does not understand the world of the spirits, but he fears them. Creb can "talk" to the spirits during self-induced hypnotic states or during a hallucinogenic drug haze. In the Clan only men are allowed to participate in religion and so the religion tends toward violence and fear.

This tendency becomes evident in the ceremonies Auel describes in the novel. The first ceremony readers see is when the Clan is still wandering and the men have separated themselves from the women and children. They do this for a specific purpose. The ceremony is based on the men begging and pleading with the spirits, exposing how weak and vulnerable humans really are. The men cannot allow women to see this ceremony because it would threaten the male dominance if women realized that men were not in control all of the time.

This is a direct attack on American social structure. Auel suggests that American men are so threatened by the power of women in the workforce and the church that they must continue discrimination against women as a method of control. The segregated ceremonies continue to grow in dis-

What Do I Read Next?

- *The Valley of the Horses* is the 1982 sequel to *The Clan of the Cave Bear*. The story follows Ayla after she leaves the Clan. Auel's second sequel, *The Mammoth Hunters,* was published in 1985. This novel deals much more with the interpersonal relationships than any technical information or physical and cultural descriptions. *The Plains of Passage* (1990) is the next book in the series.

- Naomi Miller Stokes brings Native-American legends into the modern era in her 1996 novel, *The Tree People.* Jordan Tidewater, a Native-American sheriff in Oregon, must solve a bizarre string of murders that seems to involve the spirit of an evil shaman buried alive one thousand years ago.

- *The People of Wolf* and its five sequels, written by W. Michael Gear and Kathleen O'Neale Gear, trace the history of the first Americans who follow a young warrior inspired by the spirit of the wolf. Many reviewers rate it as high or higher than Auel's series.

- *Introducing Anthropology,* edited by James Hayes and James Henslin (1975), is a standard collection of essays on anthropology as a science and cultural activity. The readings include essays by Margaret Mead, George Gaylord Simpson, Robert Adams, and Dorothy Lee.

- James Shreeve's *The Neanderthal Enigma* (1996) is a remarkably readable history of the Neanderthal people. Shreeve makes use of the latest research and presents many of the problems readers have with the image of the Neanderthal as created by Hollywood and writers like Auel. The book includes pictures and drawings of actual Neanderthal artifacts.

---

crimination and brutality throughout the novel: children are not named by their parents, but by the Mog-ur, and the Manhood ceremony involves the Mog-ur carving the boy's totem symbol into his chest with a knife; the Womanhood ceremony involves the girl being exiled from the Clan and spending at least seven days completely alone; and the mating ceremony involves the male's totem symbol being painted over the woman's, thus erasing her spiritual identity.

This violence and brutality culminates in the festivities at the Great Clan Gathering. Here, Auel is attacking contemporary Christianity in rather gross ways. First, the Cave Bear cub symbolizes the Supreme Deity on earth much like Christ did. The Cave Bear has been tamed and raised by the host Clan until he is friendly and loving. Then the Clan turns on him, attacking him with spears and killing him. The people then drink the bear's blood and eat the bear's flesh in a direct parallel to the Christian communion. Of course, Auel takes the idea of communion one step further as she has the Mog-urs eat the brains of the warrior killed during the attack on the pet bear. All of these ceremonies serve as ways for Auel to demonstrate that contemporary religions are based on fear, violence, and domination over women.

The absence of women in the religion of the Clan is perhaps the most striking aspect and the most neglected one. Both the Roman Catholic Church and the Southern Baptist Church, the two largest denominations in America, refuse to make women priests/preachers and insist on a subservient and almost nonexistent role for women in their religious services. Therefore, Auel's elimination of women from the Clan's religious life can be seen as a criticism of this aspect of modern Christianity.

However, the Clan does not allow women to participate in religion out of a need for domination, but out of fear of losing that domination. Creb remembers a time when women were allowed to participate, but it was so long ago and the Clan has changed so much that men would lose their power over women. Moreover, the spirits are all male. There is no spirit that women can pray to because women are not to speak to men until spoken to.

Again, this idea parallels the modern conception of God as male. However, by making the Clan religion male-based as well, Auel is rejecting contemporary religion. She seems to be suggesting that religions that are based on fear, violence, and domination of one gender over the other are unsuccessful, unsatisfying, and ultimately self-destructive.

In addition to critiquing American views of religion, Auel uses *The Clan of the Cave Bear* to attack American attitudes toward sex and reproduction. She creates the Clan as a people who, like many early peoples, do not understand the relationship between sex and pregnancy. For the Clan, pregnancy occurs when a woman's totem has been defeated by a man's totem. So, even in the creation of new life, the Clan is based on violence. Sex is not something that builds intimacy between hearth mates, nor is it described as something pleasurable. Sex is something women must endure and men use to "relieve their needs."

Auel's description of sexual activity attacks the stereotypical attitudes toward sex in the late 1970s and early 1980s. While the country was dancing to disco music and the sexual revolution was still going strong, the national attitudes toward sex continued to be defined by men: sex was for men's benefit and men's pleasure. Women were still conceived of as baby producers and male playthings. This is the image of female-male relationships that Auel wants to challenge.

By making Broud's sexual advances toward Ayla attacks, she shows the reader that cultural attitudes about sex have not changed. In a male-dominated society, women cannot be raped because the crime does not exist. In the Clan, any man can have sex with any woman at any time; she has no say in the matter. Sex is also performed in only one position—the woman on her hands and knees with the man coming from behind her. There is no face-to-face contact, no closeness. Sex, for the Clan, has no spiritual or emotional elements. Auel uses the sexual attitudes of the Clan to attack American attitudes toward sex, women, and the family.

Auel saves her strongest criticism for American attitudes toward the family. Although she is writing about a people who lived roughly 25,000 years ago, Auel still has them living in a modern nuclear family structure of dominate male, submissive female, and children. The gender discrimination as well as the analogy to American society is quite clear. The hearth or house belongs to the male; the female must cook, clean, and maintain the hearth, but she has no ownership in it. Women also have no choice in selecting their mates. Instead, the leader, the ultimate "father," selects a man for her. Again, she has no choice in the matter.

The mating ceremony reads almost like a modern wedding: the ceremony is held in public, the Mog-ur asks the man if he accepts the woman, and then he erases the woman's identity by drawing the totem symbol of her mate over the tattoo of her own totem symbol. The parallel between this ceremony and modern American marriage where a woman goes from being Jane Doe to Mrs. John Smith is absolutely clear. Women lose their identity in marriage. Auel argues that this is an outgrowth of a repressive, regressive, and failing social system.

The contributions of the Clan women are also generally ignored by the Clan men. Auel makes her readers aware of just how important the women's work in terms of food, clothing, and tool production is—but the Clan men do not recognize it. This is often the case in American culture as well. A housewife is defined as a woman who does not work—yet it is very expensive to hire someone to clean, cook, do the grocery shopping, and errand running that housewives are expected to do. Again Auel is attacking male cultural attitudes about the contributions and duties of women.

Even though only women can give birth, this does not give them power within the Clan. When Iza gives birth, Eba regrets that the child is a girl when she gives Brun the news. Likewise, the women are shocked that Iza asked for a girl. Whether a child lives or dies is not up to the women either. In Clan society, the men get together and "vote" on whether the child is normal or deformed. A mother can beg for the life of her child, but she has no assurance that the leader will grant her request. Another parallel to American culture is the stigma of an illegitimate birth. Ayla is not mated when she gives birth to Durc and this causes some unrest among the Clan. Children born out of wedlock are not as accepted as those who are—yet Durc will be the savior of his race.

In terms of the domestic situations of the Clan, Auel paints a rather conservative, traditional picture. Their religion, use of sex, and the family structures all bear marked resemblance to contemporary American cultural institutions. By using these structures, Auel is attacking the sexist nature of American culture. The Clan, although interesting, is ultimately unsuccessful and doomed to extinction. This rigid system of gender discrimination, religious fear, and separation of domestic tasks is what ultimately destroys the Clan. A society that is so biased toward one gender cannot survive, no matter how many generations it goes through. Auel's final statement in *The Clan of the Cave Bear* is a warning to American society that if it continues to subordinate women and ignore their spiritual, sexual, and familial needs, American culture will be just as dead as the Clan. Extinction will only be a matter of "when," no longer a question of "if."

Source: Michael Rex, in an essay for *Novels for Students,* Gale Group, 2001.

Clyde Wilcox

In the following essay, Wilcox argues that Auel's works can be considered feminist.

The Clan of the Cave Bear and the three other novels in Jean Auel's Earth's Children series are surprising best-sellers. They blend carefully researched and detailed accounts of the making of flint tools, the construction of lodges from mammoth bones, and the flora and fauna of Europe during the last Ice Age with an almost soap-opera account of the life of a blond, blue-eyed woman named Ayla. Orphaned by an earthquake at an early age, Ayla was raised by a clan of Neanderthals, who teach her to be a healer. When Ayla continues to violate clan taboos, she is exiled, where she meets another Cro-Magnon man and begins a long journey to what is now Eastern Europe to visit his home.

Recently, Bernard Gallagher has argued that *The Clan of the Cave Bear* constitutes a failed feminist novel. He reports that he initially regarded the novel as a real triumph but is now disappointed in the book. He graciously notes that he is "not suggesting, now, that Auel rewrite the ending to her novel" that sold millions of copies, inspired a rather awful film, and has led to the publication of additional books in the series. But he does suggest that the book reflects the view that relations between the sexes are "a matter of either/or. Either men are dominant or women are dominant." He sees the book primarily as a tale of the conflict between an independent and talented woman and a patriarchal culture that reviles her, yet he argues that the book contains certain elements that prevent it from fitting a feminist category.

I think that Gallagher is too hard on this novel, and that perhaps a reconsideration will enable him to again think of Auel's work as truly feminist. I will suggest that Auel's work must be considered in a wider context—that of the types of humans of which she writes, and that of the other novels in the series. Within that broader context, Auel's work can be considered feminist. Of course, there are a wide variety of feminist theories and approaches (Pateman and Gross). Auel's feminism might be described as one that entails equality of access to political power and occupations, and a blending of gender roles.

Gallagher is correct that Auel depicts women of the Neanderthal clan as quite subservient to men. Indeed, a woman of the Clan must kneel before a man and wait for a signal before she speaks, and must allow any man who wishes, to "relieve his needs" with her. Yet it is not the sexism of the Neanderthals that troubles Gallagher, for he finds Auel's account of the sexism embedded in Clan customs and language to be a truly feminist critique. Rather he makes three arguments. First, in the battle between the sexes, Ayla is given a weak and unworthy opponent. Second, Ayla is described as a classic blond-haired beauty. Finally, the novel ends with the banishment of Ayla for violating tribal taboos.

Let us consider the ending of *The Clan of the Cave Bear,* in which Ayla is banished by the new leader of the Clan. Throughout the novel, Ayla is unable to always behave in the subservient way that Neanderthal men expect. Although only Neanderthal men are allowed to hunt, Ayla teaches herself to hunt, and invents a method of using a sling that is better than that of any man. When she gives birth to a half-Neanderthal, half-Cro-Magnon child, she refuses to obey an order by the Clan leader to let it die (for it appears initially deformed because of the mixed traits of the two human species). Each of these acts leads to some sort of penalty, including a temporary banishment. Finally, she violates the order of the Clan leader and rushes to the aid of a dying man, and this leads to her final banishment and a declaration that she is "dead."

Gallagher correctly notes that Ayla's independence has led her to banishment, and to her separation from her son. He concludes that "the novel seems to suggest that male-female relationships, by their nature, involve a struggle for power that never ends, a struggle in which someone must be the slave and someone must be the master." And the message seems to be that women who seek to become the master are ultimately cut off from society.

Yet Gallagher misses one important point—this is also a clash between Cro-Magnons and Neanderthals. Gallagher notes that Auel paints a physical picture of Neanderthals that is a bit more primitive than many current anthropologists would support. Yet he ignores one other fictional characteristic of the Neanderthals—the one that is most clearly an invention of Auel. Auel exaggerates the differences between Neanderthal and Cro-Magnon skulls, where the Neanderthal had a smaller frontal lobe but an enlarged rear portion of the brain. From this, she posits the existence of a racial memory that almost dictates the actions of Neanderthals. Early in the novel, she notes that this memory had served the Neanderthals well as the ice advanced and retreated, for they could recall from an earlier period whether new vegetation was poisonous or good to eat. When confronted with a seemingly new situation that an ancestor had encountered before, a Neanderthal would simply remember the course of action that had worked in the past. Most surprising is that these memories are sex specific. Auel writes that Memories in Clan people were sex differentiated. Women had no more need of hunting lore than men had of more than rudimentary knowledge of plants. The difference in the brains of men and women was imposed by nature, and only cemented by culture. It was another of nature's attempts to limit the size of their brains in an effort to prolong the race.

These racial memories were associated with an inability to rapidly adjust to new developments. Ayla presented the clan with a challenge, for they could not understand a woman who would hunt. Women of the clan had no interest in, and no facility for, hunting because they lacked the memories. Men were similarly incapable of cooking. Although the notion of a racial memory has no basis in scientific research, the Neanderthals inhabited Europe for 100,000 years but showed no evidence of cultural accumulation—their stone tools did not become more subtle, they persisted in the use of heavy spears for thrusting instead of lighter ones for throwing, and in no Neanderthal site has there been any figurative art.

> They were slow to adapt. Inventions were accidental and often not utilized. . . . Change was accomplished only with great effort. . . . But a race with no room for learning, no room for growth, was no longer equipped for an inherently changing environment.

The Neanderthals are shown as mentally limited. When Creb, the Neanderthal spiritual leader, tries to teach Ayla a few "counting words," he is astonished that she is immediately able to grasp abstract mathematical concepts that are beyond his ability. In another passage, Creb and Ayla explore their common past and different future in a drug-induced journey. Creb sees that his people will be-

> *Auel's feminism might be described as one that entails equality of access to political power and occupations, and a blending of gender roles."*

come extinct, while Ayla's will go on to inherit the earth. Although Creb is portrayed as the most intelligent Neanderthal, Ayla is more mentally agile.

In this light, the unwillingness of the Neanderthals to accommodate Ayla's feminism is a bit more understandable. They are unable to change, and like Topol in *Fiddler on the Roof*, they bend and bend and finally break. Broud, the young leader who ultimately expels Ayla is a twisted, jealous man who had raped her to gain power over her, but the other Neanderthals who go along with the banishment are often portrayed as caring, decent individuals. They also are unable to accept or understand her behavior, for it is beyond their limited cognitive abilities. What we see in this book is not an inevitable war between the sexes, but a war between competing species of humans. Gallagher's first problem with the novel, that Broud was an inadequate foil for Ayla, misses the point. The book is not about Ayla vs. Broud, although this occupies a portion of the novel, but rather about how Neanderthals and Cro-Magnon humans would deal with an entirely new and challenging situation.

The extinction of the Neanderthals remains one of the most interesting mysteries of prehistory. Some have argued that Cro-Magnon humans killed the Neanderthals, others that the superior hunting tools enabled them to kill off some of the game on which the Neanderthals relied. Still other anthropologists have suggested that the Neanderthals and Cro-Magnon peoples interbred, although at least one anthropologist suggests that they would have been unable to produce offspring. Auel seems to suggest that the Neanderthals died out because they were unable to adapt to the end of the Ice Age, because their brains were wired to remember the past and not to plan for the future. Creb and Ayla see that the Cro-Magnon will triumph because of their greater flexibility and adaptability. Auel may be making a more general point that any society that uses past behavior as an invariable guide to present decisions will fail. Auel's novel implies that any society that rejects the innovations of its most creative citizens because of their gender, race or other characteristics, will ultimately perish.

The ending of the book remains a problem, however. Clearly Ayla's banishment is an unhappy event. In a later book she notes that she would have gladly stayed with the Clan as second woman to the jealous leader to be near her son. Is the message of the book that feminism ultimately leads to a loss of family? The last line in *The Clan of the Cave Bear* is a plaintive call of "Maamaaa!" from Ayla's son. No mother or father can read the ending of this book without a pang of sorrow.

To put this in a broader perspective, it is useful to examine the three additional books in the series that have appeared to date. In *The Valley of the Horses,* Ayla lives alone in a valley for three years. During this time, she learns to hunt with a spear, and she domesticates a horse and a cave lion and rides each in the hunt. When her future husband Jondalar suffers a deep thigh gash from her cave lion, she examines the stitching in his garments (Neanderthals did not sew) and threads together his flesh. She learns to speak (Auel depicts Neanderthals as speaking primarily in sign language—a point of some controversy today among anthropologists,) and learns to throw a spear more accurately than Jondalar. Jondalar is described as in a manner much like Ayla—tall, blond-haired, blue-eyed and very attractive. Thus Gallagher's second concern, that Ayla is described as a physical beauty, can be seen in a different light. That Ayla and Jondalar must be Aryan beauties is perhaps a concession to the soap-opera part of Auel's market, but it is not a mark of sexism. Presumably Auel believes it is necessary to have attractive characters to help fuel her somewhat predictable sex scenes in the later novels.

More importantly, Ayla meets many other Cro-Magnon people—who act and think like she does. Thus although Ayla has lost her half-Neanderthal son, she has found people like herself. Jondalar is a feminist ideal man, interested in cooking, anxious to have Ayla help with the hunt, and truly in awe of her abilities. He displays a troubling racism (or speciesism) about the Neanderthals, but he gradually comes to terms with this and accepts the Neanderthals as fully human. Ayla mourns the loss of her son throughout the next two books, although by the end of the fourth novel, she is pregnant again. It appears that the novels in this series are

building to a confrontation between her fully Cro-Magnon child and her half-Neanderthal son in the final book of the series. The banishment of Ayla can be interpreted as a rejection by a society unable to change, but it ultimately leads Ayla into a broader Cro-Magnon society of people who think and act like she does.

Consider Auel's view of gender politics among the Cro-Magnon. In the third novel *The Mammoth Hunters* the pair stay for a time on the plains with a group of Cro-Magnon hunters. This group is part of the Matutoi people, who hunt mammoths. The tribe is ruled by a headman and headwoman, who share equal power and responsibility. Decision-making is by consensus, with everyone taking a chance to speak by holding the speaking stick, and women taking an active role. The larger Matutoi people are governed by a Council of Sisters (made up of the headwomen of the tribes) and a Council of Brothers (made up of the headmen), but the women make the final decision because they are closer to the "Great Mother." All of the Cro-Magnon people encountered in these novels appear to believe in a female deity, and the Danube river is referred to as the Great Mother River.

In the fourth novel, *The Plains of Passage,* Ayla and Jondalar leave the Matutoi and journey toward Jondalar's home. They visit first the Samudoi. Women of the Samudoi take part in tribal decision-making, and men help with the cooking while women help with the hunting.

In this novel, however, is the best evidence for anti-feminism in Auel's writings, for Auel depicts a very disfunctional society ruled by women. Jondalar is captured by the S'Armunai, a tribe in which the headwoman has penned up the men of the tribe in a prison structure. The woman who heads the tribe is mad, and dislocates the legs of young boys as they pass through puberty. She challenges Jondalar to mate with her, and tries to kill him. Yet Ayla rescues him with a perfectly thrown spear. Her domesticated wolf finally kills the demented leader, and the men and women of the tribe cautiously reunite and begin to patch up a relationship.

In some ways, this section reads like a Phyllis Schlafly nightmare. Before Ayla intervenes, the women who rule this tribe torment the men, and all are starving because the entire burden of gathering food has fallen to the women. It is possible to read this story as suggesting the ultimate failure of a society in which women control government power. A more narrow reading might suggest that if angry feminists ever gained power, men would suffer from discrimination, families would be broken, and society would suffer.

Yet there is evidence within this story to suggest that Auel does not intend it as an anti-feminist parable, or at least that she does not mean to imply that a society in which women make the crucial decisions will be disfunctional. Auel does not imply in this section that women are unable to rule, for Jondalar's mother once ruled his tribe, and the Council of Sisters rule the mammoth hunters. Rather, she appears to hold that, like the Neanderthal, the S'Armunai are unable to fully function as a people without the close cooperation of men and women. Jondalar initially is stunned to learn that the tribe would prevent half of its population from helping with the hunting and gathering. Note that Jondalar is unable to free himself, and only Ayla is able to depose the mad ruler, so relief comes from a strong woman, not from a man. Interestingly, the mad woman ruler had been seriously abused by a half-Neanderthal mate, which appears to have caused her mental problems. Auel may intend this section to show that men and women must work together, regardless of previous discrimination, if society is to prosper.

Of course, there are some parts of these four novels that do not strike a consistent feminist theme. We learn that Jondalar's mother voluntarily relinquished her rule of her tribe to her son. Ayla chooses a man to rule the S'Armunai after the death of the mad woman ruler. Ayla follows Jondalar to his home, despite her preference to stay with some of the peoples they visit along the way. These are not utopian novels, and Auel writes for several seemingly distinct audiences. Yet overall, there are obvious elements of an egalitarian feminism in Auel's work.

Throughout these four novels, we see Ayla as a resourceful woman who generally does what she wants. She hunts and heals, combining the traditional masculine with the feminine. Her hunting skills astonish everyone, as do her abilities in medicine. The shamen of the tribes she visits constantly marvel at her spiritual gifts, and she appears to have genuine visions of the future. She is tough but compassionate. She domesticates a horse, a lion and a wolf. She invents surgical stitching, and many other things too numerous to mention. That she is also a beautiful blue-eyed blond does not detract from her feminist credentials.

In the later novels, she frequently confronts adversity from strength. In *The Mammoth Hunters* many Mamutoi at a large gathering of the tribes

muttered among themselves about Ayla's previous ties with the Neanderthals. Indeed, Ayla faces up to this apparently deep-seated speciesism among the Cro-Magnon at every occasion. In this novel, a half-Neanderthal child adopted by the tribe she was visiting came to the meeting, and Ayla let it be known that she had given birth to such a child. When some of the more speciesist members of the Mamutoi want to expel her, the tribe with which she stayed claims her as a member. Yet it is with a show of power that Ayla wins the battle, for she rescues a girl who appears in danger from a cave lion—the one she had domesticated. The muttering is halted when Ayla mounts and rides a lion that is as large as modern horse.

In *The Plains of Passage,* Ayla rescues Jondalar by throwing a spear that cuts the ropes that bind him—an accuracy that is almost impossible. She liberates the people of this tribe when her tame wolf kills the woman who ruled. This is a confrontation between two strong women, and Ayla wins by a real show of strength. Where Ayla left the Neanderthals in defeat, among the Cro-Magnon her drive and skills are amply rewarded. After her victory through the tough use of force, she uses her skills as a healer to begin to rebuild the tribe.

Moreover, Cro-Magnon peoples are shown as generally egalitarian in the sex roles. Jondalar is as interested in cooking as Ayla is in hunting. Women are consistently shown in real decision-making authority. In contrast, the now-extinct Neanderthals are shown as sexist and unable to accept women as equals. Those who are unable to move beyond rigid sex roles are now extinct, while the more flexible Cro-Magnon are our direct ancestors. Overall, this seems a strongly feminist message.

Gallagher can resume his respect for Auel's feminism. Her novels may not portray a prehistoric feminist utopia, but taken in context they have a strongly feminist message. She depicts a pre-history that is perhaps even more egalitarian than our present society, in which men and women must share evenly the burdens and opportunities in order for both to survive.

Source: Clyde Wilcox, "The Not-so-Failed Feminism of Jean Auel," in *Journal of Popular Culture,* Vol. 28, No. 3, Winter 1994, pp. 63–70.

Nicholas O'Connell

In the following interview, Auel discusses the research and development behind her series.

"The Venus of Willendorf," a fertility figurine from the Stone Age. Neanderthal women, having no real understanding of conception, believed the stone figure held the power to impregnate them.

[O'Connell] When you started writing the Earth's Children series, did you have any idea how popular it would become?

[Auel] No. I hoped what every writer hopes: that the first book would find a market and an audience, and maybe the second one would do a little better. That certainly has happened; it just started at a much higher level. The first printing of *The Clan of the Cave Bear* was 75,000 books. And the first printing in hardcover for *The Mammoth Hunters* was a million books. It broke the record. Somebody figured out that that would be a stack of books twenty-nine miles high.

Did you have any model in mind when you wrote these books?

No. I was just trying to write these stories. I'm still writing for myself. I'm writing the story I always wanted to read. As it turns out a whole lot of others want to read it, too. I'm not writing for critics, or to please a teacher or to please the public, or anyone else; I'm writing stories to please myself.

The first rough draft has become an outline for the *Earth's Children* series. That's why I know I'm going to have six books. People think, "She wrote *The Clan of the Cave Bear* and since it was successful, she decided to do a sequel."

But this series is not like *Clan II,* and *Rocky III* and *Jaws IV.* It is a continuation, not a repetition. I won't be telling the same story over and over again. I really did know, before I finished *The Clan of the Cave Bear,* that I had six books in the series.

Do the other books go further into Ayla's life?

All of the books feature Ayla. They are the story of her life. It's not a generational saga, one of those things where you start with the first generation and you end up with the great grandchildren. I'm trying to show the diversity, complexity and sophistication of the various cultures during the Pleistocene. Ayla's story is the thread that ties them together.

Did you base the cave dwelling described in The Clan of the Cave Bear on a particular archeological site?

Not expressly. It's more like a typical site. It was based in many ways on the cave at Shanidar in Iraq on the southern side of the Black Sea, but the setting is in the Crimea on the northern shore of the Black Sea, because there were Neanderthal caves all through that area. It typifies a Neanderthal setting.

How did you become interested in prehistoric people?

[Laughs] I wish I had a wonderful answer for that. Everyone asks, and I don't have an answer. I started out with an idea for a story. I thought it would be a short story. That was in January, 1977. I had quit my job as a credit manager. I had received an M.B.A. in 1976, so I wasn't going to school, and my kids were almost grown. I was in between, not sure what I wanted to do, in a floating state, which I hadn't been in before. I had had a very busy life.

It was eleven o'clock at night. My husband said, "C'mon, let's go to bed." I said, "Wait a minute. I want to see if I can do something."

An idea had been buzzing through my head of a girl or young woman who was living with people who were different. I was thinking prehistory, but I don't know why. I was thinking, "These people were different, but they think she's different." They were viewing her with suspicion, but she was taking care of an old man with a crippled arm, so they let her stay. This was the beginning. That night

I started to write the story. I had never written fiction before. It got to be the wee hours of the morning, I was about ten or twelve pages into it and I decided, "This is kind of fun." Characters, theme and story were starting.

But I was also frustrated because I didn't know what I was writing about. I'd want to describe something and I wouldn't know how or where they lived or what they looked like, what they wore, or what they ate, or if they had fire. I didn't have any sense of the place or the setting. So I thought, "I'll do a little research."

I started out with the Encyclopedia Britannica, and that led to books at the library. I came home with two armloads, and started reading them. I learned that the people we call Cro-Magnon were modern humans. The stereotype of Neanderthal is of a knuckle-dragging ape, but they were Homo sapiens also, quite advanced human beings.

I felt as though I'd made a discovery. "Why don't we know this? Why aren't people writing about our ancestors the way these books are depicting them?" That became the story I wanted to tell: the scientifically valid, updated version.

So you wanted to clear up this misunderstanding?

Also tell a story. It's always been the story first. I discovered that I love being a storyteller. I wanted to write a good story, but also to characterize these people in a way that is much more acceptable currently by the anthropological and archeological community.

Was it difficult to turn this archeological material into a story?

Well, any kind of writing is difficult. Basically, as I was reading those first fifty books, I began to take notes of what might be useful to the story. Then I put together a page, or page-and-a-half outline for a novel. I sat down at my typewriter, and started to tell the story to myself.

Now, if I were to compile a bibliography of my reading for the series, it would approach a thousand entries. I've also traveled to Europe, and taken classes in wilderness survival and native life ways. In terms of the research, I probably read about ten or 100 times more than I needed, until I got so comfortable with the material that I could move my characters around in the story with ease.

I wasn't thinking of getting it published. I was just thinking of the story. As I started to write it, the story started to grow and develop, and the ideas

> **I was just trying to write these stories. I'm still writing for myself. I'm writing the story I always wanted to read."**

I had picked up in the research were finding their way into it.

How long did it take you to write the rough draft?

It didn't take any more than six or seven months, from the time of the first idea to the time I finished a huge six-part manuscript that became the outline for the series. I had free time then. I didn't have any other demands on my time, except just to live and say hello and goodbye to my husband once in a while. He was really quite supportive. I became totally obsessed and involved and excited. I found myself putting in every waking moment. I'd get up and I'd almost resent taking a shower before sitting down at the typewriter. I was putting in twelve, fourteen, sixteen hours a day, seven days a week.

What happened to the rough draft?

I went back and started to read it, and it was awful. I was telling the story to myself but it wasn't coming through on the page. I thought, "My feeling and my passion are not there." So then I went back to the library to get books on how to write fiction.

After doing a lot of self-study, I started to rewrite this big mass of words. I thought I was going to cut it down. About halfway through the first of these six parts I discovered I had 100,000 words. In adding scene and dialogue and description and everything necessary to write a novel, the thing was growing. I thought, "I'm doing something wrong. At this rate I'm going to end up with a million-and-a-half words." Talk about a writer's block.

I went back and really looked at the six different parts, and realized that I had too much to cram into one novel. What I had was six different books. I can still remember telling my husband, "I've got six books," He said, "You've never written a short story, and now you're going to write six books?"

Earth's Children became the series title, and the first book became *The Clan of the Cave Bear.*

The series seems to have a very modern sensibility. Is it as much about people today as it is about prehistoric people?

It's about the struggles of human society. My characters are fully human; they have as much facility with their language as we do, which is why I started to write it in perfectly normal English, even though it would have pleased some critics if I had invented some kind of a phony construct of a language.

I think it's more accurate to show them speaking with ease. So I said, "I'm going to write this as though I am translating it from whatever language they spoke into our language." And good translators don't translate word for word, they translate idiom. There were some words I was careful with. For example, you can say, "Just a moment," but you can't say, "Just a minute."

What made these people's lives different from our own?

The world they lived in. There are a lot of things that we take for granted that hadn't been invented yet. But when Ayla in *The Clan of the Cave Bear* is five years old, she could have been anyone's five-year-old daughter today.

Because we're talking about people like ourselves, it allows me to look at ourselves from a different perspective, through a long-distance lens. I try to see what makes us human. What is basic to being human?

For example, if you plunk somebody down in a hunting-and-gathering society rather than a society where you go into your supermarket and get your meat out of a nice clean plastic package, what will be different and what will be the same? And is one society more or less violent? In most hunting-gathering societies, people feel a great deal of reverence for the animals they hunt. And we who get our packaged, sterilized meat that doesn't even bleed any more really have very little sensitivity to animals.

So there are some definite changes. But there certainly had to be some things that we suffer from, that they also suffered from.

Did you find that you admired these people?

Well, I felt that they were as human as we are, and I admired them, the same way I admire us. Unlike some people, I don't think the world is necessarily going to hell in a handbasket. I think that the human race is a very young race, and I am hoping

that we will have the sense to keep ourselves from the destruction that we are potentially capable of dealing to ourselves. For all the stereotype about the brutal savagery of our ancestors, you find almost no evidence of it in the research, not among the Neanderthals and not among the Cro-Magnon.

One of the skeletons found at that Shanidar cave was of an old man. If you read about an old man with one arm amputated at the elbow and one eye that was blind, then you have to start asking, "How did he live to be an old man?" Paleopathologists believe that he had probably been paralyzed from an early age, because there was extensive boatrophy and he was lame on that side. The paralysis may have been the reason his arm was amputated. So he was probably a paralyzed boy and at some time in his life became blind in one eye.

How does that fit in with survival of the fittest? These were Neanderthals taking care of a crippled boy and a blind and crippled old man. Evidence indicates he died in a rock fall as an old man. When I read about him I said, "Oh, my God, there's my old man with the crippled arm. There's the character in my story." That made me feel I was heading in the right direction. He became Creb.

And as you researched this book, did you find that your story grew in a lot of ways?

Exactly. And it was so much more interesting and fun to write within the modern scientific interpretation. I thought, "There's so much to write about, and I'm going to be the one to write it."

Did you do research in fields other than archeology?

Oh, yes. Many others. I would wonder, "How did they carry water? What kinds of things will carry water?" And by reading the reports of field anthropologists into more modern societies—the aborigines, the Bushmen, or the American Indians—you find out that watertight baskets will carry water, or carved wooden bowls, or water-tight stomachs.

I drew from all over the world. If it was appropriate and came together, then that's what I would use. I tried to give the sensitivity, the feeling of the hunting-gathering society.

For example, the idea of ancestor worship: when I was reading about the Australian aborigines, I learned that at one time they didn't really have a full understanding of procreation, particularly the male role in procreation. They knew a woman gave birth, but they weren't sure how she got pregnant. That led to speculation for my story.

I thought, "What if this was a time so long ago, that the male role wasn't understood by most people. What would be the result?" Well, the only parent they would know for certain would be their mother, and her mother before that, and the mother before that, and maybe somebody would think, "Who was the first mother?"

You could see how a whole mythology based on the miracle of birth could evolve. Then I remembered about all these little figurines dating back to the early Cro-Magnon period, these round, motherly women carvings. I thought, "I wonder if they aren't meant to represent a great mother sense." That's how I derived some of the culture ideas.

When you were telling a story, did you have to pick and choose among the evidence to decide what pieces to use?

Of course. For instance, did Neanderthals talk? There are two schools of thought on that. Professor Lieberman at Brown University is the proponent of the idea that there probably was some limitation in Neanderthals' ability to communicate, to talk, verbalize, and Lewis Binford finds little in the archeological record to show that they were able to make the necessary abstractions for full speech. But their cranial capacity, the size of their brains, was, on the average, larger than ours. And other scientists say that the evidence of their culture suggests that they were able to understand some abstractions. They were the first people to bury their dead with ritual and purpose. Somebody must have been thinking, "Where are we coming from and where are we going?" That gives us a clue that the way they thought might not be so different from the way we think, or at least feel. Emotions such as compassion, love and caring come through most strongly.

So they must have had, if not language, at least . . .

At least a very strong ability to communicate, which is why I came up with the sign language idea. I said, "Okay, I'll take both of these ideas and combine them. I will say, 'Yes, there was a limitation in their language, but not in their ability to communicate.'" Sign languages are very complex. I did some research into that.

So if there's a gap between pieces of evidence, you can bridge the gap with your imagination?

Yes. And sometimes I can push things out. I can go a little farther than a scientist can go, because I am writing a novel. I might stretch the bar-rier, but I don't want to break through it. I don't want to write anything that would do a disservice to the latest findings of science. I want the background to be as accurate as I can make it. If the basis is factual, then I have something for my imagination to build on.

The character of Jondalar is based on an actual skeleton found at the site called Cro-Magnon, the site that gives the name to the early race. They found five skeletons at this particular site. One of them was of a man who was 6 feet, 5 3/4 inches tall. As soon as I read that, I said, "That's got to be Ayla's man."

Does this attention to detail make the story more believable?

People say, "You're writing fiction. What do you do research for? Why don't you just make it up?" Well, in a work of fiction, even if it's a modern novel set in Washington, D.C., if you're going to mention the address of the White House, you'd better have that address right. Because if all the basic facts that you put down are as accurate as you can get them, it aids readers in suspending their sense of disbelief. As a novelist you want to have readers believe, at least while they're reading the story, that all this could be true.

Where did the information about the herbs and medicines that the people used come from?

I have a research library now of books I've purchased, and I got some of the information from public libraries. We know that they were hunting-gathering people and we know that modern hunter-gatherers are very, very familiar with their environment. Some groups can name 350 plants, know all of their stages and all of their uses. While we don't know precisely what plants Neanderthals or Cro-Magnons used, from pollen analysis and from the way we're able to tell climate, we know what plants were probably growing there because the same plants are around today. Except domestic plants were in their wild form.

Did it give the people any advantage to be closely tied to the natural world?

It would give them the advantage of being able to live in their world. They needed it to survive. That is survival in the natural world. There's also survival in New York City. If you were to take an aborigine, or a Cro-Magnon moved up in time and set him in the middle of the modern world, and if he were an adult, how would he make a living? He wouldn't have grown up in our society, or gone to school. He might have all kinds of knowledge and background but it would not be useful to him any more, and would not have the same value.

That happened in this country to native cultures when the white Europeans invaded and began to settle. For example, the Northwest Coast Indian society was a very rich culture and they built houses out of cedar planks. It is very difficult to split a log and make it into planks by hand with wedges and mauls; it takes knowledge, skill and effort, so each one of those planks had a high value.

Now, if a white settler puts in a sawmill, and suddenly they're whipping out planks at many times the number per day than a person can do by hand, the plank no longer has the same value; it has lost its meaning within Indian society. Culturally and economically the Native-American people were deprived. And that's part of the problem today, the displacement that many of them feel.

What our early ancestors knew enabled them to live and survive in their world. We wouldn't know how to follow the tracks of an animal or when they migrate, but we have to know airline schedules and how to cross a street without getting hit by a car.

Do you use elements of the Northwest landscape in your work?

Oh, absolutely. It was really kind of fun when I discovered, particularly in *The Clan of the Cave Bear,* that there's a little mountain range at the south end of the Crimea, which is a peninsula in the Black Sea, and a strip of coastland which is Russia's Riviera today. During the Ice Age that was a temperate climate. There were cold steppes to the north, but the mountain range protected the southern end. This small coastal area was a well-watered, temperate, mountainous region subject to maritime influences, not so different from the Northwest. I even discovered that azaleas grow wild there, as they do here.

Did setting the story in that particular kind of landscape create certain constraints?

Well, you can't have a story, you can't have anything, if you don't have limits, boundaries. You can't have one setting that is arctic and equatorial all at the same time. So yes, it puts limits, constraints, but those are usually fairly welcome limits. It gives you a frame to write within.

Was there an abundance of food during that period?

Most scientists and most researchers think that the last Ice Age period was probably richer than it was later during more temperate times. The glaci-

ers caused a certain kind of environment that made for open steppes, or grasslands. Those vast grasslands fed grazing animals in hundreds of thousands of millions. It was also rich in terms of the produce that was available, so there were both animal and vegetable resources.

As the glaciers retreated, the forest started to move in, and forests aren't as rich. They don't support great herds of animals. Instead, animals stay either in small family groups or alone. The deer that run through the forest don't congregate in huge herds like the bison on the plains, and they're also harder to hunt because the animals can find trees and brush to hide among. It's much easier to hunt an animal on an open plain than when it's hidden in the woods.

In forests, there's more tree-growth, but not necessarily as much variety of plant-growth. So when the glacier melted, it reduced the abundance and variety of plant species. In the late Pleistocene, after the Ice Age, evidence of much more use of fishing and shell food was found. Such climatic changes may have caused pressures toward agriculture. The great variety and abundance was gone. Some way had to be found to feed the population.

Do you get a lot of mail back from your readers?

I do get a lot of letters from readers, and I'm very grateful for them. People become quite ardent; there are readers who feel very, very strongly about these books. It's a surprise to me. I'm delighted, but I'm a little overwhelmed. I don't really know what I'm doing right.

I get letters from men and women of all ages, twelve to ninety-two, and all walks of life—engineers, scientists, marines, lawyers, teachers, and people who barely can put together a grammatical sentence.

I even get letters from prisoners in jail. The one that I didn't know quite know how to handle was a letter from a man who said he was on death row, and would I hurry up and finish *The Mammoth Hunters* so he could read it before he died? I didn't know what to say.

What do you plan to write in the future?

I intend to write all six books in the series. That's an internal pressure. I have to finish telling Ayla's story. She won't let me alone.

And after that?

I may do anything. I may write about other prehistoric people. I may change to a different part of the world. I may write about later prehistoric periods. I may write something historical. I may write something modern. I might write science fiction. I might write a horror story, or a mystery. Who knows? I've got many things that I'd like to try. What I do know now is that I want to keep on writing, but I was forty before I knew what I wanted to do when I grew up.

Why was that?

I don't know. I suspect part of it is that I couldn't have done it any earlier. There are many young people who are fine writers, but I could not have been one. I needed to live some life and gain some experiences. I couldn't have written what I did without having gone through having a family, raising children, accepting responsibility, being out there in the world, working, coming across many different kinds of people and learning how to live with them.

Source: Nicholas O'Connell, An interview with Jean Auel in *At the Field's End,* Maronda Publishers, 1987, pp. 208–19.

Lindsay Van Gelder

While praising Auel's creation of a strong female protagonist in the review below, Van Gelder faults the author for creating social interactions which are too similar to "modern" society.

I began hearing about them several years ago, always from feminist friends who said things like "You absolutely *have to* read these books." Jean M. Auel's "Earth's Children" novels—*The Clan of the Cave Bear, The Valley of Horses,* and *The Mammoth Hunters*—have since gone from feminist word-of-mouth classics to a major mainstream phenomenon. *Hunters* hit the number-one spot on the best-seller list last winter even before its official publication date, and a movie version of *Cave Bear* (starring Daryl Hannah, with a screenplay by John Sayles) has recently been released. In the era of "Rambo," Auel has given us a resourceful, *female* superhero.

She is Ayla, a prehistoric Cro-Magnon woman who is orphaned as a small child by an earthquake. Ayla, wandering alone, gets mauled by a cave lion before she is rescued by the Clan—a group of Neanderthals who also inhabited Europe during the Ice Age more than 25,000 years ago. The Cro-Magnons are the precursors of modern Europeans, and Ayla is tall, blue-eyed, and blond. The Neanderthals are short and swarthy, with no chins, ridges over their eyebrows, and flat heads; they accept Ayla—one of the group they call the Others—only with difficulty. In their eyes, she is ugly.

> Like Scarlett O'Hara and the women in Ayn Rand's novels, Ayla is, alas, a great female character who comes with some cumbersome baggage."

Clan of the Cave Bear portrays Ayla's life in the Clan, which is rigid and harsh for a girl of her spirit. Women are forbidden to hunt (although Ayla learns in secret and becomes an expert); they are taught to be submissive and required to do anything any man tells them, including putting out sexually, anytime and anywhere. (When Ayla refuses Broud, one of the Clan men, she is raped.) People of the Clan produce no art, have no spoken language (although they do communicate in sign language and have ritual storytelling and movements not unlike dance), and are physically unable to laugh or weep; they can't even learn anything new, unless their ancestors have already done it, since their brains are based not on adaptation but on racial memory (Auel's fictional theory of why the Neanderthals died out). When people need to know something about a plant or animal, they don't learn, they "remember" what their ancestors knew—and over time, male and female brains have become so differentiated that men, for example, genuinely can't "remember" how to cook. Religion is also restricted to males (and in one scene, the men ritually eat the brains of a slain Clan hero). While there are some loving (and beautifully drawn) individuals in the Clan, Ayla never entirely learns to fit in. Eventually, as a teenager, she is cast out and cursed—for the sin of talking back to the male leader, the man who raped her, and by whom she consequently has a child from whom her exile separates her.

Valley of the Horses tells the story of how Ayla survives alone for several years (during which time she tames a wild horse and a cave lion, and together they become a kind of family unit), but she ultimately encounters a man of the Others, Jondalar (also tall, blue-eyed, and blond). Through him she meets others of her own kind. *The Mammoth Hunters* is about one such tribe Jondalar and Ayla attach themselves to for a time. The Others worship the Great Earth Mother, regard rape as a sacrilege, and allow women to hunt. (Jondalar even knows how to cook, although he doesn't do it very often; he also knows how to give Ayla sexual pleasure for the first time in her life—although the 20th century feminist reader might observe that her clitoris only figures in "fore-play.") Ayla, meanwhile, seems to excel at virtually everything—hunting, healing, practical science (she invents the flint firelighter, the stitching of wounds, the threaded needle, and a special double-stone slingshot, among other things), spirituality, languages, toolmaking, sewing, cooking. She also discovers that the Others find her uncommonly beautiful. Her only problem in her dealings with Jondalar and the Others is their horror when they realize that she was raised by "flatheads"—in their view, subhuman animals. But Ayla refuses to renounce the people who saved her life.

Beyond giving us a strong female character, Auel's books are rich in technical details. We learn about the plants that an Ice Age medicine woman might use to cure different ills, how to build an earthlodge out of mammoth bones and skins, how to knap flint, how to use mashed animal brains and stale human urine to process soft, white leather, and much, much more. Auel is famous as a researcher, and she gleaned some of her survival lore firsthand on field trips into the wilds of her native Pacific North-west, where she slept in an ice cave, hunted, made arrowheads, and learned to start a fire without matches. (The author—who had five children before she was 25, went from clerical work to earning an M.B.A., and wrote her first novel when she was over 40—is something of a superwoman herself.)

And yet despite all that's positive and riveting and informative about the books, I found them problematic. Like Scarlett O'Hara and the women in Ayn Rand's novels, Ayla is, alas, a great female character who comes with some cumbersome baggage.

First of all, Auel's research into the artifacts and the ecology of the Ice Age is so first-rate that it's easy to lose sight of the fact that the rest of the story—the human relationships—is speculative fiction. At the root of what's troublesome, I suspect, is Auel's decision to make the Others as much "like us" as possible, in everything from their speech patterns to their humor to their family lives. "These men aren't that much different from your sons or your college roommates," Auel told *People*. According to another interview in *Publishers Weekly,* "I tried to show that [Jondalar and his brother Thonolan] are thoroughly modern in their emo-

tional responses, their intelligence, their psychological reactions. Anything we allow ourselves, we have to allow them." In fact, Jondalar and his brother sit around the cave talking what we would call thoroughly modern locker-room talk. ("*Markeno is right," Carlono said. "Never take [the river] for granted. This river can find some unpleasant ways to remind you to pay attention to her"* [Thonolan replies:] *"I know some women like that, don't you, Jondalar?"*).

The margins of my books are marked with dozens of similar examples of modern sexual and domestic assumptions which, when transplanted wholesale into the Ice Age, take on the nature of eternal human verities. Although nobody knows how babies are made (and although the tribe as a whole is the key survival unit), most characters pair off Noah's Ark style and form nuclear families. (A boy whose mother is single "needs a man around"—although, in fact there are lots of men a few feet away at the next hearth.) In every tribe of the Others, women have one kind of name (say a name ending with an *a*) and men have another. Among Jondalar's people, even though girls and women are allowed to hunt if they wish, only boys become men after their first kill; girls become women after they lose their virginity. Among all the tribes, Jondalar explains to Ayla, people believe that if a man of the Others rapes a Clan woman it's "not approved, but overlooked. [But] for a woman to 'share pleasures' with a flathead male is unforgivable . . . [an abomination]." (Sound familiar?)

My objection isn't necessarily that such things couldn't possibly have been true, but that there's no evidence that they were, and they often seem particularly illogical in the woman-centered cultures Auel has created. Thus, whenever Auel falls into sex-roles-as-usual, she's exercising a *choice*—and it's no more imaginative than the guys who put 1950s suburbanites in a cave and invented the Flintstones. Her Others really tell us more about ourselves than about Cro-Magnon people; indeed, Ayla is in many ways a projection of the 1980s' female ideal—a woman who brings home the bison and fries it.

The fact that the Others are so much "like us" also inform and complicates another problem—the books' subtle racism. I say "subtle" here to distinguish a different point from the more obvious Aryan blond superiority bias, although it should also be noted in fairness that a dark-skinned half-African Cro-Magnon character figures prominently in the newest book. (Unfortunately, he's cut off from African culture, having been adopted by the Others at an early age, and his blackness is merely something that looks nice next to white fox fur clothing—or Ayla's white skin.)

But more subtly, if Auel had made the Others less familiar we might have seen their conflicts with the Clan from a genuine historical perspective. As it is, although we know that the Others are wrong—that the members of the Clan *aren't* subhuman—the equation is rigged so that we automatically identify with the Others (who, we also know, are the ultimate evolutionary winners). The message that emerges is a kind of post-colonialist chauvinist liberalism: people "like us" can be secure enough in our historic destiny to tolerate "less evolved" cultures. In the new book, the character who is the only representative of the Clan is a sickly, doomed half-Clan child who reminds Ayla of the son she has lost and who needs her protection against discrimination. The character is sympathetic, but I think his sickliness is rigged. As a white North American I feel I'm already programmed to view "primitives" not as true equals, but as the inevitable "victims of progress." This character does not challenge such liberal smugness in any way.

I certainly wouldn't want Auel to provide us with Ice Age black militants or politically correct Cro-Magnon men who do exactly half the cavework, but I do wish she'd allow us some ancestors who *aren't* like our college roommates, for better or worse. In fact, I thought Auel was at her best with the Clan and with other "exotic" characters whom she perhaps doesn't expect her average reader to "relate" to. In *Horses* we meet the Shamud, a Cro-Magnon healer and religious leader who is so androgynous that Jondalar honestly can't determine his/her gender. We later learn that people like the Shamud are always channeled into the tribe's priesthood, where they suffer a certain loneliness, but are compensated by respect and knowledge. "It is not easy to be different," the Shamud explains. "But it doesn't matter—the destiny is yours. There is no other place for one who carries the essence of both man and woman in one body." This isn't exactly the stuff of liberation, but what's wonderful and convincing about Shamud is that s/he doesn't resemble any gay man, lesbian, or transsexual you've ever met; s/he is instead a logical product of a particular culture, familiar enough to be human but magically alien in a way that the singlesbarsy heterosexual characters aren't.

Auel has promised three more novels in the series. I hope that in them she'll perhaps be able to balance our present-day need for strong female characters with the genuine mysteries and complexities of the past.

Source: Lindsay Van Gelder, "Speculative Fiction," in *Ms.,* Vol. XIV, No. 9, March 1986, pp. 64, 70.

Diane S. Wood

In the essay below, Wood examines the psychological development of Auel's protagonist in the author's first two novels. She also suggests that, in spite of the strong romantic overtones of the plots, the story is a classic adventure.

By its very nature, speculative fiction has great potential to explore variations in patterns of human interaction. Jean M. Auel, in *The Clan of the Cave Bear* (1980) and its sequel *The Valley of Horses,* demonstrates how such fiction can delve into basic human problems. Set in the Ice Age near the Black Sea, the novels trace the growth and perseverance through adversity of its adolescent female protagonist. The author gives careful attention to detail and thus creates a believable portrait of the distant past. Nonetheless, the remote settings do not obscure the fact that the main character is a young woman, Ayla, caught in an essentially male-oriented world, striving for independence and self-respect. The novels question narrow definitions of masculinity and femininity to arrive at new answers which have implications for today's society.

Auel's main character represents a relatively new type of protagonist for the adventure story, the female hero. The main character of the adventure genre is traditionally male. John G. Cawelti contrasts this kind of formulaic literature with its masculine main characters to the romance which features female characters:

> The central fantasy of the adventure story is that of the hero overcoming obstacles and dangers and accomplishing some important moral mission. . . . The feminine equivalent of the adventure story is the romance. . . . The crucial defining characteristic of romance is not that it stars a female but that its organizing action is the development of a love relationship. . . . Because this is the central line of development, the romance differs from the adventure story. Adventure stories, more often than not, contain a love interest, but one distinctly subsidiary to the hero's triumph over dangers and obstacles.

The woman protagonist in Auel's novels faces the challenge of the wilderness and survives, conforming to the pattern expected of the male hero in adventure tales. Love remains secondary to heroic action. Ayla is not a heroine of romance, but, rather, a true hero. In her study of heroines in English nov-

> ... Adventure stories, more often than not, contain a love interest, but one distinctly subsidiary to the hero's triumph over dangers and obstacles."

els, Rachel M. Brownstein suggests that being a heroine necessitates a plot which ends in marriage:

The marriage plot most novels depend on is about finding validation of one's uniqueness and importance by being singled out among all other women by a man. The man's love is proof of the girl's value, and payment for it. Her search for perfect love through an incoherent, hostile wilderness of days is the plot that endows the aimless (life) with aim. Her quest is to be recognized in *all* her significance, to have her worth made real by being approved. When, at the end, this is done, she is transformed: her outward shape reflects her inner self, she is a bride, the very image of a heroine.

Ayla does not seek external validation by men but instead actively initiates the direction of the narrative without waiting for a man to take charge. She acts courageously without regard for her own safety. She not only protects children (an acceptable role for a woman), but in several instances she saves the lives of men. The creation of a female hero thus necessitates allowing the woman to assume the active, dominant role of rescuer expected in adventure fiction.

In addition to her heroic actions, Ayla possesses inherent skills which are generally associated with men. She is not passing through a "tomboy" stage, but has talents and inclinations of the opposite sex which create tension with the rest of the social order. Ayla is a *Homo sapien* adopted into a Neanderthal clan. The dexterity of her species makes her a natural hunter, an activity taboo to women of her adopted clan. Hunting is proscribed to women although it is actively encouraged for males as behavior extremely important to the survival of the group. The designation by the Neanderthals of certain behaviors as appropriate only to men runs contrary to Ayla's talents. Expression of her "masculine" nature and skill is repressed by society, resulting in a sense of personal alienation and eventually provoking rebel-

lion. According to Auel's fictional account. Neanderthal women are expressly forbidden to touch weapons. Nonetheless, Ayla teaches herself to use a sling and even invents the technique of firing two rocks in rapid succession. The challenge of the hunt beckons irresistibly despite the fact that she can show no one her kill. While outwardly seeming to conduct herself as a passive female, she secretly violates the norm of the clan. Single-minded adherence to pursuing an activity unacceptable to her sex characterizes this protagonist, and the reader is expected to perceive her tenacity as a positive trait. While she conforms in public, she does not allow others to decide what she must do in private and eventually breaks out of the rigidly narrow sex role assigned to her.

The development of these masculine pursuits results in an increase not only in Ayla's physical strength but also in her self-esteem. When Ayla masters hunting with a sling, her whole demeanor changes without her realizing it: "She didn't know there was freedom in her step, an unconscious carryover from roaming the forests and fields: pride in her bearing, from learning a difficult skill and doing it better than someone else; and a growing self-confidence in her mien." The transformation sets her apart from members of her own sex and causes her to be described in masculine terms: "As her hunting skill grew, she developed an assurance and sinewy grace unknown to Clan women. She had the silent walk of the experienced hunter, a tight muscular control of her young body, a confidence in her own reflexes and a far-seeing look in her eye." This muscular tone and development is alien to the traditional romantic heroine who never needs a muscle of her own. It is possible to see in Ayla's athletic body the new feminine ideal of the 1980s with its emphasis on participation in sports and even bodybuilding.

Male characters in the clan perceive this "masculine" female as a threat and react savagely. Auel explains how tradition calls for Neanderthal women to accept the sexual advances of any adult male of the group. Broud, a sadistic Neanderthal man who delights in repeatedly raping Ayla in the most brutal manner, embodies the resentments of the men. Dominance over the young woman forms an essential ingredient in their relationship: "Broud reveled in his newfound dominance over Ayla and used her often. . . . After a time, it was no longer painful, but Ayla detested it. And it was her hatred that Broud enjoyed. He had put her in her place, gained superiority over her, and finally found a way to make her react to him. It didn't matter that her response was negative, he preferred it. He wanted to see her cower, to see her fear, to see her force herself to submit". The anger directed by men toward her does not result in eliminating the offensive masculine inclinations or talents. Rather, it actually brings about the opposite effect, and instead of being broken into submission and passivity, Ayla is strengthened by this cruel treatment and becomes even more masculine. She undergoes stages in the life of the typical male hero, including an initiation trial similar to a male puberty rite. When Ayla uses a sling in front of clan members to save a child from a predator, she reacts instinctively without regard for possible consequences to her. The wise clan leader resolves the dilemma of an appropriate punishment for her heroic but unpardonable behavior by reducing the customary sentence to a month-long "death curse." She survives this test despite a harrowing experience in a blizzard. As a result, the clan accepts her into the ranks of hunters and her totem is symbolically marked on her thigh as would be the case with a young man at puberty. After the ceremony, the clan celebrates with the customary feast. Lest she forget her proper place, the men of the clan are careful to point out that hunting is the only male prerogative which Ayla may pursue. The leader states: "Ayla, you have made your first kill; you must now assume the responsibilities of an adult. But you are a woman, not a man, and you will be a woman always, in all ways but one. You may use only a sling, Ayla, but you are now the Woman Who Hunts". Through her courageous persistence, she earns the right to assume a male persona and enjoys increased opportunities.

The ending of *The Clan of the Cave Bear* clearly delineates Ayla's "masculine" courage and defiance as contrasted with Broud's "feminine" impulsiveness. His leadership ability and judgment are questioned. One of Broud's first acts as leader is to banish Ayla forever with a permanent "death curse," but instead of ignoring her after the curse is performed, he raises his fist in fury to her, an act of acknowledgment. Even his father realizes Broud's lack of character and gives the ultimate insult, that Ayla is more of a man than Broud is: "You still don't understand, do you? You acknowledged her, Broud, she has beaten you. She's dead, and still she won. She was a woman, and she had more courage than you, Broud, more determination, more self-control. She was more man than you are. Ayla should have been the son of my mate." There could be no harsher reproach in a society with such rigid sex-role expectations than for a man to be unfavorably compared to a woman.

The social organization of the clan fails to provide flexibility for exceptional members. Neanderthal groups, according to Auel's narrative, function because of proscribed roles maintained through racial memory. Despite inherent differences in the species, Ayla adjusts to clan life and lives happily as long as the clan has a tolerant leader. Her very nature as a *Homo sapien* arouses intense hatred in Broud and, when he finally receives power in the closing pages of the novel, she is unjustly expelled from the group. Ayla wanders northward alone, seeking others of her kind. *The Clan of the Cave Bear* ends with her being cursed and forced to leave the clan. The sequel begins with her arduous and lonely search for a new life. The plot thus advances from conflicts within society to survival alone in a hostile wilderness. Ayla's great physical stamina, her tenacity, and her basic intelligence make her story credible and her survival possible.

In *The Valley of Horses* Ayla's relationships with animals prove more satisfying than with people. She lives happily for four years with a mare and a cave lion which she raises from orphans and tames to the point where they accompany her on the hunt and allow her to ride them. This relationship between the protagonist and a horse has an erotic edge. Although she is not ignorant of the basic mechanics of sexuality, she has never felt profound yearnings. The rut of Ayla's mare provokes strange feelings in the woman which she does not understand, since sexuality among the Neanderthals is limited to the male's "relieving his needs" with the female. Ayla is distressed when her mare follows her sexual urges and freely joins a wild stallion, but since the horse, like the cave lion, is not her possession, she realizes that the mare is free to depart at will to join her own kind. In fact, Ayla envies the horse's good fortune. While the animals do not remain constantly with the young woman, they prove good companions in an otherwise lonely environment.

Whereas Ayla has certain characteristics of a male hero, she remains profoundly female. For instance, her great strength does not change her basic biological makeup. Monthly cycles still occur, and leather straps fulfill sanitary needs during menstruation. Ayla excels in traditional feminine handiwork, spending her spare time making exquisite baskets and learning how to sew. She clearly sees herself as the female in potential sexual situations with men. This heterosexual orientation remains constant throughout the novel regardless of her experiences with male brutality. She wants to find a mate/husband and raise children, but the difference between her and the typical romantic heroine is that Ayla simultaneously can accept both masculine and feminine aspects of her androgynous being. The fact that she can become a mother, for instance, does not preclude her from riding horses or hunting.

Ayla's isolation is a necessary step in allowing her to develop a more balanced sense of herself which eventually leads to her successful reintegration into a less repressive society. The changes in attitudes and experiences brought about by her separation from the group in which she was raised produce a new outlook for Ayla. The injustice she suffered as a sex object does not, however, cause her to reject all men. Indeed, the novels are *bildungsromans* exploring Ayla's nascent sexuality and her search for a meaningful relationship with a sympathetic man. She does not become sexually awakened until finding a compatible human partner in *The Valley of Horses*. She finally encounters a man who takes for granted that women hunt and make tools and that men help with food gathering and preserving. Mutual respect and admiration sparks affection between the two characters. The novel ends with the meeting of a human group, a signal of Ayla's entry into a new social order. She manages to have it all—independence and companionship—the fantasy of the modern American woman.

While Auel creates in these novels an active and heroic female figure grappling with tensions between her basic nature and her society, she also presents the difficulties males have adjusting socially. *The Valley of Horses* introduces a male protagonist, Jondalar, whose story is followed in chapters alternating with Ayla's adventures until the two finally meet and Ayla saves his life. Naturally, they fall in love. One might even say that the man's tale is the romance, since following Cawelti's definition, his preoccupation is with finding the ideal woman whereas Ayla struggles to survive and passes tests of bravery typical of the adventure story. Jondalar accompanies his brother on a journey. He would have preferred to stay at home. He serves as a companion rather than initiating action on his own as does Ayla. While he is proficient in the act of love, he does not know how to risk loving until he finds Ayla. One woman who loves him points out that he may be destined for an especially strong woman: "Maybe you haven't found the right woman. Maybe the Mother has someone special for you. She doesn't make many like you. You are really more than most women could bear. If all your love were concentrated on one, it could overwhelm her, if she wasn't one to whom the Mother gave equal gifts. Even if you did love me I'm not sure I

could live with it. If you loved a woman as much as you love your brother, she would have to be very strong." In the Ice Age world Auel creates, neither men nor women are exempt from difficulties. The author rejects the idea of dominance by either of the sexes in favor of freedom of all people.

These popular novels reflect the author's optimism regarding the resolution of the difficult problems of individual choice which plague contemporary society. Just as Ayla is isolated, present day women all too often find themselves with no role models and no positive support from society as they attempt to function in today's world. While the situation of the Ice Age is different from our own, the solutions worked out in speculative fiction mirror those that must be worked out in lives of twentieth-century women. The success of these two books as popular fiction stems from the appeal of the strength of the female hero and the positive ending to her story.

The difficulty of integrating personal and professional life can be especially challenging in a complex society. William S. Barnbridge suggests a possible effect on present society of Sword-and-Sorcery novels which applies just as well to other novels of speculative fiction such as Auel's: "While Sword-and-Sorcery imagines fantastic worlds, the analysis of alternate ascribed roles and family structures it offers may contribute indirectly to create innovation in our own society." Speculative fiction leads the way for new patterns of human interaction. In this manner, literature posits and tests creative approaches to human dilemmas, working out theoretical cases to be either accepted or rejected by the evolving social order.

Source: Diane S. Wood, "Female Heroism in the Ice Age: Jean Auel's Earth Children," in *Extrapolation*, Vol. 27, No. 1, Spring 1986, pp. 33–38.

Sources

Carlin, Margaret, "Love in the Ice Age," Review, in *The Chicago Tribune*, December 24, 1990, p. 7.

Gallagher, Bernard, "Jean Auel's *The Clan of the Cave Bear:* Failed Feminist Pre-History," in *Journal of Popular Culture*, Vol. 5, No. 1, 1991, pp. 1–18.

Libman, Norma, "'Cave Bear' Epic," Review, in *The Chicago Tribune*, December 16, 1990, p. 3.

Parks, Lisa, "Profile of Olga Soffer," in *Discovering Archaeology*, Vol. 2, No. 1, January-February 2000, pp. 26–28.

Shreeve, James, *The Neanderthal Enigma: Solving the Mystery of Modern Human Origins*, William Morrow & Company, 1995.

Straus, W. L., and A. J. E. Cave, "Pathology and Posture of Neanderthal Man," in *Quarterly Review of Biology,* Vol. 32, No. 3, 1957, pp. 348–63.

Van Gelder, Lindsay, "Speculative Fiction," in *Ms.,* Vol. 14, No. 3, March 1986, pp. 64–65.

Wayland Barber, Elizabeth, *Women's Work, the First 20,000 Years: Women, Cloth, and Society in Early Times,* W. W. Norton & Company, 1994.

Wilcox, Clyde, "The Not-So-Failed Feminism of Jean Auel," in *Journal of Popular Culture,* Vol. 28, No. 3, Winter 1994, pp. 63–70.

For Further Study

Graham, Sandy, "Making Mammoth Best Sellers," Interview, in *USA Today,* October 12, 1990, p. 6.

Auel shares her views on the Ice Age and on being a writer in this candid and personal interview.

Harrington, Maureen, "Jean Auel's Improbable Story Upstages Her Own Books," in *The Denver Post,* December 5, 1990, p. 1.

In this interview, Auel talks about her early life, how she started writing, and how the success of the Earth's Children Series has changed her life.

Hornblower, Margot, "Queen of the Ice Age Romance," Interview, in *Time Magazine,* Vol. 136, October 22, 1990, p. 88.

Hornblower interviews Auel about her life, literary success, and how she sees her work in relation to history and literature.

Pisik, Betsy, "The Mammoth Huntress and Her Prehistoric Gold Mine," in *The Washington Times,* November 20, 1990, Sec. E, p. 1.

A standard profile of Auel's literary success, but a satirical look at how authors sell out for material gain.

The Crazy Horse Electric Game

Chris Crutcher

1987

The Crazy Horse Electric Game, published in 1987, is a coming-of-age story that combines elements of sports, family dysfunction, physical disability, and social issues but also manages to infuse humor into tragic circumstances. Author Chris Crutcher specializes in young adult fiction and often draws inspiration from his work as a child and family therapist as well as his desire to give teens a dose of truth about the real world.

Crutcher received the prestigious Margaret A. Edwards Award for his young-adult writings, which, as Edwards Award committee chair Joan Atkinson told Betty Carter in *School Library Journal Online,* "bring to life the contemporary teen world including its darker side." The protagonist of *The Crazy Horse Electric Game,* Willie, lives a sheltered and somewhat charmed existence until circumstances force him to embark on a journey in order to discover how to live life under a completely different set of rules. When Willie leaves the small town of Coho, Montana, he's confronted with difficult situations that test his resilience yet also show him that he does have power and influence over his world.

The novel is told from the point of view of Willie, which reflects the influence that Harper Lee's *To Kill a Mockingbird* had on Crutcher. He admits that the strength of the main character's voice is unforgettable, which serves to make the novel synonymous with the character. Ultimately, Crutcher began writing *The Crazy Horse Electric Game* because he wanted to tell some silly jokes.

However, the story of Willie's journey does much more than provide comic relief. As Crutcher explains to Betty Carter in *School Library Journal Online,* it "give[s] hope to young adults struggling with the eternal questions of who they are and where they belong."

Author Biography

Chris Crutcher, born in the small and isolated logging town of Cascade, Idaho, on July 17, 1946, graduated from the Eastern Washington State University in 1968 and, despite what he calls his unremarkable performance as a student, later excelled as a teacher for at-risk teens at the Kennewick Dropout School in Washington State. After spending the next ten years working with troubled youth, specifically as a mental-health therapist, Crutcher became reacquainted with old college friend and writer Terry Davis. After working with Davis on his novel *Vision Quest,* Crutcher embarked on a writing career of his own, publishing his first book, *Running Loose,* in 1983. The novel was named an ALA Best Book and led to a string of successful young adult novels, which earned Crutcher a reputation for telling stories that honestly portray the life struggles of adolescents and tackle tough issues.

Despite his lack of formal training in the art of writing, Crutcher would go on to pen six novels for young adults, as well as one adult novel, over the course of his career. While his writing eventually took precedence over his work as a therapist, Crutcher still works with the Child Protection Team in Spokane, which is an organization of mental-health professionals who handle the most difficult cases. Continuing his work with disadvantaged youth gives Crutcher material for his novels, and he draws upon real-life experiences for inspiration. In fact, his mother was an alcoholic for the duration of Crutcher's adolescence, which he says gave him a real connection with troubled kids.

An avid sports enthusiast, Crutcher runs marathons, swims, and participates in triathlons, subjects that also find their way into his work. Because he undertakes difficult subject matter, Crutcher has, in the past, found himself the victim of censorship in some conservative school districts. Crutcher interprets the censorship as a desperate and shortsighted attempt to protect children from the truth, telling Betty Carter in *School Library Journal Online,* "When my books are banned,

Chris Crutcher

they're banned because people are afraid for kids to know about something I wrote about. Now, how dumb is that?"

Crutcher, who never married, still lives in Spokane, and has written screenplays for two of his novels, *Running Loose* and *The Crazy Horse Electric Game,* while *Staying Fat for Sarah Byrnes* has been optioned by Columbia Pictures. His short story "A Brief Moment in the Life of Angus Bethune" from *Athletic Shorts* was made into a major motion picture by Disney Pictures. In 2000, Crutcher received the Margaret A. Edwards Award for lifetime achievement in young-adult literature.

Plot Summary

The Championship Game

The Crazy Horse Electric Game by Chris Crutcher begins with Willie Weaver, the star pitcher for Coho, Montana's local baseball team, preparing to play the most important game of his life. Willie is blessed with a golden arm that earns him legend-like status among his friends and family, and he knows that winning the game for his team, Samson Floral, rests entirely on his shoulders. However, Willie's got the confidence to know that when he's on, nobody can touch his fastball. The whole town of Coho is counting on Willie to bring in their very first championship trophy, especially Willie's father, Big Will, who seems to be living vicariously through his son's sports triumphs and failures. Big Will's claim to fame was playing football in the '60s for the University of Washington and winning the Rose Bowl. Despite the fact that Willie knows his dad is proud of him, father and son have never been able to achieve any significant emotional connection.

On the day of the big game, Willie is on fire; no batter has reached second base, and Samson Floral is ahead 1–0 in the seventh inning. By the bottom on the ninth, however, Willie makes his first mistake of the game, putting the tying run on first just before the opposing team's big hitter steps up to the plate. When the next pitch is thrown, Willie loses his balance as the ball is hit hard toward third base. Miraculously, Willie catches the line drive on pure instinct and "etches the Crazy Horse Electric game in the mind of every citizen and ball player and coach—maybe even dog and cat—in Coho, Montana."

The Accident

With the championship under his belt, Willie is riding high for the whole summer. On a weekend getaway with his parents, his girlfriend, Jenny, and best friend, Johnny, Willie has a tragic accident while water skiing that leaves him physically disabled. The body he once had complete power over is now broken and out of his control. Willie feels ashamed, embarrassed, and frustrated over his condition. He wants to avoid everyone, but Jenny and his friends insist on bringing him back into the fold. Despite everyone's efforts to make Willie feel comfortable, their behavior has the opposite effect. Willie can't stand the pity and begins to retreat into his own world, which is wrought with depression and suicidal thoughts.

Willie's parents send him to a therapist, who tries to help Willie deal with his feelings about the accident. After a few sessions, it seems as if Willie is making some progress until he has a big blowout with Big Will, who thinks Willie isn't trying hard enough to recover. Willie feels like he's failed his father while Big Will's insensitive attitude angers Willie's mom and it creates a wide rift in the marriage. In addition to Willie's family life falling apart, he catches Jenny with a classmate and knows that she's betrayed him. That night, Willie overhears a vicious fight between his parents, fueled partly by lingering resentment over the death of

Willie's baby sister a few years ago, and he believes the only answer is to run away and release his loved ones from the burden he has put on them.

The Escape

Willie packs his bags, takes all the money he can find, and boards a Greyhound bus headed toward San Francisco. He makes it all the way to Oakland, but gets stranded late at night because the bus breaks down. Willie finds himself surrounded by a local gang who spot his cane and see him as an easy target. Despite his best efforts to escape, the gang attacks Willie, takes all his money, and leaves him battered and bleeding in the street. Willie is rescued by a local bus driver named Lacey, who takes him home and lets him stay the night.

Despite Lacey's original insistence that Willie can only stay one night, the two work out an agreement where Willie agrees to help Lacey around the house in exchange for room and board. In addition, Willie discovers that Lacey is in a dubious line of work. Lacey calls it "human relations," which Willie quickly translates. Even though Lacey is a pimp, Willie knows he's in no position to be making moral judgments. That day, Lacey calls in a favor in order to get Willie enrolled in a local school for disadvantaged and troubled teens called OMLC (One More Last Chance) High School.

OMLC

At OMLC, Willie bonds with Lisa, the physical education teacher who recruits Willie as her pet project in working toward her physical therapy degree. Willie is reluctant at first to trust her, but she makes quick progress with Willie, thus enabling him to feel less self-conscious about his broken body. He also becomes close to Andre, the school's principal, who looks after Willie like an older brother. Life with Lacey, however, doesn't go as smoothly. Late one night, Willie wakes to a fierce argument between Lacey and one of his girls, who just happens to be a classmate of Willie's. When he defends the girl and leaves Lacey unconscious, Willie is terrified that Lacey will kill him. He is set to move into the school's basement, but for some mysterious reason, Lacey tells Willie to stay.

Soon, Willie learns that he is granted permission to stay because Lacey is trying to redeem himself for a past wrong. Apparently, Lacey beat his own son so badly that he was permanently brain damaged and now lives in a hospital. Lacey is forbidden to see his own son and believes he can ease his troubled conscience by aiding Willie.

Burning Down the OMLC

As Willie continues to progress with Lisa's help and some tai chi classes, he finds his center and makes strides on the basketball court, which also gives Willie an opportunity to make friends with two other classmates, Hawk and Kato. At the same time, Andre is working hard to make decorative improvements on the school. However, the improvements are short-lived when the gang who beat up Willie months ago starts to deface the school with graffiti. Kato decides it's time to teach the gang a lesson, and with the keys to the school, makes a plan for himself, Hawk, and Willie to take down the gang when they make their next strike. The night of the rumble, Willie finds himself facing the gang alone. The gang sets the school on fire, and Willie barely escapes but manages not only to save his own life but that of the gang leader as well.

Going Home

Despite the tragedy, Andre vows to work just as hard to return the school to its old glory. Willie, inspired by Andre's vision, works so hard with Lisa that it is now almost impossible to tell that he has any physical disability. On the day of graduation, Willie makes a moving speech and thanks everyone, including Lacey, who has helped him recover. Believing his time at OMLC has run its course, Willie boards a bus and heads back to Coho, where he hopes to make amends with his friends and family. When he arrives, Willie finds that in the two years since he's been gone, so much has changed. His parents are divorced, his mother is remarried, and his father is unemployed and struggling with alcoholism. In addition, Willie's surprise reunion with Jenny is wrought with tension as she is just not ready to deal with the aftermath of Willie's sudden disappearance and unexpected return. After two lengthy and separate conversations with his parents, Willie realizes that Coho is not his home anymore. He knows it will take time to rebuild a relationship with his parents, and that someday he'll come back again, but in Coho, he still feels disabled, like he did before he left. As the novel ends, Willie takes his father's motorcycle, says goodbye, and heads back to Oakland.

Characters

Angel

Angel is a classmate at the OMLC high school and a prostitute who works for Lacey Casteel. De-

spite Willie's attempts to help her out of her situation and the fact that Willie has developed a crush on her, Angel inexplicably prefers to stay with Lacey and does not return Willie's romantic feelings.

Big Will

See William Weaver Sr.

Jenny Blackburn

Jenny is Willie Weaver's girlfriend and best friend. Also an athlete, Jenny bonds with Willie over their love of sports and competition. When Willie has his accident, it is Jenny who saves his life and remains by his side to nurse him back to health and give him all the love and support he needs. However, Jenny finds that her generosity and patience toward Willie result in jealousy and resentment on his part. While she swears to stand by Willie, the relationship comes to a tragic end when she begins dating another classmate. When Willie discovers her betrayal, Jenny tries to explain her actions, but ultimately her behavior ends the relationship permanently. Just before Willie leaves, she argues with Willie over his behavior since the accident: "You treat your friends like spit. I'd have stayed with you, Willie, if you'd have made any attempt to be decent. But no! Not Willie Weaver! If he can't be a hero, then to hell with everyone else." When Willie returns two years later, Jenny initially refuses to speak to him, but later has a conversation in which she reveals that she's too hurt and confused to tell Willie how she feels. They part ways amicably before Willie returns to Oakland.

Lacey Casteel

Lacey is a black bus driver and part-time pimp who rescues Willie one night after a gang attack. Lacey allows Willie to stay with him and enrolls Willie in a local school; however, Lacey's generosity is somewhat duplicitous. By caring for Willie, Lacey feels he can somehow redeem himself for beating his own son many years ago: "I get this idea to get me out of Hell. Raise me a white cripple kid. Can't fix all the bad shit, but maybe I make up *some*." Lacey is prone to violence and often drinks to extreme, which culminates in a physical confrontation between him and Willie. While Lacey prefers to keep his life private, he reveals parts of himself and his past to Willie, and the two make amends and develop a strong bond. Lacey struggles with his ex-wife and the son he is forbidden to see but becomes a better man through his relationship with Willie. Lacey attends Willie's graduation and is touched by Willie's public expression of gratitude toward him.

Warren Hawkins

Warren is a black student at OMLC high school and one of the toughest kids on campus. He's tall, smart, strong, and intimidating, with a short temper, a tendency to fight, and a penchant for pot smoking. However, he's also easygoing with a good sense of humor. His skills on the basketball court impress Willie, and despite their differences, the boys become allies in the fight against the street gang that tries to ruin the school.

Kato

Kato is a stocky black kid and Warren Hawk's sidekick. His eccentric sense of humor reminds Willie of an old friend back in Montana and acts as a bridge between Willie's past and present.

Lisa

Lisa is the physical education teacher at the OMLC high school. An excellent basketball player who is studying for her degree in physical therapy, Lisa takes Willie under her wing and teaches him how to build up his strength, both physically and mentally, with different exercises and the use of visualization. Her encouragement and wisdom help Willie come to terms with the accident and force him to take responsibility for his life. She tells him point-blank, "You crippled yourself because you stretched the rules till they broke. Simple as that."

Andre Porter

Andre is the principal at the OMLC high school. He accepts Willie into the school in exchange for maintenance work. Acting as a mentor for Willie, Andre guides him through some of his more difficult challenges and encourages him to reach out to the other students. It is Andre's commitment to the school and the students, as well as his determination to accept responsibility in the most desperate times, that helps Willie realize he has to keep fighting to improve his life.

Johnny Rivers

Johnny is a close friend and teammate of Willie's who reveres Willie and his athletic talent. Johnny's admiration grows after Willie's unforgettable performance in the championship game. However, after the accident, to which Johnny was a witness, the friendship becomes strained. Johnny is unable to relate to him outside of the sports arena. He tries to support his friend and invite him to par-

ties, but discovers that it's impossible to communicate with Willie: "I'm your friend, man. I wanna stay your friend, but I don't know what to *do*. Really. Just tell me what to do." Johnny watches, helpless, as Willie retreats further and further into his shell. When Willie returns to Montana, Johnny is the first person he seeks out. Even though Willie has been gone for two years, Johnny holds no hard feelings toward his old friend. Johnny welcomes Willie back but he is also the one to reveal the difficult news about Willie's parents' divorce.

Sammy

Sammy is Lisa's boyfriend and the tai chi instructor who helps Willie on his road to recovery, both physically and spiritually. He believes in "lust and passion and good old common sense. And in staying alive."

Telephone Man

Telephone Man is the first student Willie meets at OMLC high school. He is an emotionally-challenged and sensitive teenager who wears a full set of telephone repair tools on a belt around his waist. Telephone Man acts as the catalyst for the final showdown with the gang at the school. Because the gang violently attacks Telephone Man, Willie and two other students decide to fight back. This act of loyalty means the world to Telephone Man because it makes him realize that he is liked by his classmates.

Sandy Weaver

Sandy Weaver is Willie's mother. She blames herself for the death of her baby girl to SIDS (Sudden Infant Death Syndrome) a few years ago, and has never fully recovered from the loss. While she's proud of her son's accomplishments, she worries that his bravado will result in him taking his life for granted. She wishes that Willie would understand that he has been given gifts for which he should be thankful. After the accident, Sandy watches her marriage fall apart because her husband is overcome with guilt. Her relationship with William Sr. is marked by tragedy, but she criticizes her husband for his reaction to their son, saying "I don't treat our son like a leper; or worse yet, like he's invisible. He's not some possession . . . he's not a car you can take back to the dealer because it doesn't run right." When her son disappears, Sandy leaves her husband, and by the time Willie returns, she is remarried to another man. While she wishes Willie would come and live with her, Sandy understands why her son must leave again.

William Weaver Sr.

William Weaver Sr. is Willie's father and former star football player. His claim to fame is winning the Rose Bowl back in 1968. As he watches his son excel in baseball, William Sr. seems to be living vicariously through Willie's successes and failures. While proud of his son's accomplishments, William Sr. remains emotionally distant from his son and is more often imparting sports wisdom than offering fatherly support and advice. When Willie is injured in the accident, William Sr. blames himself for almost drowning his son and is unable to cope with his guilty conscience. He can't deal with Willie because he's a constant reminder of William Sr.'s mistakes. He reacts to Willie's apathy by saying, "You want to be a cripple all your life, just keep it up. When it gets a little tough, slack off." William Sr. alienates himself from his family and turns to alcohol when his marriage falls apart after Willie runs away. When Willie returns, William Sr. finds it difficult to make amends with his son, but is impressed with the way Willie has recovered.

Willie Weaver

Willie is the novel's protagonist. He is a gifted and confident baseball player and all-around athlete who pitches the local team to its first championship and, with an amazing catch, etches that particular game into the town's history. However, Willie's life changes dramatically when an accident leaves him physically disabled. Unable to deal with the physical and emotional consequences of the accident, Willie leaves rural Montana, his friends, his girlfriend, and his family behind and arrives in Oakland, California, an urban street-wise city significantly different from his hometown.

During the two years that he spends in Oakland, Willie forges friendships with various characters and graduates from an alternative high school. By working with a physical therapist and taking tai chi classes, Willie is able to regain control over his body, come to terms with the accident and how it changed his life. In his graduation speech, Willie thanks Sammy, his tai chi instructor, saying, "He talked to me, mostly without words, and I think he told me a whole lot of what I'm going to need to be an adult. He showed me how my mind and body are just different parts of the same thing and that there are no limits for either; that most of the really important answers are already inside me. . . . He taught me how to go to my gut to survive." Willie returns home to make amends with his past; however, after discovering

that his family fell apart in his absence and that his friends have moved on without him, Willie returns to Oakland to continue his new life.

Cyril Wheat

Cyril is Willie's therapist, whose unconventional style succeeds in reaching Willie in a way that no one else can. With his frank and direct manner, Cyril tells Willie, "That golden boy isn't you anymore, and as long as you keep measuring yourself up against him, you're gonna be mad as hell at *everybody*." Cyril interprets Willie's dreams and encourages him to communicate more with his family and friends. He even suggests that Willie bring his parents and his girlfriend into his office for some group sessions in order to help Willie sort through his problems. Despite the small progress Cyril makes with Willie, he can't stop him from trying to escape his problems. Once Willie leaves Montana, Cyril never sees him again.

Themes

Identity

One of the prevalent themes in the book involves how young people determine their identity as they come of age. For Willie Weaver, he identifies himself as an athlete first and foremost. Because of his talent on the baseball field and the relative ease with which he is able to master certain sports, Willie couldn't image living his life any other way. Sports are an essential element to his life; it's how he relates to his father, William Sr., who was a star football player in his day, his friends, who are also his teammates, and his girlfriend, who shares Willie's love of competition. Ironically, it is a sporting activity that takes away his physical abilities. When Willie loses power over his body and his ability to play sports in a water-skiing accident, his whole world falls apart as he can no longer relate to the people in his life. If he's not the star pitcher for the baseball team, then who is he? Willie watches as each relationship in his life suffers because of his unwillingness to accept the consequences of the accident or to make any attempt to recover. It is only when Willie travels to a place where no one knows him or who he was that he is able to find the freedom to discover who he really is.

Topics for Further Study

- Chris Crutcher has often been criticized, and sometimes censored, for tackling serious and controversial subject matter. Is it wrong for teachers and parents to ban his books? Argue for or against censorship in schools.

- Research the history of gang violence in the United States. Discuss the effects of gang violence on surrounding communities, and how the situation has changed in the last decade.

- Read Crutcher's *Ironman* and compare it with *The Crazy Horse Electric Game*. Explore the similarities and differences between the two novels and then discuss why you think *Ironman* was met with such controversy and subsequently banned.

- Define and explore some of the major elements of sports, such as competition, team work, stamina, integrity, loyalty, and cooperation, and then explain how each one directly relates to dealing with life's difficult challenges and forming one's identity.

Self-Reliance

Throughout the novel, Willie's resilience is tested several times, beginning with the accident that leaves him physically disabled. While he survives the accident, he struggles greatly with the consequences of his disability and must deal with the depression and suicidal thoughts that follow. Ultimately, Willie believes he must escape his surroundings in order to continue his life and then faces a number of challenges as a result of leaving those familiar surroundings. Once he arrives in Oakland, he suffers a violent gang attack that leaves him beaten, bloody, and broke. Yet once again, he finds the strength to survive by striking a deal with a man who offers him a place to stay free of charge. Finally, Willie's attendance at the OMLC (One More Last Chance) High School represents his final chance at survival and the ultimate test of self-reliance, which is heightened by the fact that he is surrounded by other disadvantaged individuals who face similar, difficult challenges in their struggle to survive with the limited resources they've been given.

Fate

Connected with the concept of survival is the idea of fate and the way one single moment can define a lifetime. Willie has two similar experiences that have dramatically different results. The first is his amazing play during the Crazy Horse Electric game. By making a miraculous catch to win the game, Willie becomes a minor legend in a matter of seconds. A few weeks later, during a weekend trip with his family, Willie is injured in a water-skiing accident that leaves him severely disabled. These two events are related to fate in the sense that Willie had no control over either of them. One resulted in him being a hero while the other took away the only life he ever knew. Inevitably, Willie questions why he was injured and tries to figure out whom or what to blame. He needs a reason or a purpose for his suffering. Ultimately, however, even as Willie comes to terms with the how and why of his accident, he knows the answer doesn't necessarily make him feel better about his life. Willie isn't able to move on until he accepts his situation and makes a concerted effort to recover.

Family

At the start of the novel, Willie has a traditional family that is stained by a struggle with a past tragedy. Despite the loss of a child, Willie's parents are still together and providing him with a somewhat stable home. This traditional family structure, however, is threatened after Willie's accident. Willie leaves home as a way to release his parents of the burden he has created, an act that eventually causes the end of his parents' marriage. Once Willie arrives in Oakland, he succeeds in creating another kind of family, one that is unconventional but nonetheless provides him with the support system he desperately needs. Several different characters combine to act as Willie's caretakers and substitute parents, from the man who first takes him in, Lacey Casteel, and the principal at OMLC, Andre, to his physical therapy teacher, Lisa, and his tai chi instructor, Sammy. In addition, the other students at the OMLC act as extended family members who provide Willie with loyalty and companionship. When Willie returns to Montana, he realizes that his family has fallen apart, forcing him to reconsider the concept of family. At the end of the novel, he decides to return to the home and family that he's created back in Oakland.

Style

Setting

The novel's two settings serve to greatly differentiate between Willie's life before the accident and after the accident and the spiritual journey he makes over the course of the story. In the small town of Coho, Montana, Willie leads a sheltered life in which everything comes easily to him. He is well known by the townsfolk, and the championship game turns him into a hero. However, his hero status comes too easily; he is never confronted with obstacles or major challenges. He lives a charmed life, one that is never contested, which is reflected in his safe, small-town surroundings. When Willie arrives in Oakland, he's forced to figure everything out on his own. In the tough, urban setting of Oakland, Willie is no longer the boy with the golden arm; he's just another kid down on his luck in a place filled with disadvantaged people. In this new setting, Willie learns the importance of being challenged. In his speech at graduation, he acknowledges the gift he's been given, saying, "My life is more valuable because I got knocked out of my favored spot." It's only by expanding his life experience in another setting that Willie can grow as a person.

Symbolism

Symbolism is a literary device used to instill meaning into an object. One of the symbols in this novel is a walking cane given to Willie by his teammates after the accident. It is a custom-made cane with a golden baseball for a head, reading Willie Weaver-1, Crazy Horse Electric-0, an inscription that represents Willie's shining moment. Willie uses the cane for a few weeks after the accident; he needs it to help him walk. However, even when Willie no longer physically depends on the cane, he keeps it with him, and it acts as a reminder of Willie's former glory. When Willie arrives in Oakland, the cane becomes a symbol of weakness and vulnerability. In his most desperate time of need, the cane becomes his enemy and the reason why Willie is chosen as a target. Later in the novel, as Willie begins to have some control over his life, the cane mirrors his progress and becomes a weapon that Willie uses to defend a girl whom Lacey is beating.

As Willie starts his tai chi classes, Sammy, his instructor, teaches him to use his cane to his ad-

vantage and incorporates it into Willie's balance. When Willie grows stronger, the cane comes to represent something other than the Crazy Horse Electric game. Just like Willie must learn to make allowances for his body and use what he has to the fullest extent, the cane becomes less of a symbol of who Willie used to be and more of an indication of how far he has come. In the final confrontation with the gang at the OMLC, Willie brings his cane for protection against the boys and uses it to defend himself and escape the burning building. Willie makes it out alive, but the cane gets left behind in the rubble. When he travels back to Coho, Montana, Willie arrives in town without the cane, which symbolizes that he has come full circle in his recovery.

Young Adult Literature

The Crazy Horse Electric Game is a novel that falls within the young-adult literature genre. A book is characterized as young-adult because it addresses the issues and problems of contemporary life as experienced by this particular age group. The novels within this genre often discuss many of the same questions and difficulties that teenagers must confront, such as drugs, divorce, parents, alienation, suicide, disabilities, abuse, gang violence, school, sports, and relationships. At the same time, many adolescents must deal with the transition between childhood and adulthood and the idea of discovering their identity, which is one of the main issues explored in this novel. One of the crucial elements in young-adult literature is its ability to reach its audience in a way that allows them to better understand and authenticate their own life experiences in a safe environment. It's a forum for teenagers to work through their problems without being threatened with exposure. It is also an important way to introduce teenagers to literature and create a lifelong interest in reading.

Historical Context

The War on Drugs Campaign in the 1980s

When *The Crazy Horse Electric Game* was published, President Ronald Reagan and First Lady Nancy Reagan had launched the war on drugs in America. Nancy Reagan had made it one of her personal crusades and created the slogan that urged young people to "Just Say No." As a result, "Just Say No" clubs were springing up in schools across the country. This effort was started in 1984 and continued up through President George Bush's inauguration in 1988.

In September of 1986, Ronald and Nancy Reagan gave an address from the family quarters of the White House on the subject of drug abuse. In the speech, as reported by Jacob Lamar in *Time,* Ronald Reagan said: "Drugs are menacing our society. They're threatening our values and undercutting our institutions. They're killing our children." The First Lady continued: "Today there is a drug and alcohol epidemic in this country, and no one is safe from it—not you, not me and certainly not our children, because this epidemic has their names written on it." The whole effort was widely criticized for its simplicity, its general lack of understanding of the real problems facing youth, and its superficiality. Specifically, the President's message was denounced for budgeting approximately $3 billion to fight the war on drugs but refusing to offer any real solutions to the problem. Many educators and health professionals recognized the need to create more in-depth educational programs to deal with drug use, particularly among youth with disadvantaged backgrounds and those living in decaying urban communities.

As a mental health therapist, Crutcher had first-hand experience with the issues facing disadvantaged youth. He also expressed his moral commitment to protect kids. In *School Library Journal Online,* he told Betty Carter:

> "For me, the moral thing is to set up a structure that protects kids emotionally, physically and spiritually, which is to say, 'When something hurts you, come talk to me about it. I will hear you and not punish out of fear. There's nothing you can tell me that will make me turn my back. But I'm not going to keep you in the dark about anything. I'm going to protect you from bad guys. I'm going to protect you from running out on the street . . . I'm going to do all those things, but my moral job with you is to be there and accept you.'"

Crutcher's realistic and sympathetic treatment of his characters in the novel serves to reflect the need for a more comprehensive and honest approach to the subject of drugs and the other problems teens must face in their day-to-day lives. Crutcher's effort also worked to humanize the problem. His novel shows that not every young person in America was on drugs—as implied by the perceived national crisis—and those who might experiment with drugs were not to be dismissed as junkies. He tries to emphasize that these kids have many redeeming qualities and have the ability to

contribute to society. Perhaps most evident is Crutcher's message that troubled teens desperately need support from responsible, caring adults and their communities in order to safely navigate their rocky adolescence.

Gang Violence in the 1980s

The Crazy Horse Electric Game addresses the prevalence of gang violence in the small cities of America by highlighting an Asian youth gang who terrorize the local community and school. At the time the novel was written, street gangs were spreading from the major cities such as New York, Los Angeles, and Chicago into smaller towns and cities. In 1984, there were 28,500 gang members in Los Angeles with 20,000 of those members living outside of the city. Federal researches also reported in 1984 that two-thirds of the cities reporting gang violence had populations under 500,000, which included suburbs of major cities like New Haven, Connecticut; Jackson, Mississippi; and Portsmouth, Virginia.

The spread of gangs into smaller cities was directly related to the fact that the same problems that plagued major cities, such as poverty, racial separation, youth unemployment, and broken families, were now affecting smaller cities. In addition, when youths moved from the inner cities, they often started gangs in their new surroundings. Another new problem that surfaced was that gang violence was not confined to the streets anymore; the activity often spread onto school grounds in suburban areas.

Critical Overview

When *The Crazy Horse Electric Game* was published, Chris Crutcher had already established a solid reputation for himself as a refreshing new voice of young-adult fiction that appealed to both critics and audiences. Most reviewers had praised him for addressing popular themes with adolescents, such as divorce, drugs, mental and physical handicaps, and gang violence in a manner that managed to be both humorous and unsentimental. However, critics' opinions were mixed about the effectiveness of *The Crazy Horse Electric Game.* Todd Morning, in his review in *The School Library Journal,* states:

> Willie's present-tense narration is annoying, and does not work well for this story that covers several years. The author is best in the effective description of Willie's effort to recover from his injury. But this is

the best that can be said for a novel that often seems contrived.

Roger Sutton of the *Bulletin of the Center for Children's Books* agrees with *SLJ,* saying:

> Crutcher's special brand of tough but tender machismo (used to good effect in *Running Loose*) is on uneasy ground of sentimentality here, and the thematic concerns are too obvious.

Despite these criticisms, other reviewers praised Crutcher for his development of eccentric yet truthful characters and his honest portrayal of harsh realities. Pam Spencer in *Voice of Youth Advocates* notes that "this book could have ended 'happily ever after' with Willie returning home to girlfriend and parents, all waiting for him with open arms. But tragedies don't leave a family unscarred." It is Crutcher's commitment to examining subjects with substance that led Susie Wilde of *Children's Literature* to say that "the story is a poignant telling of courage, the struggle to survive life on all levels, and an examination of values once held dear."

When Crutcher received the Margaret A. Edwards Award in 2000, he solidified his mission to continue writing about adolescence because it is such a crucial time in one's life. He told Betty Carter of *School Library Journal Online* that he writes about teenagers because "they're on the edge of having to live their lives themselves. Those initial decisions they make are really important." However, it is also Crutcher's wish to write about some of the most controversial subjects for teenagers, such as sexual abuse, which he covers in two of his books, *Running Loose* and *Chinese Handcuffs.* As a result, his works have occasionally been banned by conservative school districts. In fact, *Booklist* refused to even review *Chinese Handcuffs.* Crutcher disagrees with the idea that it's necessary to protect children from life's uglier truths and admits to dealing with these same issues in his own adolescence and suffering because of it. In an interview with Betty Carter for *School Library Journal Online,* Crutcher said:

> I had a mom who didn't want me to feel bad. She wanted me to think everything was going to be all right because she wanted them to be all right. . . . When I got out on my own, I had to take a look and say sometimes things don't turn out okay and sometimes there isn't a happily ever after, and all those things they tell you about marriage and relationships and jobs are sometimes just not the truth. . . . I don't think we should trump the bad, but there's a world out there. There's a good chance at some time in your life you're gonna run into it.

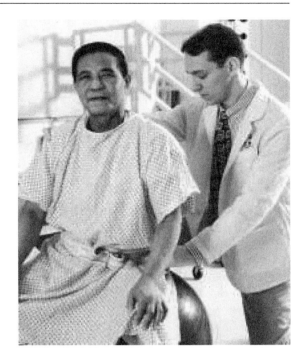

A patient works on his balance with a physical therapist. In the novel, physical therapy helps Willie to regain control of his body and eventually restore his self-respect.

Despite the censorship, or perhaps because of it, Crutcher's novels always seem to find their way into his readers' hands. While conducting a writer's workshop in Houston, Crutcher was approached by a young girl who was the victim of sexual abuse and had read *Chinese Handcuffs.* After reading the novel, the girl felt safe enough to seek help. Experiences like these give Crutcher the fuel to keep writing while refusing to shy away from the controversy that some could say has become a signature of his work. He told Heather Vogel Frederick in *Publisher's Weekly* that he knows "it's risky business letting people have their own lives, particularly if they are our children." But he's willing to take that risk because, he adds, "I'm only interested in stories that I care about. . . . If I don't feel passionate I can't write."

Criticism

Michele Drohan

Drohan is a professional editor and writer who specializes in fiction and nonfiction for young adults and children. In the following essay, she ex-

> When he asks her, 'why me?', she confronts him directly without pity and puts the blame right on his shoulders, saying, 'You crippled yourself because you stretched the rules till they broke. Simple as that.'"

plores a concept prevalent in The Crazy Horse Electric Game *and other novels in the young-adult genre, which concerns a loss of childhood innocence and the idea of confronting one's mortality during adolescence. While life's learning experiences often occur during tragic events, those hard lessons later prove invaluable as young people try to make sense of their lives.*

Critics have recognized that Chris Crutcher's *The Crazy Horse Electric Game* explores how a young man must dig deep within himself to find his inner strength. It's a story of personal courage, and the structure of the story highlights the journey that many young people must take in order to understand their place in the world. The novel is told from the point of view of an unnamed narrator, and it opens with the statement, "Sometimes he remembers it as if it were unfolding in front of him this very minute, all of it; event by amazing event. And sometimes it seems as if it all happened a long, long time ago, maybe in another lifetime." This statement implies that the protagonist, Willie Weaver, has endured a tragedy that dramatically affected his outlook on life and one that still affects him to this day. Even more compelling is the idea that the protagonist is now an old man, looking back on his life. However, it is soon revealed that the event in question occurred just two years ago when Willie was sixteen years old, reaffirming the concept that coming of age means the attainment of maturity.

Willie Weaver comes from a long line of athletes. His grandfather was a legendary athlete at Notre Dame while his father holds the distinction of playing in a winning game of the Rose Bowl in 1968. Crutcher provides this family history as a way to give readers a strong idea of Willie's sense

of entitlement to his gifts as a baseball pitcher. While Willie's life is far from perfect—his father is emotionally distant while his mother is still grieving over the loss of her infant daughter—the summer of his sixteenth year is full of promise and possibility. As Willie approaches the championship game for his team, Samson Floral, he has the kind of confidence that comes from never enduring any real obstacles in his life: "He's always been better at sports than any kid his age, so he's never felt any different than this. It's just the way things are; he's *supposed* to be a hero." Willie feels invincible as his body will do anything he asks of it and his teammates would "[sell] their souls to play on the same team as him."

Crutcher provides a moment of foreshadowing just before the game as Willie and his father have a rare moment of closeness. During the conversation, William Sr. tells his son to remember everything that happens up to and during the game. Speaking from experience, William Sr. relates the Rose Bowl as the highlight of his career and how he savored every moment because "[he] didn't know if [he'd] ever be that good at anything again." Willie listens to his father's words but does not hold them close to his heart because he knows the game will belong to him. Crutcher uses this opportunity to show Willie's bravado and naivete, and while Willie doesn't realize it, readers will understand that those very words will come back to haunt him.

Winning the game serves to bolster Willie's sense of immortality. Because he made a miraculous play and took his team to the championship, Willie has yet another reason to feel blessed. The game takes on a magical quality, which dramatically heightens Willie's sudden fall from grace. During the weekend vacation by the lake, Willie decides to take the last water-skiing run of the day, even though his body is fatigued. He pushes himself, riding high on the adrenaline that comes from the speed and power of the water. However, his shoulders begin to ache and his legs go numb, which leave him vulnerable to the water. The accident occurs quickly, and Willie is knocked unconscious. Ironically, Willie's father panics and is unable to help him, which points out another element in Crutcher's coming-of-age theme. It's the moment when children understand that their parents are fallible.

Willie is devastated by the accident and stays out of school for as long as possible. The idea of being confronted by his classmates and teammates is too much to bear. Not only will they see the full extent of Willie's disability, but it also means

Willie must face what he's lost by watching his girlfriend, Jenny, and his friends, continue to excel in sports. Willie can't help feeling that he hates his friends because they can still do all the things he can't do. Willie's sense of martyrdom grows as he searches for the reason he must endure this hardship: "He'd give anything to step back over that tiny sliver of time—the point of impact with the water ski—and be just a *hair* more cautious; back off the edge just enough. But the circumstances that allowed the Crazy Horse Electric game to be will never happen again, because he can't step back." By forcing Willie to relive the moment over and over again in his head, Crutcher highlights Willie's failure to fully accept what has happened to him.

When Willie decides the only answer to his problems is to leave Montana, it is unclear whether or not this is the right decision. This is a turning point in the novel, when Willie's actions could be interpreted as further denial and a wish to escape his problems. However, as Willie begins his journey, his thoughts fall to his girlfriend, Jenny, and her betrayal. Crutcher uses this relationship to have Willie learn one of life's more important lessons—that even the people you trust most in the world can lie. As Willie continues his journey by himself, he proceeds to learn hard lessons about life. Even though Willie's been through difficult times, he will come to realize that it's no guarantee that he's safe from further harm. Arriving in the bus terminal in Oakland, Willie is confronted by a stream of transients for whom "desperate times are the order of the day. Abandon hope is written across their faces in greasy city dirt." This gives Willie yet another epiphany—he is not special in his state of suffering. In fact, there are people in the world that have it much harder than he does.

When Willie is the victim of a violent gang attack, he thinks he'd give anything in the world to be back in Montana because "he never had any idea there was this in the world." His rude awakening to life outside his small hometown further confuses Willie, and his survival instincts begin to take shape. He understands now that he must dig deep within himself just to live another day. He has no other choice but to try and make the best of his situation. This results in his rescue by a local black bus driver and part-time pimp named Lacey Casteel. Lacey represents an opportunity for Willie, and while Willie understands that Lacey is in a dubious line of business, he realizes that he needs Lacey and he's in no position to make snap moral judgments about anyone. Lacey is quick to see that Willie is not wise to the ways of the world and jok-

What Do I Read Next?

- *The Ironman: A Novel,* by Chris Crutcher, is an intense look into the life of a seventeen-year-old athlete whose strained relationship with his father lands him in an anger management group, where he must deal with his feelings among other emotionally-challenged students.

- Carl Deuker's *Heart of a Champion* chronicles the close friendship of two boys, who bond over their love of baseball while struggling with some of life's more difficult challenges, specifically alcoholism.

- *Roughnecks* is Thomas Cochran's debut novel about a high-school senior who believes his performance on the football field is inherently connected to discovering the truth about himself.

- Chris Crutcher's *Staying Fat for Sarah Byrnes* follows the friendship between a physically-deformed girl and the boy who stays overweight for fear of losing his best friend.

ingly tells Willie that he ought to find a place close to the bus station as it would keep Willie apprised of what the world is *really* like. Willie is beginning to understand those very words: "Something changed in him after last night, after he survived what he was sure was his last second on earth, and from now on Willie Weaver's going to take whatever he has to take to survive."

When Willie enrolls in the OMLC (One More Last Chance) High School, he is surrounded by other disadvantaged kids. His friendship with the physical education teacher, Lisa, not only helps Willie regain his physical strength but it proves to Willie that once he begins to reach out to others and really try to recover, there are people he can depend on for help. It is a conversation with Lisa that helps him come to terms with his accident. When he asks her, "why me?", she confronts him directly without pity and puts the blame right on his shoulders, saying, "You crippled yourself because you stretched the rules till they broke. Sim-

ple as that." Willie is not satisfied with this explanation and mentions God, implying that if he does
exist, there is no good reason why God hurt Willie.
However, Lisa gives him the lecture of a lifetime:
"You had to go a little faster than you could, push
out there at the edge because you thought nothing
could hurt you. The rules don't slack off for
naivete. . . .You broke the rules, you got hurt."

By the end of the novel, Willie has worked so
hard to recover that it's impossible to see that he
has any disability. He has expanded his horizons,
thanks to tai chi lessons that taught him that "his
mind and body are mere extensions of each other."
By living and experiencing events that never would
have occurred had the accident never taken place,
Willie realizes how his loss of innocence has
brought him to a better place, that pain and suffering are a necessary part of life. Every moment of
his life is a part of who he is and this gives him a
power he never had. In his speech at graduation,
Willie expresses his gratitude over the fact that no
one at the school ever preached to him, but instead
"let [him] figure it out for [himself], *demanded* that
[he] figure it out for [himself]." He's ready to go
back home and face the unknown. He's not sure if
he can make it, but he knows he's strong enough
to try.

Finally, Crutcher uses the graduation speech in
order to show Willie's full transformation: "There
are lots of people . . . whose lives are protected
from the day they're born until the day they die.
But no matter how wonderful those lives seem, if
they're not contested, never put up against the wall,
then they exist inside very narrow walls, and because of that I believe they lose value, in the most
basic sense of the word." This realization is the culmination of Willie's facing his own mortality—that
it's only when you lose everything you hold dear
that you are able to really accomplish anything.
Even if he could go back to his old carefree,
charmed life, he would choose not to. The essence
of the novel puts forth some of Crutcher's own
hard-held beliefs, that you cannot protect children
from harm or stop them from falling, but you can
be there to pick them back up.

Source: Michele Drohan, in an essay for *Novels for Students,* Gale Group, 2001.

Terry Davis

*In the following essays, Davis explores the
"strong" characters and "painful" subject matter
Crutcher presents in* The Crazy Horse Electric
Game.

There's a point near the end of *The Crazy
Horse Electric Game* when Willie has gone home
to face the people and things he ran out on. He finds
his parents divorced and his mom remarried, his
dad has become a brutal drunk and tells him "I'm
not your dad," and his old girlfriend Jenny calls
him a son of a bitch. He rides up into the hills on
the motorcycle he and his dad used to ride together,
and the narrator tells us: "Willie can't believe
there's this much sadness in the world."

When we consider Crutcher's status in young
adult literature it might be hard to believe that any
of his books were ever met with disapproval or disdain. But *Crazy Horse* was, and so was *Chinese
Handcuffs. Crazy Horse* is, in fact, the only one of
Crutcher's books that wasn't a unanimous ALA
Best. He enjoys telling the story of how the novel
was effectively banned in Hawaii. In that state, he
says, a book has a chance to be reviewed twice. If
two librarians veto it, the state buys only one copy.
The first librarian who reviewed *Crazy Horse* said
it was trash, and poorly edited trash to boot, and
such an awful book that it had no right to be published. Crutcher uses the word *vicious* to describe
her commentary. The second found it well written
but so depressing that she couldn't recommend it
for young adults. Proponents of the book worked
two years to overturn this initial decision.

Crazy Horse is full of sadness, and so is life—
most of us recognize this and admit it. But to call
it "depressing" isn't a measure of the book; it's a
measure of the reader. Other readers argue that
Crazy Horse presents a positive view of life and is
uplifting because, while it imitates accurately the
painful nature of our existence, it also allows for
"one more last chance" to learn the rules that can
save us.

Art is different from life. Art—at least the storytelling art—is an imitation of life made by human beings in an attempt to bring life's complexity into focus. A story is controlled. Nothing in it
happens by chance. Yes, as the story is composed,
inspiration and intuition do strike, unconscious
forces rise to the light and bestow their surprises.
But by the time the story is ready to go out into the
world and meet its readers, it's been revised until
not just every story element but every single word
has become the result of the writer's conscious
choice.

We can be there as Willie Weaver puts on the
life jacket that's too big for him. When he pushes
the limits of his waterskiing ability, falls and gets
hit in the head with the ski, "and the life jacket slips

up, trapping his arms and head, and Willie slips into darkness" and into the brain damage that destroys what might have been a one-in-a-million athlete, we know the cause—not just the only cause we can observe but the only cause Willie could have controlled: He shouldn't have worn a life jacket that was too big. He broke the rules, and he paid.

Here's the point: God's will doesn't matter—not in a Crutcher world. Willie has no control over God's will. Willie can, however, refuse to wear a life jacket that doesn't fit; he can choose not to push his ability when he's too tired to exercise it. He can *do* something to alter possibilities; he can be a causal agent in his own life. There are things he can *control*.

Religious faith, which is to say the belief in realities beyond what we can see or understand, does not bring us control. Religious faith brings peace to some of us, but it doesn't bring control. Religious faith, in fact, is relinquishing control. And control, in a Crutcher world, is a method of salvation.

Listen once more to Crutcher speaking through another of his personas. This is Lisa, the PE teacher at One More Last Chance School, responding to Willie's question about why he got hurt:

"You mean . . . why you crippled yourself?"

Willie grimaces and nods. Lisa always words things like that; *why you crippled yourself* instead of *why you got crippled.* . . .

"You crippled yourself because you stretched the rules till they broke. Simple as that.

"God didn't cripple you, Willie. *You* did. You stretched the rules till they broke."

This question about why things happen, why the innocent suffer along with the guilty, this stuff about the nature of life is the core element in all of Crutcher's work. This core begins to glow in *Running Loose;* Crutcher puts it under greater pressure in *Stotan!;* it erupts in *The Crazy Horse Electric Game;* and the magma's heat and speed intensify as it flows through *Chinese Handcuffs* and *Staying Fat for Sarah Byrnes.* We have no obligation to believe and adopt this view of the world Crutcher presents, but if we don't see it, then we're missing what he spends so much effort trying to show and tell us.

What is this molten material flowing through the books? It's pain, the most common currency in life, a great deal more common than love. Pain is the element that allows so many readers to see their

> *Here's the point: God's will doesn't matter—not in a Crutcher world. Willie has no control over God's will. Willie can, however, refuse to wear a life jacket that doesn't fit; he can choose not to push his ability when he's too tired to exercise it."*

own lives mirrored in Crutcher's work. We are all experts in pain. Even those of us who can't articulate our pain—*especially* those—recognize it and know absolutely when a storyteller presents it accurately.

In *The Crazy Horse Electric Game* the pain starts before the action of the story. The Dragon, incarnate in sudden infant death syndrome, took Willie's sister Missy. The pain of her death haunts Willie, Big Will, and Sandy Weaver, and the fact of her death—the fact that it just happened, that it was nobody's *fault*—hovers over the story until the final moments.

What we said about *Stotan!* in relation to *Running Loose* we can say about *Crazy Horse* in relation to *Stotan!:* The same elements are here; the differences are intensity and focus. Remember what Crutcher gives as the reason his books become more and more painful: "it is the increased damage I've seen, [and] my increased awareness of what that damage is." He's speaking about the damage we do to one another, and this damage—as opposed to the damage done to us by circumstance—is what he focuses on more closely here and hereafter. In *Sarah Byrnes,* for example, the damage Virgil Byrnes did to his daughter is what fuels the central action of the story; in *Ironman* Beau Brewster's central battle is to let go of the anger that's the result of the damage his father did him.

There are the same thematic elements and similar character types, but there's also something different about *Crazy Horse.* We *feel* it in the opening sentence: "Sometimes he remembers it as if it were unfolding in front of him this very minute." What's different about this narration?

What's different is a shift in point of view. The position from which the author allows us to view the action of the story has changed. Crutcher has chosen third-person limited narration over first-person here. "Limited" refers to the degree of omniscience the narrator exercises. In this case the narrator limits to one the number of characters whose minds we're allowed to enter. He can shift focus into Willie's mind, allowing the reader to see as Willie sees and be present in his thoughts.

This change from first-person narration is another example of Crutcher's increased confidence in the craft of writing and maybe also in the magnitude of his subject matter. It takes courage and skill to abandon the first-person narrators with whom he's had so much success. These characters' voices alone are engaging enough to hook readers. But Crutcher steps outside his main character here and allows a more distanced, objective persona to tell his story. Then again we can look at this in another way: one might say that now, in third-person, Crutcher can tell the story himself—in his own voice, out of his own experience, directed by his own passions—rather than under the limitations inherent in a youthful pose.

The biggest difference this change in point of view creates is seen—is *heard,* really—in the story's tone. *Tone* refers to the storyteller's attitude toward subject matter; in *Crazy Horse,* since the narrator is no longer invested in events, the presentation of events has a more distant, objective ring. If the narration is successful, as Crutcher's is, there's no loss of emotional intensity. The source of the intensity just shifts from narrator to focal character.

An intriguing and illuminating way to consider *Crazy Horse* is as the fulfillment of Walker Dupree's musings at the conclusion of *Stotan!* We remember that Walker says if he ever makes it to adulthood and decides to turn back and help someone grow up, as a parent, teacher, or coach (or writer), he will concentrate on "dispelling myths, clearing up unreal expectations." And this is just what Crutcher does in *Crazy Horse.* Before Willie's injury changed everything, "his father was mythic to him," and part of the positive transformation that results from the way Willie's injury changes his perspective on the world is that this mythic quality gets busted.

The other word Walker uses is *expectations,* and in the book's final pages, when Willie learns about the hell his parents' lives became, we hear his mother tell him something that warrants quotation:

> "[Y]ou don't always get what you expect. I wish someone, sometime when I was growing up, would have told me what expectations would get me. . . . Our parents, schools, everyone tells us things will be a certain way when we're adults and if they're not that way, we should make them be; or at least pretend. But after a certain point that just doesn't work."

What Willie's mother says here about parents, schools, and everyone telling us things will be a certain way—and that we should *pretend* they are even if they aren't—lead us into another theme that evolves from *Stotan!,* which is the theme that to speak and act honestly is the healthiest way to live for us and for the world around us. If this isn't the major theme of *The Crazy Horse Electric Game,* it is certainly the novel's driving force.

Consider, for example, how directly it evolves from the concluding lines of *Stotan!:* "But first things first," Walker says. "Right now I've got to get dressed and go pick up Devnee. Gotta set her straight." What Walker has learned about lying—along with coming to believe that everything unsaid is a lie—is that lying unbalances the liar and the world. Walker lies to Devnee, and neither of them is able to make decisions based on "what is," because what is can no longer be perceived accurately.

The theme of honesty permeates *Crazy Horse.* As chapter 2 opens, Big Will and Willie take one of their evening rides on Big Will's 700 Honda. They wear their helmets for Willie's mom's benefit as they pull out of the driveway but take them off at the edge of town. It's dishonest, and it's also messing with "the rules." This story element wouldn't be particularly significant if Crutcher hadn't made it a part of the unity of his story by returning to it in the conclusion. Now that Willie has learned from pain and from the wisdom of others, he "thinks of strapping the helmet to the sissy bar . . . but that's just like the old days and he keeps it on." Willie won't lie now, not explicitly or by omission; and if he's going to break the rules—like Crutcher himself does by not wearing a helmet—he's not going to be surprised when the rules break him.

Willie's mom knew all along that the guys dumped their helmets. She reveals this to Willie just moments before he hurts himself waterskiing. "Don't get too taken by fast things," she says. "They can hurt you. One of these days you and your dad may have to pay for all your recklessness." Consider this and then remember what Max told Walker in *Stotan!:* "This is a world where you pay for everything you do."

Crutcher shines his honesty spotlight on Big Will again as chapter 2 closes. Willie is thinking of Missy's death and how it caused the Weaver universe to shift. "Big Will held the family together with his powerful, stoic presence," and finally time began to dull the pain. This was "something Big Will couldn't take head on, something he had to turn his back on." Here's Crutcher's point: if we turn our backs on it—on pain, on loss, on the truth— it will come back and kick the hell out of us, which is exactly what Missy's death finally does to the Weaver family. Powerful stoicism doesn't do it. Allowing ourselves to feel and to express the pain is what keeps us from being devoured by it. Crutcher tells us again and again: we can't fight the Dragon head-on, but we can go *with* him and beat him.

Cyril Wheat, the therapist Willie sees after his injury—and after the frightening reaction to the LSD he took at the party—is a Crutcher persona more Crutcher-like than most, particularly in his sense of humor and his commitment to honesty. When Willie first meets him Wheat is wearing his Gay Vegetarian Nazis for Jesus T-shirt, and when Willie gives him a look he shrugs and says, "I'm a joiner." This is vintage Crutcher humor in real life (he wears a Nuke the Children shirt), as well as in writing. Wheat's response to the events and feelings Willie recounts is this:

> "A lot of what happens now depends on truth. When you're afraid your girlfriend is going away or your friends are keeping you around just because they feel sorry for you, you have to *say* that to them."

Some of the book's most incisive and painful honesty is present in Willie's feelings about Jenny. He's accepted the manager position on her basketball team, and "he's aware that something nagging down deep in him wants Jenny to blow it." This honest portrayal of human reactions is one of the reasons people trust Crutcher as a storyteller. We all know—even those of us who can't articulate it—that this is an accurate portrait of pain.

Willie tells Cyril about his jealousy, and the therapist's response is grounded in the healing nature of the truth, in spite of how much the truth hurts: "That golden boy isn't you anymore, and as long as you keep measuring yourself up against him, you're gonna be mad as hell at *everybody. . . . And you'll lose your girl.*"

The pain becomes too much for Willie to handle when his loss of Jenny is confirmed. She couldn't muster the courage to tell Willie she liked another boy. "I didn't know what to do," she says. And Willie replies, "You . . . coulda . . . just . . . told me . . . the . . . truth." Jenny then goes on to tell him the truth that if he'd made any attempt to be decent she'd have stayed with him. "But no! Not Willie Weaver! If he can't be a hero, then to hell with everyone else." Willie "just wants to hurt her back." When he calls Jenny a bitch his life in Coho, Montana, has unraveled to the last thread. That night he steals money from his folks and catches a Greyhound west.

We need to remember that Willie is "a cripple" now. This is his physical state when he arrives in Oakland. Crutcher doesn't use the term *physically challenged,* because his commitment is to accuracy. He uses *crippled* because Willie is, indeed, "a damaged or defective object." This diction is another element in the matrix of honesty Crutcher creates. It's also important to consider in terms of story structure that if Willie isn't profoundly damaged, his recovery can't be profound or heroic enough to touch us as a great story does; if he's not brought low, he can't raise himself high.

The worst of Willie's pain isn't physical, although the beating he gets from the Jo Boys is no fun. The worst of Willie's pain is the fear and humiliation he feels now that he's been brought so low and found himself so alone. "*If I were okay, I'd beat this kid to death,*" Willie says about the gang's leader. Before he loses consciousness he realizes "he'd give anything in the world to be back in Coho." Willie never realized there was this much poverty and savagery and desolation . . . and pain in the world. Willie continues to suffer in Oakland, but this is probably his low point.

Crutcher shifts his focus slightly after Willie moves in with Lacey and enrolls at One More Last Chance School. This is a new Willie in a new world. There's so much for Willie to learn now that he's been forced into a new perspective and rendered capable of learning from it. Among the vital things he learns is the reason he's able to learn them. Crutcher makes this clear in Willie's speech to the commencement audience. He says he's aware that if they had known him back in Montana they would have hated his guts because he had everything, including people around him to protect him and make sure he didn't lose it. "And there are lots of people like that," he says, "people whose lives are protected from the day they're born until the day they die."

> But no matter how wonderful those lives seem, if they're not contested, never put up against the wall,

then they exist inside very narrow walls, and because of that I believe they lose value, in the most basic sense of the word. I guess what I'm saying is that my life is more valuable because I got knocked out of my favored spot. I can't believe I'm saying that, but I am and I know it's true. I learned it from the people who picked me up here.

We hear Crutcher's voice in the passage, of course. In a body of work packed with vital exposition, there's probably no expository passage more important than this one. Remember, again, that Crutcher has seen so much damage done. So, how do the damaged make something positive out of all their pain? We accept our new condition and the new view of the world it gives us, and we act on our new perception.

Willie's first positive contact with humanity in Oakland is Lacey Casteel, bus driver and pimp. Lacey is not a role model, but there is much to learn from him. He's capable of kindness in spite of the overriding brutality in his character. He takes Willie in after the beating, and he is sincere at the end of the story when, in his note to Big Will, he says: *"Here you boy back. He fix. Be careful how you treet him, he special. If you don't want him, send him back."*

Lacey tells Willie he's taking him in for a reason Willie doesn't know. We discover Lacey's motivation after he's helped Willie enroll at One More Last Chance. Lacey comes home drunk late one night and finds the note Willie has left him about a phone call from his former wife. Lacey says he needs to "purge his soul" and takes Willie out for a drive. "I beat my boy," he tells Willie as they drive. "Start on beatin' him. Couldn't stop. Beat my boy numb." They park and walk to a huge, dark institution, climb over the fence, and stop beneath a window too high to see into. And then in one of the most powerful scenes in Crutcher's work—reminiscent of Jeff's empty lane scene in *Stotan!* because of the power and sharpness of focus but more complex and illustrative of greater skill with prose—Lacey grabs a drainpipe and pulls himself up even with the window. Willie hears a moan and looks up to see Lacey's face go soft. Willie watches the man stare into the window through a "bottomless despair." Lacey drops to the ground and tells Willie to look. "Don' worry," Lacey says, "he don' see you." So Willie climbs on Lacey's back, stands on his shoulders, and looks in. He sees

a tall, extremely thin black boy; he could be anywhere from fifteen to forty. His long arms hang out of his plain white state-issue shirt like useless ebony twigs, their outstanding features the gnarled, twisted elbows and knuckles. . . . A narrow string of spittle

hangs from one side of his mouth, and as it lengthens, finally dropping to the floor, the boy makes no attempt to stop it. He's vacant; gone

Listen to the passage Crutcher presents as transition from Willie's visual recognition of what Lacey has done to Lacey's explanation of its consequences. This is Willie's intellectual recognition:

[T]his is *family* gone crazy. It comes in a flash the boy before him is wrecked; the man beneath his feet, desperately holding on with everything he's got to stay just above the quicksand. This is what happens when we astonish ourselves with our capacity to be vicious; when we realize so late how our expectations have betrayed us.

We hear, of course, the theme of the destructive power of expectations.

Willie feels through his feet the vibration of Lacey's sobs. Lacey falls and Willie tumbles to the ground. Lacey lies there crying. "He jus' there hauntin' me," the man says. "He there an' I can't see him; they won't let me go close." Now Willie knows that Lacey took him in to take this boy's place.

This passage is illustrative of a number of things, only a few of which we've discussed here. But too important to go unmentioned is how the passage illustrates Crutcher's growth as a writer. The writer of *Running Loose* could not have written this. It's too understated—which is to say too *restrained*—in its description; it's too complex, and it's also too wise. Crutcher has seen so much more damage now and knows so much more surely the source of it. Willie's physical healing begins at One More Last Chance. The school enhances his emotional healing also, to be sure, but Willie has hit bottom now and he's ready to start stroking back up. Crutcher makes this clear in Willie's response to the school's required resume. He was "absolutely straight" about the reasons he left home, "crystal clear in his final statement that he wasn't going back to Montana." Willie has changed: no more lies, not explicitly and not by omission. The truth does set us free, and one of the things it sets us free to do is heal ourselves.

Andre, the school's director, is another Crutcher character. His physicality, his forthright speech, his humor, and his honesty are mirrors of these qualities in Crutcher himself. Look at him and listen to him, and you'll see and hear Crutcher. Except that Andre is black and Crutcher is white. Listen, for example, to Andre describing the Last Chance students: "Some of these kids seem pretty damaged before you get to know them. Some of

The Dallas Lady Texans take on the Los Angeles Sparks in a National Women's Wheelchair Basketball tournament. In the novel, Willie learns to continue his basketball career from his wheelchair.

them seem pretty damaged *after* you get to know them, but I'm sure there are friends for you here."

And Willie does make friends at school, two of whom are women: Lisa, the PE teacher, and Angel, a fellow student and prostitute who works for Lacey. Few readers would dispute that these are "strong" women characters, but few would think of them—particularly Angel—as role models. Lisa, whom we can see as an older Elaine Ferrel from *Stotan!,* might be more overtly sexual with Sammy, the Tai Chi teacher (and a Max Il Song character) than some readers find appropriate in a school setting. And Angel isn't simply a teenage prostitute, she's a teenage prostitute resolved not to give up the trade. Willie asks Lacey to let Angel go, but Angel doesn't want out. "You think I'm a whore because of Lacey?" Angel asks. "If Lacey wasn't my pimp, I'd get someone else. I'm a whore because that's how I survive."

When we talk about "strong" characters in literature we don't mean "admirable," although strong characters are often admirable in at least some ways. Lisa is a fine athlete, for example, and it's through her coaching that Willie learns to compensate for most of the physical damage he has suffered. She's also honest, which Crutcher accents particularly in the ease and openness with which she's able to be sexual with Sammy while Willie's around.

Literary characters are referred to as "strong" when they are sharply delineated and consistent and when they know and accept themselves. Angel, for example, does not lie to herself, and she knows the source of one of the strongest currents in her personality. "You know how girls get to be whores?" she asks Willie. "Girls get to be whores when they grow up thinking sex is the only way to get anything." She then goes on to say she had sex first with her uncle when she was 7 and that it went on until she was 17. It was ugly and she hated it, but he was nice to her and gave her things she never would have gotten in another way.

Lisa and Angel are deeply tied to the unity of the story. They're important to the plot because of Lisa's role as mentor figure and Angel as the focus of Willie's romantic interest and the source of some painful information about the complexity of life. And they are integral to the theme of honesty.

It's not hard to see that *The Crazy Horse Electric Game* ventures deeper than the previous books into wild country, and we are not, of course, speaking about California here. We're speaking about the wild country of human life. In spite of language and subject matter that make it more difficult to teach in public school, it is still a novel full of victories for the damaged souls who populate it. Hawk, the basketball player who becomes Willie's friend, attends their graduation ceremony with a cast on the arm he broke protecting his mother from his drugged-out brother. Hawk stands when he receives his diploma, looks out at his father and says, "I tol' you I ain't no worthless sh—." And Telephone Man, one of Crutcher's strangest and most touching characters, "who wears a full set of telephone repair tools on his hip, giving him the appearance of an AT&T gunslinger from outer space," concludes his commencement speech by looking over at Hawk and saying, "Hawktor Doctor must really like me . . . and that's the first time anybody really liked me and I'm glad I went here."

But here's the kind of victory that makes the book most difficult for teachers and librarians in schools besieged by book *challenges*:

> [Angel] takes the diploma, looks out at the audience, then over to the graduates and simply says, "Thanks." Willie looks out to see Lacey nodding his head and clapping.

It's difficult to justify this complexity and lack of resolution to some people. Such people want Lacey and Angel, pimp and prostitute, nailed up tight in a box with the word BAD written on it. But Crutcher is wiser than that. He knows that human beings are both ghastly and glorious, and that even in their ghastliness and pain they are capable of heroic endurance, such as he implies here as Willie's bus heads out of Oakland, taking him back to Montana and more heavy jolts of sadness:

> Willie watches Lacey standing, arms folded, looking powerful and confident, without a trace of the horror in his life, and Willie marvels at the astonishing ability of human beings to go on.

Source: Terry Davis, "Yes, There Is Much Sadness in the World," in *Presenting Chris Crutcher,* Twayne Publishers, 1997, pp. 75–87.

Christine McDonnell

In the following essay, McDonnell traces Crutcher's personal background and connections to situations Crutcher explores in his novels.

Writing with vitality and authority that stems from personal experience in *Running Loose, Stotan!,* and *The Crazy Horse Electric Game* (all

Greenwillow), Chris Crutcher gives readers the inside story on young men, sports, and growing up. His heroes—sensitive, reflective young men, far from stereotypic jocks—use sports as an arena to test personal limits; to prove stamina, integrity, and identity; and to experience loyalty and cooperation as well as competition.

Louie, in *Running Loose,* is no natural athlete. "I've never been all that good. Not too big, not too fast, and a lot more desire to be a football player than to play football, if you know what I mean." Walker, the swim team captain in *Stotan!,* values his team experience over his personal achievement. "I'm part of a group of really special guys—and a girl—who happen to swim. . . . It's a lot more important to me to be a part of that group of humans than it is to be in a school of fast fish." Willie, the gifted baseball player who makes his most famous move in *The Crazy Horse Electric Game,* loses his athletic gift in a boating accident and must learn both a new way of moving and a new definition for himself. For all three, winning is not the goal; doing your best, stretching your limits, is the only true measure of success.

The vitality in these books comes from the characterization, the physical action, and quick dialogue. Crutcher gives us believable glimpses of locker rooms and practice sessions, spiced with irreverent, sometimes coarse, male humor. He shows brief awkward moments of romance in contrast with the honesty, ease, and trust of male friendships. These books are overwhelmingly male, peopled with teammates, coaches, bosses, fathers, and father figures. Women do appear as mothers, girlfriends, even as a coach, and issues of sex and love surface. In *Running Loose* the death of Louie's girlfriend is a central crisis in the book. But for the most part although women are attractive, strong, and smart, they are peripheral to the action, relegated more to fantasy than to day-to-day life.

The action scenes, the training sessions, games, and meets, provide a showcase for the strongest writing in the books. In these, Crutcher's knowledge of sports and his insight into the inner lives of young men merge. He shows not only the physical details of training and practice, the laps, exercises, drills, pacing, and strategies but also the personal experience, the pain, fatigue, exhilaration, pressures, and release. In *Running Loose* and *Stotan!* the final meets rise above simple athletic competition to take on deeper meanings. Athletes compete hoping for victory but also rejoice in one another's performances. Louie runs to prove his strength and independence in a school where his idealism and honesty have isolated him; the team in *Stotan!* swims in honor of their teammate, dying from a blood disease. In both cases the characters are supported and respected by their opponents. Competition can be unifying, not divisive. Over and over again the message is stated: don't give up; give it your best; run your own race.

"I think my job in this life is to be an observer. I'm never going to be one of those guys out there on the tip of the arrow of my time, presenting new ideas or inventing ways to get more information on a smaller chip. But I think I'll learn to see pretty well." The speaker is Walker Dupree, narrator of *Stotan!* but it could be Crutcher describing himself. Speaking directly about his writing, Crutcher said, "I want to be remembered as a storyteller, and I want to tell stories that seem real so that people will recognize something in their own lives and see the connections. We are all connected. That's what I like to explore and put into stories."

The connections between Crutcher's background and the situations he describes in his novels are numerous. Taken in order, *Running Loose, Stotan!,* and *The Crazy Horse Electric Game* give a rough outline of his life. He grew up in Cascade, Idaho, a town exactly like Trout in *Running Loose,* with wilderness nearby, deer in the backyard, driving licenses for fourteen-year-olds, and a school so small that athletes participate in every sport. He played football and basketball and ran track. "There was too much snow for baseball. The high-jumpers wore wet suits and practiced on snowdrifts." Like Louie, his father was the chairman of the school committee, a thoughtful, scientific man who appreciated independence and disliked people accepting things without questioning.

In college at Eastern Washington State, selected because the red and white of its catalog cover set it apart from others on the shelf, Chris swam competitively on a team like the one described in *Stotan!* "But the coach was even more maniacal." With his teammates he experienced a Stotan week that stretched them beyond the limits of their own endurance and forged the bonds of loyalty vividly depicted in *Stotan!*

After college Chris worked as a teacher and as director of an alternative school in Oakland, California, the model for the school described in *The Crazy Horse Electric Game.* The next stage of Chris Crutcher's life appears indirectly in his novels: fed up with waiting in lines and in traffic, he moved to Spokane where he works as a child and

> Chris Crutcher describes himself as being poorly read. 'In high school I was less than a totally serious student. I never had a burning desire to be a writer then. In fact during my four years in high school I read one novel cover to cover: *To Kill a Mockingbird* (Harper).'"

family therapist dealing with physical and sexual abuse cases. In Spokane he began to write seriously.

He now divides his week between his mental health work and his writing, enjoying the balance and contrast of the two. "In my work, the daily crisis of people's lives is so immediate. Time moves so fast. But the books are so permanent. They have their own life in time." Not surprisingly, he also makes time for running and basketball.

"I started writing late, when I recognized the need for a creative outlet in my life. Though I had read relatively little, I had always loved stories. So I gave it a go." While living in the Bay area, he experimented with fiction in a writing workshop. After moving to Spokane, he had time to develop his writing more fully. An author friend remembered one story that Chris had written earlier and suggested that he expand it. *Running Loose* was the result.

Chris Crutcher describes himself as being poorly read. "In high school I was less than a totally serious student. I never had a burning desire to be a writer then. In fact during my four years in high school I read one novel cover to cover: *To Kill a Mockingbird* (Harper)." He still doesn't read much, but through his work he hears stories every day. "I'm interested in relationships, in complexities, in seeing patterns in people's lives. I get information from other people's lives, and I put it into stories, expanding, adding more to make characters richer." Describing his writing process, he cites character as his primary source. "I start with character. Somewhere along the line I get plot. Plot comes last."

But inattention to plot in Crutcher's books is far overshadowed by the strength of characterization and dialogue, coupled with the detail and vitality of the sports scenes. Even when events are surprising, characters are consistently believable. Louie, Walker, and Willie, poised on the edge of manhood, measure themselves in sports and friendships and struggle with larger issues of integrity, dignity, and personal loss. Through their experiences, Chris Crutcher comments powerfully on the broader topic of growing up. At the end of *Stotan!* Walker speaks in a voice that echoes Chris Crutcher's own: "I think if I ever make it to adulthood, and if I decide to turn back and help someone grow up, either as a parent or a teacher or a coach, I'm going to spend most of my time dispelling myths, clearing up unreal expectations. . . . I think I'll learn to see pretty well. I think I'll know how things work—understand simple cause and effect—and, with any luck, be able to pass that on. And that's not such a bad thing."

Source: Christine McDonnell, "New Voices, New Visions: Chris Crutcher," in *Horn Book,* Vol. 64, No. 3, May 1988, pp. 332–5.

Sources

Bosc, Michael, "Street Gangs No Longer Just a Big-City Problem," in *U.S. News & World Report,* p. 108.

Carter, Betty, "Eyes Wide Open," in *School Library Journal Online,* June 2000.

Frederick, Heather Vogel, "What's Known Can't Be Known, " in *Publisher's Weekly,* February 1995, p. 183.

Lamar, Jacob V., "Rolling Out the Big Guns; The First Couple and Congress Press the Attack on Drugs," in *Time,* September 1986, p. 25.

Morning, Todd, Review, in *School Library Journal,* May 1987, p. 108.

Spencer, Pam, Review, in *Voice of Youth Advocates,* 1987.

Sutton, Roger, Review, in *Bulletin of the Center for Children's Books,* 1987.

Wilde, Susie, Review, in *Children's Literature,* 1987.

For Further Study

Davis, Terry, *Presenting Chris Crutcher,* Twayne Publishing, 1997.
    This biography explores the author's life and work.

Gallo, Donald R., ed., *Speaking for Ourselves: Autobiographical Sketches by Notable Authors of Books for Young Adults,* National Council of Teachers of English, 1990.
    A collection of autobiographical essays by young-adult authors, including Chris Crutcher, that discusses their lives and work.

Silvey, Anita, ed., *Children's Books and Their Creators,* Houghton Mifflin, 1995.
    A collection of articles that explore children's book authors and the themes of their work.

Dr. Jekyll and Mr. Hyde

Robert Louis Stevenson
1986

Robert Louis Stevenson's supernatural story *The Strange Case of Dr. Jekyll and Mr. Hyde* (most commonly known by the shortened title *Dr. Jekyll and Mr. Hyde*) became an immediate best-seller in Great Britain and America when it was published in 1886. The novel has also earned accolades from the academic community for its artistic style and penetrating psychological themes. *The Strange Case of Dr. Jekyll and Mr. Hyde* is based on the story of Edinburgh's infamous Deacon Brodie, who was discovered to have been living a double life, coupled with a dream Stevenson had one night, what he called "a fine bogey tale," about a man who drinks a potion made from a white powder and subsequently transforms into a devilish creature. The next morning, Stevenson started to write a detective/horror story in the style of those written by Edgar Allan Poe, and three days later his draft was complete. After a critical response from his wife, Stevenson threw the draft in the fire and started a new one that he completed in another three days and revised during the next six weeks. This version became, with minor alterations, the published version of the text, with its compelling illustration of one man's futile attempts to weed out the evil inclinations of his soul. Most of Stevenson's readers would agree with Stewart F. Sanderson's judgment that the complex characterization of the tortured Dr. Henry Jekyll creates "a work of extraordinary psychological depth and powerful impact."

Robert Louis Stevenson

Author Biography

Robert Louis Stevenson was born in Edinburgh, Scotland, on November 13, 1850, to Thomas, a civil engineer, and Margaret Isabella (Balfour) Stevenson. He was six years old when he first displayed his literary talents during a competition against his cousins. After the competition, one of his uncles presented him with a prize for his history of Moses. At sixteen, his father published his first work, *The Pentland Rising,* an account of a 1666 rebellion by Covenanters. Both works had a religious focus, reflecting the influence of his parents. However, while attending Edinburgh University, Stevenson denounced his Presbyterian upbringing and declared himself to be agnostic. His parents were further disappointed when he discarded his plans to become an engineer and spent a good deal of his time at the university exploring the brothels and pubs of Edinburgh. During his university years, Stevenson gained a reputation for outrageous behavior and earned the name "Velvet Jacket" for his unconventional style of dress.

Stevenson read authors like William Hazlitt and Daniel Defoe at the university and subsequently adopted their styles in his early writing. While working on his law degree, he saw several of his essays published in various periodicals. His first two books, *An Inland Voyage* (1878) and *Travels with a Donkey in the Cevennes* (1879) were based on travels that he enjoyed throughout his life. Although Stevenson earned a degree in law at the university and continued his studies in a law office in Edinburgh, he never practiced the profession, preferring instead to travel and to write. Due to the ill health that plagued him all his life, his parents supported his lifestyle and his writing career, which they considered to be a more restful occupation.

The 1883 publication of his novel *Treasure Island* brought Stevenson worldwide public acclaim. The adventure tale also earned him enough money to devote himself to his writing. Stevenson gained more attention with the publication in 1886 of *The Strange Case of Dr. Jekyll and Mr. Hyde.* He reported that the idea for the novel sprang from a dream he had about a man transforming into a monster after drinking a potion made from white powder. While dreaming this "fine bogey tale," as he called it, Stevenson started to scream and was subsequently awoken by his wife, Fanny. The next morning he began to write and three days later he had completed a first draft. After a negative response from his wife, Stevenson threw the manuscript in the fire and began a rewrite which he completed in another three-day period and revised during the next six weeks.

The subject of evil, explored so creatively in *The Strange Case of Dr. Jekyll and Mr. Hyde,* had fascinated Stevenson throughout his career and had appeared in several of his works. Although he had rejected the Calvinist doctrines his parents taught him, the focus of the interplay of good and evil continued to influence his imagination. A study of this subject in relation to the unconscious and dreams appears prominently in two of his critically acclaimed short stories, "Thrawn Janet" and "Markheim."

Stevenson died on December 3, 1894, in Apia, Samoa. Although Stevenson gained acclaim as a poet, an essayist, and a travel writer as well as a novelist, he will be remembered for his most popular works: *The Strange Case of Dr. Jekyll and Mr. Hyde,* and *Treasure Island.*

Plot Summary

Part I

The story opens with Dr. Jekyll's friend and solicitor, Gabriel John Utterson, and Utterson's distant kinsman, Mr. Enfield, taking a walk one Sunday. They find themselves passing a "certain sinister block of building" in the London district of Soho that "bore in every feature, the marks of prolonged and sordid negligence." After stopping in front of a "blistered and distained" door on this block, Mr. Enfield recalls that one evening at three he was returning home through that section of the city when he saw a man run into a little girl. He notes that "the man trampled calmly over the child's body and left her screaming on the ground." Immediately, Enfield apprehended the man and brought him back to the child and to the group that was gathering around her. Enfield admits that the suspect "was perfectly cool and made no resistance, but gave me one look, so ugly that it brought out the sweat on me." The rest of the crowd responded similarly. After ascertaining that the child was not severely harmed, Enfield directed the man to pay the family compensatory damages. The man then withdrew behind the same door at which Utterson and Enfield now find themselves and returned with a signed check. Both Utterson and Enfield comment on the mysterious air about the house. Enfield admits that he sometimes sees the man, whose name is Hyde, coming in and out of the door and that there is "something wrong with his appearance; something displeasing, something down-right detestable." He continues, "I never saw a man I so disliked, and yet I scarce know why. . . . He gives a strong feeling of deformity." Utterson claims to know the man who signed the check for Hyde, but asks his friend not to speak about the incident in the future.

That evening, Utterson puzzles over a copy of Dr. Jekyll's will with the instructions that at his death, all of his possessions were to pass into the hands of his "friend and benefactor Edward Hyde." It further states that if Dr. Jekyll unexplainably disappears for any period exceeding three calendar months, Hyde should "step into the said Henry Jekyll's shoes without further delay and free from any burthen or obligation." Unable to comprehend Jekyll's motives for writing the will, Utterson seeks advice from one of his oldest friends, Dr. Lanyon, who admits that Jekyll "began to go wrong, wrong in mind" over ten years ago and that he has not seen much of him since. Lanyon claims that he never heard of Edward Hyde.

After that night Utterson begins to "haunt the door in the by-street of shops waiting to catch a glimpse of Hyde." One night, Utterson spots the "pale and dwarfish" man who gave "an impression of deformity without any nameable malformation."

Hyde seems to know him and approaches the lawyer "with a sort of murderous mixture of timidity and boldness," speaking "with a husky, whispering and somewhat broken voice." Utterson concludes that "not all of these together could explain the . . . unknown disgust, loathing and fear" he felt toward this man who seems "hardly human." He reads the stamp of "Satan's signature" upon Hyde's face.

The next day Utterson asks Poole, Dr. Jekyll's servant, about Mr. Hyde. When Poole admits that Jekyll instructed all the servants to obey Hyde, Utterson worries about his friend's safety. Two weeks later, when Utterson brings up the subject of his will, Jekyll tells him not to worry about him.

Part II

A year later, a maid sees from her window Mr. Hyde club an older man to death. After the police find a sealed envelope at the scene addressed to Utterson, they bring it to him the next morning. Later, Utterson identifies the body as Sir Danvers Carew. Utterson also recognizes the stick the murderer used as belonging to Jekyll. When Utterson and the police go to Hyde's residence, they discover the other half of the broken stick in his ransacked rooms. The next afternoon, Utterson finds Jekyll "looking deathly sick," and with a "feverish manner." Jekyll insists he is done with Hyde, who will never be heard of again, as evidenced by a letter he claims Hyde has written. Utterson has Mr. Guest, his head clerk and an expert at handwriting analysis, compare the letter from Hyde to one from Jekyll. When Guest finds "a rather singular resemblance" between the two, Utterson concludes that Jekyll forged the note to protect Hyde.

The police investigate Hyde's past and discover "tales [that] came out of the man's cruelty, at once so callous and violent; of his vile life, of his strange associates, of the hatred that seemed to have surrounded his career." Now that the "evil influence" had been withdrawn, Jekyll enjoys "a new life." He comes out of his seclusion and renews his relations with his friends, charities, and his church. "His face seemed to open and brighten, as if with an inward consciousness of service; and for more than two months, the doctor was at peace." Soon, however, he cuts himself off from his friends. In an effort to understand Jekyll's change of heart, Utterson meets with his friend, Dr. Lanyon, whom he finds seriously ill, with "some deep-seated terror of the mind." Lanyon insists he has had a shock from which he will never recover. He tells Utterson that Jekyll is ill as well and determines to "lead a life of extreme seclusion." After Lanyon dies a few weeks later, Utterson opens an envelope Lanyon gave him and finds a sealed envelope with the instructions "not to be opened till the death or disappearance of Dr. Henry Jekyll."

Part III

One evening Poole arrives at Utterson's home and tells the lawyer that Jekyll has been shut up in his room all week. Poole is certain that there has been "foul play." When the two return to Jekyll's home and try to get him to come out of his room, Jekyll, in a changed voice, refuses. Poole tells Utterson that all week the person in the room has been begging for "some sort of medicine." Utterson breaks down the door and finds the dying Hyde "sorely contorted and still twitching." Jekyll is nowhere to be found. Utterson finds a note from Jekyll asking him to read Lanyon's letter as well as his own confession.

Lanyon's letter relates that one evening, he received a note from Jekyll exclaiming, "my life, my honour, my reason, are all at your mercy; if you fail me to-night, I am lost." Following Jekyll's instructions, Lanyon brought back to his home the contents of a drawer taken from Jekyll's study. The drawer contained a white powder, a vial of some chemical, and a book of entries recording a series of experiments. Lanyon then admitted a dwarfish man wearing clothes much too large for him, who mixed the powder and the contents of the vial. The man suggested that Lanyon watch him, for "a new province of knowledge and new avenues to fame and power shall be laid open to you, here." Lanyon agreed, commenting, "I have gone too far in the way of inexplicable services to pause before I see the end." After the man drank the potion, he transformed into Jekyll. What Jekyll then related "sickened" Lanyon's soul.

Jekyll's confession begins with his description of his "profound duplicity of life" and the shame he felt over his own "provinces of good and ill which divide and compound man's dual nature." In an effort to rid himself of his evil side, Jekyll created a potion that transformed him into Mr. Hyde. Yet he had mixed feelings about this transformation. Part of him as Hyde "felt younger, lighter, happier in body" and more free than Jekyll ever had, while at the same time he recognized this new creature as "pure evil." Jekyll continued taking the potion until one night he found himself transforming without the drug and noted that Hyde was getting stronger. He then admitted that as Hyde he killed Carew "with a transport of glee" and so had

his "lust of evil gratified and stimulated." When the transformations occurred more frequently, and Jekyll realized that eventually he would not be able to transform back into himself, he became Hyde one more time, knowing that he would then commit suicide to keep himself from the gallows.

Characters

Richard Enfield

Utterson's distant kinsman and a "well-known man about town." He is similar in temperament to Utterson. The two men enjoy Sunday walks, putting "the greatest store by these excursions, count[ing] them the chief jewel of each week." They "not only set aside occasions of pleasure, but even resisted the calls of business, that they might enjoy them uninterrupted." Enfield first alerts Utterson to the existence of Hyde.

In his book on Stevenson, Irving S. Saposnik finds Enfield "a strange, yet appropriate complement to his distant kinsman." This "well-known man about town" has a habit of "coming home from some place at the end of the world, about three o'clock of a black winter morning." Thus, according to Saposnik, he represents the "'other Victorian side of Utterson's sobriety.'"

Mr. Guest

Utterson's trustworthy head clerk. "There was no man from whom he kept fewer secrets." Since Guest was also a great student and critic of handwriting, Utterson takes him examples of Jekyll's and Hyde's handwriting, which the clerk finds bears "a rather singular resemblance" to each other.

Edward Hyde

Jekyll transforms both his physical and his moral self into Edward Hyde, a diabolical man who wallows in his wickedness. Stevenson forces readers to gain information about Hyde through the other characters in the novel, which adds to his air of mystery. Enfield insists that there is "something wrong with his appearance; something displeasing, something down-right detestable." He relates the problem many have who encounter him—an inability to get a clear vision of him: "I never saw a man I so disliked, and yet I scarce know why.... He gives a strong feeling of deformity, although I couldn't specify the point.... I can't describe him." Stevenson records the "haunting sense of unexpressed deformity with which the fugitive impressed his beholders."

Utterson expresses his inability to relate an exact description of him when he comments that Hyde "was pale and dwarfish . . . [and] gave an impression of deformity without any nameable malformation." The lawyer notes that when he met Hyde, the latter had "a sort of murderous mixture of timidity and boldness, and he spoke with a husky, whispering and somewhat broken voice. . . . Not all of these together could explain the . . . unknown disgust, loathing and fear with which Mr. Utterson regarded him." In his final estimation, Hyde seemed "hardly human" and marked with "Satan's signature."

Jekyll has a mixed response to his alter ego. When he drinks the potion and transforms into Hyde he at first admits, "I felt younger, lighter, happier in body; within I was conscious of a heady recklessness, a current of disordered sensual images running like a millrace in my fancy . . . an unknown but not an innocent freedom of the soul. I knew myself at the first breath of this new life, to be more wicked, tenfold more wicked, sold a slave to my original evil; and the thought, in that moment, braced and delighted me like wine." After this first transformation, Jekyll notices that he is smaller as Hyde, as if "the evil side of [his] nature, to which [he] had now transferred the stamping efficacy, was less robust and less developed than the good. . . . It had been much less exercised and much less exhausted. . . ." Jekyll embraces the sense of freedom he experiences as Hyde, claiming, "when I looked upon that ugly idol in the glass, I was conscious of no repugnance, rather of a leap of welcome." He understands that Hyde contains an integral part of his soul: "This too was myself. It seemed natural and human. In my eyes it bore a lovelier image of the spirit, it seemed more express and single, than the imperfect and divided countenance I had been hitherto accustomed to call mine."

Yet as Hyde unleashes all of Jekyll's repressed desires, Jekyll cannot help but label him "pure evil" and note that the evil "had left on that body an imprint of deformity and decay." He explains that "in the hands of Edward Hyde [his pleasures] began to turn toward the monstrous," and he became shocked by his "vicarious depravity." Hyde becomes more corrupt as Jekyll tries to contain him. On the evening of Carew's murder, Hyde comes out stronger than he ever had before and, as a result, he beats the helpless man "with a transport of glee." After the murder, "that child of hell had noth-

Media Adaptations

- There have been several film, television, and audio versions of *The Strange Case of Dr. Jekyll and Mr. Hyde.* The six silent films that were made from the novel were produced from 1908 to 1920. The most notable of this group was the version produced by Famous Players-Lasky Corporation, starring John Barrymore and Nita Naldi in 1920. In 1932 Paramount Publix Corp. produced a version starring Fredric March and Miriam Hopkins. Spencer Tracy and Ingrid Bergman starred in the most famous film version, Metro-Goldwyn-Mayer's production in 1941. An educational version was released by Sterling Educational Films in 1959.

- The four television productions include an adaptation by director Charles Jarrott in 1968, starring Jack Palance as Jekyll/Hyde; one by David Winters as a musical in 1973, starring Kirk Douglas; another by Alastar Reed in 1981, starring David Hemmings; and a version by Michael Lindsay-Hogg, starring Anthony Andrews. Hollywood also produced an animated version.

- Several versions have appeared on cassette in abridged as well as complete form. Naxos Audio Books produced an audio compact disc of the novel.

ing human; nothing lived in him but fear and hatred." His fear of the gallows finally prompts him to commit suicide.

Dr. Henry Jekyll

As he does with the character of Edward Hyde, Stevenson surrounds Dr. Jekyll with an air of mystery, suggesting that even his closest friends did not have a clear picture of the man. Readers learn from Jekyll's confession at the end of the book that he was troubled by what he discovered in himself— "those provinces of good and ill which divide and compound man's dual nature." He explains that throughout his life he was "inclined by nature to industry, fond of the respect of the wise and good among my fellowmen, and thus, as might have been supposed, with every guarantee of an honourable and distinguished future." Utterson considers him to be "a large, well-made, smooth-faced man of fifty" who enjoys his relations with his friends and spends his time devoted to his charities and his religion. However Jekyll admits to recognizing in himself a "certain impatient gaiety of disposition" and a failure to conquer his "aversions to the dryness of a life of study." Since he found it difficult to reconcile his baser urges with his "imperious desire to carry [his] head high and wear a more than commonly grave countenance before the public," he suppressed his "undignified" pleasures "with an almost morbid sense of shame." Thus he committed himself "to a profound duplicity of life."

This duplicity continually troubled Jekyll. He explains, "I was no more myself when I laid aside restraint and plunged in shame, than when I laboured, in the eye of day, at the furtherance of knowledge or the relief of sorrow and suffering."

Initially, Jekyll seems to have altruistic motives behind his experiments. His altruism coupled with his hubris overtakes his prudence as evidenced by his admission that "the temptation of a discovery so singular and profound at last overcame the suggestions of alarm." Looking back on the consequences of his actions, Jekyll claims, "Had I approached my discovery in a more noble spirit, had I risked the experiment while under the empire of generous or pious aspirations, all must have been otherwise, [but] at that time my virtue slumbered; my evil, kept awake by ambition, as alert and swift to seize the occasion."

When Hyde starts to appear without the aid of the potion, Jekyll's fears engulf him. He suspects that if this were "much prolonged, the balance of [his] nature might be permanently overthrown, the power of voluntary change be forfeited, and the character of Hyde become irrevocably" his. He recognizes that he is slowly losing hold of his "original and better self," and becoming slowly incorporated with his "second and worse." Jekyll develops a real horror of becoming Hyde when he recognizes, "to cast it in with Hyde, was to die to a thousand interests and aspirations, and to become . . . forever despised and friendless." As a result, he stops taking the potion and returns for a time to his old self, regaining "an inward consciousness of service." However, he does not have the strength to keep his darker side in check. After two months, he "began to be tortured with throes and longings, as of Hyde struggling after freedom" and so "in a

moment of weakness and at last, in an hour of moral weakness, I once again compounded and swallowed the transforming draught."

Dr. Hastie Lanyon

Early in the novel, when Jekyll's behavior confounds him, Utterson seeks advice from his "genial" friend Dr. Lanyon—a "healthy, dapper, red-faced gentleman" with "a boisterous and decided manner." Lanyon and Utterson are Jekyll's two oldest friends. Later in the novel, however, Lanyon's appearance and disposition change as noted by Utterson, who finds his friend seriously ill with "some deep-seated terror of the mind." The shock of facing Hyde's true identity disables him and eventually leads to his death.

Jekyll as Hyde considers Lanyon "bound to the most narrow and material views . . . [denying] the virtue of transcendental medicine." Hyde also criticizes him for not taking Jekyll's work seriously. Yet when Hyde suggests that Lanyon should watch what happens when Hyde drinks the potion so "a new province of knowledge and new avenues to fame and power shall be laid open to you, here," Lanyon agrees. His curiosity emerges in his response: "I have gone too far in the way of inexplicable services to pause before I see the end." "The moral turpitude" Hyde unveils to him, though, "sickens" his soul.

Saposnik determines Lanyon's refusal to be involved in his friend's scientific inquiries to stem from his cowardice rather than his lack of conviction. Saposnik argues that Lanyon abandons Jekyll "because he was afraid of the temptation to which he finally succumbed," the offer Hyde made to show him "a new province of knowledge and new avenues to fame and power." Commenting on Lanyon's relationship with Jekyll, Saposnik calls him "a friend in name only" whose "envy of Jekyll works in direct contrast to that which prompts Utterson to loyalty. Like Jekyll, Lanyon's outward manner belies his inner compulsions; but, unlike his colleague, he cannot struggle with their emergence."

Poole

Poole is Jekyll's servant, who provides information to Utterson about his master. Poole exhibits loyalty and concern about Jekyll's welfare.

Gabriel John Utterson

Utterson is Jekyll's "dry" lawyer and friend. Stevenson characterizes him as having "a rugged countenance that was never lighted by a smile." He is "cold, scanty and embarrassed in discourse," "backward in sentiment" "dusty, dreary and yet somehow lovable." In his discourse with others, "something eminently human beaconed from his eye; something indeed which never found its way into his talk . . . but more often and loudly in the acts of his life." "He was austere with himself, but he had an approved tolerance for others," as evidenced through his patience with Jekyll in all of his dealings with him. Utterson admits, "I incline to Cain's heresy. . . . I let my brother go to the devil in his own way."

Foreshadowing his future relationship with Jekyll, Stevenson writes, "in this character, it was frequently his fortune to be the last reputable acquaintance and the last good influence in the lives of downgoing men." Though staid and serious, he found his friends and acquaintances "liked to sit a while in his unobtrusive company, practicing for solitude, sobering their minds in the man's rich silence after the expense and strain of gaiety."

Sanderson notes Stevenson's effective use of juxtaposition as he counters the novel's "sharply focused images of violence," with Utterson's character, which Sanderson describes as "equally economical and graphic." Sanderson considers Utterson "unsmiling, unsentimental, austere, but tolerant of the peccadilloes of others, and inclined always to help rather than to reprove; a man of complete probity and conscience in matters of trust."

Saposnik argues that Stevenson presents Utterson as the novel's "moral norm." Saposnik decides that the novel opens with a focus on Utterson

> not only because he is Jekyll's confidant (the only one remaining) but because by person and profession he represents the best and worst of Victoria's social beings. Pledged to a code harsh in its application, he has not allowed its pressures to mar his sense of human need. . . . As a lawyer, he represents that legality which identifies social behavior as established law, unwritten but binding; as a judge, however, he is a combination of justice and mercy (as his names Gabriel John suggest), tempering rigidity with kindness, self-denial with compassion.

Themes

Supernaturalism

The Strange Case of Dr. Jekyll and Mr. Hyde is a fine example of supernatural fiction. Supernatural works focus on metaphysical concerns, based on the need to understand the unknown and unnameable. In primitive societies, reality that could not be comprehended was explained through folk-

tale and fable—the foundation for all supernatural works. In supernatural literature at least one of the main characters goes against the laws of nature. The themes of these works revolve around good and evil, love and hate. One overriding impulse is to regain the natural order of the universe, to escape from the world of unknown terrors and return to normal day-to-day life. Readers respond to these works with amazement, terror, or relief as the characters struggle to return to that natural order.

One type of supernatural fiction focuses on the Promethean personality. This term was taken from Greek mythology. Prometheus, the son of Iapetus and Clymene, was one of the great benefactors of mankind. According to legend, he molded mankind out of clay and water. He later stole fire from the gods and gave it to man, who was then able to learn the sciences. Zeus considered these acts to be a form of blasphemy, and so he had Prometheus chained to a mountain peak in the Caucasus. During the day an eagle would tear at his liver, which would grow back during the night, only to be eaten again the next day.

The literature that contains elements of the Promethean personality includes Mary Shelley's *Frankenstein,* Bram Stoker's *Dracula,* and Robert Louis Stevenson's *The Strange Case of Dr. Jekyll and Mr. Hyde.* Dr. Frankenstein and Dr. Jekyll are especially Promethean. They are both scientists who defy the natural laws of God and the universe in an effort to create life. In each story there is little scientific detail; the focus instead is on the consequences of "playing God." This type of literature also relies on gothic conventions, especially setting details like desolate landscapes and dark alleys.

Jekyll explains his Promethean urges when he describes the seemingly altruistic motives behind his experiments. He determines that if the evil impulses could be separated from the good,

> if each . . . could be housed in separate identities, life would be relieved of all that was unbearable; the unjust might go his way, delivered from the aspirations and remorse of his more upright twin; and the just could walk steadfastly and securely on his upward path, doing the good things in which he found his pleasure, and no longer exposed to disgrace and penitence by the hands of this extraneous evil. It was the curse of mankind that these incongruous faggots were thus bound together—that the agonized womb of consciousness, these polar twins should be continuously struggling.

Like Frankenstein, however, Jekyll's ambition overtakes his caution. In his confession Jekyll admits,

Topics for Further Study

- Research Freud's theories on sublimation and apply them to the character of Dr. Jekyll.

- Philosopher Friedrich Nietzsche was Stevenson's contemporary. Investigate Nietzsche's theories of good and evil and apply them to *The Strange Case of Dr. Jekyll and Mr. Hyde.*

- Write your own detective story or tale of the supernatural.

- Compare and contrast the structure of *The Strange Case of Dr. Jekyll and Mr. Hyde* to that of one of Edgar Allan Poe's short stories.

---

the temptation of a discovery so singular and profound at last overcame the suggestions of alarm. . . . Had I approached my discovery in a more noble spirit, had I risked the experiment while under the empire of generous or pious aspirations, all must have been otherwise, [but] at that time my virtue slumbered; my evil, kept awake by ambition, was alert and swift to seize the occasion.

Identity

Dr. Jekyll disturbs the natural order of the universe because throughout his life he struggles to accept the dual nature of his identity. He determines that all of us are plagued with this duality: "With every day, and for both sides of my intelligence, the moral and the intellectual, I thus drew steadily nearer to that truth, by whose partial discovery I have been doomed . . . that man is not truly one, but truly two. . . . I hazard the guess that man will be ultimately known for a mere polity of multifarious, incongruous and independent denizens." He explains that throughout his life he was "inclined by nature to industry, fond of the respect of the wise and good among my fellowmen, and thus, as might have been supposed, with every guarantee of an honourable and distinguished future." However Jekyll also admits to recognizing in himself a "certain impatient gaiety of disposition" and a failure to conquer his "aversions to the dryness of a life of study." Jekyll is troubled by "those provinces of

good and ill which divide and compound man's dual nature" and so determines to rid himself of his baser desires.

Change and Transformation

This need to remove the troublesome part of his identity prompts Jekyll to defy the natural laws of the universe by transforming into the diabolical Mr. Hyde. Irving S. Saposnik, in his essay on *The Strange Case of Dr. Jekyll and Mr. Hyde,* comments, "As the mirror of Jekyll's inner compulsions, he represents that shadow side of man which civilization has striven to submerge: he is a creature of primitive sensibilities loosed upon a world bent on denying him. A reminder of the barbarism which underlies civilization, he is a necessary component of human psychology which most would prefer to leave unrealized."

Freedom

Jekyll must admit to experiencing a certain sense of freedom when he transforms into this "shadow side" of himself. When he becomes Hyde he notes, "I felt younger, lighter, happier in body; within I was conscious of a heady recklessness, a current of disordered sensual images running like a millrace in my fancy . . . an unknown but not an innocent freedom of the soul." The freedom he experiences results from the release of his inner desires, which, being a respectable Victorian gentleman, he previously had to suppress.

Good and Evil

Stevenson's main focus in the novel is on this struggle between good and evil in Jekyll's soul. G. B. Stern in his book on Stevenson argues that the novel is "a symbolic portrayal of the dual nature of man, with the moral inverted: not to impress us by the victory of good over evil, but to warn us of the strength and ultimate triumph of evil over good once sin is suffered to enter human habitation."

Style

Point of View

Stevenson continually alters the point of view in *The Strange Case of Dr. Jekyll and Mr. Hyde,* which creates suspense and reinforces the novel's concentration on duplicity. The novel opens with a focus on John Gabriel Utterson, Dr. Jekyll's friend and attorney, and his gradual uncovering of the horror that lies at the heart of the story. Then the narrative immediately shifts to Utterson's friend and relative, Richard Enfield, who first informs Utterson of the existence of Edward Hyde. Enfield expresses the problem faced by those who encounter Hyde and try to describe him when he comments, "I never saw a man I so disliked, and yet I scarce know why. . . . He gives a strong feeling of deformity, although I couldn't specify the point. . . . I can't describe him." Others who see him are struck by a "haunting sense of unexpressed deformity." The characters' inability to gain a clear vision of Hyde reflects his nature. Hyde represents Jekyll's dark side, an integral part of his soul that he had repressed for years. In his assessment of Hyde, Jekyll insists, "This too was myself." Yet readers do not gain a full understanding of Hyde or Jekyll until the end of the book when Jekyll makes his confession.

Narrative

In his overview of *The Strange Case of Dr. Jekyll and Mr. Hyde* Stewart F. Sanderson comments on the construction of the narrative: "The pace of the narration, the deft way in which details supporting both the action and its unravelling are interwoven throughout the narrative, and the economy with which the story's terrifying atmosphere is created, combine to form a work of extraordinary psychological depth and powerful impact."

Irving S. Saposnik, in his book on Stevenson, also praises the novel's narrative construction:

> The three separable narrative voices—Enfield, Lanyon, Jekyll—are placed in successive order so that they add increasing rhetorical and psychological dimension to the events they describe. In contrast to other multiple narratives whose several perspectives often raise questions of subjective truth and moral ambiguity, these individual narratives in *The Strange Case of Dr. Jekyll and Mr. Hyde* provide a linear regularity of information—an incremental catalogue of attitudes toward Hyde's repulsiveness and Jekyll's decline.

Style

Several critics have praised the novel's style. Stephen Gwynn, in his book on Stevenson, insists that the novel is "a fable that lies nearer to poetry than to ordinary prose fiction." In his lecture on *The Strange Case of Dr. Jekyll and Mr. Hyde,* Vladimir Nabokov comments, "Stevenson had to rely on style very much in order to perform the trick, in order to master the two main difficulties confronting him: (1) to make the magic potion a plausible drug based on a chemist's ingredients and (2) to make Jekyll's evil side before and after the

"hydization" a believable evil." Nabokov suggests that Stevenson accomplishes these goals through his use of setting and symbolism in the novel.

Setting

Stevenson provides setting details that gain symbolic significance in the novel. His description of London helps set a mood of suspense and suggests a foreboding sense of evil. In the morning fog, London becomes

> dark like the light of some strange conflagration; and here, for a moment, the fog would be quite broken up, and a haggard shaft of daylight would glance in between the swirling wreaths. The dismal quarter of Soho seen under these changing glimpses, with its muddy ways, and slatternly passengers, and its lamps, which had never been extinguished or had been kindled afresh to combat this mournful reinvasion of darkness, seemed . . . like a district of some city in a nightmare.

Stevenson's description of the section of Soho where Hyde resides is especially ominous. As Utterson and Enfield walk through the city at the beginning of the novel, they find themselves in "a busy quarter" of London and pass a "certain sinister block of building" that "bore in every feature, the marks of prolonged and sordid negligence." The door to Hyde's quarters, in front of which the two men pause, is "blistered and distained. Tramps slouched into the recess. . . . The schoolboy had tried his knife on the mouldings; and for close on a generation, no one had appeared to drive away these random visitors or to repair their ravages."

Symbol

Stevenson uses other symbolic devices in the story, including the names "Jekyll" and "Hyde," which are of Scandinavian origin. Hyde comes from the Danish word *hide* which means "a haven" and Jekyll comes from the Danish name *Jokulle,* which means "an icicle." Nabokov argues, "Not knowing these simple derivations one would be apt to find all kinds of symbolic meanings, especially in Hyde, the most obvious being that Hyde is a kind of hiding place for Dr. Jekyll, in whom the jocular doctor and the killer are combined." Utterson's name closely fits his austere nature and relates to one of the novel's themes—the repression of personality.

Nabokov finds another important symbol in the story. The reader eventually learns that Jekyll's dissecting room, which he altered for his experiments, has become Hyde's quarters and the place where the transformations take place. Nabokov notes, "The relations of [Jekyll and Hyde] are typified by Jekyll's house, which is half Jekyll and half Hyde."

Saposnik concludes,

> the topography of *The Strange Case of Dr. Jekyll and Mr. Hyde* may be seen as a study in symbolic location, a carefully worked out series of contrasts between exterior modes and interior realities. Like much of Victorian life and letters, most of the story's action is physically internalized behind four walls. Utterson's ruminations, Lanyon's seduction, and Jekyll-Hyde's death all occur within the protective confines of what Stevenson in an essay termed "The Ideal House."

This Victorian home sheltered its inhabitants from public scrutiny.

Saposnik notes that as the action becomes more internal, so does the psychological direction of the novel:

> Although the reader's first views of the house are external, the action soon directs him to the hall, then to the study, and finally to the ominous experiments behind the closed door of the former dissection laboratory. As Poole and Utterson break down the last barrier to Jekyll's secret, they literally and metaphorically destroy his one remaining refuge; by invading his physical sanctuary, they force him into a psychological admission whose only possibility is death.

Historical Context

Benthamism

Benthamism, also known as utilitarianism, became an important ideology in Victorian society. The term came to be associated with a philosophy of Jeremy Bentham, expressed in his *Introduction to the Principles of Morals and Legislation,* that was adopted by a large portion of the Victorian middle class, affecting their habits and beliefs. By the 1820s, Benthamism gained a number of disciples who promoted his theories in theoretical debates. Supporters gained political power in the 1830s when approximately one hundred were elected to the first reformed Parliament in England.

At the core of this philosophy was the belief in "the greatest happiness for the greatest number," a phrase borrowed from Joseph Priestley, a late eighteenth-century Unitarian theologian. At the heart of this belief was the supposition that self-interest should be one's primary concern and that happiness could be attained by avoiding pain and seeking pleasure. In *Victorian People and Ideas,* Richard D. Altick explains that "utilitarianism was

. . . wholly hedonistic; it made no allowance for the promptings of conscience, or for . . . the forces of generosity, mercy, compassion, self-sacrifice, love. Benthamite ethics had nothing to do with Christian morality."

Evangelicalism

Another equally important movement in the Victorian Age was Evangelicalism, a form of Protestant pietism. Evangelicalism focused less on doctrine and more on the day-to-day lives and eventual salvation of its followers. It set rigid patterns of conduct for its practitioners to follow in order that they might find atonement for their sins. Altick notes that "the Evangelical's anxious eye was forever fixed upon the 'eternal microscope' which searched for every moral blemish and reported every motion of the soul." The religion is also noted for its inspiration of humanitarian activities during the Victorian age.

London at the End of the Nineteenth Century

Michael Sadler describes London in the latter half of the nineteenth century in his *Forlorn Sunset* (1947):

> London in the early sixties was still three parts jungle. Except for the residential and shopping areas . . . hardly a district was really "public" in the sense that ordinary folk went to and fro. . . . There was no knowing what kind of a queer patch you might strike, in what blind alley you might find yourself, to what embarrassment, insult, or even molestation you might be exposed. So the conventional middle class kept to the big thoroughfares, conscious that just behind the house-fronts to either side murmured a million hidden lives, but incurious as to their kind, and hardly aware that those who lived there were also London citizens."

Irving S. Saposnik in his article on Stevenson notes that during this period, London was

> much like its inhabitants, a macrocosm of the necessary fragmentation that Victorian man found inescapable. . . . [It] represented that division-within-essential-unity which is the very meaning of *The Strange Case of Dr. Jekyll and Mr. Hyde.* As both geographic and symbolic center, London exemplified what Stevenson called it in *New Arabian Nights,* "the great battlefield of mankind."

Reverend William Tuckniss describes London at the end of the nineteenth century as a place where

> the seeds of good and evil are brought to the highest state of maturity, and virtue and vice most rapidly developed, under the forcing influences that everywhere abound. . . . London then may be considered as the grand central focus of operations, at once the

Compare & Contrast

- **1886:** Britain annexes upper Burma after the Anglo-Burmese war, but revolutionary forces will try to regain control for several years.

  Today: The British Empire exerts its influence over only a handful of colonies, protectorates, or trust territories.

- **1886:** *Das Kapital* by Karl Marx is published in English.

  1887: "Bloody Sunday," a Socialist demonstration, erupts in Trafalgar Square.

  1926: Joseph Stalin becomes dictator of the Soviet Union. His reign of terror will last for twenty-seven years.

  1991: On December 17, president Mikhail Gorbachev orders the dissolution of the Soviet Union, and a new Commonwealth of Independent States is formed by the countries that formerly made up the USSR.

- **1882:** The Married Woman's Property Act passes in England, granting women several important rights.

  Today: Women are guaranteed equal rights under the law.

- **1901:** Queen Victoria dies and the Victorian Age ends. She is succeeded by Edward VII and the beginning of the Edwardian Age.

  Today: The British monarchy has been damaged by several scandals including the reported infidelities of Prince Charles and Lady Diana, their subsequent divorce, and her subsequent death.

---

emporium of crime and the palladium of Christianity. It is, in fact, the great arena of conflict between the powers of darkness and the ministry of heaven. . . . It is here that they join issue in the most deadly proximity, and struggle for the vantage-ground.

Critical Overview

When *The Strange Case of Dr. Jekyll and Mr. Hyde* by Robert Louis Stevenson was published in 1886, it quickly became a best seller in America and Great Britain and soon, its two main characters became part of the vocabulary of common speech. Whenever someone refers to a "Jekyll and Hyde personality," it is understood to mean someone with a combination of agreeable and disagreeable traits that appear in different situations. Since its initial publication, the work has appeared in several editions in print and has been adapted in various film, television, and audio versions. The novel has gained critical acclaim as well, especially for its narrative structure and its thematic significance.

James Ashcroft Noble, in his 1886 review of the book for *The Academy,* writes, "It is, indeed, many years since English fiction has been enriched by any work at once so weirdly imaginative in conception and so faultlessly ingenious in construction as this little tale." Celebrated novelist Henry James comments in his 1888 review for *The Century* that it has "the stamp of a really imaginative production." James praises Stevenson's artful construction of the "short, rapid, concentrated story, which is really a masterpiece of concision," and its consequential ability to sustain the reader's interest. Critic Leslie Stephen, in his 1902 assessment of the novel, finds it "able to revive the old thrill of delicious horror in one who does not care for psychical research; it has the same power of carrying one away by its imaginative intensity." In his piece on Stevenson for *Dictionary of Literary Biography,* Robert Kiely explains, "Readers of [Stevenson's] own time were exhilarated by the freshness, the unexpected directness in the midst of luscious paragraphs in which he had seemed only to be marking time. . . . Part of the appeal of the tale is, as the title suggests, its strangeness. It has its own obses-

Frederic March in the 1932 film version of the novel.

sive logic and momentum that sweep the reader along." Stewart F. Sanderson in his overview of the novel argues, "The pace of the narration, the deft way in which details supporting both the action and its unravelling are interwoven throughout the narrative, and the economy with which the story's terrifying atmosphere is created, combine to form a work of extraordinary psychological depth and powerful impact." Stephen Gwynn, in his book on Stevenson, praises the novel's style, insisting that it is "a fable that lies nearer to poetry than to ordinary prose fiction." Vladimir Nabokov, in his lecture on the book, considers it "a phenomenon of style" with "its own special enchantment."

Several critics have also celebrated Stevenson's psychological portrait of the novel's central character and his struggles with "those provinces of good and ill which divide and compound man's dual nature." Commenting on one of the novel's themes, Sanderson writes,

> the notion of evil and the frailty of conscience coincides here with Stevenson's imaginative treatment and literary craftsmanship to form a work of remarkable power; so much so, particularly as the pace quickens with Jekyll's desperate attempts to replace the failing supply of his drug, that the reader is swept forward without questioning the premises of the al-

legory or the credibility of this strange but realistic tale.

Noble echoes this assessment when he concludes that the novel has a "much larger and deeper interest than that belonging to a mere skilful narrative. It is a marvelous exploration into the recesses of human nature; and though it is more than possible that Mr. Stevenson wrote with no ethical intent, its impressiveness as a parable is equal to its fascination as a work of art." Kiely notes the allegorical nature of the story with its "warnings against intellectual pride, hypocrisy, and indifference to the power of the evil within," but claims that "the continuing attraction of *The Strange Case of Dr. Jekyll and Mr. Hyde* is of an adult's nightmare of disintegration."

James praises Stevenson's exploration of the duality that exists in human nature, commenting that "the subject is endlessly interesting, and rich in all sorts of provocation, and Mr. Stevenson is to be congratulated on having touched the core of it. . . . There is a genuine feeling for the perpetual moral question, a fresh sense of the difficulty of being good and the brutishness of being bad."

Other critics have noted how successfully the novel illuminates Victorian sensibilities. Irving S. Saposnik, in his essay on the novel, applauds its "formal complexity and its moral depth" and its intricate portrait of Victorian mores: "With characteristic haste, it plunges immediately into the center of Victorian society to dredge up a creature ever present but submerged; not the evil opponent of a contentious good but the shadow self of a half man." Focusing on Stevenson's characterization of Henry Jekyll, Saposnik notes that he is "a complex example of his age of anxiety: woefully weighed down by self-deception, cruelly a slave to his own weakness, sadly a disciple of a severe discipline, his is a voice out of 'De Profundis,' a cry of Victorian man from the depths of his self-imposed underground." Saposnik concludes, "Victorian anxieties contributed greatly to *The Strange Case of Dr. Jekyll and Mr. Hyde*'s success. The fictional paradox revealed the social paradox; Jekyll's dilemma spoke for more of his countrymen than many were willing to admit."

At the time of his death in 1894, Stevenson's literary reputation was firmly established. During the 1920s and 1930s, however, his works fell out of favor with scholars who considered them to be derivative and affected. Two decades later, critics and the public alike again praised his works. Today, the novel continues its popularity, even though

Stevenson admitted that he thought it to be the worst piece he ever wrote.

Criticism

Wendy Perkins

Perkins is an associate professor of English at Prince George's Community College in Maryland and has published several articles on British and American authors. In the following essay, she examines how The Strange Case of Dr. Jekyll and Mr. Hyde *reflects the influence of two important ideological forces in Victorian England: utilitarianism and Evangelicalism.*

Two ideologies, utilitarianism and Evangelicalism, shaped the customs and mores of Victorian society in England during the nineteenth century. In *Victorian People and Ideas,* Richard D. Altick analyzes the impact of these two forces on Victorians, concluding "together they were responsible for much that was unappealing—to some Victorians as to us—in the age's thought and manners. . . . Both left their ineradicable imprint upon the whole of the Victorian period." They also left their mark on the literature of the age. In his classic tale *The Strange Case of Dr. Jekyll and Mr. Hyde,* Robert Louis Stevenson illustrates the destructive influence that utilitarian and Evangelical ideologies could have on the lives of the Victorians. In his complex characterization of Dr. Jekyll and his alter ego, Edward Hyde, Stevenson presents a critique of middle-class Victorian society and its adoption of the tenets of these two movements.

Utilitarianism, or Benthamism, was derived from the philosophy of Jeremy Bentham, expressed in his *Introduction to the Principles of Morals and Legislation.* Utilitarians believed that self-interest should be one's primary concern and that happiness could be attained by avoiding pain and seeking pleasure. Evangelicalism, on the other hand, focused less on secular philosophy and more on the day-to-day lives and eventual salvation of its followers. In contrast to the hedonistic approach of Benthamism, Evangelicalism demanded a rigid code of conduct from its practitioners in exchange for the forgiveness of sin. It also sparked a wave of humanitarian reform that swept Great Britain during the mid-1800s.

Historian G. S. R. Kitson Clark, in his *An Expanding Society,* explains that the two ideologies

are poles apart in their intellectual postulates, but in their methods of thought and in their practical results

> When Jekyll takes the potion and transforms into Hyde, he experiences, for the first time, a free expression of his desires."

they are very much the same. In each case a hard dogmatic position is chosen and adhered to without the slightest concession to the fact that it is necessary sometimes to respect other people's opinions, and the implications of that position are put into effect remorselessly and coldly. They were fit creeds for a period of emotional tension and fanaticism.

Altick adds that in the commingling of these two ideologies in Victorian society, "a quasi-fundamentalist brand of Christianity was pitted against a vigorously skeptical, even downright anti-religious secular movement. Yet working from sometimes antithetical premises, they joined to create and rationalize what came to be known as middle-class values." Historian Elie Halevy in his *England in 1815* argues, "The fundamental paradox of English society [in the Victorian age] . . . is precisely the partial junction and combination of these two forces theoretically so hostile."

Readers first get a glimpse of one of these ideologies, Evangelicalism, in the character of Dr. Jekyll's friend and attorney Gabriel John Utterson. Stevenson describes him as "dry, cold, scanty and embarrassed in discourse," and "dusty, dreary," and notes that his face was "never lighted by a smile." His friends and acquaintances "liked to sit a while in his unobtrusive company, practicing for solitude, sobering their minds in the man's rich silence after the expense and strain of gaiety." Utterson's repressed personality and his friends' appreciation of it provide a good example of the rigid patterns of conduct followed by many middle-class Victorians who were influenced by the tenets of utilitarianism.

Yet Utterson has a human side that refuses to condemn others for not adhering to a strict code of conduct. Stevenson notes that "something eminently human beaconed from his eye; something indeed which never found its way into his talk . . . but more often and loudly in the acts of his life." Although he judged himself harshly, "he had an approved tolerance for others," as evidenced through his patience with Jekyll in all of his dealings with him. Irving S. Saposnik, in his essay on the novel,

What Do I Read Next?

- *Mary Reilly* (1990), by Valerie Martin, tells the fictional story of the young maid, Mary Reilly, sent to live and work in the house of Dr. Jekyll/Mr. Hyde.

- *Frankenstein, or the Modern Prometheus* (1818), by Mary Shelley, focuses on another man who tries to alter nature and, as a result, destroys himself.

- For another complex study of good and evil, turn to Stevenson's *Treasure Island* (1884), his first bestseller.

- Bram Stoker's classic *Dracula,* published in 1897, presents a penetrating commentary on Victorian society as well as the nature of evil.

- The psychological studies of the criminal mind presented in Edgar Allan Poe's short stories like "The Tell-Tale Heart" and "The Cask of Amontillado" also reveal the author's mastery of the detective fiction form. A good collection of his works is *The Complete Stories and Poems of Edgar Allan Poe,* published by Doubleday in 1966.

argues that Stevenson presents Utterson as the novel's "moral norm." Saposnik decides that the novel opens with a focus on Utterson

> not only because he is Jekyll's confidant (the only one remaining) but because by person and profession he represents the best and worst of Victoria's social beings. Pledged to a code harsh in its application, he has not allowed its pressures to mar his sense of human need. . . . As a lawyer, he represents that legality which identifies social behavior as established law, unwritten but binding; as a judge, however, he is a combination of justice and mercy (as his names Gabriel John suggest), tempering rigidity with kindness, self-denial with compassion.

Richard Enfield, Utterson's relative and friend, has a similar temperament to that of Utterson. In his book on Stevenson, Saposnik finds Enfield "a strange, yet appropriate complement to his distant kinsman." This "well-known man about town" has a habit of "coming home from some place at the end of the world, about three o'clock of a black winter morning." Thus, according to Saposnik, he represents the " 'other Victorian' side of Utterson's sobriety."

The negative influence of utilitarian and Evangelical ideologies becomes most apparent in Stevenson's characterization of Dr. Henry Jekyll, the novel's protagonist as well as its antagonist in his guise as Edward Hyde. Jekyll discovers within himself "those provinces of good and ill which divide and compound man's dual nature"—a state exacerbated and perhaps generated by these two main forces of Victorian society. Jekyll notes that throughout his life he was "inclined by nature to industry, fond of the respect of the wise and good among my fellowmen, and thus, as might have been supposed, with every guarantee of an honourable and distinguished future." He enjoys his relations with his friends and spends his time devoted to his charities and his church. Jekyll's dedication to humanitarian activities suggests his adoption of Evangelical doctrine. He seems also to adopt another tenet of that ideology—one that persuades followers to repress the "sinful" part of their nature. Thus when Jekyll admits to recognizing in himself a "certain impatient gaiety of disposition" and a failure to conquer his "aversions to the dryness of a life of study," his response is to try to repress those urges. His society encourages his "imperious desire to carry [his] head high and wear a more than commonly grave countenance before the public." Yet sometimes his "undignified" pleasures surface, and, as a result, he is filled "with an almost morbid sense of shame."

While Stevenson keeps the explicit nature of these "undignified" pleasures hidden, he clearly shows the effect of their existence on Jekyll, who considers them to be sinful and an expression of the "evil" side of his personality. Jekyll provides readers with a clue as to the nature of these hidden desires when he transforms into Hyde, who becomes the embodiment of his darker side. He notes with repugnance that Hyde's "every act and thought centered on self; drinking pleasure with bestial avidity from any degree of torture to another; relentless like a man of stone." Hyde clearly reflects the utilitarian devotion to hedonism and its lack of allowance for compassion, mercy, and love.

When Jekyll first considers conducting experiments in order to rid himself of his evil side, he appears to be motivated more by altruistic impulses. He considers that if the evil impulses could be separated from the good,

> if each . . . could be housed in separate identities, life would be relieved of all that was unbearable; the unjust might go his way, delivered from the aspirations and remorse of his more upright twin; and the just could walk steadfastly and securely on his upward path, doing the good things in which he found his pleasure, and no longer exposed to disgrace and penitence by the hands of this extraneous evil. It was the curse of mankind that these incongruous faggots were thus bound together—that the agonized womb of consciousness, these polar twins should be continuously struggling.

The more utilitarian side of his nature, however, soon emerges and overtakes his prudence as evidenced by his admission that "the temptation of a discovery so singular and profound at last overcame the suggestions of alarm." Looking back on the consequences of his actions, Jekyll claims, "Had I approached my discovery in a more noble spirit, had I risked the experiment while under the empire of generous or pious aspirations, all must have been otherwise, [but] at that time my virtue slumbered; my evil, kept awake by ambition, as alert and swift to seize the occasion."

The pressure Jekyll feels to conform to the dictates of society and thus to suppress his desires becomes overwhelming and inspires his decision to tamper with nature. Saposnik concludes that

> Victorian man was haunted constantly by an inescapable sense of division. As rational and sensual being, as public and private man, as civilized and bestial creature, he found himself necessarily an actor, playing only that part of himself suitable to the occasion. As both variables grew more predictable, his role became more stylized; and what was initially an occasional practice became a way of life. By 1886, the English could already be described as "Masqueraders," . . . and it is to all aspects of this existential charade that *The Strange Case of Dr. Jekyll and Mr. Hyde* addresses itself.

This duplicity continually troubles Jekyll. He explains, "I was no more myself when I laid aside restraint and plunged in shame, than when I laboured, in the eye of day, at the furtherance of knowledge or the relief of sorrow and suffering." His scientific background seems to offer him a way out.

When Jekyll takes the potion and transforms into Hyde, he experiences, for the first time, a free expression of his desires. He admits, "I felt younger, lighter, happier in body; within I was conscious of a heady recklessness, a current of disordered sensual images running like a millrace in my fancy." Even though he confesses, "I knew myself

at the first breath of this new life, to be more wicked, tenfold more wicked, sold a slave to my original evil," he also cannot deny that "the thought, in that moment, braced and delighted me like wine." This new freedom after such a lifetime of repression becomes too intoxicating for Jekyll. Expressing his joy over his new state, he reveals that he "could plod in the public eye with a load of genial respectability, and in a moment . . . strip off these lendings and spring headlong into the sea of liberty." He admits Hyde is "pure evil," and that he feels pangs of conscience after Hyde's nighttime acts of "vicarious depravity." Yet he also confesses, "when I looked upon that ugly idol in the glass, I was conscious of no repugnance, rather of a leap of welcome. This too was myself. It seemed natural and human. In my eyes it bore a lovelier image of the spirit, it seemed more express and single, than the imperfect and divided countenance I had been hitherto accustomed to call mine."

Ironically, while Jekyll suffers from having to live a double life before the transformations, he enjoys his duplicity after them. When he can give free expression to each side of his nature, he is content, even though as Hyde, his urges are becoming more and more depraved. Saposnik argues that Jekyll's continued transformations reveal his moral weakness. He concludes,

> Dedicated to an ethical rigidity more severe than Utterson's, because solely self-centered, he cannot face the necessary containment of his dual being. However he may attempt to disguise his experiments under scientific objectivity, and his actions under a macabre alter-ego, he is unable to mask his basic selfishness. . . . He has thrived upon duplicity; and his reputation has been maintained largely upon his successful ability to deceive.

When Hyde starts to appear without the aid of the potion, he suspects that if this were "much prolonged, the balance of [his] nature might be permanently overthrown, the power of voluntary change be forfeited, and the character of Hyde become irrevocably" his. He recognizes that he is slowly losing hold of his "original and better self," and gradually becoming incorporated with his "second and worse." Yet Hyde, along with Jekyll's unacceptable desires, has been repressed too long, and so takes control of Jekyll's better side.

In his final assessment of Henry Jekyll, Saposnik concludes that the doctor is a "complex example of his age of anxiety: woefully weighed down by self-deception, cruelly a slave to his own weakness, sadly a disciple of a severe discipline, his is a voice out of *De Profundis*,' a cry of Victorian

> Hyde must be hidden not simply because he is wicked but because Dr. Jekyll is a willfully good man—an example to others, like the much-admired lawyer Mr. Utterson who is 'lean, long, dusty, dreary and yet somehow [improbably?] lovable.'"

man from the depths of his self-imposed underground." Stevenson's characterization of Jekyll is so compelling to readers because it not only reflects the interaction between a man and his society, but also because it illuminates the complexity of human psychology. Henry James notes in his review of the novel that its "subject is endlessly interesting, and rich in all sorts of provocation, and Mr. Stevenson is to be congratulated on having touched the core of it. . . . There is a genuine feeling for the perpetual moral question, a fresh sense of the difficulty of being good and the brutishness of being bad."

Source: Wendy Perkins, in an essay for *Novels for Students*, Gale Group, 2001.

Joyce Carol Oates

In the following review, Oates discusses how Dr. Jekyll and Mr. Hyde illustrate the Victorian dichotomy of good versus evil.

Like such mythopoetic figures as Frankenstein, Dracula, and, even, Alice ("in Wonderland"), Dr.-Jekyll-and-Mr.Hyde has become, in the century following the publication of Robert Louis Stevenson's famous novella, what might be called an autonomous creation. That is, people who have never read the novella—people who do not in fact "read" at all—know by way of popular culture who Jekyll-Hyde is. (Though they are apt to speak of him, not altogether accurately, as two disparate beings: *Dr.* Jekyll, *Mr.* Hyde.) A character out of prose fiction, Jekyll-Hyde seems nonetheless autogenetic in the way that vampires and werewolves and (more benignly) fairies seem autogenetic: surely he has always existed in the collective imag-

ination, or, like Jack the Ripper, in actual history? (As "Dracula" is both the specific creation of the novelist Bram Stoker and a nightmare figure out of middle European history.) It is ironic that, in being so effaced, Robert Louis Stevenson has become immortalized by way of his private fantasy—which came to him, by his own testimony, unbidden, in a dream.

The Strange Case of Dr. Jekyll and Mr. Hyde (1886) will strike contemporary readers as a characteristically Victorian moral parable, not nearly so sensational (nor so piously lurid) as Stoker's *Dracula*; in the tradition, perhaps, of Mary Shelley's *Frankenstein*, in which a horrific tale is conscientiously subordinated to the author's didactic intention. Though melodramatic in conception it is not melodramatic in execution since virtually all its scenes are narrated and summarized after the fact. There is no ironic ambiguity, no Wildean subtlety, in the doomed Dr. Jekyll's confession: he presents himself to the reader as a congenital "double dealer" who has nonetheless "an almost morbid sense of shame" and who, in typically Victorian middle-class fashion, must act to dissociate "himself" (i.e., his reputation as a highly regarded physician) from his baser instincts. He can no longer bear to suppress them and it is impossible to eradicate them. His discovery that "Man is not truly one, but two" is seen to be a scientific fact, not a cause for despair. (And, in time, it may be revealed that man is "a mere polity of multifarious, incongruous and independent denizens"—which is to say that the ego contains multitudes: multiple personalities inhabit us all. It cannot be incidental that Robert Louis Stevenson was himself a man enamoured of consciously playing roles and assuming personae: his friend Arthur Symons said of him that he was "never really himself except when he was in some fantastic disguise.")

Thus Dr. Jekyll's uncivilized self, to which he gives the symbolic name Hyde, is at once the consequence of a scientific experiment (as the creation of Frankenstein's monster was a scientific experiment) and a shameless indulgence of appetites that cannot be assimilated into the propriety of everyday Victorian life. There is a sense in which Hyde, for all his monstrosity, is but an addiction like alcohol, nicotine, drugs: "The moment I choose," Dr. Jekyll says, "I can be rid of him." Hyde must be hidden not simply because he is wicked but because Dr. Jekyll is a willfully good man—an example to others, like the much-admired lawyer Mr. Utterson who is "lean, long, dusty, dreary and yet somehow [improbably?] lovable." Had the Victorian ideal been less hypocritically ideal or had Dr. Jekyll been content with a less perfect public reputation his tragedy would not have occurred. (As Wilde's Basil Hallward says in *The Picture of Dorian Gray:* "We in our madness have separated the two [body and soul] and have invented a realism that is vulgar, and an ideality that is void." The key term here is surely "madness.")

Dr. Jekyll's initial experience, however, approaches ecstasy as if he were, indeed, discovering the Kingdom of God that lies within. The magic drug causes nausea and a grinding in the bones and a "horror of the spirit that cannot be exceeded at the hour of birth or death." Then:

> I came to myself as if out of a great sickness. There was something strange in my sensations, something indescribably new and, from its very novelty, incredibly sweet. I felt younger, lighter, happier in body; within I was conscious of a heady recklessness, a current of disordered sensual images running like a mill race in my fancy, a solution of the bonds of obligation, an unknown but not an innocent freedom of the soul. I knew myself, at the first breath of this new life, to be more wicked, tenfold more wicked, sold a slave to my original evil; and the thought, in that moment, braced and delighted in me like wine.

Unlike Frankenstein's monster, who is nearly twice the size of an average man, Jekyll's monster is dwarfed: "less robust and less developed" than the good self since Jekyll's rigorously suppressed life has been the consequence of unrelenting "effort, virtue and control." (Stevenson's anatomy of the human psyche is as grim as Freud's—virtually all a "good" man's waking energies are required in beating back and denying the "badness" in him!) That Hyde's frenzied pleasures are even in part specifically sexual is never confirmed, given the Victorian cast of the narrative itself, but, to extrapolate from an incident recounted by an eyewitness, one is led to suspect they are: Hyde is observed running down a ten-year-old girl in the street and calmly trampling over her body. Much is made subsequently of the girl's "screaming"; and of the fact that money is paid to her family as recompense for her violation.

Viewed from without Hyde is detestable in the abstract: "I never saw a man I so disliked," the lawyer Enfield says, "and yet I scarce know why. He must be deformed somewhere . . . " Another witness testifies to his mysteriously intangible deformity "without any nameable malformation." But when Jekyll looks in the mirror he is conscious of no repugnance, "rather of a leap of welcome. This, too, was myself. It seemed natural and human."

When Jekyll returns to himself after having been Hyde he is plunged into wonder rather than remorse at his "vicarious depravity." The creature summoned out of his soul and sent forth to do his pleasure is a being "inherently malign and villainous; his every act and thought centered on self; drinking pleasure with bestial avidity from any degree of torture to another; relentless like a man of stone." Yet Hyde is safely *other*—"It was Hyde, after all, and Hyde alone, that was guilty."

Oscar Wilde's equally didactic but far more suggestive and poetic *The Picture of Dorian Gray* (1890) makes the disturbing point that Dorian Gray, the *unblemished* paragon of evil, "is the type of which the age is searching for, and what it is afraid it has found." (Just as Wilde's Lord Henry defends insincerity "as a method by which we can multiply our personalities.") By contrast Jekyll's Hyde is a very nearly Bosch-like creature, proclaiming his wickedness to the naked eye as if, in Utterson's words, he is a "troglodyte . . . the mere radiance of a foul soul that thus transpires through, and transfigures, its clay continent." One is reminded of nineteenth-century theories of criminology advanced by C. S. Lombroso and Henry Maudsley, among others, who argued that outward physical defects and deformities are the visible signs of inward and invisible faults: the criminal is a type that can be easily identified by experts. Dr. Jekyll is the more reprehensible in his infatuation with Hyde in that, as a well-trained physician, he should have recognized at once the telltale symptoms of mental and moral degeneracy in his alter ego's very face. By degrees, like any addict, Jekyll surrenders his autonomy. His ego ceases being "I" and splits into two distinct and eventually warring selves, which share memory as they share a common body. Only after Hyde commits murder does Jekyll make the effort to regain control; but by this time, of course, it is too late. What had been "Jekyll"—that precarious cuticle of a self, that field of tensions in perpetual opposition to desire—has irrevocably split. It is significant that the narrator of Jekyll's confession speaks of both Jekyll and Hyde as if from the outside. And with a passionate eloquence otherwise absent from Stevenson's prose:

> The powers of Hyde seemed to have grown with the sickliness of Jekyll. And certainly the hate that now divided them was equal on each side. With Jekyll, it was a thing of vital instinct. He had now seen the full deformity of that creature that shared with him some of the phenomena of consciousness, and was co-heir with him to death: and beyond these links of community, which in themselves made the most poignant part of his distress, he thought of Hyde, for all his

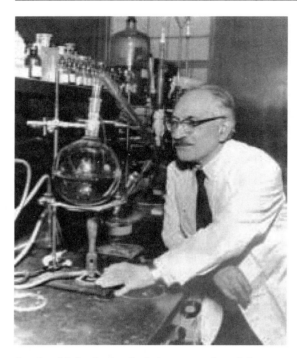

A microbiologist in the laboratory. In a lab similar to this one, Dr. Jekyll performs weeks of chemical research and experimentation trying to discover the formula for resolving man's nature into its component parts. When he tests the drug on himself, the result is the evil Mr. Hyde.

energy of life, as of something not only hellish but inorganic. This was the shocking thing; that the slime of the pit seemed to utter cries and voices; that the amorphous dust gesticulated and sinned; that what was dead, and had no shape, should usurp the offices of life. And this again, that that insurgent horror was knit to him closer than a wife, closer than an eye; lay caged in his flesh, where he heard it mutter and felt it struggle to be born; and at every hour of weakness, and in the confidence of slumber, prevailed against him, and deposed him out of life.

"Think of it," Jekyll had gloated at the start, "—I did not even exist!" And the purely metaphorical becomes literally true.

The Strange Case of Dr. Jekyll and Mr. Hyde, through stimulated by a dream, is not without its literary antecedents: among them Edgar Allan Poe's "William Wilson" (1839), in which, paradoxically, the "evil" self is the narrator and the "good" self, or conscience, the double; and Charles Dickens' uncompleted *The Mystery of Edwin Drood* (1870), in which the Choirmaster Jack Jasper, an opium addict, oscillates between "good" and "evil" impulses in his personality with an an-

guish so convincingly calibrated as to suggest that, had Dickens lived to complete the novel, it would have been one of his masterpieces—and would have made *The Strange Case of Dr. Jekyll and Mr. Hyde* redundant. Cautionary tales of malevolent, often diabolical doubles abound in folklore and oral tradition, and in Plato's *Symposium* it was whimsically suggested that each human being has a double to whom he was once *physically* attached—a bond of Eros that constituted in fact a third, and higher, sex in which male and female were conjoined.

The visionary starkness of *The Strange Case of Dr. Jekyll and Mr. Hyde* anticipates that of Freud in such late melancholy meditations as *Civilization and Its Discontents* (1929–30): there is a split in man's psyche between ego and instinct, between civilization and "nature," and the split can never be healed. Freud saw ethics as a reluctant concession of the individual to the group, veneer of a sort overlaid upon an unregenerate primordial self. The various stratagems of culture—including, not incidentally, the "sublimation" of raw aggression by way of art and science—are ultimately powerless to contain the discontent, which must erupt at certain periodic times, on a collective scale, as war. Stevenson's quintessentially Victorian parable is unique in that the protagonist initiates his tragedy of doubleness out of a fully lucid sensibility—one might say a scientific sensibility. Dr. Jekyll knows what he is doing, and why he is doing it, though he cannot, of course, know how it will turn out. What is unquestioned throughout the narrative, by either Jekyll or his circle of friends, is mankind's fallen nature: sin is *original* and *irremediable* For Hyde, though hidden, will not remain so. And when Jekyll finally destroys him he must destroy Jekyll too.

Source: Joyce Carol Oates, "Jekyll/Hyde," in *Hudson Review,* Vol. XL, No. 4, Winter 1988, pp. 603–08.

Harry M. Geduld

In the following essay excerpt, Geduld traces the intellectual and psychological environment in which Dr. Jekyll and Mr. Hyde *was first published.*

We can now see that for the Victorians, Stevenson's story expressed the anguish of humanity's compliance with the Law of Polarity, which states that all matter is a manifestation of positive and negative forces. Attempts to apply this law to the human soul stretch back at least as far as the ancient Greeks. By the mid-nineteenth century, the theory of the divided soul was complicated by Charles Darwin's popularization of evolutionary theory in *The Origin of Species* (1859) and *The Descent of Man* (1871) [Darwinism challenged the Judaeo-Christian notion that man's immoral or passionate impulses were God's device for testing human will. If human beings had direct kinship with beasts, the passions would have to be as much part of human nature as of animal nature. They would have to exist for their own fulfillment, without a divine purpose.] Among Darwin's opponents, a common reaction to this was to deny the kinship, reaffirming man's place above the beasts and the bestial, as described in the Book of Genesis. Perhaps the *excesses of Victorian restraint* that followed, represented a frantic attempt to restore mankind's previous disassociation with animal origins. The impact of Darwinism did not always produce denial and disgust, however. Stevenson's contemporary, the German philosopher Friedrich Nietzsche, insisted that "man is something that must be overcome," not by self-restraint, but by continued evolution resulting in the creation of an overman (superman). The essence of overman is described in the very title of *Beyond Good and Evil,* a work Nietzsche published in the same year as *Dr. Jekyll and Hyde.* In fact, the overman's rejection of mankind's moral values is not altogether dissimilar to Hyde's, although Hyde does not have the overman's power of creative imagination to use *his* rejection to further his own interests.

Nevertheless, the Stevenson story alone was able to produce an immediate response of mass dread. Doubtless the public angst was in part a reaction to the theme of scientific experimentation in the story. The age of modern science—and particularly modern medical science—had progressed considerably in the five years preceding the publication of *Dr. Jekyll and Mr. Hyde.* In 1881, both the germ theory and the principle of immunization were demonstrated, and between 1882 and 1885, the causes of and/or inoculations against tuberculosis, diphtheria, cholera and hydrophobia were discovered. By 1886, any medical advance by serum seemed possible. In *Modern Discoveries in Medical Psychology* (1937), Dr. Clifford Allen notes the influence this possibility had on the public's reception of Stevenson's story:

> The suggestion that there might be a drug which would enable the "good" personality to be separated from the "bad" so that sometimes the evil one was predominant and sometimes the kindly one ruled, was a new and, to most people, a horrible idea. So much excitement did the story cause that sermons were preached about it, and the more timid of the Victorians fervently hoped that the doctors who at that time

> *If human beings had direct kinship with beasts, the passions would have to be as much part of human nature as of animal nature. They would have to exist for their own fulfillment, without a divine purpose."*

seemed to be discovering everything would not unearth the mysterious drug which Stevenson made Dr. Jekyll use to free the unpleasant Mr. Hyde. . . .

The collective fear that a Jekyll-Hyde split might really happen was based on more than medical progress. Psychology, too, was fast becoming a science in which anything was possible. A case of split personality had been reported as early as 1816, and by the turn of the century, such cases and their treatment were widely known. But studies of patients suffering from multiple personalities were merely symptomatic of the unsettling facts emerging about the nature of mental functioning. Although there had long been serious speculation about a two or three part structure of the mind, there had been virtually no scientific investigation of it until the mid-nineteenth century.

In the 1840s a group of English physicians renewed scientific interest in hypnotism, a phenomenon which had been in and out of favor as a medical procedure since Mesmer's demonstration of "animal magnetism" in the eighteenth century. As hypnotism increased in popularity, so did attempts to understand it and submit it to scientific examination. One young researcher who studied the phenomenon was Sigmund Freud who went to Paris in 1885 to see the public exhibition of hypnotism by the famous neurologist, Charcot. However, it was Charcot's colleague, Pierre Janet, who first attempted to find a psychological theory that would explain hypnosis. He noted that there was a correspondence between hypnosis and hysteria, the neurosis most frequently cured by hypnosis. Hysterical symptoms, he found, could be induced as well as cured by hypnotic suggestion. Therefore, hypnosis was nothing but artificially induced hysteria. Janet concluded that hypnosis and hysteria were caused by a piece of "consciousness" that had split off from the rest of the mind. In both cases, the field of consciousness was totally absorbed by the smaller, split-off piece, while the larger bulk remained unavailable for perception. Janet thought this occurred because he believed consciousness to be composed of a multitude of sensations that are only perceived as unified during the most alert periods of mental health. Janet's ideas were developed further by the Swiss psychiatrist, Bleuler, who observed that psychotics suffer from the splitting up of consciousness into many disintegrating pieces rather than the two parts experienced by hysterics. His findings supported Janet's theory of the multiple structure of the mind.

Janet's descriptive psychology paved the way for Freud's dynamic theories of consciousness and the unconscious. Contemporaneously with Freud, although in ignorance of Freudianism, the American physician Morton Prince elaborated Janet's descriptive technique. In 1908, Prince published *The Dissociation of a Personality,* the most thorough account yet of a case of multiple personality. The patient was Sally Beauchamp who had been under treatment by Prince for seven years. She was a nurse who splintered into four personalities. The direct cause of her illness had been the trauma of seeing the face of a man she had been infatuated with—in another city—appear in a high hospital window where she worked. The sight was not an hallucination. Apparently, the man had travelled to her city, unaware that Sally Beauchamp lived there, and seeing a ladder resting against the hospital wall, had impulsively climbed up and looked in the window. (It is an interesting coincidence that Stevenson's inspiration to write the Jekyll-Hyde story also came from a dream of seeing a face in a window.) Prince used hypnosis to treat and reintegrate the shattered woman, without ever really understanding the reasons for his method's effectiveness. He used the term "co-consciousness" to describe the collections of split-off pieces of consciousness thought to embody each of his patient's separate personalities. Like Janet, he considered cases of split personalities to be extreme forms of hysteria. (In more recent times, dual and multiple personalities have been viewed as symptoms of paranoid psychosis, in which the superego is dissociated and projected in conjunction with severe psychosomatic changes in the patient's appearance. The popular confusion of multiple personality and schizophrenia is incorrect, although a schizophrenic may experience splitting as one of a variety of possible symptoms.) In any event, cases like that of Sally Beauchamp and such well-known twentieth cen-

tury examples as the cases studied in the book and screen version of *The Three Faces of Eve* (1957) and in F. R. Schreiber's 1974 novel, *Sybil,* share with the Jekyll-Hyde prototype the alternations between a puritanical personality that wants to be "good" and a childish, impulsive personality that wants to be "bad." These are generally the first two kinds of personalities to appear, even if other types eventually emerge.

Sigmund Freud published his first paper on hysteria, co-authored by Josef Breuer, in 1893. In this and the papers that followed, Freud examined the reasons why hysterics split off pieces of consciousness and forget them: the pieces contain painful or socially unacceptable or infantile ideas and wishes. (Clearly, in this instance, Stevenson anticipated Freud by allowing Hyde to represent the unacceptable ideas of Jekyll.) From this observation, Freud went on to describe the process by which an idea is forgotten or repressed as well as the process by which it might be recalled again. In later works, he developed his own theory of the mind's structure: the horizontal division between conscious and unconscious and the vertical division between ego, id, and superego.

Freud's theories were not to have any impact on the theatrical and filmic adaptations of *Dr. Jekyll and Mr. Hyde* until Freudianism became current in America in the late 1930s and 1940s. But since the MGM film version of 1941, almost all productions have taken at least a crude Freudianism into account. The MGM version notably contains a surrealistic dream sequence that accompanies Jekyll's transformation and indicates that he is in the grip of an irrational, unconscious force. Freudian sexual theory provided justification for the sexual content of many versions, although Freud's theory of infantile sexual fixations is barely suggested by the brutality of Hyde's heterosexuality. The most explicitly Freudian version of Stevenson's story to date is *I, Monster* (1971), in which the Dr. Jekyll character is a British psychoanalyst who has studied with Freud in Vienna and whose experiments are an attempt to replace psychoanalysis with a drug.

One of the most profound cultural contributions of popularized Freudianism is that it enabled society to accept the moral consequences of Darwinism. In the post-Victorian age, the sense of inner division, particularly when sexual needs are involved, has come to be regarded as normal. Hysteria is no longer the most prevalent form of neurosis, in part because sexuality no longer has to be so forcefully repressed. Our more permissive society encourages us to recognize and enjoy our kinship with animals. Sexual gratification is recommended for good mental and physical health. This has changed the modern audience's response to *Dr. Jekyll and Mr. Hyde.* We now know that drugs *can* cause extreme personality changes, and we worry about the attractiveness of these drugs to the millions of young people who use them regularly. Yet, the problem posed by Stevenson's story can still have meaning for modern audiences if the split between Jekyll and Hyde is redefined. Today, one of our pressing psychological problems concerns the duality of sex and aggression. Our desire for sexual openness (the demand of the sexual revolution) may be in conflict with our desire to suppress all hostile impulses (the demand of the cultural revolution). Whether we accept Freud's earlier theory, that aggression is a component of the sexual instinct or his later theory, published in *Beyond the Pleasure Principle* (1920), that aggression is a separate instinct coexisting with the sexual instinct, sex and aggression seem to be inextricably linked. It may well be impossible to loosen sexual inhibitions without loosening aggressive inhibitions at the same time.

The movie *Dr. Jekyll and Sister Hyde* (1971) takes this instinctual duality into account by showing that the bisexual-in-us-all (represented by the alteration of male and female personalities) also awakens the murderer-in-us-all. Thomas Berger's story "Professor Hyde" (1971) is an admission of the failure of our modern consciousness to cope with the aggressive emotions boiling over in even the weakest of us. The Hyde-in-us-all may no longer resemble Stevenson's Hyde in every respect, but the wish to separate him from our uninhibitedly humane selves may be as powerful for us as it once was for Stevenson's Jekyll.

Source: Harry M. Geduld, "Introduction," in *The Definitive* Dr. Jekyll and Mr. Hyde *Companion,* Garland Publishing, Inc., 1983, pp. 8–10.

Daniel V. Fraustino

In the following essay, Fraustino explores how two of the characters in Dr. Jekyll and Mr. Hyde *overcome both social and language convention to discover the secret of Dr. Jekyll-Mr Hyde.*

Since Robert Louis Stevenson first published *Dr. Jekyll and Mr. Hyde* almost a century ago, critics have generally regarded the work as moral allegory, a dramatization of the conflicts between Jekyll and Hyde, good and evil, split parts of a dual

> After his fatal encounter with Hyde, when he finally recognizes the real duality of man, Lanyon states: 'I have had a shock . . . and I shall never recover. It is a question of weeks. Well, life has been pleasant; I liked it; yes, sir, I used to like it. I sometimes think that if we knew all, we should be more glad to get away.'"

personality. Recent scholarship, however, disputes this reading approach, focusing on the contradictions within Jekyll's own personality, which eliminate him as a symbol of pure respectability, and on the importance of secondary characters. While Edwin Eigner [in *Robert Louis Stevenson and the Romantic Tradition*] notes that Utterson and Enfield are the first doppelgängers encountered in the novel, Masao Miyashi states that Jekyll is not really committed to goodness but to mere respectability. Miyashi further suggests that the secondary characters, formerly thought to contrast and intensify Jekyll's downfall, are in reality all "barren of ideas," "joyless," and inherently corrupt ["Dr. Jekyll and the Emergence of Mr. Hyde," *College English,* 27, 1966].

While Jekyll and Hyde are obviously disparate segments of the human personality, they are still integral parts of the whole, and Lanyon's and Utterson's failure to recognize this fact figures importantly in the novel. In *Novelists in a Changing World* Donald Stone states that there is a "buried theme" in *Jekyll and Hyde,* its key lying in the secondary characters, who are unable "to deal with the 'monster' Hyde in a normal manner." In keeping with Eigner's, Miyashi's, and Stone's revisionist focus on secondary characters, my purpose in the following paragraphs will be to discuss the novel's presentation of the two major secondary characters, Lanyon and Utterson, as they confront the truth of Jekyll and Hyde's single identity. For Stevenson's penetrating examination into his characters constitutes one of the novel's major themes: the forma-tive and often distorting effects of language and so-ciety on man's perception of himself and his world.

Dr. Hastie Lanyon is described by Jekyll as "long . . . bound to the most narrow and material views," and Stevenson seems to have selected his first name to suggest this defect. A "hide-bound pedant," Stevenson puns, Lanyon's clear intention is to block out the bimorphous reality of Hyde—the dual nature of man—so as to preserve his own social sense of man as inherently perfectible. For Lanyon man's social character is synonymous with man's essential self, hence he views Dr. Jekyll's excursion into Faustian metaphysics as a sign of moral perversion. Significantly, Lanyon is the only character in the novel who has no knowledge of Hyde's existence prior to his one fatal encounter. In a sense, Lanyon has completely alienated him-self from the Hyde within him, hence his life is shaken "to its roots" when he witnesses Hyde's metamorphosis and realizes the latter's source in Jekyll. Ironically, Lanyon's ignorance culminates in his own destruction.

Like its literary heir *Heart of Darkness, Dr. Jekyll and Mr. Hyde* suggests that society purposely cultivates self-deceit in obscuring from its Lanyons the truth about themselves. But Stevenson implies, again like Conrad, that life is not redeemable with-out its illusions. After his fatal encounter with Hyde, when he finally recognizes the real duality of man, Lanyon states: "I have had a shock . . . and I shall never recover. It is a question of weeks. Well, life has been pleasant; I liked it; yes, sir, I used to like it. I sometimes think that if we knew all, we should be more glad to get away."

Like his friend Lanyon, Utterson is a kind of guardian of orthodox knowledge. As a lawyer he has specialized knowledge of the laws by which so-ciety operates and exists. But unlike Lanyon, Ut-terson's recognition of Jekyll and Hyde's single identity is more gradual and narrated in greater de-tail. When he first hears Enfield's account of the trampling incident, Utterson becomes obsessed with seeing Hyde's face. His first response to En-field's story is to ask, "What sort of man is he to see?" This incipient mania is described at length:

> And still the figure had no *face* by which he might know it; even in his dreams, it had no *face,* or one that baffled him and melted before his eyes; and thus it was that there sprang up and grew apace in the lawyer's mind a singularly strong, almost an inordi-nate, curiosity to behold the features of the real Mr. Hyde. If he could but once set eyes on him, he thought the mystery would lighten and perhaps roll altogether

away, as was the habit of mysterious things when well examined. He might see a reason for his friend's strange preference or bondage (call it what you please) and even for the startling clause of the will. At least it would be a *face* worth seeing: the *face* of a man who was without bowels of mercy: a *face* which had but to show itself to raise up, in the mind of the unimpressionable Enfield, a spirit of enduring hatred. (emphasis supplied)

Utterson's obsession derives from his as-sumption that reality can be known by its outward form, an assumption perhaps rooted in his belief in the credibility of social appearances. Accordingly, after staking out Hyde's doorway, Utterson first asks to "let me see your face." In view of Hyde's bimorphous nature, Utterson's query is ironic, and his statement that he will now "know" Hyde some-what absurd. In the dualistic world of Jekyll and Hyde nothing can be known for sure, appearances being often misleading.

Unable to understand the enigma with which he is confronted, Utterson attempts to arbitrate re-ality by means of language, an act as perennial as art and as primitive as magic formula. Accordingly, Utterson's initial response to Enfield's narrative about the trampling is to "ask the name of that man who walked over the child." And this same preoc-cupation with definition underlies his need to find a *name* for Hyde's vague deformity. The lawyer is therefore in great "mental perplexity" because Hyde's strange physical "impression" created on onlookers is not a "nameable malformation." He ponders: "There *is* something more if I could find a name for it." Although Utterson suffers from a common human need to name and thereby control, his linguistic obsession is chronic, and, as in the case of Hastie Lanyon, his name suggests his pro-clivity. Perhaps used to the changeless regularity of legal language, Utterson may have forgotten that there is no value to words other than their arbitrary man-made one. Thus, pledging to search out Hyde, Utterson says, "If he be Mr. Hyde . . . I shall be Mr. Seek." Similarly, he dubs Jekyll "Dr. Fell" and declares to Poole, "let our name be vengeance." Fi-nally, the lawyer's obsession with words is under-lined by his concern for Hyde's lack of "fitting lan-guage" at their first interview.

For Utterson, the purely social man, words are surrogates for reality, manipulation of the former representing control of the latter. While the use of language in this way is common enough, Utterson chronically fails to discriminate between the sym-bol and the reality. Hence, in his utter confusion over the perplexing relationship between the re-spectable Dr. Jekyll and the sinister Mr. Hyde, Utterson with great wonderment reads: "Henry Jekyll, M.D., D.C.L., LL.D., F.R.S., etc." To Utterson, the words encompass the total reality, and in these symbols there is clearly no room for Hyde. But Stevenson clearly implies that words cannot satisfactorily communicate reality and that reality is not answerable to language. Thus Lanyon declares after his fatal encounter with Hyde, "I have brought on myself a punishment and a danger that I cannot name," Jekyll states that his "affairs cannot be mended by talking," and he writes in his suicide note that his situation is "nameless." Finally, prior to killing the eminent Sir Danvers, Hyde appropriately says "never a word."

Implicitly, the reality of Hyde and his relationship with Jekyll are beyond the scope of Utterson's language. If it does anything, language, a man-made apparatus, obfuscates reality rather than clarifies it. Though man's linguistic attempts to understand and control constitute an artistic activity with sources deep in the human unconscious, man deceives himself when rendering in the artificial constructs of language that which is essentially chaotic. The impossibility of the purely "social" man ever coming to grips with life's formless diversity and illogic is comically paradigmed by Utterson's ineffectual explanation to Poole of how the man behind the door writing in Jekyll's hand could be both Jekyll and someone else. The impeccable logic which Utterson uses to explain erroneously the enigma of the familiar hand and strange voice (an argument made even more farcical by the convincing repetition of *hence*) satirizes his methodology and ultimately his basic grasp of reality:

> "These are all very strange circumstances," said Mr. Utterson, "but I think I begin to see daylight. Your master, Poole, is plainly seized with one of those maladies that both torture and deform the sufferer; hence, for aught I know, the alteration of his voice; hence the mask and the avoidance of his friends; hence his eagerness to find this drug, by means of which the poor soul retains some hope of ultimate recovery— God grant that he be not deceived! There is my explanation; it is sad enough, Poole, ay, and appalling to consider; but it is plain and natural, hangs well together, and delivers us from all exorbitant alarms."

Utterson's attempt to place experience within the narrow confines of a world artificially ordered by language is what underlies his concern that his explanation be "plain," "natural," hang "well together," and deliver him from "all exorbitant alarms." Poole's reply to this last grasp at order and sanity is even more absurd in its complete lack of sophistication, yet it is not basically different from Utterson's tendency to interpret reality in the nar-

row terms in which he has been conditioned to think: "'O, sir,' cried Poole . . . 'Do you think I do not know where his head comes to in the cabinet door, where I saw him every morning of my life?'" Clearly, if truth can be known it is not found by the same measure which defines the external limits of a cabinet door. Here, Stevenson's satire on man's proclivity for concretion and hence distortion may be unmerciful but is probably directed at himself as well.

Perhaps Stevenson suggests that, unlike his early ancestors, modern man suffers from an ever-widening split in his consciousness, and we are all Lanyons, Uttersons, and Jekylls who have repressed, alienated, or otherwise estranged the Hyde within us—acts which doom us to inhabit the outskirts of reality as well as those of our own personalities. However, even this seems too optimistic for those of us who regard *Dr. Jekyll and Mr. Hyde* as Stevenson's dim statement on man's perpetual unfitness for life. An artist by nature, man is chiefly an imaginative animal who will always filter his experience through his symbols, impotently manipulating these out of a primitive impulse to control, perceiving structure where there is only the illusion of structure, and meaning where there is only fact.

Source: Daniel V. Fraustino, *"Dr. Jekyll and Mr. Hyde: Anatomy of Misperception,"* in *Arizona Quarterly,* Vol. 38, No. 3, Autumn 1982, pp. 235–40.

Sources

Altick, Richard D., *Victorian People and Ideas: A Companion for the Modern Reader of Victorian Literature,* Norton, 1973.

Gwynn, Stephen, *Robert Louis Stevenson,* Macmillan, 1939.

Halevy, Elie, *England in 1815,* Barnes and Noble, 1968.

James, Henry, "Robert Louis Stevenson," in *The Century,* Vol. XXXV, No. 6, April 1888, pp. 868–79.

Kiely, Robert, "Robert Louis Stevenson," in *Dictionary of Literary Biography, Volume 18: Victorian Novelists after 1885,* Gale, 1983, pp. 281–97.

Nabokov, Vladimir, "Robert Louis Stevenson," in *Reference Guide to English Literature,* 2d ed., edited by D. L. Kirkpatrick, St. James Press, 1991.

Noble, James Ashcroft, Review, in *The Academy,* Vol. XXIX, No. 716, January 23, 1886, p. 55.

Sadler, Michael, *Forlorn Sunset,* Constable, 1947.

Sanderson, Stewart F., "Dr. Jekyll And Mr. Hyde: Overview," in *Lectures on Literature,* edited by Fredson Bowers, Harcourt, 1980.

Saposnik, Irving S., "Robert Louis Stevenson, Chapter 6: The Anatomy of Dr. Jekyll and Mr. Hyde," in *Twayne's English Authors Series Online*, G. K. Hall & Co., 1999.

Smith, Curtis C., "Robert Louis Stevenson," in *Supernatural Fiction Writers Vol. 1*, Scribner's, 1985, pp. 307–13.

Stephen, Leslie, "Robert Louis Stevenson," in *Studies of a Biographer*, Duckworth and Co., 1902, pp. 206–46.

Stern, G. B., *Robert Louis Stevenson, British Writers Vol. 5*, British Council, 1982, pp. 383–98.

Tuckniss, Reverend William, Introduction to *London Labour and the London Poor Volume IV*, 1862.

For Further Study

Charyn, Jerome, "Afterword: Who Is Hyde," in *The Strange Case of Dr. Jekyll and Mr. Hyde*, Bantam, 1981.

Charyn offers a psychological study of Jekyll/Hyde and concludes that the character remains ambiguous.

Daiches, David, *Robert Louis Stevenson*, 1947.

An early work on Stevenson. Daiches provides a penetrating analysis of several of Stevenson's works including *The Strange Case of Dr. Jekyll and Mr. Hyde*, focusing on the author's technique.

The Grass Dancer

Susan Power

1994

The Grass Dancer grew out of a series of stories that Susan Power wrote while she was in the creative writing program at the University of Iowa. The novel was published in 1994 by Putnam and received immediate critical acclaim, and also won the 1995 PEN/ Hemingway Award for best first fiction of that year.

The book tells the story of Harley Wind Soldier, a young Sioux, and several generations of his ancestors. The novel includes nonhuman as well as human characters; the spirit world is an important part of all the stories, and ghosts and magical powers are part of the characters' everyday lives. Long-dead ancestors, such as lovers Red Dress and Ghost Horse, who lived in the nineteenth century and saw the first impact of European-American culture on their own, are still vital figures in Power's twentieth-century characters' lives.

The book's title refers to a traditional Native-American dance, and there are two kinds of grass dancing. A character in the book explains: "There's the grass dancer who prepares the field for a pow-wow the old-time way, turning the grass over with his feet to flatten it down. Then there's the spiritual dancer, who wants to learn grass secrets by imitating it, moving his body with the wind."

"I cannot tell you where characters come from," Power told Caroline Moseley in the *Princeton Weekly Bulletin.* "They come before themes; they come before action. And they sometimes take me places I don't want to go." She told Moseley that the character of Red Dress was supposed to be

evil, but when she heard Red Dress's story, she realized Red Dress had reasons for her actions. "She became a heroine, the heart and soul of the book, even though she killed some people who did not deserve to die."

When the book was published, critics praised Power's use of magic, spirits, and myth, and the way she worked them into the characters' everyday lives, showing how they perceived reality and imparting a vividly mystical quality to their often difficult existence. Dani Shapiro wrote in *People Weekly* that Power's book would "haunt readers—and perhaps [give] them pause to check the sky for ancestors of their own." A *Publishers Weekly* reviewer hailed Power as "a major talent," and in the *Los Angeles Times,* Michael Dorris praised her "series of related, beautifully told tales that unravel the intricate stitch of related lives, the far-reaching consequences of chance acts, the lasting legacies of love and jealousy."

Although Power is proud of her dual heritage, she does not want to be called a "Native-American writer." She told Moseley, "I think of myself as an American writer who happens to be Indian."

Susan Power

Author Biography

"My mother tells me the ancestors really wanted me to write *Grass Dancer,* Susan Power told a contributor to *People Weekly.* "I'm not a person of real faith—but I try to keep an open mind." *The Grass Dancer* tells the story of a young Sioux man, his teacher, and his ancestors.

Power told an interviewer from *george jr.* that both her parents contributed to her storytelling gifts. "My mother has a tremendous gift of imagination," she said, "and was always telling me stories—true tales and those she dreamed up on her own." Power's mother, Susan Dunning Power, was a Native-American activist who grew up on the Standing Rock Sioux Reservation that straddles North and South Dakota; Power's father, Carleton, was a sales representative for a publishing company. He died when she was eleven, but not before filling her with a love of reading and books by reading to her every night, even after she was old enough to read on her own.

Both of her parents also imbued her with a deep sense of her double heritage. In her childhood home, portraits of her mother's Native-American ancestors and her father's white ancestors were dis-

played. Power told Caroline Moseley in the *Princeton Weekly Bulletin,* "My great-great-grandfather, who was governor of New Hampshire during the Civil War, faced my great-great-grandfather Chief Mato Nupa (Two Bears)."

Power attended Chicago prep schools, but also went to Native-American powwows and, encouraged by her mother, worked in Native-American activist groups.

Power was born October 12, 1961, in Chicago, Illinois. She attended Radcliffe College, and later earned a law degree at the Harvard University Law School with the encouragement of her mother, who reminded her that Native Americans could use a few good lawyers on their side. However, she did not go into law after she graduated. Two summers of work in law offices had already taught her that her creative and artistic side would not be satisfied by the practice of law. She found her degree useful, however, because her carefully organized study had taught her to be a disciplined writer, instead of relying solely on inspiration.

For three years after she graduated from Harvard in 1986, she worked as a technical writer and editor, and wrote poetry during her free time. In 1989, she took a leap of faith and applied to the University of Iowa's writing program, where she was accepted. During her three years there, she published numerous short stories in literary journals, and ultimately earned a master of fine arts degree in creative writing. During her time at Iowa, she told Anne Putnam of *The Bucknellian,* she "lived, ate, slept, dreamed, breathed fiction."

She began writing *The Grass Dancer* while at Iowa, as a series of short stories. She told *george jr.* that although she was writing stories, she knew at the time that they were interconnected and that eventually they would become a novel. One of the first images she saw was that of an old Native-American woman in ceremonial dress dancing on the moon. She said, "Naturally, I wanted to know what she was doing there, and in discovering her story I realized I had written the first chapter."

The Grass Dancer was critically acclaimed, and won the 1995 PEN/Hemingway Award for the best first work of fiction of that year. Her stories have appeared in the *Atlantic Monthly, Paris Review, Story, Best American Stories of 1993, Ploughshares,* and other journals and literary anthologies.

In 1997, Power had the honor of becoming a Hodder Fellow in the Humanities. With the funds provided by the award, she began working on another novel, set in the Native-American community in Chicago, where 25,000 Native Americans now live. Titled *Strong Heart Society,* it will be published in 2001 by Putnam.

Plot Summary

1981

Pumpkin, a young Indian girl from Chicago, travels to the reservation to dance at a powwow. She is due to attend Stanford University in the fall, and because of this is the pride of the Indian community; she is also the best grass dancer at the powwow. She catches the eye of Harley Wind Soldier, a popular young man who invites her to go with him after the powwow. Several people see them go off together, including Charlene Thunder, a girl who has a crush on him. Harley takes Pumpkin to a deserted old house. It is haunted by the ghost of an old white woman who is always seen doing chores: churning butter, darning socks, sweeping the floor.

Pumpkin is as interested in Harley as he is in her, and the two of them spend the night in the house. Harley tells her of his mother's silence, and

how it has left him empty and lonely. "Nothing's here," he says, touching his chest. "My brother died a few weeks before I was born.... He took everything with him." Pumpkin tells him she has plenty of soul, and she will give him hers. She rubs her soul into him, and says, "You won't be alone now. I'm a part of you, like it or not."

The next morning, Harley sees the old ghost leaning over Pumpkin and crying, but he doesn't know why until the final day of the powwow, when Pumpkin is declared the winner of the dance competition. She moves on to the next powwow, but on the way there, she and her friends drive into a sudden storm, skid off a ledge, and die in a fiery crash. Later, Charlene Thunder, whose grandmother is a witch, wonders if her grandmother made the crash happen so that Charlene, not Pumpkin, might get to be with Harley in the end.

1977

White teacher Jeannette McVay tries to get her students to tell traditional stories. While each tells a stale story, which they think Jeannette wants to hear, they remember another, more vibrant tale that tells the truth about their lives, but which they are afraid to reveal to her or the other students. The students like her, but are wary of her because of her romanticized attitude toward them as "noble savages" and inherently spiritual people, just because they're Indian.

When Harley's turn to tell a story comes, he doesn't have any because his mother has never told him any. He makes up a story, and when he goes home, his grandfather Herod Small War asks about it and tells him a story about Ghost Horse, Harley's great-great-grandfather's brother. Ghost Horse was a *heyo'ka,* told by the spirits to do everything backward or differently from everyone else: walk backward, cry at happy occasions, laugh at funerals, run cheerfully into battle. "That one was fearless and took many risks on the battlefield," Herod says. "Your father was that way too." Harley, who knows little about his father, is fascinated and for a while he decides that he is a *heyo'ka* too. In basketball games, he shoots to miss instead of score, and wears a jacket on hot days.

1976

Herod Small War's friend Archie Iron Necklace has had a dream about the "medicine hole," a mysterious portal into the spirit world that is located in a nearby valley. The two men fast, hold a purifying sweat lodge ritual, and gather the elders together, and they hold a *Yuwipi* ceremony in which

Herod sees Archie's dream, which replicates a time long past, when Indian warriors escaped from pursuing whites by entering the hole. Herod, Archie, Harley, and Frank Pipe set out to find it, but don't succeed.

However, the trip reminds Herod that when he was a young man, he had an affair with Clara Miller, the white woman who lived in the old wooden house and who is now a ghost there. He was married at the time, but Alberta did not sleep with him often, and Clara Miller was interested in him and showed it.

A sudden storm arises, and the four men end up at Clara's old house. They spend the night there, and the ghost comes to Herod. "As a *Yuwipi* man, I had heard spirit voices and encountered dead ancestors, but a white ghost was something different altogether," he says. He asks her where the medicine hole is, and she doesn't answer, but later in a dream, the spirits tell him, "You are the medicine hole."

1969

Lydia Wind Soldier's mother, Margaret Many Wounds, is dying. Her two daughters, Lydia and Evie, come home to tend to her. They cook old Sioux recipes, make her comfortable, and listen as Margaret tells her whole life story, including the fact that their father was not a rodeo cowboy, but a Japanese-American doctor working in a prisoner of war camp in Bismarck in 1942. Margaret was working at the camp as a nurse, and she soon became pregnant. She left without telling the doctor, had her daughters, and told them that their father was a Canadian Indian who had married and then left her. Her daughters are shocked, since they had thought they were full-blood Indians all this time.

As Margaret is dying, the television shows the astronauts walking on the moon for the first time. She is not impressed: she can go there, as a spirit. As the chapter ends, she is dancing on the moon, a traditional Sioux dance. "Look at me," she says to Harley, her grandson, who is five. "Look at the magic. There is still magic in the world."

1964

Crystal Thunder, daughter of Charlene, is a high school girl who falls in love with Martin Lundstrom, a white boy who is an artist. The school and town are scandalized when Crystal and Martin start going out together, as is Mercury, who violently opposes their marriage. Crystal is pregnant, and when the baby, Charlene, is born, Mercury takes

her, working spells to keep her. Crystal says, "I do not know my daughter's name, or the shape of her face. In dreams she stands with her back to me, her hair in tight braids, stiff like black ropes." All she has of her daughter is a beaded amulet shaped like a turtle, in which Mercury put a piece of her daughter's umbilical cord; this amulet is supposed to distract evil spirits from the actual child, so they will not be able to find her and hurt her.

1961

Young white schoolteacher Jeannette McVay comes to Mercury Thunder because she has heard that Mercury knows traditional magic, and Jeannette is fascinated with traditional ways. Mercury tells Jeannette an old story of Red Dress and Ghost Horse, lovers from the nineteenth century. They never came together, but are still ghosts, searching for each other across the plains.

Partly to impress Jeannette and partly for her own reasons, Mercury decides to work love magic on Calvin Wind Soldier, who is married to Lydia. However, the magic doesn't work, because Calvin wears a belt the *Yuwipi* man, Herod Small War, gave him to protect him against such things. It's made of snakeskin, and Mercury can't get past its magic. In revenge, although she knows she can't have Calvin, she makes him have an affair with Evelyn, Lydia's sister, which results in a child, Duane, who will later be killed along with Calvin in a car wreck. Jeannette, who previously saw Mercury's magic as a sort of game and did not fully believe in it, now believes, and she's frightened by Mercury's power. She tries to leave the reservation, but can't—Mercury has placed a spell on her, and she will never be able to leave.

1954

A year after Lydia Wind Soldier finishes high school, she's working as a cook. On the way home in a snowstorm, she almost hits Calvin Wind Soldier. She takes him home, warms him and feeds him, and falls in love with him, and they get married two months later. Ghosts attend the wedding: Red Dress and others. Red Dress is looking for her lost lover, Ghost Horse, and she is interested in Calvin because he is the last direct descendant of him.

Harley stops drinking and becomes responsible, joining the tribal police, but he is haunted by his past experience as a soldier in the Korean War. He tells Lydia that during his time there, he had a vision of Red Dress, who warned him about her descendant, Mercury Thunder. "She warned me that her niece was confused, and determined to confound everyone else. She didn't want to see me trapped by that one's scheming," he tells Lydia. When he came back from Korea, Herod Small War made him a snakeskin belt to protect him from Mercury. Snakes are sacred to Red Dress and hold her energy, and Mercury can't fight them: her power is not as strong as her ancestor's. In revenge, Mercury makes Calvin have an affair with Lydia's sister Evelyn, resulting in Duane's birth. One day, Lydia notices that Duane resembles Mercury, and, spooked, tells Calvin to get him out of the house. "We'll go for a drive," he says, and on that drive, both he and Duane are killed. From that point on, she stops speaking. "They said a drunk driver was responsible for the tragedy, but I knew it was my anger and the terrible power of my voice," she says.

1935

In the midst of the Depression and Dust Bowl, Mercury Thunder is making her niece Dina a traditional Sioux dress and moccasins. Her young son Chaske is ill, and she has been a widow for two months; her husband died of tuberculosis, and now Chaske has it too. Mercury wonders if she can use her power to heal him, but realizes that she can't. "I knew we did not have the healing touch," she says sadly.

That night, a powwow is being held, but Dina's dress isn't finished yet, and Chaske needs a doctor. He coughs up blood and dies, but Dina's mother Joyce, who comes to get the dress, is unsympathetic. The doctor didn't come when her child was sick, so she is angry that Mercury thinks the doctor should come to Chaske. Angered, Mercury gives Joyce every dress in her closet, including her wedding dress. Then she sets to work beading Dina's moccasins with red beads.

She goes to Dina's house, dresses her, and tells her to dance. Dina can't stop dancing. "She danced herself into another world," Mercury says. Dina is found later, frozen in the snow, far from home. Her ghost, and Chaske's, remain close by, visiting Mercury, telling her that magic, once let loose, takes on a life of its own.

1864

Red Dress, a young Sioux woman, is apparently converted to Christianity, but this is only on the surface. She sees the crosses she wears as symbols of the Sioux Morning Star, and although she takes the Christian name Esther, she knows that she will never be the convert the priest wants. "I am Red Dress, beloved of snakes," she says. When she

was still a baby, snakes visited her and climbed on her, and a rattlesnake was her baby rattle. They are her helpers and spirit guides.

At a service held by the priest, a stranger appears, laughing at the service. He is Ghost Horse, a *heyo'ka,* or sacred clown, a position he was forced to take because he dreamed of the thunderbirds. Red Dress senses that he is lonely, set apart from ordinary life and relationships by his spiritual calling.

Red Dress's father has seen that trade with whites brings trouble and disease, so he has decided only to trade with other tribes. Her family uses traditional tools and technology, not the new metal and cloth brought by the whites. Like Ghost Horse, she has a dream that alters her life. Because of the dream, she must travel to Fort Laramie, a white stronghold.

She and her brother travel to the fort, where she gets a job by convincing the whites that she is Christian. She becomes secretary and assistant to Reverend Pyke, the post chaplain. Her brother lives nearby and hunts with local Indians. She knows the spirits have sent her to the fort for a reason, and she waits to find out what it is.

Several of the men in the cast fall in love with Red Dress, which offends her: she knows that they don't love her, they just want to use her. One night she sets out to meet her brother, and the men watch her leave. One follows her, and she enchants him and tells him what to do, using two smooth stones that are filled with power. Obedient, under her spell, he calmly hangs himself. The second man, under the stones' spell, also hangs himself. Now that two men have died, Pyke chops down the tree they hung from, saying it's evil, but of course this doesn't stop the deaths. The third man hangs himself at the fort, which is now full of fear.

Red Dress is in her brother's lodge when Reverend Pyke appears. She has not thought to put a spell on him, and he brings out a revolver and kills her. In spirit, she follows him and sees that the Sioux ancestor-spirits have punished him by making him shoot himself and die in a snowbank.

After her death, Ghost Horse goes to her father and tells him that although he and Red Dress never spoke about it, he knew she loved him, and, he says, "I request the honor of marrying your daughter's spirit, mourning her as only a devoted husband would grieve."

Ghost Horse later dies in battle, and his spirit doesn't wait to be united with Red Dress's. She is angry at this abandonment, but there's nothing she can do. Unlike him, she has never moved on to the next world, but remains in the world of the living, the Sioux people. She watches over them, only hoping that someday she will find joy.

1981

Charlene Thunder is in pain, wanting to go out with Harley, but he's still grieving over Pumpkin, who has died in the car crash. Desperate, she works some of her grandmother's love magic and ends up with six different boys in the old ruined house where the white ghost lives. After the boys leave, she sees the old white woman's ghost, and the ghost of Red Dress, who kindly advises her not to use medicine for evil, and to give it up since she doesn't understand it. Charlene agrees.

Shamed, she goes to the school guidance counselor, Jeannette McVay, and tells her that she has to change her homeroom to get away from the boys she slept with. In her new homeroom, someone leaves a present on her desk: a newspaper article about an Indian woman in Chicago who has beaded the image of Da Vinci's Last Supper, using a pattern drawn by her white husband. Charlene realizes these are her parents: they are not dead, as Mercury has always told her.

She goes to Chicago to be reunited with them, and on the way there sees Pumpkin's spirit. All this time, she has felt guilty about Pumpkin's death, thinking that Pumpkin died because of her, but Pumpkin tells her, "It wasn't your fault. These things happen. There was nothing you could do."

1982

Jeannette McVay and her husband have a baby, who looks more like a full-blood Sioux than her Sioux father, and who shows no trace of Jeannette's white heritage. Herod Small War cautions Jeannette that despite this, she must tell the girl about both sides of her lineage. "Otherwise she'll stand off-balance and walk funny and talk out of one side of her mouth. Tell her *two* stories."

Frank Pipe has decided to become assistant to Herod, and learn the *Yuwipi* ways. He is receptive to the spirit world, but knows this is a great sacrifice and responsibility; Herod believes he can do it.

Harley is still dealing with Pumpkin's death, still startled that someone as strong as she, as full of dreams and goals, could suddenly be taken out of the world. And unlike Pumpkin, he doesn't see himself as even being remotely talented. Why

should he live, when people like Pumpkin die? What he doesn't recognize is that he is gifted with a rich imagination and vision. He thinks everyone can see the spirits he sees, but they can't. Powers writes, "Harley was nearly trampled by ghosts but wholly unaware of how remarkable his vision was."

His mother, Lydia Wind Soldier, has been working on a traditional costume, a replica of a dress her great-grandmother once wore, which is now in a museum in Chicago. She plans to wear it at a powwow and show Harley, without using words, the story of his heritage. At the powwow, however, Harley gets drunk, disgusting Lydia, who slaps him.

Frank Pipe takes him home to Herod Small War's house. Herod, Frank, Archie Iron Necklace, and another man are there. They hold a sweat lodge to purify him, and he fasts for three days and asks the spirits for a vision to guide his life, alone in a hole in the ground. In his vision, spirits come and show him the long-lost medicine hole. He crawls through and meets his grandmother Margaret Many Wounds. He remembers her death—an event he's forgotten until now. "I saw you dancing on the moon," he tells her. He meets his brother Duane, and his father, who embraces him and tells him he is doing well. "We have to be careful what we say, because you're supposed to find your own answers," his father tells him. "But you are my son."

Harley also meets Ghost Horse, a beautiful and wise man who teaches him that true warriors are gentle and loving people who would give their hearts to their people. Red Dress is there too, and she tells him, "I want you to be happy, because I know what it is to be sad."

Through this vision, he finds his own strength and his own voice; he's come through a dark time in his life and is moving past it to a new life as a man. As the vision ends, he hears a strange voice singing: his own. As Powers writes, "What he heard was the music of his own voice, rising above the rest."

Characters

Evelyn

The twin sister of Lydia, Evelyn left the reservation as a young woman and moved to Minneapolis with her husband, Philbert. "You look back, you never get off the res," she tells him. Thirty years old, he is a retired rodeo bull rider, and she married him not because she loved him but because her mother told her that her father, whom she has never met, was a bull rider. Although Evie and Lydia are twins, they do not look alike: Evie is aware that Lydia is much more beautiful.

Ghost Horse

Ghost Horse is a *heyo'ka,* or sacred clown. Because he has dreamed of the thunderbirds, he must take on this role. Red Dress says of him, "His behavior was perverse: he wept at social dances, laughed at solemn events, shivered in the hot summer sun, and sweltered in frigid temperatures. He rushed into battle ahead of other warriors, treating war as play, and he always said the opposite of what he meant. I sensed he was lonely."

Martin Lundstrom

A white boy, a misfit in his high school, he walks with a limp and has been secretly making a living as an artist, drawing covers for a seed catalog, since he was fifteen. He and Crystal Thunder fall in love and get married. He is the father of Charlene Thunder.

Jeannette McVay

A white woman who has romantic notions of Indians as noble, spiritual people, she comes to the reservation to study them and ends up teaching in the reservation school. Because of one of Mercury Thunder's spells, she is soon unable ever to leave the reservation. Her students are bewildered by her exalted view of them, and although they like her, they think she's pitiful because they know she is often beaten up by her no-good Indian boyfriend. She doesn't seem to know that Native Americans live in the twentieth century like everyone else, and is continually telling them to do things in the old way of their people. She dyes her hair black in an attempt to look Indian, but even with her deep tan, it's evident that she's still white.

Frank Pipe

A friend of Harley Wind Soldier and grandson of Herod Small War, Frank is a beautiful young man, with hair so long that the ends of his sleek black braids brush his knees. He wears two silver hoops in each ear, and twists his hair into a bun when he plays basketball or thinks there will be a fight. He is small-boned, with delicate features, and dislikes this. He has two scars, one across his left eyebrow and one under his right eye, and is proud of them because they mar his otherwise feminine appearance. He does not dance in costume at powwows, because he wants to be free to leave at any time without dealing with the heavy and cumbersome beadwork, feathers, and bells.

Pumpkin

Pumpkin is a half-Sioux, half-Irish young woman from Chicago, who travels to the reservation to take part in a powwow. She received her nickname from her Irish father, who named her for her red hair. She is intellectually curious and loves to read, which sets her apart from her peers; of her graduating class in high school, she was the only girl not pregnant. Because of her reading, she feels different and no longer fits into Indian culture. She is due to attend Stanford University in the fall, and is the pride of the Indian community. She is nervous about college, knowing that she will have to leave the Indian community to go there; on her college application, she wrote, "I sometimes feel I am risking my soul by leaving the Indian community." She plans to spend the summer on the powwow circuit, dancing at as many as possible before heading back to Chicago. She is a "grass dancer," a style of dancing that is usually performed only by men, and she is the best dancer on the field, embodying the spirit of the grass as it bends and sways in the wind. Harley Wind Soldier notices her, and falls in love.

Reverend Pyke

Post Chaplain at Fort Laramie, Reverend Pyke is a stern, religious man. He is impressed by Red Dress's apparent Christianity and makes her his personal interpreter and secretary. He is an orphan and thinks of himself as "God's child. . . . No mother, no father, no strangling ties to come between me and the Lord." He sees nature as a filthy place, ruled by Satan, kills any insect he finds, and believes in the biblical notion that humans are meant to rule over all of nature.

Red Dress

Red Dress is a powerful and magical woman. Her descendant, the witch Mercury Thunder, dreamed of her as a child, and says, "I had heard her insistent voice, crackling with energy, murmuring promises of a power passed through the bloodlines from one woman to the next. I had seen her kneeling beside a fire, feeding it with objects stolen from her victims: buttons, letters, twists of hair. She sang her spells, replacing the words of an ancient honor song with those of her own choosing." Mercury also tells her niece, "She spelled one too many, and he killed her."

Herod Small War

Frank Pipe's grandfather, he is a *Yuwipi,* or dream interpreter. At the powwow in the opening chapter, he gives the invocation, or prayer, to the Great Spirit, so that the powwow can begin. He is a practical man, and believes in short, effective prayers. He does have power, but he is realistic about his humanity. "I could clear my face of any expression, retreat into my thoughts, and the people around me would wait quietly, respectfully, convinced I was experiencing a vision. Sometimes their assumption was correct, but nine times out of ten I was just spacing out."

Anna Thunder

See Mercury Thunder

Charlene Thunder

Charlene is the granddaughter of the witch Mercury Thunder. She is in love with Harley Wind Soldier. Other people are wary of her because of her grandmother's power, so she doesn't have many friends and is often lonely. She is reluctant to practice magic like her grandmother, because she would rather earn things on her own, despite the fact that prejudice against her resulting from her grandmother's behavior often thwarts her. Although she likes dancing at powwows, she no longer competes in them, because her grandmother makes sure that she wins, thus taking the joy away from competition. She identifies with the character of Darrin from the television show *Bewitched.* Just as Darrin was constantly trying to get his witch wife to stop practicing magic, she tries to get her grandmother to stop, but without success. She is in love with Harley Wind Soldier and knows she could get him by practicing love magic like her grandmother's, but she wants him to be hers of his own free will.

Charlene lives with her grandmother, who tells her that her parents ran off to a large city and became drunks, then died. However, Charlene has never seen any hard evidence of their deaths, and Mercury won't tell her where they're buried. Mercury does not believe Charlene should attend school, but thinks Charlene should simply learn what Mercury wants her to know.

Crystal Thunder

Crystal Thunder is Charlene's mother, daughter of Mercury Thunder. She marries a young white man, an artist named Martin Lundstrom, and leaves the reservation with him. She disapproves of her mother's bad magic, because it makes her an outcast in the school, and she is embarrassed by her mother's steady stream of bewitched boyfriends.

Mercury Thunder

Mercury Thunder is the grandmother of Charlene Thunder and descendant of Red Dress. She practices "bad medicine," and is known as a witch. Power writes, "Mercury believed she held her life firmly in place beneath her tongue, and she didn't spit it out here and there, in bits and pieces, diffusing its power." She was originally named Anna, but changed her name to Mercury after Charlene came home from school and explained the table of the elements to her: "An element is a substance that can't be split into smaller pieces." "That's my story," Mercury said, "I'm all of a piece." Mercury uses her magic to get her way in all things, most notably to snare men; although she is about seventy years old, she has a steady stream of dazed young lovers. "All of Mercury's lovers appeared addled, exploited by the magic she stirred with her spoons," Power writes. As a young girl, Mercury dreamed of her powerful ancestor, Red Dress, who was also a witch, indicating that she would carry on Red Dress's magic.

Calvin Wind Soldier

Husband of Lydia and father of Harley, Calvin becomes a tribal policeman. His wife Lydia stops speaking when he and their other son Duane are killed in a car crash, before Harley is born.

Harley Wind Soldier

He is the son of Lydia Wind Soldier and Calvin Wind Soldier. Lydia has not spoken since Harley's father and brother were killed in a car crash, before Harley was born. Because of her silence, he has always felt lonely and empty; as a child, he drew this empty space inside him as a black spot on his torso, to the dismay of his teachers. As he grew older, Powers writes, "The empty box didn't fill itself in the way he'd hoped. It stretched to accommodate his new size. It grew as his bones lengthened and his heart swelled." Harley dances at the powwow, wearing a costume and makeup that his father wore; because his father died before he was born, his mother showed him the patterns, without saying a word.

Lydia Wind Soldier

Lydia Wind Soldier is the mother of Harley. She has not spoken for seventeen years, since her husband and son were killed in a car crash. Her other son, Harley, has never heard her speak. The only time anyone hears her voice is at powwows, where she sings. Her sister Evie says, "People said she had the voice of a ghost. When she sang, women would carry their tape recorders to the drum to record her, and men would soften their voices to let Lydia's rise, above the dancers' heads, above the smoke of cigarettes and burning sage, some thought beyond the atmosphere to that dark place where the air is thin and Wanagi Tacanku, the Spirit Road, begins."

Themes

Magical Elements

"People in that community believe in magic, spirits and ghosts," Power told Dani Shapiro in *People Weekly,* and when ghosts, magic, and spirits appear in the book, Power and her characters treat them matter-of-factly; there is no obvious seam between the vividly sensory description of an abandoned old house and the old white woman's ghost who inhabits it. The ghost woman is usually seen doing everyday chores such as beating rugs, sweeping floors, and churning butter, a fact that only reinforces the everyday nature of the spirit realm. In other examples, Herod Ghost Horse leads a group out on horses to look for the "medicine hole," a mythical opening to another world. The description of the search is full of concrete physical details—the bottled water and sandwiches they bring, the *Star Trek* t-shirts the boys wear, the wildflowers and the heat of the sun. The medicine hole is a magical place, but Herod and the others believe that they can reach it. They don't, but Herod encounters ghosts and spirit warriors.

In another incident, Margaret Many Wounds is dying. At the same time, the television shows the astronauts walking on the moon. Margaret is unimpressed: she's been there before, in spirit. When she dies, she goes there again, and dances traditional dances there, near the astronauts' metal flag, before she moves on "toward the council fire, five steps beyond the edge of the universe."

This acceptance of the presence of spirits, magic, ghosts, and the spiritual realm, and Power's seamless treatment of them, reinforces their place in the Sioux world, where they are a normal part of everyday reality. Ghosts do not live in some other realm: they are often here, with humans. What people do in the physical world can affect the spirit world, and vice versa. Unlike the European-American world, where many people no longer believe in spirits, Power's characters don't just believe: they *know* the spirits are there.

Topics for Further Study

- In the book, Herod Small War tells Frank Pipe and Harley Wind Soldier that Christianity came to the Sioux when a steamboat came up the Missouri River, bringing the first piano to the area. "That sound made them believe about heaven better than any priest's words," he says. "After that piano and all the church music hit this tribe, there were a lot of converts." Investigate early contacts between Sioux and whites. Is this description historically accurate?

- Find out more about Sioux spiritual beliefs, specifically the *hanbdec'eya,* or vision quest, which Harley undergoes at the end of the book. What purifications do young people have to go through before they are allowed to seek a vision for their lives?

- Investigate powwow customs, costumes, and dances. What are some of the different dances, how did they develop, and what do they represent?

- Herod Small War is a holy man, but he is modest about his abilities, noting that when he appears deep in thought to others, he may simply be not paying attention. Compare his behavior and his beliefs, as shown in the book, to those of Reverend Pyke and Father La Frambois.

- Margaret's grandmother had a beautiful, intricately beaded dress that was taken to the Field Museum of Anthropology in Chicago after her death, and Charlene mentions that many of the customers for her grandmother's beadwork are white collectors of Native-American art. Do you think these artifacts belong in museums and collections, or should they remain in the hands of Native Americans? Why or why not?

Living in a Larger World

"It's hard to explain how you identify, as a part of who you are is raised with a certain world view as well as an Indian world view," Susan Power told Anne Putnam in the *Bucknellian.* She acknowl-

A wood engraving of Sioux Indians performing the Ghost Dance, a traditional dance of the Dakota Sioux whose lives the novel explores.

edged the necessity of dealing with that "certain world view," telling Putnam, "We're living in a larger world, not just an Indian world."

Power wrote in *Reinventing the Enemy's Language,*

> As the only Indian in every school I attended through twelfth grade, I knew I was different. But I didn't see it as a liability. I thought of it as an advantage. I felt I had a secret, another world I could retreat to when the dominant culture, for all its material success and political power, felt empty and meaningless. In the Indian world there were living stories: ghosts, mischievous spirits, bad medicine and good medicine, people with real problems, problems of survival. The Indian world always seemed immediate and startlingly real, a place where things happened.

In the book, this view of the Indian world as more vivid and important holds true, and so does the idea that dealing with the white world is difficult: the whites in *The Grass Dancer* all have limited world views, fueled mostly by books: anthropology texts, the Bible. Charlene is likewise immersed in her high school studies, but she uses them mainly as an escape, a screen against her grandmother Mercury, who works magic and mocks Charlene's tests and grades, telling her that Mercury's lessons and tests are more important

than those she'll endure in school. Herod Small War's teachings, and his guidance in the vision quest Harley undergoes at the end of the book, are more helpful to Harley than any amount of school. Pumpkin, who is the most educated of all the Indian characters, says that she is afraid that if she goes to school and leaves the Indian community, she will lose her soul, and the extensive reading she's done has already left her feeling alienated, cut off from her people.

Style

Flowing Backward in Time

A notable feature of the novel is that the story is told in reverse; each successive chapter goes backward in time, not forward as in most other novels. This unusual technique gives the reader a sense of the deep connections between past and present generations in Sioux belief and culture, and events in the novel reinforce this sense of the past being vividly alive. Long-dead ancestors are still active in the present life of the characters, influencing them as much or more than other living people. Red Dress and Ghost Horse interact with most of the characters in the book, either directly or through the actions of their descendants. When Harley, in despair, seeks a vision, he meets his dead grandmother, brother, father, and both Red Dress and Ghost Horse, and is blessed and guided by all of them.

Lawrence Thornton commented on this technique in the *New York Times Book Review,* noting,

> The reader responds to the narrative as if it were a series of photographs ranging from the crisp images of a Nikon to grainy daguerreotypes spotted with age. But Ms. Power's method has thematic as well as technical brio, for it also replicates the tribal sense of time and connectedness, reifying a world where ancestors are continually present in everyday life as spirits, memories and dreams.

Michael Dorris agreed, writing in the *Los Angeles Times* that, "moving a century backward from the early 1980s and reclosing the loop in the present," the book reveals the deep interconnections between the past and the present, and the human links of emotion, memory, and event that bind the characters together.

The obvious connections between different generations and ages in history also lead the reader to wonder how the people of today will influence their descendants. Just as Red Dress and Ghost Horse are still vivid presences to the current-day characters, the reader senses that Pumpkin and Harley Wind Soldier will appear in the dreams and actions of Sioux people in the distant future. This gives a sense of the continuing vitality of Native-American life, and in the *Women's Review of Books,* Linda Niemann wrote, "Power chooses to reveal indigenous history not as a record but rather as a continuing process whose outcome is still uncertain."

The Oral Tradition of Storytelling

For Native-American people traditionally, and to this day, oral storytelling is an important way of passing on values, history, and teaching to others. Powers, who heard her mother's storytelling and attended powwows where other women told hair-raising ghost stories, was raised with this tradition, which was also nourished by her father, who read stories out loud to her even after she had learned to read. *The Grass Dancer* is written in flowing, musical prose that sounds very much like that which a traditional storyteller would use, and this style is not accidental. Power told an interviewer for *george jr.,* "writing is such an oral experience for me. I have to read my work aloud over and over at both the writing and editing stages. I need to hear the language, hear the story, in order to make it live."

Historical Context

The Grass Dancer spans over a hundred years of Sioux history on the Standing Rock reservation, which straddles North and South Dakota, but it begins and ends in the present day, in 1981 and 1982, showing the continuing vitality of Native-American culture, which has become more apparent to mainstream society since the civil rights protests and Indian activism movements that began in the 1960s.

Power was touched by these movements directly, and her activist awareness of these present-day causes informs the book. She was brought up with her mother's commitment to activism on behalf of Indian people, and as a child went with her mother to sit-ins and civil rights protests. She moved back and forth from the white world of her Chicago prep schools to the Indian world of powwows and activism on the weekends. At powwows, she and her mother shared hotel rooms with older women, who told ghost stories and gave her an awareness of the richness of Sioux culture. Her encounters with her two cultures, mainstream and Sioux, inform the book and are relevant to many Native-American people today.

The book opens as Pumpkin, a young Sioux girl from Chicago, travels back to the reservation where her family has lived for generations so that she can dance in a powwow. She plans to cover the powwow circuit in the northern states for the rest of the summer, before going to school at Stanford in the fall. Because of her acceptance at the college, she is the pride of her family and community, and her sudden death in a car accident is a tragedy.

In this short chapter, Power tells the reader a great many things about current Indian life. One is that many Native Americans now live in the city; in one interview, Power estimated that there were about 25,000 Native Americans in Chicago alone. Not everyone lives on the reservation, and not everyone is a "full-blood"; Pumpkin is half Irish and half Menominee, but she is treated as Indian by everyone in the book. Another piece of information is that there are many powwows held across the country, that the dancing at them is competitive, and that it is common for young people to travel the circuit, winning prizes and money. In addition, the circuit is intertribal: Pumpkin, a Menominee girl, wins a powwow held by the Sioux.

In this chapter, Power also lets readers know that, sadly, alcohol and car crashes involving Indians are common. "So many Indians smashed themselves on the roads it was old news, but most accidents involved alcohol." In the book, six Sioux people die in car crashes: Pumpkin and her three friends, and Calvin Wind Horse and his son Duane. This is an aspect of Native-American life that is upsetting to many; Power wrote in *Reinventing the Enemy's Language* that in high school, when she wrote a story about the funeral of Big Tom, a Winnebago friend who drank himself to death, her high school English teacher told Power's mother she was worried about her, and that she thought Power should try to be more like the other students, something that was impossible for Power, since it would mean turning her back on half of her heritage.

In the closing chapter of the book, there's another powwow, this one held on the grounds of a prison. Just as in the earlier chapter, Power lets the reader know that Sioux people are just as "modern" as anyone else and experience all the same temptations of the modern world—at this last powwow, Harley gets drunk, and Frank Pipe notes that his cousin Aljoe used to be a thief before converting to Christianity, which appeals to him because of its organization and apparent lack of confusion. At the same time, the Sioux have their own rich traditions and ceremonies, such as the powwow, the *Yuwipi* ceremonies, and the vision quest that, in the end, leads Harley to begin, at long last, to heal from his emotional wounds.

Critical Overview

When *The Grass Dancer* came out, praise for Power's work was almost unanimously favorable. Power won the 1995 PEN/Hemingway Award for the best first fiction of that year, and received glowing reviews. All the reviewers were fascinated by the window into Sioux culture that the book provided, praising Power's depiction of her Native-American heritage as much as they praised her vivid, mesmerizing prose style. In *Publishers Weekly*, a reviewer wrote, "a major talent debuts with this beguiling novel," and praised Power's use of historical events such as the Apollo moon landing and the great drought on the plains during the nineteenth century, along with supernatural and spiritual events, "reinforcing the seamless connection" between these two realms. Calling her "a consummate storyteller," the reviewer also praised her use of suspense, humor, irony, and drama, and wrote, "Seduced by her humane vision and its convincing depiction, one absorbs the traditions and lore of the Sioux community with a sense of wonder."

In the *New York Times Book Review,* Lawrence Thornton remarked that Power "writes with an inventiveness that sets her writing apart from much recent American fiction. . . . Written with grace and humility, *The Grass Dancer* offers a healing vision that goes to the core of our humanity." Stephen Henighan wrote in the *Times Literary Supplement* that "this scrupulously wrought novel, deftly fusing traditional story-telling with the forms of contemporary fiction, provides a sparkling demonstration of that [Sioux] culture's continued vitality."

Caroline Moseley wrote in the *Princeton Weekly Bulletin* that the novel was "a mesmerizing tale," and that "the numinous power of the spirit world illumines the novel; the narrative flows forward and backward in time, and dead forbears—such as the 19th-century lovers Ghost Horse and Red Dress—are vital presences in daily life."

Dani Shapiro in *People Weekly* praised Power's musical, magical prose style, and in *The Bucknellian,* Anne Putnam praised the insights embodied in Power's work, which add a deeper dimension to the novel than exists in most current work.

Robert Allen Warrior, an Osage writer, was one of the few critics whose assessment of the book was not unequivocally favorable. He praised the author's "strong debut," but tempered this by remarking, "The novel exudes youthfulness, both in terms of tremendous energy and some telling unevenness, but this is a writer to watch for in the future." Warrior did not specify the nature of the "unevenness," but summed up by writing that "*The Grass Dancer* is a sometimes brilliantly told story that is well worth reading." He also drew hope from the fact that Power is clearly influenced by the excellent Native-American writers who have preceded her, most notably Louise Erdrich, Leslie Marmon Silko, and Joy Harjo, and wrote that, clearly, "new writers are learning from those who have already trod the difficult path of realizing artistic vision and are . . . honoring that earlier work."

Criticism

Kelly Winters

Winters is a freelance writer and editor and has written for a wide variety of academic and educational publishers. In the following essay, she discusses themes of cultural conflict and a spiritual world view in The Grass Dancer.

Susan Power wrote in *Reinventing the Enemy's Language* that she began writing when she was five, and that a large part of her impulse to write came from the fact that, by writing, she could "sort through the conflicting values and belief systems I was taught by being raised with one foot in the Indian world and the other in mainstream society." As the only Native American in her school classes until high school, she was keenly aware of white attitudes toward her and toward Native Americans in general.

Throughout her novel *The Grass Dancer,* Sioux characters encounter whites and white culture. Power's vivid characterization, dialogue, and storytelling style subtly, accurately, and often humorously portray various ways that whites view the Sioux, all of them based on misconceptions.

When Jeannette McVay comes to the reservation in the early 1960s, she is a starry-eyed anthropology student who wants to "go out there and meet humanity" instead of reading about people's customs in dusty books. Originally, she is sent to Herod Small War when she asks people about tribal religion and medicine people, but her feminist sensibilities are offended when he tells her she cannot participate in his sweat lodge because she is female, and can't attend his *Yuwipi* ceremony because she is menstruating. "What's the use of studying with someone like that, who excludes me, who doesn't recognize me as a full-functioning peer?," she complains to Mercury. Of course, Jeannette is not a peer of Herod Small War at all, since she doesn't share his world view or spiritual experience, but she doesn't realize that.

Like many non-Native Americans, Jeannette has preconceived notions about who Native Americans are, and about who they should be. For example, she is shocked and amused by the fact that Crystal, who is then in high school, listens to the popular singer Little Richard. "I have to get this down," she says, making notes. "A Sioux girl listening to Little Richard." It's as if, to her, Native Americans are museum pieces, with no interaction with current culture. This notion is verified by the fact that she tells Mercury Thunder that she had thought Sioux culture was dead, but that she is pleasantly surprised to find "all this activity and vitality and living mythology. I feel like I've stumbled on a secret." It's also symbolized by the beaded dress that belonged to Margaret's grandmother, which is now on display in the Field Mu-

> "'I have to get this down,' she says, making notes. 'A Sioux girl listening to Little Richard.' It's as if, to her, Native Americans are museum pieces, with no interaction with current culture."

seum in Chicago. Margaret would have loved to take that dress out, dance in it, and pass it on to future generations, but this use does not fit white notions of what is appropriate: the dress has become a dead museum piece, not a living part of culture, so now no one can use it. On display in the museum, it verifies the white visitors' impression that Sioux culture is a thing of the past.

Of course, the vibrancy of Sioux life is not a secret or a new discovery to those living it; Jeannette doesn't know it, but her attitude is much like that of the European explorers who "discovered" America, as if it was not previously "discovered" and settled by the Native Americans already living there.

In addition, Sioux culture is only fascinating to her when it fits into her comfortable notions of what it should be: she is disgusted with Herod Small War's "prejudice" against women, and she can't see Mercury as the Sioux witch she is, but must label her in terms of the Greek mythology that is familiar to her from her East Coast schooling. Mercury becomes "Aphrodite, Goddess of Desire," and this supposed familiarity and accessibility makes her all the more interesting: "You're not in some book or reclining on Mount Olympus. You're right here in the kitchen, serving me peaches!"

When Jeannette finally realizes that Mercury is not what Jeannette thought she was, that she's not some character from a book but a very powerful, selfish, and frightening woman, she flees—too late, since Mercury has already created a spell to trap her on the reservation. Like it or not, her wish to "go out there and meet humanity" has come true, and for the rest of her life, she'll be on the reservation, learning about Sioux culture.

Jeannette's views of Native Americans as a dead or dying cultural group, and simultaneously

What Do I Read Next?

- Susan Power's *Strong Heart Society* (2001), tells the stories of three Native Americans—a Sioux from South Dakota, a Vietnam veteran, and a powwow princess—in a braid of tales set in the city of Chicago.

- In *Reinventing the Enemy's Language: Contemporary Native American Women's Writings of North America* (1998), editors Joy Harjo and Gloria Bird present a collection of writings by Native-American women.

- Native-American women share their lives in the autobiographical stories presented in *American Indian Women: Telling Their Lives* (1987), edited by Gretchen M. Bataille.

- Jane B. Katz, editor, presents more true stories of Native-American women in *Messengers of the Wind: Native American Women Tell Their Life Stories* (1996).

- Paula Gunn Allen's *The Sacred Hoop: Recovering the Feminine in American Indian Traditions* (1992), first published in 1986, documents the continuing vitality of the Native-American tradition and of women's leadership within that tradition.

- In *Speaking for the Generations: Native Writers on Writing* (Sun Tracks, Vol. 35, 1998), editor Simon J. Ortiz presents nine Native-American writers who discuss the storytelling traditions of their tribes and the influence writing in English has had on their work.

- Linda Hogan's *Woman Who Watches over the World: A Native Memoir* (2001), tells the powerful story of Hogan's own family and the way in which tribal history informs her own past.

---

as a nobler, more spiritual people than whites, seems to be only a continuation of the nineteenth-century attitudes depicted in later chapters of *The Grass Dancer*. For example, Red Dress is aware that in the view of the Catholic missionary priest,

Father La Frambois, "We were already a degraded people, whom he intended to elevate, single-handedly, into the radiant realm of civilization."

Reverend Pyke shares this view, extending his vision of degradation and disorder to the entire natural world, which the Native Americans are part of: "Pyke said there was nothing natural about the natural world: it was an evil disorder requiring the cleansing hand of God." He crushes a spider's egg sac and licks his fingers clean, saying, "I've swallowed the spit of Satan." He is a deep believer in the biblical notion that humans, specifically white Europeans, were created to own and master the earth and everything on it: "Replenish the earth and subdue it, and have dominion over the fish of the sea, and over the fowl of the air, and over every living thing that moveth upon the earth." As Power makes clear, Native Americans don't share this belief, preferring to live in harmony with nature and its spiritual forces rather than "subdue" it. As Vine Deloria, Jr., the activist writer mentioned by the character Frank Pipe, wrote in his book *God Is Red: A Native View of Religion,* "We are a part of nature, not a transcendent species with no responsibility to the natural world."

Just as Jeannette is amazed and amused to see a Sioux girl listening to the popular singer Little Richard, the whites at Fort Laramie are taken aback by Red Dress's familiarity with English and her apparent conversion to Christianity. The white widow Fanny Brindle patronizingly tells Red Dress, "Do you know what they're saying about you? That you're a princess. . . . Yes, a Sioux princess with the light of the world in your heart, and a love of Jesus Christ that is so pure, your soul is white as cream. I think it's because of your remarkable English. . . . They can't conceive of it as anything but a miracle, and it is, you know. It is."

Another response to Native-American people in the book is the attempt to freeze them at some mythic time in the past, as "noble savages." This begins early, when Red Dress travels to Squaw Town and finds that the people there, unlike her own band, have accepted white trade goods. Red Dress's band is more conservative; her father, who noticed that trade with whites brought disease and dependence on them, decreed that his band would continue making bone arrowheads instead of using metal, cook with pots made of buffalo stomach lining instead of iron ones, and wear traditional buckskin clothes decorated with paint and quills, instead of beaded cloth. When Red Dress and her brother go to Squaw Town, the people there, who are now poor and unkempt, think they are the ghosts of their ancestors, and revere them because they follow the old ways.

Jeannette eventually also falls into this position. She reads to the students from a complete set of the works of the white writer James Fenimore Cooper, whose descriptions of Native Americans exasperate and bore the students—as she reads, they roll their eyes at each other, but she doesn't notice. Finally, Frank Pipe approaches her and asks, "Instead of this stuff, could we read some of that Vine Deloria?"

Jeannette has never heard of Deloria, who is a Native-American writer famous for writing activist texts such as *God Is Red: A Native View of Religion, Custer Died for Your Sins: An Indian Manifesto,* and *Beyond the Trail of Broken Treaties.* His work is much more relevant to the students, and not just because, as Frank tells her, he's their cousin. After Jeannette reads his work and that of other Native-American writers, she begins viewing her students as "royalty in exile"—an echo of the view, a hundred years earlier, of Red Dress as a "princess."

In any time period, all of the characters, both white and Sioux, are challenged by fate and by the contrast between white and native cultures. They are also constantly aware of the presence of the spirit world, which Power describes as vividly and concretely as she describes the ordinary physical world. The spirit world is not easily categorized as "good," or "evil"; like nature, it exists within and outside everyone, and includes forces that may or may not be controlled, but must be reckoned with. In every chapter, ghosts, spirits, and mysterious events occur, so much a part of ordinary life that there is no obvious dividing line between them. To Power's characters, this is reality: ghosts move among the living; a man who killed dogs is stalked and killed by the protective coyote spirit; an elder dances on the moon; a witch can make any man come to her; men can be forced to hang themselves; there is a medicine hole that leads to another reality; and a young man who fasts and prays for vision can find it and be led to a healing understanding of himself and his past.

Red Dress describes the way she is "hitched to the living and their concerns," and says, "I can bear witness to only a single moment of loss at a time. Still, hope flutters in my heart, a delicate pulse. I straddle the world and pray to Wakan Tanka that somewhere ahead of me he has planted an instant of joy." Throughout the book, characters have these moments of understanding and joy as they come to

terms with history and their own past, and as they discover secrets about their heritage. Harley's brother Duane is not his full brother, but the result of an affair between his father and his mother's sister. Lydia and Evelyn are not full-blooded Native Americans, but half-Japanese. Charlene's parents are not dead, they are alive, and her father is a white artist who designs his wife's beadwork. Crystal Thunder's father was an abusive man who disappeared. Harley meets his father and brother, filling his lifelong craving for connection and validation. Through all these events, Power shows the healing power of love, truth, and reconciliation with the past.

Source: Kelly Winters, in an essay for *Novels for Students,* Gale Group, 2001.

Stephen Henighan

In the following review, Henighan asserts that The Grass Dancer *"reassembles the history of the Sioux Indians . . . with disarming equanimity."*

The act of reclaiming a lost or suppressed cultural identity is often carried out with defiance. Histories that have been denigrated or marginalized tend to be reborn in the contentious language of rebellion. Susan Power's first novel, *The Grass Dancer,* set on a North Dakota reservation, reassembles the history of the Sioux Indians—a term Power seems to prefer to the currently favoured "Native Americans" with disarming equanimity.

Four weeks before Harley Wind Soldier's birth, his father and brother are killed by a drunken driver. The driver is white, and, though Power makes little of this detail, the accident epitomizes the offhand way in which, throughout this novel, white society wipes out the Indian past more through carelessness than malice. Harley's mother, traumatized by the accident, becomes mute; Harley grows up feeling that he has a "black, empty hole squeezed in his chest between heart and lungs". When the novel opens, in 1981, he is an introverted seventeen-year-old. At a summer pow-wow, he meets Pumpkin, a red-haired Menominee dancer of Irish ancestry. "You shouldn't ever be too arrogant or too loud about who you are", she tells Harley, in response to his anger at having been denied knowledge of his past. Before their relationship can release Harley from his stunned resentment, a second road accident claims Pumpkin's life. Her successful projection of her heritage into the hybrid reality of the present serves as a model for the stories that follow.

Sioux war chiefs.

Later chapters of the novel hop back and forth between 1961 and the early 1980s; one tale reaches back as far as the 1930s, and there is a full-blown historical re-creation of a tragic encounter between Sioux and missionaries in 1864. Each of these narratives contributes, in a subtle way, to the reader's understanding of the opening accident. Nearly all of the narrators are women. Power is anything but a racial purist; her heroines have their children by wayward Swedes and errant Japanese doctors, yet their offspring's claims to Sioux history are never in doubt. The narrating voices are tough and matter-of-fact, even when their vision elides the barrier separating life from death; spirits abound in this novel, yet their activities are depicted as unremarkable. The mingling of living and dead, like that of Indians and whites, is crucial to Power's integrated account of her community. If her various narrators all speak in similar language, at once frank and lyrical, this appears to be a strategy rather than a stylistic lapse: the complementary insights and images evoked by their respective stories forge the shared history which, in the novel's final pages, succeeds in restoring Harley Wind Soldier's sense of self.

Comparisons of *The Grass Dancer* to the work of Louise Erdrich are unavoidable. Despite the shared North Dakota settings, Indian themes and layering of voices, however, Power has succeeded in creating a universe resonant with its own obsessions. Her fiction is more introspective and less plot-driven than that of Erdrich. This novel concludes with the white woman whose meddling is indirectly responsible for the initial accident marrying and having a child with a Sioux man. Yet one of the reservation's elders discourages her from bringing up her daughter solely in the Sioux tradition: "She needs to know both sides . . . tell her two stories." Acceptance, here, grows out of a deep-seated indifference. The lure of white society fails to impress Power's Sioux characters; their culture rolls on, adapting prevailing modes to express a Sioux vision. This scrupulously wrought novel, deftly fusing traditional story-telling with the forms of contemporary fiction, provides a sparkling demonstration of that culture's continued vitality.

Source: Stephen Henighan, "The Sioux Sense of Self," in *Times Literary Supplement,* No. 4783, December 2, 1994, p. 22.

Christopher McIllroy,

In the following review, McIllroy calls The Grass Dancer *a "weaving of spells, passions, spirituality and history," and says Power exhibits an "understanding that allows compassion for white and Indian."*

Readers of Susan Power's extravagantly inventive, intellectually rigorous first novel, *The Grass Dancer,* will recognize the now-familiar territory of magic realism, but they will find themselves in a distinctively Native-American province. In Power's fictional world of the Dakota (Sioux), magic is cold fact, as much as a thundercloud or Formica tabletop. It is the "potent blood"—or "bad medicine"—of Mercury Thunder, reservation witch, that drives people to act, as much as the more conventional elements of human psychology.

The author, a member of the Standing Rock Sioux tribe, uses two tragic auto accidents as our entry into this weaving of spells, passions, spirituality and history.

In the prologue, a drunken white, distraught over his girlfriend's affair with a Dakota man, rams his car into the oncoming headlights of another, thinking they are eyes sent by "vengeful . . . Sioux ghosts." Killed in the crash are the father and older brother of yet-unborn Harley Wind Soldier.

When the novel resumes, Harley is 17, preparing for a powwow with the help of his mother, who has not spoken since the deaths. Harley applies "black-on-white teardrops" in his traditional face-painting, so that when Pumpkin, one of the novel's most appealing and poignant characters, first glimpses him, he is "crying painted tears from forehead to chin."

Pumpkin embodies the Native-American predicament of suspension between the competing values and aspirations of two cultures. An incoming Stanford freshman, she is also the grass dancer of the title—"not a girl . . . but the spirit of grass weaving its way through a mortal dancer," according to the powwow judge who awards her first prize in the traditionally male event.

Harley and Pumpkin, both loners for their different reason, spend one tender night together. Unfortunately, Harley is desired by Charlene Thunder, granddaughter of the notorious witch, Mercury Thunder. It is Mercury, we conclude, who hexes Charlene's rival, with devastating results.

In an approach reminiscent of Louise Erdrich, the Turtle Mountain Chippewa author of the trailblazing *Love Medicine,* Power lets her saga of families range-over wide stretches of time, from character to character, in shifting points of view, through a series of linked stories.

Before long, the narrative corkscrews back into the past, delving into the family suffering and loss that shaped the characters and fates of Harley Wind Soldier and Mercury Thunder. Chronology moves

> **Pumpkin embodies the Native-American predicament of suspension between the competing values and aspirations of two cultures. An incoming Stanford freshman, she is also the grass dancer of the title— 'not a girl . . . but the spirit of grass weaving its way through a mortal dancer' . . . "**

steadily backward, the 1970s, '60s, 1935. Finally, the two lines, Thunder and Wind Soldier, converge retroactively in 1864, in the legend of Mercury's ancestor Red Dress and Harley's ancestor Ghost Horse.

Red Dress, apparently Christianized, awakens to her "potent blood," at Ft. Laramie. In scenes of sinister-enchantments that are among the novel's most compelling, she induces the bluecoated enemy to hang themselves before being killed herself. The love between Red Dress and Ghost Horse, warrior and sacred clown, remains unconsummated, a "wrong of history" that Mercury will try to redress a century later with terrible consequences for the Wind Soldiers as well as for her own daughter and granddaughter.

The ferocity of Red Dress's medicine will be inherited by Mercury, but for narrower, meaner purposes. Where Red Dress has wreaked vengeance for her people, Mercury will ensnare her fellow Dakota men capriciously, as sexual toys.

What emerges from these bloody sorrows, surprisingly, is the author's attempt to overcome divisions. While honoring the implacable resistance of Red Dress to the invaders, and the struggle of her people against cultural domination, the book abounds in images and episodes of racial reconciliation; the white people work magic, too. In its treatment of gender, as well, the book suggests synthesis, Though women repeatedly heal their broken warrior-men, it is men's spiritual medicine that is most often nurturing, the women's that is cruel.

For Power there are no barriers between past and present; our ancestors live within us. In the novel's concluding two chapters, which return to the early 1980s, Charlene Thunder frees herself of her grandmother's medicine, aided by the spirit of Red Dress; visions of Ghost Horse and Red Dress help liberate Harley from his perpetual mourning.

In its effort to maintain order and clarity against the proliferation of stories, characters, images and themes, the novel achieves characterizations with a deftness and compression that become emblematic: Pumpkin's hook-shaped scar that pulses with fear; Harley Wind Soldier's painted tears and his mother's muteness; Mercury Thunder's wiry hair and wheelchair surrounded by her zombie-like, spellbound lovers. Similarly, chapter headings tend to focus on a thematic cultural icon: "The Medicine Hole," "Moonwalk," "Morse Code," "Honor Song."

At times the portraits seem anxious in their taut brilliance, hurrying to impress themselves upon us because it's time to move on, there is so much more to tell. The reliance on magic can become an easy shorthand.

Power is perceptive and nuanced in her characterizations; beneath their color and verve is a generous understanding that allows compassion for white and Indian, even for Thunder, whose evil powers originally are animated by bitter grief, hers as well as that of her people. I just wish for more time with some of Power's creations. Pumpkin, for instance, dies a sixth of the way into the book, after 30 pages' acquaintance. The pain of losing her is sharp but not the deep, transformative pain that can sear meaning into the reader.

None of this keeps the novel from moving or fascinating us—or entertaining us, either; it is frequently very funny. The flaws are those of surfeit rather than insufficiency—of talent, ideas, of things that need to be said. *The Grass Dancer* is a book of wonders.

Source: Christopher McIllroy, "Devil with a Red Dress On," in *Washington Post Book World,* Vol. 24, No. 30, July 24, 1994, pp. 3, 9.

Sources

Dorris, Michael, Review, in *Los Angeles Times,* August 14, 1994, p. E7.

Interview in *george jr.,* September 1996, online at http://www.georgejr.com/september/qapower.html (May 31, 2000).

Henighan, Stephen, Review, in *Times Literary Supplement,* December 2, 1994, p. 22.

Lynn, David H., "The Energizing, Liberating World of Multicultural Fiction: Your Culture," in *Writer's Digest,* November 1997, p. 36.

Moseley, Caroline, "Grass Dancer Evokes Past, Present," in *Princeton Daily Bulletin,* March 10, 1997.

Niemann, Linda, Review, in *Women's Review of Books,* January 1995, p. 23.

Power, Susan, Introduction to "Beaded Soles," in *Reinventing the Enemy's Language,* edited by Joy Harjo and Gloria Bird, W. W. Norton, 1997.

Review, in *Publishers Weekly,* June 6, 1994, p. 56.

Putnam, Anne, "From Heart of Chicago Fiction of Native America Arrives with Great Spirit," in *The Bucknellian,* online at http://coral.bucknell.edu/publications/bucknellian/sp97/2-20-97/lifest/1660.html (May 31, 2000).

Shapiro, Dani, "Spirit in the Sky: Talking with Susan Power," in *People Weekly,* August 8, 1994, p. 21.

Thornton, Lawrence, Review, in *New York Times Book Review,* August 21, 1994, p. 7.

Warrior, Robert Allen, Review, online at the Stanford website, http://www.stanford.edu/~warrior/grassdance.html (May 31, 2000).

For Further Study

Contreras, Dan, and Diane Morris Bernstein, *We Dance Because We Can: People of the Powwow,* Longstreet, 1996.
   Vivid photographs and profiles of powwow participants, with profiles of tribal leaders, craftspersons, and others.

Deloria, Vine, Jr., *God Is Red: A Native View of Religion,* Fulcrum, 1994.
   Deloria discusses Native-American spirituality.

Marra, Ben, and Richard Hill, *Powwow: Images along the Red Road,* Harry N. Abrams, 1996.
   Photographs and interviews of powwow dancers from many different tribes.

Less Than Zero

Bret Easton Ellis
1985

In 1985 *Less Than Zero* burst onto the literary scene. The book was a commercial success, and garnered much critical attention. As a result, its author, Bret Easton Ellis, was catapulted into the public eye. The story touches on themes of alienation, moral detachment, death, and nihilism in its portrayal of overprivileged youth in contemporary Los Angeles. Critics hailed it as the "voice of a new generation" and the "first MTV novel." The novel is narrated by Clay, a college student home on vacation, as he observes his friend slip deeper into drugs and prostitution. His detached and dispassionate view of the dissipation and corruption around him is often interpreted as a comment on modern-day society.

Author Biography

On March 7, 1964, Bret Easton Ellis was born in Los Angeles, California. He attended Bennington College in Vermont, graduating in 1986. His first novel, *Less Than Zero,* began as an assignment for a creative writing course, which was taught by the writer Joe McGinniss. Published in 1985, the novel appeared when the author was only twenty-one. It attracted much critical and popular attention, and Ellis became a very public figure. *Less Than Zero* was adapted to the screen and produced by Twentieth Century Fox in 1987.

Ellis's second novel, *The Rules of Attraction,* was published in 1987. His third novel, *American*

Bret Easton Ellis

Psycho, was published in 1991 and is perhaps his most controversial work for its portrayal of violence against women and its themes of materialism and morality. The Los Angeles chapter of the National Organization for Women boycotted the book. *American Psycho* was adapted to the screen in 2000. In 1994 he published a collection of short stories titled *Informers.* Ellis's most recent work, *Glamorama,* was published in 1999.

Plot Summary

Freeways and Billboards

A student at an East Coast college, Clay is a young man on Christmas break, spending his time off in his hometown of Los Angeles. His girlfriend, Blair, picks him up from the airport. One of her comments strikes Clay, and is worked into the rest of the novel at various key moments: "People are afraid to merge onto the freeway in Los Angeles." Clay's repetition of "people are afraid to merge" is an echo of E. M. Forster's phrase "only Connect"—the words that preface *A Passage to India*—and Ellis's phrase encapsulates the disconnected and empty life he finds back in California.

In the first section of the book Clay describes a series of parties and family meetings leading up to Christmas. He spends time with his friends Daniel, Trent, Julian and Blair; he easily falls back into the promiscuity, parties, and drugs. Clay has one-night stands with men and women, and uses cocaine frequently. Clay's relationships with his family and Blair grow more strained, and he begins repeating the key set of phrases more and more often.

Parties and Cocaine

The narrative shifts through more scenes of parties, nightclubs, and diners. In a thematically significant image, an old lady collapses from the heat at La Scala. The crowd looks on, bored. As the vignettes become more brutal and detached, Clay's memories of time he spent in Palm Springs become more poignant. He remembers closing the family home, and his grandmother's fear of death. In the house of his childhood recollections, "strange desert winds have taken over."

Clay continues to look for Julian, who owes him money. He is now spending more and more time with his dealer, Rip, in abrupt and confused vignettes of people and parties. Clay watches a televangelist preaching about redemption, and the phrase "this is a night of Deliverance" haunts him as he leaves for a meeting with Blair. Their date is awkward, and on the way home Blair hits a coyote in the road. Clay watches the animal die for ten minutes. Later he and Blair go home and have passionate sex.

Clay's cocaine use escalates and it results in more nosebleeds, just as his memories of his grandmother's cancer envision her coughing up blood. At Trent's party in Malibu, the crowd is fascinated by a snuff film depicting the brutal torture and murder of two young people. Daniel, who is aroused by the film, says he's not coming back to college with Clay because he is going to make violent sex movies. As his Los Angeles friends become stranger, Clay stops going to the psychiatrist.

The Girl on the Bed

After visiting his old elementary school, Clay finals runs into Julian, who tells him to come to Finn's house to get the money he's owed. It becomes clear that Julian is a prostitute. Clay is sent out on an appointment with him, and watches as Julian goes through with his "trick." The key phrases of the novel come together in this scene, and Clay thinks, "You can disappear here without even knowing it."

They return to Finn's and Julian tells him that he wants to stop hustling. Finn quiets his attempt to leave the business by injecting him with heroin. Clay goes to The Roxy, where the body of a drug overdose victim is being stared at by a crowd of his acquaintances. Rip asks them all if they'd like to see something that will "blow their minds": a naked and stoned twelve-year-old girl tied to the bed in Rip's bedroom. As Daniel and the rest take turns raping her, Clay leaves the house after a lame attempt to stop the abuse. Rip follows to ask what his problem is, and explains that he has, "nothing left to lose."

Leaving Los Angeles

Clay has a painful lunch with Blair. She asks if he ever loved her, and when he says no, she tells him that it's hard to love someone who doesn't care. He replies that it's too painful to care. In the final paragraph of the novel, Clay discusses a song about Los Angeles that he hears just before he returns to college. In a description that acts as a comment on his life, he explains that the song fills his head with images "so violent and malicious that they seemed to be my only point of reference for a long time afterwards. After I left."

Characters

Blair

Blair was Clay's girlfriend before he left for college. She picks him up from the airport in the opening of the novel, and they both spend most of the story unsure if they are still involved or not. They do sleep together a couple of times. In a scene near the end, Clay waits at a restaurant where he meets Blair, and she attempts to discuss their relationship; he is uncommunicative. The night before he leaves to go back to college, Blair calls him and asks him not to go.

Clay

Clay is the narrator and protagonist of the story. He is eighteen years of age, and has arrived home in Los Angeles for Christmas vacation after his first semester of college on the East Coast. Once home, he immediately falls back into his wide social circle; he begins to go from party to party, taking drugs, engaging in casual sex, and watching MTV and videos. Clay observes his social world with a detached, drug-induced passivity. There are signs that he longs for a deeper connection, shown

Media Adaptations

- *Less Than Zero* was adapted to the screen and produced by Twentieth Century Fox in 1987. The cast includes Robert Downy Jr. and James Spader.

by flashbacks to his childhood and happier times. He follows his friends and observes "the worst" in a deeper underworld of heroin addiction, prostitution and rape. The novel ends just before he goes back to college at the end of his vacation.

Clay's Father

Clay's parents are separated, and he sees his father several times over lunch at various restaurants. Clay and his father are unable to communicate with each other, and his father seems more interested in his business associates and his new car than he is in his own son.

Clay's Mother

Clay spends his vacation at home with his mother and two sisters. Clay and his mother are unable to communicate in any way, and his mother seems completely preoccupied and inattentive to her children. One night, Clay sees someone else's car parked in their driveway, indicating that his mother has brought home a man to stay the night.

Clay's Sisters

Clay has two sisters: one of whom he thinks is fifteen, and the other whom he thinks is thirteen. The lack of connection between Clay and his sisters is indicated by the fact that he never states their names.

Daniel

Daniel is a friend of Clay's from Los Angeles. He goes to college with Clay on the East Coast.

Finn

Finn is Julian's pimp and heroin dealer. When Julian tries to break free from him, he abuses him and injects him with heroin to make him passive.

Julian

Julian is an old friend of Clay's. He has become a heroin addict and a prostitute to support his addiction. Julian borrows a large sum of money from Clay, and after Clay repeatedly asks to get the money back, Julian takes him up to see Finn, his pimp and drug dealer. Julian prostitutes himself to a businessman at a hotel while Clay watches. Later, Clay accompanies Julian and Finn to a party, where Julian is required to prostitute himself again. When Julian becomes upset and does not want to do what Finn has required, Finn is physically abusive and Julian caves in to his demands.

Muriel

Muriel is a friend in Clay's social circle who is a heroin user. At one point, she is hospitalized for anorexia. After she is released from the hospital, her friends passively watch as she injects herself with heroin. Toward the end of the book, she has once again been hospitalized for anorexia.

The Psychiatrist

Clay's psychiatrist is completely self-absorbed, and therefore cannot really help him.

Rip

Clay describes Rip as his drug dealer. He is a cunning, shallow, amoral young man who has no concept that his kidnapping and rape of a young girl is wrong; instead, he considers it just a night's amusement.

Shandra

Shandra is the twelve-year-old girl whom Clay's friends have kidnapped, drugged, tied to a bed, and gang-raped repeatedly. Upon seeing her for the first time, Clay leaves the room and later gives a lame attempt to convince Rip what he is doing is wrong.

Trent

A male model, Trent is a friend of Clay's.

Themes

Death

Death is a central and recurring theme of the novel. Clay is preoccupied with death and images of death. Both Clay and his friends, however, seem to perceive images of death as a form of entertainment, no different from watching television. When

Topics for Further Study

- *Less Than Zero* makes many references to popular American music of the early 1980s. Learn more about this period in American music history. What kind of music do Ellis's characters listen to, and why are these references important to the meaning of the novel?

- *Less Than Zero* has been referred to as the first "MTV novel." The book often includes scenes in which characters are watching music videos on MTV. Learn more about the history of MTV, and other music video channels. How has MTV and the broadcasting of music video changed over the years?

- Ellis's novel includes descriptions of excessive drug use by the various characters, including Valium, heroin, cocaine, marijuana, and alcohol. Learn more about drug abuse among teenagers, and how it can affect them. What resources are available for teenagers seeking help in recovering from drug abuse? Report on these resources in your area.

- Ellis's novel *Less Than Zero* has been adapted to the screen and released as a Hollywood movie. If you have access to this film, compare and contrast it to the novel. In what ways is the meaning of the novel changed when translated onto the screen? In what was does the film adaptation add to the meaning of the novel?

a dead body is discovered in an alley, word is spread round and groups of youth go to look at the body as a curiosity. None of the characters, including Clay, seem to have any emotional response to death, and none of them consider contacting the police about the body.

Death becomes pure entertainment for Clay and his friends when they watch a "snuff" film, in which real people are killed before a camera. Again, Clay and his friends find these images intriguing and fascinating, and exhibit no human emotion whatsoever regarding the suffering and death of real human beings. Other images of death appear throughout the novel, such as the coyote Blair and Clay run over on the road, and Clay's description of house cats eaten by coyotes.

Family

Although family life is peripheral to Clay and his friends, it is a central theme of the story. All of the young people in the story come from extremely wealthy families, and many of their parents are employed in the Hollywood film industry. All of the parents in the story seem to be completely preoccupied with their careers and materialistic acquisitions, and are oblivious to their children. In fact, the parents in the story seem to be off traveling most of the time, and their children are never quite sure where their parents actually are. One of Clay's friends even has to read in a Hollywood industry periodical to find out where her mother is.

Just as none of Clay's friends are able to communicate with each other in any real way, so none of the parents in this story are able to communicate with their children. Clay's parents are separated, and his encounters with each of his parents are strained. They are oblivious to his state of mind, and he does not communicate with them. Even Clay's relationship to his sisters is distant and alienated: he's not quite sure how old they are, and doesn't seem to know their names.

Drug Abuse

Drug abuse is also a major theme of this novel. Clay and his friends seem to be almost constantly consuming drugs and seeking out more drugs. Clay frequently snorts cocaine and takes Valium. He and his friends often smoke marijuana and drink excessively. Although Clay never takes heroin, several of his friends do—including Muriel, who is anorexic, and Julian, who works for a pimp in order to maintain his addiction. Toward the end of the novel, Clay's friends have kidnapped, tied up, and gang-raped the twelve-year-old girl while injecting her with heroin. The constant drug use permeates the atmosphere of Clay's social world. Like his friends, Clay is detached from the people around him and often confused by conversations. Clay's parents are unconcerned with his drug use, as indicated when he discusses cocaine use with his sisters in front of their mother and she makes no comment about it.

Voyeurism

Voyeurism is the desire to take pleasure through detached observation and is a central theme of the novel. The most obvious instrument of voyeurism is television, usually in the form of MTV music videos, and video pornography. Through voyeurism, Clay and his friends remain detached from the world around them, and regard the death and suffering of others as merely forms of entertainment. Clay indulges himself in voyeurism when he accompanies his friend Julian when Julian prostitutes himself to a businessman in a hotel room. Clay goes along with Julian, merely to watch, because he needs to see how lowly and pathetic Julian has become.

Style

Narration

This story is narrated from the first-person point of view, meaning that the story is narrated from Clay's perspective and is limited to his thoughts and impressions of the action around him. Many critics have noted that Clay maintains a detached sense of irony in his narrative perspective. This detached tone is in part indicative of Clay's nearly constant drug use, and in part an expression of his complete sense of alienation from his own feelings, as well as from any real emotional contact with his friends and family.

Flashback Sequences

The novel is set during Clay's Christmas vacation from college. Yet interspersed with this central narrative flow of events are flashbacks to events from Clay's childhood. The flashbacks are scripted in italic type in order to set them off from the central narrative and indicate a shift in the narrative mode. Although nothing in the story directly indicates that Clay has written anything at all, the flashback sequences have a tone that suggests a personal essay or creative writing assignment for a college course.

The flashback sequences have a slightly different tone from the central narrative; they describe memories involving family interactions with relatives such as his grandparents and aunt and are less emotionally detached than the narration of the central story. Clay's memories of earlier times as described in the flashback sequences suggest a time in his life when he was more emotionally expressive and less disaffected from his family and the world around him. In the first flashback sequence, for example, Clay describes one day during his senior year of high school when he drove out to Palm

Springs where the house in which he had grown up stood run-down and unoccupied. He ends the sequence by explaining that, "I guess I went out there because I wanted to remember the way things were."

Setting

This novel is set in Los Angeles during the early 1980s. This setting is crucial to the story in several ways. Clay describes a social milieu of financially overprivileged teens who drive around in BMWs purchased by their parents, and spend countless sums of money on expensive drugs like cocaine. Ellis's novel depicts a spiritually and emotionally empty materialism of both the children and the parents in this milieu. Clay's father, for instance, is more concerned with his new car than with his own son.

The setting in LA is also important because many of Clay's friends are the children of people who work in the Hollywood film industry. The careers of the parents take them away from home much of the time, traveling to various locations for film production. Furthermore, the backdrop of the Hollywood film industry echoes a central theme of the novel, which describes a world of voyeuristic entertainment devoid of any real human contact.

Historical Context

Popular Music of the 1980s

Ellis's fiction has been noted for its many references to elements of popular American culture. This novel makes references to a number of pop musicians and bands of the early 1980s, including: Elvis Costello, the Go-Gos, Peter Gabriel, Duran Duran, INXS, Adam Ant, Sting, XTC, U2, the Fleshtones, Aerosmith, Squeeze, the Clash, the Eagles, and Fleetwood Mac. These references appear on posters and T-shirts as well as in discussion of new albums and songs, and background noise in various scenes of the novel. These references are partly what lead critics to call the novel "the voice of a new generation," as they locate the characters in a very specific historical and generational milieu of popular entertainment.

Popular Film, Television, and Magazines

Reference is also made to various movies, such as *Friday the 13th, Invasion of the Body Snatchers* and *Temple of Doom.* Several references to televi-

sion programs also appear in the novel, such as *The Twilight Zone,* a science fiction series, and *Another World,* a long-running soap opera. The titles also pick up on central themes of the novel. *Friday the 13th* and *Invasion of the Body Snatchers* are both classic horror films; their association with graphic violence, and the voyeuristic pleasures of watching graphic violence, are recurring interests of Clay and his friends. Popular magazines also figure prominently in Clay's social world of consumerism and glamour, including: *International Male, GQ,* and *Glamour.* These pop culture references together echo the book's theme of a shallow, superficial world built on the pleasures of voyeurism and consumerism.

MTV/HBO, and Betamax

Part of what makes this novel "the voice of a new generation" is the many references to newly marketed home video technology that became widely used in the early 1980s. Central to the atmosphere of the story is that televisions are often turned on to the MTV (Music TeleVision) station, featuring pop music videos. While music had been set to video or film images for promotional purposes before 1980, music videos did not become readily accessible to the public until the launching of MTV in 1981.

The *Encyclopaedia Britannica* entry on "Music Video" has captured the stylistic flavor of music videos in the early MTV era, when

performance clips had been all but superseded by a conceptual approach whose characteristic surrealism was often more stipulated than invented and whose glib stylistic hallmarks quickly became cliches: associative editing, multiple dramatized situations chosen more for their visual impact than their appropriateness, an air of significance undeterred by lack of actual meaning, and a breathtaking readiness to refer to, pilfer, and rework the 20th century's vast trove of talismanic imagery—drawn from movies, TV, painting, news photography, and so on.

MTV programming was made possible by the newly developed availability of cable television in the mid-1970s, which offered subscribers countless additional TV channels from which to choose. Characters in the novel also watch HBO (Home Box Office), a major cable station founded in 1972 by Time, Inc. In addition, characters in the novel watch videos, most often pornography, on the "betamax." The Betamax was an early version of videocassette recorder (VCR), launched by Sony in the 1970s. VHS soon dominated the market, and Betamax faded out of popularity.

Jami Gertz as Blair, Robert Downey, Jr. as Julian, and Andrew McCarthy as Clay in the 1987 film version of the novel.

Critical Overview

Ellis's first novel, *Less Than Zero* (1985), began as an assignment for a creative writing course. Upon its publication, he was both praised for his ability to capture the voice of a young generation and criticized for the novel's ambivalent sense of morality. The novel was noted for many reference to many elements of popular culture, particularly pop music. According to Peter Freese:

> The reviews of Ellis's first novel were extremely mixed. While one group of critics expressed their outraged rejection of the book's juvenile sensationalism, another group celebrated the novel as "a weirdly fascinating book" and greeted it as the authentic literary expression of a new generation.

Nonetheless, Freese contends: "However drastically the critical estimations diverged, two statements were frequently repeated: *Less Than Zero* was understood as *The Catcher in the Rye* updated for the eighties, and the slim book was classified as an 'MTV novel.'"

Freese gives a positive assessment of the novel's success as "the voice of a new generation":

> *Less Than Zero* is not only an expressive cultural document but also an accomplished narrative. It authen-

tically expresses the lifestyle of a generation nourished on the ubiquitous products of a sensation-bent entertainment industry, a generation in love with the violent and rebellious music of rock and punk, conversant with the escapist underground culture of drugs, abandoned by their pleasure-hunting, success-oriented and irresponsible parents, and haunted by a sense of impending doom.

Freese explains the title is derived from an Elvis Costello song, as indicating that "All they finally manage to effect is their physical and psychological self-destruction through drugs and prostitution, and thus it turns out that although they appear to have everything, they really have 'less than zero.'"

David Pan describes the MTV-style narrative of Ellis's novel, and its significance to the characterization of Clay, the novel's narrator and protagonist:

> The indifferent flow of images and events resembles the stream of flat images seen on television. Ellis' prose shares television's drive to continually change the image, to relentlessly keep up the pace of the action, a drive that ultimately debases the image and trivializes the action. Clay's own identity and consciousness is replaced by the string of events which, like the video images before his eyes, he seems to

have no control over, and which in the end perhaps entertain for a while, but can never really satisfy.

Freese, on the other hand, evaluates the significance of the success of Ellis's narrative style as a meaningful novelistic strategy, although he maintains that it "is no 'MTV novel.'":

> it is a tale which manages to translate the fast-paced urgency, the total lack of historical awareness, the additive impact and the macabre glitter of musical television into narrative strategies which deserve to be taken seriously as expressions of contemporary lifestyle and indications of future literary developments.

Some critics of Ellis's novel point to the passive, amoral stance of the narrator toward the events that surround him as a major weakness in the novel; others maintain that "the ironic tone" of the narrator "is unmistakable," and that this ironic distance provides a critical social perspective.

Criticism

Tabitha McIntosh-Byrd

Tabitha McIntosh-Byrd is an English literature instructor at the University of Pennsylvania. In the following essay she discusses the commodification of images and desire in Bret Easton Ellis's Less Than Zero.

In Christopher Isherwood's *Goodbye to Berlin,* the central character defines himself as a passive observer of prewar Germany by using the words, "I am a camera with its shutter open." Like the narrator of that tale, *Less Than Zero*'s narrator, Clay, positions himself as a detached observer of Los Angeles life. He and his peers are "cameras with their shutters open"—dispassionate commentators of what they see. His episodic visits to his psychiatrist bring no emotional insight, since the psychiatrist is as limited to external observation as his clients are. Rather, Clay describes a self and a world that contains no interiority—no experience or sense of itself beyond accessible surfaces. The camera view is symbiotic with its viewed object, so that Clay is both seen and seeing; object and subject at the same time. This disassociation of internal and external reality reaches greater and greater levels of psychosis as the novel develops, in a progressive move from icon to attitude to image to embodiment. The social postures of Julian, Trent, and Clay's sisters are inspired by the camera's icons, then converted into images—pornography, pho-

tography and film—and finally reified in flesh. In this way, the image (MTV, pornography) is turned into a physical practice (prostitution, torture) that carries with it the detached externality of the icon that preceded it, caused it and determined its form.

The importance and hyper-proliferation of images in the novel can be best explicated through the concept of "commodity fetishism." In "The Fetishism of the Commodity and its Secret," Marx suggests that commodity products become part of an obfuscating network of symbols that obscure the history of labor that went into their production. The "labor" at issue in *Less Than Zero* is the process of being—the act of being a living subject whose photograph can be taken, and converted into a commodity (object). In this way, images as marketed, reproduced, and reproducing commodities first obscure, and then replace the human subjects who create them. MTV, the movie industry, and fashion photography are iconic symbols that obscure their own mode of production, making the conventions and viewing models of the camera appear naturalistic.

The narrative style of *Less Than Zero* replicates these viewing models, structuring itself as a detached/observational series of jump cuts, image montages, aspect to aspect transitions, and flashbacks. This internalization of film convention is referred to explicitly as well as metatextually. At Blair's father's party, for example, Clay talks to a film student about a recent movie, asking, "Didn't it bother you the way they kept dropping characters out of the film for no reason at all?" The student replies, "Kind of, but that happens in real life." Thus, the cinematic narrative style of character development and cast have fed-back onto perceived reality, reshaping it in their own form.

Like this film student whose sense of "real life" is predicated on the continuity conventions of movies, everything in Clay's life is tainted by the camera—by the film industry, by the commodification of images, and by the facile surface level of self-representation that both demand. This relationship is indicated by the initial description of his Los Angeles bedroom. The central focus of the room, at which Clay looks "with caution," is a framed poster that hangs on the wall above the bed. Critically, the poster/image is positioned both an object for viewing, as well as an active observer in and of itself:

> It's the promotional poster for an old Elvis Costello record. Elvis looks past me, with this wry ironic smile on his lips, staring out the window . . . The eyes don't

look at me . . . They only look at whoever's standing by the window.

As he later makes clear, Clay is in the habit of going to the window so that he can be "seen" by the poster. What he does not say is even more important—that one can never be "viewed" by an image like this: its line of vision is *always* directed away from the observer.

Thus the poster is serving multiple symbolic and metaphoric functions within the novel. On the most basic level, this is a "promotional poster"—a piece of marketing ephemera that has been elevated to the status of art. In essence, Clay is decorating his life with advertising—a literalization of the media intensive atmosphere in which he moves. At the same time, the image shapes his actions and desires—forcing him to reorganize his placement within *its* field of vision in order to be seen. His uneasy positioning, repositioning, and self-abasement before the wry irony of the image thus acts as a powerful metaphor for his antagonistic and desiring relationship with the image driven world of wealthy Los Angeles.

In critical scenes, Clay's response to emotions is to externalize his perspective—to adopt a view of himself that mirrors this uneasy attempt to be the subject of his poster's vision. When Blair tries to talk about their relationship, for example, his reaction is to sort through a series of photographs of himself. The "self" whom Blair loves and the self to whom she addresses her "self," is thus entirely displaced—the image held up instead in a protective/deflective act. His critical insights are gleaned from billboards, posters and television; these are icons that he views, and that "view him back," shaping the way he thinks.

In a series of dizzying juxtapositions, Clay shifts from being the camera's object to being the camera itself: the viewed and the viewer. As viewed object he relays a nightmarish party at which a photographer is present and anorexic Muriel shoots drugs. This montage of disconnected images is linked with the phrase: "The photographer takes a picture." As viewer, Clay keeps his "shutters open" during Julian's debasement, saying "I want to see the worst." As he watches, his narrative brings together the repeated phrases that thread the novel together:

> The man rolls Julian over. *Wonder if he's for sale.* I don't close my eyes. You can disappear here without knowing it.

"Disappear Here" is the message on a billboard that Clay passes early in the novel. By introducing

> In this way, the image (MTV, pornography) is turned into a physical practice (prostitution, torture) that carries with it the detached externality of the icon that preceded it, caused it and determined its form."

it at this point, Julian's prostitution is linked to the wider exchange base of consumer culture, and both are shown in a symbiotic relationship with the viewer. In this critical scene, then, Clay ties together the desire to view, the impact of advertising, the economic purpose of viewing, and the essentially exploitative basis of pleasure/desire. If Julian is a "fetishized" commodity, this scene uncovers the intellectual, semiotic, and emotional labor that produced him.

Though Julian, Clay and the other male characters are thus maimed by "camera eyes," the most violent effects are reserved for female characters. The degradation of women in cinematic viewing is shown in a continuum of effect throughout the novel, a process best understood through the notion of "the gaze." Laura Mulvey's extremely influential 1975 essay, "Visual Pleasure and Narrative Cinema," describes the image of woman in Hollywood cinema as the passive object for the active male gaze. In her analysis, this "pleasure of the male gaze" is threatened by the woman's representation as a signifier of castration. She argues that two unconscious responses alleviate this fear. The first is a process of sadistic voyeurism, which denigrates the woman, and the second is a process of "fetishistic scopophilia." Fetishistic scopophilia overvalues the woman's physical appearance, thus "controlling" her.

The female images in *Less than Zero* are layered in increasingly horrific permutations of subjection to the male gaze. Clay's nameless sisters act as the initial stage. Viewers rather than viewed objects, these girls read GQ with muted pornography playing on the television. The fashionable, viewing, and cultural forces at play here are critically

What Do I Read Next?

- *The Rules of Attraction* (1985) is another novel written by Bret Easton Ellis. This is his second novel and concerns a love triangle among three students at an East Coast college.

- James Joyce's *A Portrait of the Artist as a Young Man* (1916) is considered to be the greatest *bildungsroman* in the English language. In this story, Stephen Daedalus is completing his studies at Trinity College in Dublin, Ireland, but is distracted by aesthetic questions and the temptations of the flesh.

- Ellis's controversial novel, *American Psycho* (1991), has been recently made into a popular movie of the same name. It chronicles the activities of a psychotic serial killer in Manhattan and is set in the early 1980s.

- Lisa Alther's 1976 bestseller, *Kinflicks,* chronicles the story of a young woman who discovers the joys of liberation and sexual experimentation in the 1960s.

- *The Catcher in the Rye* (1951) is a classic novel written by J. D. Salinger. Some critics have compared Ellis's fiction to this American novel of alienated youth in the 1950s.

---

different to those in Clay's domestic space. His overriding image of aspirational self—the poster—haunts him by his inability to be seen, signifying a masculinity that always escapes self-awareness and satisfactory representation.

On the other hand, his sisters have surrounded themselves with a highly functional version of gender identity in which representations of the female are inextricable from representations of the passive female body as an eroticized object of viewing. The role of sex in advertising is made obvious in this scene by its juxtaposition with staged sex. The set of sexual images is muted in the same way that scopophilic consumer culture is metaphorically "soundless"—apparently unobtrusive, yet consis-

tently and overwhelmingly concerned with presenting the female body for scrutiny. This "gazed upon" object of the female body to sell movies, clothes, commodities, and lifestyles means that Clay's sisters have surrounded themselves with icons totally opposed to the "wry irony" of the Costello poster. Unlike that framed icon, their model for identification is supremely accessible, both to the gaze and to the satiation of desire. The female self is reduced to a form, used as an object/commodity in both their reading and viewing matter. Pornography, fashion and advertising are tied together as scopophilic mechanisms, and, crucially, they are shown to be mechanisms that reproduce themselves.

This downward spiral of self-reproduction is indicated by the progressive destruction that is wrought upon the object of the scopophilic gaze throughout the novel. Clay's sisters are contrasted with the snuff-film victim, and then the drugged and tortured girl in Rip's apartment. The progression demarcated is that from warping of the self through endless viewing, reviewing, enactment and reenactment of a commodified version of reality—the movie camera's object as lived experience. Women shift from being the consumers of images (viewers), to being the subject of commodities (people in films), to being themselves commodifiable forces (used to sell things), and finally to being commodities themselves (things).

The cinematic male gaze transforms the consensual actress of the sound stage into the pornographic object of desire that loops endlessly in the sisters' bedroom. In turn, this image of desired object is intensified into a more "real" version of itself—the ultimate cinema verite of the snuff film. This progression of greater and greater imposition of control/gaze is finally and horribly reified in the tied body of the girl in Rip's bedroom. Drugged, shaved, voiceless and powerless, she is a reified, literalized version of the process to which the female self is subjected. As the precursor to this episode makes clear, the culture of cinema necessitates, causes, and is caused by this brutality.

Critically, Daniel's decision to stay in L.A. comes after he's been aroused by the snuff film. In a conversation with Clay, he explains what he's been thinking about: a pretty young girl who's "shot full of smack," taken to a party and "gangbanged." Clay assumes he's talking about real life. Daniel corrects him. It's a "good idea for a screenplay" and it's the reason he's not going back—he's "going to write this screenplay, see?" Several pages later, he and the other male characters do just that—"write this screenplay" by "gangbanging" a child.

The image of the girl on the bed is more than a symbolic stand-in for the role of women in an image-obsessed society. She also acts as the victim of a process to which all of the "once children" of Clay's world have been subjected by their culture. She acts thus both as an object on which to express desire, as well as an avatar of the Beverly Hills self—a corporeal manifestation of the self-hatred, self-exploitation, and self-destruction which drives Julian, Trent, and Daniel, and which is symbolized for Clay by haunting visions of tortured and burning children on the freeways. Crucially, this destruction, self-destruction and exploitation proceeds from and is preceded by imagery. As Clay says at the close of his story:

> These images stayed with me even after I left the city. Images so violent and malicious that they seemed to be my only point of reference for a long time afterwards.

Source: Tabitha McIntosh-Byrd, in an essay for *Novels for Students,* Gale Group, 2001.

Peter Freese

In the following essay, Freese contemplates the narrative qualities and social commentary of Less Than Zero.

In 1985, a twenty-year-old Bennington College undergraduate named Bret Easton Ellis published a book which, as rumour has it, he had typed on his bedroom floor in about a month and which he entitled *Less Than Zero.* The young man, who had grown up in Sherman Oaks as the son of a well-to-do real estate analyst, wrote about what he seemed to know well from personal experience: the aimlessness and *angst* of rich Los Angeles youngsters in their hectic world of drugs, casual sex and violence. In a surprisingly short time his lurid tale about "the seamy underside of the preppy handbook" turned into a craze in Los Angeles and a must on many American campuses. The movie rights were secured by independent producer Marvin Worth before the novel had even appeared in the stores, and Penguin Books bought the paperback rights for $100,000. Meanwhile the film has been released, and the book is out in a fast-selling German translation. Ellis has followed his successful debut with a second novel, *The Rules of Attraction* (1987), which the blurb of the paperback edition describes as dealing with "the couplings and capitulations, the dramas and the downfalls of American college life in the 1980s" and which

> " To cultural critics of shirt-sleeved free enterprise the novel offers devastating proof of their charges, and it strikingly illustrates Neil Postman's thesis that we are amusing ourselves to death in our mendacious age of show business."

reads like a fictional confirmation of Allan Bloom's crushing diagnosis of contemporary student life in his controversial bestseller *The Closing of the American Mind.*

The reviews of Ellis' first novel were extremely mixed. While one group of critics expressed their outraged rejection of the book's juvenile sensationalism conveyed, as one aggravated reviewer put it, "in the inarticulate style of a petulant suburban punk," another group celebrated the novel as "a weirdly fascinating book" and greeted it as the authentic literary expression of a new generation. However drastically the critical estimations diverged, two statements were frequently repeated: *Less Than Zero* was understood as *The Catcher in the Rye* updated for the eighties, and the slim book was classified as an 'MTV novel.'

Whereas the first argument can be easily disproved—Ellis' protagonist is definitely no new Holden Caulfield but rather a latter-day male Sally Hayes—the second argument raises some intriguing questions. Has the ubiquitous mass medium of Music Television with its incessant flow of video clips, its devotion to glittering surfaces, its limitation to the immediate present, and the reduction of its 'stories' to the short attention span of contemporary youth really found its verbal equivalent in a new narrative style? Is it feasible to say that "you don't so much read [*Less Than Zero*] as you watch and listen to it unfold"? and is "reading it [. . .] like watching MTV"? Has the young debutante actually managed to develop a new narrative voice geared to the lifestyle and the experiential reality of a particular segment of today's young generation?

Since so far no critic has subjected the supposedly ephemeral novel to the close scrutiny necessary to either confirm or disprove the trendy phrases of hurried reviewers, these questions remain as yet unanswered. And they are difficult to answer because the referential context within which Ellis' novel unfolds combines the hero worship, fashion cults and behavioral codes of a rapidly changing youth culture with the hermetic habits and expressions of an underground drug scene. Consequently, the traditional literary critic has a hard time unravelling the significance of rock lyrics and behavioral or conversational gambits which do not belong to his cultural code and he is too easily tempted to dismiss the laconically understated first-person narration of Ellis' protagonist as just another example of pervasive triviality and cultural decay. Quite obviously, *Less Than Zero* is no masterpiece, but, apart from its significance as a cultural document, it deserves closer scrutiny as a narrative which is more artfully structured than a first reading reveals.

> "Where are we going?" I asked. "I don't know," he said. "Just driving." "But this road doesn't go anywhere," I told him. "That doesn't matter." "What does?" I asked, after a little while. "Just that we're on it, dude," he said.

The action of *Less Than Zero* can be easily summarized: Clay, an eighteen-year-old freshman, comes back from his first term at a college in New Hampshire to spend his Christmas vacation with his broken-up wealthy family in Los Angeles. During the month he stays in his hometown, he whiles away his time at endless parties and in fashionable restaurants and nightspots, sleeps indiscriminately with the boys and girls that belong to his over-privileged set of bored adolescents, constantly drinks and smokes, sniffs cocaine to get high and takes Valium to come down again, aimlessly drives around sprawling Los Angeles in his expensive car, mindlessly watches television, listens to pop songs on the ubiquitous stereos, and plays senseless games in video arcades. In between he visits his fashionable psychiatrist, who cannot help him, and tries to avoid contact with his parents, with whom he cannot communicate. Clay's frantic search for cheap thrills leads to nothing but boredom and a pervasive sense of anomie and desperation.

Clay's aimless meandering between beach houses in Malibu and extravagant villas in the Hollywood Hills, guarded mansions in Bel Air and expensive bungalows in Palm Springs conveys an image of a world which is characterized by frantic hedonism and pathetic futility. The interchangeable members of his clique turn out to be alienated youths who have nothing to look forward to because they know and own everything. They take their Porsches, BMWs and Mercedes for granted, assume that it is their natural right to go to the most expensive colleges and universities, and have tried every sexual variation and experimented with every available drug. These boys and girls, whose lives revolve around the newest fads, who talk about the state of their suntan with the intensity of theologians discussing God, and whose cultural horizon is confined to current pop songs and movies, are deprived of the stability provided by functioning families. Their parents, divorced or separated, occupied by their passing affairs, intent on their success in the Hollywood industry, and obsessed by their futile attempts at preserving eternal youth, have no time for and no interest in their children, have never provided them with a functioning value system, and try to absolve themselves of their responsibility by generously writing cheques. Consequently, their children enjoy every privilege money can buy, but their anarchic liberty is tainted by rootlessness and the complete absence of any sense of belonging. For all the young drifters contact with their dealer is much more important than any other relationship. Human decency and care are unknown factors in this world of drug-induced euphoria, and the ever-changing partners for both hetero-and homosexual sex are either shown off as status symbols or simply used as objects of instant gratification.

The young men and women with their well-tanned bodies and stylish clothes pretend to themselves and others that they are rebels against the money-orientated life of their parents. But they are rebels without a cause, who shy away from bodily labour, intellectual exertion and emotional commitment alike and who act out their phony rebellion by spending the money of those they pretend to despise. All they finally manage to effect is their physical and psychological self-destruction through drugs and prostitution, and thus it turns out that although they appear to have everything, they really have "less than zero."

Clay's dealer Rip, for example, who had earlier complained that "there's not a whole lot to do anymore", tries to get some new 'kick' by drugging and sexually abusing a twelve-year-old girl in the most sadistic fashion. When Clay halfheartedly remonstrates that this is not right, Rip states, "If you want something, you have the right to take it. If you want to do something, you have the right to do it"; he dismisses Clay's objection that he has everything with the plaintive assertion: "I don't have anything to lose". Young Alana, who has just gone through an abortion, knowledgeably confides in Clay, "I think we've all lost some sort of feeling". Lindsay reports to his exhilarated peers "how he hasn't met anyone for the past four months who's over nineteen", and Kim tells Clay that she had thought her mother was in England but she recently read in *Variety* that she is actually in Hawaii. Julian, the spoilt youngster with his expensive Porsche who peddles drugs to children to finance his costly habit, ambiguously observes, "I'm just so sick of dealing with people", and Clay, after looking for new records in a well-stocked store, comes to the realization, "I don't find anything I want that I don't already have".

These statements illustrate a lifestyle which is both repellent and pitiable. They demonstrate that, as a cultural document about the consequences of affluence and permissiveness, the ceaseless search for success and the influence of sensation-seeking mass media, *Less Than Zero* is a frightening admission of social failure. To cultural critics of shirt-sleeved free enterprise the novel offers devastating proof of their charges, and it strikingly illustrates Neil Postman's thesis that we are amusing ourselves to death in our mendacious age of show business.

> "The young Americans [. . .] have abandoned all concealment; and when they are most themselves, nearest to their central concerns, turn frankly to Pop forms—[. . .] they choose the genre most associated with exploitation by the mass media: notably, the Western, Science Fiction and Pornography."
>
> (Leslie Fiedler, "Cross the Border—Close That Gap: Post-Modernism")

Considered as a 'literary' text, Ellis' novel appears to be a rather artless tale, which makes use of the genuinely American tradition of vernacular first-person narration, employs the elementary story line of a chronological sequence of events in the form of a loosely structured urban picaresque, and limits itself to a simple concatenation of brief narrative passages and extended dialogues rendered in direct speech. The reader's initial impression of formlessness and contingency is underscored by the fact that the 208 pages of the novel are divided into 108 very short chapters with an average length of less than two pages. These chapters are obviously geared to the limited attention span of both the drug-impaired narrator himself and the readers he addresses. Each chapter presents a self-sufficient slice-of-life, a short 'take,' as it were, defined in space and time and unfolding as a visible action, with the available 'actions' limited to partying,

watching television, driving around, taking drugs, having sex, eating out, and talking at cross purposes. The chapters often switch abruptly from one place and time of action to another, and as it is up to the reader to connect them, they provide the necessary orientation by opening with exact temporal and/or spatial pointers like "it's two in the morning and hot and we're at the Edge" or "I'm sitting in my psychiatrist's office the next day". Thus the outward pattern of the novel might well be compared to the rapid sequence of video clips as they abruptly and unceasingly follow each other on Music Television.

Behind the artless surface of Clay's fast-paced tale, however, lies a structure that provides the novel with some unexpected coherence and additional meaning. Ellis makes his eighteen-year-old protagonist tell his story in the present tense. This strategy is meant to enhance the immediacy and confessional urgency of Clay's tale. While it certainly achieves the desired effect, it necessarily deprives the story of historical depth and disconnects Clay's frantic present from the past which alone could help to explain it. Such a lack of continuity characterizes the hedonistic existence of all the novel's actors with their hectic search for instant gratification, and thus Ellis' choice of narrative tense turns out to be an appropriate formal correlative of his *sujet*. But obviously Ellis knows that a novel is supposed to deal with life in its developmental unfolding, and he achieves at least some semblance of temporal depth by presenting 12 of his 108 chapters as 'memory' chapters which deal with selected aspects of Clay's earlier life. In deference to the uninitiated reader, these chapters, which necessarily use the past tense, are printed in italics and thus made immediately recognizable as 'inserts' providing some explanatory material which the reader has to relate to the present state of affairs. These chapters also announce their function by opening with temporal pointers like "during the end of my senior year" or "last summer". They deal with "the way things were" and thereby conjure up some vague image of a time when the family was still intact—with the grandparents alive, the parents not yet separated, and Clay's love affair with Blair still flourishing. But the 'memory' chapters are already suffused with ominous signs and intimations of bad things to come. They thus serve the double function of providing a foil against which to understand Clay's present malaise and of offering some tentative explanation why an erstwhile happy youth has turned into a passive wreck haunted by disorientation, anxiety and despair.

While the outwardly unstructured sequence of chapters in the present tense turns out to be the appropriate formal equivalent of the fact that in spite of all the actors' hectic activities nothing significant can happen in their lives, the twelve interspersed 'memory' chapters in the past tense suggest a historical dimension and introduce a developmental aspect into the novel. Of course, this rather superficial attempt at a point-and-counterpoint structure is hardly a great achievement, but it points to a group of structural strategies which are meant to translate a sequence of chapters merely added to one another into a causally unfolding whole and which therefore deserve a detailed investigation.

On closer scrutiny, the dizzying spiral of Clay's desperate search for pleasure and diversion in the metropolitan purgatory of *ennui* and *angst* reveals some inner logic. This logic depends on the two strands of the novel's kaleidoscopic action which are concerned with the gradual breakup of Clay's relationship with his girlfriend Blair and with his witnessing the development of his erstwhile school friend Julian into a drug addict and male prostitute. The loss of the only person Clay felt close to and the frightening decline of his best friend constitute the two strands which dominate the action of the novel. Although these strands are often interrupted and superseded by other events, they provide the threads which keep the action together and give the four weeks of Clay's life to which *Less Than Zero* is limited some coherence and meaning. Thus, it is no accident that at the very beginning of the novel Clay is picked up at LAX by Blair and that the first thing he finds in his room is a message from Julian asking him to phone back. And thus it is equally logical that the last conversation he has before leaving is his 'final' talk with Blair and that the last important event during his holiday is his witnessing of Julian's degradation.

Since it would go against the grimly 'cool' attitude sported by Clay and his group to discuss personal problems in detail and to show true feelings openly, the ritualistically understated verbal and gestural delivery of both the narrator and the novel's actors prevents the real issues of the book from being expressed directly. Consequently, the reader has to proceed on mere hints and oblique clues. It is against this background that Ellis artfully employs a set of iterative images and muted references to make his point. Here again an analogy to the video clips of MTV and the patterns of rock lyrics proves helpful, because these iterative images work like the refrains of songs and convey their messages through repetition and variation.

The opening sentence of the novel—"People are afraid to merge on freeways in Los Angeles"— an observation made by Blair which "stays in [Clay's] mind for an uncomfortably long time" and occupies him for reasons he cannot name, is an outstanding example of Ellis' associative technique. Given a prominent position at the very beginning of the novel, the sentence is soon repeated verbatim and then taken up again with "on freeways in Los Angeles" left out. Thus, right at the beginning, the conversational remark about people's behavior in traffic turns into a general comment on the human situation—"people are afraid to merge"—and thereby assumes a more general significance. When Blair drops Clay at his house, "nobody's home": his mother and sisters have gone shopping instead of waiting for him on his first return from an eastern college. They are "afraid to merge," and when Clay goes to his room in the empty house, it is small wonder that he "still can hear that people are afraid to merge and tr[ies] to get over the sentence, blank it out".

Seven short chapters later, Clay is returning from a shopping trip with his mother and sisters and listening to their gossip. Talking about a young man, they mention that his house is for sale, and the older sister nastily remarks, "I wonder if he's for sale". For the moment, this is just a passing slanderous remark, but two chapters later Clay, sitting in a restaurant, feels he is being stared at by a stranger and comments, "all I can think is either he doesn't see me or I'm not here. I don't know why I think that. People are afraid to merge. *Wonder if he's for sale*". Here two hitherto unrelated observations are brought together and suddenly acquire a new meaning. The general comment about people's fear to communicate and the nasty quip about a young man's sexual availability for money are applied to a stranger whose insistent stare Clay interprets as an attempt to make a pass at him. In connection these statements render the insight that people might try to buy sexual contact unencumbered by personal commitment for the very reason that they are afraid to 'merge.' Two chapters later, Clay stops at a traffic light on Sunset Boulevard and sees a billboard. "All it says is 'Disappear Here' and even though it's probably an ad for some resort, it still freaks me out a little". In the context established so far, the slogan 'Disappear Here' can be understood as referring back to Clay's observation under the gaze of the staring stranger that possibly

"I'm not here", and while the link is yet rather tentative, it soon becomes obvious.

A few days later, a sleepless Clay thinks "about the billboard on Sunset and the way Julian looked past me at Cafe Casino". By now he has not only heard nasty comments about Julian's state but has also met him without being able to find out from his strangely reluctant friend what his message had been about. He has deduced from Julian's behaviour and his way of avoiding eye-contact that his unrevealed problems might have to do with his drug addiction and that he might already be selling himself to acquire the money for his habit. The probability of such a development—and this is another of Ellis' strategies—is obliquely insinuated when Julian tells Clay that he has been to a Tom Petty concert and heard him sing a former favourite song of theirs—"*Straight into darkness, we went straight into darkness, out over that line*".

Thus, the different and initially unrelated images can begin to coalesce when Clay spends Christmas Eve with his embarrassed parents in an expensive restaurant. Bored by the phony familiarity of the two strangers claiming to be his parents and "semistoned" on cocaine, he falls into an associative reverie: "I think about Blair alone in her bed stroking that stupid black cat and the billboard that says 'Disappear Here' and Julian's eyes and wonder if he's for sale and people are afraid to merge". Here, then, Clay thinks about his former girlfriend Blair with whom he would like to 'merge,' and about Julian who might be "for sale," that is, willing to 'merge' for money because he has gone "straight into darkness," crossed "that line" of drug addiction and therefore is well on his way towards 'disappearing here.'

A few days later, Clay is lying listlessly on the beach and staring "out at the expanse of sand that meets the water, where the land ends. Disappear here". By now the clever advertising slogan has assumed crucial significance and turned into an obsessive concern for Clay. And when one relates the young man's unhappy stare into nothingness to one of the mottos of the novel, a quotation from a Led Zeppelin song that reads "There's a feeling I get when I look to the West . . . ," the extent of Clay's hopelessness becomes painfully obvious. Walt Whitman, "facing west from California's shores," could still seek "what is yet unfound" and speculate about "the circle almost circled"; a century later the heroine of Thomas Pynchon's *The Crying of Lot 49,* a novel about the Californian subcultures of the sixties, was sustained by her belief in "some

principle of the sea as redemption for Southern California" in spite of her recognition that the American Dream had turned into a nightmare. For Clay, however, the traditional promise of westward expansion has completely evaporated. Having substituted the last, the inner frontier to be reached only on drug-induced 'trips,' for the vanished frontier of the West, all he can see is an "expanse of sand that meets the water" and all he can think of is "Disappear Here".

After the combination of 'disappearing' and being 'for sale' has been mentioned once more and is thus kept alive even for the undiscerning reader, the cluster of images gains its final impact in the two crucial scenes which deal with Julian's downfall. Driven by his "need to see the worst", Clay accompanies his friend to a hotel to watch a stranger make love to Julian: "The man rolls Julian over. *Wonder if he's for sale.* I don't close my eyes. You can disappear here without knowing it". This is the ultimate degradation brought about by the need for drugs. Julian's 'disappearing' into the abyss of sexual exploitation, his self-betrayal through prostitution and the loss of his human dignity graphically illustrate what happens when one goes "*straight into darkness, out over that line* ". A little later on the same day, Julian makes a final and desperate attempt to rebel against his drug-dealing pimp. But cynical Finn, on whose desk stands "this glass paperweight with a small fish trapped in it, its eyes staring out helplessly", knows his power and easily quenches his employee's rebellion by giving him an injection: "Disappear Here. The syringe fills with blood. [. . .] Wonder if he's for sale. People are afraid to merge. To merge". By now the three originally unrelated phrases about disappearing, being for sale and fearing to merge have acquired manifold meanings through repetition and variation within different contexts. By simply combining them Clay can express his terror and despair about the hopelessness of a self-destructive generation suffocating on the terrible combination of spiritual poverty and material abundance.

But this does not end Ellis' artful manipulation of his few simple but effective images. When Clay meets Blair for a last time before his return to the East, their meeting takes place in a restaurant on Sunset. And while Blair takes her former boyfriend to account for his negligent behavior, "I look at her, waiting for her to go on, looking up at the billboard. Disappear Here". On the surface, Clay will soon follow the injunction of the advertising slogan and 'disappear'—"After I left" are the final words of the novel—but on a metaphorical level he has 'left' long ago by withdrawing into the narcissistic no-man's-land of drug-induced apathy and self-pity. Ellis obliquely conveys this fact by making Blair reproach her former boyfriend that "it was like you weren't there. [. . .] You were never there".

From Clay's casual comment on a stranger's stare at the beginning of the novel—"either he doesn't see me or I'm not here"—to the book's final scene in which "for one blinding moment [Clay] see[s] [him]self clearly" and the person closest to him charges him with never being there, he has been afraid to 'merge,' has run away from the risks and problems of human companionship and 'disappeared' into the dream world of cocaine and the false security of tranquilizers. The billboard slogan, then, supposedly advertising "some resort," proves true in an unexpected way. Functioning like the refrain of a pop song to which some new meaning accrues after every stanza, it sums up the cowardly retreat of Clay and his clique into the escape world of drugs and 'kicks,' their withdrawal from a socially useful and fulfilled existence into "some resort" of their sick imagination. It proves a highly effective strategy of providing the understated and scarcely verbalized problems of the rather incoherent narrator and his peers with some deeper meaning.

Another variation of the point-and-counterpoint strategy is Ellis' use of a background of ominous signs and catastrophes serving as a foil against which to evaluate the hectic foreground activities of Clay and his friends. Coming home, the first thing Clay sees are some workmen "lifting the remains of palm trees that have fallen during the winds". This is an early and as yet inconspicuous reminder of the ubiquity of death and decay, which is taken up when Clay reminisces about the old house in Palm Springs as full of "empty beer cans that were scattered all over the dead lawn and the windows that were all smashed and broken". In the nocturnal silence of the Hollywood hills Clay can "hear the sound of coyotes howling and dogs barking and palm trees shaking in the wind up in the hills". Time and again there are passing references to the "damage the storm caused", the sudden torrential rains that wash houses down, the fact that cats cannot be let out at night because "there's a chance that the coyotes will eat them", or someone finding "a rattlesnake floating" in his swimming pool. Nature cannot be domesticated and will lash back at the thoughtless humans who exploit and ruin it. An earthquake is the most obvious reminder of the fact that Los Angeles is situated on the San Andreas Fault and that the pleasure-seeking activities of its rich denizens are a dance on the volcano.

But society is also in a state of threatening unrest and imbalance. When Clay and Rip have a talk about the quality of their suntans, "an old woman, holding an umbrella, falls to her knees on the other side of the street". On their way to yet another party, the young drifters "pass a poor woman with dirty, wild hair and a Bullock's bag sitting by her side full of yellowed newspapers. She's squatting on a sidewalk by the freeway"—by the freeway, that is, on which people are afraid to 'merge.' When the clique goes to the City Cafe, "there's an old man in ragged clothing and an old black hat on, talking to himself, standing in front and when we pull up, he scowls at us". Shopping-bag ladies, loitering bums and elderly people breaking down in the streets are a constant reminder of poverty and misery, pain and illness; and throughout the novel one hears ambulances passing by and police sirens howling in the distance.

Clay remembers driving around Palm Springs and coming upon "a Toyota parked at this strange, crooked angle, its hood open, flames pouring out of the engine," and for a long time he has "these visions of a child, not yet dead, lying across the flames, burning". This is when he starts collecting newspaper clippings about violent accidents, sadistic cruelties, and brutal crimes. He collects "a lot of clippings [. . .] because, I guess, there were a lot to be collected". This aspect of a society driven by violence and brutality is obvious in the novel. The pornographic activities of Clay's clique find their equivalent in the daily crime statistics of Los Angeles. When Clay buys some magazines, "the checkout clerk is talking about murder statistics"; when the family comes home from their expensive Christmas dinner, "on Little Santa Monica, a car lays overturned, its windows broken"; when Rip and Clay drive along winding Mulholland, Rip gleefully points out "the number of wrecked cars at the bottom of the hill"; and before Clay leaves his hometown, he coolly enumerates the following incidents:

> Before I left, a woman had her throat slit and was thrown from a moving car in Venice; a series of fires raged out of control in Chatsworth, the work of an arsonist; a man in Encino killed his wife and two children. Four teenagers, none of whom I knew, died in a car accident on Pacific Coast Highway.

All through the novel, then, there are constant reminders of natural catastrophes and disasters, of violent crimes and terrible accidents, of old age, illness and death. They conjure up the general state of a society divided into the obscenely rich and the unspeakably poor and provide the overall background against which the hedonistic dance of pleasure and withdrawal of Clay and his clique has to be seen.

> "For Los Angeles, more than any other city, belongs to the mass media. What is known around the nation as the L.A. Scene exists chiefly as images on a screen or TV tube, as four-color magazine photos, as old radio jokes, as new songs that survive only a matter of weeks."
>
> (Thomas Pynchon, "A Journey Into the Mind of Watts")

Of crucial importance to a better understanding of the youngsters' thoughtlessness and inconsideration, their ruthless pursuit of pleasure, and their violence and inhumanity is the formative influence exerted upon them by the ubiquitous mass media devoted to the lurid, the sensational, the gruesome and the horrible in their cynical attempt to reach a surfeited audience. As early as 1961, Philip Roth observed that "the American writer in the middle of the 20th century has his hands full in trying to understand, and then describe, and then make *credible* much of the American reality" and complained that "the actuality is continually outdoing our talents, and [that] the culture tosses up figures almost daily that are the envy of any novelist." A few years later Bruce Jay Friedman spoke of "a fading line between fantasy and reality," stated that *The New York Times* with its daily reports on the most unbelievable events had become "the source and fountain and bible of black humour," and concluded that a writer who wanted to reach a "surprise-proof generation" needed to use a "new, one-foot-in-the-asylum style of fiction" to catch the attention of his audience.

These observations certainly apply to *Less Than Zero,* and whoever thinks that Ellis' novel is given to undue exaggerations just needs to read the *Los Angeles Times* to learn better. The list of drugs consumed by Clay and his friends offers a faithful replica of the existing drug scene and testifies to the fact that in Hollywood "the white kid digs hallucination simply because he is conditioned to believe so much in escape, escape as an integral part of life, because the white L.A. Scene makes accessible to him so many different forms of it." Then too, the countless references to films, television plays, video clips and pop songs conjure up an actual youth culture with its hectic media events. The general atmosphere evoked by these references is one of abandonment, revolt and brutality, even bes-

tiality, of a vicarious release of aggression and sadistic urges through fantasies of violence and pornography, and of an all-pervasive ecstasy of doom and destruction.

Clay's thirteen-and fifteen-year-old sisters habitually watch "porno films on the Betamax". Clay buys porno magazines, and his aroused clique gleefully watch a sadistic blue movie and agree that the mutilations and castrations it shows must be "real" because somebody "paid fifteen thousand for it". Kim and Blair insist on going to a movie "about this group of young pretty sorority girls who get their throats slit and are thrown into a pool," but bored Clay watches "just the gory parts". Pornography, then, is ubiquitous: Rip's sadistic violation of a twelve-year-old girl is just his individual acting out of the media events to which he is constantly exposed; and the animalization of humans which results from this exposure is graphically illustrated when Clay says about one of the girls waiting to be admitted to a nightclub that she "stares at me and smiles, her wet lips, covered with this pink garish lipstick, part and she bares her upper teeth like she was some sort of dog or wolf, growling, about to attack".

On the car radio a group called "Killer Pussy" sings a song entitled "Teenage Enema Nurses in Bondage", and when Clay's outraged mother asks whether they have to hear this, her under-age daughters insist on listening to it. At a concert of The Grimsoles, the singers throw live rats out into the audience. One day Clay wakes up to a song entitled "Artificial Insemination", and he frequently listens to songs like "Do You Really Want to Hurt Me?", "Hungry Like the Wolf" or "Tainted Love". The Clash sing about "Somebody Got Murdered"; and at a party everybody expectantly waits for the songs "Sex and Dying in High Society" and "Adult Books" to be performed. A video bootleg of *Indiana Jones and the Temple of Doom* is traded for high prices (pp. 34, 90). Other films or TV plays referred to are *Alien, The Invasion of the Body Snatchers, Beastman!, Star Raider, War of the Worlds, The Twilight Zone,* and "the new *Friday the 13th* movie". Even the video games with which Clay and his friends while away their time seem only to "deal with beetles and bees and moths and snakes and mosquitoes and frogs drowning and mad spiders eating large purple video flies [. . .] and the images are hard to shake off". Small wonder, then, that when somebody disappears in Bel Air there are hysterical speculations about "some kind of monster, [. . .] a werewolf"; that Spit, who wears "a skull earring," assures a friend, "You know I don't keep dead animals in my room anymore"; and that Rip "carries a plastic eyeball in his mouth". The unceasing onslaught of outrageous science-fiction horrors and ever more violent pornography has made people callous and insensitive. A "huge green skull leering at drivers from a billboard on Sunset, hooded, holding a pyx, bony fingers beckoning" advertises some new 'kick'; "little girls" sing about an earthquake in Los Angeles and announce *"My surfboard's ready for the tidal wave [. . .] Smack, smack, I fell in a crack [. . .] Now I'm part of the debris"*. When Clay, whose first action is to switch on MTV whenever he is alone, refers in passing to "a video on cable of buildings being blown up in slow motion and in black and white", or when he enters somebody else's house and finds a girl "watching some movie about cave men" and describes his exit by saying, "Some caveman gets thrown off a cliff and I split", the continual presence of images of violence and destruction is quite incidentally evoked as something which everybody takes for granted.

The ubiquitous presence of sensational films and videos that thrive on sadistic violence and all-encompassing destruction, on gruesome fantasies of man-animal transformations and intergalactic warfare, on outrageous sexual abuse and the thrills of a final cataclysm pervades *Less Than Zero,* and this presence becomes all the more striking as it stands in absurd contrast to such faddish accessories of wealth as Giorgio Armani sweaters and Calvin Klein jeans, Gucci loafers, Louis Vuitton luggage, and Wayfarers sunglasses. Leslie Fiedler's assertion that the new 'Pop novel' thrives on the genres most associated with exploitation by the mass media, namely the Western, Science Fiction, and Pornography, is fully borne out by Ellis' tale, which makes use of these fields not only as the 'cultural' background to its foreground action, but also as the target of its obliquely presented exposure of social grievances.

> "[. . .] she thinks of the Heat Death of the Universe. A logarithmic of those late summer days, [. . .] the heat pressing, bloating, doing violence. The Los Angeles sky becomes so filled and bleached with detritus that it loses all colour and silvers like a mirror, reflecting back the fricasseeing earth. [. . .] She imagines the whole of New York City melting like a Dali into a great chocolate mass, a great soup, the Great Soup of New York."
>
> (Pamela Zoline, "The Heat Death of the Universe")
>
> "What it is is, most of the things we say, I guess, are mostly noise."
>
> (Thomas Pynchon, "Entropy")

It is obvious that the manifold references to a spiritually sick culture and the illnesses it has bred in a sizeable segment of its affluent young generation create a pervasive sense of impending doom, a cataclysmic feeling of last days which Clay and his friends use as an alibi for their refusal to grow up and face reality. This sense of doom is related to the traditional notion of the Christian apocalypse when Clay starts "watching religious programs on cable TV because [he is] tired of watching videos". The first show he sees happens to be especially pertinent to his world because it presents some fervent preachers "talking about Led Zeppelin records, saying that, if they're played backwards, they 'possess alarming passages about the devil'". Again, this is no invention of Ellis' but the show depicts an actual record-burning campaign of a Pentecostal group. The programme is ironically related to the novel's action when the worried preacher declares that he will go on fighting satanic rock music since it is detrimental to youth and "the young are the future of this country". At another occasion a televangelist promises that Jesus "will come through the eye of that television screen" and thereby involuntarily reveals that even the Christian message has been commercialized and trivialized by the mass media. Clay is desperate enough to wait "for something to happen", but, of course, nothing happens; and again it is highly ironic that all the helpless youth can remember are the preacher's words "Let this be a night of Deliverance".

The apocalyptic implications of *Less Than Zero,* however, are only of marginal importance, because Ellis' kaleidoscopic whirl of disparate 'takes' and the iterative images relating them is infused with a competing motif providing his verbal "videos [. . .] flash[ing] by" with some deeper significance. This motif is that of entropy in both its thermodynamic sense of the 'heat death' of the universe and its cybernetic sense of increasing informational attrition. One day, Clay and a friend of his meet the girl Ronnette. She tells them that she had

> this dream, see, where I saw the whole world melt. I was standing on La Cienega and from there I could see the whole world and it was melting and it was just so strong and realistic like. And so I thought, Well, if this dream comes true, how can I stop it, you know?

On the surface, of course, this is just a drug-induced hallucination, but it so obviously points to the traditional motif of the 'heat death' of the universe that it becomes an indicator of some larger significance. Such an assumption is borne out by many further references. Clay remembers, for example, "last Christmas" in Palm Springs when it was so unbelievably hot that "the metal grids in the crosswalk signs were twisting, writhing, actually melting in the heat". When he witnesses a car accident, he is haunted by a vision of "a kid burning, melting, on the engine". Going out into the oppressive heat, he experiences the sun as "huge and burning, an orange monster", and on another occasion he stands on a hill, "overlooking the smog-soaked, baking Valley and feeling the hot winds returning and the dust swirling at my feet and the sun, gigantic, a ball of fire, rising over it". He reads the paper, "at twilight," and finds "a story about how a local man tried to bury himself alive in his backyard because it was 'so hot, too hot'". And when he hears a harsh and bitter song about Los Angeles, he hallucinates "images of people, teenagers my own age, looking up from the asphalt and being blinded by the sun". At the house of Finn, the pimp, he sees a young surfer dividing his attention between reading the back of a Captain Crunch cereal box and watching *The Twilight Zone* on television, and on the huge screen "Rod Serling's staring at us and tells us that we have just entered The Twilight Zone and though I don't want to believe it, it's just so surreal that I know it's true".

It is a genuine achievement of Ellis' novel that its whirl of interrelated 'clips' is so surreal that it achieves the frightening impact of authenticity and truth. It is a world in which, in a fashionable nightspot, someone has "written 'Help Me' over and over in red crayon on the table in a childish scrawl", thus revealing the amount of loneliness and despair behind the glittering facade of mindless pleasure; in which the vanity number plates of rich people's cars read "CLIMAXX" and "DECLINE", thus achieving a significance their owners are probably unaware of; and in which bathroom graffiti spell out "Gloom Rules"—such a world has already entered the 'twilight zone' of chaos and inertia, in which the available energy has been spent and the entropy of the system is moving towards a maximum. Therefore, the atmosphere which pervades *Less Than Zero* is not that of apocalypse, that is, of an impending Last Judgment which will bring both death and rebirth, an end and a new beginning, but that of entropy with its irreversible movement towards final chaos and decay.

On the informational level, as worked out by Shannon and Brillouin, popularized by Wiener and brilliantly put to literary use by Thomas Pynchon, the concept of entropy as a gradual reduction of communicable information is also implemented in

Ellis' novel. The numerous dialogues between Clay and his friends never become a real exchange of ideas or opinions. They constitute frightening examples of the speechlessness of an almost autistic generation living in a world in which true meaning has long been buried under the relentless onslaught of never-ceasing 'information.' The entropic movement from diversity to similarity, from difference to sameness is strikingly illustrated by the uniformity and interchangeability of the young people.

In Clay's circles, one of the most important prerequisites for being 'in' is the correct tan: Blair's U.S.C. friends, "all tan and blond", Blair's father's boyfriend, who is "really young and blond and tan", Clay's father, who is "completely tan and has had a hair transplant", Dimitri, who "is really tan and has short blond hair", and Clay himself, who comes back from the East looking "pale" and quickly decides that he "need[s] to work on [his] tan"—anybody who wants to be accepted has to have the correct complexion. When Clay goes to a party, he comments, "There are mostly young boys in the house and they seem to be in every room and they all look the same: thin, tan bodies, short blond hair, blank look in the blue eyes, same empty toneless voices, and then I start to wonder if I look exactly like them". Of course, he does. The similarity and interchangeability of the standardized youths is not only another indication of the failure of their phony revolt in the name of liberation from social pressures, but also the sign of a far advanced entropic movement from difference to sameness. On a deeper level, then, the frantic punk-yuppie-video hunt for instant pleasure on a volcano that can erupt any moment, under a sun which is a gigantic "ball of fire" and "an orange monster" threatening to melt the whole world, is revealed as a last desperate exertion before the final and imminent onset of maximum entropy and the appearance of the ultimate chaos of inertia.

In Thomas Pynchon's *Gravity's Rainbow* there is a reference to "those emptying days brilliant and deep, especially at dawn, with blue shadows to seal its passage, to try to bring events to Absolute Zero," which occurs in the first book entitled "Beyond the Zero." With Pynchon one can safely assume that this is a reference to Walther Hermann Nernst's Third Law of Thermodynamics, concerning the zero entropy to be achieved at a temperature of absolute zero which, however, one cannot reach. With Ellis, however, the "Zero" appears to be just a metaphor of ultimacy indicating that the irresistible movement from distinction and differentiation to sameness and interchangeability has run its course, that an irreversible and universal 'merging' other than the desirable one of human interaction is about to occur, and that the energy necessary for survival is on the verge of 'disappearing here.'

It is in this context that the novel's title achieves its metaphorical significance, which is underscored by a fact which is not mentioned but which the youthful reader is expected to know. In his room Clay has "the promotional poster for an old Elvis Costello record [. . .] on the wall above [his] bed". This record is one of the most successful songs Costello ever produced, namely, "Less Than Zero." The novel's title, then, is an unacknowledged quotation, and its allusion to a song by a leading representative of the British punk and new wave explosion is another indication that Ellis' referential context is not that of 'mainstream' literature but of contemporary pop culture. Costello's song refers to "Mr. Oswald with his swastika tattoo" and obliquely relates President Kennedy's assassination to general social decay by stating that "Mr Oswald said he had an understanding with the law / He said he heard about a couple living in the USA / He said they traded in their baby for a Chevrolet." The refrain of the song reads:

> Turn out the TV,
> No one of them will suspect it.
> Then your mother won't detect it,
> So your father won't know.
> They think that I got no respect,
> But every film means less than zero.

Costello's song, then, conjures up the very atmosphere of a world violently out of joint and drifting towards ultimate chaos, filled with the ubiquitous 'noise' of the mass media and pervaded by a desire for the release of death, which also pervades *Less Than Zero*. Consequently, the novel's title is a programmatic statement which places the book within the wider context of a youthful punk and rock revolt.

> "The facts even when beaded on a chain, still did not have real order. Events did not flow. The facts were separate and haphazard and random even as they happened, episodic, broken, no smooth transitions, no sense of events unfolding from prior events."
>
> (Tim O'Brien, *Going After Cacciato*)

When Salinger's Holden Caulfield declared his rebellion against a "phony" adult world in the name of the few things he considered "nice," his position constituted a psychologically believable stance in spite of his adolescent obfuscation. This is why a whole young generation could identify with him and venerate him as their spokesman. With Ellis' Clay, however, the situation is different. Paul Gray

was certainly right when he observed in his *Time* review that Ellis' "efforts to distance Clay, the narrator, from all the other zombies is unsuccessful" and that "ultimately, Ellis' novel is anchored to a hero who stands for nothing." Clay is bound to remain an unconvincing character because his creator's choice of the present tense deprives him of historical depth and results in a complete lack of narrative distance between Clay's behavior as 'experiencing I' and his stance as 'narrative I.' Moreover, there is a disturbing tension between his languidly understated, indifferent and drug-impaired registering of his and his clique's meaningless life on the one hand and the rare instances in which he achieves the distance necessary for meaningful narration on the other. Admittedly, he has, rather inexplicably, mustered enough energy to leave his group and attempt a new beginning at an eastern college, he is content with 'only' sniffing cocaine and has not yet "mainlined"; he chides Rip for his sadistic behavior, cannot stand the pornographic movie to its cruel end, and rejects the invitation to rape the drugged girl. His recurring crying fits are obviously meant to indicate that he is conscious of his malaise, and in the end he knows that "it was time to go back. I had been home a long time". But the tension between his unprepared assertions of self-recognition—"the sun bursts into my eyes and for one blinding moment I see myself clearly"— and his immediately adjacent expressions of indifference and inertia—"Nothing makes me happy. I like nothing"—remains unresolved, and he never assumes the stature of a rounded personality.

Such shortcomings are typical of a first novel and are the necessary corollaries of the narrative perspective chosen by Ellis. Nevertheless, *Less Than Zero* is not only an expressive cultural document but also an accomplished narrative. It authentically expresses the lifestyle of a generation nourished on the ubiquitous products of a sensation-bent entertainment industry, a generation in love with the violent and rebellious music of rock and punk, conversant with the escapist underground culture of drugs, abandoned by their pleasure-hunting, success-orientated and irresponsible parents, and haunted by a sense of impending doom. *Less Than Zero,* then, is no *Catcher in the Rye* of the eighties. But the unwarranted comparison can alert us to the enormous and frightening changes that have occurred in the less than four decades between the appearance of Salinger's and Ellis' novels. And despite the reviewers' rash assertions, *Less Than Zero* is no 'MTV novel,' a genre which due to the differences between visual and verbal texts will remain impossible. But it is a tale which manages to translate the fast-paced urgency, the total lack of historical awareness, the additive impact and the macabre glitter of musical television into narrative strategies which deserve to be taken seriously as expressions of a contemporary lifestyle and indications of future literary developments.

Source: Peter Freese, "Bret Easton Ellis, Less Than Zero: Entropy in the 'MTV Novel'?," in *Modes of Narrative,* Konigshausen & Neumann, 1990, pp. 68–87.

David Pan

In the following essay, Pan looks at the stylistic features of Less Than Zero *in relationship to the visual media of television, video and film.*

The first question which comes to mind in reading Ellis' best-seller, *Less Than Zero,* is "Is Los Angeles really like that?" This astonishment betrays not only the vague feeling that one has somehow missed out on all the action in Los Angeles, but also the compulsion to continue reading in order to experience, at least vicariously, all the sordid details of life in the American "elite." This voyeuristic query fits perfectly into the framework of a book in which the closest thing to a plot is the attempt of Clay, the first person narrator, "to see the worst" and in which the characters continually try to certify the authenticity of their experiences. After watching a snuff film, the characters voice the same concern as the readers:

"Yeah, I think it's real too," the other boy says, easing himself into the jacuzzi. "It's gotta be."

"Yeah?" Trent asks, a little hopefully.

"I mean, like how can you fake a castration? They cut the balls off that guy real slowly. You can't fake that," the boy says.

The voyeuristic impulse which grips the snuff film viewers and forces the question, "Is it real?" is the same impulse which propelled *Less Than Zero* to its best-seller status, fueling suspicions of its essentially trashy novel character. But the question "Is it real?" in addition to revealing the voyeuristic stance of the questioner, also expresses a certain incredulity that the scenes depicted might not be fiction, but reality. *Less Than Zero* might really be a journalistic account. Either way, both the pulp fiction and journalistic qualities of the book tend to disqualify it from being real "literature." Yet, even though it has succeeded as a pulp novel and has become, in its abysmal Hollywood filming, a piece of journalistic evidence for crusaders in the war on drugs, it is clear that *Less Than Zero*

> Not only is Clay the example of the passive television viewer who lives his life like he watches a video, he is also the critic of this same attitude, ironically describing the teenagers bathed in images."

is not just pulp fiction or journalism. It is also a critique. Whether this critique is successful hinges on the question constantly haunting critics of culture of how to criticize the banal without becoming it. For the primary reason for studying the products of mass culture is their popularity, and to the extent that critics do not share the enthusiasm of the populace, they are also excluded from a true understanding of the influence and significance of mass culture. The successful critic must both identify with the duped cultural consumer and also maintain a reflective stance. Though unable to achieve a satisfactory solution, *Less Than Zero* does make the attempt.

In the novel, the first person narrator, Clay, continuously high on drugs, alcohol or both, wanders from nightclub to nightclub and party to party, mingling with "blond-haired pretty male models," standing mesmerized before video screens, and sleeping with most anybody, male or female, who seems to take a passing interest in him. He is less a character than a spectator of all that happens to him, passively and indifferently accepting everything around him as if he were watching it on TV. The prose style underlines Clay's virtual lack of individual identity. Though Clay is the first person narrator throughout the novel, his consciousness is at times so inobtrusive that most passages read as if written in the third person. That the reader loses track of the first person narrator in the midst of the action does not merely demonstrate the unreflecting mentality of "Clay" who, presumably faithful to the name, compliantly accepts any situation he happens to find himself in. The indifferent flow of images and events resembles the stream of flat images seen on television. Ellis' prose shares television's drive to continually change the image, to relentlessly keep up the pace of the action, a drive which ultimately debases the image and trivializes the action. Clay's own identity and consciousness is replaced by the string of events which, like the video images before his eyes, he seems to have no control over, and which in the end perhaps entertain for a while, but can never really satisfy. Accordingly, Clay's displays of discontent correspond to the sort of dazed and disgusted feeling one has after having sat in front of the television until three in the morning, and which, if one is like Clay, can quickly be remedied by taking another Valium.

Yet, Clay is not always a passive observer without a conscious perspective of his own. In sharp contrast to this virtual absence of consciousness, Clay at other times demonstrates the same ironic distance which Ellis himself expresses in describing his peers at Bennington College. This attitude becomes obvious in passages where the ironic tone is unmistakable, but at the same time, entirely incompatible with the passive attitude which Clay otherwise displays. Sensing that his MTV prose style threatens to become as banal as MTV itself, Ellis attempts to use such ironic passages to make Clay into a critic. Not only is Clay the example of the passive television viewer who lives his life like he watches a video, he is also the critic of this same attitude, ironically describing the teenagers bathed in images. By combining both perspectives in one character, Ellis attempts an "immanent" critique of mass culture, i.e., from the "inside." This "insider," however, has an implausibly schizophrenic consciousness. Clay as the passive spectator accepts his surroundings as real and submits to their logic, no matter how artificial, distorted, or manipulative. Clay as critic takes the exact opposite tack by completely rejecting through irony the very same object which the spectator so uncritically accepts. Ellis' depiction of Clay as a totally passive media construct takes the logic of the spectator too seriously by denying Clay the participation and feeling which the culture industry manipulates, but never completely eliminates. On the other hand, Clay's rejection of the media world is a failure to take it seriously. The rejection is too facile, as if his critical self could simply erase his voyeuristic self without a trace and his return to an Eastern college at the end of the book could leave "LA decadence" far behind.

Finally, *Less Than Zero*'s deadpan, state-of-the-art "MTV" prose demonstrates a problem which is shared by a specific sector of 1980s American culture, the David Byrne mixture of parody and hip cynicism. A conversation in *Less Than Zero* illustrates the problem:

"Yeah, *Beastman!* that was pretty good," the film student says to me. "See it?"

I nod, looking over at Blair. I didn't like *Beastman!* and I ask the film student, "Didn't it bother you the way they just kept dropping characters out of the film for no reason at all?"

The film student pauses and says, "Kind of, but that happens in real life . . . "

A characteristic of the film which would normally be considered "bad art" acquires new meaning because it turns out to be a characteristic of "bad reality." But whether the film reproduces bad reality because it is simply unconscious of its inadequacy or it is actually trying to parody reality, the film, as well as *Less Than Zero* itself, falls prey to the same problem. In either case, the resort to a reproduction of clichés in reality demonstrates both a lack of inventiveness and a fascination with the inane which numbs one's sense for the healthy. For even as parody, such a film would contribute to the omni-presence of that which it should resist by failing in its representation of reality to present positive aspects and alternatives within the dominant order. As much as the present media environment might testify to the contrary, reality is not merely "less than zero." Positive elements exist as well, both in reality and as not yet fulfilled possibilities. *Less Than Zero*'s suppression of those elements is a capitulation before the media's depiction.

Though he never gets beyond a clichéd description of the two extremes of voyeur and critic and his attempt at combining them in Clay fails to illuminate the complexity of the problem, Ellis' attempt at problematizing the relationship between the two attitudes, whether successful or not, demonstrates the present quandary of American media critics. For as Christa Bürger notes, "even in cases where they find themselves in opposition to contemporary society and culture, they see this society and culture simultaneously as a history which they seek to appropriate as their own." These critics attempt to combine the perspectives of the media "voyeur" and the media "critic." The voyeur is fascinated by that which he sees and allows himself to be led along by the images and the action. The engendering of a voyeuristic attitude is the sign of all successful forms of mass culture: e.g., Hollywood movies, network broadcasting and best-seller novels. Their success lies in their ability to indeed tap real desires and needs and give them expression. At the same time their insidiousness lies in their channeling of the expression of these desires into forms which end up preventing their fulfillment. The critic on the other hand remains distant from the images and refuses to become caught up in the fascination. The critic seeks thereby to expose the subjugation which this fascination means for both viewer and viewed alike. But it is precisely the distance of the critic from the object of criticism which often makes the criticism, on the one hand, unfeeling, and, on the other hand, uninformed. Clay, as ruthless critic of mass media, is certainly guilty of the first charge, and, in spite of his complicity with the captive spectators, voices a critique which is extraordinarily oblivious of their situation. By depicting its characters as totally subsumed within their lifestyle and impossible to differentiate from each other, *Less Than Zero* confirms rather than resists the stereotyped images. But even a critique of mass media which begins as an informed analysis of the spectator often denies the voyeuristic impulse which threatens the analysis. For this analysis has as its basis the same frustrated desire to attain something real which compels the voyeur. The critic after all seeks the "realization" of that which he finds lacking in the object of criticism.

Which brings us back to the question "Is it real?" At first, this question which the boys in *Less Than Zero* pose about the snuff film does not seem to fit into the logic of voyeurism at all. A voyeur is supposed to be so fascinated by the images and the action that the constructedness and artificiality of what is being viewed remain unconsidered and, in the end, irrelevant. So long as the desired effect (emotional high, suspense, excitement, shock, sexual stimulation, thirst, hunger) is achieved in the receiver, the image has been successful, regardless of whether there is any "reality" to the image. This should apply as well to the snuff film as it does to a TV thriller, a Hollywood movie, a Coca-Cola commercial, or a network news broadcast. In all these examples the images are oriented toward drawing in their viewers and riveting their attention, thereby maintaining sales and improving ratings. The question of the reality behind the images is of secondary concern, often times even irrelevant.

For the critic as well, the question of an outside reality does not seem to always be an issue. In *Amusing Ourselves to Death,* Postman argues that the very logic of the video medium, independent of any other outside factors, threatens to destroy the possibility of rational debate and argumentation in practically every area of public society. In Postman's eyes, the video medium dictates the characteristics of that which is shown through it. The emphasis on immediate images, the need to constantly

change the images, and the compulsion to pull elements out of their contexts are unavoidable characteristics of television programming. These properties prevent sustained thought on the part of the viewer and even dissolve the fundamental concept of contradiction upon which all logical thinking is based. According to Postman, the inevitable consequence of the rise of the video media has been the deterioration of political debate in the US. As evidence, Postman contrasts the televised debates between Reagan and Mondale in the 1984 presidential elections with the 1858 Lincoln-Douglas debates in Illinois. Whereas the Lincoln-Douglas debates were marked by complex argumentation and positions which could be critically studied and further discussed, the emphasis in the Reagan-Mondale debates was on appearances and on a rhetoric reminiscent of television advertising. Postman contends that the change in the character of political debate is a result of the rise of the electronic media. As clear as the contrast is which Postman demonstrates, the conclusion which he draws fails to penetrate to the core of the problem. Because Postman ascribes such overwhelming power to the video medium and holds the medium itself principally responsible for the deterioration of American politics and education, he never discusses the relationship between the television image and an outside reality, a relationship which is crucial for the role of television images in our society. For as Noam Chomsky has pointed out, the spectators of televised sporting events, for example, are extremely well-informed, intellectually sophisticated, and not at all interested in appearances, but rather in concrete results. "I think this concentration on such topics as sports [wrote Noam Chomsky, in *The Progressive,* July 1987] makes a certain degree of sense. The way the system is set up there is virtually nothing people can do anyway, without a degree of organization that's far beyond anything that exists now, to influence the real world. They might as well live in a fantasy world, and that's in fact what they do. I'm sure they're using their common sense and intellectual skills, but in an area which has no meaning and probably thrives because it has no meaning . . . " The problem lies not with a medium which in itself leads to the imbecility of its users, but in the structuring of this medium in a way which excludes the populace from participation in debate about real social issues.

Television in the US demonstrates the absence of such active participation. Whatever the viewers might think or do, their thoughts and actions will have virtually no effect upon that which happens on the screen, in "TV land." However, this lack of participation is not caused by the medium itself, but by the current implementation of this medium within a context of decreasing public debate. The lack of active participation on the part of the typical television viewer in fact mirrors and reinforces the lack of active participation within which typical US "citizens" exist within their society. For the fascination of television viewers is predicated upon their boredom, a boredom which is a result of their exclusion from a participatory role, both in the action on the screen and in their society. The failure of society to provide its members with opportunities for active participation—the state and corporate bureaucratization of modern society—leads to a permanent state of boredom which drives a person to turn on the television set. Bureaucratization of society is the precondition for the development and expansion of the culture industry.

But because the television does not offer anything essentially different than a passive relationship to uncontrollable events either, the boredom which turned on the television in the first place constantly threatens to overtake the viewer again while watching. Consequently, the first rule of American television programming is that the images must constantly entertain the viewer to the point where not only the boredom of the viewer's passive position in front of the television is forgotten, but also the initial boredom in society which drove the viewer to buy the television and turn it on in the first place. This obligation to entertain is not inherent to the video medium itself, as Postman argues, but to the specific situation of American television programming, manifesting itself in its most successful forms as an ability to fascinate viewers, turning them into "voyeurs." For what separates a normal "viewer" from a true "voyeur" is this fascination which allows the voyeur to vicariously participate in the images and the action. This participation remains, however, on the level of voyeurism—the fascination functions, on the one hand, as a passive participation of the viewer with the viewed object which, on the other hand, is based upon the viewer's exclusion from a truly active participatory relationship to this same object. The inability of the typical citizen to influence decision-making in society is the prerequisite for the power the image attains by providing a replacement for such true participation. The citizen, frustrated in the attempt to achieve this goal, accepts the artificial media substitute which distracts the viewer from the original desire for participation to such an extent that it is displaced into a desire for spectacles and diversionary entertainment.

This voyeuristic attitude has become so far-reaching that it has overtaken not only the television viewer but also the television critic. Neil Postman directs his criticism against the medium and does not consider the programming at all. According to Postman, the programming itself cannot be successfully criticized because it has no other alternative but to create the fascination which is demanded by the logic of its medium. He compares the advent of television to the invention of the printing press. Both are technological advances which actually change the character of truth, according to Postman's invocation of Marshall McLuhan's slogan, "the medium is the message." In Postman's perspective, if the invention of a written language and the Gutenberg press necessarily made truth into something written, expository, and argumentative instead of oral, mnemonic, and aphoristic, the invention of television has made truth into something necessarily visual, spectacular, and entertaining. At this point, Postman's argument, in its attempt to be a strict analysis of the video medium, demonstrates its own participation in the same passive, voyeuristic attitude which it should be criticizing. Postman's description of the development of human technology from the alphabet to the television set, as well as his excusing of television programming because it is merely obeying the logic of its medium, recalls the same attitude which prevails over the television viewer. By viewing both the development of technology and of television programming as if they were occurring on a screen, totally beyond the control of the viewer, he fails to recognize possibilities for interaction with other aspects of society, possibilities which can radically alter the "logic" of television. He in effect affirms these developments by participating in them in the same passive, fascinated way that voyeurs "participate" vicariously in that which they are watching. In both cases the participation is an affirmation of the object which questions neither the relation of the viewer to the object—Postman himself never mentions the voyeuristic quality of this relationship—nor the extent to which the object both hides and betrays a reality more important than the object itself.

The failure of Postman and the television voyeur to perceive this reality leads in both cases to the assumption that this reality does not exist. With the television voyeur this assumption takes the form of a fascination with the image which considers the question of the reality of this image as either irrelevant or senseless. The level of fascination is the primary interest. With Postman this assumption expresses itself in the belief that truth itself changes according to the medium. "The medium is the message," and there is no reality behind the medium. Hence Postman cannot even conceive of the possibility that television's fascination might be grounded in a reality separate from it— the bureaucratization of modern society.

In spite of such denials, however, the question "Is it real?" continues to recur. For the television viewers, the question is an expression of the inadequacy of the pure image in satisfying their desires. For Postman, who implicitly asks a similar question by undertaking a critique of television at all, this question signals the sense of loss remaining after the disappearance of the message in the medium and the withering of public debate in society. If it were not for this sense of loss, Postman would have to embrace television as the bringer of a new age in truth, and all his humanist worries about a society without political debate would be obsolete concerns from out of the antiquated medium of written language. A critique of television would be senseless because the advent of the video medium would be inevitable and unstoppable, as open to criticism and human decision as the movement of the stars in the sky or, in Postman's perspective, the play of images on the screen.

That Postman senses such a loss in spite of his own argument is to be explained by the fact that the phenomenon he is describing is only a part of a larger process of bureaucratization in American society. But Postman's fascination with the logic of the video medium itself causes him to overlook the social prerequisites for television's exploitation of a passive voyeuristic attitude. It is also this oversight which explains his lame liberal solution to the problem which he sees as being confined to the effects of television. His solution is a change in educational policy which would teach children to be "critical viewers." Postman fails to demand changes in television programming and in the bureaucratic organization of both the television industry and American society in general. He thus demonstrates the same paralyzing despair in the face of the power of technological developments and the bureaucratization of society as the despair which draws the voyeur to the image.

An article in the *New York Times* describing a shootout in Miami between FBI agents and two suspected robbers reported that "A few cars traveling on the street merely slowed and steered around the stalled vehicles as the agents and the robbery suspects exchanged fire. Several witnesses later said they had believed at first they had come across the filming of a scene from the television show *Miami Vice.* Because the witnesses consider reality as if it were an image, the actual shootout is no longer a part of direct experience which has any consequences for those experiencing the event. The motorists could ignore the shooting and steer around just as if it were a television show to be switched off. The stance toward reality becomes a passive one. According to Susan Sontag, whereas "philosophers since Plato" have insisted upon the distinction between image and reality, both a "primitive" sensibility and the "modern" one do without such a distinction. "But the true modern primitivism is not to regard the image as a real thing; photographic images are hardly that real. It is common now for people to insist about their experience of a violent event in which they were caught up—a plane crash, a shoot-out, a terrorist bombing—that 'it seemed like a movie'." As the "Miami Vice" incident demonstrates, Sontag's observation about the transformation of reality into an image is certainly to be taken seriously. The actual development of the video media and the resultant change in the way reality is actually perceived implacably demonstrate that the relationship between image and reality has fundamentally changed since the advent of photographic images. But in her ardor to show that the "powers of photography have in effect de-Platonized our understanding of reality, making it less and less plausible to reflect upon our experience according to the distinction between images and things, between copies and originals," she neglects to develop the distinction between the "primitive" treatment of images as reality and the "modern" treatment of reality as image. For the "primitive," by elevating image to the level of reality, maintains an active relationship to both image and reality and is a participant in both, subject to their influence and able to influence them in turn. An image is not merely an imitation, but an emblem, a talisman, which embodies otherwise unseen powers and which is to be respected as such. The "modern primitive," however, by reducing both reality and image to the level of a TV image, maintains a passive relationship to both reality and image and is a helpless spectator of both. Not only is "Miami Vice" an imitation, but the actual shootout cannot be taken seriously either. Instead of being able to consider both images and thereby also the metaphysical as serious components of a heterogeneous reality, the "modern primitive" reduces everything to the level of impotent images, shorn of any real significance.

This repression of an active relationship to both image and reality eventually feeds into a latent aggression. The resulting violence comes to light in the fascination of the snuff film viewers in *Less Than Zero*. The passive fascination of these viewers at first fits in with the earlier model of alienation from real participation. The viewers embrace a passive voyeuristic stance which robs them of a direct participation in reality. The boy being castrated and the boy watching the castration do not stand in direct relation to each other. It is only the relationship of their roles which influences each of them. The first boy is not being castrated because one particular boy wanted to watch, but because of the general existence of such a desire. He does not ever see the real viewer, but only the camera, an abstraction of this viewer. The boy who watches is not fascinated by the castration of a particular boy, but by the thought of such a thing happening at all. The original castration was an act of violence performed for the benefit of the camera and, ultimately, of the viewers. Once the event is transferred to the screen, it becomes a spectacle and the questions of intervention, practical action, and morality become irrelevant. Instead, the effects of the images on the viewer become the primary concern.

The frightening aspect of this development is that, together with the stimulation which the snuff film viewers in *Less Than Zero* experience in watching the film is a nonchalance which carries over into their reactions to "real" events. The characters discover a dead body in an alley and carry out the gang rape of a 12-year-old girl with the same detached and yet rapt fascination with which they view a film. Not only that, but their actions actually mimic the actions which they originally see on film. Not only does pure stimulation become the primary concern in watching a film, stimulation, not participation, becomes the essential characteristic of all experience. This change in the character of experience leads in turn to a horrifying revision of the meaning of participation for the snuff film viewers. Whereas the television viewer's passive fascination provides a replacement for direct experience, and the underlying longing for a participatory situation is thus forgotten, the snuff film viewers have reached the point where participation has been redefined as subjugation. In this new sense, the snuff film viewers push for more participation. The thrill which accompanies the young boys' hope in *Less Than Zero* that the cas-

tration was "real" is the horrifying expression of a desire on the part of the voyeur to stop being a voyeur and become a participant. For if a young boy had truly been castrated in order to make the snuff film, then the voyeurs have the assurance that their collective gaze, by creating the demand for such a castration, actually did have a real effect on that which they see. The absolute boundary which the screen creates between viewer and viewed, preventing the development of any direct relationship between the two, would have been overcome. But in the case of our snuff film viewers, the breakdown of the absolute boundary between viewer and viewed, far from being the fulfillment of the dream of a participatory democracy, becomes the blueprint for the torture chamber.

The move from passive fascination to active aggression can be traced in the historical development of the forms of mass culture. [Russell] Berman [in *Telos,* Winter 1984–85] has provided a detailed analysis of this development. Without going into details, it will suffice to note that, in the 1980s, the passification which the image once enforced becomes coupled with a simultaneous unleashing of latent aggression. "The increasingly violent character of culture industrial manipulation is evident not only in the bloodlust of films like *Friday the Thirteenth* and *Halloween,* but in the murderous sociability portrayed in daytime soap operas or prime time series (*Dallas, Dynasty*) in contrast with which the television figures of the 1950s and 1960s seem endearing in their naive accounts of humanistic values." What differentiates the snuff film viewer from the previous description of the television viewer is that the television viewer's passive and "naive" identification derives from an empathy with the characters or the action. Such empathy, the most "endearing" aspect of the television viewer, is missing from the snuff film viewer, as it is from the sadist-torturer. *Leave It to Beaver, Friday the Thirteenth,* and the snuff film are stages in a development in which the viewer gains more and more distance from the action—at first totally empathizing with the characters, and by the end deriving only stimulation from the effects of the images. In this development there remains an essential tie between the voyeur who must settle for a vicarious fulfillment of desire and the snuff film viewer who, unsatisfied with vicarious fulfillment, begins to demand a direct participation which takes the form of a violent subjugation. The fulfillment of desire expresses itself as violent aggression. As Berman argues, "the attack on erotic restriction has turned into its opposite: the restriction of eros to universal competitiveness and a weakening of the structures with which eros held thanatos in check. The modernist promise of unlimited pleasure has been realized as a constantly increasing aggressive potential . . . " While Berman here emphasizes the proximity of eros and thanatos—the voyeur and the snuff film viewer—he also relates how this aggressive potential feeds into bureaucratic structures which contain equally destructive impulses.

It turns out, however, that this aggressive potential is also an element of the critic. The element of empathy differentiating the naiveté of the television viewer from the violence of the snuff film viewer, a sign of compassion, was what also caused the television viewers to lose themselves in the television plot in the first place, thereby giving up on social action in reality. The empathy and identification with another's situation, a sign of compassion, leads in this case to both an alienation from one's own situation and a consequent inability to actively criticize this situation. It was precisely this problem against which modernists such as Benjamin and Brecht directed their aesthetics. Through the use of techniques such as montage, distraction, or interruption of dialogue, they sought to break down the identification of the viewer with the characters in order that the viewer might develop a critical stance. But the elimination of identification in the fostering of a critical audience corresponds with the elimination of empathy in the genesis of the snuff film viewer.

This unexpected congruence underlines the fact that the problem of the spectator is twofold and paradoxical. For in both the case of the voyeur and that of the critic, the result is "less than zero." On the one hand, when images become "larger than life," as they do for the voyeur, reality becomes less than the "zero" of the televised image. On the other hand, when the voyeur has no sympathy in the eyes of the critic, the critic's lack of feeling, his cold castration of the voyeur, is even less appealing than the "zero" of the voyeur's passive fascination. But this cold contempt which the critic too often directs against the voyeur, resulting in a cynical despair, is primarily a result of the critic's failure to identify with and encourage those aspects of the voyeur

which are not determined by the video medium. Analyses of film and video which do not recognize the primary role of an outside reality for the development and logic of video must remain trapped within the strict dichotomy of spectator and critic. The successful merging of these two poles and the attainment of something more than that which is being presented on the screen can only come about when this basic question concerning video, "Is it real?" is answered with "Of course not. It's only Hollywood."

Source: David Pan, "Wishing for More," in *Telos,* No. 76, Summer 1988, pp. 143–54.

Sources

Freese, Peter, "Bret Easton Ellis, *Less Than Zero:* Entropy in the 'MTV Novel'?" in *Modes of Narrative,* Konigshausen & Neumann, 1990, pp. 68–87.

Pan, David, "Wishing for More," in *Telos,* No. 76, Summer 1988, pp. 143–54.

For Further Study

Baughman, Judith, *American Decades: 1980–1989,* Gale, March 1996.

> This is primarily an outline of events that happened in the United States during the 1980s. The book focuses on the arts, education, government and politics, law, and sports.

Coupland, Douglas, *Generation X: Tales for an Accelerated Culture,* St. Martin's Press, October 1992.

> This book contains several stories about the culture and attitudes of people born in the 1970s and 1980s.

Sewall, Gilbert, ed., *The Eighties: A Reader,* Perseus Books, November 1998.

> This ultraconservative book covers an array of articles that deal with the politics and culture of the 1980s.

Winter, Gibson, *America in Search of Its Soul,* Morehouse Publishing Company, November 1996.

> This book takes an in-depth look into the lives of today's young people through social, ethical and spiritual views.

The Return of the Native

Thomas Hardy

1878

The Return of the Native is Thomas Hardy's sixth novel and probably his best known. In fact, many critics assert that Eustacia Vye is one of the most memorable characters in English literature. The story focuses on the lives and loves of residents in the fictional county of Wessex, England, an area which was based on the rural area where Hardy was raised.

When the book was published in 1878, it met with mixed reviews. Some commentators praised Hardy's vivid descriptions of the geographical landscapes, especially those in the first chapter. Others felt that his portrayal of the local characters was shallow and unconvincing. Yet other critics objected to the sexual relationships in the novel. The charge that he wrote about sexual relationships purely for sensationalism hurt Hardy to such a degree that he quit writing novels by 1895, although he continued to live another thirty-three years.

Author Biography

Thomas Hardy was born in Higher Bockhampton, in Dorsetshire, England, on July 2, 1840. His father and grandfather were master masons, and it was expected that he would be one also; but as a young man he excelled in his academic studies, learning Latin and Greek and studying poetry. At age sixteen, he left school to be an apprentice architect in nearby Dorchester.

Thomas Hardy

In 1862, he moved to London to work with a noted architect. It was then that he started writing in his spare time. His first love was poetry, but he had trouble getting his work published. In 1868 he returned to Dorset as an architect. He began writing novels, publishing the first one, *Desperate Remedies,* in 1871. The three novels that he wrote over the next three years were successful, so that after publishing *Far From the Madding Crowd* in serial form in 1874, he was able to quit architecture.

Hardy's work met with commercial and critical success. However, starting with *The Return of the Native* in 1878, Hardy's fiction began to gain a reputation for its salacious treatment of sexual relationships. When *Tess of the D'Urbervilles* was published in book form in 1891, he included scenes that had been cut out of the magazine serialization because they were considered too scandalous. As a result, Hardy became a controversial figure. With the publication of *Jude the Obscure,* critical and popular opinion began to turn against him.

Because of this negative publicity, Hardy quit writing novels more than thirty years before his death. After 1895, he concentrated all of his literary efforts on poetry. He published the poems that had been rejected early in his career, along with new works: *Wessex Poems* (1898) and *Poems of the Past and Present* (1902). After his wife's death in 1912, he published a book of short, bitter poems about marriage, *Satire of Circumstances;* yet additional poems published later showed a fond and tender remembrances for their courtship and early years. In 1914 he married Florence Emily Dugdale, who had been his secretary for years.

Between 1898 and his death in 1928, he published eight volumes of poetry. As a senior literary figure, he was an influence on many twentieth-century writers, such as Ezra Pound, William Butler Yeats, and Virginia Woolf. After a short illness, Hardy died on January 11, 1928. His ashes are buried in the Poet's Corner of Westminster Abbey, London, next to those of Charles Dickens. His heart was removed and buried separately in Dorset.

Plot Summary

Book First: The Three Women

This novel opens with a sweeping view of the Egdon Heath countryside, providing descriptions of the landscape and some sense of its history. In the next chapter, an old man—later identified as Eustacia Vye's grandfather—meets a red dye salesman, known as a reddleman. They briefly discuss Thomasin's marriage, and the old man infers from the reddleman that the wedding has been postponed.

In town, Thomasin meets her aunt and explains that her wedding was called off because of a mix-up with the license. They go to the tavern and receive assurance from Damon Wildeve, her fiancé, that he will marry Thomasin in a day or two. When the locals show up to sing to the newlyweds, they are forced to pretend that the marriage occurred.

After everyone leaves that night, Wildeve sees a bonfire up on the hill nearby the Vye house. Eustacia Vye, the exotic beauty who lives there, has heard from her grandfather that the marriage did not take place. She lit the fire, which was not unusual because many people celebrated Guy Fawkes Day with bonfires. Yet this was the same way she had attracted Wildeve the previous year; he had come to her house and they had begun a passionate affair. Confused, he goes to Eustacia again. After his visit, Wildeve decides that he does not want to marry Thomasin after all.

Diggory Venn, the reddleman, has been in love with Thomasin since childhood. He finds out about Eustacia and tries to get her to leave town.

Thomasin's aunt, Mrs. Yeobright, tells Wildeve her niece is thinking of marrying Venn. When she hears this news, Eustacia decides that Wildeve is not as attractive as she had thought; she begins to have doubts about her relationship with him. Meanwhile, news comes that Mrs. Yeobright's son, Clym, has returned from Paris.

Book Second: The Arrival

Clym's arrival is important news to the locals, who remember what a bright, promising boy he was. Bored with Wildeve, Eustacia becomes infatuated with Clym. On the night that the drama troupe is going to put on a Christmas play, Eustacia finally meets Clym, although she keeps her identity hidden. She is so preoccupied with Clym that she fails to show up to tell Wildeve whether she will run off with him or not. Diggory Venn pressures her to leave Wildeve alone, and so she writes Wildeve a letter saying that she will not be involved with him anymore.

As soon as Venn admits that he is not engaged to Thomasin, Wildeve rushes to her house and sets a wedding date. When Thomasin and Wildeve get married, the witness to their wedding is Eustacia Vye—she just happenes to be in the churchyard when a witness is needed.

Book Third: The Fascination

Clym's Christmas holiday at home turns into an extended stay. He considers his life in the diamond trade in Paris to be superficial, and formulates a plan to open a school in the heath where he can teach the poor children who otherwise would get no education. He finally meets Eustacia, and is impressed with her beauty and intelligence. He informs his mother that Eustacia could be a part of his heath school.

Yet in fact, his mother doubts that Clym is serious about being a teacher at all. She accuses him of being interested in the young woman romantically. Eustacia does not like his plan to open a local school either; she sees none of the charm of Egdon Heath, and instead wants to go to Paris with him. When Clym proposes, she accepts, thinking that she can change his mind after their marriage.

After a fight with his mother, Clym marries Eustacia. In protest, his mother does not even attend. Yet she decides to send a local boy to the wedding with a hundred guineas. On the way, Wildeve dupes the boy into gambling and takes all of the money, which he considers half his anyway;

Diggory Venn, who has been following him, gambles with Wildeve and wins the money from him.

Book Fourth: The Closed Door

Not knowing that the money was meant for Thomasin and Clym, Venn gives it all to Thomasin. Mrs. Yeobright assumes that Wildeve gave the money to Eustacia, his old lover. Mrs. Yeobright and Eustacia have a bitter argument.

Studying late into the night to become a schoolmaster, Clym damages his eyes and is told to quit reading for a while. Rather than staying idle, he takes a job as a furze cutter. Being married to a furze cutter is exactly the fate that Eustacia thought she was avoiding by marrying a worldly diamond merchant from Paris. As a result, she is humiliated. Depressed about her life, she goes to a local dance and meets her old flame, Wildeve. He is now rich from an inheritance from a distant relative—just the kind of man she would have wanted to marry. Yet she refuses to get involved with him.

Wildeve cannot get Eustacia out of his mind. He goes to her house at night, but Diggory Venn plants traps along the path. To avoid Venn, Wildeve goes to the house one afternoon. That happens to be the afternoon that Mrs. Yeobright has decided to visit Clym and Eustacia's house for the first time.

With Clym exhausted and sleeping on the couch, Wildeve arrives and Eustacia invites him into the living room. Just as they decide that they will not have an affair together, Mrs. Yeobright knocks at the door. Eustacia ushers Wildeve to the back door. When she checks the front door, Eustacia finds that Mrs. Yeobright has left.

On the way back to her house, Mrs. Yeobright walks with a young boy from the area, Johnny, telling him that her son has broken her heart. He leaves her when she sits down at the side of the trail to rest. That night, after work, Clym decides to visit his mother and settle their differences. He finds her lying on the side of the road, unable to talk. Local people determine that she has been bitten by a snake. They try to cure the bite.

Meanwhile, Wildeve has returned to the house to say goodbye to Eustacia. She has him walk her to join Clym and Mrs. Yeobright. They come across the people trying to revive the sick women and Eustacia is afraid to let anyone know she is there. Mrs. Yeobright dies, and the boy she was walking with tells Clym that she said that afternoon that her son had broken her heart.

Book Fifth: The Discovery

In mourning, Clym is overcome with sorrow and grief until he finds out more about his mother's last day. It is then that he learns that there was another man in the house, and that Eustacia looked out the window at Mrs. Yeobright when she was knocking. He accuses her of having an affair, so she moves back into her grandfather's house. Wildeve comes to her and asks her to go away with him, but she refuses to be unfaithful to Clym. When he asks if there is anything he can do for her, she says he can arrange transportation to the port town of Budmouth, where she can catch a ship.

Thomasin convinces Clym to forgive Eustacia, but she has already left. That night, Wildeve tells Thomasin that he has to go away for a while; she sees him take a huge roll of bills, indicating that he is going for a long time. Thomasin tells Clym that she thinks Wildeve and Eustacia are running away together. After he goes to stop them, she goes out into the storm too. Lost, she comes across Diggory Venn's wagon and he helps her in the search. Just as Clym finds Wildeve's coach, they hear a body fall into the river near the dam. Both men jump in to save Eustacia. When Venn arrives he jumps in too, pulling out Clym and Wildeve. Wildeve and Eustacia are dead, but the doctor is able to revive Clym. He blames himself for her death in addition to the death of his mother.

Book Sixth: Aftercourses

One year later, Clym lives with Thomasin and her daughter in his mother's old house. Diggory Venn has made enough money selling reddle to buy a large dairy farm. He asks Thomasin to marry him, but she thinks that he has become too isolated to be a good husband. Just as Clym is thinking that he should probably ask Thomasin to marry him, she tells him that she would like to marry Venn. Venn and Thomasin marry and Clym becomes a famous preacher.

Characters

Christian Cantle

Christian is a shy, ineffectual young man, nervous around women. Entrusted to go to Clym's house on his wedding day and deliver a gift—one hundred guineas that are to be divided between Clym and Thomasin—Christian loses the money to Wildeve in a game of dice.

Media Adaptations

- *Return of the Native* was adapted as a television presentation for the Hallmark Hall of Fame series in 1994, starring Clive Owen, Catherine Zeta-Jones, and Joan Plowright. The television movie was directed by Jack Gold and released as a video in 1999 by Hallmark Home Entertainment.

- Audio Partners Publishing Company has an unabridged, 12-tape edition of actor Alan Rickman reading the novel which was produced in 1999.

Grandfer Cantle

Grandfer (a title that is local dialect for "Grandfather") represents the lively spirit of the simple country people. At almost seventy, he is eager to dance, sing, joke, and tell exaggerated stories.

Charley

Charley is a local man who cares for Eustacia. After Eustacia has argued with Clym and gone back to her grandfather's house, Charley takes care of her. He makes a fire for her and feeds her, and when he sees that she has looked too long and sorrowfully at the pistols, he sneaks through a window and takes them away to hide them.

Olly Dowden

A local woman, Olly is a besom maker. Wildeve takes a bottle of wine to her sick husband one night, using the visit as an excuse when he goes to see Eustacia.

Humphrey

Humphrey is a furze-cutter. When Clym decides to go into the business of cutting furze, he borrows Humphrey's old equipment.

Johnny Nunsuch

Johnny is a young boy who lives near Captain Vye's house. At the beginning of the novel, Eustacia pays him to tend the bonfire that she uses to signal Wildeve. He sees Wildeve talking to Eustacia and tells Venn about it. Johnny later walks with Mrs. Yeobright after she leaves Clym's cottage at Alderworth.

Susan Nunsuch

Susan is Johnny's mother. A superstitious woman, she believes that Eustacia is a witch and blames her for her children's illnesses.

Diggory Venn

Venn is a local man that has been in love with Thomasin since childhood. As such, he frequently works behind the scenes to protect her and assure her happiness. He is called the "reddleman" because he deals in reddle, a dye used by sheep farmers; as a result of handling it, his clothes, skin, and everything he owns are dyed red, giving him a devilish look. It is Venn who brings Thomasin back to town after her marriage to Wildeve is delayed. When he finds out that Wildeve has been seeing Eustacia, Venn pressures him to marry Thomasin; though it means he cannot have Thomasin for himself, it would be the best thing for her reputation. Moreover, he offers to arrange a job for Eustacia so that Wildeve will go back to Thomasin and make her happy.

After Wildeve wins the money that Christian was supposed to deliver to Clym and Thomasin, Venn wins it back and gives it to Thomasin. When Wildeve has run off with Eustacia, Venn helps Thomasin find them. It is Venn who saves Clym's life by pulling him out of the water. When he has saved up enough money, Diggory Venn quits the reddle business and buys a dairy farm. Eventually he proposes to Thomasin and they marry.

Captain Vye

Captain Vye is Eustacia's grandfather.

Eustacia Vye

Eustacia is local woman and one of the major characters of the novel. She is exotic, beautiful, ambitious, and eager to leave Egdon Heath. Much of the action in this story revolves around the fact that men find Eustacia so unnaturally attractive that there are even rumors of her being a witch. Born and raised in the seaside resort of Budmouth, Eustacia's father was a musician from the island of Corfu, in the Ionian Sea. Eustacia was educated and raised in a cosmopolitan environment, but after her parents died her grandfather brought her to Egdon Heath.

She is forced to find the excitement she craves in her relationships with men. She has an affair with Wildeve, but cuts it off after he breaks his engagement to Thomasin. She falls in love with Clym before meeting him, almost solely on the fact that he had a successful career in Paris. While courting, Clym is adamant about the fact that he plans to stay in the country and open a small school, but Eustacia believes she can change his mind later. When Clym takes a job cutting furze, Eustacia resents him.

Soon after Eustacia marries, Wildeve inherits a fortune. Eustacia feels she has married the wrong man. This feeling intensifies when Clym accuses her of causing his mother's death. Wildeve offers to take her away, but Eustacia insists on remaining faithful to her wedding vows. She does accept a ride to the port town. Tragically, she drowns in the reservoir, and there is a question whether her death might have been a suicide.

Damon Wildeve

Wildeve is a wild young man. Engaged to Thomasin, he has a long-standing affair with Eustacia. In fact, he decides to drop Thomasin for Eustacia; instead, Eustacia breaks off their affair and he marries Thomasin. Not surprisingly, he isn't a very good husband. Just as Eustacia is feeling that her marriage to Clym is boring and difficult, Wildeve inherits a fortune; they meet at a dance and find each other exciting all over again. When she separates from Clym, Wildeve offers Eustacia anything that his money can offer, but she declines. At the end of the novel, he drowns in the reservoir trying to save her.

Clemson Yeobright

The "native" of the novel's title, Clemson (also known as Clym) is a local boy who has returned to Egdon Heath after a successful career in Paris. He is sick of city life, and looks forward to starting a local school. Not long after he returns, he meets Eustacia and marries her. He thinks that Eustacia supports his plan to start a school, and is shocked when he realizes that she doesn't. While studying to be a teacher, Clym damages his eyes. Because he cannot read until they heal, he takes a job cutting furze, which is what most of the local men do for a living.

After his mother's death, he feels guilty and blames himself. When he finds out that Eustacia did not let his mother in the house because she was talking with Wildeve, he accuses his wife of having an affair and blames her for his mother's death.

After Eustacia's death, he lives with Thomasin and considers marrying her. When he realizes that she will be happy married to Diggory Venn, Clym becomes an open-air preacher and becomes famous by talking to the field workers in language that they understand.

Clym Yeobright

See Clemson Yeobright

Mrs. Yeobright

Clym's mother, Mrs. Yeobright, represents conventional Victorian values in the novel. For example, when Wildeve postpones the marriage, she feels that Thomasin's honor is at stake; to save her niece's reputation, she pressures Wildeve to fulfill his commitment. Mrs. Yeobright also objects to her son Clym marrying Eustacia, considering the young woman a "bad girl." She does not attend their wedding, but gives him his inheritance as a present. When she receives no thanks for it, she reaches the conclusion that Wildeve gave the money to Eustacia. When Eustacia denies knowing anything about it, the two women have a fight.

To reconcile with her son, Mrs. Yeobright travels to Clym's house, but by mistake, no one lets her in. Mrs. Yeobright walks home feeling that she has been turned away, and on the way a snake bites her. Clym finds her on the path that night, dying.

Thomasin Yeobright

Thomasin is Clym Yeobright's cousin. She is in love with the charismatic Wildeve and is disappointed when he puts off their marriage. She considers marrying Diggory Venn, the reddleman who is in love with her. Yet she takes his devotion for granted and is still attracted to Wildeve. Eventually she does marry Wildeve, but their union is not a happy one. After her husband dies, she marries Diggory Venn, who has become a wealthy dairy farmer.

Themes

Time

The role of time and the effect of its passage are major themes in the novel. As the story spans eighteen months, the landscape of the heath remains unchanged—that consistency is reflected in the people who live on the heath for generation after generation. They are creatures of tradition, following the same wedding rituals, the same harvest rituals, the same holiday traditions and the same folk remedies (such as the traditional cure for an adder's bite) that has been handed down to them. Sometimes traditional beliefs lead to hostility, like the fear of Eustacia Vye being a witch.

The characters who encounter difficulty are the ones who are not content to live in rhythm with country life. Most notably, Eustacia is impatient with life on the heath, wishing for the "bustle" of Paris. Wildeve is also bored with life on the heath. When he inherits a large sum of money, he plans to tour the world. Clym is the most divided character in the novel; Eustacia assumes that he is too worldly to settle down in the country, but he is able to appreciate the beauty of the land's timelessness.

> [W]hen he looked from the heights on his way he could not help indulging in a barbarous satisfaction at observing that, in some of the attempts at reclamation from waste, tillage, after holding on for a year or two, had receded again in despair, the ferns and furze-tufts stubbornly reasserting themselves.

Nature

Hardy introduces his readers to the landscape of Egdon Heath before introducing any characters. This emphasizes the important role that the natural landscape will play in the story. His description of the natural setting can be taken as symbolic of the people who live there—"neither ghastly, hateful, nor ugly: neither commonplace, unmeaning nor tame; but, like man, slighted and enduring." It can also be taken as a simple acknowledgment that people come to resemble the place where they live.

For instance, the extreme heat of the August day when Mrs. Yeobright is turned away from Clym's cottage may be perceived as symbolic of her turmoil. Hardy addresses this issue directly when he has Eustacia wander out into a violent storm on the night of her greatest mental anguish: "Never was harmony more perfect than that between the chaos of her mind and the chaos of the world without." If the people of Egdon Heath seem carefree, it is because they are comfortable in their surroundings.

The character who appears to be most in tune with nature's mysteries is Diggory Venn. He does not look like a human because of the red dye that has seeped into his skin and hair, and he does not operate by the rules of human interaction, instead appearing and disappearing mysteriously at night. It is not surprising that in the end he becomes a dairy farmer—making his living with domesticated animals, in harmony with nature but not completely subject to its whims.

Topics for Further Study

- The events of this story take place in the 1840s. Determine how rural England changed between that time and the time of the book's publication in 1878. What factors account for such a change?

- At the beginning of the book, Thomasin and her aunt are worried about her reputation when she comes home unmarried. Investigate Victorian social customs. Discuss how things have changed since Victorian times. In your opinion, have they changed for the better or for the worse?

- The legendary figures of the American West, including Jesse James and Billy the Kid, were active in 1878 when this book was published. Explain the relationship between the wilderness of Egdon Heath and the wilderness of the West as fictional settings.

- Some of the people of Egdon Heath consider Eustacia Vye to be a witch because of her exotic looks and behavior. Research other women in history who have been charged with witchcraft, and draw comparisons between them and Eustacia.

Conscience

The characters in *The Return of the Native* are motivated by their consciences more than any other driving force. Their attempts to avoid social confrontation are not guided by concern about what others will think, but by what harm they will do to others. This is evident in the opening chapters, with Thomasin's return after her aborted attempt to be married; although eloping is considered shameful, Thomasin and Wildeve are unconcerned about that social stigma, which is quickly forgotten anyway.

On the other hand, Wildeve is unwilling to go through with his wedding to Thomasin when he feels that he might end up regretting it and longing for Eustacia. When they do marry, it is not to satisfy the social requirement, but because of Wildeve's failed romantic life. Diggory Venn is driven to assure Thomasin's happiness, passing up opportunities that could benefit him in order to protect her. Telling her about Wildeve's involvement with Eustacia might make her forget Wildeve—thereby clearing the way for him—but Venn cannot hurt her. So he keeps silent.

Late in the novel, when Eustacia realizes that Wildeve has become the rich, worldly husband that she always wanted, she does not run away with him because she cannot hurt Clym. At her house, he says that he could not abandon his wife either, but later, when Eustacia is leaving town, he is willing to run away with her, still making sure that Thomasin will receive half of his inheritance.

Style

Point of View

This novel is told from the third-person point of view, which means that the narrator is a disembodied voice, referring to each character as "he" or "she." However, the narrative is not omniscient. This means that the narrator looks at the story unfolding from different points of view, but when it settles on any particular viewpoint it stays consistent, if only for a short amount of time. When new information is introduced into the story, that information is initially understood only in terms of the narrator's point of view at the time.

For instance, when Wildeve first appears, readers are not told who he is; his character is revealed by what he says. Clym is a mystery for Eustacia to fantasize about long before his thoughts are related. In fact, even when they do talk outside of the Christmas party, the narrative shifts from her perspective to his then back to hers. Giving readers access to just one person's experience at a time is called "limited omniscience."

By limiting the flow of information to the reader, Hardy is able to create a sense of mystery in the story. This is accomplished because the motivations and intentions of the characters are not always immediately clear. When Hardy wants to convey theories and opinions, he frequently presents a scene in which several of the local characters are gathered together and talking while doing something else. This occurs in the bonfire scene in the chapter called "The Custom of the Country" and in the later chapter where people gather and discuss the best way to deal with a snakebite. A contrast to this is the scene of hauling the bucket out of the well: general knowledge of the subject of bucket retrieval is conveyed directly from the narrator to the reader here, rather than through the conversation of the locals.

Structure

This book was written for magazine serialization, and this is reflected in its structure. Actions occur within specific episodes, and future developments in the story are foreshadowed. Chapters end with lines that are meant to raise curiosity, a technique that is effective to keep readers of novels turning the pages. Moreover, it was meant to inspire excitement so the reader would buy the next month's installment.

A good example of this technique is when Thomasin returns unmarried from Angelbury. The chapter ends with her aunt asking, "Now Thomasin . . . what's the meaning of this disgraceful performance?" Readers know that the explanation will follow, but it does not follow right away. Viewers of television—where shows are regularly scheduled in weekly installments—are very familiar with this technique.

Critics have also contended that this book is structured like a Shakespearean drama. Most of Shakespeare's plays were organized in five acts, with a climactic conclusion in the last act. Although *The Return of the Native* is presented in six books, most critics agree that its artistic structure only requires five—the sixth was added to please general audiences that wanted to see everything turn out all right in the end. A clue to the book's debt to Shakespeare is the reference to *King Lear,* one of Shakespeare's greatest tragedies, in the introduction.

Symbolism

The names of Thomas Hardy's characters are almost always symbolic of their functions within his novels, and the names in *The Return of the Native* are no exception. "Wildeve" suggests someone on the verge, or eve, of wildness, while his first name, Damon, is commonplace enough to suggest that he will never break out of the mold.

Eustacia is derived from the word "eustacy," which means a change in the level of the sea all around the world, indicating the immense changes that she is set to bring into the lives of the people on the heath and beyond. It also rings of the prefix "eu-," which has an Latin meaning of "good" and an Old Norse meaning "to want," and from "ecstasy." Her last name, "Vye," indicates the character's combative stance toward the world.

Clym's last name, "Yeobright," combines the word "yeoman" which indicates a servant or underling with the indication of his natural intelligence, or brightness. There are minor characters here also given names that are common words that appear in dictionaries, such as "Nunsuch" (normally spelled "nonesuch"), "Christian," and "Fairway."

Setting

The sweeping topographical and historical description of Egdon Heath that opens this book is considered to be one of the finest extended descriptions in all of English literature. The importance of this setting to the events of the novel cannot be overemphasized. It is the land's flatness and barrenness that has made it useless for development, which means that the civilized world has passed it by. The residents of the heath are isolated and possess their own distinct culture, separate from the rest of the world.

Eustacia is feared by the ordinary people and alluring to Wildeve and Clym for the same reason, because she keeps herself separate from the ordinary people; she is treated as if she has supernatural powers, as if she can transcend the land's hard demands. Clym is treated as an almost mystical personage because he has been to Paris, even though there is no indication that in Paris he was treated as anything more than a jeweler's clerk. The only way for people of the heath to gain wealth is to inherit it from far away, as Wildeve does, or to earn it in other places, as Diggory Venn does.

Historical Context

The Victorian Age

Today, Victorianism is thought of as another word for sexual repression. Yet the Victorian Age (1839–1901) was also a period of profound social commentary and social developments. The literature of the time addressed such significant issues as the growth of English democracy, the education of the masses, and the impact of industrialization on the working class.

One constant of the Victorian Era was that it was a time of an increased sense of social responsibility. In her early days on the throne, Victoria was viewed as liberal in her beliefs. A marked change came in 1840, when she married Albert, her mother's nephew and prince of Saxe-Colburg Gotha. Albert was conservative, moralistic, and prudish; Victoria adopted similar attitudes. After

Compare & Contrast

- **1840s:** Milk production in dairy farming is all done by hand.

  1878: The first commercial milking machines are produced in Auburn, New York.

  Today: Dairy farming is automated. Cows are kept in small enclosures that allow no room to move and seldom come into contact with humans.

- **1840s:** The typewriter is a new invention. Patented in 1843, it uses the concept of the moving carriage to make letters strike evenly.

  1878: The typewriter is greatly improved when the Remington Arms Company added a shift key that would allow the same document to include lower—and upper—case characters.

  Today: Typewriters are practically obsolete. Word processing makes any desktop system capable of professional-quality graphics.

- **1840s:** The first rail lines are just beginning to connect major urban areas, with passenger train travel starting in the 1830s. The only transportation available to inhabitants of Egdon Heath is primitive, such as horse-drawn carriages.

  1878: Railways are common across the English countryside. They link cities and allow travel to even isolated areas.

  Today: With automobiles providing convenient personal transportation, travel to any point in England is quick and easy.

- **1840s:** Human behavior is a matter for speculation by philosophers and fiction writers.

  1878: The first laboratory for experimental psychology is opened by Wilhelm Max Wundt, making a science out of the study of the mind.

  Today: The latest developments in psychology have been in the area of treating depressions and violent behavior with mood-altering drugs.

---

his death in 1861 she reigned for another forty years and never remarried. Her personality influenced all of society and set the tone for the age. In a way it provided a moral compass that provided a sense of constancy in a turbulent time.

Politically, the era was characterized by a prolonged economic boom. England reigned as a prosperous and dominant world superpower. In 1853, England, the Ottoman Empire, the Kingdom of Sardinia, and France fought a military conflict against Russia, in what was known as the Crimean War. It was fought to keep Russia from widening their influence in the Ottoman Empire and the Middle East. The conflict ended with the Treaty of Paris, signed on March 30, 1856.

The novelist most commonly associated with the Victorian Age is Charles Dickens (1812–1870), whose books were modest about sexual relations; yet, they are aggressive in portraying the wretched social conditions of urban life. Thomas Hardy is also associated with the era, even though his works were considered controversial and even prurient according to Victorian standards. Hardy's sexual openness in portraying Eustacia's and Wildeve's lust for each other even when they are married to others was viewed as shocking. It certainly violated the sensibilities of the time, and earned Hardy a legion of detractors who looked on his works as a form of pornography.

Critical Overview

Before it was even published as a novel, *The Return of the Native* had already been rejected by Leslie Stephen, the editor of the prestigious *Cornhill Magazine*. Stephen objected to the hint of ex-

Map of the fictional county of Wessex, England, which Hardy created for the novel's setting and is based on the rural area where he was raised.

tramarital sex and found it inappropriate for a family magazine. The serial ran in *Belgravia*, which, according to Desmond Hawkins, Hardy found to be an inferior publication.

The initial critical response to the novel was mixed. A review in *Athenaeum* deemed it "distinctly inferior to anything of his we have yet read." The reviewer also took issue with the language used by the characters, which seemed "pitched throughout in too high a key to suit the talkers." That same month critic W. E. Henley reviewed the book in *The Academy.* He found the work highly artificial but was reluctant to say so, because Hardy himself seemed sincere. On a positive note, he praised the opening descriptions of the heath and of Eustacia to be among the best things written in the English language—but that was not enough to make up for the weaknesses. Henley summarized all that was good and bad about Hardy's work in one seemingly endless sentence:

> . . . that he rarely makes you laugh and never makes you cry, and that his books are valuable and interesting rather as the outcome of a certain mind than as pictures of society or studies in human nature; that his tragedy is arbitrary and accidental rather than heroic and inevitable; and that, rare artist as he is, there is something wanting in his personality, and he is not quite a great man.

More than a decade later, Francis Adams pointed out the same strengths and weaknesses. Of Hardy's characterization of the dialogue of country maids, he wrote, "Nothing more ridiculous than this has been done by any writer of anything approaching ability in our time, and it is as false in characterization as it is absurd in conception." He went on to praise Hardy's artistic gift for making characters' environments reflect in their personalities, "a single harmonious growth of spiritual and natural circumstances."

Negative critical responses did not seem to trouble Hardy as much as the artistic constraints of having to please Victorian sensibilities. In 1894, the first book-length analyses of Hardy's fiction were published: Lionel Johnson's *The Art of Thomas Hardy* and Annie Macdonell's *Thomas Hardy.* Hardy mentioned them in a letter to a friend that year: " . . . are too laudatory. They are not in bad taste as a whole, if one concedes that they had to be written, which I do not." It is generally accepted that he wrote no novels after 1895 because of the changes that he had to make to every piece in order to tone down any suggestion of sexual passion.

In the decade after his death, Hardy's reputation declined. His fiction was too outdated to hold much interest—it was half a century since *Return of the Native,* and in the meantime modernism had redefined literary tastes. T. S. Eliot asserted that Hardy was "indifferent even to the prescripts of good writing: he wrote sometimes overpoweringly well, but always very carelessly; at times his style touches sublimity without ever having passed through the stage of being good."

His literary reputation soon revived, though, when critics started to take a new look at his work after the celebration of the hundredth anniversary of his birth in 1940. Since then, his six major novels—*Far From the Madding Crowd, Return of the Native, The Mayor of Casterbridge, The Woodlanders, Tess of the D'Urbervilles,* and *Jude the Obscure*—have held significant places in the ranks of English-language literature.

Criticism

David Kelly

Kelly is an instructor of Creative Writing and Literature at Oakton Community College in Illinois. In the following essay, he examines how the timelessness of Egdon Heath actually helps support the plot's reliance on chance.

Upon delving into any number of essays focused on Thomas Hardy's *The Return of the Native,* one is almost certain to come across a few important issues. The first issue is the character of the setting, Egdon Heath, which Hardy establishes in that long, lovely description in the first chapter and then comes back to throughout the book. More than most novels, even the bulk of Victorian romances, this book uses the setting as a character, a living presence, and not just as a buffer to linger over in between scenes. It seldom fails to impress. Critics who do not think much of Hardy's attributes as a novelist will usually point out, to soften the tone of their criticism, how he brings Egdon Heath to life—it's their way of paying homage to the man whose literary reputation is firmly established. Similarly, critics often point out his greatest weakness as a fiction writer: that he often stretched credibility too far by expecting his readers to believe that awkward twists in the plot happened because of coincidence.

These two outstanding aspects of *The Return of the Native,* though often mentioned just in passing and almost always separately, are in fact supports bracing one another—wedges of the same

frame that Hardy used to present a unified worldview. The timelessness of the heath, and the unlikely confluence of the events that go on there, blend to create a unique place where nature itself is unnatural.

Stories, of course, have to happen somewhere; moreover, the stories that are the most artistically sound use their settings to manifest what is happening to the characters. Some novels, especially if they are set in the present and under familiar circumstances, can take their settings for granted, offering up names of towns and streets and occasional descriptions of the surroundings. When the location will probably be unfamiliar—most notably in science fiction or fantasy or historical fiction—the writer is obliged to paint a fuller landscape. What is notable about *The Return of the Native* is that Hardy could have effectively set the scene with far less detail than he did in fact use. It is a desolate area; the people there live as their ancestors did; the railroad has not arrived yet. That covers all that needs to be covered.

Instead, he opens the book with a haunting description that extends from sky to ground, from dark to light, and from the present to the past. Other novels occur in settings that have evolved in ways corresponding to the laws of history, but the rules of physics don't apply to Egdon Heath.

In his study of Hardy's career, Richard Carpenter cites John Patterson as identifying the heath as Limbo or the Cimmeron of Homer—places that are balanced between this world and Hades—not miserable but certainly not places of life. Hardy writes that the heath has the ability to "retard the dawn, sadden noon, anticipate the frowning of storms scarcely generated, and intensify the opacity of a moonless midnight to a cause and dread." The character of this place is so crucial to telling this story that it is expanded across six pages, which is an incredible amount of space for a novelist to spend on a description of anything. Also telling is the fact that it is situated first in the book, establishing its importance before any specific human characters are introduced.

Carpenter describes this setting as more than an image: it is a convenient narrative tool, allowing Hardy's characters to summon one another across miles with signal fires and also to bump into each other unexpectedly as they wander the twisted paths through the furze. "By confining nearly all of his action to its terrain," he writes, Hardy "achieves a unity of place which markedly aids in the creation of dramatic effects." It is a handy setting for events that have to be brought together in order to make the story work, but it is in no way a superbly successful one. If Egdon Heath were flawless in drawing readers into the novel's magical spell, the reader would be left feeling completely satisfied about the reality and inevitability of what he or she is told goes on there. Instead, the reader is left conscious of the hand of the author as coincidences abound, apparently there only for his storytelling convenience.

Stories always depend on coincidental events. Hardy appears to not have recognized the boundary that separates "did not anticipate" from "*could not anticipate*"—and that line, wide as the Mississippi River, separates tragedy from potboiler. A turn of events like Clym Yeobright's semi-blindness, for example, seems to materialize pretty quickly in the story, but it follows naturally from Clym's sudden dedication to be a great educator, which follows from his impulsive high-minded character, and is therefore grounded in the story.

Diggory Venn *always* shows up unexpectedly and fortuitously, so the reader can accept him as either a supernatural presence or an extremely prepared guardian. Eustacia and Wildeve are drawn together by a similar restlessness, so it is no wonder that their internal clocks would direct them both to the East Egdon "gipsying" at the same time. The adder that bites Mrs. Yeobright is the natural result of life on the heath. Eustacia is devious enough to loiter outside of the chapel when Wildeve is marrying, so there is no stretch of reality in her being the wedding's witness.

Even the event that starts the whole novel into motion—the canceled marriage between Thomasin and Wildeve—seems only to be a matter of coincidence to the people in the book. Readers recognize this as one of those psychological non-accidents, reflecting the fact that one of these two subconsciously wanted the ceremony abandoned— although it is unclear whether the hesitant party is Thomasin, who changed towns suddenly at the last moment, or Wildeve, who forgot to change the license.

These coincidences can all be explained, and they even afford readers some fun in recognizing that life in the novel can be as unruly and unpredictable as it is in the world. Other coincidences are harder to swallow. Readers who can get past the idea that Mrs. Yeobright and Wildeve and Johnny Nunsuch all arrive at the cottage at the same time still have to accept the fact that Clym would happen to choose that particular night, after

> **The timelessness of the heath, and the unlikely confluence of the events that go on there, blend to create a unique place where nature itself is unnatural."**

months, to visit his estranged mother's house. Wildeve's fortune arrives out of nowhere, just in time for Eustacia to notice him again. The strangest of all, perhaps, is Fairway showing up late the night Eustacia is leaving, almost as an afterthought, with Clym's letter: it is hard enough to believe that he would happen to write when she happens to be leaving, but having a very minor character show up and say he had forgotten the letter until the drama is mounting shows a truly half-hearted effort on the part of the writer to simulate reality.

All readers of conscience are left to wonder how much the heath's wonderful, unique character can be allowed to account for the gaps in the story's credibility. To some extent, a lot: the otherworldliness that is so richly established allows Egdon Heath to excuse itself from any standards of behavior that are generally expected. If the laws of evolution are suspended there, then the laws of chance must be so too, since the one leads to the other. The same glitch that has left the heath unaltered for a thousand years also makes it possible for money to rain down unexpectedly from a previously unknown source, or for Diggory Venn to show up whenever his appearance would help the story.

In fact, Hardy not only flaunts the fact that chance rules, but he actually uses the readers' diminished expectations as part of the story's fabric. The characters who have any sense of the outside world become impatient with the slow, staid pace at Egdon Heath and they try taking fate into their own hands, creating tragedy. These characters include Eustacia and Clym, who has lived in Paris, the capital of the civilized world. Wildeve, an educated man, is able to sense a world beyond the heath, but he lacks the fortitude to do anything about it. When he inherits a lot of money later in the novel, he makes plans to break free of the heath

What Do I Read Next?

- All of Hardy's other novels are well-respected, but *Tess of the D'Urbervilles,* published in 1891, is particularly like *Return of the Native* in theme and setting.

- One of the greatest novelists of Hardy's time was George Meredith, an author known for his psychological insights. His *Diana of the Cross-ways* (1885) is about a woman who has an affair and is accused of giving away secrets to her lover.

- Margaret Mitchell's 1936 romance set during the Civil War, *Gone With the Wind,* is an epic story about longing and survival. The protagonist of the novel, Scarlett O'Hara, possesses many of the same traits as Eustacia Vye: she is proud, ambitious, restless, and driven by love.

- George Eliot (the pen name of Mary Ann Evans) wrote similar stories about life in rural England. *The Mill on the Floss* was published in 1860 and it concerns the trials of a sensitive young woman, facing rejection by her family.

- The definitive biography of Thomas Hardy is Martin Seymour-Smith's *Hardy* (1994), which includes exhaustive detail and comprehensive insight.

and traverse the globe, but this hope is what leads to the tragedy at the book's end. Wildeve and Eustacia find out that the law of the heath is not outside of nature, that it *is* their nature.

Trying to change is what causes trouble in an environment where change is the one thing that cannot happen; and, because their energies cannot produce the results that were intended, the force expended careens off into the void and then bounces back in ways not expected. Readers who accept the fact that time has passed the heath by do not have to strain too hard to see that the same mysterious force that stops time is not universal—that the real-world passions of Eustacia and Yeobright and

Wildeve will bring loose energy into the place and create chaos.

The question at the center of all of this is whether Thomas Hardy is the force that made the heath, or if the novel's unique elements can be accounted for naturally. One thing that is certain is that Hardy felt that the Egdon Heath he presented was a description, not a creation. Photographs and the testimony of other writers who came after him seem to bear out this idea, that the place before the arrival of technology was just as it had been for thousands of years. In old pictures, it looks just as desolate as the moon would look if it grew weeds. However, the old photos were shot with the theme of desolation in mind, thanks to Hardy: he observed the land and then added the idea that it willed itself to not change. Today, that area in the south of England is plenty inhabited, as cultivated as any other, proving, if such is necessary, that it had no magic aura that sealed it. Thomas Hardy, like any good novelist, saw a unique situation and took advantage of that opportunity to create his own mythology.

Much as I try, I cannot find causes for the strikingly bold "coincidences" I have mentioned, but I do feel that they belong in the novel. The same property that made Egdon Heath unique also allows characters in the book to stroll up with letters sent long ago, or to all decide at once to go to the same place. Like early physicists, the readers' job might be to identify the unseen currents and principles that make actions lead to unexpected results in this one field; or, like early theologians, the reader might just have to accept the fact that all that occurs is related. The degree to which Hardy's surprises are or are not believable goes beyond the events themselves and depends on how much one believes in the author and his world.

Source: David Kelly, in an essay for *Novels for Students,* Gale Group, 2001.

Avrom Fleishman

Fleishman is an American educator who has written extensively on the English novel. In the following excerpt, he analyzes the nature of Egdon Heath.

One would search long for a commentator on *The Return of the Native* who has failed to locate the story of Clym Yeobright and Eustacia Vye in the elaborated space of its landscape. Still it may be said that Egdon Heath has not been recognized as a figure in its own right—in both narrative senses of "figure," as person and as trope. One of the closest observers of the novel, John Paterson, has listed [in his essay "The 'Poetics' of *The Return of the Native*"] some of the heath's associations: " . . . it is a stage grand enough to bear the weight of gods and heroes; more specifically still, it is the prison-house of Prometheus, the fire-bearing benefactor of mankind." Paterson and others have supported such identifications by quoting the novel's repeated attribution of Promethean characteristics to the major characters. Hardy is never one to make his classical allusions evasively; the demonic rebelliousness of Eustacia and the bonded martyrdom of Clym are steadily projected upon the heath in the mode of scenic amplification. Yet the felt connection between the human actors and their inanimate setting exceeds the scope of metonymic associations like the scene-act ratio of Kenneth Burke. The ruling passions of the protagonists in *The Return* and the awesome powers of the heath need to be treated as forces of a like nature—the heath manifesting the same impulses as do the fictional characters.

To return to the setting of Hardy's first major novel is to seize his imagination at an originative position, where his sense of the past and his complex feelings about modern life intersected at a place with which he identified himself. Throughout his career, Hardy was inclined to express his strong response to the history-laden landscape of his shire in images of a special kind—special, that is, when compared with those of other Victorian novelists but commonplace in the tradition of local observers with a bent for narrative explanation. He was born, it will be recalled, in a cottage on the edge of the fourteen miles or so of high ground that has come to be identified with Egdon Heath, and he built his home, Max Gate, near its southwest flank five years after writing *The Return*. In 1878, the year the novel was published, the Folk-Lore Society was founded in London, and at about this date Hardy joined the Dorset Natural History and Antiquarian Field Club. To the latter he also delivered a paper on "Some Romano-British Relics Found at Max Gate, Dorchester"—found, that is, during the digging of foundations for his house. These delvings in the earth encouraged Hardy in a long series of reflections on the presence underfoot of a many-layered past: beginning as early as the passage in *The Return* on Clym's attendance at the opening of a barrow (book III, chapter iii); continuing with the account of unearthed Roman skeletons in *The Mayor of Casterbridge* (chapter xi); and developing a fine blend of fascination and detachment in poems like "The Roman Gravemounds" and "The Clasped Skeletons."

> These poems call to mind others in which one of the most familiar features of Hardy's style, personification, is employed in its mode of gigantism."

The sense of the past, it has been abundantly demonstrated, touches Hardy's work at innumerable points, but one may be isolated for the present discussion: his adumbration of an animate (or once-animate) being dormant in the earth, whether in the form of a buried skeleton incarnating the ghosts of the past, or of a quasi-human figure underlying or constituting certain topographical features (usually hills), or of a *genius loci* residing not in an aerial or other evanescent medium but in the soil of the place itself. It will be seen that some such preternatural beliefs are at work amid the rationalist skepticism which Hardy tried to maintain and that, while his own beliefs are not to be equated with those of the peasants in his tales, his absorption in them resembles the intellectual sympathy which modern anthropologists and folklorists have been recommending.

The prime instances of buried figures in the Hardy country are, quite naturally, those associated with a number of massive formations which surpass anything comparable in the southwest—the region of England perhaps most densely populated by ancient remains. Foremost is Maiden Castle, a Celtic hillfort a few miles south of Dorchester, which Hardy described as "an enormous many-limbed organism of an antediluvian time . . . lying lifeless, and covered with a thin green cloth, which hides its substance, while revealing its contour." Comparable in fame and grandeur is the Cerne Abbas giant, with his club and explicit phallus, on a hill seven miles north of Dorchester in a region Hardy favored for his rambles; it is mentioned in *Tess of the d'Urbervilles* and other writings, most saliently when described by the local peasantry in *The Dynasts* as a malevolent ogre, comparable to Napoleon.

Besides those and other gigantic erections in the vicinity, like Stonehenge, additional outcroppings of the land contour Hardy's writings. In a poem titled "The Moth-Signal," specifically set on

Egdon Heath and reminiscent of an incident in *The Return,* the waywardness of modern domestic life is seen from the perspective of a dweller in the earth:

> Then grinned the Ancient Briton
> From the tumulus treed with pine:
> "So, hearts are thwartly smitten
> In these days as in mine!"

Hardy takes up the point of view of an inhabitant of the heath in a more personal way in another poem, "*A Meeting with Despair*" (noted in the manuscript as set on Egdon Heath):

> As evening shaped I found me on a moor
> Sight shunned to entertain:
> The black lean land, of featureless contour,
> Was like a tract in pain.
> "This scene, like my own life," I said, "is one
> Where many glooms abide;
> Toned by its fortune to a deadly dun—
> Lightless on every side."
>
> . . . .
>
> Against the horizon's dim-discerned wheel
> A form rose, strange of mould:
> That he was hideous, hopeless, I could feel
> Rather than could behold.

Although Hardy metaphorically identifies the pattern and tone of his life with the heath's, he resists the insinuations of the apparition—named "Despair" in the title but referred to only as "the Thing" in the poem itself—so as to argue that the glowing sunset portends better prospects for the future. In a voice we recognize as that of the stupid giant of fairy tales, his interlocutor replies, "Yea—but await awhile! . . . Ho-ho!— / Now look aloft and see!" More striking, perhaps, than either the poem's finale (with the loss of light and portent of defeat) or the similarities between its treatment of Egdon Heath and the novel's is the encounter with an abiding presence there—the black lean land, featureless, in pain, from which a hideous, hopeless form arises.

These poems call to mind others in which one of the most familiar features of Hardy's style, personification, is employed in its mode of gigantism. The best-known instance of this trope is found in "The Darkling Thrush": "The land's sharp features seemed to be / The Century's corpse outleant. . . ." In the periodical publication of the poem, its original title emphasized this figure rather than the thrush: "By the Century's Deathbed" enforces the idea not simply of a localized spirit but of the entire earth as a body suffering a secular decline. A more sharply focused version of this image occurs in the poem "By the Earth's Corpse" (from the

same volume as "The Darkling Thrush"), in which Time and "the Lord" conduct a dialogue on the themes of guilt and repetition, while placed like mourners near "this globe, now cold / As lunar land and sea," at some future time "when flesh / And herb but fossils be, / And, all extinct, their piteous dust / Revolves obliviously. . . . "

The most highly developed vision of the earth as an organic, vaguely human being is, however, that of *The Dynasts.* A stage direction of the "Fore Scene" is justly famous for its panoramic sweep, anticipating (but still surpassing) the movement of the camera eye in epically scaled movies:

> The nether sky opens, and Europe is disclosed as a prone and emaciated figure, the Alps shaping like a backbone, and the branching mountain-chains like ribs, the peninsular plateau of Spain forming a head. . . . The point of view then sinks downwards through space, and draws near to the surface of the perturbed countries, where the peoples, distressed by events which they did not cause, are seen writhing, crawling, heaving, and vibrating in their various cities and nationalities.

With the return to this vision in the "After Scene," Europe is "beheld again as a prone and emaciated figure. . . . The lowlands look like a grey-green garment half-thrown off, and the sea around like a disturbed bed on which the figure lies." In this instance, human forms in the mass join with geographical features to create the image of a total organism: the earth itself (or its European portion) as a giant, going through the stages of awakening, struggle, and exhaustion—a composite being living out the disturbances and sufferings of humankind.

Is it this (or a related) giant who confronts the reader from the title of the opening chapter of *The Return:* "A Face on which Time makes but Little Impression"? The rhetoric of the so-called pathetic fallacy suggests that it is a creature on the scale of the earth: it "wore the appearance of an instalment of night" and, reciprocally, "the face of the heath by its mere complexion added half an hour to evening." Not only are vital reflexes, human apparel, and personal physiognomy suggested, but the sustained comparison of Egdon Heath and mankind is raised from mere analogy to essential identity:

> It was at present a place perfectly accordant with man's nature—neither ghastly, hateful, nor ugly: neither commonplace, unmeaning, nor tame; but, like man, slighted and enduring; and withal singularly colossal and mysterious in its swarthy monotony. As with some persons who have long lived apart, solitude seemed to look out of its countenance. It had a lonely face, suggesting tragical possibilities.

It is on the basis of this profound identity that the epithets used for the heath come to resonate like personal designations: "Haggard Egdon," "the untameable, Ishmaelitish thing that Egdon now was," "the people changed, yet Egdon remained." In the most pathetic of these characterizations, the place is defined in relation to other natural forces in a style usually reserved for romantic fiction: "Then Egdon was aroused to reciprocity; for the storm was its lover, and the wind its friend." But the role hardly suits a figure that has emerged as not merely humanized but on a larger-than-individual scale: "singularly colossal and mysterious in its swarthy monotony." Such a colossus can be a hero only of a special sort.

In inventing the name itself, Hardy seems to have had in mind not a place-name but a personal one. Its closest analogue is a forename: *Egbert,* from Old English *ecg* ("sword") and *bryght* ("bright")—the latter term also appearing in the chief surname used in the novel. *Egdon* would be its derivable opposite: the second syllable is equivalent to *dun,* the word used since Anglo-Saxon times to describe the natural shades of landscape, animals, and atmosphere in a dull, brown grey range. (But compare the Celtic name of Maiden Castle: *mai dun* ["strong hill"].) Etymology resolves nothing, but this name goes beyond the expansive suggestiveness of well-wrought place-names in fiction, encouraging instead the identification of a personal presence by a favored technique of characterization.

If these two processes are indeed comparable—if a somewhat amorphous terrain is presented here in the manner in which fictional characters are conventionally introduced—we shall have to revise our expectations of the role of landscape in this novel more radically than we may be prepared to do. Landscape is not satisfied to act in *The Return of the Native* as a background, with human subjects in the foreground (although some positioning of people against a background of natural elements is at work, e.g., in the chapter entitled "The Figure against the Sky"). Instead, Egdon Heath becomes one of the principal agents of the action, a protagonist in the classical sense of the dramatic actor, and probably the most memorable figure to emerge from the events. The title of the novel has been given some new turns in recent criticism, so as to widen its reference beyond the donnée of Clym's return to Wessex. If its individual implications are taken seriously, the title refers somewhat sardonically to Clym's return to the native state in the course of the action; it also suggests more broadly the heath's renewed prominence in the life of the characters and of the modern age generally. "The Return of the Native" would name, then, a story about Egdon Heath.

The operation of these narrative traits makes the term "personification" no longer adequate to describe the process by which Egdon Heath is generated by the text. When natural categories are fixed, one may speak about the ascription of human characteristics to inanimate beings or about the representation of an abstract or other impersonal entity in human terms. But Egdon is not so clear-cut: it is never given as entirely on one side of the animate/inanimate polarity before being assimilated to the other. Even in the opening chapter, the metaphoric expressions by which it is rendered human are immediately posited as literal (or as leading to literal statements about the heath's role in human psychology): "Then [in storms, etc.] it became the home of strange phantoms; and it was found to be the hitherto unrecognized original of those wild regions of obscurity which are vaguely felt to be compassing us about in midnight dreams of flight and disaster, and are never thought of after the dream till revived by scenes like this." Without drawing conclusions about Hardy's version of the unconscious, we find his prose moving from the metaphoric level (movement of storms / movement of phantoms), to statements that posit the heath as the original model of dream landscapes, to a final suggestion of its function as a permanent index of the unconscious "regions" of the mind itself. So steadily cumulative is this assimilation of the heath to the animate level that toward the close of the novel, as intensity of style mounts in tempo with intensity of action, we are prepared to take in stride such passages as this: "Skirting the pool [Eustacia] followed the path towards Rainbarrow, occasionally stumbling over twisted furze-roots, tufts of rushes, or oozing lumps of fleshy fungi, which at this season lay scattered about the heath like the rotten liver and lungs of some colossal animal." While it is Eustacia who is stumbling toward her death, it is the heath that is seen here as a dismembered giant—neither clearly human nor, as Lawrence thought, merely bestial but a "colossal animal" who is martyred and distributed in a spectacular way.

While the interconnections of the animate and the inanimate must be deduced from the rhetorical modes of the opening chapter, later passages state their inherent identity in the heath with some urgency. The chief of these occurs in the first description of Eustacia Vye:

There the form stood, motionless as the hill beneath. Above the plain rose the hill, above the hill rose the barrow, and above the barrow rose the figure. Above the figure was nothing that could be mapped elsewhere than on a celestial globe.

Such a perfect, delicate, and necessary finish did the figure give to the dark pile of hills that it seemed to be the only obvious justification of their outline. Without it, there was the dome without the lantern; with it the architectural demands of the mass were satisfied. The scene was strangely homogeneous, in that the value, the upland, the barrow, and the figure above it amounted only to unity. Looking at this or that member of the group was not observing a complete thing, but a fraction of a thing.

Hardy employs the term "organic" in the next sentence to describe the internal relations of the "entire motionless structure"; we may apply it equally to the tenor of his thinking in this passage. Although the human figure is to be regarded esthetically as a "necessary finish" and a satisfaction of an "architectural" demand, it is more fundamentally a "fraction" of a larger "unity." Nor is the heath complete without the person: it needs it as its "obvious justification," to become a "homogeneous" being in its own right. The text speaks of this organic unity of the human and the nonhuman "members" of Egdon Heath as "a thing" and elsewhere adds, "a thing majestic without severity, impressive without showiness, emphatic in its admonitions, grand in its simplicity."

Although Eustacia is most striking in her unwilling assimilation into Egdon Heath, other characters exhibit a spectrum of possible relations to it, ranging from identification to detachment. Although the gigantic "thing" takes in both human beings and the heath, there are a number of possible modes of integration, which various characters explore. The peasants live in wary observance of the land and its seasons, but their limited mentalities are none too gently satirized in Hardy's folkish chapters. The reddleman, Diggory Venn, shows himself adroit not only in the world of commercial and (eventually) erotic competition but is especially competent among the highways and byways of the heath. (It is noteworthy that he gets no particular credit for this intimacy with the heath, as measured by the conventions of heroic stature; given Hardy's view of him as an "isolated and weird character"— in the "Author's Note" of 1912—he is scarcely ennobled by his numerous displays of omnicompetence.) It is Clym who displays the most complex relation to the heath, being the one who exercises a series of considered choices in the matter. In his first characterization, his constitution or generation

by the place is stressed: "If any one knew the heath well it was Clym. He was permeated with its scenes, with its substance, and with its odours. He might be said to be its product." At the end of his series of ideological shifts and personal misfortunes, he stands before the heath in an alien position, as of one face impervious to another: ". . . there was only the imperturbable countenance of the heath, which, having defied the cataclysmal onsets of centuries, reduced to insignificance by its seamed and antique features the wildest turmoil of a single man." But the most extreme separation from the heath—indistinguishable from a kind of rationalistic stupidity—is represented by the pragmatic objectivity of Thomasin Yeobright: ". . . Egdon in the mass was no monster whatever, but impersonal open ground. Her fears of the place were rational, her dislikes of its worst moods reasonable."

Despite their differences, the characters have a common connection with the heath, a unity of fate that is consistently figured in allusions to Prometheus: "Every night [the heath's] Titanic form seemed to await something; but it had waited thus, unmoved, during so many centuries, through the crises of so many things, that it could only be imagined to await one last crisis—the final overthrow." The iconography of Prometheus chained to a mountain in the Caucasus is strikingly transmuted in this and similar passages: the *scene* of suffering becomes the sufferer (Egdon is not Caucasian but Titanic), while at least part of the demigod's character is ascribed to the land itself in its "unmoved" martyrdom. Yet the myth's primary orientation toward apocalypse (the final overthrow of Zeus) is, as we shall see, fully employed in *The Return*.

The heath's Promethean, long-suffering form of resistance is picked up in the characterization of the human actors but is resourcefully applied as a differentiating factor. The peasants' lighting of fires to celebrate Guy Fawkes Day, although localized as a modern British survival of the ritual death and rebirth of the year, is seen as the expression of a universal need: "Moreover to light a fire is the instinctive and resistant act of man when, at the winter ingress, the curfew is sounded throughout Nature. It indicates a spontaneous, Promethean rebelliousness against the fiat that this recurrent season shall bring foul times, cold darkness, misery and death. Black chaos comes, and the fettered gods of the earth say, Let there be light." Here humans, heath, and Titans are seen on the same side, resisting—or at least protesting—an imposition from without, the fiat of a being or realm

The novel's setting reflects Hardy's memories of Egdon Heath, an expanse of English heathland like that pictured above.

representing black chaos, winter, and death. Humanity joins with the land itself in "Promethean rebelliousness," and it is with one voice that they register their counterfiat; theirs is the voice of the "fettered gods" or Titans, which proclaims light—a biblical equivalent for the Promethean fire that is the subject of this passage.

The chief characters are, however, subtly distinguished in their articulations of this rebellion and thus in their associations with the band of "fettered gods." Eustacia is described from the first in terms derived from the preceding passage: "Egdon was her Hades, and since coming there she had imbibed much of what was dark in its tone, though inwardly and eternally unreconciled thereto. Her appearance accorded well with this smouldering rebelliousness. . . . A true Tartarean dignity sat upon her brow . . ." The term found in both passages, "rebelliousness," is linked to its consequences of banishment or living burial, whether of humans in Hades or of Titans in Tartarus (the variability of mythological traditions is exploited here to make these roughly equivalent terms for confinement in the earth). It is notable that this passage begins by emphasizing Eustacia's unwilling bondage in Egdon, the setting of her unsatisfactory station in life, but it gradually identifies her with the heath insofar as

the latter, too, is unreconciled to its bound condition under the fiat of the ruling gods.

Precisely the opposite shift occurs in the course of Clym's characterization: beginning as one fully at home on the heath—"its product"—he becomes so thoroughly acclimated in his return to the soil that he renounces rebelliousness: "Now, don't you suppose, my inexperienced girl, that I cannot rebel, in high Promethean fashion, against the gods and fate as well as you. I have felt more steam and smoke of that sort than you have ever heard of. But the more I see of life the more do I perceive that there is nothing particularly great in its greatest walks, and therefore nothing particularly small in mine of furzecutting." Clym's liberal renunciation of the Promethean stance is part of an explicit cultural theme in the novel, concerned with the vulnerability of the modern mind by virtue of its skeptical intelligence, its loss of traditional, organizing mythologies (a loss and a vulnerability in which Hardy felt himself implicated). But Clym's career also involves a break with the creaturely tendency to rebellion against earthbound suffering, a separation from the Titanic "fettered gods" with whom Eustacia, involuntarily, associates herself. And it is this loss of Promethean vision that is his true undoing, for he sees "nothing particularly great in

> A long train of disillusive centuries have shown the defects of natural law and the quandary in which their operation has placed man. Life causes one to set aside the vision of what ought to be and induces a listless making the best of the world as it is."

[life's] greatest walks" or, by the same token, in the heath's.

Source: Avrom Fleishman, "The Buried Giant of Egdon Heath: An Archeology of Folklore in *The Return of the Native,*" in *Fiction and the Ways of Knowing: Essays on British Novelists,* University of Texas Press, 1978, pp. 110–22.

Harvey Curtis Webster

In the following excerpt Webster suggests that according to Hardy, human effort, governed by natural law in a "Chance-guided universe," goes "from one mistake to another," and this gives the novel its pessimistic and bleak outlook.

The Return of the Native is the most pessimistic of [Hardy's] early novels. From the first description of Egdon Heath until the close of the story, this dreary and unfertile waste seems to symbolize the indifference with which Nature views the pathetic fate of human beings. Occasionally the reader is likely to look upon the long-enduring barrenness and apparent purposelessness of the heath as a sign of its kinship to man, to feel that it is like man, slighted and enduring. More frequently, its somber beauty, which, Hardy tells us, is the only kind of beauty that thinking mankind can any longer appreciate, reminds us that man is of no more significance than an insect against its far-extending barrenness. It is the unsympathetic background for the human scene. What happens to man is not its concern. Like the forces of Nature, it has participated passively in man's slow and unhappy progress through disillusive centuries, unconcerned with the joys or sorrows of petty humankind.

What the dreary atmosphere of Egdon Heath makes us feel, the author's interpolations emphasize. The modern facial expression portrays a "view of life as a thing to be put up with." A long train of disillusive centuries have shown the defects of natural law and the quandary in which their operation has placed man. Life causes one to set aside the vision of what ought to be and induces a listless making the best of the world as it is.

More than in any other Hardy novel, we feel the power of the forces that control man's destiny. Heartless Circumstance, this time *not* viewed as an environment that can be contended against, has placed Eustacia Vye in a situation in which her gifts are a plague rather than a blessing. Natural law leads man from one mistake to another. Chance, in the shape of accident and coincidence, joins itself with these other unsympathetic powers to assure man's unhappiness. . . . Undoubtedly Hardy believes that there is nothing actively malign in Egdon Heath, in natural law, or in the play of Circumstance or accident; but the very indifference of these forces to the fate of human beings results in such unhappiness that we are likely to assume that sinister gods control the action.

Against the somber atmosphere of an indifferent and Chance-guided universe, the characters move in accordance with natural law. Eustacia's physical attractiveness compels the love of Charley, Clym, and Wildeve. By a similar force Eustacia is drawn to Wildeve and Clym. None of them is fitted for each other, but their imaginations cause them to believe that their ideas of each other are real. Disillusionment and pain result.

Source: Harvey Curtis Webster, in *On a Darkling Plain: The Art and Thought of Thomas Hardy,* University of Chicago Press, 1947, pp. 120–21.

Joseph Warren Beach

In the following excerpt, Beach emphasizes the action and reaction ("suggestive of physics and dynamics") of the feelings of Hardy's characters, and the heath as representative of natural forces that are indifferent or antagonistic to human will.

[With] *The Return of the Native,* Hardy has taken up a theme which involves a clear-cut issue in the minds of the leading characters, and especially in the mind of Eustacia, which is the main stage of the drama. It is her stifled longing for spiritual expansion which leads her to play with the love of Wildeve, which causes her later to throw him over for the greater promise of Clym, which leads her back again to Wildeve, and at last—with the loss of all hope—to suicide. In every case it requires but the smallest outlay of incident to provoke the most lively play of feeling; and the play of feeling—the opposition of desires—is embodied here, in true dramatic fashion, in talk rather than in acts. It takes nothing more than the return of Thomasin from town unwed to set going the whole series of dialogues which make up the substance of the first book, dialogues in which Wildeve and Mrs. Yeobright, Venn and Eustacia, Eustacia and Wildeve do nothing more than fence with one another, each maneuvering for position in a breathless game of well-matched antagonists. These are scenes in the true dramatic sense, not in the popular sense that calls for violence and surprising action.

In the third book the main thing that happens is a quarrel between Clym and his mother over Eustacia. The wedding itself is not presented, having no dramatic value. The dramatic value of the book is indicated in its caption, "The Fascination," the drama lying in the resistless attraction to one another of two persons so far apart in mind.

Never before in Hardy had the machinery of action been so masked and subordinated. Never again perhaps was it to occupy a place of so little prominence in his work. It is only once or twice in Meredith, and more generally in the later novels of James, that we find so great a volume of emotional energy released by events of so little objective importance. Only in them is found a greater economy of incident; and many more readers will testify to the dramatic intensity of *The Native* than to that of *The Egoist* or *The Golden Bowl.*

The whole course of the story was conceived by the author in terms suggestive of physics and dynamics. Each step in the plot represents the balance and reaction of forces expressible almost in algebraic formulas. Many readers have been impressed with the strong scientific coloring of Hardy's mind: with his tendency to view both external nature and the human heart with the sharpness and hard precision of a naturalist, and to record the phenomena observed with some of the abstractness of the summarizing philosopher.

The division of a novel into parts is always a significant indication of an author's interest in the logical massing of his material, in the larger architectonics of his work. It is very little used by novelists like Dickens; very much used by novelists like George Eliot, Victor Hugo, Henry James, and . . . Mr. Walpole. It generally implies a bias for the "dramatic," in so far as it involves the grouping of the subject-matter around certain characters or

> **The division of a novel into parts is always a significant indication of an author's interest in the logical massing of his material, in the larger architectonics of his work."**

great moments in the action, as that of a play is grouped in the several acts. In *The Native* this is especially notable.

These five books are like the five acts of a classic play. And in each book the scenes are largely grouped around certain points in time so as to suggest the classic continuity within the several acts.

What we are concerned with here is the unity of tone—the steadiness with which the heath makes us feel its dark and overshadowing presence, so that men and women are but slight figures in a giant landscape, the insect-fauna of its somber flora. Mr. Hardy was bold enough to begin this grave history with an entire chapter devoted to a description of the heath at twilight; and his choice of a title for the second chapter but serves to signalize the littleness and frailty of man upon the great stage of inhospitable nature: "Humanity appears upon the scene, hand in hand with trouble." It is very quietly and without word or gesture that humanity makes its appearance, like a slow-moving shadow.

It is thus that Egdon takes its place as the dominating force of the tragedy, as well as its appropriate and impressive setting. So that the unity of place, in itself an artistic value, is but the counterpart of a unity of action rooted and bedded in a precious oneness of theme. Instead of being, as in *Far from the Madding Crowd,* brought together arbitrarily to make out the prescribed materials of a novel, plot and setting here are one, growing equally and simultaneously out of the dramatic idea expressed in the title. For the first—and almost for the last—time in the work of Hardy, the discriminating reader is delighted with the complete absence of mechanical contrivance. Contrivance there is as never before in his work, the loving contrivance of an artist bent on making everything right in an orderly composition; the long-range contrivance of an architect concerned to have every part in place in an edifice that shall stand well based and well proportioned, with meaning in every line.

The determinist may be equally impressed with the helplessness of man in the grip of strange forces, physical and psychical. But he is distinguished from the fatalist by his concern with the causes that are the links in the chain of necessity. Determinism is the scientific counterpart of fatalism, and throws more light on destiny by virtue of its diligence in the searching out of natural law. Mr. Hardy is rather a determinist than a fatalist. When he speaks most directly and unmistakably for himself, it is to insist on the universal working of the laws of cause and effect.

The point in which determinism and fatalism agree is the helplessness of the individual will against the will in things. Only the determinist conceives the will in things as the sum of the natural forces with which we have to cope, whereas the fatalist tends to a more religious interpretation of that will as truly and literally a *will,* an arbitrary power, a personal force like our own. Sometimes Mr. Hardy allows his characters the bitter comfort of that personal interpretation.

What gives rise to such notions is the ironic discrepancy between what we seek and what we secure, between what we do and what follows from it. We have control of so very few of the factors that go to determine our fortunes that we can hardly help imagining behind the scene a capricious and malignant contriver of contretemps.

Source: Joseph Warren Beach, in *The Technique of Thomas Hardy,* University of Chicago Press, 1922, pp. 93–4, 96–7, 101, 105, 228–9.

Sources

Adams, Francis, Review of *Tess of the D'Urbervilles,* in *The Fortnightly Review,* Vol. LII, No. CCVII, July 1891, pp. 19–22.

Carpenter, Richard, *Thomas Hardy,* Twayne Publishers, Boston, 1964.

Eliot, T. S., *After Strange Gods: A Primer of Modern Heresy,* Harcourt & Brace, 1934.

Hawkins, Desmond, "The Native Returns 1876–1878," Barnes & Noble Books, 1976, p. 76.

Henley, W. E., Review, in *The Academy,* Vol. XIV, No. 343, November 30, 1878, p. 517.

Page, Norman O., "The Return of the Native," in *Reference Guide to English Literature,* edited by D. L. Kirkpatrick, St. James Press, 1991.

Review, in *The Athenaeum,* November 23, 1878, p. 654.

Taylor, Richard, "Thomas Hardy: A Reader's Guide," in *Thomas Hardy: The Writer and His Background,* St. Martin's Press, 1980, pp. 219–58.

For Further Study

Brooks, Jean R., "*The Return of the Native:* A Novel of Environment," in *Modern Critical Views: Thomas Hardy,* edited by Harold Bloom, Chelsea House, 1987, pp. 55–72.
   Analyzes the novel's most conspicuous literary theme.

Davidson, Donald, "The Traditional Basis of Thomas Hardy's Fiction," in *Hardy: A Collection of Critical Essays,* edited by Albert J. Guerard, Prentice-Hall, 1963, pp. 10–23.
   Identifies elements of the oral tradition of rural England in *The Return of the Native* and other works.

Hands, Timothy, "'Yea, Great and Good, Thee, Thee we hail': Hardy and the Ideas of his Time," in *Thomas Hardy,* St. Martin's Press, 1995.
   Traces the philosophical movements of the late nineteenth century and evaluates their influences in Hardy's works.

Hawkins, Desmond, *Hardy the Novelist,* David & Charles, 1965.
   This respected analysis offers a strong background to students who are becoming acquainted with Hardy's fiction.

Hillis Miller, J., "The Dance of Desire," in *Thomas Hardy: Distance and Desire,* The Belknap Press of Harvard University Press, 1970, pp. 144–75.
   Considers the themes of desire and longing in Hardy's novel.

Hornback, Bert G., *The Metaphor of Chance: Vision and Technique in the Work of Thomas Hardy,* Ohio University Press, 1971.
   Exploration of Hardy's narrative technique.

Mickelson, Anne Z., "The Marriage Trap," in *Thomas Hardy's Women and Men: The Defeat of Nature,* The Scarecrow Press, Inc., 1976.
   A feminist reading of Eustacia Vye.

Sumner, Rosemary, *Thomas Hardy: Psychological Novelist,* St. Martin's Press, 1981.
   Discusses the treatment of psychological issues in Hardy's work.

A Room with a View

E. M. Forster
1908

An essayist, lecturer, tutor to the working class, and travel guide, Edward Morgan Forster is recognized chiefly for his five novels published up to 1924. For those works, Forster has been proclaimed one of the greatest novelists of the twentieth century though he has no school of followers or even an obvious apostle. Instead, Forster holds his position of influence on the novel in solitude. Though Forster would not approve of his works being adapted to film, a renewed appreciation of Forster in the late twentieth century coincided with film adaptations of his works.

Forster's belief in personal relationships and his experience as a globetrotter allowed him to be a staunch advocate of multiculturalism long before the term came into academic vogue. His stories and writings are rife with a permissive transgression of social, racial, sexual, and cultural strictures. Forster's egalitarianism found a large audience during a time when his intellectual contemporaries were elitist, conservative, and still trying to transition from Victorian to Modern England.

Forster contributes to this transition with his third novel, *Room with a View*, which he started in 1902 but did not publish until 1908. In this novel, Lucy finds completeness in an ending of unabashed happiness after journeying through a story of textbook comic structure. She has found love, adulthood, and happiness—all things lacking in the beginning. The work celebrates youth, nature, and the comic or Greek spirit with Lucy a light that illuminates a path for both men and women to follow.

E. M. Forster

Lucy, with her husband, takes the best of radical politics and Victorian society and makes a place of equanimity.

Author Biography

Forster, born in London on January 1, 1879, was raised by his mother, Alice Clara Whichelo Forster (known as Lily), two aunts, and a grandmother. His father, an architect named Edmund Morgan, died of consumption in 1880. Forster spent a happy childhood at Rooksnest, a house in Hertfordshire his mother rented, which provided the material for Forster's 1910 novel *Howards End.* Boarding school, however, was a misery. In 1890, Forster attended Kent House, a prep school in Eastbourne, but harassment led to his transfer to The Grange. When that proved intolerable, Lily moved to Tonbridge in 1893 and Forster became a day boy at Tonbridge School, where he finished prep school. While attending Tonbridge, Forster had his first taste of travel when he joined his mother on a tour of churches in 1895.

Marianne Thornton, a great-aunt, bequeathed Forster monetary independence. He used some of this money, beginning in 1897, to attend King's College, Cambridge. Forster thrived in the liberating atmosphere of the university where he belonged to the Cambridge Conversazione Society, also known as the Apostles. Among these friends, Forster learned that being homosexual was not abnormal. After a period of travel, Forster joined his old friends for avant-garde discussions as a member of the Bloomsbury Group. At school, he achieved an unsatisfactory second-class honors degree in classics followed by one of the same rank in history. He was awarded an M.A. in 1910.

Disappointed by his academic rank, Forster accepted his mother's plan to delay the future by travelling. In Italy, their stay in a Florentine pension inspired Forster to begin work, in 1902, on the "Lucy" novel, which would eventually become *A Room with a View.* He returned to England briefly before he began a life abroad with a journey to Greece in 1903. This expedition was followed by travels to Germany, South Africa, and the United States. Forster's visits to India resulted in several works, most notably a 1924 novel, *A Passage to India.*

During World War I, Forster volunteered as a searcher for the Red Cross in Egypt. He interviewed convalescent soldiers in order to gain information about missing persons. While in Egypt, Forster made a name for himself as an essayist and travel writer under the pseudonym Pharos (for the ancient lighthouse). These writings gave way to *Alexandria: A History and a Guide,* followed by a book that collected essays from the period.

At the age of forty-six, Forster separated from his mother and rented a flat of his own in London. He began a relationship with Robert Buckingham which became a lasting friendship when Robert married in 1931. For the next thirty-nine years, Forster remained a respected essayist and literary critic. After his death June 7, 1970, from a series of strokes, *Maurice,* a largely autobiographical novel whose protagonist grapples with the trials of being gay, was published in accordance with Forster's will. A seventh novel that Forster never completed, *Arctic Summer,* was published in 1980.

Plot Summary

Italy

When Lucy Honeychurch and Charlotte Bartlett arrive at the Bertolini Pension, the women are upset that their rooms view a courtyard instead of the promised view of Florence. An uncouth man, Mr. Emerson, offers to swap rooms but Charlotte refuses. Clergyman Beebe, however, rescues the situation and the swap takes place. Lucy, a young woman in Italy for the first time, wants to take in all the sights but is slowed down by Charlotte, her spinsterly chaperone. Fortunately, another English tourist, Miss Lavish, offers to take her to Santa Croce. After an exciting walk, Miss Lavish abandons Lucy who enters the church alone.

Since Miss Lavish kept the guidebook, Lucy finds herself "in Santa Croce with No Baedeker." She has no choice but to tour the church in remembrance of what she has read. By accident, Lucy meets the Emersons, who show her how to enjoy the church with their own unfiltered senses. Lucy insists on points the book had highlighted but "the pernicious charm of Italy worked on her, and, instead of acquiring information, she began to be happy." While his son, George, is at a distance, Mr. Emerson proposes that Lucy take an interest in him. Despite this insult, Mr. Emerson helps her to not have the proper aesthetic experience. Rather, she is "inflated spiritually," "thoroughly happy, and having a splendid time."

Invigorated by a rainy afternoon spent playing the piano, Lucy avoids being ensnared by Pension gossip with Beebe and Miss Catherine Alan and walks into the now sunny Florence. After purchasing some photos of famous paintings, Lucy witnesses passion boil over into murder in the Piazza della Signoria. As an Italian is knifed, he looks to Lucy and opens his mouth as if to give a message "and a stream of red came out." Lucy faints and her pictures are soiled with blood. George, who happens to be in the Piazza, rescues Lucy and tosses the besmirched photos into the River Arno. Art has met life and "something happen[ed] to the living: they had come to a situation where character tells, and where Childhood enters upon the branching paths of Youth." While they recover, they watch the River Arno.

Lucy's confrontation with reality disables any chance of a "return to the old life!" Fearful of her feelings for George, she shops with Charlotte the next day instead of joining a tourist excursion. They run into Miss Lavish in the Piazza trying to salvage the murder scene for use in her novel. Lucy and Charlotte leave her and bump into Mr. Eager, who invites them on a drive—a treat he reserves for the most deserving—to view Fiesole. Mr. Beebe manages to be included on the trip but fails to consult with Mr. Eager before doubling the party to include

the undeserving. Despite careful planning, Lucy finds herself in a carriage with Mr. Eager and the two people he disapproves of the most: Mr. Emerson, for killing his wife, and Miss Lavish, "a shoddy lady writer."

Mr. Eager proposes that they discover the very spot where Alessio Baldovinetti made his Tuscan landscapes. They go to the bluff with this in mind but instead of rediscovery, Lucy falls into a bed of violets and George—enraptured by the beauty of the scenery and the lovely woman lying in flowers before him—imprudently kisses Lucy. This leads Charlotte into paranoid delusions that Lucy will be exposed to others as the beloved of George, a man of the lower class who did not have such permission.

The party returns to Florence during a storm and whatever "game" was being played on the hillside has been "lost." A Miltonic lightning bolt seals off the possibility of return to the garden where play and liberty were possible. Charlotte, who witnessed the kiss, ponders over who else knows. George chooses to remain in nature, and walks back. The storm's violence allows the party one brief moment of lost self-control but then they recover their roles. Charlotte struggles to recover Lucy from being like the Emersons; Lucy wants "to be truthful."

Worried that George may strike again, Charlotte packs Lucy off to Rome where they have a miserable time with the Vyse family. Cecil Vyse, induced to take the two women to St. Peter's, notices Lucy as more than a commonplace English tourist. He sees that Italy has given her "light" and "shadow" and made her a "woman of Leonardo," a body for intellectual admiration, not engagement. Cecil wants to purchase her.

England

Back at Windy Corner in England, Lucy accepts Cecil as her "fiasco" and society is pleased with the impending match. Believing he has purchased Lucy, Cecil considers how to finish Lucy's education while he dreams of ways to redecorate the drawing-room at Windy Corner as "more distinctive." Lucy's brother, Freddy, and Beebe are inwardly disappointed; even Mrs. Honeychurch shows signs of disillusionment with Cecil, her dream son-in-law. This results from his reaction to suffering through an announcement party. He hypothesizes that engagements should be private—like a business transaction. In the ensuing discussion, Lucy shows her brain and pains Cecil: he wants to look at his Leonardo, not see her in moral judgment amongst Michelangelo's figures in the Sistine Chapel.

Walking home, the party runs into Sir Harry Otway, who has cottages to rent. After a discussion of the ramifications of the cottages, Cecil disapproves of the knight alone to Lucy, who begins to wonder if anything from her hometown can meet with Cecil's approval. Chiding her for always leading him on the road, the lovers take the path through the woods. As they near Windy Corner, Cecil attempts to be romantic and asks Lucy if he might kiss her but "passion should believe itself irresistible." Their kiss proves to be a failure. Strangely, it leads Lucy to pronounce the name Emerson.

In an attempt to pull a prank on the knight, Cecil arranges for the Emersons—a pair he meets mispronouncing names in the art galleries in London—to take a cottage on his recommendation. This angers Lucy, who had been trying to bring Miss Alans to the same cottage. As the Emersons arrive, Lucy and Cecil leave to visit Mrs. Vyse in London. There, Lucy glimpses her future life of playing piano for grandchildren. Mrs. Vyse comforts her when she awakes from a nightmare about a kiss.

Back at Windy Corner, Lucy, Cecil, and Mrs. Honeychurch are on their way to visit a neighbor when they run into Freddy, George, and Beebe in the midst of bathing in the Sacred Lake. Instead of a proper social encounter with George, for which Lucy had spent hours rehearsing, Lucy bows to him while he is half-naked. She finds him beautiful and clearly more her type than the contracted Vyse.

During a dinner party, Vyse refuses to play tennis and Lucy seizes on the refusal as indicative of Vyse generally and breaks off the engagement. What really set her off, however, was Cecil's insistent reading from a romance novel written by Miss Lavish and another uninvited kiss from George. The novel happens to have a scene in it made up of information that Charlotte provided about the kiss at Fiesole. Having been betrayed by Charlotte, Lucy plays the piano as she thinks about her next step.

Back to Italy

Lucy decides to catch up with Miss Alans in Greece. Tickets in hand, Lucy encounters Mr. Emerson in Beebe's rectory and he brings her to her senses. Lucy extracts herself from the muddle she has created and accepts union with George. They return to the Pension in Florence to enjoy a room with a view.

Characters

The Miss Alans

Miss Theresa and Miss Catherine Alan are normally referred to as "the Miss Alans who stood for good breeding." They are yet another example of what Lucy might become by following Charlotte. They have chosen independence but within the confines of society's rules. They can remain single but they gain little in doing so. They are dull people who see the world as a book. They travel to read the great book and learn about life but they cannot live for themselves. They cannot be passionate living people. They must be staid, demure, and carry their guidebooks. They are part of the Army of Darkness.

Lucy is actually en route to join them when she confronts Mr. Emerson. At this moment, the Greek spirit, in the form of life with George, can be hers but she thinks she wants to study past Greek civilization. Fortunately, she chooses to live life now.

Charlotte Bartlett

Cousin Charlotte is not as rich as Lucy and travels with monetary help from Lucy's mother. In return for this help, Charlotte tries to impart her wisdom to Lucy by acting as chaperone. Instead, she comes off as a self-serving spinster who loves to play the role of "prematurely aged martyr." Charlotte is also a prude, absurdly so. Charlotte successfully manipulates Lucy into a successful match with Cecil. When this proves obviously stifling to her protégé, Charlotte orchestrates an escape route in the form of independence and travel to Greece. The Comic Muse has the last laugh, however, and Charlotte's visit to church allows Lucy to converse with Mr. Emerson who convinces her to marry George. The happy couple wonder whether Charlotte intended the fortuitous meeting.

Arthur Beebe

At first appearance, Beebe seems to be a tolerant man hoping to see Lucy blossom in all the glory she can possibly attain as a young woman. Through the course of the novel, however, Beebe reveals that he wants Lucy to become a gothic statue—celibate, religious, and proper. Mr. Beebe thinks people are "better detached." As his name suggests, Beebe is a drone worker for the hive. He is a clergyman who ministers to the needs of the hive's proper functioning. Lucy, for Beebe, is a problem.

Mr. Beebe has a theory about Lucy which he shares with Cecil while he doesn't know of the couple's engagement. Some day, Beebe thinks, Lucy's musical ability will merge with her quiet living. Then she will be both "heroically good, heroically bad." He pictures her in his diary as a kite whose string is held by Miss Bartlett. In the next picture of the Lucy series, the string breaks. Mr. Beebe, therefore, is disappointed when he hears that Lucy is to marry Cecil. In the end, when he hears that Lucy loves George, Beebe shows her a genuine concern for the first time. However, his feelings about the idea of Lucy's life with George remain ambiguous; he only wants to help Lucy.

Minnie Beebe

Mr. Beebe has taken charge of the education of his niece, Minnie. The little girl looks to Lucy as a role model and shows that she has Emersonian potential when she insists on sitting outside at the pub.

Cuthbert Eager

Mr. Eager serves as chaplain to the English expatriates living around Florence as well as to the tourists. However, he helps to keep the two groups separate. The expatriates jealously guard their knowledge and access to the real Florence from the ignorant tourists with their Baedekers. Every so often, a tourist will appear in Florence who is above-average. Only such select people are taken by Mr. Eager to the expatriate group. Lucy receives such an invitation. However, the inclusion of others on the outing by Mr. Beebe dissuades Mr. Eager from taking her to "tea at a Renaissance villa."

George Emerson

The younger Emerson, George, "has a view too." Though freed of the molds of religion by his father's enlightened scheme of education, George is a classic melancholic depressed by too much knowledge. Mr. Beebe reveals several of the works George has imbibed—books that easily lead one to a despondent view of life. Reflecting the Freudian airs of the time, George's melancholia can be cured by sex. Happily, Mr. Emerson sees very quickly, Lucy's problem can also be solved by sex. The two young people are introduced and love takes over.

George scoffs at a society that wants to bar him from kissing a woman when he wants to and running through suburbia naked. "He had sighed among the tombs at Santa Croce because things wouldn't fit; . . . after the death of that obscure Italian he had leant over the parapet by the Arno and

Media Adaptations

- In 1950, Stephen Tait and Kenneth Allcott adapted *A Room with a View* to the stage. The play was produced in Cambridge and published by Edward Arnold in 1951.

- Cinecom released a film adaptation of *A Room with a View* produced by Merchant-Ivory Productions in 1986. Using an adaptation by Ruth Prawer Jhabvala, James Ivory directed the film. Nominated for eight Academy Awards, the film won three: for screenplay, costume design, and set design. The cast included the notable Daniel Day-Lewis (Cecil), Helena Bonham Carter (Lucy), and Julian Sands (George).

said to [Lucy]: "I shall want to live, I tell you." Playing tennis he shows that he wants to live and in doing so seems to shine like the sun. By the end of the novel, George and Lucy will, like Phaeton and Phoebus, show that life must be lived in the fullness of the moment.

Mr. Emerson

Mr. Emerson has a distinct view which frees him from answering to a specific social order or mechanic clique. Mr. Emerson is a man of the Enlightenment who values experience and science and, in his thoughts about education, conjures Jean-Jacques Rousseau. Taken together, Mr. Emerson—in comic theory terms—is the wise elder who comes off as an angry old man. He views his purpose in life as that of a teacher—he wants to free the minds of the young so they will make decisions and personal philosophies based on experience, not the dictates of society. He reveals this in his encounter with the child in Santa Croce. Mr. Emerson is horrified that a child plays in the dark of a church instead of running around in the sunshine. Mr. Emerson "is kind to people because he loves them." Such honesty horrifies members of society who are accustomed to the awful machinations of women like Charlotte and men like Cecil.

Mr. Emerson looms large in the novel, for his singular gesture of room-swapping disrupts the ritual of society beyond recovery. The Emersons have the rooms with a view—they can see the beauty of Italy and the role of passion in life. By giving his room to Lucy, Mr. Emerson lets her taste this view—a view she will come to adopt as her own. His reasons for doing so allow a discussion of the assumptions underlying the view held by society—thus, on the matters of religion, gender, education, art, and music, Mr. Emerson shows Lucy that there are alternatives.

Freddy Honeychurch

As with Lucy, society assumes that Freddy will take his rightful place and become Lord of Windy Corner. Charlotte, in Part I, presents Freddy as the chivalrous type who would defend his sister's honor against any who might dare sully it. However, Freddy fails at chivalrous calculating. Thus, in his amusement over Cecil's medieval request for his sister's hand, he replies rashly; "Take her or leave her; it's no business of mine!" But Freddy does not pose such thoughts intellectually—Freddy acts in the heat of the moment. Freddy embodies the comic spirit—he is a "seize the day" type of character. His response to Cecil and other social blunders indicate this. While Mr. Beebe theorizes the Garden of Eden, Freddy asks, "what about this bathe?" Enough talk, says Freddy, let's have fun.

Still, Freddy tries to gain an education in manners though he merely acquires bruises. His endless self-consciousness about the way in which he handled Cecil pains him. Freddy doesn't like Cecil but he adores his sister. He tries to emulate Cecil once he knows him but George disrupts Freddy's education. George also encourages Freddy's natural philosophy. Freddy believes in the notion of "freedom of the individual"—so long as nobody else is hurt.

Lucy Honeychurch

Lucy, the protagonist, is from a middle-class family accidentally brought up in society through association with bluebloods. Her coming of age involves an achievement of wisdom, or view, of life. In the process, she unsuccessfully attempts to mold herself into a proper woman to please her mother, her teacher (Charlotte), and her fairy-tale suitor (Cecil). Within this route, she might have emulated the Miss Alans who represent a kind of feminine freedom within the rules of Cecil's world. Instead, she becomes "a rebel who desired, not a wider dwelling-room, but equality beside the man she loved." Her decision costs her to "break the whole of life." By accomplishing such destruction and deriving genuine happiness, she becomes a beacon to others; she shows that women can have a view alongside a man.

Lucy's name announces her allegorical status. Her name comes from the Latin word for light. Throughout the novel Lucy cannot help but love light (especially sunlight), nature, and views of pretty scenes. However, the world which longs to possess her is the "army of darkness." There, bourgeois rules, fashion, and rooms are the views that must be enjoyed. Such a life of shadows does not accommodate members of the light. Lucy's challenge in the novel is to stay true to herself and have a clear view or be a proper woman and be snuffed out. Throughout the work, Lucy's journey toward her true nature as a light is revealed in the degree to which she stands in the shadows. Her final epiphany, of course, finds her fumbling in the dark before Mr. Emerson. This darkest and most trying of hours gives way to the brilliance of happiness with George.

Mrs. Honeychurch

Widowed mother of Lucy and Freddy, Mrs. Honeychurch is mistress of Windy Corner. The house was a speculative venture on the part of her husband, an honest solicitor, but its early existence in what was becoming a suburb of London made the newly arrived aristocracy regard the Honeychurches as old blood. By the time they learned of the error, it was too late and the middle-class family had been raised to the upper class.

Mrs. Honeychurch is an antifeminist who mistrusts passion. Despite being in charge of her own household, she glories in doing what she can to uphold traditional gender roles. She gets worked up about women who do not take up their proper place, saying "beware of women altogether"—especially women writers. She compliments men as embodiments of their chivalrous role. Aware of the change that occurs in Lucy around music, Mrs. Honeychurch hopes Lucy will "never live a duet."

Eleanor Lavish

The stock phrase "Miss Lavish is so original" is used several times to describe this representative of early-twentieth-century liberated woman. Society members perceive her as being a radical, wise woman of the world and they tolerate her as such. This tolerance and encouragement symbolize the traditional ability of the upper classes to purchase and enjoy the superficially subversive artists, artwork, or person. Miss Lavish, in a way, plays the role of fool. She may appear to understand how lifeless society is but she can't bear to leave the courtroom. She remains the clown, not a spout of wisdom, because she doesn't care about others. Mr. Emerson, her opposite, does care and does succeed in saving a soul from society's vise.

As a novelist, Miss Lavish mirrors Forster. Her novel about an Italian romance uses Lucy as inspirational material. The book should entrap Lucy in the "army of darkness" but the opposite happens. Lucy sees herself incompletely in that artwork and sets about finishing her creation of herself.

Harry Otway

A member of the local aristocracy in Sussex and a friend of the Honeychurch family, Sir Harry Otway has recently purchased the Cissie and Albert cottages from Mr. Flack. These two cottages, to many in the area, have ruined the traditional main street. In late-twentieth-century parlance, the cottages are sprawl constructions that are hurriedly built without regard to the established aesthetic. Otway's inability to prevent their construction brought him much criticism from his peers. He now hopes to assuage the predicament by finding good tenants. Proper, in this case, is homogenous. Otway hopes to find a certain tenant with the right class, race, and ethnic identities. Such screening will become a mainstay of suburbs as they try to keep out blacks in the course of the twentieth century. In terms of the novel, Otway represents another failure of an otherwise likable person to keep pace with the times. Significantly, it is Cecil who "helps" him complete the search.

Phaethon

Phaethon, in Greek mythology, was allowed by his father, Helios, to drive the sun chariot for a day. Unable to control the horses, the chariot began to burn the earth until Zeus' thunderbolt knocked Phaethon into the river Po. He is the mythological counterpart to George, a railroad worker, who will succeed in driving a new chariot in a new way.

Phoebe

The driver of the carriage on the outing to Fiesole begs permission to pick up his "sister." As it turns out, Phoebe is his girlfriend and they proceed to behave as young lovers, right under Mr. Eager's nose. Her name conjures the Titan daughter of Uranus and Gaea in Greek mythology who signifies brightness and the moon. Thus, she is a symbol of femininity and of the passion of the night with all the mystery such symbolism affords. Phoebe is Lucy's counterpart; Lucy becomes a beacon for others to follow when escaping from the "army of darkness."

Cecil Vyse

"Appearing late in the story, Cecil . . . was medieval. Like a Gothic statue. [Whose] head . . . was tilted a little higher than the usual level of vision, he resembled those fastidious saints who guard the portals of a French cathedral." More importantly, Cecil represents masculine sexuality as seated in Rome to oppose the passionate sexuality represented by George in Renaissance Florence. Rome, as seat of the Pope, represents the heart of Europe's dark medieval traditions within the universe of Forster's novel. As a representative of the gothic, Cecil invokes the traditions of chivalry, celibacy, rules, sins, and the stringent attitudes that allowed witches to be burned—misogynistic and fearful of bodily passion. Cecil is a Victorian mother's dream and he has thrice asked Lucy for her hand in marriage. Lucy does say yes, on the very day in fact that Sir Harry Otway finds tenants for his rental property. Cecil makes this connection and it is appropriate because Cecil views relationships in feudal terms. For Cecil, Lucy is an artwork whose possession will aggrandize his self-worth.

Mrs. Vyse

Cecil's mother represents the crushed light that Lucy might become. "Mrs. Vyse was a nice woman, but her personality, like many another's had been swamped by London . . . the too vast orb of fate had crushed her." She, unabashedly, reveals the intentions of the society people arrayed against the Emersons' and Lucy's natural inclinations. To Cecil she orders, "make her one of us." As a woman of society, her judgment on whether a person will "do" is sacrosanct and Lucy steadily wins her approbation.

Themes

The Body

Forster investigates ideas about gender by showing how the body exists as a site of societal contest. A body that has been claimed by society as, for example, female due to its reproductive abilities will have definite strictures placed upon it. Likewise, a male body has certain freedoms which he can sacrifice in order to show himself more civilized. Beebe, as usual, unconscious of having put his finger on it, nicely cuts to the point himself with a rich summary. "Can you picture a lady who has been introduced to another lady by a third lady opening civilities with 'How do you do? Come and have a bathe'? And yet you will tell me that the sexes are equal." Men have certain privileges denied to women and the continuation of this paradox depends on Lucy becoming a woman like Charlotte.

Women like Charlotte exhibit absurd prudishness about male flesh while using the body to censure young women. They hold up the "medieval lady," who loathed all physical elements, especially her own flesh, as the ideal. Charlotte displays this stance early through her shock over George's admittance that his father bathes. She also betrays her ideas when she refers to naked Venus as "a pity." Charlotte desires a world of chivalry where men donned armor to amuse well-dressed ladies. The distance between men and women is, thus, well maintained. Charlotte uses her body against Lucy constantly. For example, she wins their fight at Fiesole by sitting on the wet ground and tries to physically reclaim her from George beneath the carriage rug. Lucy learns that Charlotte's view, like that of Mrs. Honeychurch, depends on viewing the male body as something extraordinary. However, she realizes that men, like women, are just human. After realizing this, she accepts Mr. Emerson's idea of "direct desire" with which she robs "the body of its taint." This frees her from the "medieval lady" for she accepts that "love is of the body."

George comes alive when nude. The pond where he bathes with Freddy and Beebe acts like "a spell" from a "chalice" that resuscitates his spirit. He abhors civilization's distaste for the body and longs to live a balanced life. However, in keeping with his father's teaching, George knows that women must also enjoy the body. Only then can men and women be "comrades" and enter Eden together. Cecil, however, embodies the perfect male Vyse. He gives up the ability to play lawn tennis and reads from a book in order to show he is more civilized.

Travel

Travel enables the English person of an open mind to taste life and, thereby, begin to live. As Miss Lavish says, to Italy "one comes for life." All too often, the largest obstacle in this process is also the first one confronted by the traveler. The English hotel simply recreates England and allows the English tourist to stay English. His vacation, then, consists of collecting evidence of having been there: "The narrowness and superficiality of the Anglo-Saxon tourist is nothing less than a menace." Lucy comments to Charlotte that there is no difference between a Bloomsbury boarding house in London and the Pension. The same social rules, people, clothes, and paintings surround them. Only in surroundings completely foreign to the pension and London will Lucy possibly learn anything. Different surroundings are important but contact with different people is intrinsic.

The characters reveal their ability to discover themselves in their attitude toward travel and the use of the Baedeker. For example, Miss Lavish is the type of tourist who believes she owns the place and likewise believes that there is nothing about her that needs perfecting. Charlotte is terribly lonely, clingy, and loves to play the emotional martyr in her personal relationships. Likewise, she views traveling as an endless series of chores. Cecil, a proclaimed Italophile, understands as little about Italy as he does about himself though he gives off airs of knowing both. Lucy and George, however, learn little about Italy in comparison but they have a good time and become better people for it. This, Forster indicates, should be the goal of every journey—self-discovery.

Taste and Manners

"Tact!" is the very thing the Emersons disdain but which lubricates the societal hive. Manners, taste, and tact are the very things that muddle Lucy's brain. She spends hours rehearsing bows and statements, and interpreting the actions of others. She wants to "do"; to be approved of by high-standing members of society and, if she tries hard enough, by the queen bee—Mrs. Vyse. At the start of the novel, Lucy has "not yet acquired decency" but she hopes to do so by the end of her Italian tour with Miss Bartlett, her teacher. The education is not without its hardships; one of Charlotte's early lessons ended Lucy's bathing in the Sacred Lake. To be a Lady is to give up on manly prerogatives like public bathing.

In the storm on the return from Fiesole, the result of such an education is glimpsed. The various party members lose control of themselves and act naturally. They act in "unladylike" or "unmanly" ways. Lucy is quickly acquiring such unnatural abilities but "she was not better able to stifle emotions of which the conventions and the world would disapprove." An educated lady can violate natural inclinations and always act properly. Ultimately,

Topics For Further Study

- Forster's theory of marital comradeship has been said to be a homosexual viewpoint masked by a heterosexual story. Do you agree or disagree?

- Forster identified readily with Renaissance figures. Research the Neoplatonist Gemistus Pletho or the Italian mathematician Girolamo Cardano and read Forster's essay on either one. What comparisons can be made between these Renaissance figures and Forster?

- The Greek Spirit or the Comic Muse are composed of profound human musings. Taking George's book shelf as a guide (Byron, Butler, Gibbon, Schopenhauer, and Nietzsche) as well as the novel itself, define Mr. Emerson's understanding of the Greek Spirit.

- In the novel, the potential liberating effects of art must be guarded against. This is done by aesthetic education, not censorship. How has the battle over the impact of media on youth changed? What can be learned from Forster on this issue?

- Botticelli's "Birth of Venus" was celebrated in the novel as a moment of body appreciation— not an example of exploitation. Feminists in Forster's day, and still today, disagree. Research the arguments on both sides using Forster's novel and Lynda Nead's *The Female Nude.* Which do you find most persuasive?

- Read Forster's own travel books or early National Geographics to ascertain the conditions a traveler faced in Forster's time. What does Forster believe to be the value of travel? Compare this to the goal of package tours and the ability to eat at McDonald's in any city on the planet. Is Forster's sense of travel possible in, for example, the Florence of today?

---

she will become a nearly "medieval lady," and as "mechanical" as Mrs. Vyse.

Fortunately, comic forces intervene and Lucy sees the world of Vyse as "nonsense." It helped that throughout her progress on the path to being ladylike, she was always conscious of how unnatural it was. She succeeded in being a lady only when she concentrated and remembered to perform properly. Otherwise, she was as truthful as the Emersons— who would not "do."

Art

Art, in the novel, can inspire characters to live more passionately. Therefore, paintings, literary works, and musical pieces exist as gauges of a character's open-mindedness. By thinking about art and its role in society, a character reveals his or her view of whether life should be experienced naturally or aesthetically, directly or in its written form. For example, as they begin the drive to Fiesole, Mr. Eager points out a beautiful cottage, which happens to be owned by an Englishwoman. To some, the cottage becomes exciting only when Mr. Eager points out that some believe it to be the place of a scene from Boccaccio's *Decameron.* The literary connection enhances the aesthetic enjoyment of the cottage and displaces the natural reaction. Books act this way throughout the novel. Book knowledge overrides natural inclination. Not surprisingly, Cecil hopes to finish Lucy's education with books. The base of aesthetic living, then, is to know how to respond to a given situation by collating one's knowledge.

Paintings work in the same way. Lucy hopes her guidebook will enable her to have the proper response to the frescoes in Santa Croce. Instead, the Emersons react from their experience. Likewise, Lucy reacts to Botticelli's "Birth of Venus" from her own experience. She purchases a copy of the painting in a fit of rebellion. Charlotte disapproved of the painting because Venus is naked. Purchasing photographs, however, does not satisfy Lucy—she wants to recapture the passion the artist felt in the painting.

Performance becomes the key to recapturing the Renaissance spirit. Miss Lavish comes off as a villain for her writing and yet she offers Lucy a hint: Anyone can accomplish a work of art. Lucy also performs: "Lucy never knew her desires so clearly as after music." The performance of a beautiful work—much like the reading of a good book—can help to illuminate desires. In other words, when Lucy is engaged with life—playing tennis, piano, or kissing—she becomes fully alive. Artworks can show the way, but Lucy must play.

Style

Leitmotif

A term that literary criticism borrows from music describes the technical repetition of key phrases or ideas in association with persons or places. The device can also assume larger proportions when, for example, an action is repeated with different portents. Forster employs leitmotif throughout his novels.

Swimming and violets are George's simple signifiers. The device becomes more intricate with Lucy. She employs music as her leitmotif. Lucy's playing affords an opportunity for other people to glimpse her real personality. The pieces she chooses to play have far reaching effects. Beethoven means something different from Schuman. Lucy's inability to play Wagner signals the novel's larger comedic struggle. The piece she cannot play comes from Wagner's operatic adaptation of the Holy Grail legend. Forster's novel is full of references to the tale and these references are leitmotifs.

Place becomes a leitmotif governing the novel's structure. Italy, at both the beginning and end, is a place of passion, youth, and possibility. The dark phase of the novel when Lucy is most endangered of joining the "army of darkness" takes place in England; far in the north, England is the seat of cold Victorianism. The leitmotif of physical intimacy reveals the position of opposing character. Lucy's kisses with her mother are mechanical. Hand brushings with Mr. Emerson are genuine but Charlotte's embrace is a betrayal. Kissing, of course, becomes the most potent act. George's kiss sets her ablaze. Cecil's kiss makes her feel awful and awkward.

Comedy

Forster makes no secret about this technique. He ascribes the structural theory of the novel to George Meredith at the moment when Cecil thinks he is scoring a victory for the Comic Muse. Meredith put forth his comic theory in an 1877 lecture, "On Comedy and the Uses of the Comic Spirit." He said, in part, "now comedy is the fountain of good sense; not the less perfectly sound on account of the sparkle: and comedy lifts women to a station offering them free play for their wit. As they usually show it, when they have it, on the side of good sense. The higher the comedy, the more prominent the part they enjoy in it." He then goes on to discuss classic works of comedy and the role that women play. Dorine in Moliere's *Tartuffe* is one example. That Lucy plays the most prominent part indicates that the novel is of the highest order; it wants nothing less than to save mankind. In "Le Rire," Henri Bergson, a contemporary of Forster, pointed out that comedy arises wherever the living are encrusted with the mechanical. Bergson argued that where humans become bogged down in ritualized habits, rules, or patterns that deaden vitality, comedy arises to offer a corrective. By viewing themselves in a comedic light, people feel better and sometimes seek to live better.

The comic structure originates in springtime ritual. The deadening pattern of winter is disrupted by a change in temperature which results in the rejuvenation of living things. This phenomenon is transcribed into society, which is laboring under a very dull and unchanging pattern of existence. The disrupting element, often referred to as the Comic Muse or Comic Force, can take the form of a stranger, a fool, or a revelation of knowledge. In *A Room with a View,* the typical rite of initiation of a young woman into "medieval lady" is disrupted by the interference of Mr. Emerson. The hive of society attempts to counter his disruption using Charlotte, Beebe, and others. They only make the problem larger and soon the mechanisms that had hitherto gone unquestioned become exposed and look "brown" against the violent beauty of the Italian landscape.

The disruption to the norm is important to begin the process but does not guarantee a comedic ending. The characters in the midst of the muddle must experience some form of raw nature and intellectual epiphany. Lucy experiences the forces of nature when she witnesses the murder, is drenched in a storm, confronts George at the Sacred Lake, and compares kisses. Mr. Emerson gives her philosophic questions that lead to her tear-filled awakening in Beebe's rectory.

Comedy, in its basic structure, also demands a sacrifice before allowing rebirth, redemption, or spring. Lucy, the Christ figure of this novel, sacrifices her family, friends, and her sought-after place in society. In doing so, she achieves the happy life of eternal spring. George is also saved and they become a new Adam and Eve who can remake society. More than just laughter, comedy shows its audience how to break with mechanical restraints and live naturally once again. As Mr. Emerson says, "let us rather love one another, and work and rejoice. I don't believe in this world sorrow."

Symbolism

Forster employs symbolism to bolster his comic structure. Nearly allegorical names serve to cement the position of certain characters. Beebe, like his insect namesake and the sign over the pub door where he conspires with Charlotte, gathers pollen—young people—into the hive where they become proper communal members, like Mrs. Honeychurch. The Vyses are at the top of the hive. Like their name, they are gripped and squeezed by their own rules. Mrs. Vyse is described, in fact, as a machine who is all but dead. Cecil is well on his way to his mother's stature for already he cannot play—he is too tight. The Vyse society has many names; they are the "the army of darkness" and they appear "brown"—the color of Charlotte after the first kiss.

Clothing, as the accoutrements of society, is symbolic. When George and Lucy meet at the Sacred Lake, they meet amidst strewn clothes, the shambles of civilization. In the last scene, a lone sock stands for the rules of Vyse that should have been left in England. Lucy is tempted to mend it. Instead, George helps her to put it down and join him at the window to take in the view.

Historical Context

Edwardian Age

King Edward VII, known as Bertie, ascended the throne at the death of his mother, Queen Victoria, in 1901. Bertie turned the monarchy into a national pageant. He opened the parliament in 1902, worked hard to improve foreign relations (including the entente with France that allowed for the Anglo-French alliance), and gave every encouragement to military reform. Domestically, Bertie championed tolerance by going out of his way to show that Jews and Indian princes were not, by nature, inferior to himself. Bertie's love of pageantry ensured that people noticed this attitude and British society grew more tolerant.

By 1906, Bertie's health showed signs of decline while a constitutional crisis brewed. The question arose as to whether the Lords or the House of Commons should deal with financing the arms race with Germany. As the dispute flared in 1909, Bertie vacationed in France although elections were imminent. He returned to political chaos, succumbed to bronchitis, and died in the spring of 1910.

The British Empire

At the end of the nineteenth century, Britain ruled an empire that encircled the globe. However, the degree to which Britain controlled the areas of the map it marked in pink or red was questionable or in decline. Exacerbating Britain's anxiety, European nations increasingly challenged her hegemony. The most brazen was Germany and the most worrisome was Russia. Britain sought to pacify her challengers. She successfully formed an alliance with France through trade concessions and military agreements. The United States, clearly on its way to being a great industrial power, was pacified and war between the two nations became unthinkable if not quite impossible. Challenges in other areas of the Empire (namely, Ireland, Palestine, Africa, and India) were not so easily dealt with.

At home, the suffragette movement had taken its demands to the streets. Through various militant displays, women publicized their demand for the right to vote. They did not win this right until 1918; New Zealand was the first nation to grant suffrage to women in 1893, while the United States granted the right in 1920. Trade unionists and a very strife-ridden parliament made the latter half of the first decade tumultuous. This strife would lead to a series of strikes in 1911 and 1912. Still, by the eve of World War I, Britain was the wealthiest and most powerful nation on earth.

Italy

Since the Renaissance, wealthy Europeans and salaried intellectuals have traveled to Italy in order to regain the knowledge and riches of Roman civilization. During the eighteenth century, Italy rivaled France as the necessary stop for any gentleman completing his education with a Grand Tour. This interest in Italy—its ancient ruins, museums, and art treasures—continued into the nineteenth century. The strength of the British currency and

Compare & Contrast

- **1908:** Based on an arrangement with Russia, Austria annexes Bosnia and Herzegovina. This disrupts Serbia's plans for a Greater Serbia including the two provinces. Britain and France thwart Russia's gain of the promised access to the Dardanelles and Bosporus straits. Austria denies any secret arrangements and the Balkan fuse is set to explode as World War I.

  Today: With the collapse of Yugoslavia, Balkan provinces again struggle for control. At the close of the twentieth century, Serbia has been isolated for its attempt to annex and ethnically cleanse Kosovo.

- **1908:** Before it annexes Hawaii in 1898 and colonizes the Philippines a year later, the United States possesses a military just capable of dealing with indigenous tribes, the Mexican army, and Spain. America's stance is defensive, although the world powers know that the United States has the capacity as soon as it finds the will.

  Today: The United States has the largest military-industrial complex in the world. On paper, the United States can fight two full-fledged wars simultaneously. This military might is matched by a consumer and financial base that dominates global markets.

- **1908:** The West views China as a source of riches so long as the country can be controlled.

  Today: The view of China by the West has not changed. The United States hopes to edge out its competitors and gain preferred access to China's vast population for its goods and services.

- **1908:** Europe and the United States account for nearly all industrial production. Europe depends on Africa, Asia, and the Americas for its raw materials and food. Europe begins industrializing its colonies by building railways, mining centers, and factories.

  Today: Europe and the United States lead the world in finance, service, and legislative sectors but have given up ground in manufacturing and production.

- **1908:** The heterosexual ceremony of marriage allows no mutations. Due to industrialization, women and men can choose to be single. In addition, the social atmosphere allows nontraditional relationships.

  Today: The Big Three automotive companies in the United States have extended spousal health-care benefits to their gay employees. Homosexual marriage, meanwhile, is gaining acceptance in parts of the West.

---

the money accruing to its upper classes enabled a lively tourist trade in Italy. This is the basis for Forster's *A Room with a View* but its depictions of Italians as the passionate idyllic peasants of old is false. Italy during Forster's sojourn was caught in the throes of modernization.

Officially adopting a modern parliamentary system in 1861, Italy still had to overcome centuries of international intervention, internal strife, the Catholic Church, and an underdeveloped economy. For the first fifty years, barely two percent of the population had the right to vote. However, the industrial regions in the north grew their economy at a phenomenal rate and, in southern Italy, the number of literate people began to outnumber the illiterate. By the eve of WWI, Italy's yearly steel output had gone from negligible to nearly one million metric tons and the nation was a producer of cars, typewriters, motorcycles, silk, and fertilizer.

These successes concentrated in the north; many Italians from the rest of the peninsula sought opportunity elsewhere. More than half a million Italians left the country each year of the first decade of the century. Many went overseas and a majority to the United States. In addition to its lopsided development, Italy adopted imperial ambitions beyond its abilities. This led to the humiliating defeat of the Italian army by the Abyssinians at Adowa in

Julian Sands and Helena Bonham Carter in the 1986 film version of the novel.

1896. Italy's policy of irredentism—a desire to control areas inhabited by people speaking the same language outside national boundaries—led it to attempt annexation of Trieste and Tripoli. Failure in these areas by 1912 added fuel to the fire that would implode as World War I.

Avant-Garde

Though the term has been applied to numerous epochs and movements, as a label for a specific period it denotes the bridge from post-impressionism through cubism to surrealism (roughly 1906–1930). The avant-garde was a series of art movements whose practitioners saw themselves leading society to better and better plateaus through art. Usually this meant remaking society with socialist or Marxist doctrine. At minimum, the artist of the avant-garde saw himself as an interpreter of the place of the individual in an industrial world.

The Italian poet Filippo Tommaso Marinetti began one such movement, futurism. Marinetti believed that industrialization was the only means for Italy to achieve its ambition to become a world power. He wanted Italy to destroy its museums and build factories in their place. He further believed that a consumerist society was the ultimate form of living. He therefore advocated a state of war (the purest state of consumption by any society) that would eventually destroy relics of the past and spawn new machines. Many adherents of futurism died during World War I and Marinetti went to work for Benito Mussolini.

In England, the most famous avant-garde movement was the Bloomsbury Group. This group was composed of Cambridge Apostles, including Forster, who had moved to London. The group met alternatively at the homes of Virginia Woolf and Vanessa Bell in the Bloomsbury district adjacent to the British Museum beginning in 1907. The group's early discussions centered around the agnostic ponderings of G. E. Moore's *Principia Ethica* and the *Principia Mathematica* by A. N. Whitehead and Bertrand Russell. The group survived World War I but disintegrated by 1930.

Critical Overview

Critically, *A Room with a View* has been treated as a fine example of travel literature, character development, satire, comedy, writing style, and a modernization of ancient myths. Forster's novel was immediately popular with readers and early reviewers praised the novel, enjoying the Jane Austen-style observation of human society. Acclaim began with a review in the *Morning Leader* (October 30, 1908) which declared the work the best of the year. C. F. G. Masterman's review in *The Nation* plugged the work because it deftly satirized Edwardian England. Virginia Woolf, writing for the *Times Literary Supplement* in her article "The Novels of E. M. Forster," and collected in *The Death of the Moth and other Essays,* declared the book a wonder for its beauty. However, Forster's friend also criticized Forster's characters as unsatisfying. Later critics have not agreed with Woolf.

Writing almost sixty years later, Jeffrey Meyers thought the characters exactly fulfilled their functions. In "The Paintings in Forster's Italian Novels," Meyers discusses how character response to Giotto's fresco, "The Ascension of St. John," "reverberates throughout the novel." Their "aesthetic responses become identified with moral issues" that are hashed out in the novel. Meyers furthers his claim by noting that Forster believed in art as a means for people to learn how to take up the Emerson view and celebrate life. The characters satisfy this principle to the degree to which they proceed to adopt a new view.

A Room with a View cemented Forster's reputation as a writer that began with his short stories and his first two novels. The third novel won him the compliment of being Austen-like in his observational ability and gained him admittance to a line of comic writers from Fielding to Dickens. Frederick C. Crewes comments, in his "Comic Spirit," that Forster and Austen's "comedy is generated by ironic contrasts between what is superficially 'proper' and what is truly reasonable." Land, in his *E. M. Forster,* writes that Forster doesn't simply write about class or race "but rather like Jane Austen he uses the attitudes and habits of a class as a framework or image for the exploration of human behavior." At the same time, the novel found him accused of writing melodrama.

"Technically," writes Walter Allen in *The Modern Novel,* Forster's work—except *A Passage to India*—"are as melodramatic as any in Victorian fiction." Forster is redeemed, for Allen, by his personal attitude whose pure humanism allows him a tone as pure as Fielding or Thackeray. A few years later, Forster defender Joseph Epstein responded in his review for the *New York Times Book Review.* "Technically . . . Forster's novels form a connection between the ethical-culture and traditional forms of the 19th century novelists and the main preoccupation of the novelists of the 20th—Forster takes up, that is, where George Eliot leaves off and

leaves off where D. H. Lawrence takes up." But, he goes on to say that placing Forster there "is really not to place him at all." For Forster looms so large in English letters that he transcends it. Forster, for Epstein, rooted himself in his nation's character and remained decent about it. Though Forster, like Jonathan Swift and Samuel Butler, satirizes his nation through fantasies, he never humiliates his characters.

Forster attempted to deal with timeless themes by modernizing ancient myths. Lionel Trilling, in his *E. M. Forster,* uncovers Forster's secret way of doing this when he notices that there is a "barricade" in each of Forster's novels. "The opposed forces on each side are Good and Evil in the forms of Life and Death. Light and Darkness. Fertility and Sterility . . . all the great absolutes that are so dull when discussed by themselves" are made interesting in Forster because he uses the "comic manner." Forster wrote in light of the comic theory being developed in his day by George Meredith, Sigmund Freud, and others. This theory holds that characters who have too much of an absolute within them need to be adjusted—usually, as Northrop Frye says, by a chaotic clash with nature. John Lucas deftly shows how this works in *Room with a View* as well as the essential role music plays in the novel.

In his essay "Wagner and Forster," Lucas first places Forster's novel in its cultural milieu. He describes how Wagner dominated European arts at the close of the nineteenth century. He also notes the importance that Forster himself ascribed to the art of music. He relates these two facts to the dynamics of the novel. Thus Wagner's *Parsifal*—a retelling of the Grail legend with only one major change—is shown to be a guide to deconstructing the text. Also, music proves to be the only available technique to wire in the problems Lucy faced. By making her a pianist, Forster can quickly build up her character in notes familiar to the music fans of 1908. To the reader of today, this element is easily forgotten but in 1908, playing Beethoven or Mozart was a crucial distinction. According to Lucas, Lucy's "transition from Beethoven through Schumann to Mozart . . . [prefigures] her decline into a probable future of middle-class sterility." The call for Parsifal, but Lucy's inability to deliver as George steps into the room, is, therefore, an essential scene to the novel's denouement. Lucy cannot play the score of a work in which she plays the lead role.

In light of *Maurice,* critical interest in Forster's third novel was revived by gender identification theory. For example, Claude J. Summers, in his *E. M. Forster,* declares the novel "a bold festival of domestic comedy and sexual celebration; *A Room with a View* assimilates into a heterosexual plot the ideology of homosexual comradeship." Summers' essentialism, fortunately, becomes rational in the hands of other critics who point out that Forster's sexual identity motivated his insight into Edwardian personal relationships. Forster, soon after the publication of the novel, worried that it already appeared dated. By all accounts, *A Room with a View* remains one of the best Edwardian novels and a novel whose observations on human nature retain relevance.

> Industrial progress can be a boon so long as its goal is to make human lives better; industrial progress cannot be, for Forster, an end in itself. In other words, humans cannot be bound to machines. The choice depends upon our view of things, a problem as old as Plato's room."

Criticism

Jeremy W. Hubbell

Hubbell has an M. Litt. from the University of Aberdeen, Scotland, and currently seeks a Ph.D. in history at the State University of New York at Stony Brook. This essay purports that the place of technology in civilization haunts A Room with a View.

Though they had profited handsomely by industrialization, Britain's upper classes did not view technology with the enthusiasm characteristic of Americans. They still held to the feudal or "medieval" view, which held that profit should accumulate in their pockets—they saw themselves as the center of the universe. Technology, for the elite, achieved a good investment return, which they enjoyed, but it also increased the prosperity of the lower classes. Gains in productivity allowed for healthier wage packets while union action shortened the workweek. Thus, members of the working class began to play sports on their off days, women went shopping in arcades built with new building technology, families rode bikes and went on outings to museums and parks. The elite did not meet this alteration bravely and continued to insist on class separation. This tension is at the heart of E. M. Forster's novel *A Room with a View,* whose message of ultimate compromise includes dismantling the nature versus civilization dichotomy. Cecil Vyse, who offers a speech to Lucy Honeychurch to the effect that the classes ought to intermingle, notes that the rabble are even eating better so that "the physique of the lower-middle classes was improving at a most appalling rate."

Before industrialization accelerated in the eighteenth century, Europeans regarded themselves as warring against nature for their very lives. That changed when the Renaissance revived science and took advantage of medieval mechanics. Attitudes altered as civilization gained the upper hand and began to control nature. By the nineteenth century, control was all but attained and philosophic figures like Thomas Carlyle began to suggest a new attitude of harmony. They declared that the battle was over; civilization and its technics were harmonious parts of nature, not at war with it. Theories of evolution helped bolster the idea that by cooperating with nature, humans would prosper in both wealth and health. One technology stands out in this period and in Forster's novel because it was the growth engine of the nineteenth century economy, the steam engine atop a wheel carriage.

The rich invested heavily in the railroad in the late nineteenth century and they received handsome rewards. However, the railroad allowed unprecedented social mobility and created an entirely new class of rich people. Walt Whitman captured the appreciation of this technology in his 1851 poem, "To a Locomotive in Winter." There, the locomotive was a beautiful creature set free in nature. The railroad quickly became more than just a creature; it became a liberator of people and latent potential. The railroads enabled greater prosperity for all people which led, of course, to increased mingling of the classes. The railroad, as Ralph Waldo Emerson put it in "The Young American," "is the magician's rod, in its power to evoke sleeping energies of land and water." Emerson celebrated technology because it enables people to further their abilities to

What Do I Read Next?

- The first novel of Forster's Italian series, *Where Angels Fear to Tread* (1905), sequentially follows from *A Room with a View*. The novel anticipates the themes Forster would explore in his later works through a story about two journeys to Italy. On the first, an English widow, Lilia Herriton, goes to Italy, falls in love with an Italian, and dies in childbirth. Fearing the idea that this child should grow up Italian causes another journey to Italy to be made by English people. The goal of this journey is to recover the baby.

- Set in Cambridge, Forster's *The Longest Journey* sits in the middle of the Italian series. In this novel, the comfortable university world is forever disjointed for young Rick Elliot when he falls in love with Agnes Pembroke. The novel captures the essence of university life in turn-of-the-century Britain as well as the experience of tea with a dowager.

- With some autobiographical touches, Forster memorialized the house of his youth, Rooksnest, in his fourth novel, published in 1910, *Howards End.* Here, the children of the Wilcoxes try to ignore the note by their mother, Ruth, which bequeathed the house to Margaret Schlegal. Margaret marries Ruth's surviving husband, Henry, and gains the house regardless. After a series of traumas, Margaret and an ailing Henry return to the house.

- The 1924 work *Passage to India* was the last novel Forster published and it has been widely acclaimed as his best work. The novel examines the themes of race and colony through the problems that develop when Adela Questad, an Englishwoman, accuses Dr. Aziz, an Indian, of attacking her on an outing. During the trial, Dr. Aziz befriends Cecil Fielding but colonialism impossibly complicates their relationship.

- Iris Murdoch has been favorably compared with Forster. *A Severed Head,* from 1976, displays Murdoch's abilities to observe humanity in its complexities. In this novel, Martin Lynch-Gibbon believes he can have both a wife and a mistress but when his wife leaves him his sense of reality crumbles.

- *Portrait of a Lady,* by Henry James, was first published in three volumes in 1881. This work about a young American woman, Isabel Archer, who is "doing" Europe has many points of comparison and contrast with *A Room with a View.* James' heroine becomes a victim of her provincialism as she is the focus of an examination of American values.

- A very different approach to analyzing relationships and society appeared in 1925 from Forster's friend Virginia Woolf. Written under the influence of James Joyce, *Mrs. Dalloway* follows the title character through one June day as she confronts her surroundings and remembers the past.

- After Forster, the person most responsible for creating the stereotypical early twentieth-century British gentlemen is P. G. Wodehouse. His ninety-some stories concern the chaos of society life as experienced by Bertie Wooster and his manservant, the original butler, Jeeves. The first of Wodehouse's success was the 1913 novel *Something New.*

- Quite easily, the domestic scene did not exist before Jane Austen and certainly the genre of spoiled rich kid depends on her 1815 novel, *Emma.* Emma Woodhouse thinks she knows what is best for everyone in her provincial society and she attempts to resolve fates accordingly. Her plot lines are not exactly carried out and she finds herself married in the end to George Knightley.

- The 1988 Pulitzer Prize winner by Anne Tyler, *Breathing Lessons,* is an American domestic comedy set, appropriately, in the car. The Morans display their familial difficulties through flashbacks as they travel to an old friend's funeral.

open up land to agriculture and the progress of civilization. Only by the employment of technology can people build a Garden of Eden where everyone is fed and clothed—a garden, after all, employs cutting-edge agricultural technology. That is the message of Forster's book, a realization that the American spirit is a good one and Britain would do well to learn from it. Britain, as the novel shows, may not be able to Americanize because of people like the Vyses and, therefore, places like Italy might be the better place for that spirit.

The discussion of technological advance occurs at several points in the novel. While in Florence, Mr. Eager notes the way in which trams enable people of the lower classes to take outings in the countryside. However, the reality of a working person's life justifies Mr. Eager's pity for them. Still, trams enable the "poor" to walk where only the rich had previously. Sir Harry Otway enunciates the anxieties of the rich to Mr. Vyse. He fears, he says, that he will rent to the wrong sort of person because the physical barriers that had kept the rich apart have been overrun. The rich had always been able to afford the time and expense of country estates, but both time and expense were being leveled by the railroad. "The train service has improved—a fatal improvement, to my mind. And what are five miles from a station in these days of bicycles?" He worries that the bike and the train will enable the working-class man to afford a home away from the toxicity of industry (cars will soon make the matter worse). His fears are realized when the Emersons, the working-class heroes of the novel, move in. Though only Mrs. Honeychurch makes the connection, Mr. Emerson, who was a mechanic before going into journalism for socialist organs, follows the teachings of the American philosopher already mentioned. George, appropriately, works as a clerk for a railroad company. Otway had hoped for a bank clerk, an occupation he understood, but in the new economy, suggests Forster, the railroad clerk becomes the victor.

The novel assesses the anxiety of the wealthy classes in terms of its inability to change its view of life by which is meant, philosophies of life or interpretations of the universe—how things work. The rich, like Otway and Vyse, are conservative; they want class separations maintained with themselves at the top according to the medieval ideals. They see nature as something to be controlled for their benefit as it was in feudal times. They can be thought of "as in a room" or protected by "fences" and ensconced in palaces and churches. Members of this view "have no profession." Instead, they

manage and accumulate wealth—the Vyses are parasites whose salary is made up of dividends. The Emersons are liberals, meaning they believe in individual rights and democratic institutions. They are humanists and base their judgments about society on empirical data "of," not from (as in stolen), nature. Thus, they can be thought of as a view without obstructing walls. People who share the Emersons' view live by their own labor and they enjoy bodily pleasure. Reason governs their behavior.

In Freudian terms, a person of cathexis focuses his mind toward one goal or view of life. Such a person can be described as anal or unyielding. This person frequently becomes the center of a comedy whose end is his catharsis. That is, events and experiences of disruption force the person of cathexion to see things differently and realize he had been narrow-minded. A catharsis is, literally, a release of psychic energy, a release from being anal, which allows for a readjusted and more balanced psyche. Forster's comedy is different. The Vyses cannot help but live up to their name, which conjures the Latin verb "to see." Vyse also conjures the mechanical apparatus, the vise. As the leading members of society, such allusions are fitting. The Vyses stick to their rules and view of society normally described as hive-like. The blending of the biologic and mechanical is no accident. The society which the Vyses lead is, in modern parlance, like the Borgs from Gene Rodenberry's *Star Trek* series. They attach people to their system after a period of molding. In terms of the history of technics, the society of Vyse is a megamachine whose purpose is to maintain its members and itself by acquisition of new members and adamant adherence to decorum. The cathected are not saved by the story; hope lies in the young who have not yet made up their view.

Forster hated the megamachine of the Vyses'. In a short story written after *A Room with a View* he was even more vitriolic in his characterization of this tendency in humans to live in cathexion. In "The Machine Stops," a machine does all of society's work so that the humans can sit in their rooms away from each other and continually fabricate aesthetic systems. The body is left to atrophy. However, Forster does not foresee total divorce from the body and, therefore, maintains the hope of reconnecting with the body or giving the room a view. The Emersons are that hope. They are part of the middle class whose physique has improved with industrialization. They believe in communal recreation of the Garden where technology does not take over society but positively aids people in their lives. The Emersons, in their ideal, can be thought of as a utopic view of boundless progress. Forster, a pragmatist, believes in a compromise made possible by Lucy who, as light, can bring the two worlds together. She brings music, art, and literature to match George's modern philosophy and technology.

The marriage of the two views happens in Florence—one of the cities responsible for the change in Europe described as the Renaissance. That epoch of rediscovery held out the possibility of compromise from the outset. A historical example of this can be found in the efforts of a man who lived in Florence during the Renaissance and arguably has had the greatest view of the cosmos. His very name has become a synonym for clear sight. His sight would not be obfuscated by religious doctrine or doubt but fueled by Baconian practice. Galileo Galilei, court mathematician to the Medici, had the clearest view of all the Renaissance thinkers and it was straight up. His observations led to the downfall of the old geocentric view of the universe and the rise of a heliocentric view of the universe. Forster's location of his novel about views and technological attitudes was appropriately placed in Florence. Forster's sense of compromise matches Galileo's, who did not want to overthrow or disagree with the Catholic Church (the story often told about his "trial"). Instead, Galileo believed he utilized his God-given talents to explore God's wondrous creations in order to glorify the Catholic faith. Galileo failed to observe a separation between religion and science.

"It was the old, old battle of the room with a view." The statement stands like a thesis within a theory about human nature. While it appears to announce that there is nothing new in the Lucy problem, it also luxuriates in the timelessness within the problem. Industrial progress can be a boon so long as its goal is to make human lives better; industrial progress cannot be, for Forster, an end in itself. In other words, humans cannot be bound to machines. The choice depends upon our view of things, a problem as old as Plato's room. The old, old battle is over whether or not humans will stay looking at the shadows on the wall or go out of the cave. The Emersons remind the reader that "there is only one perfect view—the view of the sky straight over our heads, and . . . all these other views on earth are but bungled copies of it." Forster celebrated life and sunlight but he was not against technology. Forster, writing at a time when Europe had created a science of fatigue and was obsessed with industrial efficiency, points out that the important things

are to observe nature as our forebears did. And maybe observe and pay attention to each other. Machines, as critics of Taylorism were quick to see, can numb the senses of the human worker. Forster wants that worker to be able to have fun in the sun once in a while far from "the world of motor cars."

Source: Jeremy W. Hubbell, in an essay for *Novels for Students,* Gale Group, 2001.

Twayne Authors Series

The following essay analyzes the structure of A Room with a View *and Lucy's journey toward enlightenment.*

Forster began *A Room with a View* (1908) before *Where Angels Fear to Tread* (1905) and finished it after *The Longest Journey* (1907). Since it is the most halcyon and direct of his novels and since it was the work with which he started, we shall begin with it. Though it is his least complex book, it is his most Jane Austen-like and perhaps his most delightful. As in the earlier-published *Angels,* Italy acts as the chief source of vitality, and the two novels reflect the intense impact that the South made upon him in his early twenties. In *Room,* after the characters return to England in Part II, Italy retreats to the background but still acts as a formative influence.

In any case, Italy is the main force which in Part I of *Room* contributes to Lucy Honeychurch's liberation. The conventional Reverend Beebe reluctantly acknowledges the intuitive wisdom of Italians though it chiefly annoys him: "They pry everywhere, they see everything, and they know what we want before we know it ourselves." So "Phaethon," the driver of the carriage taking the English to the hills above Florence, reads Lucy's heart and directs her to George Emerson rather than to the Reverends Beebe and Eager when she asks in faltering Italian "where the good men are." Both Italy and the English countrywide encourage a free and open existence as compared to cramped, stereotyped, middle-class British life. The primary impression produced by the novel, the prevalence of wind and air and sunlight, establishes, as in George Meredith, the primary role of nature as redemptive power.

The English and Italian settings, rendered with complete immediacy, reveal Forster's sensitivity to place. Houses and buildings take on life in his fiction: the church of Santa Croce and the Pension Bertolini in Florence, for example, and Windy Corner, a Surrey country house. The Florentine pension and the Surrey house focus the action in the two sections of the novel. Chapter 1 presents at the Pension almost all the actors who figure in Part I: Lucy; Charlotte Bartlett, her "proper" chaperone; George Emerson, a troubled but vital young man; his father, the prophetic proponent of the free and natural life like that advocated by the American Ralph Waldo Emerson; the Reverend Mr. Beebe, the ascetically inclined but socially agreeable clergyman of Summer Street near Windy Corner; Eleanor Lavish, an "emancipated" novelist whose unconventionality is superficial; and the Misses Alan, elderly and genteel lady travellers. Only the snobbish chaplain to the English colony, the Reverend Cuthbert Eager, remains for Chapter 5.

The opening chapter of Part II introduces at Windy Comer all the other principles: Mrs. Honeychurch, Lucy's impulsive and affectionate mother and an endearing portrait of Forster's maternal grandmother whom he loved intensely; Freddy, Lucy's playful but instinctively sound brother; and Cecil Vyse, a "medieval" young man to whom Lucy has become engaged after his third proposal. She breaks her engagement when Mr. Emerson convinces her that she really loves his son. In the concluding chapter, Lucy and George return for their honeymoon to the Pension Bertolini which provides a frame for the novel and a reminder of Italy's pervasive power.

Structure depends upon a number of encounters between Lucy and George which revise her staid outlook. In Chapter I the Emersons offer the ladies their room with a view; and, before retiring, the now restless Lucy gazes beyond the Arno at the hills which betoken the freedom that she has not yet achieved. In Chapter 2 George appears in the Church of Santa Croce at his most lugubrious, and Lucy disdainfully pities him; but in Chapter 4 he reveals his potential strength as he supports her in his arms when she faints after witnessing a quarrel between two Italians over money, a quarrel that results in the sudden murder of one of them. After Lucy's "rescue," she and George gaze at the Arno flowing beneath them and respond to its mystery and promise (though with her rational mind, Lucy is later ashamed that she has given herself away to this extent). With the death of the Italian, Lucy feels that she, too, has "crossed some spiritual boundary," though she is not sure at the moment just what it may be. When they go back to Florence for their honeymoon, it is as if to place themselves under the spell of a force—the river—that has never ceased to exert itself. In Italy violence enlarges Lucy's horizons, and she now feels that something has indeed "happened to the living."

> **The picture connects with the Italian springtime, the pagan atmosphere of the novel, and the birth of love in Lucy's soul. Just as the blood of the murdered man defiles the pictures, so Lucy would, through her own blindness and obstinacy, do violence to her instincts."**

In Chapter 4 Forster also suggests the effete quality of the casual tourist's culture when Lucy buys photographs of works by the great masters. Reality impinges upon the pictures when the dying man's blood spatters them and when George throws them into the Arno to have them, as it were, washed pure in its waters. The principal picture, Botticelli's *The Birth of Venus,* has symbolic meaning that is at once lucid and profound. The picture connects with the Italian springtime, the pagan atmosphere of the novel, and the birth of love in Lucy's soul. Just as the blood of the murdered man defiles the pictures, so Lucy would, through her own blindness and obstinacy, do violence to her instincts. Just as the soiled photographs return to the water that has given birth to Venus, so Lucy must immerse herself in elemental passion, in order to cleanse her soul and to attain a new life. The birth of the goddess and the death of the Italian man also suggest the nearness of love and death as the most fundamental and mysterious of our experiences.

Lucy has another encounter with George when in Chapter 6 the Bertolini guests go for a drive above Fiesole. Lucy discovers that her standards have altered and that she does not know how to account for the change. She doubts that Miss Lavish is an artist and that Mr. Beebe is spiritual, but previously she would have been less critical. She judges them by a new criterion. Vital energy, she thinks, should animate them, but she finds them lacking in warmth and spontaneity, qualities that she has begun unconsciously to associate with George. Lucy is a woman who registers the effects of an emotional awakening before she can acknowledge its existence and cause. The Arno Valley is once more present in the distance from above Fiesole when George kisses Lucy after she surprises him on the bank covered with violets. Going against the dictates of instinct, Lucy seeks the advice of her proper chaperone, Miss Bartlett, who dismisses George, and the ladies depart forthwith from Rome where Lucy first meets Cecil Vyse.

Encounters with George also organize the narrative in Part II, although in the first chapters it is Cecil Vyse, Lucy's fiance (or "fiasco" as Freddy calls him), who dominates. Another kiss, Cecil's self-conscious one in Chapter 9, contrasts with George's spontaneous embraces. Cecil not only takes the place temporarily of George as his temperamental opposite, but assumes in Part II the role of Charlotte Bartlett as exemplar of the proprieties. In Chapter 12 Lucy regains contact with George as he emerges like a pagan god from "The Sacred Lake," a charming country pool near Windy Corner, and emanates all of nature's freshness.

Part II is a contest between George and Cecil for the control of Lucy's inner being. In Chapter 15 a kiss again enlivens the novel. George has just beaten Lucy at tennis; while the contestants rest, Cecil reads from Miss Lavish's novel, which features an incident similar to George's first kissing of Lucy on the heights over Florence. Miss Lavish had learned of the incident through the duplicity of Charlotte Bartlett who had enjoined Lucy to tell no one about it, even her mother. The memory of this scene arouses George, and he kisses Lucy in a copse close to Windy Corner. The outraged Lucy again does violence to her true self; she retreats from the light of truth and passion and prepares to enter "the vast armies of the benighted". After this second kiss and the lies that she tells about herself to George, Cecil, Mr. Beebe, her mother, and Mr. Emerson, pretense all but conquers her. In Florence, after George's kiss, she had realized how difficult it was to be truthful, but by this point she has become less conscientious.

The overall movement of the novel results in enlightenment for Lucy, after several divagations into falsehood. With one side of her nature she responds to passion as it concenters in George; with another, she aligns herself with upholders of Victorian social standards, Charlotte Bartlett and Cecil Vyse. With unremitting force Lucy's instincts carry her toward a larger life than these mentors will allow. Finally, Mr. Emerson sweeps away her accumulated errors of perception when he divines her love for George, instructs her about the sanctity of passion, and gives her the courage to claim the man she loves.

From the beginning Italy is a subversive influence, causing Lucy's well-known world to break up; and in its place the "magic city" of Florence elicits all that is unpredictable. Passionate, vibrant, violent Italy all but overwhelms Lucy. Her sympathies for "Phaethon," the coach-driver, startle her, as he embraces his "Persephone" on the drive to Fiesole. If she had been able to see more clearly, she would have recognized a god in George Emerson, who would, for his part, have seen in a liberated Lucy a real goddess. Before he kissed her in the hills, she had seemed "as one who had fallen out of heaven"; and, before her inhibitions stifled her, Lucy could identify him with "heroes—gods—the nonsense of schoolgirls". Later when she greets him at "The Sacred Lake," she thinks of herself as bowing "to gods, the heroes, to the nonsense of school girls! She had bowed across the rubbish that cumbers the world". And George was here a "Michelangelesque" figure, the essence of heroic vitality; earlier he had similarly appeared to her as a figure appropriate to "the ceiling of the Sistine Chapel, carrying a burden of acorns". But, in repudiating George a second time, she turns from a god incarnate to the academic study of Greek mythology as she prepares for her journey to Greece with the Misses Alan. She is rejecting in the actuality a god, knowledge of whose counterparts she is pursuing in the abstract.

In order to intensify Lucy's conflict with convention and to convey the force of her muted passion, Forster uses imagery drawn from music. Music lifts her out of herself and permits her to see, at least for the moment, the irrelevance of prescriptive standards: "She was then no longer either deferential or patronizing; no longer either a rebel or a slave". By force of will, she transforms Beethoven's tragic sonatas, for example, into expressions of triumph. Lucy, moreover, instinctively suits her music to her mood or situation. In Italy where she can acknowledge the elemental, she leans toward Beethoven. When she plays for Cecil and his guests in London, she performs the decorous Schumann, who suggests to her "the sadness of the incomplete." It is as if she has some intimations that she is now denying the demands of life, and so cannot play her beloved Beethoven in these artificial surroundings. At Windy Corner she plays the erotic garden music from Gluck's *Armide* and makes her audience restless (as if they reflect her own conflicts), and she also finds it impossible to play the sensual garden sequence from *Parsifal* in George's presence, since she is sexually distraught at this time. When she plans to renounce the call of passion, she indulges in the artifices (for her) of Mozart.

Forster suggests Lucy's progress toward enlightenment in terms of light and shadow images (these are so numerous that full discussion is not possible). Light and darkness suffuse natural phenomena, as these respectively signify freedom and inner fulfillment or bondage and human waywardness. Forster also associates light with the Emersons to the extent that father and son represent spiritual truth. In Italy Mr. Emerson urges Lucy to expose her thoughts to the sunlight rather than keep them in the depths of her nature. She resists full illumination, however, because she resists as yet the full promptings of instinct. George is, like Lucy, in danger of spiritual disablement, and he will enter the abyss if Lucy does not return his love, his father tells her in England. Lucy, in fact, will condemn herself by her evasions and lies to "marching in the armies of darkness", so long as she resists the truth about herself.

Though the clouds of pessimism often surround George, he becomes a source of light to Lucy. Both darkness and bright light characterize her encounter with him in the Piazza Signoria. To correspond with the crime that takes place there, the Piazza is in shadow and the tower of the palace arises out of a sinister gloom. Yet the tower is emblematic of the sexuality that Lucy experiences and represses, rising as it does "out of the lower darkness like a pillar of toughened gold. It seemed no longer a tower, no longer supported by earth, but some unattainable treasure throbbing m the tranquil sky". In Surrey George's kindness to his father strikes Lucy as "sunlight touching a vast landscape—a touch of the morning sun". He has just said that "there is a certain amount of kindness, just as there is a certain amount of light," and that one "should stand in it for all you are worth, facing the sunshine." When he wins at tennis from Lucy, he is brilliant against the sunlight, godlike in appearance. In defending himself in Surrey after he kisses her, he emphasizes how his love had been kindled when he saw her the day that he bathed in the Sacred Lake; the life-giving water and the glorious sunlight combined to make her beauty overwhelming. It is with this sunlight, too, that Forster identifies George and suggests that he is a Phaethon figure.

After she breaks the engagement with Cecil, Lucy realizes that George has gone into darkness; but she does not yet perceive that by her denial of sex she is fashioning an "armour of falsehood" and

is about to go into darkness herself. She now becomes as one who sins "against passion and truth", or against Eros and Pallas Athena. She resists taking others into her confidence lest inner exploration result in self-knowledge and "that king of terrors—Light", the light that her own name (from the Latin, *lux,* meaning light) signifies and that she must acknowledge to become her true self. But for the intervention of Mr. Emerson, Lucy would stay in darkness. He gives her "a sense of deities reconciled"; he enables her, in short, to balance the claims of Eros and Pallas Athena, of sense and soul.

George, who is in part a nature god, is at his most vital seen against the expanses of the Florentine and English hills. Appropriately enough, his earliest memory is the inspiriting landscape seen from Hindhead in company with his mother and father, a prospect which unified the family in deepest understanding. In symbolic terms, both the Emersons now have, and have always had, "the view" that Lucy must acquire. External nature is always seen in motion, as if it too is in protest against Cecil's static existence and in sympathy with George's dynamic energies. Kinetic and auditory images dominate so that nature seems always active rather than passive. The Arno River after a storm bounds on like a lion, and at several points it murmurs a promise of a free and open existence for the lovers. In Surrey and Sussex the atmosphere, comprising "the intolerable tides of heaven," is always in motion. Glorious lateral views dominate the region; but this landscape becomes ominous as Lucy represses sexual passion. The sounds and movements of nature intensify to register their protest as Lucy denies life and love. Now the sky goes wild; the winds roar through pine trees; and gray clouds, charging across the heavens, obscure the white ones and the blue sky, "as the roaring tides of darkness" set in. The novel closes on a serene note, however, with nature's forces finding fruition in human beings, as Lucy on her honeymoon surrenders not only to George but to the Florentine spring and to the Arno's whispers.

When Mr. Emerson counsels Lucy toward the novel's end, he emphasizes the difficulties of life, the continual presence of muddles, and the consequent need to clear them away; he quotes a friend of his (actually Samuel Butler): "Life is a public performance on the violin, in which you must learn the instrument as you go along". Lucy acquires now a sense of the complexities of life; and she finds that she cannot plan for it and know in advance its contingencies. This lesson she learns from her first meeting with George in Surrey, for she had not thought of meeting him when he is happy and exuberant, as a godlike being at the Sacred Lake against the background of verdant nature. Lucy herself shines with intensity throughout the novel, with the result that a rather ordinary young woman is transfigured into a radiant presence, the resolution of whose conflicts becomes a matter of genuine urgency.

George is designedly less complex than Lucy, since he need not so much modify his values as gain the courage to assert them. Early in the novel George gives Lucy "the feeling of greyness, of tragedy that might only find solution in the night", though Forster fails to establish the precise intellectual grounds for his pessimism. Forster misses in George some opportunity to convey the complicated mentality of a young man suffering from a *Weltschmerz* characteristic of the late Victorian age and induced, among other forces, by the loss of a dynamic religious faith. But George is, on the whole, a successful creation, an archetypal personage embodying the freshness, the power, and the passion of youth.

Lucy's chief mentor and George's father, Mr. Emerson, evinces a rousing candor that is refreshing, but on the whole Forster conceived him with less decisiveness and complexity than the novel demands. His valetudinarianism, for example, is too far removed from the vitality attributed to him, and his message is too direct to be aesthetically compelling. But what damages Mr. Emerson as a presence chiefly is the dated quality of some of his ideas, ideas which reveal how shallow he is when he assumes that he is being profound. In his scathing remarks about the Reverend Eager's Giotto lecture, in the Church of Santa Croce, Mr. Emerson exhibits a literalness of mind not far different from the fundamentalism he criticizes. Thus, he asserts that an edifice built by faith means that the workmen were underpaid and that Giotto's *Ascension of Saint John* is ridiculous because a "fat man in blue" could not be "shooting into the sky like an air-balloon". It is therefore difficult to agree with Forster that Mr. Emerson is "profoundly religious," for he seems to operate on the surface, rather than at the depths, of religious issues.

Forster's great success in the novel is with his rendition of the humorous and satirically envisioned persons. Some of them—the Reverend Eager, Mrs. Honeychurch, and Eleanor Lavish—Foster presents in brief, through epigrammatic summary or through their spoken words. He tells us, for instance, all we have to know of Reverend Eager, in this account of his unctuous ministrations

for transient visitors: " . . . it was his avowed custom to select those of his migratory sheep who seemed worthy, and give them a few hours in the pastures of the permanent". The portrait is made complete when Eager discourses patronizingly upon the way in which the "lower-class" Emersons have risen: "Generally, one has only sympathy with their success. The desire for education and for social advance—in these things there is something not wholly vile. There are some working men whom one would be very willing to see out here in Florence—little as they would make of it". Reverend Eager's apparent generosity, in fact, masks feelings of snobbishness, contempt, and exclusiveness.

But it is with Lucy's antagonists that Forster does best: Charlotte Bartlett and Cecil Vyse. Although he presents them satirically, he also sees them sympathetically; as a result, his humor at their expense is genial as well as satiric. Charlotte and Cecil are misguided, they are hypocrites, and they extinguish the generous instincts; they cause unhappiness and they propagate darkness. But, since they are not conscious of wrongdoing, Forster not only tolerates them but feels affection for them. As a consequence, he fully delineates them; and they become large-scale figures even if they are not complex individuals who develop dynamically.

Charlotte is given to excessive propriety and is deficient, therefore, in graciousness, kindness, and consideration. Her hypocrisies are the source of much fine comedy, as is her penchant for the irrelevant. Specious and superficial incidents and ideas gain ascendancy in her mind and allow her thereby to evade uncomfortable realities that a conscientious individual would feel obliged to facet. She is able to rationalize any occurrence in her own favor. Thus she stresses Miss Lavish's perfidy in using for her novel Lucy's being kissed by George on the Florentine heights. As a result, Charlotte diverts attention from her own perfidy in telling Miss Lavish in the first place: "Never again shall Eleanor Lavish be friend of mine". Her incompetence as a person who is "practical without ability" is the source of much humor. Her packing in Florence is protracted further than it ought to be, she is unable to pay the driver at Windy Corner because she arrives without small change and then becomes confused in her monetary calculations, and she "impedes" Mrs. Honeychurch with offers of help in tying up dahlias after a night of storm. Her sense of decorum is outlandish, as she recoils from George's casual mention in Chapter 1 that his father "is in his bath," and only she could be quite

A 19th-century English country house like the one in the novel.

so thorough a martyr in her home to a "tiresome" boiler.

The portrait of Cecil is equally authoritative. He is the diffident man who finds it difficult to become emotionally involved even with an attractive woman. Forster describes him as resembling a "fastidious saint" in the facade of a French cathedral and as being by temperament self-conscious and ascetic. His courtship follows the are from "patronizing civility" to "a profound uneasiness." The uneasiness arises when Lucy threatens to become vital and dynamic, to be more than a Leonardesque work of art. Cecil calls himself a disciple of George Meredith, agreeing with his mentor that the cause of comedy and the cause of truth are identical, though Cecil cannot realize that he will be the individual, in the course of his engagement to Lucy, to be unmasked as self-server and hypocrite.

George Emerson appraises well his adversary. He perceives that Cecil "kills," when it comes to people, by misjudging or undervaluing them, by playing tricks on them instead of cherishing "the most sacred form of life that he can find", and by being snobbish and supercilious toward those inferior to him in station and income. Accordingly, Cecil patronizes Lucy when she confuses two Italian painters, winces when Mr. Emerson mispronounces the names of artists, becomes bored and disdainful of the Honeychurches for whom "eggs, boilers, hydrangeas, maids" form part of reality, and fails to see that it is sometimes an act of kindness for a bad player to make a fourth at tennis. In short, as with Meredith's Sir Willoughby Patterne, Cecil is an egoist, with the egoist's inability to see himself as he is, with the egoist's tendency to assume that other people exist to minister to his well-being. Something of the large dimensions of Sir Willoughby inheres in Cecil's portrait, though Lucy hardly attains the dimensions of Clara Middleton, her prototype in *The Egoist*.

Northrop Frye's discussion of the *mythos* of comedy illuminates *A Room with a View* which is the only Forster narrative that can be fully assimilated to these ideas of Frye's. This *mythos* devolves about the central characters attainment of a new society after the influence of those who obstruct their free development has been neutralized (Charlotte Bartlett and Cecil Vyse are the "blocking" figures in *Room*). There transpires a new life for the hero and the heroine as they move "from a society controlled by habit, ritual bondage, arbitrary law and the older characters to a society controlled by youth and pragmatic freedom," under the aegis of "a benevolent grandfather,"—Mr Emerson in this novel. There are also occurs a visit to "the green world" of romance, to the healing powers of nature, as George and Lucy participate in their ritualistic honeymoon beside the life-restoring Arno River before they return, reinvigorated, to middle-class life in England. If anything, the mythic and archetypal—and romance—aspects of Forster's imagined universe are even more to the fore in his subsequent fiction.

Source: "A Sense of Deities Reconciled: *A Room with a View*," in *Twaynes Authors Series: Twayne English Authors,* Twayne, 1999.

Eric Haralson

In the following essay excerpt. Haralson analyzes the homoerotic elements of the Sacred Lake episode in A Room with a View.

A Room with a View, published in the same year as Forster's meeting of James, gives a convenient gauge of his progress along his different novelistic "road," as well as an inventory of the obstacles lying in it. In this monitory tale in which young lovers transcend "the rubbish that cumbers the world," obstructing both emotional and physical expression, old Mr. Emerson's much-quoted pronouncement that "love is of the body" seems a staunch rebuttal of the austerity that Forster disliked in James. Further, the novel (unlike James's) boasts characters whose clothes explicitly "take off," as with the three men who disport themselves in the Sacred Lake, a scene memorably circulated in popular culture through the Merchant Ivory film adaptation. Already in 1908, that is, Forster found himself searching—in the terms of Bristow's analysis—for "a public and plausible form" of representing homoeroticism in unobjectionable relation to both heterosexist taste and feminine authority; and already his text betrayed a crisis of representation, remaining "regulated—if not, by necessity, mystified—by profoundly heteronormative assumptions". As a narrative hot spot, the bathing scene conveys Forster's sense of the male body, in especial, as a "restless captive of culture" that "animates and disrupts the social order" and that the social order struggles always to recontain. Yet just as the clothes that "take off" eventually go back on—"To us shall all flesh turn in the end," they taunt from the lakeshore, countermanding the Thoreauvian dictum on the Emersons' wardrobe—Forster is ultimately compelled to cloak his critique of the "normal" in the garb of the normal, thus risking the same "cocooning and muffling" he deplored in James.

Before addressing the Sacred Lake episode in detail, however, it will be useful to review Forster's

characterization of his three bathers—Fredd), Honeychurch, George Emerson, and the clergyman Mr. Beebe—and of the negative countertype Cecil Vyse, who will show up with his intended, Lucy Honeychurch, and her mother to put "a confining and depressing end to the affair," as Samuel Hynes says. Young Freddy, whose letters to his sister Lucy are "full of athletics and biology" and who is seen "studying a small manual of anatomy," can easily be pegged as the earnest, hail-fellow-well-met creature of such homosocial institutions as the British public school and (prospectively) the medical establishment. Forster has fun with Freddy's efforts to sever the maternal apron strings ("Oh, do keep quiet, mother . . . and let a man do some work") and permits Cecil to sneer at him as the sort of muscular-Christian "healthy person . . . who has made England what she is," but Freddy also scores points for his glad animal movements: "Apooshoo, apooshoo, apooshoo . . . Water's simply ripping".

In George Emerson, who will dislodge Vyse as Lucy's true mate, Forster tests out a prototype of the new-age male—a character, as Bristow writes, who incorporates "an idiosyncratic blend of cultural interests . . . where the appreciation of art and 'love . . . of the body' are not separate". Yet, although George is dedicated to securing the heterosexual love-plot, and will emerge from his dip "bare-chested" and "radiant" to smite Lucy's vision, Forster simultaneously invites another frame and another kind of gaze—not only by annexing the post-Whitmanian tradition of bathing-boys scenes but also, and less obviously, by stocking George's library with his own early readings of a homoerotic hue, notably Samuel Butler's *The Way of All Flesh* and A. E. Housman's *A Shropshire Lad,* which, as Forster said, "mingled with my own late adolescence and turned inward upon me".

Completing the trio, the "stout but attractive" Mr. Beebe is a slightly more hopeful incarnation of the Victorian bachelor figure whose line of descent, as Eve Kosofsky Sedgwick has shown, includes John Marcher of "The Beast in the Jungle" (1903) and other "poor sensitive gentlemen" whose psychic constitution opens onto homosexual panic, it not homosexual possibility In a tactful but no longer difficult allusion, Forster notes that Beebe has "rather profound reasons" for responding coolly to women and for seeing them as objects of strictly anthropological curiosity, even though as a "feminized" man of the cloth he lives mainly among them. Forster's indirection in describing Beebe, moreover, is inscribed in the cleric's own manner of commentary—or what Freddy calls his "funny way, when you never quite know what he means." Not coincidentally, what puzzles Freddy's amiable but restricted mind is Beebe's contention that Vyse can only *impersonate* a (hetero)romantic suitor, being in actuality "an ideal bachelor . . . like me—better detached." And even though Forster satirizes Charlotte Bartlett's lament to Lucy, bemoaning the death of chivalry ("Oh, for a real man! . . . Oh, for your brother!"), Charlotte's sense of Beebe as "hopeless" in this regard also tags him as exemplifying another style of masculinity.

An extra emphasis on "masculinity" is warranted here, for Forster takes pains to discriminate between Mr. Beebe and Cecil Vyse as, respectively, the hearty and mostly *sympathetic* "ideal bachelor"—one who, as Charlotte primly objects, "laughs just like an ordinary man"—and the repugnant variety, one of the "despicable and regressive species of mocking intellectuals" who combined, for Forster, a precious Paterian-Jamesian aestheticism with a Wildean lassitude and antiathleticism ("I have no profession," says Cecil, "It is another example of my decadence". It is Beebe, after all, who analogizes Vyse to a Gothic statue, implying "celibacy," where a Greek statue implies "fruition"—who perceives, in a word, that Vyse is insufficiently masculine for *either* heterosexual or "masculine love" (as it will be named in *Maurice*) and thus perniciously opposed to the currents that replenish and "fructify every hour of life". In this way, too, Beebe distinguishes himself from the novel's other clergyman, the Reverend Cuthbert Eager, who fatuously praises Giotto's frescoes for being "untroubled by the snares of anatomy" and for avoiding the corporeal "taint of the Renaissance". Beebe's consent to strip and swim, then, aligns him provisionally with the adversaries of "drawing-room twaddle" and genteel Baedeker discourse (echoes of Lamb House, to Forster's ear), which chastely applauds Giotto's "tactile values" and holds that "a pity in art . . . signified the nude"—as in Charlotte's disdain for *another* water-borne being, Botticelli's Venus. Like Mr. Emerson, who pontificates about the paradise to be regained when "we no longer despise our bodies," like Lucy Honeychurch, who "by touch . . . come[s] to her desire" and "entertain[s] an image that [has] physical beauty," but decidedly *unlike* Cecil Vyse with his "depths of prudishness," Beebe votes for—and with—the body at the Sacred Lake.

What makes the lake sacred in Forster's fable is no great mystery, although here again the level of popular, heteronormative signification and reception shades into more covert "messages" and a

> **Might stopping this one step shy of fully 'carnal embracement'—a last-ditch reticence encountered in all of Forster's fiction, including *Maurice*—involve renewed concessions to a spiritualized 'love' that is always in peril of being (re)engulfed in heteronormativity?"**

queerer take on the scene As a medium of more or less *generic* lubrication, tumescence, nakedness—and notice that Lucy, too, had bathed there until "found out" and reclaimed for gentility by Charlotte—the take emblematizes Mr. Emerson's projected paradise on earth: "set in its little alp of green . . . [it was] large enough to contain the human body, and pure enough to reflect the sky". Further, to the extent that the episode advances George's conquest of Lucy, the lake reprises the riverine bed of violets in which they first kissed in Italy—that ejaculative "primal source whence beauty gushed out" to "irrigate" the grass with "spots of azure foam". At this level, both the hyperidealized scenery—the "beautiful emerald path, tempting the feet towards the central pool"—and the sacramentalized passion it induces ("a call to the blood . . . a momentary chalice for youth") subserve an Eden whose beckonings and indulgences wear a look familiarly heterosexual, or at the very least "neutral". To put this another way, Forster's obligatory insistence on scenic "purity" and, by extension, on the innocent frolicsomeness of his male bathers does little to retard the normative thrust of the narrative or to disturb the normative valence of the "floods of love . . . burst[ing] forth in tumult" that it seeks to celebrate.

Yet as we remarked in sorting through George Emerson's library, in which Housman huddles next to Nietzsche, the heralded bathing scene manages to gesture toward a different call to the blood and a different kind of sexual immersion as well. As hinted by the unidentified "aromatic plant" flourishing near the pond's "flooded margin"—almost certainly a tribute to Whitman's calamus, or sweet-flag—Forster provides a comic, if inevitably veiled, variant of the "greenwood" fantasy of masculine love that concludes *Maurice.* In a setting "beyond the intrusion of man" and nestled in the bosom of nature—in an aqueous vessel, no less, that conjures up both seminal and amniotic associations—Freddy, George, and Mr. Beebe find a social space where not only anticorporeality but also heterosexist presumption and regulation are put in suspense—where for a moment, in the parlance of *Maurice,* the Law slumbers. Whether "rotat[ing] in the pool breast high"—in Forster's campy depiction—like "the nymphs in Gotterdammerung," or "play[ing] at being Indians," or kicking their bundled clothes like schoolboys at soccer, or "twinkl[ing] into the trees," the three men try on alternative genders, ethnicities, and social roles in a temperate carnival of deviance. In fact, they even try on each other's costumes in a homoerotically coded sequence of exchanges: Freddy, who significantly cannot see the repressed Cecil Vyse "wearing another fellow's cap", here makes off with Beebe's waistcoat, while George dons Beebe's "wide-awake hat" and ends up wearing Freddy's "bags." These often phallically connotative swappings and sharings, in turn, culminate in a figurative instance of male-male conception when Freddy announces, giddily: "I've swallowed a pollywog. It wriggleth in my tummy".

But as we know—and as Forster, for all his lighthearted treatment, underscores—the Law only slumbers, soon to arouse and reinstate itself, as the amalgamated powers of the maternal, the domestic, the female-amative, and the bourgeois-respectable intervene to terminate this idyl of masculine adhesiveness. Freddy's weak protest against the restoration of conventional rule ("Look here, mother, a fellow must wash, . . . and if another fellow—") is quelled when Mrs. Honeychurch declares that, being naked, he is "in no position to argue" and gains his compliance by means of a time-honored token of motherly concern: "All these colds come of not drying thoroughly." Meanwhile George, in all his "barechested" radiance, gets carefully reinvested in the heterosexual paradigm, calling Lucy to her romantic fate "with the shout of the morning star," and Mr. Beebe finds himself painfully recalled to reality and propriety, imaging—in his paranoia—that "every pine-tree [is] a Rural Dean".

Perhaps most telling, from the standpoint of Forster's adjudication of masculinities, is his casting of Cecil as unwittingly arrayed with the feminine forces of normalization—a notion embedded in Beebe's sentinel cry of alarm, "Hi! Hi! *Ladies!*," which seems to collapse Vyse with his female companions. By now well-established as a condescending poseur who "believe[s] that women revere men for their manliness," Vyse here shows even more sharply as a walking parody of the English patriarch, "who always felt he must lead women, though he knew not whither, and protect them, though he knew not against what". To this ersatz version of an already corrupt gender style the Merchant Ivory film furnishes an added accent as Cecil—gloriously overplayed, as hardly seemed possible, by Daniel Day-Lewis—bushwhacks through the bracken, "ladies" in tow, in quest of new territory to colonize on behalf of the constrained body, male privilege, and imperial aggrandizement. We may confidently speculate that Forster, whose later novels criticize just such a "desire for possessions [and] creditable appendages," would have appreciated this touch.

A *Room with a View* might be read then as a concerted attempt to reject what Forster saw as the mistaken scheme of values informing James's oeuvre, as well as a critique of the sociopolitical context that surrounded and conditioned those writings. In a calculated riposte to authors like James, who believed fiction should delineate the "elementary passions . . . in a spirit of intellectual superiority" and who anticipated modernist misgivings about sentimentalism's "connection to a sexual body", Forster set out to give his third novel a "stifling human quality"—to make it "sogged with humanity" (in the aptly fluid terms of *Aspects of the Novel*) and *not* to deny the "sentimentality . . . lurk[ing] in the background" of much readerly pleasure. As I began this essay by suggesting—and as would become apparent in the experiment of *Maurice*—one powerful (if still hidden) motive of Forster's campaign to make a great good place for the body and naked feeling in fiction was the hope of clearing a narrative field for homosexual subjectivity—for the "generous recognition of an emotion and . . . the reintegration of something primitive into the common stock". Not only did the "common stuff" that Forster missed in James's characters need to be reanimated in the conversation of culture, but that same move should open a way toward acceptance of less common—or rather, less commonly acknowledged—sexualities as well.

In the final analysis, though, we must ask whether *A Room with a view* accomplishes or even effectively predicts such a "rout of . . . civilization" in this more ambitious sense or whether instead—as queer theory posits, and as Forster would perceive with growing acuity—certain costs attach to the traditional "marital teleology of the comic text" with its policing of nonnormative masculinities. If one means to contest the cultural position that Forster found inadequately contested in James by asserting that love is "of the body," why stipulate (as Mr. Emerson does) that love is "not the body"? Might stopping this one step shy of fully "carnal embracement"—a last-ditch reticence encountered in all of Forster's fiction, including *Maurice*—involve renewed concessions to a spiritualized "love" that is always in peril of being (re)engulfed in heteronormativity? Doesn't *A Room with a View* forfeit something *politically* vital by deferring to the usual script with its "idiotic use of marriage as a finale," as Forster wrote in *Aspects of the Novel,* repeating an opinion he held even at the time of the novel's composition? Or if one *does* nod, in the same work, toward other possible desires and consummations, how much gets changed, in the realm of the real, when the nod is only to those in the know?

The rhetorical posture of such a line of inquiry is perhaps unavoidably invidious, and as we have seen, Forster's private ruminations were not without self-doubt and self-recrimination on this score. Yet to charge "queer Forster" with not being queer *enough*—or with failing decisively to subvert heterosexist narrative conventions—would seem to miss the point. For how, in fairness, was one to "reveal the hidden life at its source" when "mutual secrecy" had always been the enabling premise of society, and especially when the state and its agencies of sexual regulation made one pay with one's body for certain disclosures? To leave Forster's perennial quarrel with Henry James simply in the region of psychobiography—the influence of somebody upon somebody, to adapt Woolf—would be to neglect the *collective* testimonial of their works to the efficacy and resilience of homophobia in what is called, evidently without conscious irony, the life of man.

Source: Eric Haralson, *Queer Forster,* edited by Robert K. Martin and George Piggford, The University of Chicago Press, 1997, pp. 66–72.

Sources

Allen, Walter, *The Modern Novel,* Dutton, 1964, pp. 36–7.

Crewes, Frederick C., "Comic Spirit," in his *E. M. Forster: The Perils of Humanism,* Princeton University Press, 1962.

Emerson, Ralph Waldo, "The Young American," in *Complete Works,* Vol. 1, Houghton Mifflin, 1903, p. 364.

Epstein, Joseph, Review, in *New York Times Book Review,* October 10, 1971, pp. 1–2, 28–9.

Frye, Northrop, *Anatomy of Criticism: Four Essays,* Princeton University Press, 1957.

Land, Stephen K., *Challenge and Conventionality in the Fiction of E. M. Forster,* AMS Studies in Modern Literature, No. 19, AMS Press, 1990.

Lucas, John, "Wagner and Forster: *Parsifal* and *A Room with a View,*" in *ELH,* Vol. 33, Issue 1, March 1966, pp. 92–117.

Masterman, C. F. G., "The Half-Hidden Life," in *The Nation,* November 28, 1908, pp. 352, 354.

McDowell, Frederick P. W., *E. M. Forster,* Twayne Publishers, 1982.

Meredith, George, "On Comedy and the Uses of the Comic Spirit," in *Comedy: An Essay on Comedy,* edited by Wylie Sypher, Peter Smith Publishers, 1983.

Meyers, Jeffrey, "The Paintings in Forster's Italian Novels," in *London Magazine,* February/March 1974, pp. 46–62.

Review in the *Morning Leader,* October 30, 1908.

Summers, Claude J., *E. M. Forster,* Frederick Ungar Publishing Co., 1983, 406 p.

Trilling, Lionel, "E. M. Forster," in *New Directions,* 2d ed., 1964.

Woolf, Virginia, "The Novels of E. M. Forster," in *The Death of the Moth and Other Essays,* Harcourt, Brace, Jovanovich, 1942.

For Further Study

Adams, Henry, *The Education of Henry Adams,* Oxford University Press, 1999.
    The greatest representative of its genre, Adams' 1906 autobiographical *bildungsroman* grapples with the themes of the corruption of humanity. In one chapter, "The Dynamo and the Virgin," he compares the figure who unified the Middle Ages, the Virgin Mary, with the technological enthusiasm of the dawn of the twentieth century. Adams fears that modernism will devolve humans into greedy beasts incapable of appreciating those finer elements of civilization—such as art.

Ellman, Richard, "Edwardians and Late Victorians," edited by Richard Ellman, Columbia University Press, 1960.
    Ellman's volume reveals the differences between the Edwardians and the Victorians. Philosophically, the Edwardians sought to create a more modern view of the world, though it was not modern enough for some.

Forster, E. M., *Aspects of the Novel,* 1927.
    Forster was the first novelist invited to deliver a Cambridge University Clark Lectures series and his se-

ries remains the most well-known. The lectures he delivered were gathered together as *Aspects of the Novel* in 1927. Forster argued in favor of remembering that a novel represents life, that it is not a dead work of art.

Frye, Northrop, *Anatomy of Criticism: Four Essays,* Princeton University Press, 1957.

Frye's work, and others like it, has helped to show the way in which cultural artifacts, like literature, are a part of a greater record of human civilization. In this work, Frye attempts to reveal the taxonomy of literature. For Frye, the literature of the West has historically utilized the same structural principles although it moves, chronologically, from pure myth to works of realism. In the "Third Essay," he diagrams the four basic patterns: romance, comedy, tragedy, and satire. Frye's work almost accomplishes the scientific analysis of literature that Forster's contemporaries, like George Meredith, desired.

Nead, Lynda, *The Female Nude: Art, Obscenity, and Sexuality,* Routledge, 1992.

The dominating discussion in *A Room with a View* hovers around the way women are viewed by society, or should be viewed. The depiction of women in artworks, Nead argues, has been historically constructed out of the long-running aesthetic debate and that depiction impacts women. She begins her discussion with a violent act by a suffragist against a painting of Venus in 1914. The work gradually journeys to female artists who are reacting to the artistic tradition.

Nye, David E., *American Technological Sublime,* MIT Press, 1994.

Nye traces the evolution of America's attitude toward technology back to the eighteenth-century aesthetic discussion of the sublime. Nye shows that technology does not have its own agency but must be championed and utilized by farsighted individuals.

Wagner, Richard, *Parzival,* directed by Hans-Jürgen Syberberg, Image Entertainment, 1999.

Early in the thirteenth century, Wolfram von Eschenbach used the unfinished epic poem by Chretien de Troyes to introduce Germans to the Grail legend. At the end of the nineteenth century, Richard Wagner—one of the most famous composers of his day—adapted the story to the stage in the form of his last opera. Elements of this story can be seen in Forster's *Room with a View* whose heroine, Lucy, cannot perform the piece for her suitor, Cecil. Image Entertainment has produced a DVD of Syberberg's 1988 production.

Walkowitz, Judith, *City of Dreadful Delight: Narratives of Sexual Danger in Late-Victorian London,* University of Chicago Press, 1992.

Late-nineteenth-century London was a dynamic period which ushered in recognizable consumerist habits. These habits were altering social customs governing young women especially and new dangers cropped up attempting to maintain traditional gender roles. Walkowitz examines the murders ascribed to the elusive Jack the Ripper and their social fallout in this book. She hypothesizes the underlying reason as a cultural habit of anxiety over women who venture out into the city alone.

The Stone Angel

Margaret Laurence
1964

Although Margaret Laurence had been publishing fiction for a decade before *The Stone Angel* was published in 1964, it was this novel that first won her a wide and appreciative audience.

In ninety-year-old Hagar Shipley, the restless, crotchety, and proud protagonist, Laurence creates a memorable character who reveals what it is like to be very old, physically frail, dependent on others, and tormented by memories of the past. Laurence also movingly depicts the sudden dawning of realization in Hagar's mind of where she has gone wrong in life, and what has been the cause of her unhappiness. The novel suggests there is hope that even those most set in their ways can find the inspiration to change for the better, and that change, even at the last stage of life, is never wasted.

The Stone Angel is also a realistic portrayal of life in the prairie towns of western Canada from the late nineteenth century to the Depression of the 1930s and beyond. Laurence went on to write four more books set in the same region, and these, together with *The Stone Angel,* are collectively known as the Manawaka series. Critics regard the series as one of the finest achievements in contemporary Canadian fiction. *The Stone Angel* in particular has continued to win respect for its structure, in which present and past are interlinked, its language, which captures the forms of Canadian speech of the period, and the universality of its theme, which at its broadest is one character's search for self-understanding and redemption.

Margaret Laurence

Author Biography

Margaret Laurence was born Jean Margaret Wemyss on July 18, 1926, in the small town of Neepawa, Manitoba, Canada, to Robert Wemyss and Verna Simpson Wemyss. Like Jason Currie, Hagar's father in *The Stone Angel,* Laurence's father was of Scottish protestant ancestry. And just as Hagar is raised without a mother, Laurence's mother died when Laurence was four. She was raised by her aunt, Margaret Campbell Simpson.

In 1944 Laurence won a scholarship to study English at United College in Winnipeg, where she published poetry and stories in the college paper. After graduation she worked as a reporter for *The Winnipeg Citizen,* and in 1949 she married Jack Laurence, a civil engineer. In 1950 her husband's work took him to the British protectorate of Somaliland (now Somalia) in Africa. In 1954, Laurence published a translation of Somali poetry, *A Tree for Poverty.* After living in Ghana from 1952 to 1957, the Laurences returned to Canada. Laurence's first novel, *This Side Jordan* (1960), and her collection of short stories, *The Tomorrow-Tamer* (1963) were both set in Ghana.

In 1962, Laurence separated from her husband and moved to England with her two children. Two years later, *The Stone Angel* was published. The fictional town of Manawaka in which much of the story takes place is based on the Neepawa of Laurence's childhood and youth. *The Stone Angel* was the first of five books by Laurence that have become known as her Manawaka series, which together create a realistic picture of the small Canadian town in the prairies from the late nineteenth century to the 1960s. The other four books are *A Jest of God* (1966), which won the Governor General's Literary Award for fiction and was adapted for the screen as *Rachel, Rachel* (1968); *The Fire-Dwellers* (1969); the semi-autobiographical collection of short stories *A Bird in the House* (1970), and *The Diviners* (1974). *The Diviners* was controversial, and in 1976 and 1978 attempts were made by religious conservatives to have it removed from the high school curriculum in Ontario.

In addition to the Manawaka novels that made her famous, Laurence wrote a critical work, *Long Drums and Cannons: Nigerian Dramatists and Novelists 1952–1966* (1968), a memoir, and several novels for children, including *Jason's Quest* (1970), *The Olden Days Coat* (1979), *Six Darn Cows* (1979), and *The Christmas Birthday Story* (1980).

In 1969, Laurence became writer-in-residence at the University of Toronto, and in 1973, after accepting a similar position at the University of Western Ontario, she moved back to Canada permanently, settling in Lakefield, Ontario. In 1974, she became writer-in-residence at Trent University.

Laurence died of cancer on January 5, 1987.

Plot Summary

Chapter 1

Ninety-year-old Hagar Shipley, who lives with her son Marvin and his wife, Doris, reminisces about her childhood in Manawaka, a fictional town in western Canada. She grew up in a large house with a stern father, her brothers, Matt and Daniel, and the housekeeper, Auntie Doll. She recalls the day Daniel fell through the ice while skating. He was rescued but developed a fever and died.

The narrative returns to the present. Over tea, Marvin says he is considering selling the house and buying something smaller. Hagar insists that the house is hers. Marvin reminds her that she made it out to him when he took over her business affairs, but Hagar still regards it as her own.

Chapter 2

Hagar is visited by the minister, Mr. Troy, but she has little patience with him. The narrative then returns to Hagar's youth. She recalls being sent to an academy for young ladies in Toronto. She hoped to become a schoolteacher, but her father insisted that she keep the accounts at his store. Hagar met Brampton Shipley at a dance, and married him against her father's wishes.

Back in the present, Hagar discovers that Marvin and Doris are planning to move her to a nursing home. Later, she reminisces again, this time about the death of her brother Matt, and how her father cut her out of his will.

After another episode in the present, in which it is clear that Hagar is forgetful and confused, she gazes at the photographs in her room. This prompts more reminiscence, of shopping trips with her husband, in which Bram's boorish behavior made her ashamed of him.

Marvin and Doris try to persuade Hagar that she will receive better care at the nursing home. Hagar wonders whether they will be able to force her to move.

Chapter 3

In the doctor's office, Hagar recalls how Bram boasted about how successful he would be. He planned to switch from farming to raising horses, but he was not a good businessman and nothing ever came of his plans.

When Hagar sees Dr. Corby, she loathes the physical examination. After supper, Marvin and Doris take her for a drive in the country, but Hagar is alarmed when she discovers they are visiting the nursing home. While there, Hagar finds fault with everything. She meets two residents of the home, Miss Tyrrwhitt, whom she dislikes, and Mrs. Steiner, to whom she takes a liking. She also recalls the birth of her first son, Marvin, and for a moment thinks a man in the summer house is her late husband.

Chapter 4

As she waits in the hospital for x-rays to be taken, Hagar returns to memories of her marriage. While her life was filled with household chores, her husband would often prefer to spend time duck-shooting or drinking.

The doctor recommends that Hagar be admitted to the nursing home, but she still resists. She recalls her second son, John, who used to get into fights at school and engaged in dangerous games with his friends. She recalls how, after watching Bram create an embarrassing scene in the store formerly owned by her father, she decided to leave him.

Back in the present, Marvin tells Hagar she must move into the nursing home in a week's time.

Chapter 5

Hagar makes plans to flee before she can be taken to the home. Then the narrative returns to her decision to leave Bram, who had no objections to her departure.

Putting her plan of escape into action, Hagar cashes her old-age pension check, buys food supplies and takes a bus to a quiet place called Shadow Point. Once in the countryside she finds an abandoned building, near to the fish cannery, long since closed. It is in a valley near the sea. She inspects it with approval. Her new abode leads into another flashback, to her memories of her life after she left Bram, when she worked as a housekeeper for an elderly man, Mr. Oatley.

Chapter 6

Hagar wakes in her makeshift home. She shivers in the cold as she lies on a mildewed, damp mattress.

The narrative goes back to Hagar's life during the Great Depression of the 1930s. John found it hard to find work, and returned to Manawaka to live with his father. Two years later, Bram became sick, and Hagar returned to live at the family home. Drought and economic depression had hit the region, and Hagar found their house in poor condition. Bram was so sick he did not recognize her, and it was John who cared for his father until his death.

Chapter 7

Hagar wakes in the morning feeling sore. She drinks from a pail of rain water, and then walks down a path to the sea. She encounters two children playing, but when they see her they run away. She walks through a wooded area and rests on a fallen tree trunk, where she recalls her life with John after Bram died. Their relationship was a quarrelsome one. Eventually, when Hagar returned to Mr. Oatley's house, John refused to accompany her. Returning the following year, Hagar learned that John planned to marry Arlene Simmons. Hagar disapproved of the match.

The chapter ends in the present, with Hagar walking to the cannery.

Chapter 8

Hagar explores the cannery and settles herself on some old boxes. A seagull flies around the room; Hagar throws a box at the bird, injuring it. At night, a man enters the cannery. He is Murray Lees, who says he has come to the cannery for some peace and quiet. As they drink the bottle of wine Lees has brought with him, Lees tells Hagar about how his son was killed in a fire at the family home.

The narrative returns to the past. Hagar relates how John and Arlene were killed when John bet his friend he could drive a truck across a railroad bridge. They were hit by a freight train. Hagar returned to Mr. Oatley's house.

In the cannery, Lees has been listening to her story and commiserates with her. They spend the night together, leaning against boxes. Lees comforts Hagar when she wakes up in the night sick.

Chapter 9

In the morning, Hagar finds that Lees has gone. He returns with Marvin and Doris, who express relief that Hagar is safe. Suffering from exposure, Hagar is taken to the hospital, where she lies in a ward of about thirty women, complaining about the lack of privacy. At first Hagar dislikes the patients in the adjoining beds, but later finds she has something in common with Elva Jardine, who comes from a town close to Manawaka. They exchange news of people they knew. When Marvin and Doris visit, they tell Hagar that Tina, her granddaughter, is getting married. Hagar pulls a sapphire ring from her finger, and asks Doris to give it to Tina.

Chapter 10

Hagar is moved into a semi-private room, which she shares with Sandra Wong, a sixteen-year-old girl who is to have her appendix out. Hagar tries to calm Sandra's fears. Doris visits with Mr. Troy. The clergyman sings a hymn, and the words make Hagar realize that her unhappiness in life has been caused by her pride. Later, she receives a visit from her grandson. In the night, Sandra is in pain. Hagar fetches a bedpan for her, struggling the few steps to the bathroom and back. A nurse arrives and is horrified to find Hagar out of bed, but when the nurse leaves, Hagar and Sandra laugh together about the incident. Marvin visits, and Hagar tells him he has always been good to her. Finally, Hagar, close to death, holds a glass of water in her hands and is ready to drink. The novel ends at this point.

Characters

Daniel Currie

Daniel Currie is the son of Jason Currie. He is four years older than his sister, Hagar. Called Dan by his family, he is delicate, lazy, and often in poor health. He dies at the age of eighteen of a fever after falling into an icy river.

Jason Currie

Jason Currie is Hagar's father. He was born in Scotland to a good family but his father lost all his money in a business deal. Currie immigrated to Canada from the Scottish Highlands with nothing to his name. However, he worked extremely hard, and as owner of Currie's General Store in Manawaka, he became wealthy. Stern, authoritarian, and a harsh disciplinarian, Currie prides himself on being a self-made man and he expects others to conform to the high standards he sets for himself. He is impatient with his sons, and refuses to let Hagar become a schoolteacher. He regards Hagar's husband, Bram, as lazy, and cuts Hagar off without a penny in his will. While stern at home, he is public-spirited, donating money for the building of a new church, and leaving all his wealth to the town.

Matt Currie

Matt Currie is the first son of Jason Currie, and Hagar's brother. He works hard in his father's store but he is clumsy. Ambitious, he dreams of becoming a lawyer or buying a ship and entering the tea trade. He marries Mavis McVitie and moves away from Manawaka. He dies of influenza while still a young man.

Lottie Dreiser

Lottie Dreiser is Hagar's childhood friend. She was born out of wedlock and is mercilessly teased because of it. The boys call her "No-Name." Lottie and Hagar never really like each other. Lottie marries Telford Simmons and she meets Hagar again when Hagar pays her a visit to express disapproval of her son John's plans to marry Lottie's daughter, Arlene.

Elva Jardine

Thin, tiny, and old, Elva Jardine is a patient in the same ward of the hospital that Hagar is admitted to. She talks a lot and tries to befriend Hagar, who slowly warms to her.

Murray F. Lees

Murray F. Lees is a middle-aged man who goes to the fish cannery at Shadow Point to find some peace and quiet. He meets Hagar there and they share their experiences of life. Lees has worked for an insurance company for twenty years. He tells the story of how his son was killed in a fire at the family home when he and his wife were out at a meeting of the Redeemer's Advocate, a Christian sect that preached the end of the world was imminent.

Mr. Oatley

Mr. Oatley is the owner of the house that Hagar lives in with her son John after she leaves her husband. He is a kind, elderly man, and Hagar is his housekeeper. When he dies he leaves Hagar some money in his will.

Henry Pearl

A big farm boy, Henry Pearl is one of Hagar's childhood friends. He marries and has three sons. He brings Hagar the news of John's accident and drives her to the hospital.

Mrs. Reilly

Mrs. Reilly is a patient in the hospital ward with Hagar. She is very large, and speaks in a melodious tone.

Bramford Shipley

Bramford Shipley is a widower who marries Hagar. Bram is tall, black-haired, and bearded, and a good dancer, but he is also vulgar in speech and manner, and largely uneducated; he never reads a book. Fourteen years older than Hagar, he has two daughters, Jess and Gladys, by his previous wife, Clara, and he fathers two sons with Hagar. He has plans to prosper and start a business raising horses, but he is lazy and never applies himself consistently. Nor does he have a good head for business. Eventually he makes himself a laughingstock because his big plans never come to anything. However, Bram does not care what others think of him and he acquires a low reputation in Manawaka. On one occasion he is threatened with jail by a policeman for relieving himself on the steps of Currie's General Store. Bram has more affection for his horses than for the people in his life. He is deeply affected by the death of his favorite stallion, Soldier, but cares nothing when his wife leaves him. Several years after Hagar's departure, Bram becomes sick, and his son John looks after him. When Hagar returns to live at his house, he is so

Media Adaptations

- A version of *The Stone Angel* on audiocassette is available from Northwest Passages, 628 Penzer Street Kamloops, BC, V2C 3G5, Canada. Web site: www.nwpassages.com

ill he does not recognize her, saying only that she reminds him of Clara, his first wife.

Doris Shipley

Doris Shipley is Marvin's wife, and Hagar's daughter-in-law. In her early sixties, Doris has the principal responsibility for looking after Hagar. She finds this increasingly difficult, and takes every opportunity to point out, with as much tact as she can manage, that Hagar has become a burden. It is Doris who has to push Marvin into moving Hagar into a nursing home. However, while she is caring for Hagar, Doris fulfills her duty as well as she is able, and she finds comfort in religion. Hagar regards Doris as unintelligent and rarely has a good word to say about her.

Hagar Shipley

Hagar Shipley is the ninety-year-old narrator of the novel. Irascible, uncharitable, and impatient with the faults of others, she fears that she is about to lose her independence by being placed in a nursing home by her son Marvin and his wife, Doris. Although tough-minded, she is physically frail, often in pain, forgetful, and confused. She speaks impulsively and sometimes regrets her harsh words even as she speaks them. She often surprises herself by crying without warning. Hagar lives as much in the past as the present. Her memories go back as far as when she was six years old, being brought up by her father, Jason Currie, a stern disciplinarian, who would on occasion beat her with a ruler or a birch twig. Hagar's mother died giving birth to her, and the female influence in the house came from the housekeeper, Auntie Doll. Although Hagar was brought up in a religious household, she has always been skeptical about religion. She received a good education at an academy in Toronto, and she prizes the ability to speak correctly, criticizing and correcting those who do not. As a tall, black-haired, handsome young woman she had pride and willfulness. She married beneath her, to the coarse Bram Shipley, in defiance of her father's wishes. After twenty-four years of marriage, during which she gives birth to two sons, Marvin and John, she once again asserts her independence by leaving her husband and taking a job in another town as a housekeeper. Although she dotes on her younger son, John, Hagar's negative attitude towards others eventually alienates him, and he returns to live with his father. Even as a ninety-year-old, Hagar retains her independence of spirit, fleeing her home and taking refuge in an abandoned building near the sea. But at the end of the novel she realizes that it is her pride that has stopped her from achieving happiness or peace of mind. Her son Marvin sums up Hagar's character when he calls her a "holy terror."

Jess Shipley

Jess Shipley is the daughter of Bram Shipley by his first marriage, to Clara. Hagar does not get along well with her, and they argue about where Bram should be buried.

John Shipley

John Shipley is Hagar's second son. He is nearly ten years younger than his brother Marvin, and is Hagar's favorite. Handsome, with straight black hair, John is inquisitive, a quick learner, and possesses a lot of energy. As a child he often tells lies and gets into fights at school. When he is a teenager he makes friends with the Tonnerre boys whom Hagar distrusts. As a young man, John tires of putting up with Hagar's negative frame of mind and returns to Manawaka to live with his father, Bram Shipley, whom he takes care of until Bram's death. John plans to marry Arlene Simmons but they are both killed after he takes on a bet that he can drive a truck across a railroad bridge. The truck gets hit by a freight train.

Marvin Shipley

Marvin Shipley is Hagar's son, married to Doris. A plodding, unimaginative man of nearly sixty-five who has settled for a quiet, respectable life, Marvin makes a living selling house paint. He dislikes conflict and tries to keep the peace in the family, but he often feels caught between Doris and Hagar, who sometimes exchange sharp words. He has to summon all his courage to inform Hagar that

she is being moved to a nursing home. Marvin was never very close to his mother as a boy. Hagar hardly regarded him as her own child, and he has none of her restless and cantankerous spirit. When he was seventeen, Marvin joined the army and fought in World War I. After the war he did not return to Manawaka but worked as a logger on the coast, and then as a longshoreman. He and Doris have a son, Steven, and a daughter, Tina. Hagar frequently thinks disparagingly of Marvin. In her eyes, he is a slow thinker who finds it difficult to express himself verbally.

Steven Shipley

Steven Shipley is Hagar's grandson. He is an architect and visits Hagar in the hospital. Hagar is fond of him.

Tina Shipley

Tina is Hagar's granddaughter who has recently moved out of the family home. She does not appear directly in the novel, but Hagar refers to her with affection.

Arlene Simmons

Arlene Simmons is the daughter of Lottie and Telford Simmons. Fair-haired and pretty, she becomes the girlfriend of John Shipley, and they plan to marry. Arlene is killed along with John when the truck John is driving across a railroad bridge is hit by a train.

Billy Simmons

Billy Simmons is the owner of the funeral home in Manawaka when Hagar is a child. He is poor and has a reputation for drinking too much.

Telford Simmons

Telford Simmons is the son of Billy Simmons. As a boy he has curly hair and a slight stammer. Later he becomes a bank manager and mayor of Manawaka.

Mrs. Steiner

Mrs. Steiner is a talkative resident of Silverthreads Nursing Home. Hagar meets her when she visits the home.

Auntie Doll Stonehouse

Auntie Doll, a widow, is Jason Currie's housekeeper while Hagar is growing up. She takes care of the three Currie children, acting as a surrogate mother.

Charlotte Tappen

A doctor's daughter, Charlotte is Hagar's best friend when they are children. She and her mother put on a wedding reception for Hagar.

Tonnerre Boys

The Tonnerre boys are three brothers who become friends with John Shipley. Their father, Jules, was friends with Matt Currie. The Tonnerres are "half-breeds," a mixture of French Canadian and Indian blood.

Mr. Troy

Mr. Troy is a young clergyman who visits Hagar several times at the request of Doris. He attempts to chat politely, but Hagar is impatient with his religious platitudes.

Sandra Wong

Sandra Wong is a sixteen-year-old girl of Asian ancestry. She shares a room in the hospital with Hagar, and undergoes surgery for the removal of her appendix.

Themes

Pride

The dominant theme of *The Stone Angel* is that of pride. As Hagar herself realizes in a moment of insight near the end of the novel, "Pride was my wilderness, and the demon that led me there was fear." By pride, Hagar means a number of related qualities, such as stubbornness, rebelliousness, willfulness, and a refusal simply to respond naturally to her own feelings. Pride made her cover up her real emotions and reactions to people and events. She was always too concerned with what others would think. In old age she says, "What do I care now what people say? I cared too long."

The novel is strewn with examples of Hagar's pride. As a girl, she refuses to cry when she is whipped by her father, and he grudgingly admits she has "backbone." As a young woman, she is unbending. When her dying brother Dan, delirious, calls out for his deceased mother, Matt tries to persuade Hagar to don her mother's old shawl and pretend to be her, in order to comfort her brother. But Hagar, although she wants to, cannot bring herself to do this. She cannot bear to imitate the frailty of the woman who died giving birth to her, because she prides herself too much on her own strength. Later, pride also stops Hagar from enjoying sexual

relations with her husband. She never lets him know when she feels pleasurable sensations, because she is ashamed of such feelings. "I prided myself on keeping my pride intact, like some maidenhead," she says.

Hagar is very concerned about keeping up appearances in front of other people. She is always aware that she received an education at a private academy and therefore knows how to behave. She looks down on those who do not speak or behave well, and this includes her own husband. She refuses to go to church after Bram has embarrassed her there with his rude comments. And in old age Hagar recalls how on countless occasions she would say to Bram, "Hush. Hush. Don't you know everyone can hear?"

Hagar's pride also results in the suppression of her real feelings. When her son John dies, she refuses to cry in front of the nurse; she will not allow a stranger to see her emotions. But then when she is alone, she finds that she is unable to cry at all. Similarly, she will not show her emotions to her first son, Marvin, when he departs to fight in World War I: "I wanted all at once to hold him tightly, plead with him, against all reason and reality, not to go. But I did not want to embarrass both of us, nor have him think I'd taken leave of my senses."

Aging

The indignities, infirmities, and fears associated with old age are continually present in the novel. Hagar must bear many things. Her memory, although razor-sharp when she recalls the events of her youth and middle age, falters when it comes to the immediate past. She forgets, for example, that her granddaughter, Tina, left the home more than a month ago, and asks Doris whether she will be home for supper. She confuses the name of her doctor with that of the doctor who practiced in Manawaka when she was a child.

Hagar has many physical problems, including an unexplained pain under her ribs which is sometimes so severe it takes her breath away. She falls frequently and also suffers from constipation and incontinence. Unaware of the latter, she accuses Doris of making it up. Her physical problems and senility have made her a danger to herself, although she does not know this until Marvin points out that one night she left a cigarette burning and it fell out of the ashtray. When Marvin and Doris tell Hagar they plan to get a sitter so they can go out one evening, she reacts so angrily to the notion that,

Topics for Further Study

- Research the topic of elder care. What are some typical problems that arise when people care for an elderly parent, and how are these shown in *The Stone Angel?*

- Investigate the aging process and how it affects short- and long-term memory. How are these changes reflected in *The Stone Angel?*

- Research the history of Manitoba and describe how it was affected by the Great Depression in the 1930s. How accurately is this reflected in what happens to Manawaka in *The Stone Angel?*

- Describe your response to Hagar Shipley. Does your reaction to her change during the course of the novel, and if so, in what way?

---

like a child, she needs a sitter, that they change their minds about going out.

In her old age, Hagar dislikes her appearance. She regards her overweight, unreliable body with disgust, and as she glances sideways in a mirror she sees:

> [A] puffed face purple with veins as though someone had scribbled over the skin with an indelible pencil. The skin itself is the silverish white of the creatures one fancies must live under the sea where the sun never reaches. Below the eyes the shadows look as though two soft black petals had been stuck there. The hair which should by rights be black is yellowed white, like damask stored too long in a damp basement.

Alienation

As a consequence of her pride, Hagar has cut herself off from the natural flow of human sympathies. In her old age, trapped in her own negative perceptions and long habits of mind, she is unable to relate harmoniously with others. She is suspicious of people's motives and rejects their attempts to be pleasant. Sometimes she would like to be more reasonable, but a bitter or sarcastic remark will escape her mouth instead, in spite of herself.

Hagar's extreme alienation, the product of a closed heart, sometimes produces unexpected effects. Because she rejects others, she expects them in turn to reject her, so a simple act of kindness from someone else may produce a sudden burst of tears, as when a girl gives up her seat for Hagar on a bus.

Hagar's alienation finds expression in her attitude to religion and to God. She never declares herself to be an atheist, but she has no belief that the universe is under the care of a loving God. She admits to Mr. Troy, the minister, that she has never been able to pray, and she pours scorn on the literalistic Christian picture of heaven: "Even if heaven were real, and measured as Revelation says, so many cubits this way and that, how gimcrack a place it would be, crammed with its pavements of gold, its gates of pearl and topaz, like a gigantic chunk of costume jewelry." Nor does Hagar accept the religious belief that everything that happens in life is for the best: "I don't and never shall, not even if I'm damned for it."

Towards the end of the novel, Hagar makes two small but significant steps that lessen her alienation. She tells Marvin that he has always been good to her, because she senses that that is what he needs to hear; she no longer thinks entirely of her own needs. And though it costs her considerable effort, she fetches a bedpan to ease the discomfort of Sandra Wong, her sixteen-year-old fellow patient in the hospital.

Style

Setting

The present-day setting of the novel, in an unnamed town in Canada, is unremarkable, but Hagar's memories of Manawaka over the years presents a rich portrait of small-town western Canada in the early days of settlement and in the Depression era.

While Hagar is a child, Manawaka is just being established. Hagar's father built the first store in the town, and the house Hagar grows up in is only the second brick house to be constructed in Manawaka; most of the other houses are still poorly built shacks and shanties. Early Manawaka is bleak and isolated. Hagar describes the immediate environment: "the bald-headed prairie stretching out west of us with nothing to speak of except couchgrass or clans of chittering gophers or the gray-green poplar bluffs." It is a harsh, unforgiving environment, in which the temperature in winter sometimes drops to forty degrees below zero.

There are many glimpses of life as it was lived in the last decades of the nineteenth century. In the absence of modern techniques of refrigeration, for example, Manawaka has a town icehouse, where ice blocks cut from the river in winter are stored all summer under sawdust.

Manawaka is a farming community, and in the 1930s there is a drought which has a devastating effect on the town. Machinery stands idle and rusting, and the whole environment presents a sad sight:

> The prairie had a hushed look. Rippled dust lay across the fields. The square frame houses squatted exposed, drabber than before, and some of the windows were boarded over like bandaged eyes. Barbed wire fences had tippled flimsily and not been set to rights. The Russian thistle flourished, emblem of want, and farmers cut it and fed it to their own lean cattle.

Point of View

The novel is written in the first person, and is narrated by Hagar. This means that everything is seen from her point of view. It is her thoughts, memories, and impressions that make up the novel; there is no direct information about what other characters are thinking and feeling. They must be understood by their words and actions as Hagar reports them. Of course, Hagar is often a biased witness. It is clear that Marvin and Doris, as they try to do what is best for Hagar, are worth more than the contempt that Hagar heaps upon them.

The limitation of the first-person point of view is that it can only relate events in which the narrator is a direct participant. In *The Stone Angel,* the author overcomes this limitation on several occasions by having Hagar overhear conversations between others. One example is when she takes some family treasures to Jess, her husband's daughter by his first marriage. She stops outside the kitchen and overhears a conversation between Jess and John, Hagar's son.

Structure

The narrative weaves back and forth between the present and the past through the technique of the flashback. Usually, the transition is prompted by something in the present that triggers Hagar's memory. For example, the nursing home she is taken to visit reminds her of a hospital, which prompts a reminiscence about the birth of her first son.

Hagar's memories are presented in chronological order. Many critics found fault with this aspect of the novel, pointing out that memories are more random and haphazard; they do not usually occur strictly in chronological order. Laurence was aware of this problem. She wrote in an essay, "Gadgetry or Growing: Form and Voice in the Novel":

> In some ways I would have liked Hagar's memories to be haphazard. But I felt that, considering the great number of years these memories spanned, the result of such a method would be to make the novel too confusing for the reader. I am still not sure that I decided the right way when I decided to place Hagar's memories in chronological order.

Imagery

The imagery in the novel is frequently drawn from the animal world. Often this is used by Hagar to present a person in an unflattering light. One of Hagar's main targets is Doris, "who heaves and strains like a calving cow"; or is seen "puffing and sighing like a like a sow in labor." Doris gapes at Marvin "like a flounder"; her voice squeaks "like a breathless mouse."

Sometimes this type of simile is used to comic effect, as when Hagar recalls that her husband "used to snort and rumble like a great gray walrus." Sometimes it is directed at Hagar herself, as when she describes herself as a "fenced cow meeting only the barbed wire whichever way she turns," or when she glares at the doctor "like an old malevolent crow, perched silent on a fence."

Symbolism

The recurring bird imagery sometimes acquires symbolic importance, as when Hagar injures a sea gull and it lies on the ground beating its wings helplessly. The sea gull symbolizes Hagar's own state of non-freedom. The bird batters itself "in the terrible rage of not being able to do what it is compelled to do," an apt description of the reality of Hagar's life, in which her desire to live independently, which her pride demands, is no longer possible.

Another symbol is the stone angel that stands over the family plot at the Manawaka cemetery. The novel opens with a description of how this white marble statue was brought from Italy by Hagar's father at great cost. It dwarfs all the other monuments in the cemetery, and is a symbol of her father's pride, which Hagar inherited.

The stone angel also symbolizes Hagar herself. Like stone, Hagar is hard and will not bend. When her son dies, she is "transformed to stone" and can-

Compare & Contrast

- **1890s:** Presbyterian clergyman Ralph Connor, one of the earliest of Canadian writers of the West, writes best-selling novels that draw on his Scottish heritage.

  1940s: Distinctive Canadian fiction, celebrating Canadian identity, begins to emerge in the work of Sinclair Ross and Hugh MacLennan.

  1960s: Margaret Laurence writes most of the Manawaka series.

  Today: Canadian writers such as Alice Munro and Margaret Atwood are in the forefront of world literature.

- **1890s:** The economy in Manitoba is based on agriculture, with manufacturing and transportation later becoming important.

  1930s: One out of every four workers is unemployed, and Manitoba is devastated by drought.

  Today: Agriculture remains the backbone of rural Manitoba, where wheat is the most important crop, followed by barley and canola.

- **1890s:** Educational opportunities for women are very limited. Like Hagar Shipley, women typically work unpaid in the home, looking after the children and performing household tasks.

  1930s: Fewer than four percent of Canadian women work outside the home.

  1960s: The women's movement emerges, calling for equality with men.

  Today: Over ten percent of women in Canada hold a university degree. Women make up more than fifty-three percent of full-time undergraduate students at Canadian universities, and account for forty-five percent of the Canadian labor force. However, in many jobs they continue to earn less than men.

not weep. Like the stone angel, which was carved with blank eyeballs, Hagar is blind, in that she can view things only from her own self-centered point of view. She lacks insight into herself.

Historical Context

An Authentic Canadian Literature

Laurence once declared that Canadian literature came of age around the time of World War II. It was then that Canadian writers ceased to look to British or American writers for models, but created stories based on Canadian themes and Canadian identity, using specifically Canadian language. One notable example was Sinclair Ross, whose novel *As for Me and My House* (1941) is set in a prairie town during the Great Depression of the 1930s. Laurence, who thought of herself as a prairie writer, acknowledged Ross's work as an influence on her own.

Laurence also named Hugh MacLennan as belonging to that first generation of Canadian-inspired writers. MacLennan's first novel was published in 1941, and he is also noted for his strong sense of place and Canadianness.

Laurence placed herself among the second generation of these specifically Canadian writers, but commented that during the 1960s and 1970s, which includes the time when *The Stone Angel* was written, it was still a struggle for such writers to gain appreciation. She said in an interview with Alan Twigg in 1981, "[I]n those days we never valued what we had as a nation. For instance, when I was in high school we never read one Canadian book. Then at university I studied the contemporary novel but all the writers were American. This was when Hugh MacLennan and Gabrielle Roy were writing some of their finest work."

By the 1980s, this had changed. In the same interview, Laurence said, "Now there's a whole new generation of Canadian writers who can almost take this 'valuing' of ourselves for granted. I like to keep reminding them that we owe a lot to that generation of writers before me. They worked in terrific isolation. A book wasn't considered any good if it didn't get a seal of approval in London or New York."

The Origins of Manawaka

The Canadian quality of Laurence's work is most noticeable in the flashback portions of *The Stone Angel* that take place in the fictional town of Manawaka. Manawaka is based on Neepawa, the prairie town in southern Manitoba that Laurence grew up in during the 1930s.

Neepawa was established in the late nineteenth century by Scottish settlers who made their way west from Ontario. The first general store was built in 1880 (in the novel, Jason Currie builds the first general store in Manawaka), and the decision of the Manitoba and Northwestern Railway to build a station in Neepawa ensured that the town would flourish. Laurence's own grandfather was the lawyer who incorporated the new town in 1883. The population then was 308.

Although Laurence commented that Manawaka is an amalgam of many prairie towns and is not to be wholly identified with Neepawa, two Manawaka landmarks which appear in *The Stone Angel* do have their real-life counterparts. Neepawa's Whitemud River, where Laurence skated as a child, becomes in the novel Wachakwa River, where Hagar's brother Dan falls through the ice. And the cemetery on the hill where the stone angel stands is based on the Riverside Cemetery in Neepawa.

Early Neepawa, like Manawaka, was a close-knit community steeped in its Scottish Presbyterian heritage that emphasized hard work and religious faith. In the novel, this heritage is embodied in Jason Currie, who was born in the Highlands of Scotland. Like many of the early settlers of Neepawa, he made his way from Ontario without a penny to his name, hoping for a new beginning in the West. Hagar recalls the "Scots burr" of his voice, and the rigid work ethic to which he adhered. Currie, who never missed a church service, embodied the qualities of self-reliance, self-discipline, orderliness, social conservatism, and dour, Calvinist religious faith that characterized these settlers of the Canadian west.

Such hardiness of body and soul served Neepawa well in the early days. By the mid-1890s the town was thriving. The area was a wheat-growing region—Neepawa is a Cree Indian word meaning

"land of plenty"—and Neepawa served as an agricultural trading center. In *The Stone Angel,* a few years after Hagar marries, "all the farms had bumper wheat crops . . . the Red Fife growing so well in the Wachakwa valley." Local industries in Neepawa included lumber milling, farm equipment manufacturing, and dairy goods production. In the novel, Hagar sells eggs for extra income to the Manawaka Creamery and to town families.

Critical Overview

When *The Stone Angel* was first published in 1964, most reviewers recognized it as a major achievement. Robertson Davies, in *The New York Times Book Review,* praised Laurence's insight into character as well as her "freshness of approach . . . her gift for significant detail." The most notable quality of the novel, according to Davies, is "her form and style. . . . She has chosen to relate the story of Hagar in a series of flashbacks, and in the work of writers whose sense of form is defective this device can be wearisome and confusing. Mrs. Laurence slips in and out of the past with the greatest of ease, without arousing any doubts of chronology." Davies also admires the language of the novel, its "good firm vocabulary, congruous with the mind of Hagar herself." Honor Tracy, in *New Republic,* bestowed equally high praise: "It is [Laurence's] admirable achievement to strike, with an equally sure touch, the peculiar note and the universal: she gives us a portrait of a remarkable character and at the same time the picture of old age itself." A reviewer for *Time* described *The Stone Angel* as "one of the most convincing—and the most touching portraits of an unregenerate sinner declining into senility since Sara Monday went to her reward in Joyce Cary's *The Horse's Mouth.*"

One of the few dissenting voices was an anonymous reviewer for London's *Times Literary Supplement,* who wrote: "It is a bleak, forbidding book. The life-denying qualities of the character which dominates it spread a chill over its pages, and in choosing to tell the story in the first person—a vast, senile soliloquy—Mrs. Laurence puts a strong check on her genuine creative gifts."

More than any other single work, *The Stone Angel* established Laurence's reputation not only in her native Canada but in the United States and internationally. The novel has stood the test of time. In 1981, Patricia Morley, in her book *Margaret Laurence,* referred to it as "Laurence's best known

The angel statue that stands over the Shipley family plot at the Manawaka cemetery is an important symbol in the novel, and also represents Hagar herself, who is hard as stone and will not bend.

and most deeply respected work, a novel hailed as a Canadian classic."

The portrayal of the character of Hagar has generally been the most admired aspect of the novel. William New, in the introduction to the 1968 edition of the book, wrote: "So sympathetically has Margaret Laurence created Hagar that we see the world through her. In following the track of her mind as it travels back and forth in its personal narrative, we are moved—not only with her, but also by her—and we come at least to understand a little more about being alive."

More recent critics have explored *The Stone Angel* from a number of different angles. Feminist critics have been attracted to it because of the strong character of Hagar. Brenda Beckman-Long, in *"The Stone Angel* as a Feminine Confessional Novel,"* has identified the novel as a "feminine confessional narrative that gives voice to a peculiarly feminine experience." Helen M. Buss, in *Mother and Daughter Relationships in the Manawaka Works of Margaret Laurence,* has taken the approach of archetypal criticism, examining the novel in terms of the mother archetype as first identified by Carl Jung: "As Hagar moves toward the unconsciousness of death she reaches for acceptance of the mother on

three levels: her memory of the personal mother; the rescue of her own repressed feminine self; and the experience of the numinosity of the Great Mother."

In addition to the accolades of critics, *The Stone Angel* has had an influence on later Canadian writers. David Staines, in his essay on Laurence in *Dictionary of Literary Biography,* points out that writers such as Jack Hodgins and Dave Godfrey saw in Laurence a model for what they were trying to achieve in their own work: "Hodgins acknowledges the importance of the novel as the first he read with a voice and a world directly related to his western sympathies."

Because of its compelling portrait of the problems associated with old age, *The Stone Angel* has also been used as a training text in geriatric nursing schools.

Criticism

Bryan Aubrey

Aubrey holds a Ph.D. in English and has published many articles on twentieth-century litera-

ture. In the following essay, he explores the spiritual journey of Hagar Shipley in The Stone Angel.

Poor Hagar Shipley. Unreconciled to old age and approaching death, relentlessly critical, unable to reach out to others, always ready to think the worst of people, Hagar is a stone angel indeed. Imprisoned in her own mind, she is unable to bring light to herself or to those around her. However, although the weight of the novel is on the negative aspects of Hagar's behavior, she eventually goes some way towards breaking down the walls she has built around her, and finding redemption.

The word *redemption* is appropriate because there are biblical echoes that suggest the novel may be interpreted as a spiritual journey. In an interview with Rosemary Sullivan, Laurence commented, "My novel in some way or other parallels the story of the Biblical Hagar who is cast out into the wilderness. . . . The natural frame of reference [is] the Biblical one."

In Genesis, Hagar is an Egyptian slave who bears a son to Abraham, then quarrels with Abraham's wife, Sarah, and is temporarily cast into the wilderness. The story is turned into an allegory by St. Paul in his letter to the Galatians (4:22–31), in which Hagar represents bondage to the flesh, without the knowledge of divine grace, whereas Sarah represents freedom.

Seen in this light, Hagar in *The Stone Angel* is a wanderer in exile, cut off from the experience of connection to God and to others. Her task, although she may not consciously realize it, is to break out of her isolation, to return to true human community that will take her beyond the confines of her own skin.

Hagar's difficult, halting spiritual journey begins about halfway through the novel, when she concocts a hare-brained scheme to thwart Marvin and Doris's plan to put her in a nursing home. She flees to a quiet place in the country. As she sits down on a toppled tree trunk she realizes that she likes this spot in the open air and muses, "Perhaps I've come here not to hide but to seek. If I sit quietly, willing my heart to cross over, will it obey?"

This is the most urgent question for Hagar to consider. Although consciously she may be referring to her own demise, her heart must "cross over" in another sense—to express compassion for others—before she can reach the safe oblivion of death. Only then will she have learned the lesson of how to live in freedom.

> **A few moments after giving the ring, she gets impatient and regrets her generosity. Never for a moment does the novelist imply that transformation is easy, or that the long habits of the past can simply be discarded without a trace."**

These lessons initially come to her obliquely through several incidents involving the natural world. As she looks down at the moss-covered tree trunk on which she sits, Hagar notices some fungus, "the velvety underside a mushroom color," and reaches down to touch it. She finds that "it takes and retains my fingerprint." After a long reverie, she comes to herself and finds that she is holding "a hairy slab of coarse moss in one hand." At her feet, a "blind slug hunches itself against one of my shoes." In these small symbolic ways, Hagar is reconnecting herself to life through the forms of the natural world.

Shortly after this, when she takes shelter in an abandoned fish cannery, Hagar notices half a dozen june bugs at her feet. They are dead, but they retain their natural beauty: "Their backs are green and luminous, with a sharp metallic line down the center, and their bellies shimmer with pure copper. If I've unearthed jewels, the least I can do is wear them." She arranges the june bugs in her hair, looks into her purse mirror and finds the effect pleasing: "They liven my gray, transform me."

The effect is rather like the garland of flowers that adorns the head of Shakespeare's *King Lear,* when he too goes through a painful experience of spiritual rebirth. Significant also is the fact that in order to put the bugs in her hair, Hagar must first remove the "prim domestic hat sprouting cultivated flowers" that she is wearing. She casts off the artificial in favor of the natural. This positive step harks back to the beginning of the novel, when in the description of the neatly kept cemetery, the artificial, civilized world of Manawaka's respectable citizens is contrasted unfavorably with the wild freedom of nature. The "wild and gaudy flowers" that grow untended, and have always done so, are more alluring than the "pompous blossoms" of the "portly peonies" that have been planted there. Man's desire to control his environment, to be "civilized" and orderly, leads only to rigid conformity and repression of the natural impulses of life.

Another moment of catharsis arrives when Hagar, still in the fish cannery, relates to Murray Lees, her unexpected visitor, the story of the death of her son John. She finds herself weeping over an event that took place over thirty years ago, something she was unable to do at the time. It is clear that Hagar is on a painful road of healing by coming to terms with her past and her true feelings.

When Hagar enters the hospital, her world shrinks to a single hospital ward, then to a semi-private room. She makes a dark joke about the next room (her coffin) being the smallest of all. And yet as her outer world shrinks, her inner world, painfully, in fits and starts, begins to expand.

But progress is slow. When Marvin visits, Hagar is surprised at how pleased she is to see him, but is unable to tell him so. What comes out of her mouth instead is a long list of complaints. A short while later, she complains about the bland diet she had been put on. But this time she is more reflective, wondering why she always needs someone to blame when things are not as she thinks they should be. Then in another moment of calmness she realizes that Marvin is concerned about Doris's health problems simply because he is fond of her. Hagar knows that this is only natural, "But it seems unfamiliar to me, hard to recognize or accept."

Another significant moment comes in the hospital ward. Initially, Hagar loathes being there, but eventually she discovers that Elva Jardine, the patient in the adjoining bed, comes from a town close to Manawaka, and they have some acquaintances in common. The fact that when Hagar is moved to a semi-private room she feels a sense of loss, as if she has been cast out, suggests that her brief friendship with Elva has served as a reminder of the links formed by human community, the barrier such community erects against the utter solitude of each human life.

Hagar also finds it in herself to recognize the links between generations. In an act of sudden generosity, she gives her mother's sapphire ring, which means a great deal to her, to her granddaughter.

There is nothing sentimental in any of these small steps that Hagar takes toward freeing herself from her mental prison. For most of the time, she remains her usual crotchety, unregenerate self. A few moments after giving the ring, she gets impatient and regrets her generosity. Never for a moment does the novelist imply that transformation is easy, or that the long habits of the past can simply be discarded without a trace.

Whatever are the forces that are gathering to aid Hagar in these last days of her life—and the agnostic Hagar would not be one to speculate—they finally produce a moment of self-realization. As Mr. Troy, whom she has always ridiculed, sings a hymn to her about rejoicing, she realizes that that must be what she has always wanted to do, but has never been able:

> Every good joy I might have held, in my man or any child of mine or even the plain light of morning, of walking the earth, all were forced to a standstill by some brake of proper appearances. . . . When did I ever speak the heart's truth?

> Pride was my wilderness, and the demon that led me on was fear. I was alone, never anything else, and never free, for I carried my chains within me, and they spread out from me and shackled all that I touched.

This realization is bitter because Hagar knows that nothing can erase the errors of the past. But it is a breakthrough nonetheless.

Hagar's redemptive journey culminates in two incidents. First, she befriends Sandra, a sixteen-year-old girl who shares Hagar's hospital room. When Sandra needs a bedpan in the middle of the night, and cannot summon a nurse, Hagar struggles the few steps to the bathroom to fetch it for her. She shuffles and lurches, gets out of breath, almost falls, and ignores stabs of pain. But she is determined to succeed. Nothing compels her to do this, other than concern for another person. After a nurse arrives and reproaches her, Hagar and Sandra laugh together over the incident. As Patricia Morley points out in *Margaret Laurence,* the pronoun "we" occurs four times in as many lines (such as "Convulsed with our paining laughter, we bellow and wheeze. And then we peacefully sleep") which makes it clear that at least for a moment, Hagar has overcome her sense of separation from others.

The second incident is a moment of rare intimacy between Hagar and Marvin. Her son apologizes for being impatient with her and clasps her hand. Hagar realizes what he needs to hear and tells him that he has always been good to her. She is at last able to see a situation from a point of view other than her own, understanding that "I . . . can only release myself by releasing him."

Later Hagar decides that these two acts—helping Sandra and comforting Marvin—are the only two free acts she has performed in all her ninety years of life.

As the novel closes, there are hints of metamorphosis. Earlier images of Hagar in the hospital suggest entrapment: she is caught "like a fish in a net"; she feels "like a trussed fowl." But now she lies in a "cocoon," which suggests the possibility of transformation, of rebirth.

Another hint of a subtle alteration in Hagar's condition is the cluster of references to angels. Hagar's words to Marvin quoted earlier allude to the biblical story of Jacob wrestling with the angel and demanding a blessing. Hagar views Marvin as Jacob and acknowledges that she is casting herself strangely as the angel. A flashback follows in which Hagar recalls a visit to the cemetery where the stone angel presides over the family plot. Then she speculates about whether life in another realm after death will be surprising in ways that she cannot imagine, just as a newborn baby must be surprised when he discovers that life on earth requires him to breathe. "If it happened that way, I'd pass out in amazement. Can angels faint?" Hagar asks herself, a question which seems to associate her at long last with the other half of the stone angel image of the title. Hagar has been like stone, hard and impenetrable, for long enough; now, perhaps it is time for her to reflect the other side of the image—messenger of truth, symbol of the eternal operation of divine love and light in the human world. It is not that stubborn Hagar herself becomes angelic, but she has pushed open a door just wide enough for light to penetrate. No longer stone, she expresses something more fluid, and it is appropriate that the final transformative image is of water. Hagar's last act is to hold in her hands a full glass of water, wresting it away from a nurse who tries to hold it for her. This is much more than a final affirmation of independence and dignity; for the glass of water held freely at life's end surely also symbolizes the inexhaustible "living water" of the New Testament that signifies divine grace, for grace, like Hagar's glass of water, is also "To be had for the taking."

Source: Bryan Aubrey, in an essay for *Novels for Students,* Gale Group, 2001.

Constance Rooke

In the following essay excerpt, Rooke analyzes The Stone Angel *from a feminist perspective, focusing on Hagar's male relationship.*

> We judge her less harshly than we might because we acknowledge the power of those forces which have worked against her. At the same time, we admire Hagar's pride precisely because it is a form (however twisted) of resistance to those forces—a statement, in fact, that Hagar Shipley is her own woman."

The Stone Angel is a carefully organized novel which operates on two obvious levels: the present time of the novel which takes us through Hagar's last days on earth, and the past time of memory which moves us in strict chronological order through the major events of her life to explain the old woman whom we see now. In support of this structure, we are made to sense the physically decrepit Hagar as a mask behind which the true Hagar continues to reside. The novel is also elaborately based upon the biblical stories of Hagar and Jacob and upon sacramental patterns of confession and communion, so that the reader may well arrive at yet another sense of the novel's two dimensions: in the foreground (both past and present) we have the realistic tale of a woman's pride, and in the background (where confirmations or hidden meanings are supposed to lie) a Christian context within which we are to measure the significance of that pride. Thus, we might suppose that Hagar's pride is something like Eve's and that it is seen by the author as reprehensible, the cause of her fall from the garden. Yet here we falter. In the realistic foregound we feel that Hagar's pride is not merely her downfall, but also her salvation—and we may question what sense to make of that within the religious context. Our difficulty is compounded by Hagar's refusal to capitulate finally to that insistent religious dimension. While she does clearly make certain accommodations, it is equally apparent that Hagar approaches her death still in the spirit of those lines from Dylan Thomas which Laurence employs as epigraph: "Do not go gentle into that good night. / Rage, rage against the dying of the light."

The difficulty which has been described here comes from our expectation that background and foreground should cohere, and perhaps from an assumption that any extensive use of the Bible and sacraments will very probably signal belief. Some of this difficulty can be resolved if we approach *The Stone Angel* from a feminist perspective. If we consider the role of Christianity in Hagar's life as a woman, we may find another justification for the weight which is given to Christianity in this novel and a partial explanation for Hagar's resistance to it. We will also discover another significant area of backgrounding, an area of feminist concern which explains or corrects our vision of the foreground in which a woman is chastised for her mistreatment of men. These various backgrounds—the past time of the novel, the religious and feminist dimensions—must be considered together if we are to understand *The Stone Angel* as a whole. They cohere as an historical explanation of how Hagar came to be the woman she is at the point of death.

The feminist dimension of *The Stone Angel* can be described as a kind of backgrounding because there is almost no overt consideration of these themes, and because the foreground may seem to be occupied with antithetical ideas. If Hagar is Everywoman, she is apparently a woman on trial for her crimes against men. Indeed, Hagar sees in the woods of Shadow Point the imaginary props and players for a jury trial in which she will summarily be found guilty; her sense of guilt is also indicated when she finds an old scale with its weights missing. But if the trial were a fair one and her attorney as eloquent as Margaret Laurence, there is little question that Hagar would be let off on compassionate grounds. *The Stone Angel* is told in the first person, by Hagar Shipley—so that Laurence must do all her pleading behind the scenes. In that background she prepares a devastating brief, a full-scale feminist analysis which operates as counterweight to the crime of pride. While she admits Hagar's share of responsibility, Laurence also cites patriarchal society as a kind of instigating culprit; and she argues that men and women alike have been injured by the forces which lead to Hagar's intractable, compensatory pride. The novel avoids polemic by this fortunate circumstance, that Hagar cannot herself articulate (because historically she does not know) the feminist view of her case. Thus, Laurence is compelled to embody these ideas rather than to discuss them, and she does so ultimately in defence of her heroine.

Hagar is consistently identified with the stone angel which is the central image of the novel, indicative obviously of her pride and blindness. But the angel is in fact a monument to Hagar's mother, "who relinquished her feeble ghost as [Hagar] gained [her] stubborn one." The association between angel and mother will require our careful attention, for it is obscured by Jason Currie's evident lack of interest in his dead wife and by our knowledge that the stone angel is essentially a monument to his own pride. Indeed, so thoroughly has she been obliterated that even her name is missing from the text. Hagar has supplanted her mother, rejected her image, and chosen instead to mirror her father's pride. But in the shadow of that stone angel which she becomes is another angel, ministering and mild—the kind of woman we take her mother to have been.

This stone angel is an imported creature, not anything original to the Canadian soil. The would-be pharaoh Jason Currie has purchased it from Italy, presumably because he thinks he can establish his pre-eminence in Manawaka only through an image crafted abroad. Clearly his is the colonial sensibility which looks to the old world for its values and for a continuation of class privilege. By the time Hagar is an old woman, Jason's pretensions (like those of Ozymandias) will have turned to dust: the Currie-Shipley stone will be recognized by a new generation as simply Canadian, marking the graves of two pioneering families with little to choose between them. The angel itself is "askew and tilted"; and even marble does not last forever—as we know from the description of Hagar's aged skin: "too white . . . too dry, powdery as blown dust when the rains failed, flaking with dryness as an old bone will flake and chalk, left out in a sun that grinds bone and flesh and earth to dust as though in a mortar of fire with a pestle of crushing light." In the light of truth, which is partly the recognition of our common mortality, the proud marble angel will finally be dissolved. But there is another angel which also must be laid to rest. And that is the image which Jason Currie seems to have imported from Britain: the Victorian image of woman as "The Angel in the House," a seminal conception of the Victorian era which is celebrated in Coventry Patmore's poem of the same name. This angel is soft, but it is ironically as rigid in conception as the marble image which Jason Currie erects over the corpse of a wife driven to an early grave—a woman puzzled, we may suppose, that her accommodation to the feminine ideal has served her no better than this. The stone angel in this sense expresses Jason

Currie's privilege as a *man,* as well as the privilege he enjoys as a man of substance. Jason had little use for women, and little reverence for those feminine virtues which inspired men like John Ruskin or Coventry Patmore to such absurd heights of idolatry; but he shared their more significant belief in male superiority, and he accepted their notions of what behaviour and what education were appropriate for a lady.

Hagar very naturally wishes to exhibit whatever qualities are consistent with her pride and are admired by others. Her nearest judge is Jason, who encourages the male virtues in her and neglects certain of the feminine virtues which he will expect her eventually to display. Proud of her refusal to cry in the scene where he beats her with a ruler, Jason remarks that she has a "backbone" and takes after him. He is proud also of her intelligence, but wishes it had been granted to his sons instead. So Hagar is courageous, proud, brainy—everything that her father admires; and she is also female, so that these virtues are perceived as useless. Moreover, they prevent the subservience which Jason ultimately expects of her. The tender virtues are not developed in Hagar: she perceives them only as weakness, a malleability which is unacceptable to her sense of self. She repudiates the silliness of other girls, dislikes anything flimsy or gutless. Only when she becomes aware of the standard which holds Lottie Drieser's china doll prettiness superior to her own strong-boned handsomeness does Hagar begin to share her father's view that a genetic irony has transpired in the Currie family: *she* should have inherited her mother's "daintiness", and the "graceful unspirited boys" should have had their father's ox-like strength. Symbolically, however, Hagar's backbone and other insistent bones preserve her from the repulsive formlessness which is stereotypically assigned to women, even as they condemn her in another sense to the rigidity of a stone angel.

In particular, Hagar loathes the vulnerability which she associates with the image of her mother, and which she perceives is equally despised by her father. Jason Currie would occasionally squeeze out a tear at the thought of his late wife, for the edification of "the matrons of the town, who found a tear for the female dead a reassuring tribute to thankless motherhood." Margaret Laurence reminds us here of the perils which attended childbirth in the days before antibiotics, and which required that women be rather forcibly locked into a notion of themselves as mothers to the race. Hagar has no wish to be a martyr; thus she approaches the

What Do I Read Next?

- *When I Am an Old Woman I Shall Wear Purple* (1991), edited by Sandra Martz, is a collection of prose, poetry, and photographs that explores the aging process in women in a positive light.

- Barbara Pym's novel *Quartet in Autumn* (1977) explores with wry humor and gentle irony the lives of four single people in their sixties. In the face of solitude and aging, they do their best to construct meaningful lives.

- William Shakespeare's *King Lear* (1605–06) is a harrowing play about an eighty-year-old king who is cast out by two of his daughters, and through extreme suffering finally attains a measure of wisdom and redemption.

- "Today Is Sunday," one of the stories in Peter Ho Davies' collection *Equal Love* (2000), is interesting because it revolves around a situation that occurs twice in *The Stone Angel,* when a character pretends to be a cherished relative of a delirious or dying person in order to offer the sick person comfort.

- *The Jest of God* (1966), the second novel in Margaret Laurence's Manawaka series, is about Rachel Cameron, a lonely teacher who eventually learns how to come to terms with her anxiety and confusion.

- *Aging 00/01,* 13th ed. (1999), by Harold Cox, is a collection of press articles that discuss a variety of problems and solutions related to aging in today's society.

- Betty Friedan's *The Fountain of Age* (1994) presents a new look at how society views aging. It shows that myths of inevitable decline are outdated, and that life can continue to be full of growth and happiness even as people age.

birth of her first son reluctantly, convinced it will be the death of her. Often in the novel, images of the birth process seem repulsive—as when Hagar observes the "mammoth matriarchal fly . . . labouring obscenely to squeeze out of herself her white and clustered eggs." As a child Hagar refuses to be lulled by her father's crocodile tears; she knows that her mother was "the brood mare who lay beneath [the monument] because she'd proved no match for his stud." So Jason Currie pays his token dues to womankind in pretending to honour his wife for her status as victim, but Hagar—instead of feeling compassion or anger on her mother's behalf—merely shares in his contempt for the biological slavery of women.

Jason's wife, in the daguerreotype which Hagar keeps of her, is "a spindly and anxious girl . . . [who] peers perplexed out of her little frame, wondering how on earth to please." That little frame is, of course, the straitjacket which Hagar wishes to avoid in her own life. It requires of women that they live to please others, and it is clearly pernicious. But Hagar reacts too extremely, becoming hidebound in pride—so that only at the point of death can she engage in "truly free" acts of maternal tenderness. The first of these, involving the pursuit of a bedpan for her young room-mate in the hospital, is possible only because Hagar has been liberated from an actual straitjacket. The second of her free acts also signifies a release from constriction and a motherly reaching out to others, as Hagar breaks the death hold of her wrestling match with Marvin (in the role of Jacob) to give her son the angel's blessing. Although she does not remember her mother in these last hours of life, Hagar as she approaches her own grave has achieved something like a reconciliation with that other angel. So it is that Hagar's last thought, as she holds the glass of water triumphantly in her own hands, taking what is there to be had, is "There. There." These are the mother words, which she has failed to supply for others in their deepest need—and which should have been as free as water. At least three times before in the novel these words have appeared, once when she thought but could not say them to Bram, once when she was trying to calm herself into remembering the name of Shadow Point, and once when she congratulated herself for standing upright in the woods: "There. There." Motherless, Hagar has for nearly all her life been unable to give a mother's love and consolation to the people who needed her. In these last words, she appears as mother to herself: it is a beautiful resolution of her independence and her need. . . .

We come now to one of the most insistent themes of the novel. Hagar is unable to let Bram know the satisfaction she feels in their lovemaking; her pride as a lady forbids any admission of that kind, so that ironically she cannot profit fully

from her choice of a virile man. Immediately following her memory of this forced coldness in Bram's bed, Hagar is seen as an old woman lying flat on her back and "cold as winter" in another bed, remembering how children lie down in snow to make "the outline of an angel with spread wings." Significantly crafted in childhood, this snow angel recalls obviously the whiteness and chill of marble as well as the chastity of the Victorian angel. The root cause of Hagar's dilemma is religion, by way of Jason—for her father's dour Presbyterianism holds that sexuality is evil. Accordingly, his affair with "No-Name Lottie Drieser's mother" is perceived as dirty, something to be concealed from decent folk. Jason's partner in crime is a Victorian stereotype, abused and dwelling in shadows: "her face soft and blank as though she expected nothing out of life . . . she began to trudge up the hill." Because women like this exist, others may remain pure . . . so absurdly pure in fact, that Hagar is condemned to enter marriage with absolutely no information about what will happen on her wedding night. The sum of Jason's teaching is that " 'Men have terrible thoughts,' " a notion which explains in part (for there are also economic motives) the Victorian allocation of chastity to women: as angels they must compensate for the bestiality of men, keeping humanity as far as possible out of Satan's grasp. Particularly was the lady to be unimpassioned, while women of a lower order (harlots and half-breeds) might be lascivious in the service of any man who chose to risk perdition. Hagar is not devout, but she is Presbyterian and Victorian enough to associate sex with stable beasts and the lower classes, with men who cannot help themselves, and with ladies least of all. In this way is her body victimized—not that she must endure her husband's embrace, but that she may not labour in love for their mutual satisfaction. She is paid for her sacrifice in being known as a lady. Again and again, Hagar relinquishes her claim to a full humanity—always in order that she may remain a lady, always failing to perceive that this apparent superiority is a ruse.

Hagar's exposure to genteel poetry and art have also contributed to her view of love as asexual: "Love, I fancied, must consist of words and deeds delicate as lavender sachets, not like things he did sprawled on the high white bedstead that rattled like a train." Bram has proven more rough Indian than Hagar had any reason to suspect. She brings to his house a print by Holman Hunt which she had acquired in the East (always the avenue for Victoriana): "I did so much admire the knight and lady's swooning adoration, until one day I saw the coyness of the pair, playing at passion, and in a fury I dropped the picture, gilt frame and all, into the slough, feeling it had betrayed me." Significantly, this picture is juxtaposed against another of horses—which Bram dislikes, despite his passion for horses, because he is annoyed that Hagar prefers the picture of the thing to the reality. The horses here (recalling Jason as stud to his wife's broodmare) obviously signify the truth of sexuality, in contrast to the myth which is perpetrated in Holman Hunt's picture. But Hagar knows that she has been betrayed, is angered not by the harsh reality of love so much as by the fact that lies such as these pale images of Holman Hunt have cut her off from authentic passion.

Hagar enters in her marriage to Bram a new kind of subjugation. She has escaped the destiny of Victorian females who sacrifice everything to their parents, a fate like that of the poor Manawaka spinster whose tomb inscription reads: *"Rest in peace. From toil, surcease. Regina Weese."* But sexual experience is not liberating for her, and the work site must perform for a houseful of men is still drudgery. That ox-like strength she would once have exchanged for daintiness takes her through twenty-four years of hard labour in which she becomes increasingly like Bram's first wife. Clara Shipley, "inarticulate as a stabled beast," was fat, her voice gruff as a man's; likewise, Hagar gains bulk (for lack, she believes, of a proper lady's corset) and wears a man's overcoat without remembering to object. But internally she remains Hagar Currie. She is contemptuous of Bram's daughters by Clara, coarse women who cannot in any way transcend their condition. At the same time, she is reduced in the fashion of all such farm wives to cheating her husband on the egg money and never questions that what little Bram's farm makes is not his own entirely. She is Hagar the Egyptian bondwoman of *Genesis*, no happier in her servitude than was that other Hagar. Always she rejects the satisfactions of martyrdom, the support which Clara Shipley received from what Hagar calls her "morbid motto": *"No Cross No Crown."* Even as an old woman, Hagar will recoil from the martyrish attitudes of her daughter-in-law, despising that slavish Christianity which looks for its reward in another world. Hagar is too proud to grovel for profit, and we may honour her for that—even as we deplore her failure to appreciate the labours of Doris, and of those other women with whom she denied kinship.

Finally, Hagar decides to leave Bram. The offence of her pride has become unendurable, and she is anxious to provide another sort of environment for John, the favoured son in whom she believes the Currie heritage will flower. Ironically, she must become a servant in earnest—a woman in uniform, no longer veiled as daughter or wife—in order to earn money and to live in the sort of house she thinks is appropriate for a Currie. Also ironically, her new position echoes that of Auntie Doll, housekeeper to the Curries, in relation to whom Hagar had supposed herself "quite different . . . a different sort entirely." That she has gone from bad to worse is suggested by the peculiarly unsavoury manner in which Mr. Oatley, her employer, has made his fortune: he has shipped Oriental wives into Canada, allowing them to plummet through the false bottom of the vessel whenever Immigration became suspicious. This grisly practice obtrudes oddly in the book, until we realize that it announces the author's concern with the wrongs which have been perpetrated against women by male society.

In a male fortress, then, a house founded on the death of women, Hagar lives quietly with John and at night (but only then) yearns for the body of her husband. She has resumed a version of the place she held in Jason Currie's house, and in her retreat to such spurious prestige has re-created for John the prison of her own childhood. John is deprived of Bram, as the Currie brothers were deprived of their father's love; and he is raised to hold himself aloof in pride, in circumstances which reveal the foolishness of pride. When the Depression strikes and his prospects are reduced to zero, John returns to Manawaka. There he presides over the death of Bram, caring for him as Matt had for Dan—again as a substitute for Hagar, who comes finally but is not recognized. This is a kind of retribution for her unwillingness at Dan's death to bend and assume another's role: now Bram, the one person who called her Hagar, mistakes her for "his fat and cowlike first wife," Clara.

During this and a subsequent visit to Manawaka, Hagar observes the love which is growing up between John and Arlene Simmons, who is Lottie Drieser's daughter. Arlene's position in Manawaka society is superior to John's, a neat reversal of the time when Hagar could hold herself superior to Lottie. Thus, John thinks at first that he is Bram-like for Arlene, illicit and therefore attractive as an opportunity for rebellion. But Arlene is free of such considerations. She has abandoned the sense of class superiority and with it the sense of sex as something a woman cannot enjoy without demeaning herself. She loves John and is capable of redeeming him for a life of joy—not of changing him exactly, as Hagar (thinking of Bram) warns her that she cannot, but of being open to him in such a way that John will change and grow of his own volition. That "stiff black seed on the page" of her *Sweet Pea Reader,* at which Hagar had stared as a child, hoping it would "swell and blossom into something different, something rare," shows signs of doing just that in the relationship of Arlene and Hagar's son. Seeing how freely Arlene can show her passion to John, Hagar finds it "incredible that such a spate of unapologetic life should flourish in this mean and crabbed world"—incredible perhaps, but for an instant she believes in this new, miraculous life for men and women.

Then she conspires with Lottie to separate their children, symbolically to stamp out their life, just as once before she stood by as Lottie trampled on the chicks emerging from their shells; in both cases death is accomplished presumably for the good of its victims. In the same punishing spirit, Jason Currie had claimed that he beat his daughter for her own good; thus he forbade her marriage to Bram. In fact his motive was self-interested, and the motive is what counts. Hagar, in need of water (her well in the wilderness) at Shadow Point, will quote Coleridge and ask "What albatross did I slay, for mercy's sake?" She will wound a gull (the spirit of love) and think "I'd gladly kill it, but I can't bring myself to go near enough." The significance of this seems to be that Hagar's fastidious pride keeps her from an act of mercy, as it had when she refused to wear the plaid shawl to ease Dan's death. In causing the separation of John and Arlene, however, their mothers do not kill "for mercy's sake," but for their own. John (whose mother will not allow him independent life) regresses to the recklessness of an embittered child and kills both himself and Arlene in a car crash. Their life is coolly stamped out. And Hagar's albatross, the guilt she feels for John's death, will be appeased only when Hagar in the role of the ancient mariner can look into her heart and admit the failure of love.

The circumstances surrounding John's death are repressed by Hagar (and kept from the reader) until the turning and gathering point of the novel, which occurs at Shadow Point. Hagar has run away from her house in Vancouver because Marvin and Doris intend to put her in the nursing home which Hagar the Egyptian thinks of as "a mausoleum": she is running still from incarceration, from any imposed image of herself as feeble or subject to another's will. Twice before Hagar had fled—from

her father's mausoleum to Bram's house, and from there to Mr. Oatley's death-like mansion in Vancouver. Her destination now repeats the flight to Bram's house. The abandoned house in which she first seeks shelter is unpainted, as the Shipley place had been; but now Hagar takes satisfaction in its weathered state, thinking how Marvin (the proper son, who sells house paint) would disapprove as once she relished Jason Currie's disapproval. Her second shelter, the cannery, with its "rusted and unrecognizable machinery" and the "skeleton" of a fishboat, also recalls the Shipley place, where "rusty machinery stood like aged bodies gradually expiring from exposure, ribs turned to the sun." These connections are important, because at Shadow Point Hagar will confront the deaths associated with the drought-plagued Shipley place—Bram's death, and finally John's. Hagar, we may remember, is herself a figure of the drought: her aged skin is "powdery as blown dust when the rains failed . . . left out in a sun that grinds bone and flesh and earth to dust as though in a mortar of fire with a pestle of light." But she will also, when she has suffered enough of such fiery enlightenment, be granted the mercy of water before her own death comes in fact.

Significantly, she must descend a stairway to arrive at the place where her genuine freedom will begin. There may be echoes here of that staircase she climbed up in Jason's house to begin her tenure as his chatelaine. Now, as the stone angel topples, as a lady would come down from her pedestal, so Hagar laboriously descends the half-rotted steps which lead to the beach. "It's not a proper stairway, actually"—it is returning to its natural condition, just as Hagar, "feeling slightly dizzy," abandons propriety to enter the depths of her own nature. On the way down these steps she feels the "goatsbeard brush satyr-like" against her—as Bram had done when they met; and she sees a kind of wildflower called the Star of Bethlehem, which (together with the Pan images) implies the spiritual rebirth which is waiting for her at Shadow Point. She delights in thinking of herself as Meg Merrilies, from the poem by Keats—an old gypsy woman (common, by the world's reckoning) whose house was "out of doors," whose "book" (like Hagar's) was "a churchyard tomb." It is as Meg *Merrilies* that she will encounter *Murray Lees,* her spiritual double, and drink the wine which is referred to in Keats' poem. They will exhibit toward one another something of that easegiving generosity which is also contained in the poem: "She plaited mats o' rushes, / And gave them to the cottagers /

She met among the bushes." Old Meg is compassionate; she sings and decks her hair with garlands (as Hagar does with June bugs); she rejoices in nature; and she dies. The model of womanhood she offers to Hagar on the eve of her own death is also one of independence and of undiminished pride: "Old Meg was brave as Margaret Queen/And tall as Amazon." This is the resolution of compassion and pride which Hagar seeks.

On the beach, Hagar sees a small boy and girl playing house. These children are later compared to John and Arlene, and there is also a connection with Hagar and Murray Lees, who take up residence together in the cannery. The girl is nagging at the boy, fussing about appearances; and Hagar wants to warn her that she will lose him if she continues to be so critical, so niggardly of praise. Again, the drought metaphor is employed: *The branches will wither, the roots they will die, / You'll be all forsaken and you'll never know why.*" When she intervenes, however, the children cling to one another—and this show of unity makes Hagar think that she has underestimated them, as clearly she does in the case of John and Arlene. Rather strangely, Hagar has claimed that she was herself forsaken: "I never left them. It was the other way around, I swear it." In any case, she is at last beginning to know why. She acknowledges here that love is the water required for growth, and that false pride can kill as surely as the drought. When love fails, each partner is forsaken; both lose, and blame is not the crucial issue.

The turning point comes with the arrival of Murray F. Lees. Almost her first remark to him is "'I hope you'll excuse my appearance,'" but soon Hagar relaxes enough to share his wine and listen to his tale. What she hears is essentially her own story: a tale in which religion plays an important role, where the chief villains are a concern for appearances and the denial of sexuality, and where the catastrophe involves the loss of a son. Murray's story is about two women, his mother and his wife. Rose Ferney was his mother's name, "'A delicate name, she used to say,'" but Rose was in fact as tough as a morning glory vine. Ironically, Hagar fails to see herself in Rose: "'Fancy spending your life worrying what people were thinking. She must have had a rather weak character.'" The point, of course, is that the proverbial clinging vine takes many forms, both strong and weak; the frailty of women can be deceptive (as in the case of Rose or Lottie), and the tenacity which is shown in an obsessive regard for appearances is also weakness.

Murray's grandfather was a circuit rider, an evangelist who greatly embarrassed his Anglican daughter-in-law; yet Murray preferred "'hellfire to [his mother's] lavender talcum,'" and became himself a Redeemer's Advocate. The passion of that sect became still more attractive when he met Lou at Bible Camp, for here it seemed was a religion in which "'prayer and *that*'" were not the "'odd combination'" which Hagar thinks they are. Then Lou got pregnant and began to worry (as Murray's mother always had) about her reputation. They married, but her concern grew with the arrival of a child too big to be premature—and her heart went out of sex. She thought that God was punishing her, and her religion became (like Jason's Presbyterianism) a denial of the flesh. But the real punishment came for Lou and Murray, as it had for Hagar, in the *death* of their son—and not his birth, which was the fruit of love. Thus, the child is killed in a fire while Lou is in the tabernacle with Murray, "'begging for the keys of heaven.'" They are punished symbolically, as Hagar is throughout her life and especially in John's death, for the denial of sexuality which Laurence opposes so vehemently in this novel. In Lou's original sensuality and its demise, we see clearly what Laurence believes has been done to women in the name of religion and propriety; in Murray's deprivation at the change in his wife, we see how this process has worked also to the disadvantage of the male.

Hagar does not come to any conscious realization of her error in listening to Murray's story. But it works on her subconsciously, as in a sort of dream she admits the guilt which is parallel to Murray's, and he assumes the role of John in order to forgive her. She also exhibits forgiveness toward Murray, first in trying to assuage his guilt over the fire, and second in pardoning him for the broken promise which brings Marvin and Doris to the cannery. Strictly speaking, Hagar is wrong when she tells Murray that "'No one's to blame'" for his son's death. Yet there are times when compassion requires us to act and speak not strictly in accordance with some ideal of truth, but with a clear sense of the other's plight. That same generosity in which Hagar has failed so often, and which she is learning with such difficulty now, must in the end be applied to her. We judge her less harshly than we might because we acknowledge the power of those forces which have worked against her. At the same time, we admire Hagar's pride precisely because it is a form (however twisted) of resistance to those forces—a statement, in fact, that Hagar Shipley is her own woman. She will not beg at

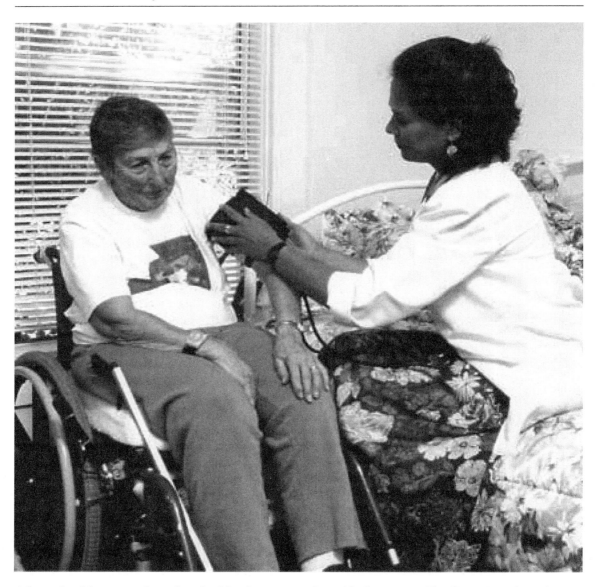

A home healthcare worker takes the blood pressure of an elderly woman. The Stone Angel *is often used by instructors of geriatric nursing, who value Laurence's illumination of the mental and physical impairments associated with aging.*

heaven's gate, or cite excuses; if there is a God, he must take her as we do—for better or worse.

With the arrival of Marvin and Doris at the cannery, we learn that Hagar is dying. She is taken to a hospital, where her pride seems to be thriving still as she insists that Marvin get her a private room. A ward full of helpless women, where you sleep "as you would in a barracks or a potter's field, cheek-by-jowl with heaven knows who all," is not the place for Hagar. Although she has just been comforted by a night in the proximity of Murray

Lees, "Nothing is ever changed at a single stroke." In fact, the ward is exactly what Hagar needs, and she is kept there long enough to make friends with Elva Jardine, a common *woman*—as if to repeat in another key her experience of comradeship with Murray Lees. It is at this point in the novel that the theme of sisterhood becomes apparent. After a lifetime of despising women, Hagar is at last compelled to join the ranks of her own sex. Her democratization (the lessening of class pride) takes the form of a movement toward her fellow women in order to suggest that Hagar has turned to pride of class partly as an escape from the humiliations of her sex.

Elva Jardine recalls Mrs. Steiner, the woman at Silverthreads Nursing Home who had seemed briefly to hold out the promise of friendship for Hagar. It was she who spoke of the comfort to be had from daughters (a point also made by Lottie), and who articulated Hagar's own astonishment at the way a woman's body can travel from puberty through childbirth to menopause with such harrowing speed that the *mind* seems left behind at every stage, aghast and wondering. Hagar liked Mrs. Steiner immediately, but saw her as a trap designed to make Silverthreads and resignation seem attractive. She ran from that "oriental shrug" which accompanied Mrs. Steiner's ironic question: "'Where will you go? You got someplace to go?'" Having run from "oriental" (or submissive) womanhood as far as she was able, Hagar at last can run no more; the body is insistent, and now what it insists upon is death. Thus, she confronts her *human* fate simultaneously with her identity as woman, which she recognizes through Elva and other women in the hospital. It is important for Laurence that Hagar should make this connection before she dies.

Hagar doesn't like Elva immediately, for her pride interferes, and she recoils as usual from the sort of woman who seems "flimsy as moth wings." But Elva is tough in spirit, as well as compassionate toward other women and tender in the love she exhibits toward her husband. All of this is a lesson for Hagar, one that strikes to her roots because Elva (by a fortunate coincidence) is from Manawaka. Thus, Hagar can return in imagination to claim Bram instead of Jason (whom she might have used to impress Elva) and to admit through Elva her kinship with those common women of Manawaka she had once denied. Like Mrs. Steiner, Elva Jardine faces her own imminent death as a woman and with courage, revealing to Hagar that the two are not at odds. And she offers another lesson in the way she handles the indignities of bowel and bladder which have been so oppressive to Hagar in her infirmity. She struggles to the bathroom on her "'own two pins,'" but will accept help when she needs it—as well as *offer* help, in the shape of a bedpan for Mrs. Dobereiner. Hagar proves that she has learned what Elva has to teach when (valiantly, but with an appreciation of absurdity) she gets the bedpan for Sandra Wong, her final room-mate. Those bedsheets which Doris washed so frequently, without complaining to Hagar until the end, are recalled by

these events—so that we have a sense of many women joining together to admit the realities of the body, and to deal with the indignities that oppose them.

In Sandra Wong, Hagar confronts the changes which have occurred in women's lives. Laurence makes her Chinese so that Hagar can imagine her as "the granddaughter of one of the small footbound women whom Mr. Oatley smuggled in, when Oriental wives were frowned upon." But Sandra "speaks just like Tina," Hagar's own liberated granddaughter—which places Hagar squarely in that generation of women whose feet were bound. The corset of a lady was more appealing to Hagar, and would seem more natural; but it is not dissimilar in function, as both forms of binding work to restrict the movements of women and reduce their size. And all of this occurs for the delectation of the male, whose vanity is flattered by an implicit comparison to his own superior mobility and stature, while ironically the vanity of woman is provoked to make her collaborate in the process of diminution. In effect, woman turns to self-love in order to avoid self-hatred; she defeats herself in order to save herself when she embraces pride of class or personal vanity as her defence. This image of constriction (the footbinding) connects with that straitjacket of pride from which Hagar must be released in order to get the bedpan for Sandra and to bless Marvin—her two "truly free" acts—and so reveals the deep interpenetration of these themes in the novel. Hagar's own complicity is further implied when she thinks, "Maybe I owe my house to her grandmother's passage money. There's a thought." She does not pursue that thought, but we may—and we realize that Hagar's mistake has been to join forces with the oppressor (all that Jason Currie has represented in the way of patriarchal, Victorian arrogance), and that she has done so for her own profit, although that profit has been illusory. In fact, she has been deformed as badly as those other women from whom she had hoped to dissociate herself. As their feet were crippled, so in her compensatory pride Hagar has been kept from the natural, healthy development of feeling which was her birthright as a woman and as a human being.

Hagar welcomes the changes which have come about for women, that the young nurse has training which allows her independence and that Sandra Wong can refer knowledgeably to hysterectomies, but she knows that nothing changes all at once: "The plagues go on from generation to generation." With Tina, however, it seems that progress has been made, for contrary to her grandmother's expectation, Tina has found "a man who'll bear her independence," and Hagar sends her a sapphire ring as a wedding present. With this ring, the novel comes a full circle. It had belonged to Hagar's despised mother, and should have gone (as Hagar tells Doris in a gesture of reconciliation) to her despised daughter-in-law first of all. It might also have gone to Arlene, of course, if Hagar had possessed the wisdom then that she shows now in sending the ring to Tina. Hagar does not envision here a future for women without men, but a situation in which both men and women will be free to love one another and to respect each other's needs. She cannot undo the past. She will not deny the person she has been. But in the act of ring-giving, Hagar succeeds in linking four generations of women with some faith that whatever plagues continue, of pride or other oppression, there will also be increasing joy.

Source: Constance Rooke, "A Feminist Reading of *The Stone Angel,*" in *Canadian Literature,* Vol. 93, Summer 1982, pp. 26–41.

Sources

Beckman-Long, Brenda, "*The Stone Angel* as a Feminine Confessional Novel," in *Challenging Territory: The Writing of Margaret Laurence,* edited by Christian Riegel, University of Alberta Press, 1997, p. 48.

Buss, Helen M., *Mother and Daughter Relationships in the Manawaka Works of Margaret Laurence,* University of Victoria Press, 1985, p. 11.

Davies, Robertson, Review, in *New York Times Book Review,* June 14, 1964, p. 4.

Laurence, Margaret, "Gadgetry or Growing: Form and Voice in the Novel," in *A Place to Stand On: Essays by and about Margaret Laurence,* edited by George Woodcock, NeWest Press, 1983, p. 83.

Laurence, Margaret, "Sources," in *Margaret Laurence,* edited by William New, McGraw-Hill Ryerson, 1977, p. 15.

Morley, Patricia, *Margaret Laurence,* Twayne, 1981, pp. 78, 81.

New, William, ed., *Margaret Laurence,* McGraw-Hill Ryerson, 1977, pp. 141–42.

Staines, David, "Margaret Laurence," in *Dictionary of Literary Biography, Volume 53: Canadian Writers Since 1960,* first series, edited by W. H. New, Gale, 1986, pp. 261–69.

Sullivan, Rosemary, "An Interview with Margaret Laurence," in *A Place to Stand On: Essays by and about Margaret Laurence,* edited by George Woodcock, NeWest Press, 1983 p. 68.

Review, in *Time,* July 24, 1964.

Review, in *Times Literary Supplement,* March 19, 1964.

Tracy, Honor, Review, in *New Republic,* June 20, 1964, p. 19.

Twigg, Alan, "Canadian Literature: Margaret Laurence," in *For Openers: Conversations with 24 Canadian Writers,* Harbour Publishing, 1981, pp. 261–71.

For Further Study

Cameron, Donald, *Conversations with Canadian Novelists,* Macmillan of Canada, 1973.
    Includes "The Black Celt Speaks of Freedom," an interview with Laurence.

Coger, Greta M. K. McCormick, ed., *New Perspectives on Margaret Laurence: Poetic Narrative, Multiculturalism, and Feminism,* Greenwood Press, 1996.
    Eighteen essays on all aspects of Laurence's work, including three on *The Stone Angel,* suitable for advanced students.

Gibson, Graeme, *Eleven Canadian Novelists,* Toronto, 1973.
    This includes a wide-ranging interview with Margaret Laurence, as well as with other Canadian authors, including Margaret Atwood, Alice Munro, and Mordecai Richler.

Kuester, Hildegard, *The Crafting of Chaos: Narrative Structure in Margaret Laurence's The Stone Angel and The Diviners,* Rodopi, 1994.
    The chapter on *The Stone Angel* is scholarly but readable, and includes an interesting section on the genesis of the novel, in which Kuester examines an earlier typescript version and compares it to the final version.

Lennox, John, and Ruth Panofsky, eds., *Selected Letters of Margaret Laurence and Adele Wiseman,* University of Toronto Press, 1997.
    Laurence conducted a forty-year correspondence with her friend and fellow novelist Adele Wiseman, and nearly four hundred of those letters are included here. There are numerous comments about *The Stone Angel.*

Morley, Patricia, *Margaret Laurence: The Long Journey Home,* McGill-Queens University Press, 1991.
    A biographical and critical study which shows the links between Laurence's African and Canadian writing and her evolving sociopolitical concerns.

Thomas, Clara, *The Manawaka World of Margaret Laurence,* McClelland and Stewart, 1976.
    This readable survey of Laurence's fiction is one of the best introductions to her work.

Watership Down

Richard Adams
1972

Watership Down was first published in 1972, when Richard Adams had almost given up on having it published at all without resorting to paying for the publication out of his own pocket. The book, which originally began as a series of stories Adams told to his two young daughters on long car trips, was originally published by a small press, Rex Collings, and then reprinted by Penguin as a juvenile title, and by Macmillan as an adult title. Surprisingly, Adams's tale of a band of adventurous rabbits became a huge success, and eventually won the Guardian Award and the Carnegie Medal. The book's success led to a great surge in the publication of other fantasies set in animal communities. Adams was not the first writer to use animals as his main characters, and noted that the animal stories of Ernest Thompson Seton served as inspiration for the book. However, *Watership Down* had the rare distinction of being read by both children and adults and of receiving wide critical acclaim. In the *International Companion Encyclopedia of Children's Literature,* Peter Hunt called the book "the most successful single postwar [World War II] animal story."

Watership Down is not a sweet fable about bunnies; it's a gritty, often frightening tale, in which characters die or become injured and these facts of life are not disguised. Hunt quoted an interview with Adams, in which Adams said of his writing style, "I derived early the idea that one must at all costs tell the truth to children, not so much about mere physical pain and fear, but about the

Richard Adams

really unanswerable things—what [writer] Thomas Hardy called 'the essential grimness of the human situation.'" Paradoxically, Adams chose a tale about rabbits to do just that.

Author Biography

Richard George Adams originally began telling the story of *Watership Down* to his two young daughters, Juliet and Rosamund, during long car trips. A civil servant in Britain's Department of Environment, Adams was interested in nature and concerned about the environment, and these interests are strongly apparent in the book, which tells the story of a group of rabbits who are forced from their home by real estate development.

Adams's daughters insisted that he publish the book, which took two years to write, but it was rejected by thirteen major publishers. Discouraged, Adams considered paying a publisher to print the book, but then heard of Rex Collings, a small publisher who had just produced a book about animal characters. Rex Collings accepted *Watership Down* and agreed to print 2,000 copies. From this modest beginning, the novel's merits spread by word of mouth among avid readers, and it was later reprinted by Penguin and Macmillan, with huge success. The book won the Guardian Award and the Carnegie Medal, and it is regarded by many as a classic of fantasy.

Richard George Adams was born May 9, 1920, in Newbury, Berkshire, England, where the book is set, and attended Bradfield College in Worcester. He received a B.A. in modern history there and earned an M.A. at Worcester College, Oxford. He served in the British Army from 1940 to 1945, and then obtained a post as a civil servant in the Ministry of Housing and Local Government in London, and was assistant secretary of the Department of the Environment until 1974, when he became a full-time writer. He has been a writer-in-residence at the University of Florida in Gainesville and at Hollins College in Virginia. In addition, he has served as president of the Royal Society for Prevention of Cruelty to Animals. He and his family have lived in London and in a cottage near the Berkshire Downs, where the events in *Watership Down* take place.

Since writing *Watership Down*, Adams has written many other books, including *Shardik, The Plague Dogs, The Girl in a Swing, Maia, Traveller,* and many other titles, including nature guides and collections of fables. He has also written an autobiography, *The Day Gone By.*

Plot Summary

A Vision of Blood

Watership Down tells the story of a small group of rabbits who leave their home, Sandleford Warren, at the urging of Fiver, a young, small rabbit who has the gift of clairvoyance and who has a vision in which the entire field where the warren is located is covered in blood. His vision is correct: the area is soon to be bulldozed and developed, and the warren will be destroyed by humans. Although most of the rabbits think they are safe and ignore Fiver's warning, a few believe him, and they set out, led by Fiver's brother Hazel, a calm and modest yearling. They head south, toward the far-off hills Fiver says will be a safe home.

Dangers along the Way

They face various hazards posed by predatory animals, such as a badger, a dog, crows, and foxes; by terrain, as they cross the Enborne River; and by humans, who have guns and cars. At a temporary rest stop, they are digging rough shelters in a meadow near the river when a well-fed, aristocratic rabbit named Cowslip appears and invites them to join his warren, which is not far off. This invitation is strange and contrary to rabbit ways, and they are initially suspicious, but eventually decide to go with him to the warren.

Too Good to Be True

The new warren is a strange place: the rabbits there are all as sleek and rich as Cowslip, and they provide the wanderers with comfortable burrows and good food, but they also all seem vaguely sad, and none of them will ever answer a direct question. This secrecy is disturbing to Hazel, Fiver, and the others, but since they can find nothing obviously wrong with the warren, they are tempted to stay there. The temptation lasts until they find out that the warren's apparent safety from predators and its abundant supply of food are the work of a nearby farmer, who leaves food out for the rabbits and shoots predators that would hunt them, but who also occasionally kills some for his own use. The rabbits in the burrow have chosen safety and wealth in exchange for their freedom and perhaps their lives, but when Bigwig, a strong and capable member of the wanderers, is caught in a snare, the wanderers realize the danger they are in and head out. Strawberry, a member of the new warren whose mate has been recently snared, also decides this price is too great to pay, and joins them.

A New Home on Watership Down

At Fiver's urging, the group climbs a high hill, known as Watership Down, and within a grove of beeches, begins digging the warren that will be its permanent home. The site is ideal: high and remote, so the rabbits can see predators from far away, and at some distance from the dangerous humans. Although these male rabbits are not accustomed to digging warrens—a task usually undertaken by female rabbits—the work makes them realize that they have become a strong team and that Hazel is a compassionate, intelligent, and capable leader. Shortly after they move in, two straggling survivors show up—rabbits who did not follow Hazel's initial warning and who stayed in the original warren, and who were there when humans poisoned and bulldozed it. These survivors are Holly, former captain of the Sandleford security force, or Owsla, and Bluebell, a young rabbit with a never-ending supply of bad jokes.

Plans for the Future

Although the rabbits now have a new home, they soon realize that their community will not last long without female rabbits and future generations to sustain it. They discover Kehaar, a wounded seagull who is lingering in the neighborhood until his wing heals, and make friends with him. In gratitude, when he is healed he agrees to fly around and reconnoiter the landscape, then come back and tell them where they can find female rabbits, or does. He reports two locations: Nuthanger Farm, where tame rabbits are kept in cages, and Efrafa, a large wild rabbit warren to the south.

The rabbits decide to send Holly and some others to that warren so that he can ask for does. While they are gone, Hazel and a small rabbit, Pipkin, go to the farm. Although they succeed in liberating two tame does there, Hazel is wounded and lost in a drainage pipe, and is only found and healed through Fiver's second sight.

Efrafa

Holly and his group return, badly shaken by their experiences at Efrafa, the large warren. The warren is a totalitarian dictatorship, run by General Woundwort, a strong and ruthless rabbit who refuses their request for does and also tries to trap and keep them in Efrafa, which is a closed society.

Hazel, undaunted, devises a plan. Bigwig goes to Efrafa, pretending to be a loner who is looking for a new home in a strong society. He infiltrates the Efrafa secret police and is accepted by Woundwort, and meanwhile works to find does who are dissident and who would be willing to leave Efrafa. These are not hard to find, because it's such an oppressive society, but getting them out safely is the challenge, as the warren is highly regulated and every move is watched. With Kehaar's help, the rabbits pass news and strategy back and forth between Bigwig and Hazel, and plan the escape from Efrafa.

A Valiant Escape

With the help of a thunderstorm, Kehaar, and a boat that a human has left on the river, Bigwig and the others run a frightening and nick-of-time course away from Woundwort and his ruthless security officers. Even after they arrive home, they find that Woundwort and his forces are still pursuing them and plan to lay siege and battle them until they are dead, in order to get the dissident does back. The enemy rabbits start digging into the new warren, and Bigwig leads the fight against them valiantly; he is almost killed by Woundwort. Hazel and other rabbits run to Nuthanger Farm, where they gnaw through the watchdog's rope and then lead him back to the warren, where he attacks Woundwort and his minions. Woundwort is killed, although his body is never found. Hazel, who was wounded back at the farm, is found by a little farm girl, nursed back to health, and brought back to the warren in a car by the girl and a local doctor who advises her that he is a wild rabbit and will be happier in the wild; thus, he returns in triumph.

The Efrafan survivors of the raid are allowed to join the Watership Down warren, and the group of rabbits, now safe, grows and prospers. By the end of the book, future generations of rabbits listen in awe to the tales of their forebears, mingled with frightening stories of General Woundwort and the rabbits' age-old mythologies.

Characters

Bigwig

Bigwig is a large, powerfully built rabbit, originally a member of his home warren's "Owsla," or police force. His name, Thlayli, literally means "furhead," a reference to the distinctive thick growth of fur on the top of his head. At first, the other rabbits are wary of him; when Hazel brings up his plan to leave the home warren, he is taken aback when Bigwig volunteers to come along. Adams writes, "The last thing Hazel had expected was the immediate support of a member of the Owsla. It crossed his mind that although Bigwig would certainly be a useful rabbit in a tight corner, he would also be a difficult one to get along with. He certainly would not want to do what he was told—or even asked—by an outskirter."

Although Bigwig is used to being respected and has a tendency to throw his weight around, as the rabbits' adventure progresses, he proves that he certainly is "a useful rabbit in a tight corner." In the new warren, the rabbits realize that they need female rabbits to carry on, or their community will not live beyond one generation. Bigwig's major role in the book involves his leadership of an expedition to an enemy warren to get doe rabbits, during which he shows not only great courage and physical strength, but also quick yet calm thinking. In the expedition, he goes alone to the warren, called Efrafa, pretending to be a loner looking for a new home in a disciplined community. Having ingratiated himself with the secret police there and pretending to be an enthusiastic member of their group, he makes friends with a dissident female rabbit, Hyzenthlay, and uses the cover of a thunderstorm and the help of a seagull, Kehaar, to lead a group of ten discontented does to safety. The escape is fraught with danger, but the group makes it to the new warren.

Arriving at their new home on Watership Down, Bigwig and the does settle in to recover from their exhausting trek, but soon find that General Woundwort, leader of Efrafa, has followed them and intends to battle over the does. Laying siege to their burrow, he sets his forces to work digging into the Watership Down warren, and Bigwig comes to its defense. He is almost killed in a personal fight with Woundwort, but in the end, with the help of all the rabbits and a dog, the Watership Down rabbits win the battle.

By the end of the book, through all these adventures, Bigwig has matured into a fair but still powerful figure in the new warren, under the leadership of Hazel. Described as "a hulking veteran, lop-eared and scarred from nose to haunch," in the final pages of the book he is teaching the new young rabbits of the warren how to deal with cats and other hazards, as a sort of benevolent old soldier.

Blackberry

Blackberry is a very clever rabbit, whose mind is quick and inventive. When the group has to cross a river, he notices an old sign on the bank and realizes that it must have drifted downstream: therefore, it must float. He also realizes that if a rabbit stands on it, the rabbit will float too: the wood can serve as a raft. Most of the other rabbits are not able to understand this, but they trust his intelligence and are able to use the wood to cross the river. Later, they use a boat in a similar manner to escape pursuit by General Woundwort and his forces. Blackberry also figures out how to open a cage that holds some does on a farm, and later participates in a dangerous quest to release a dog tied on a nearby farm and lead it to attack Woundwort and his forces.

Cowslip

Cowslip offers the wandering group shelter at his warren. When they meet him, they see that he is "a big fellow, sleek and handsome. His fur shone and his claws and teeth were in perfect condition. . . . There was a curious, rather unnatural gentleness about the way in which he waited for them to come nearer. . . . He had the air of an aristocrat." Despite this, he also has an aura of sadness about him, which puzzles the wanderers. They are further puzzled by the inhabitants of his warren, who are all equally well-fed, equally sad, and who produce art, architecture, and poetry, all of which are foreign to the rougher, traveling band of rabbits. He invites them to stay in his warren, saying that there is plenty of empty space in it, and they will be welcome there.

This puzzles them, since rabbits are usually more territorial, and eventually they discover that the good food and safety from animal predators come at a price. A nearby farmer, noticing the warren of rabbits, puts out food for them and kills predators, thus ensuring their safety, but periodically he also snares and kills some of them to sell in the market. The rabbits in the warren are aware of the price they pay, but are too comfortable to want to change it; the farmer only takes a few, and each rabbit hopes and assumes it will be someone else. Cowslip, in inviting them, knows that they will probably be killed, since they don't know about the snares—so his invitation is a death sentence in disguise. Fiver feels the menace, but his vision of the danger is not clear enough to prevent Bigwig from being caught in one of the snares.

Fiver

Fiver is an undersized rabbit, the "runt" of a large litter, whose rabbit name, "Hrairoo," literally means "Little Thousand," or "the smallest of many." Although stunted in size, Fiver is large in spirit and has a prophetic gift: he is clairvoyant, and often sees events at a distance or in the future. Because of this gift, he is often high-strung and sen-

Media Adaptations

- *Watership Down* was adapted as an animated motion picture, produced by Martin Rosen of Nepenthe Productions and directed by John Hubley and Martin Rosen, in 1978. Voice actors included Joss Ackland as the Black Rabbit, Richard Briers as Fiver, Michael Graham-Cox as Bigwig, Micheal Hordern as Frith and the narrator, and John Hurt as Hazel.

sitive; Adams writes, "He was small, with wide, staring eyes and a way of raising and turning his head which suggests not so much caution as a kind of ceaseless, nervous tension."

As the reader finds out, Fiver has a reason to be tense: he has had horrible visions of destruction. He sees the field where their warren is located covered with blood, and feels an overwhelming sense of death and danger all around them. He tells his brother Hazel about these visions, and urges that all the rabbits immediately evacuate the warren and go elsewhere. Because rabbit society is hierarchical, they must go see the Chief Rabbit and try to convince him; without his support, little can be done. The Chief Rabbit is reasonably fair, but has grown complacent in his leadership and is not inclined to listen to the ravings of a runt, especially since there is no concrete evidence of danger. The rabbits are content, there are no predators, the weather is good—in his mind, Fiver is to be pitied and patronized, not believed.

However, of course Fiver is right, and Hazel, who knows him well, believes him. With a small group of other rabbits, they leave the old warren at Sandleford and set out across country looking for a new home. Fiver has seen it in a vision, and it is a high, clean hill, known as Watership Down, from which they can see predators long before the predators see them, find abundant food, and be far from the developments of humans. As the rabbits travel, Fiver urges them on, even when they're reluctant, led astray, or attacked by enemies. Fiver's prophetic gifts, and his storytelling ability, save them more than once; his visions lead them to safety, warn them of danger, suggest new ways of coping with trouble, and offer hope when, rationally, there is none.

Fiver's gift is passed on to one of his offspring, a young rabbit who shows signs of his clairvoyance. Hazel, who has become leader of the new warren largely because of his faith in Fiver's gifts, says that as long as there are rabbits with this gift in the warren, the community as a whole will do well.

Hazel

Hazel is the leader of the rabbits who escape from Sandleford Warren after his brother Fiver warns that it will soon be destroyed; although other rabbits, including the Chief Rabbit of Sandleford, are skeptical about Fiver's warning, Hazel believes his brother and makes plans to leave. Hazel is a yearling and has not yet become a strong figure in the warren, although, as Adams writes, "He looked as though he knew how to take care of himself. There was a shrewd, buoyant air about him as he sat up, looked around and rubbed both paws over his nose." Hazel is calm, steady, and modest, as well as compassionate and fair, and as leader of the group, he encourages democratic discussion and listening to all the members of the group before making a decision. He does not always make good decisions—one that leads to trouble is his decision to get female rabbits from a nearby farm—but in general, he has balanced judgment. Eventually, he becomes the much-loved and respected leader, or Chief Rabbit, of the new warren on Watership Down.

At the end of the book, an epilogue shows Hazel lying half-asleep in his burrow when a shining stranger appears and summons him out into the spring sunshine. Although Adams does not state this explicitly, the text implies that this stranger is Lord Frith, the rabbit god, summoning him to the next world; evidently Hazel, having lived a long, eventful, and good life, has a peaceful death. As he passes some does and young rabbits on his way out, Adams writes, "he stopped for a moment to watch his rabbits and to try to get used to the extraordinary feeling that strength and speed were flowing inexhaustibly out of him into their sleek young bodies and healthy senses."

Holly

Holly is the captain of the Owsla, or security force, at the Sandleford Warren, under the leadership of the Chief Rabbit. He does not leave with the original group of rabbits, and in fact tries to arrest Bigwig and prevent him from leaving. When the bulldozers come and humans pipe poison gas into the warren, Holly escapes with one other survivor, a jester named Bluebell, and eventually finds the wanderers and joins Hazel's warren. He was originally deeply against their leaving Sandleford, but once he sees that they were right, he becomes an equally strong supporter of the new warren and Hazel's leadership in it, and even apologizes to Bigwig for trying to arrest him. He leads the initial expedition to Efrafa to get female rabbits, and barely escapes—without the does—but despite this experience is a strong fighter and leader throughout the book.

Hrairoo

See Fiver

Kehaar

Kehaar is a seagull who has been grounded by an injured wing near the Watership Down warren. When the rabbits find him, they are afraid of him at first, because most large birds prey on rabbits, but he is weak from starvation, and Hazel decides that they will help him and thus make an ally of him. Eventually, Hazel hopes, the bird can fly far and wide, find female rabbits, and tell the Watership Down rabbits where they are so that they can go get them and bring them back to join the warren. Kehaar is tough, blunt, intelligent, and social, and he is lonely now that the rest of his flock has migrated far away; although he has never socialized with rabbits before, he is happy to have others to talk to and perfectly willing to help them. He eventually finds does—at nearby Nuthanger Farm and at Efrafa. In their later confrontation with the rabbits of Efrafa, Kehaar acts as scout and spy, telling them of the enemy rabbits' movements and whereabouts as well as the layout of the terrain and carrying news back and forth from Bigwig, who is living undercover at Efrafa, and the other rabbits. He also attacks General Woundwort during his epic chase of Bigwig.

Strawberry

Strawberry is a large buck rabbit, a member of the highly civilized warren kept by a local farmer, and until his mate is killed by the farmer's snare, is a supporter of its system. When the Watership Down rabbits decide to leave, he comes with them, having realized that the price of food and safety—his mate's life—is too high to pay. He would rather live free, in the wild, and later proves to be a useful scout and fighter and a dependable member of the community.

Thlayli

See Bigwig

The Threarah

Also known as the Chief Rabbit, he is the leader of Sandleford Warren, and he has grown complacent in his power. When Hazel and Fiver come to him and tell him of Fiver's vision that the warren will be destroyed, he patronizes them and ignores their warning. "These rabbits," he says later, "who claim to have the second sight—I've known one or two in my time. But it's not usually advisable to take much notice of them." When he finds out that several rabbits have left, he sends the Sandleford security force after them, but when they come back empty-handed, he says there is no point in looking further. When Fiver's prophecy comes true and the warren is destroyed, two rabbits escape and eventually meet up with the Watership Down rabbits, but the Chief is not one of them; he does not survive the disaster.

General Woundwort

General Woundwort is the totalitarian dictator of the evil warren of Efrafa, a closed society which rabbits may enter but never leave. Like similar human societies, it has a repressive force of secret police and elaborate, brutal laws, and punishes infractions of them with torture and death. Woundwort was orphaned in infancy, grew up without love or community, and ended up savage, brutal, and with a lust for power and control. He is "almost as big as a hare and there's something about his mere presence that frightens you, as if blood and fighting and killing were all just part of the day's work to him." Woundwort forced himself into a small warren, quickly took control of it, and in time organized it into the feared warren of Efrafa. Supposedly, the elaborate repressive system of this warren is a method of keeping the rabbits from being detected and killed by humans and other enemies, and the members of the warren at first accepted this rationale. Woundwort established a ruling Council and strong-handed Owsla, both of which obeyed his commands without question. However, by the time the rabbits from Watership Down arrive, Efrafa has become overcrowded, and some rabbits are chafing against Woundwort's repressive regime.

After lengthy battles, Woundwort is finally defeated when the Watership Down rabbits lead a dog to attack him. His death is as brutal as his life was; at the end, as the dog bears down on him, he screams to his forces, "Come back, you fools! Dogs aren't dangerous! Come back and fight!" His body is never found, and eventually he becomes a sort of "bogey-man" to the local rabbits. Adams writes, "And mother rabbits would tell their kittens that if they did not do as they were told, the General would get them—the General who was first cousin to the Black Rabbit himself. Such was Woundwort's monument: and perhaps it would not have displeased him."

Themes

The Natural World and Development

A major concern in the book is the devastation of the natural world that results from human development of the land. The book's action begins when humans post a notice in the field where the rabbits live; it reads:

> THIS IDEALLY SITUATED ESTATE, COMPRISING SIX ACRES OF EXCELLENT BUILDING LAND, IS TO BE DEVELOPED WITH HIGH CLASS MODERN RESIDENCES BY SUTCH AND MARTIN, LIMITED, OF NEWBURY, BERKS.

In a harrowing chapter, one of the two survivors of the poisoning and bulldozing of the rabbits' home warren tells of the cold destruction, and the rabbits' realization that the humans killed them, as another rabbit said, "just because we were in their way. They killed us to suit themselves."

Throughout the book, the rabbits are keenly aware of humans and their disastrous effects. When they cross a road, Adams vividly describes the disgusting smells of cigarettes, tar, gasoline, and exhaust, as well as the rabbits' nauseated response to them. The cars on the road can run faster than any rabbit—something highly unnatural—and when they pass a rabbit, they don't seem to notice the rabbit at all. Machinelike, they stay on the road, and machinelike, they don't slow down for animals. This lesson of human senselessness and lack of connection or care is borne out by the presence of a smashed piece of roadkill—a hedgehog that is now "a flattened, bloody mass of brown prickles and white fur, with small black feet and snout crushed round the edges."

Humans are associated with this senseless, machinelike response to the world, which leads to callous death; they are also associated with some of the worst enemies of rabbits: cats and dogs. In contrast, Adams lovingly and vividly describes the natural world in great detail. Almost every page of the book contains passages on nature that are as vivid

Topics For Further Study

- How is General Woundwort like other dictators in human history? What methods does he use to control his community, and how are these similar to methods that have been used in repressive regimes throughout history? Do you think that his experience of an unhappy youth fully explains his actions?

- When the Watership Down rabbits meet Cowslip, they find that his community has highly developed art, poetry, and architecture, and that these rabbits look down on the religious beliefs and mythological tales the less-sophisticated Watership Down rabbits share. Are there parallels between these rabbit societies and others in human history? For instance, when Europeans first met native people throughout the world, how did they view the spiritual beliefs and customs of these people in comparison to their own?

- The rabbits in Cowslip's warren pay a price for their high standard of living: they have lost their freedom. If someone offered you all the wealth and comfort you ever dreamed of in exchange for your freedom (and perhaps someday, your life or that of someone you love), would you take it? Why or why not?

- *Watership Down* speaks strongly against development, and strongly for the preservation of the environment and the habitat of animals. In the book, the animals are the heroes and humans are shortsighted and greedy. Is there a place near you that has been destroyed by development, as the rabbits' home warren was? What was it like before, and what is it like now? Are shopping malls, suburban developments, parking lots, golf courses, and other places worth the price of losing wild land?

- Adams creates a whole world for his rabbit characters, with its own language, customs, mythology, and spiritual beliefs. These are based loosely on real, observed characteristics of rabbits as described by naturalist R. M. Lockley, whom Adams often quotes in the book. Choose an animal of your own and invent a language and society for it, basing these on real characteristics of the animal as described by naturalists.

---

as those written by any naturalist and that allow the reader to step into the rabbits' world. In fact the book begins, "The primroses were over. Toward the edge of the wood, where the ground became open and sloped down to an old fence and a brambly ditch beyond, only a few fading patches of pale yellow still showed among the dog's mercury and oak-tree roots. On the other side of the fence, the ground was full of rabbit holes. . . ."

Throughout the book, descriptions of natural beauty and rabbit life are contrasted with the disastrous effects of humanity. The first warren is utterly destroyed by development. Cowslip's warren, where the rabbits are fat and leisurely, is owned by a farmer, who kills rabbits to sell for meat. Efrafa, the totalitarian dictatorship, became that way partly in response to hazards—if humans didn't know the rabbits were there, they couldn't kill them, so General Woundwort instituted an increasingly repressive series of controls to keep the warren a secret. Kehaar the seagull is wounded by a farmer's pet cat, and so is Hazel.

The rabbits' only chance for permanent safety lies in getting as far away from humans as possible—to the remote, high country of Watership Down. What Adams does not bring up is the question of whether increasing development will eventually reach even there—if the rabbits' safe home will one day, like the first warren, be destroyed to make way for human building.

Democracy versus Totalitarianism

The book clearly contrasts two forms of leadership—democratic versus totalitarian. Under Hazel's leadership, discussion, openness, and equal participation among all members of the warren is encouraged. In the closed warren of Efrafa, General Woundwort's word is law, and any discussion is immediately punished.

In Efrafa, each rabbit is "marked," and its behavior is strictly regulated; as Holly explains, "They bite them, deep, and under the chin or in a haunch or forepaw. Then they can be told by the scar for the rest of their lives. You mustn't be found above ground [to feed or excrete waste] unless it's the right time of day for your Mark." Each Mark has a captain who oversees this and punishes infractions, and if a Mark can't go aboveground because a man or a predator is near, it must wait until the next day. To prevent the spread of infection—and dissension—rabbits are not allowed to visit another Mark's burrows without permission, which is seldom granted.

The warren's Owsla, or police, patrol the countryside, watching out for predators. When they find strange rabbits, they bring them back to Efrafa or, if they won't come back, kill them so that they don't attract the attention of humans or other predators to the area.

Supposedly, this system arose because General Woundwort, who took control of the warren, wanted to ensure its safety from predators. However, in exchange for safety from outside enemies, the rabbits now are constantly threatened and oppressed from within, by those in power. As a result, most of the rabbits in the warren can't do anything but what they're told to do; they've never been out of the warren, never smelled an enemy, and never learned to think independently.

Those who do think independently are severely punished. In a chilling incident, Bigwig meets Blackavar, a rabbit who tried to leave Efrafa. Guarded by rabbit officers, he stands at the entrance to a burrow, where all can see him. As Adams writes, "He was dreadfully mutilated. His ears were nothing but shapeless shreds, ragged at the edges, seamed with ill-knit scars and beaded here and there with lumps of proud, bare flesh. One eyelid was misshapen and closed askew." He has been held here for a month, forced to explain to all who ask that this torture and mutilation was his punishment for attempting to leave, and thus instilling fear and obedience in other possible rebels.

Style

Myths and Tales

A most unusual feature of the book is its depiction of rabbits' mythological and spiritual life.

Throughout *Watership Down,* chapters telling tales of rabbit adventures are interspersed with stories of another kind—legends from the rabbit mythology. The rabbits tell each other tales of how the first rabbit, El-ahrairah, received a white tail and strong back legs from Frith, the sun god, and at the same time, was marked as prey for many other animals. "All the world will be your enemy, Prince with a Thousand Enemies, and whenever they catch you, they will kill you. But first they must catch you, digger, listener, runner, prince with the swift warning." Other stories tell how El-ahrairah stole the king's lettuce; how he was put on trial for stealing Prince Rainbow's carrots; how, when his people were under siege, he went to the Black Rabbit of Inle (Death personified) and offered his own life in exchange for the safety of his people; how he outwitted a huge dog, and other tales. All these stories serve to reinforce the rabbits' sense of a shared heritage. They also reinforce the rabbits' view of themselves as fast, cunning, compassionate, and community-minded. Traditional rabbit virtues are like old-fashioned human ones: the hero El-ahrairah is ready to help his companions, give up his own life for them, and fight for what he believes in. At the same time, he is quick, cunning, has a bright sense of humor, and is a consummate storyteller, all traits the rabbits value highly. These myths help bond the rabbits together in times of trouble, and also inspire them with ideas to use in their own difficulties.

Naturalistic Detail

Another feature, as notable as Adams's use of myth and exactly opposite from it, is his use of closely observed, factual details of rabbit life and nature. Many of the epigrams preceding chapters are drawn from the naturalist R. M. Lockley's book *The Private Life of the Rabbit,* which Adams also cites in his acknowledgments. Adams clearly used this book to inspire and inform his descriptions of rabbit behavior and "customs." He was also a keen observer of many other aspects of natural phenomena, including weather, flowering times, the movements and appearance of insects, and the habitats of various birds and plants. A list of all the birds, plants, animals, and insects he mentions would probably comprise a relatively complete field guide to the part of England where the story is set.

As the rabbits travel across country, Adams also keenly observes and describes the smells, textures, and fauna of the different territories they cover, from the damp river bank to the mysterious and dangerous forest, to the peaty, boggy, rocky upland, to the high, clean height of Watership Down. All these places are real—though of course the characters are not—and these rich details serve to ground the reader in Adams's setting, give the story authority, and encourage the reader to believe in the "truth" of the tale.

Animal Communication

Another interesting feature of the book is that in Adams's world, rabbits can communicate with each other and with other animals, although communication with other animals takes place through a sort of universal pidgin, or primitive language, which all the animals use when talking to other species. The one "animal" who cannot understand the rabbits, and whom the rabbits can't understand, is the human. In Adams's world, humans are outside the natural order and even in opposition to it—their presence almost invariably leads to death and destruction. (The one exception to this is Lucy, the farmer's daughter, who saves Hazel and insists that the doctor bring him back to the warren in his car; perhaps this is because she is a child, and therefore still innocent and perhaps closer to the animals than adult humans are.) The book reverses the usual perception of animals as "dumb" creatures that cannot feel or communicate; in it, humans are the senseless, speechless ones. They kill without thinking, and unlike natural predators such as foxes who kill to survive, they simply roll on in their cars, or build their developments, without even noticing the devastation they've caused.

Historical Context

A Created World

Watership Down is set in the larger human world of Berkshire in England, but the historical time in which it takes place is vague. The events clearly take place sometime in the second half of the twentieth century, since cars and trucks are commonplace, and age-old fields and farms are threatened by development. However, Adams is not interested in the human world or in human history. The rabbits are the focus of the story, and of course don't know of historical events in the human world, so this aspect of the story is deliberately left vague. This gives the book an immediacy and refreshing lack of datedness that it would not have if Adams had identified the time period: the book could be taking place now, or in the 1970s, when Adams wrote it.

The rabbits do have a history and a culture of their own, although their immediate history is not as detailed, since they don't write anything down. Rabbits may have heard stories of their grandfathers or grandmothers, but their history seldom goes back farther than that; events taking place any time earlier than that gradually become part of the mythic age of El-ahrairah, the rabbits' clever, trickster hero.

The book is set in an actual area in England; Adams writes in a note at the beginning that "Nuthanger Farm is a real place, like all the other places in the book," but that the few humans mentioned in it are fictitious. In addition, Adams's close observation of place makes it evident that the places mentioned are real. Since the book was written almost three decades ago, it would be interesting for a reader, or for Adams, to go back now and note whether the landscape has changed—whether Watership Down is still safe from development, or whether the real farms, fields, and forests the fictional rabbits traveled through have changed through human intervention.

The culture of the Watership Down rabbits is similar to some traditional human cultures, with an emphasis on oral tradition and on tribal/community values such as heroism, self-sacrifice, community, family, and compassion, as well as democracy. Like human societies, however, rabbit culture and government differ from warren to warren, and as the rabbits discover, Efrafa is a physically and spiritually oppressive dictatorship. At the time Adams wrote the book, many nations lived under this type of system, most notably the Soviet Union and Eastern European countries, on which Efrafa seems to be modeled. The Cold War was still a very important factor in European and American consciousness, and people outside those countries were well aware that torture, killing, and imprisonment of dissidents was commonplace. Like Efrafa, these countries justified this oppression of their citizens with the rationale that their tight control was for the ultimate security and safety of all. Since Adams wrote *Watership Down,* the governments of many of these countries have become more democratic, but dictatorships still exist in many places in the world and the example of Efrafa is still relevant. Just as in Efrafa, history has shown that in these countries there will always be dissidents, attempts to escape, and discontent.

Critical Overview

People have probably been telling stories about animals since time began. Some of the earliest

Scene from the 1978 animated version of the novel.

known animal stories are the fables of Aesop, a slave who lived in Greece around 500 B.C. He told stories about animals, which had morals illustrating lessons and aspects of human life. Since then, many authors have told and written stories in which animals could speak and talk, and in which they have their own societies. Some early, and still well known, animal stories include Rudyard Kipling's *Just So Stories* and *Jungle Book,* Joel Chandler Harris's *Uncle Remus* stories, Kenneth Grahame's *The Wind in the Willows,* and George Orwell's *Animal Farm.* However, these stories were not realistic in the sense that they did not take into account the actual biology and behavior of the animals: the characters were basically humans in animal form.

The first realistically told animal story was *Bambi,* by Felix Salten, a Hungarian journalist. Unlike the more famous Disney film, the book is not sentimental, but is, as Cathi Dunn MacRae wrote in *Presenting Young Adult Fantasy Fiction,* "a sensitive study of a deer's natural life. Joy and fear are basic expressions for Bambi and his forest companions; death is part of life. Salten's respect for animals' experience was revolutionary."

Like Salten, Adams bases his rabbit society on many real characteristics of the biology and behavior of rabbits, particularly as they are described by naturalist R. M. Lockley in his classic *The Private Life of the Rabbit,* whom Adams often quotes in the epigraphs of chapters in the book.

In *A Reader's Guide to Fantasy,* Baird Searles, Beth Meacham, and Michael Franklin wrote that *Watership Down* "caused a sensation" when it came out, mainly because, unlike previous works such as *Bambi,* the book tells the rabbits' story in an epic context, and includes excerpts from the rabbit mythology. They also write, "There is also a healthy dose of satiric allegory, which fortunately does not dominate the novel."

Adams's success led to many others following in his footsteps and writing what have since become known as "animal fantasies." According to MacRae, this type of writing has several characteristics, including: (1) language and the ability to communicate with other species; (2) a culture that is not based on human values; (3) a visionary leader who senses dangers and leads the group toward change; (4) an underlying sense that animals are superior to brutal humans; and (5) a struggle for survival against a force, often of human origin, that threatens their way of life. As MacRae noted, *Watership Down* has been so successful, and incorporated these traits so completely, that "few animal fantasies escape comparison."

Critics have differed, however, on how effective the use of these typical conventions really is.

In *Fantasy Literature: A Core Collection and Reference Guide,* Marshall B. Tymn, Kenneth J. Zahorski, and Robert H. Boyer wrote that the main reason for the success of the book is that people are charmed by stories of animals that can talk. "This charm," they wrote, "as well as the spell of a well-told tale, is what has made [the book] so popular."

Peter Hunt wrote in the *International Companion Encyclopedia of Children's Literature,* "Its intricate depiction of a rabbit community and the characterization of its (mainly male) protagonists have enough contact with realism to make the book seem entirely credible."

However, in *Fantasy and Mimesis: Responses to Reality in Western Literature,* Kathryn Hume wrote that in her opinion, the book starts out attempting to enter rabbit minds, "but quickly lets the lapine [rabbit] vocabulary . . . substitute for real strangeness, while the plot degenerates into the adventures of animals with human brains. . . . The novelty and strangeness which entering a rabbit's mind should entail quickly disappears. The fantasy of this adventure is only skin deep; the minds and characters of these furry humans are but little touched by newness or originality."

In *National Review,* D. Keith Mano wrote in response to another critic's comment that the book did not fit any known formula, "Nonsense: it fits five or six. This bunny squad could be a John Wayne platoon of GIs. The foresighted, tactful rabbit leader. The fast rabbit. The clever rabbit. The blustery, hard-fighting noncom rabbit. . . . *Watership Down* is pleasant enough, but it has about the same intellectual firepower as *Dumbo.* . . . This is an okay book; well enough written. But it is grossly overrated."

Despite the criticisms of Mano and others, readers loved the book, sending it to the best-seller lists and leading it to be regarded as a classic of modern fantasy. In the *New York Review of Books,* Alison Lurie wrote that the reason the book was so successful and so loved was that unlike many contemporary novels, which feature sad, cynical, or nasty characters, *Watership Down* celebrates characters "who have honor and courage and dignity, who will risk their lives for others, [and] whose love for their families and friends and community is enduring and effective."

The book's popularity has endured, and since its publication, there has been a surge in the publication of animal fantasies; readers can now read books starring sentient horses, foxes, cats, and many other animals, thanks to Adams's groundbreaking work.

Criticism

Kelly Winters

Winters is a freelance writer and editor and has written for a wide variety of academic and educational publishers. In the following essay, she discusses themes of the hero's journey in Richard Adams's Watership Down.

Throughout prehistory and history, people have told stories of wanderers who, seeking a better life, travel through adversity, danger, and hardship to a new home. Richard Adams's *Watership Down* is a classic example of this "quest" story, and in his epigrams to the chapters, Adams pays homage to previous literary quests, citing John Bunyan's *Pilgrim's Progress;* Sir Thomas Malory's *Le Morte d'Arthur* about the quests of noble knights; the *Epic of Gilgamesh,* one of the earliest quest stories known; Joseph Campbell's *The Hero with a Thousand Faces,* which examines quest myths and stories worldwide; and Walter de la Mare's poem *"The Pilgrim,"* and in the text, he mentions that "Odysseus [the mythical Greek wanderer] might have borrowed a trick or two from the rabbit hero."

In the classic quest, according to Joseph Campbell in *Hero with a Thousand Faces,* the hero, in this case Hazel, is called to leave home and begin a new life. Fiver's prophetic vision, which is sparked by the human scent of a cigarette butt lying in the grass, is of the field where they live, covered with blood. This sense of the imminent, violent destruction of their old life leads Hazel, Fiver, and a few other rabbits to leave their comfortable warren—where no danger is yet evident—in search of a new home, which Fiver intuits will be a high, clean hill, far from humans and other dangers. Joseph Campbell calls this stage of the journey "the call to adventure," and writes that this call "signifies that destiny has summoned the hero and transferred his spiritual center of gravity from within the pale of his society to a zone unknown."

This means that the journeyers can no longer count on things they previously did, and that once they leave home, they must contend with a variety of dangers, both seen and unseen, some physical, some psychological. Like other wanderers, the rabbits must break out of their accustomed patterns of thought and try new things—such as crossing a river on a raft made of an old wooden notice board, digging a home for themselves, and making friends with a mouse and a seagull; must escape from predators such as dogs and foxes, and must contend with subtle, hidden dangers. When the sleek, ultracivilized rabbit Cowslip invites them to his wealthy warren, at first they are lulled by its prosperity and peace, and by the physical health and ease of its inhabitants. They are in great danger, but none of them know it except Fiver, whose intuition tells him this is a dangerous place and that death is near. They finally discover, almost too late, that a nearby farmer is snaring the rabbits, but not before Bigwig is snared and almost killed. Campbell calls this phase of the journey "the road of trials," and tells of the tests, ordeals, and dangers that other heroes faced in dreams, literature, and myths from all over the world.

The rabbits finally leave the treacherous warren and make their exhausted way to Watership Down, where they begin digging a new home. No quest is that easy, however; as Campbell wrote, "The original departure into the land of trials represented only the beginning of the long and really perilous path." The rabbits realize that it's not enough to find a home; they must also secure a future for themselves, and without families and offspring this is impossible. They need to find female rabbits, and this need sparks two perilous expeditions: one to a nearby farm where humans and dangerous cats and dogs lurk, the other to Efrafa, a repressive, totalitarian warren from which no rabbit has ever escaped alive. Like the larger journey to Watership Down, both of these journeys are fraught with perils, ordeals, and trials involving predators, treacherous terrain, doubt, and fear. In the end, both expeditions succeed, but not without great cost; rabbits are injured and changed forever, and some are killed. Like many heroes of the great quest myths, the rabbits face the presence of death, and although they survive, they are never the same.

They also grow through their adventures. Hazel matures from a yearling with potential into a calm, wise, balanced, and beloved leader. Bigwig mellows from a rather overbearing type into a seasoned, compassionate, and protective old soldier who is loved by the young rabbits, and Fiver's prophetic and intuitive gifts are respected as the ultimate source of guidance and safety in the warren. "As long as we've got some of that," Hazel says of this gift, "I dare say we'll be all right."

> " Like many heroes of the great quest myths, the rabbits face the presence of death, and although they survive, they are never the same."

Journeyers in all ages will recognize this pattern. Even in modern times, those who take to the road undergo these same phases of leaving home, facing trials and dangers, and sometimes even death, and of being buoyed up by intuition, a connection to mystery, and coincidence. In *The Archetype of Pilgrimage,* Jean Dalby Clift and Wallace B. Clift quote Alan Nichols, who rode a bicycle through Central Asia and was lost in a blizzard: "I accepted the fact that I was going to die. . . . I told myself I would fight to survive as long as I could. I prayed. After a time, the first of my miracles occurred. The snow storm stopped, the wind died down, and the sky cleared leaving only a huge full moon in the sky. I took that to be a sign that I would survive."

This is remarkably similar to the tale of the rabbits in *Watership Down,* who tell stories of their gods and heroes and draw upon their strength in dangerous times. When Holly, Silver, Buckthorn, and Strawberry escape from Efrafa, they experiences a miracle in the form of a train that thunders down the track they have just crossed and cuts off the rabbit soldiers pursuing them. When Hazel is shot by men and left bleeding to death in a drainage ditch, he is found and saved only because Fiver, in a vision, sees where he is and summons help.

At Efrafa, the danger is both physical and mental—rabbits are tortured and killed, and they are also deprived of free speech and the right to think independently. In a harrowing scene, the dissident Blackavar is exposed for all to see, his ears ripped to shreds, as he pathetically mumbles his crime: wanting to leave Efrafa. Bigwig courageously goes to Efrafa and, with the help of the other rabbits and the seagull Kehaar, manages to escape, bringing female rabbits from Efrafa with him. A very similar, but true, story of an escape from a totalitarian prison is told in Slavomir Rawicz's gripping book, *The Long Walk: The True Story of a Trek to Free-*

What Do I Read Next?

- *Tales from Watership Down,* by Richard Adams (1998), continues the story of *Watership Down* and includes new tales from the rabbit mythology.

- Richard Adams's *The Plague Dogs* (1978) tells of the adventures of two dogs who escape from an animal experimentation laboratory.

- In Richard Adams's heroic saga of a mythical past, *Shardik* (1975), people worship a giant bear.

- *Traveller* (1988), by Richard Adams, tells the story of the Civil War from the point of view of General Robert E. Lee's horse, whose name was Traveller.

- In Brian Jacques's *Redwall* (1998), the one-eyed rat warlord, Cluny the Scourge, is hell-bent on destroying the tranquillity of Redwall Abbey as he prepares to fight a bloody battle for its ownership.

- *Mossflower,* by Brian Jacques (1998), is the story of how mouse Martin the Warrior and his woodland friends fight ruthless wild cats for leadership of the abbey and Mossflower Woods.

- In Brian Jacques's *Marlfox* (2000), when marlfoxes steal the precious tapestry of Martin the Warrior, the children of warrior squirrels must follow in their fathers' heroic footsteps to recover it.

---

dom, in which Rawicz describes his and his companions' three-thousand-mile trek across Siberia, through China and the Gobi Desert of Mongolia and across the Himalayas to India in the early 1940s, after their escape from a Siberian prison camp in the Soviet Union. Like the rabbits in Efrafa, Rawicz learned early on that "the prisoner was left in no doubt that a deviation off course to right or left would mean death from the carbine or pistol of the guards marching two paces behind

him." Blackavar, who likewise is always accompanied by two burly guards, tells Bigwig what he has been taught to say: "Every Mark should see how I have been punished as I deserve for my treachery in trying to leave the warren."

Another aspect of the classic journey is that when the journey is over, the journeyer must share the story with others, thus inspiring them. At the end of the book, the rabbit Vilthuril tells the young rabbits the story of the wandering rabbits' adventure, except that now it has been incorporated into the rabbits' body of myth; Hazel and the others have become the rabbit hero El-ahrairah and his people, and Cowslip's wealthy, civilized warren is now a place where all the rabbits "were in the power of a wicked spell. They wore shining collars round their necks and sang like the birds and some of them could fly." Likewise, Kehaar the seagull has become "a great white bird which spoke to [El-ahrairah] and blessed him."

Just because the rabbits' true story has become amplified into myth, however, does not mean that it is now distorted. As Gregg Levoy wrote in *Callings,* "myths may not be literally true, but they are psychologically true. The pattern of breaking away from home, undergoing trials, and experiencing change and growth as a result is something that everyone, in every age and culture, can relate to and learn from. Perhaps this is one of the reasons for the success of *Watership Down.*" Levoy wrote that two similar stories, the *Odyssey* and *The Wizard of Oz,* are not just the stories of Odysseus and of Dorothy, and in the same way, *Watership Down* is the story of everyone who struggles to find the way home. Above all, Levoy noted, these and similar quest stories are "stories of transformation: from chaos to form, from being lost to finding our way. They describe the stages of life, the initiations we all go through as we move from one level to another: child to adult, young to old, single to married, cowardly to courageous, life to death, death to life."

Source: Kelly Winters, in an essay for *Novels for Students,* Gale Group, 2001.

Jane Resh Thomas

In the following essay, Thomas explores the limited, stereotypical portrayal of the female characters in Watership Down.

Writers of fantasy enjoy the incomparable opportunity to create the world anew, but they suffer from the same problem as Archimedes, who said he could move the world with a system of levers if only he were given a place to stand apart. In creating the new world of *Watership Down* (Macmillan), Richard Adams stands squarely in the old one. His novel draws upon not only epic and picaresque literary traditions but also an anti-feminist social tradition which, removed from the usual human context and imposed upon rabbits, is eerie in its clarity.

Watership Down well deserves the Carnegie Medal and the praise it has won from critics and reviewers, for Adams has created a splendid story, admirable for its originality as much as for its craft. Since the stereotype to which the female characters conform dictates their colorlessness and limits their social range, they are so peripheral they are scarcely noticeable. Its anti-feminist bias, therefore, damages the novel in only a minor way.

A literary work may survive such flaws as peripheral prejudice or cruelty or racism. It is important that the soldier in Andersen's "The Tinderbox" gratuitously murders the old woman and does so with impunity; it is important that the elephants in the Babar books sometimes seem more human than the "savages." But despite what may be viewed as ethical lapses, these stories still merit qualified praise. Just so, it is important that in *Watership Down*, Richard Adams has grafted exalted human spirits to the rabbit bodies of his male characters and has made the females mere rabbits. The males are superhuman and the females subhuman, creatures who occupy only a utilitarian place in the novel's world. That fact is important, notwithstanding the artistic merit of the work as a whole.

Adams' band of rabbit refugees who escape the poison gas and bulldozers of a housing project are not the sweet bunny rabbits that have accompanied the treacle into the nursery ever since imitators first bowdlerized Beatrix Potter's miniature hair-raisers. No. The refugees are literal rabbits, subject to the dictates of biology, to the compulsions of their reproductive impulses, their hunger, and their need for shelter. So they recognize and name every plant they encounter, or they feel inborn terror when they smell a dog approaching.

The refugees owe their survival and the establishment of a new warren to the variety of their talents. They exhibit admirable human traits—bravery to support their daring; the common-sense kind of wisdom; originality; reverence for history tempered by flexibility; compassion. The group includes a bard, a politician, a seer, a soldier, and even an intellectual. As they travel together, they improvise a new community which not only ac-

> **Although it seems odd that Adams counters an ugly totalitarian society with a system where females are merely interchangeable ciphers, one easily ignores that discrepancy too, because the females are unessential baggage, present only to motivate the male characters, not necessary to the story for their own individual sakes."**

commodates but values their great differences. Thus, it seems an enormously civilized and humane society, an association of equals whose personal gifts are recognized. But the members of this civilized society are all males.

To my mind, a just community is a cooperative venture which enriches individual lives instead of restricting them for the supposed good of the group. Even when membership is exclusive, one can admire fictitious community where one finds it—in a rathole with Mole and Ratty in *The Wind in the Willows* (Scribner) or on a journey through Mirkwood in *The Hobbit* (Houghton)—if one ignores any deprived class. So Kenneth Grahame and J. R. R. Tolkien wisely avoid the intrusion of females into the fraternity, just as cultivated gentlemen lock the massive doors of their oak-and-leather clubs. The illusion of civilization, of equalitarian warmth and respect, could hardly be maintained in the presence of a declassed group.

Richard Adams himself avoids that problem throughout the first half of *Watership Down*, which describes the itinerants' perilous journey. Like Grahame and Tolkien, he simply omits females from consciousness. However, when the rabbit troupe settle down, they begin to long for female companionship, a longing based on afterthought.

For one thing, they'd like to have some females around to do the work: In established warrens, nubile females do all of the serious digging. Adams has so skillfully bridged the distance between rabbits and people that, whoever digs the burrows in rabbit reality, one easily draws conclusions from Adams' rabbit fiction about the appropriate roles of men and women. The girl who rescues chief Hazel from a barnyard cat's jaws receives her orders from men with a lapine docility that reinforces this rabbit/human connection.

Additional considerations also bring females to the refugees' minds. As Hazel observes, "We have no does—not one—and no does means no kittens and in a few years no warren." The narrator further explains the need for females after Hazel kidnaps two does from Nuthanger Farm:

> The kind of ideas that have become natural to many male human beings in thinking of females—ideas of protection, fidelity, romantic love and so on—are, of course, unknown to rabbits, although rabbits certainly do form exclusive attachments. . . . However, they are not romantic and it came naturally to Hazel and Holly to consider the two Nuthanger does simply as breeding stock for the warren. Although the males are rarely called bucks but are individually designated by name and collectively referred to as *rabbits,* the females are usually called *does,* a distinction analogous to the classifications *people* and *women* with reference to human males and females. For all its subtlety, that is a psychologically charged distinction, as Simone de Beauvoir suggested when she wrote that there are two classes of people, human beings and women. When women try to be human beings, she said, they are accused of acting like men.

Furthermore, the narrator makes it clear that only two alternatives exist in relations between sexes, the human way of romantic idolatry or the rabbit way of animal husbandry. In either case, the female is deprived of anything like the participation granted male members of the brotherhood by virtue of their maleness. Consorting with females seems to be an onerous necessity.

Eventually the refugees act on their longing and raid Efrafa, a neighboring rabbit police state. Of the ten does who willingly escape the totalitarian rule of General Woundwort, only two are even superficially characterized. One is a scatter-brained youngster who reveals the escape plan by chattering uncontrollably to Efrafan officers. All of the others, except Hyzenthlay, are powerless to act on their own initiative—paralyzed by fear at every critical turn.

Only Hyzenthlay possesses courage or dignity. She is a seer, gifted like the male Fiver, with prophetic vision. And like Dandelion, the refugees' bard, she is an artist, a poet whose lament resembles primitive poetry. But her artistic energies, like her determination to escape, are biologically di-

rected, for what she laments is lost opportunities for reproduction. Although the males' sex makes demands upon them, as do their needs for food and shelter, sex does not dictate every form and detail of their lives. But Hyzenthlay is first and only a female, with her poetry seeming merely an aspect of her femaleness. Indeed, since her talents are neither admired nor even noticed, the rabbits of Hazel's warren consult her only as mate, not as prophet or bard. With motherhood, her poetry apparently ends.

A male victim of Efrafan violence says without correction when a fox kills one of the females, "What's a doe more or less?" He accepts the leader's decisions automatically, even forgetting his own opinions if they differ from those of the chief. Asked if her thought processes are like those of the Efrafan male, Hyzenthlay cryptically replies, "I'm a doe." After her brief heroism in the run for freedom, Hyzenthlay turns, in accordance with her sexual definition, to the roles of mate and mother. Her presence on stage is so brief, though, it hardly matters.

Watership Down survives the flawed characterization and the discrepancy between the richness of the male rabbits' lives and the spiritual penury of the females'. Although it seems odd that Adams counters an ugly totalitarian society with a system where females are merely interchangeable ciphers, one easily ignores that discrepancy too, because the females are unessential baggage, present only to motivate the male characters, not necessary to the story for their own individual sakes.

All of this is important, like the murder of Andersen's expendable old woman and like the beastiality of Babar's black neighbors. Within the framework of an otherwise delightful story, Richard Adams has embodied an anti-feminism which deprives his female characters of the spiritual fruit of community.

Source: Jane Resh Thomas, "Old Worlds and New: Anti-Feminism in *Watership Down*," in Horn Book, Vol. 50, No. 4, August 1974, pp. 405–08.

Aidan Chambers

In the following essay, Chambers discusses the origin of Watership Down, *and deems the novel deeply moving and vividly memorable."*

Watership Down is presently a name to conjure with. An extraordinary feat of sustained narrative, the novel appeared in England towards the end of 1972. The coterie critics got excited before it was even published, the reviewers duly raved, and everyone who bothers at all about children's books (and some who don't) have now formed extreme opinions—this being one of those books about which it is not easy, if at all possible, to be neutral. I've no doubt that, as with Alice, the hobbits, and Batman, there'll be cultishness to cope with before long.

I gather Macmillan is bringing it out in the States, and I shall be fascinated to discover the kind of response this quintessentially English book stirs in American commentators. As I wouldn't want to steal one rumble of their thunder, my instinctive impulse to launch into a detailed revelation of all that makes this epic novel so unusual is as instinctively frustrated. Nevertheless, I cannot possibly report on children's books in this country without saying something about it, however tantalizing, however premature it might be.

Watership Down was written by Richard Adams, who, it turns out, is an official in the Department of the Environment—a biographical nicety not without ironic overtones, as may become clear in a moment. He is new to the ranks of published authors; has, I fancy, spent years on his novel; and hawked the bulky manuscript round numerous reputable houses—all of which turned it down and must now be suffering agonies of belated regret—before finding his way to the desk of Rex Collings.

Mr. Collings is one of a new breed. Until recently an editor with a monolith firm, he decided to opt out from literary factory production dominated by accountants and to set up on his own in faith and hope, if not on—or even in—charity. There are a number of people trying the same optimistic gambit just now, and one cannot but applaud their efforts to revivify literary publishing.

According to his own somewhat sugary publicity, Mr. Collings was forced at bowler point to read the daunting manuscript by its desperate author, found himself hooked by the end of the first chapter, and thereafter took the undoubtedly courageous step (for such a young firm) of publishing the fat volume. Unfortunately, his courage was not matched by his production skills: He designed an ugly edition, with cramped typography and dressed in an appallingly inept dust-jacket. The outward and visible appearance doubtless turned off more readers than were turned on.

The hardback edition is, in fact, four hundred and thirteen pages thick, fifty chapters and one map long, and is all about rabbits. Now, lapine fantasy is not my literary cup of tea—be it for children or

A man reaches into a rabbit burrow. In the 1950s, British farmers began taking a serious look at the damage to their crops caused by rabbits. The Pests Act of 1954 paved the way for Rabbit Clearance Societies, which provided teams of experts that came onto agricultural lands to kill overabundant rabbit populations.

not, and I question whether *Watership Down* was ever really intended for children until the question of publication arose. Rabbits, to my mind, are best left to their own rodent activities. And had I not had to review the tome, I would certainly have given it the go-by. (Will one ever learn to judge books, like people, only after listening a while! For sure, first impressions were utterly deceptive in this case, and ugliness only jacket deep.)

What next took me aback was that a quotation from Aeschylus's *Agamemnon* stood sentinel at the head of Chapter One, a lost Victorian device made the more startling because it was quoted in the original Greek. I flipped the pages. Quotations sprouted like thorny, protective hedges at the beginning of every chapter, taken from sources as disparate as the aforementioned classic to bits from R. M. Lockley's erudite treatise on your true and living bunny.

Disconsolate, a reviewer in professional straits, I set to work. But work it remained for only a page or two. Thereafter, I was an addict. I could have stayed on *Watership Down* (which, incidentally, is a real and visitable part of chalky Hampshire, as are all the places named in the book) as long as Mr. Adams wished to keep me there. Four hundred and thirteen pages seemed, when they were finished, a less than generous amount. Absorbing, sensational, staggeringly unexpected, flawed to the point of critical disaster, brilliant, exciting, evocative (the sense of place and atmosphere, climate and season is beautifully achieved), English to the last full-stop, tough, gentle, bloodshot, violent, satisfying, humorous. The list of epithets, superlatives, qualifiers, paradoxes, and blazoned blooming nouns could cover the rest of the space allotted me.

In sum, *Watership Down,* though not a comfortable nor even a lovely book, is deeply moving and vividly memorable in the way that all "good" books, all works of true art, are: They implant themselves—some by main force, others by subtle injection—into the living tissues of your being, to remain there, illuminating your view of life ever after. Most obviously and least importantly, rabbits will never be the same again for me, a warren never again be simply a collection of messy holes in the ground. But to say that is to say little. There are some who speak of allegory and hint at many hidden and profound meanings burrowed beneath the surface of the narrative. They may well be right. But I suspect there are as many different tunnels of meaning as one cares to dig. So, to return for now to the pleasantly simple and obvious: I shall never again watch a bobbed and white-lined tail stub its way across a field in pursuit of a hedge without believing it belongs to a lapine guerrilla from the warren Mr. Adams biographs in such rich and intimate detail.

The story is what one might expect had *Wind in the Willows* been written after two World Wars, various marks of nuclear bomb, the Korean and Vietnam obscenities, and half-a-dozen other hells created by the inexhaustibly evil powers of Man. In fact, the tale begins with a deliberate act of demolition, when human beings destroy an ancient warren in order to clear a building site, inadvertently leaving alive a handful of ill-assorted rabbits to wander the countryside as refugees. Despite all the calamities that befall luckless Toad, no one ever dreamt Toad Hall would be bulldozed. And putting the pick into the medieval rooms inhabited by Badger would have been unthinkable. But that was 1908. And 1908 is gone, *Wind in the Willows* with

it. *Watership Down,* if none the wiser than that wise and lovely book, is a great deal better informed.

But I must stop. To go on would be to spoil things for your own reviewers. Let me finish by mentioning that Puffin paperbacks will soon be publishing the book in better and more attractive clothes. Then we shall very soon discover how much it is a children's book children will read, and how much it is enjoyed by adults only.

Source: Aidan Chambers, "Letter from England: Great Leaping Lapins!," in *Horn Book,* Vol. 49, No. 2, June 1973, pp. 253–55.

Sources

Campbell, Joseph, *Hero with a Thousand Faces,* Bollingen, 1949.

Clift, Jean Dalby, and Wallace B. Clift, *The Archetype of Pilgrimage,* Paulist Press, 1996.

Hume, Kathryn, *Fantasy and Mimesis: Responses to Reality in Western Literature,* Methuen, 1984.

Hunt, Peter, ed., *International Companion Encyclopedia of Children's Literature,* Routledge, 1996.

Levoy, Gregg, *Callings,* Three Rivers Press, 1997.

Lurie, Alison, Review, in *New York Review of Books,* April 18, 1974.

MacRae, Cathi Dunn, *Presenting Young Adult Fantasy Fiction,* Twayne Publishers, 1998.

Mano, D. Keith, Review, in *National Review,* April 26, 1974.

Rawicz, Slavomir, *The Long Walk: The True Story of a Trek to Freedom,* Lyons Press, 1956.

Searles, Baird, Beth Meacham, and Michael Franklin, *A Reader's Guide to Fantasy,* Facts on File, 1982.

Tymn, Marshall B., Kenneth J. Zahorski, and Robert H. Boyer, *Fantasy Literature: A Core Collection and Reference Guide,* R. R. Bowker, 1979.

For Further Study

Adams, Richard, *The Day Gone By,* Century Hutchinson, 1990.
    Adams's autobiography.

Helbig, Alethea K., and Agnes Regan Perkins, *Dictionary of British Children's Fiction: Books of Recognized Merit,* Vol. 1: A–M, Greenwood Press, 1989.
    Provides a biography of Adams.

Smith, Elliot Fremont, Review, in *New York,* March 4, 1974.
    Review of *Watership Down.*

Glossary of Literary Terms

A

Abstract: As an adjective applied to writing or literary works, abstract refers to words or phrases that name things not knowable through the five senses.

Aestheticism: A literary and artistic movement of the nineteenth century. Followers of the movement believed that art should not be mixed with social, political, or moral teaching. The statement "art for art's sake" is a good summary of aestheticism. The movement had its roots in France, but it gained widespread importance in England in the last half of the nineteenth century, where it helped change the Victorian practice of including moral lessons in literature.

Allegory: A narrative technique in which characters representing things or abstract ideas are used to convey a message or teach a lesson. Allegory is typically used to teach moral, ethical, or religious lessons but is sometimes used for satiric or political purposes.

Allusion: A reference to a familiar literary or historical person or event, used to make an idea more easily understood.

Analogy: A comparison of two things made to explain something unfamiliar through its similarities to something familiar, or to prove one point based on the acceptedness of another. Similes and metaphors are types of analogies.

Antagonist: The major character in a narrative or drama who works against the hero or protagonist.

Anthropomorphism: The presentation of animals or objects in human shape or with human characteristics. The term is derived from the Greek word for "human form."

Antihero: A central character in a work of literature who lacks traditional heroic qualities such as courage, physical prowess, and fortitude. Antiheroes typically distrust conventional values and are unable to commit themselves to any ideals. They generally feel helpless in a world over which they have no control. Antiheroes usually accept, and often celebrate, their positions as social outcasts.

Apprenticeship Novel: See *Bildungsroman*

Archetype: The word archetype is commonly used to describe an original pattern or model from which all other things of the same kind are made. This term was introduced to literary criticism from the psychology of Carl Jung. It expresses Jung's theory that behind every person's "unconscious," or repressed memories of the past, lies the "collective unconscious" of the human race: memories of the countless typical experiences of our ancestors. These memories are said to prompt illogical associations that trigger powerful emotions in the reader. Often, the emotional process is primitive, even primordial. Archetypes are the literary images that grow out of the "collective unconscious." They appear in literature as incidents and plots that repeat basic patterns of life. They may also appear as stereotyped characters.

Avant-garde: French term meaning "vanguard." It is used in literary criticism to describe new writing that rejects traditional approaches to literature in favor of innovations in style or content.

B

Beat Movement: A period featuring a group of American poets and novelists of the 1950s and 1960s—including Jack Kerouac, Allen Ginsberg, Gregory Corso, William S. Burroughs, and Lawrence Ferlinghetti—who rejected established social and literary values. Using such techniques as stream of consciousness writing and jazz-influenced free verse and focusing on unusual or abnormal states of mind—generated by religious ecstasy or the use of drugs—the Beat writers aimed to create works that were unconventional in both form and subject matter.

Bildungsroman: A German word meaning "novel of development." The *bildungsroman* is a study of the maturation of a youthful character, typically brought about through a series of social or sexual encounters that lead to self-awareness. *Bildungsroman* is used interchangeably with *erziehungsroman*, a novel of initiation and education. When a *bildungsroman* is concerned with the development of an artist (as in James Joyce's *A Portrait of the Artist as a Young Man*), it is often termed a *kunstlerroman*. Also known as Apprenticeship Novel, Coming of Age Novel, *Erziehungsroman*, or *Kunstlerroman*.

Black Aesthetic Movement: A period of artistic and literary development among African Americans in the 1960s and early 1970s. This was the first major African-American artistic movement since the Harlem Renaissance and was closely paralleled by the civil rights and black power movements. The black aesthetic writers attempted to produce works of art that would be meaningful to the black masses. Key figures in black aesthetics included one of its founders, poet and playwright Amiri Baraka, formerly known as LeRoi Jones; poet and essayist Haki R. Madhubuti, formerly Don L. Lee; poet and playwright Sonia Sanchez; and dramatist Ed Bullins. Also known as Black Arts Movement.

Black Humor: Writing that places grotesque elements side by side with humorous ones in an attempt to shock the reader, forcing him or her to laugh at the horrifying reality of a disordered world. Also known as Black Comedy.

Burlesque: Any literary work that uses exaggeration to make its subject appear ridiculous, either by treating a trivial subject with profound seriousness or by treating a dignified subject frivolously. The word "burlesque" may also be used as an adjective, as in "burlesque show," to mean "striptease act."

C

Character: Broadly speaking, a person in a literary work. The actions of characters are what constitute the plot of a story, novel, or poem. There are numerous types of characters, ranging from simple, stereotypical figures to intricate, multifaceted ones. In the techniques of anthropomorphism and personification, animals—and even places or things—can assume aspects of character. "Characterization" is the process by which an author creates vivid, believable characters in a work of art. This may be done in a variety of ways, including (1) direct description of the character by the narrator; (2) the direct presentation of the speech, thoughts, or actions of the character; and (3) the responses of other characters to the character. The term "character" also refers to a form originated by the ancient Greek writer Theophrastus that later became popular in the seventeenth and eighteenth centuries. It is a short essay or sketch of a person who prominently displays a specific attribute or quality, such as miserliness or ambition.

Climax: The turning point in a narrative, the moment when the conflict is at its most intense. Typically, the structure of stories, novels, and plays is one of rising action, in which tension builds to the climax, followed by falling action, in which tension lessens as the story moves to its conclusion.

Colloquialism: A word, phrase, or form of pronunciation that is acceptable in casual conversation but not in formal, written communication. It is considered more acceptable than slang.

Coming of Age Novel: See *Bildungsroman*

Concrete: Concrete is the opposite of abstract, and refers to a thing that actually exists or a description that allows the reader to experience an object or concept with the senses.

Connotation: The impression that a word gives beyond its defined meaning. Connotations may be universally understood or may be significant only to a certain group.

Convention: Any widely accepted literary device, style, or form.

D

Denotation: The definition of a word, apart from the impressions or feelings it creates (connotations) in the reader.

Denouement: A French word meaning "the unknotting." In literary criticism, it denotes the resolution of conflict in fiction or drama. The *denouement* follows the climax and provides an outcome to the primary plot situation as well as an explanation of secondary plot complications. The *denouement* often involves a character's recognition of his or her state of mind or moral condition. Also known as Falling Action.

Description: Descriptive writing is intended to allow a reader to picture the scene or setting in which the action of a story takes place. The form this description takes often evokes an intended emotional response—a dark, spooky graveyard will evoke fear, and a peaceful, sunny meadow will evoke calmness.

Dialogue: In its widest sense, dialogue is simply conversation between people in a literary work; in its most restricted sense, it refers specifically to the speech of characters in a drama. As a specific literary genre, a "dialogue" is a composition in which characters debate an issue or idea.

Diction: The selection and arrangement of words in a literary work. Either or both may vary depending on the desired effect. There are four general types of diction: "formal," used in scholarly or lofty writing; "informal," used in relaxed but educated conversation; "colloquial," used in everyday speech; and "slang," containing newly coined words and other terms not accepted in formal usage.

Didactic: A term used to describe works of literature that aim to teach some moral, religious, political, or practical lesson. Although didactic elements are often found in artistically pleasing works, the term "didactic" usually refers to literature in which the message is more important than the form. The term may also be used to criticize a work that the critic finds "overly didactic," that is, heavy-handed in its delivery of a lesson.

Doppelganger: A literary technique by which a character is duplicated (usually in the form of an alter ego, though sometimes as a ghostly counterpart) or divided into two distinct, usually opposite personalities. The use of this character device is widespread in nineteenth- and twentieth-century literature, and indicates a growing awareness among authors that the "self" is really a composite of many "selves." Also known as The Double.

Double Entendre: A corruption of a French phrase meaning "double meaning." The term is used to indicate a word or phrase that is deliberately ambiguous, especially when one of the meanings is risqué or improper.

Dramatic Irony: Occurs when the audience of a play or the reader of a work of literature knows something that a character in the work itself does not know. The irony is in the contrast between the intended meaning of the statements or actions of a character and the additional information understood by the audience.

Dystopia: An imaginary place in a work of fiction where the characters lead dehumanized, fearful lives.

E

Edwardian: Describes cultural conventions identified with the period of the reign of Edward VII of England (1901-1910). Writers of the Edwardian Age typically displayed a strong reaction against the propriety and conservatism of the Victorian Age. Their work often exhibits distrust of authority in religion, politics, and art and expresses strong doubts about the soundness of conventional values.

Empathy: A sense of shared experience, including emotional and physical feelings, with someone or something other than oneself. Empathy is often used to describe the response of a reader to a literary character.

Enlightenment, The: An eighteenth-century philosophical movement. It began in France but had a wide impact throughout Europe and America. Thinkers of the Enlightenment valued reason and believed that both the individual and society could achieve a state of perfection. Corresponding to this essentially humanist vision was a resistance to religious authority.

Epigram: A saying that makes the speaker's point quickly and concisely. Often used to preface a novel.

Epilogue: A concluding statement or section of a literary work. In dramas, particularly those of the seventeenth and eighteenth centuries, the epilogue is a closing speech, often in verse, delivered by an actor at the end of a play and spoken directly to the audience.

Epiphany: A sudden revelation of truth inspired by a seemingly trivial incident.

Episode: An incident that forms part of a story and is significantly related to it. Episodes may be either self-contained narratives or events that depend on a larger context for their sense and importance.

Epistolary Novel: A novel in the form of letters. The form was particularly popular in the eighteenth century.

Epithet: A word or phrase, often disparaging or abusive, that expresses a character trait of someone or something.

Existentialism: A predominantly twentieth-century philosophy concerned with the nature and perception of human existence. There are two major strains of existentialist thought: atheistic and Christian. Followers of atheistic existentialism believe that the individual is alone in a godless universe and that the basic human condition is one of suffering and loneliness. Nevertheless, because there are no fixed values, individuals can create their own characters—indeed, they can shape themselves—through the exercise of free will. The atheistic strain culminates in and is popularly associated with the works of Jean-Paul Sartre. The Christian existentialists, on the other hand, believe that only in God may people find freedom from life's anguish. The two strains hold certain beliefs in common: that existence cannot be fully understood or described through empirical effort; that anguish is a universal element of life; that individuals must bear responsibility for their actions; and that there is no common standard of behavior or perception for religious and ethical matters.

Expatriates: See *Expatriatism*

Expatriatism: The practice of leaving one's country to live for an extended period in another country.

Exposition: Writing intended to explain the nature of an idea, thing, or theme. Expository writing is often combined with description, narration, or argument. In dramatic writing, the exposition is the introductory material which presents the characters, setting, and tone of the play.

Expressionism: An indistinct literary term, originally used to describe an early twentieth-century school of German painting. The term applies to almost any mode of unconventional, highly subjective writing that distorts reality in some way.

F

Fable: A prose or verse narrative intended to convey a moral. Animals or inanimate objects with human characteristics often serve as characters in fables.

Falling Action: See *Denouement*

Fantasy: A literary form related to mythology and folklore. Fantasy literature is typically set in non-existent realms and features supernatural beings.

Farce: A type of comedy characterized by broad humor, outlandish incidents, and often vulgar subject matter.

***Femme fatale*:** A French phrase with the literal translation "fatal woman." A *femme fatale* is a sensuous, alluring woman who often leads men into danger or trouble.

Fiction: Any story that is the product of imagination rather than a documentation of fact. Characters and events in such narratives may be based in real life but their ultimate form and configuration is a creation of the author.

Figurative Language: A technique in writing in which the author temporarily interrupts the order, construction, or meaning of the writing for a particular effect. This interruption takes the form of one or more figures of speech such as hyperbole, irony, or simile. Figurative language is the opposite of literal language, in which every word is truthful, accurate, and free of exaggeration or embellishment.

Figures of Speech: Writing that differs from customary conventions for construction, meaning, order, or significance for the purpose of a special meaning or effect. There are two major types of figures of speech: rhetorical figures, which do not make changes in the meaning of the words, and tropes, which do.

***Fin de siecle*:** A French term meaning "end of the century." The term is used to denote the last decade of the nineteenth century, a transition period when writers and other artists abandoned old conventions and looked for new techniques and objectives.

First Person: See *Point of View*

Flashback: A device used in literature to present action that occurred before the beginning of the story. Flashbacks are often introduced as the dreams or recollections of one or more characters.

Foil: A character in a work of literature whose physical or psychological qualities contrast strongly with, and therefore highlight, the corresponding qualities of another character.

Folklore: Traditions and myths preserved in a culture or group of people. Typically, these are passed on by word of mouth in various forms—such as legends, songs, and proverbs—or preserved in customs and ceremonies. This term was first used by W. J. Thoms in 1846.

Folktale: A story originating in oral tradition. Folktales fall into a variety of categories, including legends, ghost stories, fairy tales, fables, and anecdotes based on historical figures and events.

Foreshadowing: A device used in literature to create expectation or to set up an explanation of later developments.

Form: The pattern or construction of a work which identifies its genre and distinguishes it from other genres.

G

Genre: A category of literary work. In critical theory, genre may refer to both the content of a given work—tragedy, comedy, pastoral—and to its form, such as poetry, novel, or drama.

Gilded Age: A period in American history during the 1870s characterized by political corruption and materialism. A number of important novels of social and political criticism were written during this time.

Gothicism: In literary criticism, works characterized by a taste for the medieval or morbidly attractive. A gothic novel prominently features elements of horror, the supernatural, gloom, and violence: clanking chains, terror, charnel houses, ghosts, medieval castles, and mysteriously slamming doors. The term "gothic novel" is also applied to novels that lack elements of the traditional Gothic setting but that create a similar atmosphere of terror or dread.

Grotesque: In literary criticism, the subject matter of a work or a style of expression characterized by exaggeration, deformity, freakishness, and disorder. The grotesque often includes an element of comic absurdity.

H

Harlem Renaissance: The Harlem Renaissance of the 1920s is generally considered the first significant movement of black writers and artists in the United States. During this period, new and established black writers published more fiction and poetry than ever before, the first influential black literary journals were established, and black authors and artists received their first widespread recognition and serious critical appraisal. Among the major writers associated with this period are Claude McKay, Jean Toomer, Countee Cullen, Langston Hughes, Arna Bontemps, Nella Larsen, and Zora Neale Hurston. Also known as Negro Renaissance and New Negro Movement.

Hero/Heroine: The principal sympathetic character (male or female) in a literary work. Heroes and heroines typically exhibit admirable traits: idealism, courage, and integrity, for example.

Holocaust Literature: Literature influenced by or written about the Holocaust of World War II. Such literature includes true stories of survival in concentration camps, escape, and life after the war, as well as fictional works and poetry.

Humanism: A philosophy that places faith in the dignity of humankind and rejects the medieval perception of the individual as a weak, fallen creature. "Humanists" typically believe in the perfectibility of human nature and view reason and education as the means to that end.

Hyperbole: In literary criticism, deliberate exaggeration used to achieve an effect.

I

Idiom: A word construction or verbal expression closely associated with a given language.

Image: A concrete representation of an object or sensory experience. Typically, such a representation helps evoke the feelings associated with the object or experience itself. Images are either "literal" or "figurative." Literal images are especially concrete and involve little or no extension of the obvious meaning of the words used to express them. Figurative images do not follow the literal meaning of the words exactly. Images in literature are usually visual, but the term "image" can also refer to the representation of any sensory experience.

Imagery: The array of images in a literary work. Also, figurative language.

In medias res: A Latin term meaning "in the middle of things." It refers to the technique of beginning a story at its midpoint and then using various flashback devices to reveal previous action.

Interior Monologue: A narrative technique in which characters' thoughts are revealed in a way that appears to be uncontrolled by the author. The interior monologue typically aims to reveal the inner self of a character. It portrays emotional experiences as they occur at both a conscious and unconscious level. Images are often used to represent sensations or emotions.

Irony: In literary criticism, the effect of language in which the intended meaning is the opposite of what is stated.

J

Jargon: Language that is used or understood only by a select group of people. Jargon may refer to terminology used in a certain profession, such as computer jargon, or it may refer to any nonsensical language that is not understood by most people.

L

Leitmotiv: See *Motif*

Literal Language: An author uses literal language when he or she writes without exaggerating or embellishing the subject matter and without any tools of figurative language.

Lost Generation: A term first used by Gertrude Stein to describe the post-World War I generation of American writers: men and women haunted by a sense of betrayal and emptiness brought about by the destructiveness of the war.

M

Mannerism: Exaggerated, artificial adherence to a literary manner or style. Also, a popular style of the visual arts of late sixteenth-century Europe that was marked by elongation of the human form and by intentional spatial distortion. Literary works that are self-consciously high-toned and artistic are often said to be "mannered."

Metaphor: A figure of speech that expresses an idea through the image of another object. Metaphors suggest the essence of the first object by identifying it with certain qualities of the second object.

Modernism: Modern literary practices. Also, the principles of a literary school that lasted from roughly the beginning of the twentieth century until the end of World War II. Modernism is defined by its rejection of the literary conventions of the nineteenth century and by its opposition to conventional morality, taste, traditions, and economic values.

Mood: The prevailing emotions of a work or of the author in his or her creation of the work. The mood of a work is not always what might be expected based on its subject matter.

Motif: A theme, character type, image, metaphor, or other verbal element that recurs throughout a single work of literature or occurs in a number of different works over a period of time. Also known as *Motiv* or *Leitmotiv*.

Myth: An anonymous tale emerging from the traditional beliefs of a culture or social unit. Myths use supernatural explanations for natural phenomena. They may also explain cosmic issues like creation and death. Collections of myths, known as mythologies, are common to all cultures and nations, but the best-known myths belong to the Norse, Roman, and Greek mythologies.

N

Narration: The telling of a series of events, real or invented. A narration may be either a simple narrative, in which the events are recounted chronologically, or a narrative with a plot, in which the account is given in a style reflecting the author's artistic concept of the story. Narration is sometimes used as a synonym for "storyline."

Narrative: A verse or prose accounting of an event or sequence of events, real or invented. The term is also used as an adjective in the sense "method of narration." For example, in literary criticism, the expression "narrative technique" usually refers to the way the author structures and presents his or her story.

Narrator: The teller of a story. The narrator may be the author or a character in the story through whom the author speaks.

Naturalism: A literary movement of the late nineteenth and early twentieth centuries. The movement's major theorist, French novelist Emile Zola, envisioned a type of fiction that would examine human life with the objectivity of scientific inquiry. The Naturalists typically viewed human beings as either the products of "biological determinism," ruled by hereditary instincts and engaged in an endless struggle for survival, or as the products of "socioeconomic determinism," ruled by social and economic forces beyond their control. In their works, the Naturalists generally ignored the highest levels of society and focused on degradation: poverty, alcoholism, prostitution, insanity, and disease.

Noble Savage: The idea that primitive man is noble and good but becomes evil and corrupted as he becomes civilized. The concept of the noble savage originated in the Renaissance period but is more closely identified with such later writers as

Jean-Jacques Rousseau and Aphra Behn. See also Primitivism.

Novel of Ideas: A novel in which the examination of intellectual issues and concepts takes precedence over characterization or a traditional storyline.

Novel of Manners: A novel that examines the customs and mores of a cultural group.

Novel: A long fictional narrative written in prose, which developed from the novella and other early forms of narrative. A novel is usually organized under a plot or theme with a focus on character development and action.

Novella: An Italian term meaning "story." This term has been especially used to describe fourteenth-century Italian tales, but it also refers to modern short novels.

O

Objective Correlative: An outward set of objects, a situation, or a chain of events corresponding to an inward experience and evoking this experience in the reader. The term frequently appears in modern criticism in discussions of authors' intended effects on the emotional responses of readers.

Objectivity: A quality in writing characterized by the absence of the author's opinion or feeling about the subject matter. Objectivity is an important factor in criticism.

Oedipus Complex: A son's amorous obsession with his mother. The phrase is derived from the story of the ancient Theban hero Oedipus, who unknowingly killed his father and married his mother.

Omniscience: See *Point of View*

Onomatopoeia: The use of words whose sounds express or suggest their meaning. In its simplest sense, onomatopoeia may be represented by words that mimic the sounds they denote such as "hiss" or "meow." At a more subtle level, the pattern and rhythm of sounds and rhymes of a line or poem may be onomatopoeic.

Oxymoron: A phrase combining two contradictory terms. Oxymorons may be intentional or unintentional.

P

Parable: A story intended to teach a moral lesson or answer an ethical question.

Paradox: A statement that appears illogical or contradictory at first, but may actually point to an underlying truth.

Parallelism: A method of comparison of two ideas in which each is developed in the same grammatical structure.

Parody: In literary criticism, this term refers to an imitation of a serious literary work or the signature style of a particular author in a ridiculous manner. A typical parody adopts the style of the original and applies it to an inappropriate subject for humorous effect. Parody is a form of satire and could be considered the literary equivalent of a caricature or cartoon.

Pastoral: A term derived from the Latin word "pastor," meaning shepherd. A pastoral is a literary composition on a rural theme. The conventions of the pastoral were originated by the third-century Greek poet Theocritus, who wrote about the experiences, love affairs, and pastimes of Sicilian shepherds. In a pastoral, characters and language of a courtly nature are often placed in a simple setting. The term pastoral is also used to classify dramas, elegies, and lyrics that exhibit the use of country settings and shepherd characters.

Pen Name: See *Pseudonym*

Persona: A Latin term meaning "mask." *Personae* are the characters in a fictional work of literature. The *persona* generally functions as a mask through which the author tells a story in a voice other than his or her own. A *persona* is usually either a character in a story who acts as a narrator or an "implied author," a voice created by the author to act as the narrator for himself or herself.

Personification: A figure of speech that gives human qualities to abstract ideas, animals, and inanimate objects. Also known as *Prosopopoeia*.

Picaresque Novel: Episodic fiction depicting the adventures of a roguish central character ("picaro" is Spanish for "rogue"). The picaresque hero is commonly a low-born but clever individual who wanders into and out of various affairs of love, danger, and farcical intrigue. These involvements may take place at all social levels and typically present a humorous and wide-ranging satire of a given society.

Plagiarism: Claiming another person's written material as one's own. Plagiarism can take the form of direct, word-for-word copying or the theft of the substance or idea of the work.

Plot: In literary criticism, this term refers to the pattern of events in a narrative or drama. In its simplest sense, the plot guides the author in composing the work and helps the reader follow the work. Typically, plots exhibit causality and unity and have a beginning, a middle, and an end. Sometimes, however, a plot may consist of a series of disconnected events, in which case it is known as an "episodic plot."

Poetic Justice: An outcome in a literary work, not necessarily a poem, in which the good are rewarded and the evil are punished, especially in ways that particularly fit their virtues or crimes.

Poetic License: Distortions of fact and literary convention made by a writer—not always a poet—for the sake of the effect gained. Poetic license is closely related to the concept of "artistic freedom."

Poetics: This term has two closely related meanings. It denotes (1) an aesthetic theory in literary criticism about the essence of poetry or (2) rules prescribing the proper methods, content, style, or diction of poetry. The term poetics may also refer to theories about literature in general, not just poetry.

Point of View: The narrative perspective from which a literary work is presented to the reader. There are four traditional points of view. The "third person omniscient" gives the reader a "godlike" perspective, unrestricted by time or place, from which to see actions and look into the minds of characters. This allows the author to comment openly on characters and events in the work. The "third person" point of view presents the events of the story from outside of any single character's perception, much like the omniscient point of view, but the reader must understand the action as it takes place and without any special insight into characters' minds or motivations. The "first person" or "personal" point of view relates events as they are perceived by a single character. The main character "tells" the story and may offer opinions about the action and characters which differ from those of the author. Much less common than omniscient, third person, and first person is the "second person" point of view, wherein the author tells the story as if it is happening to the reader.

Polemic: A work in which the author takes a stand on a controversial subject, such as abortion or religion. Such works are often extremely argumentative or provocative.

Pornography: Writing intended to provoke feelings of lust in the reader. Such works are often condemned by critics and teachers, but those which can be shown to have literary value are viewed less harshly.

Post-Aesthetic Movement: An artistic response made by African Americans to the black aesthetic movement of the 1960s and early '70s. Writers since that time have adopted a somewhat different tone in their work, with less emphasis placed on the disparity between black and white in the United States. In the words of post-aesthetic authors such as Toni Morrison, John Edgar Wideman, and Kristin Hunter, African Americans are portrayed as looking inward for answers to their own questions, rather than always looking to the outside world.

Postmodernism: Writing from the 1960s forward characterized by experimentation and continuing to apply some of the fundamentals of modernism, which included existentialism and alienation. Postmodernists have gone a step further in the rejection of tradition begun with the modernists by also rejecting traditional forms, preferring the anti-novel over the novel and the antihero over the hero.

Primitivism: The belief that primitive peoples were nobler and less flawed than civilized peoples because they had not been subjected to the tainting influence of society. See also Noble Savage.

Prologue: An introductory section of a literary work. It often contains information establishing the situation of the characters or presents information about the setting, time period, or action. In drama, the prologue is spoken by a chorus or by one of the principal characters.

Prose: A literary medium that attempts to mirror the language of everyday speech. It is distinguished from poetry by its use of unmetered, unrhymed language consisting of logically related sentences. Prose is usually grouped into paragraphs that form a cohesive whole such as an essay or a novel.

Prosopopoeia: See *Personification*

Protagonist: The central character of a story who serves as a focus for its themes and incidents and as the principal rationale for its development. The protagonist is sometimes referred to in discussions of modern literature as the hero or antihero.

Protest Fiction: Protest fiction has as its primary purpose the protesting of some social injustice, such as racism or discrimination.

Proverb: A brief, sage saying that expresses a truth about life in a striking manner.

Pseudonym: A name assumed by a writer, most often intended to prevent his or her identification as the author of a work. Two or more authors may work together under one pseudonym, or an author may use a different name for each genre he or she publishes in. Some publishing companies maintain "house pseudonyms," under which any number of authors may write installations in a series. Some authors also choose a pseudonym over their real names the way an actor may use a stage name.

Pun: A play on words that have similar sounds but different meanings.

R

Realism: A nineteenth-century European literary movement that sought to portray familiar characters, situations, and settings in a realistic manner. This was done primarily by using an objective narrative point of view and through the buildup of accurate detail. The standard for success of any realistic work depends on how faithfully it transfers common experience into fictional forms. The realistic method may be altered or extended, as in stream of consciousness writing, to record highly subjective experience.

Repartee: Conversation featuring snappy retorts and witticisms.

Resolution: The portion of a story following the climax, in which the conflict is resolved. See also *Denouement*.

Rhetoric: In literary criticism, this term denotes the art of ethical persuasion. In its strictest sense, rhetoric adheres to various principles developed since classical times for arranging facts and ideas in a clear, persuasive, appealing manner. The term is also used to refer to effective prose in general and theories of or methods for composing effective prose.

Rhetorical Question: A question intended to provoke thought, but not an expressed answer, in the reader. It is most commonly used in oratory and other persuasive genres.

Rising Action: The part of a drama where the plot becomes increasingly complicated. Rising action leads up to the climax, or turning point, of a drama.

Roman a clef: A French phrase meaning "novel with a key." It refers to a narrative in which real persons are portrayed under fictitious names.

Romance: A broad term, usually denoting a narrative with exotic, exaggerated, often idealized characters, scenes, and themes.

Romanticism: This term has two widely accepted meanings. In historical criticism, it refers to a European intellectual and artistic movement of the late eighteenth and early nineteenth centuries that sought greater freedom of personal expression than that allowed by the strict rules of literary form and logic of the eighteenth-century neoclassicists. The Romantics preferred emotional and imaginative expression to rational analysis. They considered the individual to be at the center of all experience and so placed him or her at the center of their art. The Romantics believed that the creative imagination reveals nobler truths—unique feelings and attitudes—than those that could be discovered by logic or by scientific examination. Both the natural world and the state of childhood were important sources for revelations of "eternal truths." "Romanticism" is also used as a general term to refer to a type of sensibility found in all periods of literary history and usually considered to be in opposition to the principles of classicism. In this sense, Romanticism signifies any work or philosophy in which the exotic or dreamlike figure strongly, or that is devoted to individualistic expression, self-analysis, or a pursuit of a higher realm of knowledge than can be discovered by human reason.

Romantics: See *Romanticism*

S

Satire: A work that uses ridicule, humor, and wit to criticize and provoke change in human nature and institutions. There are two major types of satire: "formal" or "direct" satire speaks directly to the reader or to a character in the work; "indirect" satire relies upon the ridiculous behavior of its characters to make its point. Formal satire is further divided into two manners: the "Horatian," which ridicules gently, and the "Juvenalian," which derides its subjects harshly and bitterly.

Science Fiction: A type of narrative about or based upon real or imagined scientific theories and technology. Science fiction is often peopled with alien creatures and set on other planets or in different dimensions.

Second Person: See *Point of View*

Setting: The time, place, and culture in which the action of a narrative takes place. The elements of setting may include geographic location, characters' physical and mental environments, prevailing cultural attitudes, or the historical time in which the action takes place.

Simile: A comparison, usually using "like" or "as", of two essentially dissimilar things, as in "coffee as cold as ice" or "He sounded like a broken record."

Slang: A type of informal verbal communication that is generally unacceptable for formal writing. Slang words and phrases are often colorful exaggerations used to emphasize the speaker's point; they may also be shortened versions of an often-used word or phrase.

Slave Narrative: Autobiographical accounts of American slave life as told by escaped slaves. These works first appeared during the abolition movement of the 1830s through the 1850s.

Socialist Realism: The Socialist Realism school of literary theory was proposed by Maxim Gorky and established as a dogma by the first Soviet Congress of Writers. It demanded adherence to a communist worldview in works of literature. Its doctrines required an objective viewpoint comprehensible to the working classes and themes of social struggle featuring strong proletarian heroes. Also known as Social Realism.

Stereotype: A stereotype was originally the name for a duplication made during the printing process; this led to its modern definition as a person or thing that is (or is assumed to be) the same as all others of its type.

Stream of Consciousness: A narrative technique for rendering the inward experience of a character. This technique is designed to give the impression of an ever-changing series of thoughts, emotions, images, and memories in the spontaneous and seemingly illogical order that they occur in life.

Structure: The form taken by a piece of literature. The structure may be made obvious for ease of understanding, as in nonfiction works, or may be obscured for artistic purposes, as in some poetry or seemingly "unstructured" prose.

Sturm und Drang: A German term meaning "storm and stress." It refers to a German literary movement of the 1770s and 1780s that reacted against the order and rationalism of the enlightenment, focusing instead on the intense experience of extraordinary individuals.

Style: A writer's distinctive manner of arranging words to suit his or her ideas and purpose in writing. The unique imprint of the author's personality upon his or her writing, style is the product of an author's way of arranging ideas and his or her use of diction, different sentence structures, rhythm, figures of speech, rhetorical principles, and other elements of composition.

Subjectivity: Writing that expresses the author's personal feelings about his subject, and which may or may not include factual information about the subject.

Subplot: A secondary story in a narrative. A subplot may serve as a motivating or complicating force for the main plot of the work, or it may provide emphasis for, or relief from, the main plot.

Surrealism: A term introduced to criticism by Guillaume Apollinaire and later adopted by Andre Breton. It refers to a French literary and artistic movement founded in the 1920s. The Surrealists sought to express unconscious thoughts and feelings in their works. The best-known technique used for achieving this aim was automatic writing—transcriptions of spontaneous outpourings from the unconscious. The Surrealists proposed to unify the contrary levels of conscious and unconscious, dream and reality, objectivity and subjectivity into a new level of "super-realism."

Suspense: A literary device in which the author maintains the audience's attention through the buildup of events, the outcome of which will soon be revealed.

Symbol: Something that suggests or stands for something else without losing its original identity. In literature, symbols combine their literal meaning with the suggestion of an abstract concept. Literary symbols are of two types: those that carry complex associations of meaning no matter what their contexts, and those that derive their suggestive meaning from their functions in specific literary works.

Symbolism: This term has two widely accepted meanings. In historical criticism, it denotes an early modernist literary movement initiated in France during the nineteenth century that reacted against the prevailing standards of realism. Writers in this movement aimed to evoke, indirectly and symbolically, an order of being beyond the material world of the five senses. Poetic expression of personal emotion figured strongly in the movement, typically by means of a private set of symbols uniquely identifiable with the individual poet. The principal aim of the Symbolists was to express in words the highly complex feelings that grew out of everyday contact with the world. In a broader sense, the term "symbolism" refers to the use of one object to represent another.

T

Tall Tale: A humorous tale told in a straightforward, credible tone but relating absolutely impossible events or feats of the characters. Such tales were commonly told of frontier adventures during the settlement of the west in the United States.

Theme: The main point of a work of literature. The term is used interchangeably with thesis.

Thesis: A thesis is both an essay and the point argued in the essay. Thesis novels and thesis plays share the quality of containing a thesis which is supported through the action of the story.

Third Person: See *Point of View*

Tone: The author's attitude toward his or her audience may be deduced from the tone of the work. A formal tone may create distance or convey politeness, while an informal tone may encourage a friendly, intimate, or intrusive feeling in the reader. The author's attitude toward his or her subject matter may also be deduced from the tone of the words he or she uses in discussing it.

Transcendentalism: An American philosophical and religious movement, based in New England from around 1835 until the Civil War. Transcendentalism was a form of American romanticism that had its roots abroad in the works of Thomas Carlyle, Samuel Coleridge, and Johann Wolfgang von Goethe. The Transcendentalists stressed the importance of intuition and subjective experience in communication with God. They rejected religious dogma and texts in favor of mysticism and scientific naturalism. They pursued truths that lie beyond the "colorless" realms perceived by reason and the senses and were active social reformers in public education, women's rights, and the abolition of slavery.

U

Urban Realism: A branch of realist writing that attempts to accurately reflect the often harsh facts of modern urban existence.

Utopia: A fictional perfect place, such as "paradise" or "heaven."

V

Verisimilitude: Literally, the appearance of truth. In literary criticism, the term refers to aspects of a work of literature that seem true to the reader.

Victorian: Refers broadly to the reign of Queen Victoria of England (1837-1901) and to anything with qualities typical of that era. For example, the qualities of smug narrowmindedness, bourgeois materialism, faith in social progress, and priggish morality are often considered Victorian. This stereotype is contradicted by such dramatic intellectual developments as the theories of Charles Darwin, Karl Marx, and Sigmund Freud (which stirred strong debates in England) and the critical attitudes of serious Victorian writers like Charles Dickens and George Eliot. In literature, the Victorian Period was the great age of the English novel, and the latter part of the era saw the rise of movements such as decadence and symbolism. Also known as Victorian Age and Victorian Period.

W

Weltanschauung: A German term referring to a person's worldview or philosophy.

Weltschmerz: A German term meaning "world pain." It describes a sense of anguish about the nature of existence, usually associated with a melancholy, pessimistic attitude.

Z

Zeitgeist: A German term meaning "spirit of the time." It refers to the moral and intellectual trends of a given era.

Cumulative Author/Title Index

Cumulative Nationality/Ethnicity Index

African American

Angelou, Maya
  I Know Why the Caged Bird Sings: V2
Baldwin, James
  Go Tell It on the Mountain: V4
Ellison, Ralph
  Invisible Man: V2
Gaines, Ernest J.
  The Autobiography of Miss Jane Pittman: V5
Haley, Alex
  Roots: The Story of an American Family: V9
Hurston, Zora Neale
  Their Eyes Were Watching God: V3
Kincaid, Jamaica
  Annie John: V3
Morrison, Toni
  Beloved: V6
  The Bluest Eye: V1
  Song of Solomom: V8
Naylor, Gloria
  Mama Day: V7
  The Women of Brewster Place: V4
Shange, Ntozake
  Betsey Brown: V11
Toomer, Jean
  Cane: V11
Walker, Alice
  The Color Purple: V5
Wright, Richard
  Black Boy: V1

Algerian

Camus, Albert
  The Stranger: V6

American

Allison, Dorothy
  Bastard Out of Carolina: V11
Alvarez, Julia
  How the García Girls Lost Their Accents: V5
Anderson, Sherwood
  Winesburg, Ohio: V4
Angelou, Maya
  I Know Why the Caged Bird Sings: V2
Auel, Jean
  The Clan of the Cave Bear: V11
Bradbury, Ray
  Fahrenheit 451: V1
Brown, Rita Mae
  Rubyfruit Jungle: V9
Butler, Octavia
  Kindred: V8
Card, Orson Scott
  Ender's Game: V5
Cather, Willa
  My Ántonia: V2
Chopin, Kate
  The Awakening: V3
Cisneros, Sandra
  The House on Mango Street: V2
Clavell, James du Maresq
  Shogun: A Novel of Japan: V10
Clemens, Samuel
  The Adventures of Huckleberry Finn: V1
  The Adventures of Tom Sawyer: V6
Conroy, Frank
  Body and Soul: V11

Cooper, James Fenimore
  The Last of the Mohicans: V9
Cormier, Robert
  The Chocolate War: V2
Crane, Stephen
  The Red Badge of Courage: V4
Crutcher, Chris
  The Crazy Horse Electric Game: V11
Dick, Philip K.
  Do Androids Dream of Electric Sheep?: V5
Dickey, James
  Deliverance: V9
Didion, Joan
  Democracy: V3
Doctorow, E. L.
  Ragtime: V6
Dorris, Michael
  A Yellow Raft in Blue Water: V3
Dreiser, Theodore
  Sister Carrie: V8
Ellis, Bret Easton
  Less Than Zero: V11
Ellison, Ralph
  Invisible Man: V2
Erdrich, Louise
  Love Medicine: V5
Faulkner, William
  As I Lay Dying: V8
  The Sound and the Fury: V4
Fitzgerald, F. Scott
  The Great Gatsby: V2
Flagg, Fannie
  Fried Green Tomatoes at the Whistle Stop Café: V7

Asian American

Asian Canadian

Australian

British

Subject/Theme Index

Upper Class
   The Age of Innocence: 3, 7, 11

V

Voyeurism
   Less Than Zero: 241

W

War, the Military, and Soldier Life
   Appointment in Samarra: 31–33

Betsey Brown: 85, 88–89
Body and Soul: 97, 101–104
Cane: 126–128, 130
The Grass Dancer: 219, 221–224,
   228–229, 235–236
A Room with a View: 295–297
Wealth
   The Age of Innocence: 9–11
Western Hemisphere
   Betsey Brown: 90
Wildlife

The Clan of the Cave Bear:
   147–148, 152, 154, 158,
   160–161, 163–164, 166–169
Less Than Zero: 251–255
The Stone Angel: 315–316, 321,
   323
Watership Down: 337, 339, 343,
   345–348
World War I
   Appointment in Samarra: 26, 31–33
   A Room with a View: 295–297

T 70219